◄§ The Propriety of Liberty ◊►

❧ The Propriety of Liberty ❧

PERSONS, PASSIONS AND JUDGEMENT
IN MODERN POLITICAL THOUGHT

Duncan Kelly

PRINCETON UNIVERSITY PRESS

PRINCETON AND OXFORD

Copyright 2011 © by Princeton University Press
Published by Princeton University Press, 41 William Street,
Princeton, New Jersey 08540
In the United Kingdom: Princeton University Press, 6 Oxford Street,
Woodstock, Oxfordshire OX20 1TW

press.princeton.edu

Library of Congress Cataloging-in-Publication Data

Kelly, Duncan.
The propriety of liberty : persons, passions and judgement
in modern political thought / Duncan Kelly.
p. cm.
Includes bibliographical references and index.
ISBN 978-0-691-14313-2 (hardcover : alk. paper)
1. Liberty. 2. Liberty—History. 3. Political science—History.
I. Title.
JC585.K39   2011
320.01'1—dc22   2010022371

British Library Cataloging-in-Publication Data is available

This book has been composed in Sabon

Printed on acid-free paper. ∞

Printed in the United States of America

10 9 8 7 6 5 4 3 2 1

FOR RACHEL, FELIX, LESLEY AND JOCK

Contents

Acknowledgements

It is a pleasure to be able to thank those institutions and individuals who have been crucial to the research for and writing of this book, and without my family, none of it would have been done at all. This book is for them. In a more academic vein I owe an early debt to friends and colleagues in the Department of Politics at the University of Sheffield, where the preliminary drafts of my argument were first sketched out. I am now equally happy to be able to thank colleagues in the Department of Politics and International Studies at the University of Cambridge for helping me to settle in to an exceptionally rewarding new environment. At the same time, many colleagues and friends in other faculties in Cambridge have been terrifically helpful. The Master and Fellows of Jesus College, Cambridge, welcomed me into the Fellowship and have provided me with an excellent and collegial place to think, and a quiet room in which to work.

The library staffs in the rare books section of Sheffield University library, and particularly those associated with Inter Library Loans, have my thanks for their courtesy and work in providing me with material. Equally, the many librarians and library resources in Cambridge have made the task of completing the book easier than it might otherwise have been. Thanks also are due to the staff of the rare books and manuscripts rooms at the British Library, the Bodleian Library, and University of Oxford, to the University Libraries and archivists at Glasgow and Edinburgh, and to the National Library of Scotland in Edinburgh. My thanks for help and much needed advice go to the staff in the western manuscripts reading room of the Archives Nationales, as well as to the staff of the Bibliothèque Nationale, in Paris. At the beginning of my research, I was fortunate to be able to return to the Staatsbibliothek in Munich, and once again was able to make use of its excellent resources. All of these institutions provide exceptional services for visiting scholars.

For their generous financial support, I am deeply grateful to the British Academy for awarding me two small grants during the course of my research, which made travel to archives and institutions both possible and pleasurable. I am similarly grateful to the Academy for funding a symposium that I organized under the title 'Lineages of Empire', where much engaging discussion of questions related to parts of this book took place. Indeed, some of the papers given there have since been published together as a volume in the *Proceedings of the British Academy*. I should also like to thank the University of Sheffield once again, for providing two small grants to enable further archival and library-based research. Finally, my sincere thanks to the Arts and Humanities Research Council for the award of a period of matching leave, which enabled me to finish the full draft of this manuscript unencumbered by teaching and administrative commitments.

A great many people have commented on parts of the work, whether in the form it now takes, or as lectures, academic papers and conference presentations over the past several years in Cambridge, Columbia, Glasgow, London, Newcastle, Oakland, Oslo, Oxford, Portland, Pyrgos, Sheffield, Sussex, Walla Walla, Warwick, Washington DC, and York. My particular thanks, however, must go to a group of senior students at Whitman College, who graciously persevered with what turned out to be some of my earliest and most rudimentary thinking on this topic, for both their earnest questioning and their sincere encouragement. Since then, many other talented students in both Sheffield and Cambridge have forced me to think hard about what I mean by some of the issues raised in this book, whether inadvertently or explicitly, and I have learned much from the give-and-take of ideas in supervisions.

My editor at Princeton University Press, Ian Malcolm, has been tremendous and tremendously encouraging about the whole project during its long gestation, and I am deeply grateful for his advice and conversation throughout. The two anonymous referees he commissioned to report on the manuscript have my thanks too, and even if I have not always followed their advice, the book would have been considerably poorer without my having been forced to consider it. In similar fashion, I am very grateful to Richard Isomaki for his splendid copyediting.

A large number of friends and colleagues have discussed relevant work with me or read and commented on my thoughts, sent materials pertinent to my topic, engaged in interesting conversation or simply provided scholarly inspiration in their own right. Indeed, although naming (sadly) cannot absolve me of any of those errors that remain, I do hope it will at least constitute something of a public thank-you, with my apologies to anyone who has inadvertently been missed. So, my thanks to Katharine Adeney, Carolina Armanteros, David Armitage, Patrick Baert, Duncan Bell, Richard Bourke, Chris Brooke, Thom Brooks, Mike Braddick, Jimmy Burns, Dan Carey, Clare Chambers, James Clackson, Janet Coleman, Kyriakos Demetriou, Biancamaria Fontana, Andrew Gamble, Douglas Dow, John Dunn, Sam Fleischacker, Rebecca Flemming, Michael Freeden, Fabian Freyenhagen, Andrew Gamble, Peter Garnsey, Raymond Geuss, Peter Ghosh, Mark Goldie, Knud Haakonssen, Iain Hampsher-Monk, Geoff Harcourt, Edward Harpham, Ian Harris, Joel Isaac, Tony and Clare Heron, Istvan Hont, Ben Jackson, Susan James, Stuart Jones, Colin Kidd, Jim Kloppenberg, Melissa Lane, Mary Laven, Charlie Lees,

Jörn Leonhard, Noel Malcolm, Peter Mandler, Karuna Mantena, Jeanne Morefield, John Morrow, Sarah Mortimer, Véronique Mottier, Sam Moyn, Jan Werner Müller, Peter Miller, Michael Neu, Peter Nicholson, Mike O'Brien, Jon Parkin, Phil Parvin, Emile Perreau-Saussine, Jennifer Pitts, Andrew Rehfeld, David Runciman, Magnus Ryan, Alberto de Sanctis, Melissa Schwartzberg, Ruth Scurr, Quentin Skinner, Mike Sonenscher, Céline Spector, Tim Stanton, Marc Stears, Bob Stern, Benjamin Thompson, Helen Thompson, John Thompson, Keith Tribe, Richard Tuck, Jim Tully, Colin Tyler, Nadia Urbinati, Andrew Vincent, Ben Wempe, Richard Whatmore, Geraint Williams, Donald Winch, and Alex Zakaras.

Parts of this book have appeared elsewhere, though they are revised and (sometimes significantly) updated here. A version of chapter 1 appeared as 'The Propriety of Liberty and the Quality of Responsible Agency', in C. Miqueu and M. Chamie (eds.) *Locke's Political Liberty: Readings and Misreadings* (= *Studies on Voltaire and the Eighteenth Century*, 2009:04), Voltaire Foundation: Oxford, 2009, pp. 97–125. I am grateful for permission to re-use this material from the Voltaire Foundation, Oxford. Similarly, an earlier version of chapter 5 appeared as 'Idealism and Revolution: T. H. Green's *Four Lectures on the English Commonwealth*', *History of Political Thought*, vol. 27, no. 3 (2006), pp. 505–42. I am grateful for permission to re-use the material from Imprint Academic, Exeter. Finally, for their permission to use as my cover illustration an image of the etching in their possession by Hieronymus Wierix, *The Fall of Man* (*after Ambrosius Francken the Elder*), 1578, I am especially grateful to the Samek Art Gallery of Bucknell University, Lewisburg, PA. And for those who might read this book without a dust jacket, this particular image is available to view on the website of the Samek Gallery. Finally, for her extra help in arranging the image transfer and copyright, my particular thanks go to Tracy Graham.

Cambridge, *January 2010*

Abbreviations

AHR	*American Historical Review*
AN	Archives Nationales
APSR	*American Political Science Review*
BJHP	*British Journal for the History of Philosophy*
BL	British Library
BN	Bibliothèque National
CSSH	*Comparative Studies in Society and History*
CW	*Collected Works*
ECT	*An Essay Concerning Toleration and Other Writings on Law and Politics, 1667–1683*
EHR	*English Historical Review*
EJPT	*European Journal of Political Theory*
EPM	*Enquiries concerning Human Understanding and concerning the Principles of Morals*
EPS	*Essays on Philosophical Subjects*
ER	*Edinburgh Review*
HEI	*History of European Ideas*
HJ	*Historical Journal*
HPT	*History of Political Thought*
HWJ	*History Workshop Journal*
JBS	*Journal of British Studies*
JHI	*Journal of the History of Ideas*
JHP	*Journal of the History of Philosophy*
JLH	*Journal of Legal History*
JMH	*Journal of Modern History*
JoPh	*Journal of Philosophy*
JPP	*Journal of Political Philosophy*
LRBL	*Lectures on Rhetoric and Belles Lettres*
MIH	*Modern Intellectual History*
OC	*Oeuvres Complètes*
ODNB	*Oxford Dictionary of National Biography*
OPM	*Oeuvres philosophiques et morales*
P&P	*Past and Present*
PAS	*Proceedings of the Aristotelian Society*
PBA	*Proceedings of the British Academy*
PhilSt	*Philosophical Studies*
PhW	*Philosophical Works*

PMLA	*Proceedings of the Modern Language Association*
PPA	*Philosophy and Public Affairs*
PS	*Political Studies*
PT	*Political Theory*
PW	*Political Writings*
QdS	*Quaderni di Storia*
SVEC	*Studies on Voltaire and the Eighteenth Century*
THN	*A Treatise of Human Nature*
TMS	*Theory of Moral Sentiments*
TPM	*The Philological Museum*
TPR	*The Philosophical Review*
TRHS	*Transactions of the Royal Historical Society*
UCP	*University of Chicago Press*
WMQ	*William and Mary Quarterly*
WN	*Wealth of Nations*

❧ The Propriety of Liberty ☙

The Propriety of Liberty

This is an intellectual history of some of the major ways in which the idea of liberty was understood by John Locke, Charles Louis Secondat, Baron de la Brède et de Montesquieu, Adam Smith, John Stuart Mill and Thomas Hill Green. It might well then be asked what could possibly be said that merits yet another book on these thinkers in general, and on the topic of liberty especially. For a great many people have written on any one or all of these men, and often with specific reference to the idea of liberty. My answer to this reasonable question is simple, but perhaps surprising. It seems to me that despite the agglomeration of commentary and critique, indeed perhaps because of it, many interpreters have missed something absolutely crucial. This is particularly the case amongst those who have been keen to incorporate these writers into a canon of modern liberalism, and who often tend to read the concerns of contemporary liberal political theory backwards onto these putative founders of such a tradition. In this reading, what is typically missed is the relentless focus of these writers on the way in which the quality of individual agency is related to an understanding of freedom. My central claim is that the writers discussed in this book typically conceive of liberty as a form of propriety, or appropriate agency. Although they do not cultivate explicit theories of liberty as propriety, my use of the term 'propriety' with reference to liberty is designed to illustrate the connections between governed conduct and free agency that are central to each of these writers. Because of these connections, the arguments about liberty they present are inextricably linked to questions about the nature of personhood, the passions and judgement.

This means that at least part of my story concerns the intellectual history of what some modern philosophers have referred to as 'agency-freedom'. Agency-freedom is the capacity of individuals to choose between alternative courses of action internally, and then act on their choices both in private and in public, and to be recognized or judged as being responsible for those actions. Analytically separable from claims about well-being, for example, agency-freedom thus understood is a relatively simple idea. It nevertheless has a complex and deeply rooted intellectual history.[1] For example, the interconnections between power and control in the agency view of freedom are central to an idea of liberty as propriety or responsible agency. In what follows I shall try to trace how and why the writers I am interested in think about liberty in terms of the quality of what contemporary philosophers might call agency-freedom or even autonomy, because this focus on the quality of agency highlights the close connections between individual and political liberty that all of them take to be crucial.

As the subtitle to my story indicates, in exploring this topic one must be aware of the way in which political liberty has often been seen as a complex balance between claims about personhood, passions and judgement. Therefore, and for the sake of clarity in what might otherwise be a rather complicated narrative, let me try to present the central thesis of the book as sharply as possible. Taking my cue from a thought outlined most explicitly by Adam Smith, the propriety of agency-freedom refers to the judgement of action in terms of justice or injustice. This connection between propriety and justice points in turn to deeper sources of value that lie behind these judgements, and whose sources are found in our moral motivations. For the writers in this book, the predominant sources of such moral motivations are found in the passions. Therefore, the relationship between personhood and the passions, more specifically between passions and the judgements of agency undertaken by persons, is central to the overall account. The agency-freedom of persons takes place in societies, societies governed by conventional rules of justice that have developed over time. Therefore, and because of this cognate concern with the internal as well as external dimensions of individual agency, there is an analogy between the quality of agency undertaken by citizens and the quality of agency undertaken by individuals. Good men and good citizens combine in this narrative, which is why the account of the propriety of liberty reveals a quite clearly moralized conception of freedom. Indeed, although technically separable, the judgements of the rightness or wrongness of actions for Smith seem to be the basis for his account of our capacity to sympathize with action at the same time. Any adequate theory of moral and political judgement must incorporate both propriety and sympathy in Smith's sense, and it seems to me that the spirit (if not always the exact letter) of his own argument is to understand them as interdependent.[2] In this sense, sympathy with the propriety of agency is already always governed by conventional public standards of appropriateness, which receive their general expression in strict understandings of justice or right. This is where the interplay between political liberty and

---

[1] Sen 1985, esp. pp. 203–12; cf. Griffin 1986; Pettit 2001.
[2] Cf. Raphael 2007, esp. pp. 21–25.

the quality of agency is most apparent, and where, it seems to me, that Smith simply expresses more explicitly what had been just as important to Locke and Montesquieu before him, and to Mill and Green after him. Because of this interplay between public and private, or between political liberty and self-regulation, the relationship between persons, passions and judgement structures my discussion of liberty as propriety.

Put simply, for the writers discussed in this book there is a reciprocal relationship between political liberty and individual agency. This means that although what is deemed appropriate or just in one polity might not be so in another, how we should think about questions of justice and liberty could, nevertheless, have universal application. If justice determines the external standard of propriety, individuals are free if they make appropriate judgements about which actions to pursue in the face of conflicting internal and external pressures. In the public realm of action, moreover, these writers continually ask how a free agent must act in order that other agents recognize them as free, so that the quality of their action might in turn be judged. In their various answers, it seems to me, the focus on propriety in action, or the quality of agency, is what determines the judgement of freedom. Political liberty is the freedom accorded to citizens who balance their own private desires with the public requirements of justice and decorum, and citizens who act in accordance with justice and decorum are those who have political liberty. It is a circular argument, but it means that justice is both the standard of propriety and an expression of it, so that political liberty consists in doing what one should do in accordance with shared standards of judgement that are rooted in motivations of passionate individuals. This general application of the term 'propriety' is my own, but is an amalgamation of concerns treated sometimes separately in Smith's analysis in particular. Yet it seems to me to capture something crucial about the ways in which political liberty relates to the quality of agency more generally. In fact, beginning with Locke there is a very clear development of an extant language of self-propriety as independence, moving towards a discussion of rational freedom. I have already noted, in fact, how liberty as propriety typically presents itself as a moralized (and on occasion moralistic) view of freedom. This is unsurprising, however, given that it attempts to reconcile the moral responsibility of the free person with the political responsibility of the free citizen.

In developing this argument, my aim is to justify this focus by showing how political liberty is related to the capacity of an individual to act freely as a person. To do this means that my book is an attempt to write an intellectual history of these ideas over time. Thus, the capacity of an agent to act freely depends on an account of his or her personhood, which in turn (for some more explicitly than others) means a focus on the nature of the will. This view does not collapse into an atomistic conception of liberty, however, where a free person is an individual chooser who resides outside of any social context. Rather the understanding of autonomy or free agency in operation here is always governed by social and political considerations. This context frames the extent to which agents can be judged, and indeed held responsible, for their actions as free persons because the restraints upon their liberty are grounded in the shared understandings of justice that bind citizens together. To revise a classic trope, both good men and good citizens want to act justly, even if part of the reason for this orientation is because acting justly is seen as instrumentally valuable. All persons want to avoid either causing, or correlatively feeling, resentment, because although resentment is the appropriate response to injustice, because of its force it is also a threat to the very fabric of political order.

Free agency is therefore akin to rational action, but this does not mean that it is simply instrumentally rational action. Indeed, it is not clear that one can even talk sensibly of rationality as purely instrumental.[3] Instead, free agency here assumes a conception of rationality that views the justification for action in the choices made by individuals not simply by virtue of their having reasons for acting, nor in their having desires that those reasons express. Instead it is a form of volitionally responsible action. This means that agency-freedom is the capacity to determine what we want to do based on those things we identify with or care about, independently of the actual choices available to us at any one time, and which we can ourselves provide reasons for pursuing.[4] This way of putting the point about volitional and discursive control, which is derived from contemporary philosophy of action, nevertheless captures quite neatly the type of freedom the writers under consideration in this book took to be crucial. More importantly, though, such an argument allows for the fact that one develops a sense of what constitutes appropriate action over time, as one develops as a person and as a citizen in a political society. Volitional capacity requires both internal and external judgement, and it is always located in the wider context of our relationships with others who judge us and who hold us responsible. This situation has manifest consequences for our understanding of the relationship between our status as persons ruled by passions that require regulation and justification, and the degree to which we are politically free. Indeed, this book might well be seen as a limited attempt to provide another historical rendering of those problems of action that contemporary rational choice theory deems

[3] Sen 2002a, esp. p. 4; Raz 2005, pp. 2–28.

[4] Jay-Wallace 2006, esp. pp. 58–62; also Frankfurt 2004, pp. 16f, 26, 39ff, 61, 79ff; see too Mendus 1999, esp. pp. 72ff; Wollheim 1999, pp. 130–35, 212–15.

as central, but intellectually problematic. The question is not just how, but why it might be thought rational for people to act co-operatively with one another without the threat of (illegitimate) coercion.[5] This co-operation could simply result from moral and political identification with general rules of justice and appropriateness, or freedom as convention. What sets the writers in this book apart, perhaps quite obviously, is that the developmental aspect of their arguments often stands in some tension with the conceptual demands of contemporary moral and political philosophy. Its synthesis of persons, passions and judgement, however, encompasses many of the issues at the centre of contemporary accounts of freedom and agency.

Precisely because these writers suggest that political liberty is a form of appropriate or governed conduct, many subsequent critics have wanted to reject it. They claim that such arguments do little more than equate right reason with polite conduct, and in their own terms did little more than allow liberalism to become the ideological lubricant oiling the wheels of a rapacious and unjust modern commercial capitalism. This historical claim in its strong forms seems to me only to be justified through a partial reading of the texts, for these are texts which actually provide deep-seated and profoundly serious engagements with the paradoxes of political liberty in modern society. The criticism also neglects the extent to which the writers under consideration understood liberty to be progressive, or developmental, not fixed or teleological. What this book tries to show is that political liberty, as it came to be thought of through this focus on propriety, goes beyond the standard accounts of modern liberalism provided by most studies of political ideologies. Put bluntly, contemporary liberalism often seems to misunderstand its intellectual history.

Equally, and as already implied, there are those who reject or who have rejected this way of thinking precisely because of its attempt to relate individual moral agency and general theories of politics in defence of a moralized conception of freedom. It is on this basis that contemporary political philosophy, particularly that underpinning recent discussions of liberal and republican conceptions of freedom, often turns away from these writers.[6] Nevertheless, I hope to show that there is nothing necessarily debilitating about a moralized conception of freedom in the terms outlined by the writers discussed here. More polemically, perhaps, it might be argued that in their focus on the relationship between passions, judgements and individual action, rather than simply the range of conjunctively possible actions available to an agent at a particular time, these writers offer a much richer analysis of freedom than that found in

[5] Hollis 1998, esp. pp. 54–60, 160–63; cf. Gray 2000, ch. 4; Tuck 2008.
[6] Maynor and Laborde 2008, esp. chs. 2–5.

contemporary analytical political theory. A related aim of this book is to show how polarized contemporary debates between liberalism and republicanism have led to a rather bizarre presentation of various writers as theorists of, variously, negative, positive, republican or, on occasion neo-Roman conceptions of liberty. In reconciling theories of agency with theories of politics, the arguments examined in this book all clearly sought to transcend such oppositions, for they encompass elements of all of these analytically separate categories. However, this does not automatically mean that they clearly present some kind of synthesis of liberal republicanism either.[7] Rather, if the study of political thought and intellectual history can show the limitations of our contemporary political and philosophical thinking about liberty through the use of these shared traditions themselves, then perhaps it will provide resources for those who wish to develop still further arguments about the politics of agency. It might also show the value of historical reflection to the otherwise abstract arguments about reasoning and judgement prevalent in most of the contemporary philosophy of rational action, and to the relationship between reasons, judgements and agency.

The Self at Liberty

As I have said, arguments about freedom covered by these writers typically refer to the idea that agency is motivated by passion, that the passions are natural but potentially irrational, and only with their control or volitional regulation (very few writers sought their complete extirpation) could one talk about individual freedom of action. This view relates in two ways to the third element of my subtitle, judgement. First, passions are not just more or less active or passive states determined by our reactions to particular objects, although of course they are these. Fundamental to the argument outlined in this book is the classically inspired idea that our passions also express particular value judgements by prompting our reactions in the first place. The argument does not go so far, though, as to claim that judgements are literally expressive of our passions. Various contemporary writers also reject strongly expressivist accounts of the emotions, but there are in fact many ways in which the writers considered here could be aligned with current discussions of the emotions.[8] This is because the issue of how our passions are caused, manipulated, controlled and shaped is central to them all. Second, and in related fash-

---

[7] Cf. Kalyvas and Katznelson 2008; Sullivan 2004.

[8] Strawson 1968, pp. 71–96; cf. Jay-Wallace 1994, esp. pp. 74–83. See too James 1983, esp. p. 170.

ion, the connections between personhood and judgement are structured around an awareness of how the passions actually constitute something like a narrative about a life. They inform the presentation of self that develops in and through time, as well as underpinning the sort of 'civil inattention' we expect in the public sphere. It is, in other words, a continual project that might be construed in broad terms as self-fashioning.[9] These sorts of questions remain central to our own reflections on the nature of individual and political judgement as well, and in particular their relationship to the passions.[10]

There has been a marked increase over recent years in the production of studies attempting to chart, in various ways, the origins, sources, or making of the modern self, and of studies devoted to the importance of the passions in classical, medieval and early-modern history and philosophy. Whether inspired by the search for the particular 'technologies' of selfhood, or in seeking to highlight conceptual innovations in the nature of modern, as opposed to pre-modern, selfhood, there has been little explicit discussion of the relationship between liberty and selfhood in the terms that concern me within the history of modern political thought.[11] Put another way, the genealogy that I shall present is a variation on the theme made famous by Albert Hirschman, and latterly reinterpreted by many historians of self-interest and natural jurisprudence, about a movement from the passions to interests.[12] It may also, as a genealogy, have implications for those who have taken up the academic challenge laid down by Robert Nozick, to explore the conceptual ambiguities of self-ownership and its origins in Locke.[13]

Here, most would probably agree with Gerry Cohen when he states that theories of self-ownership thus understood do not and cannot refer to metaphysical claims about the ownership of a self, but rather refer to bodily integrity and freedom from the requirement to provide service to others. One implication of what I try to show in this book is that if one were to look to Locke for a defence of self-ownership, it is precisely a metaphysical claim about the capacity of persons to have something like ownership of a self that one would find. This view, apart from any other claims about the usefulness or otherwise of the very idea of self-ownership, is partly why his thought remains perplexing for contempo-

[9] See Nussbaum 2000, pp. 27–30, 80–84; cf. Goldie 2000, esp. pp. 72ff, 92ff, 125, 130, 133; Goffman 1959; Geuss 2001, pp. 13ff.

[10] Sabl 2002, esp. pp. 299–325; Beiner 1983, esp. pp. 135–44; Thompson 2005, esp. chs. 9–10; Urbinati 2006, esp. pp. 115–19; Philp 2007, pp. 106f; see too Weber 1994, esp. p. 362; Krause 2008.

[11] Though see Foucault 1986, esp. pp. 43–67, 90–95.

[12] Hirschman 1977; Force 2004.

[13] Nozick 1974.

rary political theory and why a little more is said about it in the coda to the book, chapter 6.[14] In cases such as these, contemporary political theory once more often seems to neglect the richness of its own intellectual history.

This is a book, then, which aims to provide a modest reminder of the richness of that intellectual history by focusing particularly on the idea of liberty as propriety. But because my concerns lie with what well-known writers do with their arguments about persons, passions and political judgement when they present political liberty as a form of propriety, something should be said about how this view of liberty relates to more recent historical reflection on the idea of freedom. In fact, recent historical engagement with the question of how freedom and the self are related has yielded significant rewards for earlier periods as well as being suggestive for later discussions.[15] My concern is therefore less with the rise of a distinctively modern self in terms of an increased focus on interiority and self-cultivation.[16] The book would be even longer and less self-contained had the modern self and its attendant sources been my subject.[17] What I am more interested in is how the intellectual history of political thinking in the period covered here might, on its own terms, challenge the ways in which conventional and contemporary arguments about liberty have come to be understood and applied. One of the ironies of this focus, however, is that my narrative of persons, passions, judgement and liberty quite closely tracks the direction in which some more recent republican political theory is moving.[18]

In contemporary debates about liberty, a principal focus has been the idea that freedom is best understood as non-domination, or as independence from arbitrary power. The normative trump card in this claim is that freedom becomes both a form of anti-power and a theory of responsible action. In its philosophical presentation, as well as in certain historical debates, the so-called unfreedom of a person (paradigmatically a slave) results from the person's being under the arbitrary will or power of another. From this it follows that even if the slave has the most benevolent of masters, there is no way that he or she could be said to be free. Even the potential rather than the actual exercise of the master's power is enough to negate any claim by the slave to having the status of a free

[14] Cohen 1995, pp. 68f and n. 4, 211, 236f.

[15] James 1997; Sorabji 1999; cf. Nussbaum 2001. See too Williams 1993, esp. pp. 81–85, 89ff, 219–23; cf. Dodds 1963, esp. pp. 35ff.

[16] Berlin 2001; cf. Taylor 1996; Wahrman 2004.

[17] Seigel 2005; see too Martin and Barresi 2005; cf. Sorabji 2006.

[18] Pettit 1997, p. 41; 2001, esp. pp. 102f, 132–44, 152. For an acute but sympathetic critique, see Markell 2008, esp. pp. 16–24; cf. Waldron 2007, esp. pp. 155, 158f.

person.[19] One can still have many liberties or freedoms under such a regime, and indeed one might never in fact be interfered with, but one cannot be said to be free or at liberty according to this republican vision. Contemporary 'pure negative' liberty theorists reject this argument in favour of focusing on the range of actions conjunctively available to an agent at any moment. By so doing, they claim that liberalism can incorporate the republican worries about slavishness, servility and self-censorship that are said to decrease freedom even in the absence of direct interference. This is because it already recognizes that the options available to the slave are clearly fewer because of this perceived need to monitor action in light of status. The slave may therefore be more or less free at particular moments, or time slices.

The republican counter is simply that this response fails to recognize the absolute character of the relationship between freedom and status. For republicanism, the slave can never be free, and that is that. Nevertheless, whether or not either of these branches of political theory is right to suggest that what one misses, the other already sees, or that what one sees is irrelevant to thinking about freedom, all my own account claims is that the framework of liberty as propriety already contains much of that which is considered distinctive within both republicanism and contemporary liberalism thus outlined. Because of this fullness, it offers many of the resources needed to present an argument about freedom as the capacity to be held responsible for one's actions within a well-ordered polity. It similarly reflects upon the corrupting and choice-reducing effects of conformity, arbitrary power and inequality in terms of the moral sentiments. Indeed, it also attempts to reconcile a focus on liberty with a consideration of the background assumptions of what is valued in a polity, such as justice or property rights, which many accounts of freedom often either simply assume or in fact stand opposed to.[20]

LIBERTY AND POLITICAL THEORY

Many of the writers treated in these pages have been allocated central positions in histories of modern liberalism, even though the avowedly liberal type of freedom they are most-often taken to express rather misses the point that unites them all. This point is a concern with the relationship between the nature of persons and the quality of agency, or between the passions that both cause and constrain our liberty and action, and

[19] See Skinner 2002, esp. pp. 238–47, 255ff, 264; cf. Skinner 1997, pp. 22, 54ff; Skinner 2008, ch. 1; cf. Nelson 2005, esp. pp. 64–67.
[20] Waldron 2007, pp. 152f.

which also affect our judgement. Current discussions, whether historical or normative, are still dominated by what are now quite conventional historiographic and philosophical assumptions. Building on the brief outline of liberalism and republicanism in the previous section, one could say that for most contemporary writers the concept of liberty is typically defined in one of three distinct ways. As a negative proposition, one might be said to be free in the absence of some form of impediment or of coercion, particularly of the will.[21] By contrast (and if it is to be coherent), a positive conception of liberty claims that true freedom is a quest for rational control over the will in the name of perfectibility, or the realization of an inner essence.[22]

Isaiah Berlin of course famously rejected the utility of this positive understanding of liberty, seeing it in the historical context of his own lecture as a prelude to totalitarianism.[23] His account did at least present positive liberty as a distinctive concept in its own right, a claim that has had many detractors but some persuasive defenders. And at first glance, if there were a connection to the idea of liberty as a form of propriety and contemporary accounts of liberty, it would seem to be most intimately related to positive freedom thus understood. However, such connections are not quite so clear. Freedom as a form of propriety requires neither positive self-realization nor the positing of some inner essence, even if it demands self-regulation that is to some degree difficult or unnatural. Indeed, the reasons for its escaping such requirements are in large part due to the conventional and modest ends that most of the writers discussed in this book sought to attain, in terms of outlining the shared civil liberties of citizens in a polity. These writers are therefore also distant from the plausible criticism levelled at contemporary accounts of freedom, which are often held to obfuscate a difficult, but centrally important, political question. That question is one of how and when we might really know (and by implication adequately measure) whether someone is actually more or less free.[24] It is true that this is not a question these writers really try to answer directly, except in the most general historical-sociological terms, and those terms largely have to do with a now somewhat hackneyed and clichéd understanding of European distinctiveness in contrast to Eastern despotism or New World primitivism.

Another, different attempt to discern something approaching a third concept of liberty has also been adumbrated. This is slightly different from the variant of negative freedom outlined by republican writers al-

[21] Berlin 1988, esp. p. 121.
[22] Baldwin 1984, pp. 125–42.
[23] Riley 2001, pp. 283–95; cf. Kelly 2002, pp. 29–45.
[24] Steiner 1974–75, pp. 33–50.

ready mentioned, for whom freedom is the absence of dependence or arbitrary power. Instead, in recent writing about Adam Smith and Immanuel Kant in particular, the idea of liberty has been associated principally with the capacity of agents to acquire and implement good judgement, based on their effective capacity to reason well about the situation they find themselves in.[25] A similarly normative argument about John Locke has been made in terms of seeing liberty in his work as an attempt to bolster rational deliberation under conditions of both personal and political uncertainty. Still further scholarship has been devoted to uncovering the scaffolding that supports a normative theory of rational care for the self and others in terms of sympathy and empathy between persons.[26] These considerations begin to get closer to the type of liberty that is uncovered in this book, showing that a variety of intellectual sources lie behind arguments about normativity and freedom addressed by the propriety of liberty.[27]

One might counter that none of this sounds much like an ideal of freedom, particularly if by freedom is understood autonomy, power, desire or authenticity. Indeed, the writers in this book are often presented as focusing precisely on the regulation of autonomy as an ideal, and as such are held up as exponents of what might be thought of as a self-policing and hence conservative concept of negative liberty.[28] In response, these writers clearly think that political liberty is both an 'opportunity' and an 'exercise' concept, but they go further to investigate what sorts of constraints count as legitimate limitations on freedom, and what sorts of possibilities might be expressive of liberty.[29] To this end, they consider the quality of agency in terms of an agent's fitness to be held responsible, and then according to shared moral understandings or judgements rooted in conventional justice. Their arguments in fact synthesize claims about liberty with discussions of autonomy, desire, power and authenticity all at the same time.[30] Of course, in saying this, one might simply want to conclude with the response presented most powerfully by MacCallum, where the liberty of an agent is always said to be of a triadic character. That is to say that freedom is always to be understood as the liberty *of* an agent, *from* someone or something else, *to* do something.[31] What is of interest thereafter, however, is the question of who constitutes an agent, what the nature and type of restraint agents may be subject to is, what the ends sought

---

[25] Fleischacker 1999, pp. 151f.
[26] Yaffe 1999; Darwall 2002, esp. ch. 3.
[27] Pocock 2003; cf. Nelson 2004.
[28] Geuss 2005, esp. pp. 71ff, 77.
[29] Taylor 1979, esp. pp. 180–83; cf. Carter 1999, pp. 153–56.
[30] Cf. Geuss 2005, pp. 15f.
[31] MacCallum 1972, pp. 174–93.

are, and how the quality of their agency is understood. If this book is at all correct, then one major understanding of these relationships in the intellectual history of modern political theory could be considered under the heading of propriety. This understanding would at least allow us to get beyond the historically unrealistic positioning of thinkers like Hobbes and Rousseau within the traditional rubric of negative and positive freedom, to understand better the complexities of the natural law tradition, and perhaps even to banish the dichotomy completely.[32]

STRUCTURE

Given these claims, my story begins with the figure of John Locke. His account is of a freedom that is both more than negative, and less than positive, freedom as traditionally understood. It is freedom as appropriate conduct within the framework of justice understood ideally as natural law, and conventionally as an artifice of human construction. His account of political liberty as freedom from tyrannical government and arbitrary power, individual slavery and coercion is well known to generations of political theorists. But when we explore the relationship between his conception of propriety, which for Locke means a mixture of conventional use (particularly in language), appropriation and ownership in common, but which also connotes ideas of dignity, justice and right, the Lockean view of liberty becomes more complex. My first chapter illustrates in more detail what this means, and suggests that his account of liberty is inextricably linked with his understanding of the quality of responsible agency. Part of my concern is with aspects of Locke's political theory that have usually been approached through study of the *Two Treatises of Government*, but which can better be seen from the slightly different angle of vision provided by *An Essay concerning Human Understanding*. One aim here is to show how the two projects can be reconciled by focusing on liberty and responsible action.

There is also, as is well known, a theological foundation to Locke's work, which is discussed in chapter 1 and which helps to explain part of his interest in translating several of the major essays of the seventeenth-century French Jansenist Pierre Nicole. Nicole's ideas had an important effect on the nature of Enlightenment and even late-modern political thought.[33] His concern with the relationship between self-love, natural

---

[32] Berlin 1988, pp. 123–54, esp. pp. 146, 152ff; cf. p. 124; for practical illustrations of the historical anomalies in Berlin's analysis, see the accounts of various scholars in Tuck 1999, pp. 197–207; cf. Hochstrasser 1993, pp. 289–308.

[33] Hundert 1994; cf. Schneewind 1998, esp. pp. 273, 275–79, 326ff, 390.

law and political judgement certainly also had a profound impact upon Locke's intellectual development. This means that Locke's account of liberty needs to be considered in terms not only of the freedom of the will from coercion, but also in terms of the relationship of the will to the causes of action and to judgements about those actions and their appropriateness. Such concerns thereby help to locate Locke's arguments about the will and human freedom within classical questions of judgement, self-cultivation and self-propriety, all of which are fundamental to the idea of what it means to be a responsible agent in a political society. They also locate him at the foundation of a particular development in thinking about liberty that is both important historically, and which has powerful connections to contemporary theories of agency and rationality.

The second chapter takes up these themes by way of a detailed consideration of the political thought of Montesquieu, focusing on the ways in which he relates the question of agency to theories of politics. Like Locke, whom he is often paired with in histories of liberalism, he was an adversary of the perceived wisdom (if not always the reality) of contemporary Hobbism. He argued against the idea of natural man's lack of sociability, and of the state of nature as a state of war. His complex relationship to Hobbes's political ideas explains the cast of part of his argument about variations in liberty between different peoples, discussions that would of course have important consequences for the ways in which Rousseau, among others, would come to terms with his intellectual heritage. According to Rousseau, those like Grotius (whom he termed the 'master of all the savants' in the never to be established discipline of 'true political theory') were ultimately inferior to Montesquieu. For Montesquieu was the 'creator' of the 'grand and useless' science of politics, and someone who helped Rousseau think through aspects of his own tangled relationship with Diderot and Hobbism.[34] Yet apart from providing a fruitful series of explicitly political arguments with which Rousseau would engage, Montesquieu also outlined an account of the relationship between the passions and action. It mirrored in important respects the Platonic analogy between the city and the soul, but more obviously developed an Aristotelian-inflected argument about the relationship between justice and agency. His discussion of passion and action was also given a peculiarly French colouring through his engagement with, and Stoic-inspired critique of, the classic account of the passions of the soul provided by Descartes. These elements of Montesquieu's political theory of liberty as

[34] Rousseau 1969, vol. 4, p. 836; Diderot 1779, p. 589; see too Wokler 1975, pp. 55–111.

propriety are less often discussed than they should be, so they are given adequate space in my own treatment.

Montesquieu's work also dovetailed with debates about the relationship between judgement and taste, which highlights again the general concern amongst the theorists of liberty as propriety with the relationship between history and normativity, or how rational agency can be understood historically and contextually. This concern came through as much in his thoughts on taste and aesthetics as it did in his engagement with a well-established tradition of natural jurisprudence. It was, moreover, in his discussion of the general 'spirit' of the laws, in which he included such factors as climate, religion, and politics, that Montesquieu provided a profound addition to modern natural law theory and to contemporary French scholarship, particularly the work of the Jansenist Jean Domat.[35] And although Domat is only cited once directly in Montesquieu's works, he is a major background presence in Montesquieu's similarly styled treatise. Montesquieu's caution in avoiding explicit reference to Jansenist ideas in the context of early eighteenth-century France is completely understandable.[36] What is of still more interest in this chapter, however, is Montesquieu's account of the development of the passions and their specific expressions. It offers a crucial if still relatively underexplored foundation to his thinking about the psychology and the politics of agency, which is designed to foster moderation as the basis of freedom. In this chapter, moderation is a direct analogue for propriety.

In his discussion of the passions, Montesquieu was drawn into a theoretical and historical narrative concerning the nature of self-love, in an attempt to come to terms with the legacy of Augustinian attacks on human sociability and weakness. Alongside this topic, Montesquieu also developed a keen interest in the problems of contingency and chance in modern political thought, problems that had also begun to be developed in the discussions of writers such as Nicole and his fellow Jansenist Antoine Arnauld, and which were applied in contexts as diverse as gambling and elections. They bore heavily on the subsequent development of thinking about the art and nature of statecraft, which Montesquieu took over and adapted. His discussion was clearly also informed by contemporary criticisms of universal monarchy in general and the rule of Louis XIV in particular. In the context of the Seven Years' War in mid-eighteenth-century Europe, Montesquieu developed a balance sheet of the decline of Rome and the problems of universal monarchy that would set the tone for sub-

---

[35] Domat 1722, esp. vol. 1, ch. 11.
[36] Cf. Montesquieu 1964a, p. 811; in general, Doyle 2000; Jones 2006, esp. pp. 21ff.

sequent discussion. In this effort he was, moreover, part of the crucially important revival of Tacitus in the eighteenth century.[37]

These frameworks all informed Montesquieu's thoughts on the relationship between the state and the economy, and most centrally the important debates about luxury that developed within its contours and which many others have focused on. For that reason this book only deals with these issues where they can most clearly be related to liberty as propriety.[38] This orientation moves the discussion some way towards conceiving liberty as rational self-deliberation and tempered or responsible agency. The relationship between liberty and the cultivation of a sense of personhood or personality that can learn how to be free and act according to inner balance and harmony, or more classically *aequabilitas*, is nevertheless central to both. Indeed, this seems to be part of a broader and quite traditional concern to reconcile the spheres of the good and the useful, or *honestum* and *utile*, through the promotion of decorum or tranquillity at the level of the individual as well as the state, or legislator.[39]

Propriety therefore has a twofold sense. One meaning concerns something like the quality of agency that one owns oneself, or that one can be held responsible for as an autonomous agent. It is underpinned by the idea that only a certain type of agency, predicated upon a discrete conception of personhood, can do the work required by an individual who is said to be at liberty to act, and hence able to deliberate about how to act appropriately. Secondly, propriety refers to shared or intersubjective judgements about the propriety of particular actions, rooted in a common conception of justice. As with Locke's account, for Montesquieu a recognition of the fragility of common life and trust between individuals leads him to focus on the cognate judgements of propriety, namely dignity and right or just conduct, that structure his analysis of liberty. Putting judgement first, as it were, underscores much of what Montesquieu and the other writers in this tradition are doing: they are explicitly challenging the idea of a sharp dichotomy between reason and the passions, and typically favouring in fact the latter over the former.

Chapter 3 discusses the work of Adam Smith, focusing on his account of the interrelationship between liberty and agency, propriety and judgement, and the passions that motivate our actions. It was through Scottish writers more generally that a discussion of the sources of human motivation in terms of sympathy and benevolence came to the forefront, and this was in no small measure a result of the pervasive influence of Montesquieu and other French theorists of sentiments, which ran along-

[37] Burke 1991, pp. 479–98.
[38] Hont 2006, pp. 379–418.
[39] Moore 2002, pp. 365–86.

side a domestic tradition of thinking about moral sense.[40] In this regard, however, the very limited discussions of one figure who might have been expected to receive significant treatment in this book should be noted. My reflections on David Hume are only fleeting and partial, even though his discussion of the 'noble resentment' that underscores justice provides some of the relevant intellectual foundations to the narrative. For it is Adam Smith who I think offers a more profound and relevant discussion of the relationship between the passions and judgement in the development of a complicated theory where propriety underscores justice, and where justice is the foundation of political liberty. Indeed, although Hume has been more historically significant as a moral philosopher, it is in the work of Smith that we find most explicitly the idea of acting or agency analysed according to the double meaning of propriety. Indeed, Smith is perhaps the ideal exemplar of the propriety of liberty as agency-freedom, for he is quite clear about the primacy of the individual person or agent in political analysis, and he founds his entire theory of judgement and jurisprudence upon propriety and sympathy.

While it has long been clear that the work of Locke and Montesquieu developed in part through engagement with French debates about the passions and political judgement, many scholars have incorporated these questions into their discussions of natural jurisprudence in general, and particularly upon its theoretical narratives about the stages of human progress from barbarism to civility. Smith too would elaborate this succession in developing his own four-stage theory of civilization and progress.[41] As with my discussion of Locke and Montesquieu, however, I shall develop some of the implications suggested by such scholarship, but only to the extent that it informs Smith's theory of politics in relating liberty to propriety. In this context, the more ambivalent tenor of Smith's arguments about trade, commerce, ambition and particularly empire are brought to the forefront. For although he recognizes the positive interrelationship between ambition and emulation, the pathological distortion of our moral sentiments that accompanies such developments receives equal consideration in his work. More generally still, how individuals come to appropriate their sentiments and to judge the calibre of their actions and interactions with others is critical to the argument expounded in this book, and it is at the heart of Smith's project.[42] Therefore the complex connections between sympathy, the passions, and propriety are variously outlined in this chapter, and an argument put forward to the

[40] For example Pouilly 1766, esp. pp. 233ff; on whom, see Golden 1951; Smith 1976, *TMS*, p. 14.

[41] Hont 2005, esp. chs. 1, 5.

[42] Cf. Griswold 1999; Rothschild 2001.

effect that Smith defends a notion of 'persuasive mediocrity', in his assessment of the propriety of free agency. It is a corollary of what he called the system of natural liberty, and is an expression of our natural desire to persuade, emulate and indeed to dominate.

The next part of the book begins with an assessment of the relationship between character and civilization, and takes my narrative well into the nineteenth century. Chapters 4 and 5 focus on two giants of the political theory of modern liberalism. Chapter 4 explores the political thought of John Stuart Mill, suggesting that he developed an argument about liberty as a property of cultivated character or personhood, within a framework governed by assumptions about the development of modern civilization and the centrality of justice. This is an extension not only of the British and French contexts out of which his work developed, but also of the classically Greek (and occasionally Roman) historical political theories that he brought to bear on contemporary arguments about politics and society. For Mill, the relationship between propriety and freedom is perhaps best explained by focusing on propriety as the property of a cultivated individual who can act appropriately both in public and in private. He seems to suggest that the quality of such agency can be explored through the internal sanctions that individuals place upon themselves, and which then go on to buttress the external sanctions applied to responsible agents by shared norms of justice. Through an exploration of some of the various ways in which Mill's arguments develop, I then try to press home the connections, both historical and conceptual, that link Mill to the genealogy outlined in the first half of the book. Mill presents a synthesis of the contested legacies of eighteenth- and nineteenth-century political thinking in an original manner, whilst he simultaneously tries to reorient discussions of liberty towards the cultivation of character through processes of education, civic engagement and political reform. Yet even though liberty is an inherent property or capacity of persons according to Mill's arguments, how it is capable of being actualized in a modern world (in particular by those he takes to be 'civilized' peoples) is his central problem. Like many others, he wondered how freedom could be upheld in a world subject to the overbearing despotism of custom and bureaucratic capitalism on the one hand, and an Atlantic world engaged in colonial enterprises on the other.

It is normally suggested that Mill's discussion of liberty is a negative theory of freedom, returning us to the starting point of this introduction. Conversely, one of the most apposite exponents of a theory of true or positive freedom is T. H. Green. What I wish to argue in the fifth chapter is that there is rather more to the story than this bipolarity. Green certainly does suggest, albeit in idealist rather than jurisprudential language, that freedom is an inherent property of personhood capable of being moulded and directed by the passions. He further suggests that this idea of self-realization is only possible under properly defined external (or legally codified), and internally robust, conditions of self-development. Whether or not the idea of liberty as self-realization is analytically coherent in its own terms, Green's position as the concluding figure in this book is doubly appropriate, because the idea of freedom as a property of personhood correctly understood locates Green directly in the intellectual lineage traced here. A nineteenth-century interpreter of the English Revolution, and a lecturer on the logic of Mill and Kant and the moralists of the eighteenth century, he combines elements of everything discussed in this book. Furthermore, Green's early thought is especially interesting, for not only does he present a particular theory of freedom that seems to be different, but which is in fact quite similar in fundamentals to those outlined by other writers in this book, he also develops a novel thesis about the prerequisites for the realization of true human freedom that is not wholly conjectural, and which offers both an historical and indeed historicist argument for the origins of modern liberty. That the anterior requirement for real or true freedom is the negative liberty of legal or constitutional freedom is clear. So too is the fact that behind all of this theory one must have an account of freedom as the capacity of willing agents to deliberate between particular courses of action they might or might not choose. A crucial further question for Green concerned the real historical origins of this idea, and my argument suggests that his answer is to be found in his relatively little focused-upon lectures on the English Revolution. Delivered in 1867, the year of the third Reform Act in England, these lectures help to structure his account of freedom and provide it with a distinctive focus. Moreover, in taking the discussion back to the English Commonwealth, the book returns at least in part to moral, political and theological debates with which Locke, the starting point of the study, was closely engaged.

A natural conclusion of the Reformation, Green claimed that the English Commonwealth saw English exceptionalism and specifically English liberty develop most clearly in opposition to continental absolutism. If this reaction makes for the distinctive character of modern Britain, according to Green, then by exploring the political theory of liberty he provides in the context of contemporary debates about freedom and history in mid-Victorian England, a slightly different picture of his political thinking emerges. It is one at least as rich as, and hopefully more satisfying than, those interpretations that focus exclusively on the excavation of his posthumously published lectures on obligation and ethics. For not only does the discussion return the story to the seventeenth century in particular, it also pays attention to claims made before Green became Green, so to speak, the figure better known to generations of political theorists precisely for his lectures on obligation and liberal legislation. The early Green reconciles many of the different claims about liberty and propriety in ways that never quite again receive this level of synthesis, and that is why the book ends with him. By way of conclusion, a short and final coda to the book offers some thoughts on the ways in which the idea of liberty as propriety relates to, and might also have implications for, particular issues in contemporary political theory. These concern self-ownership, the relationship between personhood, character and responsibility, and finally, the idea of the state as a person in its own right.

The overall structure of the book is designed to highlight both the chronological and the thematic development of a particular way of thinking about liberty from Locke to Green. It is an attempt to present an historically sensitive genealogy of an idea of liberty as propriety, predominantly in British political thought, where liberty was understood as the property of a person who can, in the double sense of the term 'propriety', both act appropriately and govern his or her own conduct according to standards of propriety and justice. Clearly such questions about the nature and extent of individual liberty, the sense of justice, of responsible agency and political judgement, remain crucial to our own age. Considerations of ownership and control in an era of increasing global economic and political instability, alongside questions of intellectual conformism and dependence, continue to structure much of our public political discourse. Equally, the relationship between the passions that guide us and our ability to subject them to internal and external control remains central to much contemporary political thought and action. Reflection on the propriety of liberty seems in part to cover all of these concerns, but although it remains close to various contemporary concerns, it also has a deep and complex history. It is to this history that my discussion now turns.

CHAPTER ONE

'That glorious fabrick of liberty': John Locke, the Propriety of Liberty and the Quality of Responsible Agency

My story begins with a problem, because I want to make two claims that might well be seen as contradictory. The first is that John Locke's political theory of liberty is based on an idea of propriety, or appropriate agency, which is itself underpinned by his analysis of justice as an expression of natural law. On its own this is perhaps not too problematic an assertion, given Locke's celebrated argument that one achieves freedom as a person upon reaching a 'State of Maturity'. Only then can one properly appreciate the true extent of the law, and how far it appropriately limits your actions and increases your freedom, because free action is regulated agency. Maturity is foundational to responsible and free action under law, because law extends freedom by removing arbitrary power and upholding an impartial administration of justice in the interests of the '*Peace, Safety* and *publick good* of the People'.[1] I shall argue that this analysis of liberty had an important impact on a major strand of the subsequent development of modern political theory. This second claim, however, comes with some difficulties attached. For it is an exceptionally complicated task to be clear about the legacy of Locke's political ideas. In one sense, modern liberalism has adopted the superstructure of Locke's political theory, but rejected its basis in natural law and theology. The implication is clear. It looks rather like the historical Locke is someone who cannot speak to the needs of a modern and secular political theory unless perhaps we focus on the contingent character of political trust that he addresses.[2] That Locke's work exhibits a tension between human freedom and an apparently determinate natural law was not a problem that escaped him. But this simply amplifies the quandary facing sympathetic readers of Locke who perhaps like the politics but have no taste for the theology. This is because it was a quandary that Locke found impossible to navigate both intellectually and practically. His own anguish can be seen in a relatively late letter written to William Molyneux, where he claimed that due to

[1] Locke 1988, II, §§ 59, 57, 131, pp. 307, 306, 353.
[2] Dunn 1969, p. 267; Dunn 1990, esp. pp. 34–37, 41ff.

the 'weakness of my understanding', he simultaneously held that 'there is omnipotence and omniscience in God, our maker, and I cannot have a clearer perception of anything, than that I am free; yet I cannot make freedom in man consistent with omnipotence and omniscience in God, though I am as fully persuaded of both, as of any truths I most firmly assent to'. He had, he continued, 'long since given off the consideration of that question, resolving all into this short conclusion; that if it be possible for God to make a free agent, then man is free, though I see not the way of it'.[3] In fact Locke wrote to his father much earlier that he had also 'long since learnd not to rely on men', but still wondered if he could differentiate between 'the goblins of warre and bloud' all around, and recognize instead 'that glorious fabrick of liberty and happinesse' when it appeared.[4] My aim is to explore the ramifications of these tensions and the way they inform Locke's defence of political liberty. This means that my focus is quite specific.

PROPRIETY, PRUDENCE AND INTERPRETATION

The claim about weakness of understanding is a clue to the puzzle of how to think about the relationship between liberty and morality in Locke's work, or so I shall suggest. This is because although morality is, for Locke, in theory rationally demonstrable, in practice it is often very far from clear and something we only learn how to orient ourselves towards as we cultivate ourselves as persons over the course of a lifetime.[5] The twin claims he wished to uphold ultimately forced Locke to conclude that the best life was a life led in pursuit of Christian redemption, and that only those who received grace through revelation, rather than reason, could be certain of salvation. The move was made towards the end of his life, when he began to focus explicitly on the character of revealed religion and the figure of Christ as an exemplar. However, even at that late stage he could still recognize the truth of human uncertainty in judgement and action. Because of this intellectual as well as practical fragility, Locke defended a form of civil prudence, at the levels both of the individual and of the state, that could simultaneously erect and defend a system of government whose function was to promote the ends of man as laid down by the God of Creation, and in a manner as close to conformity as possible with the requirements of justice. Neither philosophy nor a science

[3] Locke, Letter 1592, to William Molyneux, January 26, 1693, in Locke 1976–89, vol. 4, pp. 623–28, at pp. 625ff; discussed in Dunn 1969, p. 193.
[4] Locke, Letter 59, to Locke, sen., June 22, 1659, in Locke 2002, pp. 6f.
[5] Locke 1984, I. iii. 1, pp. 65f.

of politics could complete this task on its own, for there is quite literally no way of convincing all the people all of time. As Rousseau would later paraphrase, if the people couldn't be convinced, they could nevertheless be persuaded. Yet only a rare few individuals actually had the time or the inclination to work this reasoning out for themselves. Others needed to be persuaded by arguments that they could not fathom. So Christianity and revealed religion were given the exemplary task of enlightening individuals where rational persuasion alone was insufficient.[6]

The theme of civil prudence was central to the early as well as the later Locke, and can sometimes seem to stand in for the idea of propriety understood as conventional, appropriate or responsible agency. In fact, both his political and his philosophical writings suggest that with civility, prudence and reason, a well-governed life could be the pursuit of 'Industrious and Rational' agents.[7] Indeed, it seems to me that prudence is largely analogous with propriety in Locke's mind, and one can be a free agent on his account only if propriety replaces simple self-interest as the spur to action. Otherwise one is simply an unthinking slave to the passions who cannot be said to act freely, and hence responsibly, in accordance with the requirements of both civil and natural law. In making such claims, Locke drew upon distinctive arguments about the nature of persons as agents, about their capacity to act at liberty and to choose courses of action that reconciled their own happiness to the needs of a community governed by rules of justice, and to pursue self-preservation in line with the duties of natural law. However, the ways in which our judgements could be rationalized, either through philosophy (which was partial), opinion and reputation (which were contingent and contextual), or political authority, all seemed to point away from a universally obliging form of natural law. Hence it was not at all unsurprising that even close friends such as James Tyrrell thought his analysis left one with something ultimately similar to a Hobbist political theory. In 1690, when Locke eventually published the *Essay*, this was still a highly charged claim. Certainly by the time he published *The Reasonableness of Christianity* in 1695, he had rejected the idea of a natural law prior to Christ in favour of a revealed religion. However, this move away from an avowedly Hobbist position only came at the expense of being thought of as too closely aligned (in the eyes of many) with the heterodox and anti-Trinitarian Socinians.[8]

The theological radicalism of Socinian arguments, however, were reconciled by major adherents into a defence of quite conventional natural

[6] Locke 1997k, pp. 319f; also Marshall 2006, pp. 710f.

[7] Locke 1988, II, § 34, p. 291.

[8] Tuck 1990a, pp. 153–71, esp. pp. 162, 163, 165ff. For detail, see Marshall 2000, esp. pp.145–49, 152, 155f, on the Socinian tenor of much of Locke's reading *c.* 1679–82; also

jurisprudential claims about the primacy of self-preservation.[9] To this was added a 'humanitarian' requirement to ameliorate poor social conditions in order to allow all God's creatures to develop their potential as far as possible.[10] In Locke's case, the idea of charity did similar intellectual work.[11] In general, though, his intellectual history is bound up with a series of moves that attempt to pursue the apparently irreconcilable claims of free human agency with divine omnipotence through natural law. His best solution, it seems to me, was to think of human freedom as a form of responsible agency, with the analogue of political liberty as appropriately regulated civic conduct. This is simply another way of saying that he thought of liberty as a form of propriety in action, where propriety refers to the capacity of persons to act freely both as individuals and as citizens under law. In fact, free agents are capable of governing their conduct towards the appropriate ends of civil prudence under law, because their judgements about the role of passionately motivated actions are determined by the standards of justice. As I have already tried to indicate, liberty as propriety here works as something like shorthand for responsible or appropriate agency, governed by the connections between individual persons, passions and judgement in Locke's understanding of political liberty. There is no explicit theory of liberty as propriety in Locke, but although the phrasing is mine, it seems to capture the distinctiveness of his attempt to reconcile the psychology and the politics of free agency.

Thus, while the question of how he passed from the one extreme to the other, from Hobbism to Socinianism, and with what consequences remains a difficult issue, it is clearly one that might have radical implications for how we think about his legacy. This is because the move from the early disquisitions on natural law to a broad Socinianism is oriented around the polestars of the *Essay* and the *Two Treatises*. In this discussion, I would like to suggest that interpreting these texts, and especially the *Essay*, in terms of Locke's focus on the requirements of responsible and free agency, constitutes the best part of what Locke's legacy could still mean for us and what it did mean for his successors. Before proceeding further, though, I should add one caveat. My analysis will not focus on the account of property given seminal formulation in Locke's *Second*

Mortimer 2009, esp. pp. 194–97. On Locke and Tyrell, see Gough 1976, esp. pp. 585ff, 588f, 593.

[9] Tuck 1999, pp. 106f; Grotius 2004, pp. 37, 52; Dunn 1969, pp. 87–95. Cf. Wootton 1989, esp. pp. 44–47.

[10] Kott 1957, esp. pp. 140–43, 214; also Schløsler 1994, pp. 305–8; Nuovo 2000, pp. 190ff.

[11] Locke 1988, I. iv, § 42, p. 170; II, §§ 30, 27, 6, pp. 290f, 287f, 270f; Harris 2000, pp. 68–72, and esp. p. 72 n. 63; also Coleman 2004, pp. 134ff; Boyd 2002, esp. pp. 48–52; Waldron 2002, pp. 177–87; Lamb and Thompson 2009, pp. 229–52.

Treatise. This is partly because it has been the subject of such intense investigation into the dating of the texts and his method of composition.[12] This is particularly so as it pertains to questions of colonialism.[13] Equally, it is because Locke's analysis of the ownership of property and goods, or the holding of dominium over others, remains secondary to the account of liberty as a form of responsible and self-regulating agency that this book is principally concerned with. I shall approach Locke's theory of liberty from a different angle of vision, through a lens that might be helpfully understood as self-propriety. Later, I shall make detailed reference to Locke's account of personhood and the idea of liberty, in order to show the broadly Ciceronian character of his reflections, and to highlight his cognate attempts to reconcile the useful (*utile*) with the moral (*honestum*), which *decorum* is supposed to facilitate. In order to develop this discussion, I shall begin by focusing on what is still a relatively neglected element in Locke's intellectual development, namely his engagement with Pierre Nicole's analysis of civility and the morality of self-interest.

John Locke and Pierre Nicole: Language, Prudence and the Propriety of the Passions

Whilst in France during 1676, Locke translated three of the famous *Essais de Morale* of Pierre Nicole, those on the means of preserving civil peace, on the existence of God, and on the weakness of man.[14] This reading of Nicole would prove central to his analysis of human freedom and responsible agency, and Locke's interest in a Jansenist political thinker who attempted to bring together elements of Thomism with the *politique* Augustinianism of Jansenius among others, is clarified by his reaching of similar conclusions albeit from slightly different premises.[15] Alongside Nicole, Locke understood conventional human opinion as the driving force of individual agency. For Nicole, this conception was a neo-

---

[12] Locke 1686, pp. 315–40; Locke 1720; Goldgar 1995, pp. 119f, 125, 142; cf. Savonius 2004, p. 56 n. 51. See also Dacome, esp. pp. 606–14, 621, 623; Martin and Barresi, pp. 12–29.

[13] See Armitage 2004, esp. pp. 606, 610–16; Arneil 1996, esp. pp. 69, 72f; J. R. Milton 1995, pp. 356–90; cf. Tuck 1999, esp. pp. 103, 166–87; Alexandrowicz 1967, pp. 46ff; Tuck 1979, pp. 59–64, 79, 172f; Tully 1980, esp. pp. 79, 114ff, 118–24; Buckle 1991, p. 190; Farr 1986, pp. 263–90. PRO 30/24/47/3 is the pocket book copy of the *Fundamental Constitutions* with emendations in Locke's hand.

[14] According to Lough 1953, p. 111, Locke bought, through a Mr. Wall, Nicole's *Essay Morale* on Tuesday, September 29, 1676; cf. Lough 1953, p. 202. Nicole 1677 is a contemporary English translation by a 'person of quality'; on the *Essais* in general, see Keohane 1980, pp. 293–303.

[15] See Orcibal 1989, esp. pp. 239, 240 n. 113, 243; cf. Orcibal 1954, pp. 1077–85.

Augustinian recognition of the capacity of pride and self-interest to mimic the duties of charity. Locke's claim, made in his *Essay*, about the reasonable sources of probable knowledge rooted in opinion and probability, similarly suggested a bifurcation between the true laws of morality and the everyday actions of most people. Nicole then attempted to show how public virtue could therefore be manufactured through the wise regulation of private selfishness by a powerful legislator. In turn, Locke's mature analysis also attempted to promote reconciliation between 'self-interest and the Conveniences of this Life', and the ultimate plan of divine morality. In the absence of innate ideas implanted on the minds of men, the most obvious freedom of agency is permitted, according to Locke, to the extent that natural laws can be and are often transgressed.[16] But this fact did not prove the case against Locke's other claim, that with reason as our guide, our moral action could in principle (if not always in practice) be as capable of rational demonstration as mathematical proof.[17] Locke allowed consistently for human error, and for the truly paradoxical capacity of free agents to transgress moral laws, the source of which they sought in human convention but which were in fact expressions of the 'Will and Law of a God, who sees Men in the dark'.[18] Indeed, Locke consistently highlighted the importance of custom, tradition and experience as the forces that lead men to live in accordance with social propriety in his criticisms of Edward Stillingfleet, and which help to discipline the will, aid deliberation and hence make the right or responsible choices.[19] The connection here carried over into Locke's much later distillation of his thoughts on legitimate rule against those like Stillingfleet and George Hickes.[20] But in explaining his understanding of man as a 'dependent intelligent being', Locke took law to be a relationship of dependence between man and God as much as between citizen and sovereign.[21] Nevertheless, the figure of the legislator was of central importance to both Locke and Nicole, and for Nicole, the Prince was there to provide guidance that would mimic the effects, if not the reality, of charity given the opacity of human judgement about the true nature of human dependence.[22] The impartial legislator of Locke's *Second Treatise* certainly recalls this function, with the end of political power being the defence of property, which

[16] Locke 1984, I. iii. 6, pp. 68f.

[17] Locke 1984, IV. xii. 8, p. 643; Locke 1954, I, p. 85; IV, pp. 100–103, 128; Dunn 1969, 87–95.

[18] Locke 1984, I. iii. 5, p. 69.

[19] MS. Locke c. 34, fos. 158–60; Stanton 2007, pp. 143–72; Marshall 1994, pp. 105ff; cf. Yaffe 1999, pp. 23, 79ff.

[20] Stillingfleet 1689, pp. 4, 11, 30; Hickes 1692, p. 22; cf. Hoekstra 2004, pp. 67ff.

[21] Locke 1997n, pp. 328f.

[22] James 1972, esp. pp. 113, 150ff, 156–61; also Parrish 2007, esp. pp. 202f.

is to say a defence of a right to anything in line with the requirements of the Golden Rule laid down by the Creator.[23] In this he seems to have built upon the extant concerns of radical Presbyterian writers who had long discussed the distinction between force and right, and the account is closely aligned with George Lawson's *Politica sacra et civilis*, published around 1660. In a theme analogous to that of this book, the opening of Lawson's study asserted that 'propriety is the ground of power, and power of government; and there are many degrees of propriety, so there are of power'. But there is only 'one supreme and universal power', and 'blessed and eternal God can only challenge as his due'.[24] Lockean property or propriety is an equally capacious category, and as had Lawson, Locke also developed well-known arguments from natural jurisprudence and so-called monarchomach political theories, particularly concerning the original 'negative community' of mankind.[25]

Overlapping contexts governed the common interests of Locke and Nicole, both temporally and intellectually. The religious intolerance of the Restoration, for example, was fuelled by argument over true religion. Whereas St. Augustine was the 'lifeblood of Restoration polemic', the Jansenist problem of grace and salvation clearly motivated Nicole. The problem of human depravity and continental absolutism were therefore central to both Locke and Nicole. Earlier debates that Locke had engaged in over what was termed *adiaphora*, or the question of whether and how human and civil intervention in 'matters indifferent' to the sovereign were justifiable, had actually been a long-running concern in the complex political and theological arguments of the early seventeenth century.[26] Locke had argued these points explicitly in the *First Tract on Government* of 1660 and in debates with Edward Bagshaw. In fact the first edition of Bagshaw's treatise on this matter had suggested that a major presupposition of things indifferent was the 'Outward Circumstances of our Actions: which the Law of God hath left Free and Arbitrary'.[27] Later editions argued that the magistrate '*hath no Power to impose things doubtful and disputable in the Service of God*', and that '*if he doth impose, we cannot lawfully obey him*'.[28] Locke's response, the first of two tracts on

---

[23] Locke 1988, II, §§ 169f, 135, pp. 380ff, 358; cf. Locke 1988, I. 9, § 86, pp. 205f; I. 9, § 92, pp. 209f.

[24] Lawson 1992, p. 8; ch. 1, § 1, p. 15.

[25] Philodemius [pseud.] 1649, pp. 7f, 11, 24–28; for the general context, see Friedeburg 2002, esp. pp. 256–62. Cf. Franklin 1968, pp. 64ff, 67ff; cf. pp. 125f; Waldron 1988, esp. pp. 233–41; Tully 1993, esp. pp. 168f, 98; Brito-Viera 2003, pp. 361–77, on negative community arguments. See also Harrison and Laslett 1971, nos. 1695, 1696, 1697.

[26] Rose 2005, esp. pp. 603, 605f, 612f; Stanton 2006, p. 94.

[27] Bagshaw 1660, p. 2.

[28] Bagshaw 1660a, p. 3. Emphasis in original.

this topic, did not reach a wider audience than those copies he circulated privately. They remained unpublished until the nineteenth century, so they did not have much in the way of real influence on many of the arguments discussed in this book. But what they highlight is the longevity of Locke's ideas about the relationship between toleration and civil or legal authority, and they complicate the view of Locke's transformation from a royalist apologist into the Locke more recognizable to contemporary liberalism. How far he would travel on the issue can be seen in this early, near Erastian demotion of religious to civil authority.[29] A letter written in December 1660 amplifies the connection, repeating a line from the *First Tract* where Locke stated that 'it being sufficient to my purpose that the supreme magistrate of every nation what way soever created, must necessarily have an absolute and arbitrary power over all the indifferent actions of his people'.[30]

In these early writings, he was explicit that there is little talk of polities beyond the 'government of the Jews' in scripture, and the reason for this is that 'God doth nowhere by distinct and particular prescriptions set down rules of government and bounds to the magistrate's authority'.[31] In fact, in a clear presaging of later concerns in the *Essay* over language and polity, in the *First Tract* we find Locke arguing that 'one form of government was not like to fit all people', but that mankind was 'sufficiently instructed in the necessity of laws' through nature.[32] The critique of priestcraft that pervades Locke's political thought places him at the foundation of 'true' Whiggism, while his focus on the importance of education, internal civility (as opposed to external flattery) and virtuous conduct grounds his analysis of civil society.[33] Meanwhile, however, his discussion of toleration some seven years later develops several of these points more concisely. Internal belief is not capable of being coerced by the civil magistrate, because governmental power has to do with external force coupled with right, not internal compulsion of the will. In fact, the understanding itself cannot be subject to external compulsion, it is determined by 'inward persuasion of the mind' not from magisterial

---

[29] Goldie 1993, esp. pp. 216, 219; Rose 2005, p. 619; Cranston 1985, esp. pp. 58–63; Laslett 1988, esp. pp. 70–77.

[30] Locke, Letter 108, to [Gabriel Towerson?] [Pensford or Oxford], December 11, 1660, in Locke 2002, pp. 22–23; Locke 1997, p. 9.

[31] Locke 1997, p. 51.

[32] Locke 1997a, pp. 54–78; cf. Waldron 2002, p. 195.

[33] Locke 1989, §§ 67, 114, 143, 145, pp. 125, 174, 202, 206. For wider discussion, see Goldie 1980a, esp. pp. 208, 214; also Goldie 1980, pp. 516ff, on Locke's purchasing of the popular radical Whig pamphlets surrounding the Allegiance Controversy and the Exclusion crisis, and his location in a part of the 'whiggish left-wing ... insisting that the [Tory] *de facto* case was no part of true whiggism' (p. 516); cf. Peltonen 2005, esp. pp. 400ff.

pressure.[34] A manuscript on civil and ecclesiastical power from 1674 makes essentially the same point, suggesting that although the 'laws of religious society' are 'immutable, not subject to any authority of the society', at the same time 'no external punishment, i.e. deprivation or diminution of the goods of *this* life, belongs to the church'.[35] Locke's later justifications for calculable legislative power underpinned by a common or conventional standard surely have their roots in these early theological debates, but he also changed his mind about things. He opposed both toleration and resistance in the *First Tract*, advocated toleration but not resistance in his early essay on toleration, and finally supported both toleration and resistance when he came to write the bulk of the *Two Treatises* in the early 1680s.[36] By that time, Locke would use a different lesson from political Hebraism about the nature of government. This aimed to show, given the example of Jephtha he rather contradictorily applied, how men would have to give account of themselves to the 'Supream judge of all men' on the 'great Day' of reckoning for actions undertaken in the absence of a judge on earth. But whilst on earth, they could and should trust their own judgement.[37]

Some of this had to do with questions of toleration and the extent of civil government, whilst another side had to do with the relationship between church and state. Statements that the church was a spiritual association which, nevertheless, had both an ancient secular history and a spiritual link to Christ were combined with the temporal and earthly based political argument that the church was also itself a form of commonwealth, or at least a '"state" church bound to the institutions of the realm.' Combined and properly ordered, this idea of something like a confessional *civitas* or ecclesiastical polity, reconciling Roman *imperium* with Christian *sacerdotium*, was central to the pamphlet literature on the relationship between ecclesiology and political thought.[38] When Locke moved from discussion of *adiaphora* towards questions of toleration, then, he had to shift ground more explicitly onto the terrain of those interested in whether conscience was free or not. Here, Locke's most effective opponent, Jonas Proast, effectively recast the Augustinian argument that conscience could (and should) be coerced. Locke agreed that there was a 'true' religion, but he could not countenance coercion to fa-

---

[34] Locke 2006, pp. 270–75, 278–82, 287ff, 293–96, 136ff; cf. Locke 1988, II, §§ 8–9, pp. 272f; §§ 135–42, pp. 357–63; Locke 1968, esp. pp. 99ff, 103–9, 123–31.

[35] Locke 1997d, quotations from pp. 218, 219, emphasis added; cf. Locke 1997b, p. 204.

[36] Marshall 2006, p. 5.

[37] Locke 1988, II, § 21, p. 282; for wider difficulties in Locke's political Hebraism, see Rehfeld 2008, esp. pp. 71, 76, 79.

[38] Prior 2005, pp. 861f, 875; cf. Collinson 1979, pp. 205–29; Questier 1997, pp. 311–29.

cilitate its promotion, in what is an interestingly Hobbesian-sounding argument.[39]

However, Locke could equally never bring himself fully to commit to the apparently Hobbesian resolution, that sovereign authority legitimately curtails judgement; instead he sought the proper limits of sovereign power in freedom of conscience and a general Christian concern with the potential for eternal damnation that would motivate individuals to act responsibly.[40] But if he could not countenance Hobbes's *Leviathan* as a solution, it is certainly clear that the necessity for toleration on the part of a civil magistrate, particularly in terms of the private religious sentiments of citizens that did not affect directly the public pronouncements of the sovereign, are pivots around which both Hobbesian and Lockean politics turn.[41] These concerns with religious persecution (along with the problematic position of James II in the English context) exerted a considerable effect.[42] Although the multi-confessional alliance against James II and Louis XIV was grounded in more than just worries about universal monarchy, Locke would later appear to tie together these concerns in placing the *Two Treatises of Government* under the guise of an appeal to William III as the 'great restorer', a usurper of religious tyranny, a *de facto* ruler and a safeguard against absolutist political rule.[43] He was also to be a break from the Calvinist moral stranglehold on European politics, as Locke's continental reception highlighted.[44] His time in Holland amongst the Huguenot community, and indeed the proximity of certain of his views with the writings of Pierre Bayle, has often been remarked upon in this context (although there is some dispute as to whether they ever actually met).[45] Both interestingly rejected Hobbes publicly, but differed over the possibility of a society of virtuous atheists.[46] Bayle's tol-

---

[39] Goldie 1991, pp. 336, also 338f, and esp. 363–67 (on Locke's critic, Jonas Proast); cf. Goldie 1993a, pp. 143–71. See too Dunn 1993, esp. pp. 177f, 185; Savonius 2004, esp. p. 67.

[40] Locke 1984, I. iii. 5, p. 68; see also Wootton 1989, p. 57; Marshall 1994, pp. 97 n. 34, 101ff.

[41] Tuck 1990a, pp. 167f; Locke 2006a, esp. pp. 343, 355 (citing Grotius to argue that promissory oaths are denied by Christ), 365ff; also Locke 1988, II, § 98, p. 333. For the Whig contexts, see Ashcraft 1986, pp. 120ff; cf. Marshall 1994, pp. 86–89.

[42] Goldie 1992, esp. pp. 569f, 584ff; Franklin 1968, p. 97.

[43] Locke 1988, p. 137; cf. Stillingfleet 1689; Pincus 1995, esp. pp. 47ff, 59; Farr and Roberts 1985, pp. 395, 397; Marshall 1994, p. 91.

[44] Savonius 2004, pp. 72, 74; Labrousse 1982, esp. pp. 236ff; Dodge 1947; Tuck 1999, pp. 181f.

[45] Pierre Bayle, Letter to Vincent Minutoli, entry for September 24, 1693, in Pierre Bayle, *Oeuvres Diverses*, vol. 4, p. 700, discussed and cited in Hutchinson 1991, p. 16.

[46] Locke owned a copy of Bayle's 'Lettre à M. L. A. D. C. de Sorbonne, où il est prouvé par plusieurs raisons tirées de la philosophie et de la théologie que les comètes ne sont point

eration was rooted in a mixture of sexual libertinism and universalism, alongside a strong state capable of upholding political order.[47] Indeed, although both legitimize resistance, Bayle's analysis was more radical than was Locke's assertion of individual rights, and seems to lead necessarily towards an atheism that Locke could not accept.[48]

Locke's focus on toleration and civil propriety also has a complex foundation in his reflections on language. In his work, civil discourse absolutely requires the capacity to speak freely and truthfully according to shared standards of meaning, even though such conventional agreement or understanding is always precarious. It is something akin to a civic minimum, which, if pushed, might legitimately stretch as far as providing a right of resistance to illegitimate authority, or once more to an appeal to the judgement of Heaven.[49] There are obviously classical roots to this reviving of the idea of speech as rational deliberation, based upon trust and conventional propriety in judgement, and Locke's early French editors and translators like Jean Le Clerc did much to draw out this background. Indeed, Le Clerc took up Locke's account of liberty and the requirements of truthfulness in particular as a guide to understanding and explaining the judgements of historians, presenting his own compendium of historical and conceptual political theory in a work expressly titled *Parrhasiana*.[50] The idea of *parrhasia* buttressed the idea of the virtuous citizen as one capable of speaking freely, and the image of the frank speaker, or *Parrhasiastes*, was certainly as central to contemporary theories of freedom of speech in England as it had been to Greek self-understanding.[51]

Nicole's *Essais* as a whole highlighted the Jansenist trope that man was weak through pride, and only through the strength that God could provide would man be able even to begin to think beyond simple hedonism. There was no guarantee of salvation, but free agency could pursue right action and at least attempt to overcome the natural depravity of the human condition. However, and consonant with his dual recognition of divine omniscience and free agency, Nicole thought that humans were

le presage d'aucun malheur', Cologne, 1682; for details see Harrison and Laslett 1971, no. 237[a], p. 82; also Marshall 2006, pp. 698ff.

[47] Labrousse 1983, pp. 84f, 75; cf. Wootton 1997, esp. pp. 198ff, 210ff, 213 n. 30, 220f, 223f; Lennon 1997, esp. pp. 187f, 190f; Simonutti 2007, esp. pp. 53f.

[48] See Mori 1999; Kilcullen 1988, esp. pp. 54–105.

[49] Locke 1988, II, § 168, pp. 379f; §§ 224–25, pp. 414f.

[50] Le Clerc 1699, p. 131; cf. Grafton 2007, pp. 11ff, 28.

[51] Monoson 2000, esp. pp. 54–57, is exceptionally interesting; see too Raaflaub 2004, esp. pp. 100ff, 257; Pitkin 1988, esp. pp. 532ff. Cf. Colclough 2005, esp. ch. 1; Foucault 2005, pp. 364–68, 371–411.

easily deluded. Because the individual can 'move severall parts of this engine' (namely the soul and body) 'which obey his will' (*de remuer certaines parties de sa machine qui obéissent à sa volonté*), Nicole suggested (in Locke's translation) that 'Self-love [*l'amour propre*] is the mother, & nurse, of this extravagant [*présompteuse*] Idea' that individuals are therefore autonomous.[52] As his own notes on the subject reiterated, Locke also thought that laws could not be based solely on the idea of self-interest. If they were, it would give full rein to the passions at the expense of that regulated conduct, which alone permits individuals to live peacefully with others in civil society. Indeed, using laws to motivate appropriate conduct was central to Locke's project because laws were public methods of governing the actions of individuals whose inclinations were at root driven by hedonistic motives.

Laws also have the potential to overcome the problems of arbitrariness better than a motivational focus on moral rectitude alone, which was a weakness he perceived at the heart of the 'heathen' form of Ciceronian ethics he otherwise so admired.[53] It was given philosophical consideration in the *Essay*, where Locke discussed religion as not only the cause of much human strife, but also generally beyond the faculties of human understanding. Therefore government and civil authority have to act as the guarantors of right action, in so far as that is possible in this world.[54] The analysis was of a piece with the appeal to heaven outlined in the *Second Treatise*. Nevertheless, Locke left the problems deliberately open-ended. It seems that he could not satisfactorily resolve the issue of why a certain few virtuous men might be able to overcome the progressive increase in human depravity that had occurred since the Fall, even if one could reasonably reject the doctrine of original sin. Allowing for human error and partiality of judgement, Locke could only claim that although knowledge of natural law is in principle available to all, because of the experiential development of sense perception even this knowledge is subject to potential misrepresentations by our 'phansy'. This theme of the mismatch between perception and reality was also extensively discussed in the *Essay*, and some have seen in it an Epicurean-inspired argument

[52] Locke 2000b, p. 55; cf. Locke 2000b, 2. IV, § 18, p. 59: 'The least vessell crack'd [*le moindre vaisseau qui se rompt*] ... is enough to ruin the whole oeconomy'. Quotations refer first to the number/part of the discourse, second to the chapter within the discourse, and third to the particular numbered sections therein. Cf. Nicole 1677, §§ XIII, XIV, XIX, pp. 8, 10, 15.

[53] Locke 1983, p. 39; 1988, § 219, pp. 410f; also Dunn 1969, pp. 50f; Halldenius 2003, esp. pp. 267, 270; Marshall 1994, esp. p. 302.

[54] Marshall 1994, pp. 89, 93–94 n. 30.

about the nature of matter, substance and ideas.[55] But as Locke's use of Nicole and his early lectures on natural law clearly show, he had already given this problem considerable independent thought.[56] In contemporary notes, he discussed the questions of atheism and the unproven immortality of the soul in terms that closely recalled Pascal's *Pensées*, a work that had been radically assessed, edited and incorporated by the Port-Royal Jansenists.[57] Locke clearly knew about all of this.[58] Indeed, he wrote that 'it would make a man very wary how he embraces an opinion where there is such unequal odds [of 'infinite misery' or 'annihilation'] and where the consequences are of such moment and so infinitely different'.[59] Recourse to probability was insufficient, however, as Locke wished to move beyond the idea of a wager on salvation to prove the existence of God.[60] This was partly because one could have no certainty over the 'eternity' of torment in Hell. It was also because of his belief that natural law should ground obligation more securely than could chance, and partly because of the hypothetical character of probability.[61] In much the same way, he thought social existence could only have meaning if one learns (for it is not innately known) that behind us lies the 'Hand of the Almighty visibly held up, and prepared to take Vengeance' for breaches of duty.[62] Concomitantly, political authority is given to those whom we can legitimately trust, because civil politics must be assumed to pursue the public good. This is how Locke justified trusting the judgement of rulers, and how he attempted (rather by the back door) to deflect potentially radical criticisms of arbitrary political power in his justification of political prerogative. In fact, his response to these radical critics closely recalls Hobbes's deflection of similar opposition, in his account of minimally rational agents authorizing actions through leaders allegedly for

[55] Cf. Michael and Michael 1990, p. 395; Walmsley 2003, esp. p. 428 n. 53. See too Wilson 2008; Brandt Bolton 1983, pp. 353–75.

[56] Locke 1954, Essay IV, p. 149; Locke 2000b, 2. XI, § 47, p. 91; Locke 1990, vol. 1, *Draft 'A'*, §§ 8, 27, 39–42, 43, pp. 18ff, 47f, 66–74, 75; *Draft 'B'*, § 72, p. 176; cf. Locke 1984, III. xi. 24–25, pp. 520–23.

[57] McKenna 1999, esp. pp. 53ff, 127–53, 155ff, pp. 160ff. Cf. Miel 1969, pp. 181f.

[58] J. R. Milton 2001, esp. pp. 231f; Lough 1958, esp. pp. 247f. Locke's copy was the 1674 reissue of the fourth edition, published in Paris in 1671.

[59] Locke 1997f, pp. 245f; Wootton 1989, pp. 52f.

[60] Locke 1990, vol. 1, *Draft 'B'*, § 94, pp. 229f; Locke 1984, IV. x. 6, pp. 621. For discussion see Ayers 1981, esp. pp. 217, 219f, 234f, 238ff, 242f, 246; von Leyden 1971, pp. 41–55. Locke 2000b, 2. XV, § 67, p. 113, anglicized Nicole's Latin rendering of Psalm 38. 6, in his translation as, '*My substance is as noe thing before thee*' [ET SUBSTANTIA *mea tanquam nihilum ante te*]. Emphases in original. Cf. Nicole 1677, § LXVIII, p. 62.

[61] Walker 1964, pp. 73–93; Wootton 1989, pp. 52f.

[62] Locke 1984, I. iii. 13, p. 74.

their own good.[63] This further complicated Locke's utility for later, particularly radical, writers as well.[64]

In his notebooks for 1677 Locke was reflecting on the nature of knowledge, the will and study in Jansenist-inspired terms, suggesting that an awareness of God would lead anyone to the conclusion that the 'happiness & misery' of any future state 'depends on the ordering of our selves in our actions in the/his view of our probationorship' in this life.[65] The reiteration of this fact in the *Essay*, where our 'State of Mediocrity and Probationership' was duly noted, meant that for Locke we must at least make do with probability in our assumptions about morality drawn from natural law in our actions in this world. It is on this basis that we must, if we are to act at liberty, exercise our judgement.[66] However, when one examines Locke's familiarity with the origins of these debates, it is striking how his political theory both emerged at particular moments of high tension, but also remained parasitic upon his medical studies.[67] His work with Thomas Sydenham was particularly important in this regard.[68] Indeed the combination of practice and experience in the fields of both medicine and politics seemed to suit him.[69] Equally, the medical discussions clearly fed into his philosophical consideration of mechanism. But although these contexts are important, and there is much written on them (as evidenced in these relatively few footnotes) they are somewhat tangential to my major theme.[70]

In general terms Locke thought that 'Nature' had placed into human beings a desire for pleasure and an aversion to pain, and that these 'are indeed innate practical Principles, which (as practical principles ought)

[63] Locke 1988, II, §§ 159–60, 164, pp. 374f, 377; cf. Skinner 2009, esp. pp. 124f, for sharp criticism.

[64] Cf. Dunn 1969a, esp. p. 57.

[65] MS Locke f. 2, p. 49.

[66] Locke 1984, IV. xiv. 2, p. 652; see also Darwall 1995, pp. 164, 167.

[67] J. R. Milton 1994, esp. pp. 36–39; von Leyden 1954, p. 24. See too Walmsley 1998, p. 33; cf. pp. 209ff, 245, 251; Ayliffe Ivye, Letter 97, to John Locke, May 20, 1660, in Locke 1976–89, vol. 1, pp. 146f; J. R. Milton 2001, esp. pp. 224ff, 228–31.

[68] Sydenham 1991, esp. pp. 51–67, 68–95, 116–39, 177f; Ms. Locke c. 29, f. 27. See also Dewhurst 1963, pp. 10–15; Meynell 1996, pp. 65–74; 1993, esp. p. 331; 2006, esp. pp. 95, 97–100, 101–10. Cf. Stewart 1981, pp. 19–44; J. R. Milton 2001, pp. 229f.

[69] PRO 30/24/47/2 fos. 31–38, 47–56. See too Meynell 1994, pp. 65–73; Walmsley 1988, transcribes the key documents on pp. 260–69 (*Respirationis Usis*); 272–85 (*Anatomia*); 286–95 (*De Arte Medica*), 390–93 (*Morbus*); cf. pp. 95–108. See also Walmsley 2000, pp. 366–93; 2003, esp. pp. 418–24.

[70] Cf. Walmsley 2006, pp. 331–35; J. R. Milton 2001, p. 228. See also Frank 1980, pp. 186ff, discussed in Walmsley 2003, p. 418 n. 8; also Meynell 1997, pp. 473–86; 1993, pp. 245–67. See Walmsley 1998, p. 48 n. 54, for Locke's award of a King's Pardon assuring his receipt of a BM, though not a DM, in 1675.

do continue constantly to operate and influence all our Actions, without ceasing'. They are 'Inclinations of the Appetite to good, not Impressions of truth on the Understanding', and although there are 'natural tendencies imprinted on the Minds of Men' this 'makes nothing for innate Characters on the Mind, which are to be the Principles of Knowledge, regulating our Practice'.[71] The ways in which such hedonistic concerns could be reconciled with the demands of morality and appropriately regulated conduct required a form of self-propriety that many have seen as a Christianized Epicureanism, similar in form, if not in substance, to Gassendi's analysis.[72] Locke undertook some consideration of Gassendi's *Life of Peireske*, which was in his library and which he used both as a biographical guide and also (perhaps) for its eloquent illustration of the life of the mind as a cultured and civilizing process that appealed to his broader Ciceronian sympathies.[73] He also had a copy of the *Syntagma philosophicum*, and a concern with Gassendi seems to line up with his contemporaneous readings of Descartes and Spinoza.[74] But his early readers knew that he rejected 'Oxford Peripatetick' philosophy, and it was equally 'well known he was no *Cartesian*'.[75] Moreover, there is considerable dispute about the precise content of Locke's use of Descartes, Gassendi, and Lucretian or otherwise updated forms of Epicureanism. These disputes relate to how we might understand the embodied character of Locke's political theory.[76] Indeed, serious early Lockean scholars like Barbeyrac also expressly considered why and how Locke might even be seen as a Spinozist because of his analysis of substance and its properties, or *propria*.[77] Yet despite these conflicting demands, Locke's claims not only

[71] Locke 1984, I. iii. 3, p. 67; MS Locke f. 2, pp. 42–53; cf. Carey 2006, p. 43.

[72] J. R. Milton 2000, pp. 94ff, 97–102 (on Bernier particularly).

[73] J. R. Milton 2000, esp. pp. 91f, 97; Miller 2000, esp. pp. 16f, 21, 45–48, 62f, 146f; cf. Marshall 1994, pp. 163f.

[74] Ms. Locke f. 27, p. 5; BL. Add. MS 32544, fo. 177; Harrison and Laslett 1971, no. 2755, p. 238; Joy 1987, pp. 198, 293, n. 27 (on the *Syntagma*), 41–65 (on the *Life of Peiresc* and universal history). Cf. Michael and Michael 1990, pp. 382, 389–93, 395ff; J. R. Milton 2000, pp. 102ff.

[75] Le Clerc 1706, p. 2; see Harrison and Laslett 1971, nos. 2742, 2518, p. 238.

[76] See Osler 1994, esp. pp. 62f, 66–72; also Kroll 1984, pp. 339–59; cf. Locke, Letter 830, to Lady Masham, September 15, 1685[?], in Locke 1976–89, vol. 2, pp. 734–38; Jones 1989, pp. 169f, 178ff, 191ff.

[77] Jean Barbeyrac, Letter to Pierre Desmaizeaux, May 4, 1706, BL Add. Ms. 4281, fo. 21: 'Ce que vous dites du Spinozisme du feu Mr Locke ... Puis que vous avez de *très-bonnes raisons de croire que Mr. Locke avoit cette pensée*, il faut que cela paroisse ou par quelcun [*sic*] de ses Ouvrages Posthumes, ou par des Conversations Particulières où il aît declaré ses sentimens là-dessus. Je ne vois pas qu'on puisse [?] vien conclurre de tel de son *Essai sur l'Entend*'. Emphasis in original. See also the discussion of a year later from Barbeyrac, Letter to Desmaizeaux, May 7, 1707, BL Add. Ms. 4281, fo. 22^v: 'Quoi qu'il en soit, je n'ai point prétendu de penser que Mr. Locke fût Spinoza à tous égards: ce que je disais, ne tom-

sit well with broader attempts to reconcile theological reflection with civility, and to modify Cicero in order to reconcile the *honestum* with the *utile*.[78] They also complement his use of Nicole in developing an account of self-propriety.[79] Perhaps this is quite enough to try to make sense of.

Whilst Locke's worries about the sources of civil and political strife were to be found in attempts to constrain and delimit religious opinion, he was faithful to the argument that a principal source of disruption was a cause internal to man, and that was self-love or self-interest. It was, he wrote, quite 'evident, how much Men love to deceive, and be deceived', and post-lapsarian man illustrated this keenly, as Wierix's representation on the cover of this book suggests.[80] Locke's use of Nicole pointed in the same direction, at the same time as it developed certain conventional jurisprudential arguments.[81] Indeed, taking as its starting point the biblical idea that men should seek peace, the third of Nicole's *Essais* was explicitly concerned with the ways (*des moyens*) of preserving peace between men. At a very general opening level, Nicole had suggested that mankind shares the world in common and that therefore the whole of the world is the city of man. Furthermore, he made the point that Locke along with others would repeat in numerous treatises: 'The necessitys, & wants of life drive men into societys, & keepe them there togeather, & plainly evince, that societys are according to the will of god'.[82] It also formed the basis of Locke's solution to the problem of how natural rights and self-preservation could be made to cohere with the idea of divine law and the grand design of a Creator, as illustrated in the *Two Treatises*.[83] His translations of Nicole, then, were undertaken as part of a wider project of 'showing how men could be made to perform their duties of service to other men' whilst they remained hedonistic and would not be rewarded on earth for such action.[84] As Nicole had argued, civil peace was best achieved through mankind's bending its own will towards the will of

---

boit que sur l'unité de Substance, qui appler [*sic*] grand principe de Spinoza'. There is brief notice in Thomson 2008, p. 143; cf. Hunter 2004, pp. 694–97.

[78] J. R. Milton 2001, p. 226; Lough 1953a, p. 17; Lough 1953, p. 230; also Walker 1964, pp. 75f, 93ff, on Locke as English Arian.

[79] See MS Locke f. 1, pp. 367–70, cited in Yolton 2000, p. 2; cf. Jacovides 2007, esp. pp. 488–95, 504f, 507f; see too Hampsher-Monk 1977, esp. pp. 403, 406–9, 411, 413, 415ff; Losonsky 2001, esp. pp. 92–95.

[80] Locke 1984, III. x. 34, p. 508.

[81] Schuurman 2001, esp. pp. 450–54, 456–60, 462; Yolton 1959. See also Nadler 1989, p. 20; Gaukroger 1997, pp. 343, 345f. See also Hont 2005, esp. pp. 47–51.

[82] Locke 2000c, 3. I, §§ 1–3, pp. 118f; 3. I, § 90, p. 191. His notebook for Monday, February 8, 1677, MS Locke f. 2, esp. pp. 44f, 49, shows him thinking about this question at this time in precisely Nicole's terms.

[83] Harris 2007, esp. pp. 145ff, 164.

[84] Marshall 1994, p. 189.

God, doing so voluntarily, and thereby fulfilling duties to fellow citizens by interacting with them according to propriety and at peace, or at least as often as was humanly possible.[85] This was, once more, the true nature of charity, and the basis of our love for others is to be found in the 'inclination to serve them'.[86] The idea of justice as analogous with divine service was of course a central tenet of Christian moralism, and from it Locke could relate his theology to politics by focusing on how the justice of the magistrate was limited by the authorization granted to him by the people to defend their property or right as an impartial umpire.[87] This was part of the providential design of government as much as it was Machiavellian and modern.[88] And as Montesquieu would also later reiterate, Locke thought the political esotericism outlined by Machiavellians like Naudé was increasingly irrelevant.[89] Legitimate political authority, which is always rooted in man's lack of power relative to God, necessarily places limits on the proper scope of governmental power.[90]

Given this sort of argument, according to Locke the principal concern of the good citizen was part of a wider project that has aptly been termed 'governing conduct'.[91] The good citizen certainly does not take offence inappropriately, much less would he or she desire to give offence to others. At the same time the propriety of prudence provides a means to achieving the ends of happiness, tranquillity, health, wealth, power, reputation and favour, explicitly through 'self-knowledge; mastery of one's

[85] Locke 2000c, 3. III, §§ 15–16, p. 131; 3. IV, §§ 20–23, p. 135ff, on the causes of 'difference and aversion' amongst men, namely from either 'Contradicting their opinion, or Crosseing their passions' given the naturally hedonistic desire for 'superiority' over others.

[86] Locke 2000c, 3. III, §§ 12–13, p. 129; cf. 3. XI, § 14, p. 129: 'If we doe not actually doe them good, we ought to forbear at least doeing them any harme'.

[87] Marshall 1994, pp. 201–4, 209ff, 235ff, 280f; Tuck 1999, esp. pp. 168 n. 6, 172–79; Cromartie 2000, esp. pp. 63ff; Tuck 1993, p. 151.

[88] Cf. Rahe 2008, p. 52 n. 126.

[89] Naudé 1679 esp. pp. 52f: 'la Prudence comme une vertu morale & politique'; see too Naudé 1679, pp. 57f; Naudé 1662, pp. 204, 207, 209, 218, 220; Tuck 1993, p. 93. Cf. Dunn 1969, pp. 163, 128 n. 1; Locke 1954, pp. 275ff, for the relevant manuscript sources (MS Locke d. 10, pp. 111, 137, 139; MS Locke f. 1, August 24–26, 1676, pp. 415–21); also Keohane 1980, pp. 145f, 157, 171–74.

[90] Locke 1988, II. xv, § 171, pp. 381f; discussion in Harris 2000, pp. 74f; cf. Harris 2007, pp. 149f, 152ff.

[91] Tully 1993, p. 224. See Locke 2000c, 3. IX, 52, p. 161, on the 'Ascendant' or 'imperious' method of contradicting opinion, to be avoided; cf. Locke 2000c, 3. X, § 60, p. 167, where this is less a fault 'in gray hairs [*viellard*] a superior or a person of quality then in a young man an inferiour or one of meane condition [*peu de considération*]'; 3. IX, § 54, p. 163, on delivering 'opinions dogmatically'; 3. IX, §§ 57–58. pp. 165f, on showing passion, contempt, and insult; 3. X, § 61, p. 169, on 'Schollars ... [who] assume to themselves a power of talking magisterially of all things'; 3. X, § 62, p. 169, on being 'positive' and having 'good stock' ['*Pour parler donc avec autorité & décisivement, il faut avoir la science; & la créance tout ensemble*']; cf. Locke 2000c, 3. XII, §§ 69, 71, 72–73, pp. 175, 177–78; 3/2. I, § 1, p. 195.

passions'.[92] At root, says Locke translating Nicole, 'we procure our owne peace [*la paix à soi-même*] within, by governing well our thoughts & passions. By this internall peace, establishd in our selves, we contribute to the quiet of society'.[93] Governed conduct promotes peace internally, while externally such conduct under the law provides the foundation for our liberty. Avoiding both hating others, and being the subject of others' hatred, was therefore of paramount importance, and this was to be achieved by coming to understand how one should engage in conversation and dialogue with fellow citizens without the distortions of 'false rhetoric'.[94] Within this distinction between the particular ends of the orator and the general ends of the virtuous life stands Locke's classical recognition, that the foundations of civil society are compromised by semantic instability.[95]

This need for linguistic propriety, a prerequisite for the internal peace required to maintain social order, is just as Nicole had also proposed. Indeed, the double meaning of propriety, as both conventional use in language, and (with its French and Latin derivations of *proprieté* and *proprietas*) of a peculiarity or specificity of possession, or as a measure of accuracy or justness, continued through Locke well into the eighteenth century. Johnson's *Dictionary* explicitly referenced it in his own entry on the topic.[96] But Locke was happy enough for the time being with Nicole's claim that in practical terms, the capacity to generate love and respect through the use of reason, as a God-given faculty, would place human relationships on a sure footing.[97] His own solution was grounded in a contract of faith or trust; as he argued, *fides vinculum societatis*. What this idea implied, though, was that tolerance of religious viewpoints fed into a wider scheme for the preservation of a regulated society through linguistic openness and discussion. Civil discourse was the solution to the

---

[92] Quotations from Locke 1997c, p. 215; for the incorrect dating of the manuscript, see Abrams 1967, pp. 245–46; cf. J. R. Milton 1998, pp. 105–7.

[93] Locke 2000c, 3. I, § 4, p. 119; cf. 3. II, § 5, p. 121: 'Men ordinarily, in the conduct of their lives, governe them selves, neither by ffaith, nor Reason. But heedlessly give them selves up to the impressions of objects, that come their way; or the received opinions of those with whome they converse'.

[94] Locke 2000c, 3. V, § 27, p. 141; cf. 3. V, § 33, p. 145; 3. VI, § 36, p. 147, on the origins of false beliefs through the influence of 'leading men'. See too Ms. Locke f. 1, 'Spelling', *Journal*, August 15, 1676, pp. 402–6, in Locke 1954, pp. 256f: 'I cannot forbear to think that charity to men may well make us less tender of the genealogies of words'.

[95] Dawson 2005, esp. pp. 402, 405f, more generally pp. 401–11, 416ff, 420ff; cf. Locke 1984, III. ii. 5, p. 407, on the 'perverting of the use of words' by those who make words stand 'for any thing, but those Ideas we have in our own Minds'. See then Plato 1997, 384c, p. 103; Aristotle 1984, 1359^{b}10 (p. 2160), 1360^{a}24–25 (p. 2162), 1365^{b}22–26 (p. 2173).

[96] Johnson 1755, s.v. 'PROPRIETY'.

[97] Locke 2000c, 3. XIV, § 88, p. 189: 'Tis civility which by the senses sends in effectuall convictions'. Cf. Locke 1997l, p. 321.

problem of those 'quarrells' which 'spring commonly from our indiscreet stirring of other mens passions'.[98] In fact, the passion of love (a topic absolutely central to the Cambridge Platonists whom Locke knew well) could be the balm for such 'frenzied engagements'.[99]

However, probability in judgement provides the grounds for our experience of the world. Therefore rhetoric, 'that powerful instrument of Error and Deceit', can directly affect the actual liberty of an agent through its capacity to 'move the passions, and thereby mislead the Judgement'.[100] For 'he is certainly the most subjected, the most enslaved', says Locke, 'who is so in his Understanding'. Such persons lack the capacity to judge on what grounds of probability they should give their assent to, or actually reject, certain courses of action.[101] This incapacity in turn has critical implications for the quality of their agency and their responsibility or otherwise for it.[102] Politically similar concerns were mapped onto a discussion of the adequacy of judgement in the *Second Treatise*, where representatives in the legislature are supposed to listen to both sides of a debate impartially prior to reaching a decision, although their judgement may be impaired by rhetoric.[103] Thus, the private and the public, or the internal and external elements of liberty as propriety are both affected by the power of words. This circumstance relates directly to the claim that liberty is required for the understanding, and that persons have liberty to be held responsible for their actions only through their capacity to deliberate between choices and suspend their judgement before acting. Therefore judgements are deliberations based on trust according to truthful or appropriate reasons in the face of uncertainty. In this process, each individual is 'Judge for himself', as Locke put it in the *Second Treatise*, in a claim with important ramifications for the relationship between liberty and the will.[104]

Equally, Locke's account of philosophical enquiry directly considers the import of ordinary speech or language, which requires us to retrieve simple modes or ideas in order to make sense of particular claims. His crucial point is that confusion over particular words threatens to distort claims about knowledge, and thus produce both error and uncertainty. The solution to this very real problem is a resort to the claim that natural

---

[98] Locke 2000c, 3. II, § 7, p. 123; 3. II, § 9, p. 125; cf. MS Locke f. 2, entry for Monday, February 8, 1677, pp. 50f.

[99] Locke 2000c, 3. II, § 10, p. 127: 'l'amour éteient toutes les malignes passions: & ce sont celle-là qui troublent notre repos'. See too Locke 1984, II. xx. 3, pp. 230.

[100] Locke 1984, III. x. 34, p. 508.

[101] Locke 1984, IV. xx. 6, p. 711.

[102] See Locke 1984, IV. xv. 5, p. 656; IV. xix. 4, p. 660; cf. IV. xix. 14, p. 704.

[103] Locke 1988, § 222, p. 413.

[104] Locke 1988, II, § 22, pp. 283f.

law allows us, if we use our faculties correctly, to determine for ourselves rules that are 'intelligible to all mankind' and which should govern appropriate conduct in the quest for knowledge.[105] This is what allows him to further claim that although the essence of certain forms of bodies or substance might remain unknown, this is not so with morality, which '*is capable of Demonstration*, as well as Mathematicks'. The mixed 'modes' and 'substances' relevant to moral argument are such that to allow for clarity in definition, 'their divers Natures are not so much enquir'd into, as supposed'. This offers a structure of understanding that makes our everyday lives comprehensible.[106] Indeed, his famous worry about the 'gaudy dress' that philosophical discussion must metaphorically wear during public discussions illustrates his point about the necessary requirements of conventional understanding.[107] Linguistic impropriety threatens stability at the most basic level of human intercourse, and thereby poses a threat to civil prudence because speech is always open to manipulation and misunderstanding, which in turn actively promotes untrustworthiness. If we cannot ground even our speech on a sure footing, then there is little hope that we can successfully and peaceably communicate with one another. To overcome this danger requires a very particular focus on judgement and convention, because for civil society to function, our conduct must be appropriately regulated.[108]

So, if self-love initially tells us that fault always lies elsewhere, and that we should correct others rather than look to ourselves, then it is our self-love that needs to be counteracted and the 'contrairety' between our own dispositions and those of others, which needs to be rethought if aversion is to be tempered.[109] This can best be done by adhering to prudence, which 'requires us to take a quite contrary course, & quit the thoughts [*le dessein chimérique*] of correcting others. The right way is, to endeavour to secure our peace by reforming our selves, & to establish our quiet upon the government of our own passions'.[110] Understanding our place in the world under God allows us the potential to transform our myriad 'occasions of complaint', for what we truly love are the 'contrarys' of our baser emotions such as incivility, resentment and distrust. We can and

[105] Locke 1984, III. ix. 22–23, pp. 489f. My thanks to Tim Stanton for advice here.

[106] Locke 1984, III. ix. 16, p. 516.

[107] Locke 1984, II. xxi. 20, pp. 243f; for wider discussion, see Aarsleff 1982; Dawson 2007.

[108] Schuurman 2003; 2001, esp. pp. 457f; cf. Walmsley 1998, pp. 49f n. 57; J. R. Milton 1984, pp. 25–34.

[109] Locke 2000c, 3/2. V, § 39, p. 229.

[110] Locke 2000c, 3/2. I, §§ 2–3, on the initial reaction afforded by self-love; the quotation is from 3/2. I, § 5, p. 197.

should look instead to civility, affection, esteem and gratitude.[111] This relates once more to our judgement. The reasons we should give for our assent to particular claims that cannot be based in knowledge, but in ideas only, means that 'this fleeting state of Action and Blindness we are in, should make us more busy and careful to inform our selves, than constrain others'.[112] Our own vanity binds us doubly, however, because it forces us to present only a partial image of ourselves to the world, thereby encouraging the self-deceiving notion that we are free from those defects we try to hide from others. The 'esteeme, that soe elevates us' is 'noe thing but an opinion raised upon the consideration of some small part of our selves'.[113] Opinion too is related to civility and promotes it not only because it is a duty, but also because our desire for the good opinion of others motivates us to act civilly even if it is true that this motive is based on an assessment of our own self-interest. Therefore, an argument is being made that the development of character is predicated on a desire for individual approbation and that this desire can be used to foster a virtuous disposition and the following of God's will.[114] Our reason is, after all, 'natural *Revelation*', according to Locke, in a thought that would have a lengthy afterlife in the theories of rational dissent and in the radical catechisms offered by John Toland in his *Pantheisticon*, for the 'Socratic-Society', for example.[115] Yet reason is also problematic, and as Locke would suggest, 'the three great things that govern mankind are reason, passion, and superstition ... [for they act] most powerfully and produce the greatest mischiefs'.[116]

'Men hate in generall the Selfish & Coviteous, the Proud & Presumptious', not because they are necessarily unjust, but because they reflect a distinct lack of propriety and force us to consider ourselves in ways which we do not find attractive. Nevertheless, Nicole continued, even when men love us, it is not really us, but a projection of us whom they love because (in Locke's translation) they 'phansy us others then we are, & soe fall in love with us: & painting us in their imaginations with good qualitys, which we have not, & without the ill ones, that we have, place their af-

---

[111] Locke 2000c, 3/2. I, § 13, p. 205 (on love of civil passions).

[112] Locke 1984, IV. xvi. 5, p. 660.

[113] Locke 2000c, 3/2. II, §§ 17–18, p. 209 (on vanity and self-deception); cf. Locke 2000c, 3/2. II, §§ 19–21; 3/2. III, §§ 22–24, 35–37, pp. 211–13, 226f (on the fleeting and uncertain character of esteem); also 3/2. IV, §§ 29–30, pp. 219f.

[114] Harris 1994, pp. 282ff, 287ff; cf. Locke 2000b, 2. XIV, § 61: 'the vertues purely humane are but weaknesses'; Locke 2000b, 2. XV, § 65, p. 109: 'noe thing discovers the power of grace [more] then the weaknesse of man'.

[115] Locke 1984, IV. xix. 4, p. 698; cf. Price 1991, esp. pp. 140, 144, 166; Price 1769, esp. pp. 47ff, 61f; Toland 1751, p. 84: 'PRES[ident?]: "There's as wide a Difference between *Liberty* and *Licentiousness*." RESP[onse?]. "As between *Liberty* and Slavery."'

[116] MS. Locke f. 5, p. 59, May 16, 1681; cf. Locke 1954, p. 204; Locke 1984, IV. 20. 12, pp. 714f; II. 33. 9, p. 397; IV. xii. 11, p. 646.

fection on a thing very different from us. In their hatred they doe just the same'.[117] Our own concupiscence, which Locke renders as 'naturall inclinations', leads us down this path where our 'peevishnesse' simply 'rises from some foolish passion' and the 'passions spring from the weaknesse of our mindes'.[118] This could then be historicized, and Locke talked of a period of 'Innocence and Sincerity' something like a 'Golden Age' prior to the time when 'evil concupiscence, had corrupted Mens minds into a Mistake of true Power and Honour'.[119] Natural wants drive us to society, and because of the 'inconveniencies of that condition, and the love, and want of Society', people quickly became 'united and incorporated' so that they might 'continue together'.[120] This claim was presented as a way of explaining the origins of political society , but it remained heavily indebted to the theological premises of his argument.[121] There are always dangers, because true love and a proper adaptation to the path laid down by God requires us to reject comparisons, which can only lead to aversion in this world. Instead, we are advised to focus on the heavenly rewards of the next world, as recompense for our fallen lives and continual unease and disquiet in this one.[122] If these themes reconceptualize the Jansenist-Augustinian notion of the misguided will acting through concupiscence, they highlight something of Locke's major debt to Nicole's analysis of the human condition. However, they would prompt still further reflections by Locke on the role of the will in securing our freedom.

LIBERTY AND THE WILL

As I have already suggested, many contemporary theories of agency take their cue from the intuition that the way we think about freedom depends upon our view of autonomy and responsibility, and that responsibility in turn is grounded in reactive attitudes, particularly attitudes of resentment.[123] Cognate puzzles, such as whether one must be an autonomous

---

[117] Locke 2000c, 3/2. V, § 41, p. 231; 3/2. XI, §§ 74–75, 77, pp. 255, 257.

[118] Locke 2000b, 2. XI, § 51, p. 95; cf. Locke 1988, II, § 111, pp. 342f.

[119] Locke 1988, II. viii, §§ 108, 110, 111, pp. 339f, 341ff; cf. Shklar 1985, pp. 49ff; Waldron 1988, p. 171.

[120] Locke 1988, II. vii, § 77, pp. 318f; II. viii, § 101, p. 334.

[121] Dunn 1969, esp. pp. 154f, 171ff; cf. Waldron 2002, p. 81; Tully 1993, pp. 214ff; Ivison 1997a, pp. 132f.

[122] Moreover, it is 'yet more unreasonable' to be 'vexed that others treat us with indifferency [*l'indifférence pour nous*]', whilst love itself 'lays on us an obligation to certain dutys of difficult permanence'. Locke 2000c, 3/2. VI, §§ 41, 42, p. 233; also 3/2. VII, § 52, p. 241; cf. Locke 2000b, 2. XII, § 52, p. 97, on the partial nature of any given 'state of tranquility' in the world. See also Marshall 1994, pp. 183–93.

[123] Strawson 1968, pp. 71–96; cf. Jay-Wallace 1994, esp. pp. 74–83; Jay-Wallace 2007, pp. 295–318.

agent in order to be morally responsible, or whether one can be both autonomous and not morally responsible for action, or indeed whether the relationship between these two fields is contingent, are the sorts of puzzles that engaged Locke as much as they do contemporary philosophy.[124] In the *Essay*, Locke builds on his account of the passions to suggest that our volitions are fundamentally caused by feelings of uneasiness, disquiet, or pain that we feel in our mind. This is our will, or the 'power of Volition', which is 'much more distinct from *Desire*'.[125] For desire, in fact, is moved 'by happiness and that alone', and happiness and misery are but the extremes of those impressions made upon us by delight and joy on the one hand, and torment and sorrow on the other.[126] As he wrote, 'Pleasure and Pain, and that which causes them, Good and Evil, are the hinges on which our Passions turn'.[127]

There are two interesting positions here, one relating to the foundations of Locke's account, and the other relating directly to his understanding of the passions. A wry inkling of the connection between the passions and temporal happiness might be gleaned from the *oration funèbre* Locke gave for his students at the end of his period as Censor in Moral Philosophy at Christ Church, Oxford in 1664. The title he spoke to was, 'Can Anyone by Nature be happy in this life?' And although the answer to the question was a resounding no, his critical appraisal of Epicureanism was of a piece with a rejection of the main schools of philosophy. There was doubtless some irony in Locke's rendition, and he must have been playing to his audience somewhat. But he nevertheless suggested that the laws of nature are not privileges of the happy and content, but instead 'the fetters whereby the wretched are detained in this life'. Aristotle, the Stoics and the Epicureans had all been wrong, especially in their various attempts to 'despoil' men of their passions; 'to anyone striving after happiness the earth is just what it was to Alexander: it is a prison, and too narrow for a mind destined for higher ends'.[128] Because of this, it is perhaps not surprising that many have understood Locke's prominent thoughts on hedonism to be a development of neo-Epicurean philosophy as a search for tranquillity.[129] But the reconciliation of hedonism with earthly tranquillity, and the close interrelationship between propriety as a form of both property and appropriation, and hence a category of right

[124] Oshana 2008, esp. pp. 193–96; McKenna 2008, pp. 222ff; Beauchamp 2008, pp. 325ff.

[125] Locke 1984, II. xxi. 30, p. 250.

[126] Locke 1984, II. xxi. 41, p. 258.

[127] Locke 1984, II. xx. 3, pp. 229f; cf. Locke 1984, II. xx. 5–6, p. 230; 1997g, pp. 300f; also Tully 1993, pp. 207f.

[128] Locke 1954a, quotations from pp. 221, 223, 231.

[129] Joy 1987, p. 222; cf. Carey 2006, pp. 46f nn. 25f.

and justice, more obviously sends us back to Locke's most prized book, Cicero's *De Officiis*. It was a text that played a wide role in his thought, particularly his later moral and educational writing.[130] I should first like to focus on Locke's account of the will, however, in order to go on and show how these Ciceronian concerns develop in his work.

As Locke glosses his theme, 'Uneasiness determines the Will'.[131] If the will is so determined, it is this fact which 'sets us upon those Actions, we perform'. Correlatively 'by *Pleasure* and *Pain*, *Delight* and *Uneasiness*', Locke means not only bodily feelings but also 'whatsoever *Delight* or *Uneasiness* is felt by us'.[132] Such actions are determined by the will, itself properly caused by uneasiness about the relationship between pleasure and pain perceived by our minds, and from which it follows that issues of uneasiness are determined by the desire for the most positive good that our 'All-wise Maker' has given to us. Correlatively we are also motivated by our desire to remove our uneasiness in order to promote our happiness, because our will is given volition by the most pressing uneasiness we face.[133] Moreover, this is 'not an imperfection in Man, it is the highest perfection of intellectual Natures', and it is simply a fact that because we reflect and consider different possible goods and desires, our will comes to be activated or determined and our actions prompted by them.[134] Our actions are grounded in our experience, and therefore rooted in our conventional and limited judgement. Equally, our actions can only be free if we have both the choice and the capacity to either act or to refrain from acting; in the language of modern philosophy, Locke suggests that liberty is autonomy. It 'consists solely in a power to act or not to act according to the determination of the will', but at the same time only makes sense in a social context. Thus, liberty 'should not and cannot even be supported in a state in which it is manifest that a man as a free agent cannot act since liberty, as I have said, consists solely in the power to act or not to act consequent on, and accruing in, the determination of the will'.[135]

As learning and reflecting creatures, we therefore have liberty to the extent that we are able to propose the 'suspension of any desire, before the will be determined to action, and the action (which follows that determination) done, we have opportunity to examine, view, and judge, of

[130] Locke 1989, esp. §§ 41–42, 45, 54, 56, 94, 98; see too Marshall 1994, esp. pp. 301–15; Mitsis 2003, pp. 45–61.

[131] Locke 1984, II. xxi. 31, pp. 250f; also II. xx. 3, p. 230.

[132] Locke 1984, II. xxi. 31, p. 251; II. xxi. 15, p. 232; Locke 1997e, p. 244; 1997m, p. 321.

[133] Locke 1984, II. xxi. 34, p. 252; cf. II. xxi. 37, pp. 254f, II. xxi. 39–40, pp. 256ff.

[134] Locke 1984, II. xxi. 30, note to § 30, p. 251; II. xxi. 46, p. 262.

[135] Locke, Letter 2925, to Philippus van Limborch, May 21, 1701, in Locke 1976–89, vol. 7, pp. 325–30, at pp. 328, 329; cf. Oshana 2008, p. 199.

the good or evil of what we are going to do'. This fact is both the 'end and the use of our *Liberty*; and the farther we are removed from such a determination, the nearer we are to Misery and Slavery'.[136] '*Liberty* is a power to act or not to act according as the Mind directs'.[137] True liberty, then, consists in the following by intellectual beings of their true happiness, which is their greatest good, but such liberty is not always used effectively because of faulty judgement. That is, people frequently 'take not that to be necessary to their Happiness, which really is so'.[138] In the second edition of the *Essay*, Locke made as clear as he could the implications of this analysis.[139] Unease is prompted by desire, unease causes willing, and through willing individuals can be said to set upon a course of action, or to have an agency that relates to their identity. Thus, the will is ultimately determined by a passion, though in an immediate sense the passions that produce desire are both mostly negative (hence their leading towards uneasiness) and remain unfocused without the wider import of the will.[140]

In contrast to the standard opposition between reason and the passions, here a combination of desire and reasoned volition produces action, for the will on its own is not self-determining.[141] Locke certainly does not want to say that when we talk of liberty or freedom we are attributing our capacity to act or to forebear from acting as freedom of the will. This would be to attribute a power—which is a capacity of thinking, reasoning agents, and of them only—to another power, namely the will. And although uneasiness is typically equated with 'desire' in the *Essay*, in other places Locke recognizes that different passions will also give rise to it. This suggests that desire is either an all-encompassing term for the passions (apart from love) in Locke's mind, or that desire and uneasiness do not mean the same thing at all times.[142] If there is fluidity or ambiguity here, it helps to explain Locke's suggestion that sometimes our minds are completely taken over by particular affective states that limit our freedom, such as the 'pain of the Rack', love, anger, or any other 'violent' passion.[143] He concludes, however, by reiterating his claim that the will is simply a '*Power* which the mind has, thus to order the

[136] Locke 1984, II. xxi. 48, p. 264; the political implications of slavery as a state of war are sketched in Locke 1988, II, § 24, pp. 284f; it is unclear whether Locke intends us to think of ourselves as slaves to our passions if we fail to act at liberty and hence in a state of war. Cf. Scott 1992, pp. 581f.

[137] Locke 1984, II. xxi. 71, pp. 282f.

[138] Locke 1984, II. xxi. 68, p. 279.

[139] Locke 1984, II. xxi. 71, pp. 282f.

[140] Locke 1984, II. xxi. 4, p. 235.

[141] James 1997, pp. 279f; cf. Cromartie 2000, pp. 64f.

[142] Harris 2005, p. 29 n. 18.

[143] Locke 1984, II. xxi. 53, pp. 267f.

consideration of any *Idea*, or the forbearing to consider it'. Therefore, 'to prefer the motion of any part of the body to its rest, and *vice versâ* in any particular instance is that which we call the *Will*'.[144] Our judgement may go '*amiss*', simply because our own minds cannot cope with having to gauge future pleasures and pains in direct comparison with our present uneasiness. It is another illustration of the weakness of the human condition that such future discounting (as many later theorists, particularly utilitarians, would suggest) is so thoroughly problematic.[145] But the close connections between judgement and assent, the passions, and the liberty of deliberation, all coalesce in Locke's political thinking around the idea of responsible agency.

Locke continued, arguing that the 'actual exercise of that power, by directing any particular action, or its forbearance is that which we call *Volition* or *Willing*'. If we forebear from particular actions through the command of our own mind, then such actions are '*Voluntary*'. But what is 'performed without such a thought of the mind is called *Involuntary*'.[146] This is the reason why issues of both moral good and evil simply express the relationship between voluntary acts and the law for Locke, and why his account seems to hover uneasily between voluntarism and volitional determinism.[147] Indeed, trying to keep the will and desire separate but related as two components of the actual, lived experience of freedom that every individual agent can identify with is crucial to his project.[148] In later correspondence with Limborch he clarified some of these changes further, focusing once more on the relationship between liberty and power, and the extent to which free action depends upon the idea of an agent acting with a power, or acting against a judgement of his or her understanding; that is, acting self-contradictorily.[149] In fact, Locke had just a few years earlier replied to Le Clerc that there were three 'considerations' necessary to an understanding of liberty. First, 'ordinary and successive uneasinesses' affect our day-to-day lives and 'for the most part determine the will but with a power still of suspending'. Second, we must recognize the 'Violent uneasinesse which the minde cannot resist nor away with'. Third, there are the 'great number of litle and very indifferent actions which mix themselves with those of greater moment and fill up as it were the litle empty spaces of our time'. When this happens, the will is

---

[144] Locke 1984, II. xxi. 5, p. 236.

[145] Locke 1984, II, xxi. 64, p. 276.

[146] Locke 1984, II. xxi. 6, pp. 236f.

[147] Chappell 1994, esp. pp. 102f, 109ff, 113, 118f.

[148] Locke 1984, II. xxi. 29, p. 249; cf. Harris 2005, pp. 27, 29ff.

[149] Locke, Letter 2925, to Philippus van Limborch, May 21, 1701, in Locke 1976–89, vol. 7, pp. 325–30, at p. 329: 'Liberty cannot consist in a power of determining an action of willing contrary to the judgement of the understanding'.

determined without reference to good or evil, but such events are themselves unimportant and resemble a 'deliberation about trifles'.[150] If we are to understand the subtleties of Locke's account of liberty, however, we must ask where his account fits with his discussions of personhood and judgement.

PERSONS, PASSIONS AND JUDGEMENT

Although Locke said that the Stoics were wrong to try to extirpate the passions, were wrong to think that we have innate ideas of virtue, and were certainly wrong to think that the figure of the sage could be anything other than an unfeeling monster, there may be a case for thinking that Locke has simply moved the goalposts. In classical Stoic philosophy, the passions are mistakes about values, where the affections of the soul are 'nothing by aberrations of human reason'.[151] This means that the two primary passions of fear (*phobos*) and desire (*epithumia*), alongside the two reactive passions of pain (*lupē*) and pleasure (*hedonē*) are all nevertheless reactions to impressions, and although they may seem appropriate in the eyes of the agent in the throes of a particular passion, they are not. Therefore, although passions certainly arise from things we do care about, from our own care of the self to anger and rage, what is necessary for a well-ordered life is to try to minimize the impact of these misdirected feelings about what is valuable and live instead a regulated life (*apatheia*). This goal requires we choose what is appropriate (*kathēkon*), and the criterion of appropriateness is that which is in line with our nature, though on its own this standard is only a necessary, and not a sufficient condition of undertaking morally right actions. We are required also to cultivate our own character through a process of education, a therapeutic set of procedures designed ultimately to make us act rationally and hence happily. If we act irrationally, we act falsely, and this fact leads us to be governed by those passions produced by excessive impulses (*hormē*) that in turn lead to unnatural movements in the soul. Within this process, however, 'our moral progress is typified not by the extirpation of all emotion and desire, but by the occurrence of desires and feelings which are dispositions of a governing-principle increasingly consistent with right reason'.[152] Though exceptionally difficult to achieve, actions undertaken

---

[150] Locke, Letter 1798, to Jean Le Clerc [Oates?], October 9, 1694, in Locke 1976–89, pp. 159f; cf. Jean Le Clerc, Letter 1767, to Locke, August 2/12, 1694, in Locke 1976–89, pp. 103–5; Darwall 1995, pp. 162f, 169ff.

[151] Frede 1986, p. 98.

[152] Long 1974, p. 177.

through right reason are sharply contrasted with the passionate character of the human condition in general, which typically gives rise to disorders, or diseases of the soul that require therapeutic treatment. In an argument that would have profound implications, these four principal passions (of pleasure, pain or distress, fear and desire), are those that most people are prone to but which need to be regulated if our true good or happiness is to be achieved, and if we are to properly control our fears.[153]

If passions are often mistaken judgements, the idea that one can ever extirpate the passions therefore seems to go too far in conflating different Stoic propositions.[154] Such immunity is simply impossible. For as well as not simply being about the extirpation of the passions as such, what is hinted at in broad Stoic doctrine is that attention be paid to one's reaction to the causes of the passions in the first place and also therefore to the idea of aiming always to follow right reason (*logos*) in one's actions, even if this aim is not always achieved.[155] Thus, the causes of the passions are rooted in sensation, but these first prompt our so-called preliminary passions, or *propatheia*, which are the instant reactions we feel that we cannot control. What the sage will do here, that the majority will not, is judge whether these *propatheia* are important or not to the issue of human happiness, and act accordingly.[156] He will be guided by knowledge and experience, which has been developed by education and cultivation rather than mere opinion, and he will therefore act constantly and act politically, for the wise man will act for the common good of the community. Such 'reasonable emotions' for the Stoic are neither good nor bad, but simply indifferent, though in the appropriation of our actions to our own rational nature, a process often termed *oikeiōsis* (*οικειοσισ*) and outlined by Cicero in particular, such emotions can still lead to normative conflicts between individuals over particular relationships and choices.[157] This is because *oikeiōsis* appears to contain both social and individual characteristics, namely a coming to terms with what is appropriate to nature in the community, but also a personal element that allows us to try to perfect our own nature as best we can. This criterion of 'propriety' was, and is, flexible. It could even be used to justify a neo-Stoic withdrawal

[153] Cicero 1927, 4. 6. 12; discussion in James 1993, esp. pp. 294ff.

[154] Sorabji 2002, pp. 195ff.

[155] Garver 2006.

[156] Locke 1984, I. ii. 5, p. 48, on the opinion that primary characters or *koinai ennoia* are 'stamped on the Mind of man'; cf. I. iv. 15, p. 93, showing that even ideas of God cannot be thought to have been implanted except perhaps by those extremely rare '*wise Men* of all Nations [who] came to *have true Conceptions* of the Unity and Infinity *of the Deity*'. But this, importantly, 'excludes universality of Consent in any thing'.

[157] Cicero 1967, III. iv–v. 16–17, pp. 233–37; Annas 1995, p. 275; see too Frede 1986, p. 95; Reydams-Schils 2002, esp. pp. 232–36, revised Reydams-Schils 2005, ch. 2.

from a contemporary corrupt politics, as the use of Seneca in England shows.[158] At this point, though, I should like to return to the relationship between Locke's account of the will and the conception of personhood that can be found in Cicero's *De Officiis*.

In the first book of *De Officiis*, Cicero laid down the four ways in which one can think about the nature of personhood. He begins with the well-known presupposition that the idea of personality stems from the noun *persona*, traditionally the idea of the mask. The various personae with which one presents oneself to the world are tied to wider questions of what constitutes *decorum*, or what is fitting and appropriate for human beings, and in turn they offer an understanding of how propriety in both individual and social contexts might be able to reconcile claims of the *honestum*, or what is good, with the *utile*, the useful or beneficial. These claims have paramount importance for our understanding of later eighteenth-century writers, and the theatrical lineage did not go unnoticed.[159] But they equally importantly provide a context for Locke's ethics. Locke uses his philosophical discussion of qualities to determine what we mean when we use the term 'person' to refer to a general sense of the species to which that noun refers; he is most interested in the nature of individual personality, although both issues are foundational to the Ciceronian account.

In Cicero's updating of earlier discussions, we all bear two personae (*prosopon*). One, universal and common to all, consists in rationality and the capacity for moral choice and self-direction. Another equally 'natural' persona is that which is peculiar to us. To achieve *decorum* in general, and *aequabilitas* in particular, we must submit to both our general rational natures and our specific personal attributes. A third persona refers to the social position in which individuals find themselves, and a fourth consists in our own personal choice and the direction we give our lives through the vocation we choose. Moreover, although this fragmentation of individual identity into multiple personae might seem to threaten the avowedly Stoic concern with the unity of a person's sense of identity through appreciation of one's nature, it remains integral to the four-personae doctrine that these different masks 'can and must be made to cohere and coalesce by the self-directing moral agent, through the kind of choices that give his life the unity and consistency (*aequabilitas*) that is an integral component of *decorum*'.[160] As individual persons, we must choose what 'fits' with our nature best, in order to achieve our

---

[158] Seneca 1928, p. 242. For the background, see Salmon 1989, pp. 199–225; Tuck 1993, pp. 50ff, 104–19.

[159] Moore 2002, pp. 365–86.

[160] Cicero 1991, bk. 1, §§ 107, 110–12, 115, 119, pp. 42–46; discussion in Gill 1988, p. 177. See also Rorty 1990, pp. 21–38; Long 2006, esp. pp. 326ff.

own peace, or *decorum*. Persons act well when they act appropriately according to their status, nature and place in a wider hierarchy, as well as according to their own desires.[161] Our actions must therefore remain appropriate, while we can in fact 'appropriate' our actions to our own selves, in line with the doctrine of *oikeiōsis*. This idea will be rehearsed in a still more modern updating of the doctrine in the work of Adam Smith, and perhaps provides some foundation for Nietzsche's even later claim that everything which is truly 'deep' loves (*liebt*) masks, rather than direct appearance. Indeed, the capacity to wear appropriate masks and change one's personae as circumstances direct is the hallmark of the free.[162] In Locke it also often seems that the idea of decorum is closely related to that of virtue, but this 'virtue' simply equates to the free individual who is able to forebear from acting until a choice has been made about the quality of the action itself. The Stoic concern with the coincidence between reason and nature in the well-ordered and appropriately considered action, or between *logos* and *physis*, is mirrored in Locke's account of virtuous action and the causes of action in the uneasiness prompted by our passions.

There are certainly also close connections between Cicero's and Locke's arguments on property and personhood. Locke, of course, made the point explicitly when talking of individuals as having that 'Property which Men have in their Persons as well as Goods'. To talk of property is to talk of a right to anything, which is to say that it is a claim about justice, which then motivates the attempt to reconcile a narrative about the origins of government with a defence of property rights and what others called 'political arithmetick'.[163] The foundational importance of Epictetus's doctrine of self-ownership has often been noted in this context, as the ownership of an autonomous mind that has nothing to do with material possessions, but conceives of property as that which is truly and necessarily our own. Here, something like *oikeiōsis* as applied to the instinctual ability of animals towards self-preservation could provide an analogy (in terms of the 'cradle' argument) for Stoic notions of human self-consciousness. For when reflection upon the human animal begins, various stages of a life cycle are posited that render certain forms of appropriation appropriate at particular moments. This Stoic conception is underpinned with the idea of a developmental sense of personal identity that persists through time, but which also develops through it.[164] Given the intimate connections between this sort of appropriation of one's ac-

---

[161] Frede 2008, esp. pp. 157f, 161–66.

[162] Nietzsche 1968, §§ 40, 289, pp. 53, 244.

[163] Locke 1988, II, § 173, p. 383; Petty 1690, ch. 1, § 3; Goldie 2005, p. 15; cf. Long 2006a, pp. 342f.

[164] Long 2006a, pp. 345f, 351–57.

tions in the development of oneself as a person, and the foundations of
material property, the two themes coalesce around the question of justice. Justice is appropriate to the extent that it governs our own conduct
(as something like self-consciousness), and our social and economic interactions with other individuals.[165] For Locke, justice or just action is
that which conforms to the standards of propriety and which guarantees
through impartial legislation the rights of persons, and this guarantee of
a right is correlate with property, because property or propriety is simply
a right to something.[166] Justice is both the supreme and the most difficult
virtue to establish, but it is from justice that all duties to preserve rights
flow; indeed one needs 'upright' rather than 'learned' men to administer
such justice, given that 'most of the wrong judgments that are given in the
world are rather the faults of the will then of the understanding'. Justice
is therefore grounded in the fact that our rights as persons and our rights
towards others all stem from the workmanship of God.[167] Locke had elsewhere rejected the account of justice as pure utility, but understood well
its connections with both property and appropriate conduct. Instead, he
retained the foundational construction of pleasure and pain as the motivation for action within his defence of natural law.[168] Thus, our right to
liberty is simply construed as part of the wider duty of self-preservation,
even though self-preservation on Locke's reading is itself bound up with
the requirements of human and commercial prosperity and cultivation. It
is both self- and other-regarding, and must in fact be so if it is to cohere
with the dictates of the Golden Rule.[169] Civility (including the idea of loving one's neighbour) thus stems from justice, and justice as the defence of
one's right to any thing (that is, to property) is grounded in a theological
politics. Government functions to preserve property, in order that duties of self-preservation can be reconciled with providential design.[170] Yet
Locke here moves beyond Cicero towards his analysis of property rights
grounded in cultivation and the mixing of labour with an object. That
claim has no basis in Cicero's discussion of the origins of private property
in first, and then lengthy, occupation. Indeed, later writers like Thomas
Rutherforth would criticize Locke's use of it.[171]

If my argument is at all correct, then the distance between Locke's political theory and a modified Stoicism, or rather Ciceronianism, is not at

[165] Long 2006a, p. 357.
[166] Locke 1988, II, §§ 5, 219, pp. 270, 411.
[167] Quotations in Locke 2006b, p. 388; see too Locke 1997g, pp. 267ff; Locke 1988, I.
iv, § 39, pp. 167f; see too Harris 2000, pp. 49ff.
[168] von Leyden 1954, p. 39; cf. Tuck 1999, p. 169.
[169] Harris 2000, pp. 54–59.
[170] Locke 1988, II. vii, § 94, pp. 329f; Harris 2000, pp. 63–66.
[171] Cf. Cicero 1991, bk. 2, §§ 73–74, 78–83, pp. 92f, 95ff; Locke 1988, II, §§ 27–28, pp.
288f; Garnsey 2008, esp. pp. 113–18, 142ff; Sonenscher 2008, p. 230 n. 66.

all far. This is particularly pertinent given the importance of the addition of beneficence to the arguments about the paramount virtue of justice in both Cicero and Locke. It also accords with some recent scholarship, which notes that what Cicero proposed in 44 BC after the Ides of March was not the restoration of liberty after tyranny, but a reconceptualized account of freedom. Possessing liberty is not the absence of *dominatio*, but rather self-control over the power of *dominatus*, whether in terms of passion or reason, or of the power or *dominatus* of legitimate rule. This is a strongly Greek-inflected construction.[172] If I am right, moreover, Locke might well be seen as a particularly astute commentator on the Grecian implications of Cicero's politics concerning justice, trust and self-propriety, at least as much as he was astute concerning Cicero's Roman arguments about property.[173] What the 'heathen' Cicero could not offer Locke, as has already been suggested, was an argument that made sense of his theological commitments and motivations. And as it related to Locke's account of personhood, contemporary discussions of the Trinity filled in that gap. In answering questions similar to Hobbes's concerning the representation of the three personae of the Trinity, and rejecting the Trinity on broadly Socinian grounds, Locke explicitly engaged with different discussions of the nature of identity and personhood. In so doing he developed four distinct positions. First, he claimed that personal identity was consciousness through time, so that a person was distinct from a self. It was a position he argued for against the views of William Sherlock, for whom soul and person were the same, and Robert South, his contemporary at (and later canon of) Christ Church, for whom person, man, and self were coterminous. Second, Locke promoted a new and constitutive role for consciousness that would bring unity to personal identity. Third, against Sherlock again, Locke suggested in fact that that natural consciousness could not explain the unity of the Godhead as three distinct persons. Fourth, Locke did not suggest that a person was the same as an object, so that individuality of the self was presupposed for consciousness, but not for personal identity. Thus, personhood and selfhood could be disentangled. Yet although Locke certainly seems to have had Trinitarian debates and Sherlock's arguments in mind when writing his discussion of identity, these theologically inspired engagements were fundamentally in line with what he had been arguing in the *Essay* as well.[174] As is well known, Locke tried to assure his readers that immortality depended upon God, that mortalism was likely, but that debates about the

---

[172] Arena 2007, pp. 49–73; 2007a, pp. 59–63.

[173] See Atkins 1990, esp. pp. 264, 266ff, 276, 280; cf. Wood 1991.

[174] Thiel 2000, esp. pp. 241, 238f; cf. pp. 225f, 228f, 230f, 243; see also Locke 1997i, pp. 313–17; Sherlock 1691; discussion in Dunn 1969, p. 148 n. 1.

material or immaterial character of the soul were typically insufficient to prove the case.[175]

Such arguments were also clearly filtered through Locke's engagement with the main theses of Cambridge Platonism, especially those referring to the 'light of reason' implanted in human souls by God, and the 'active sagacity' of the mind in learning from its 'connatural' ideas.[176] Locke too conceived of the 'light of reason' as illustrating the obvious precepts of natural religion when properly understood; he also used the common metaphors of illumination and the light of the mind to indicate truth in the quest for knowledge.[177] He also, as did Montesquieu after him, thought hard about the implications of Malebranche's accounts of truth; in this case, however, he ended up mired in polemic with another critic, John Norris, particularly through his relations with Damaris Masham.[178] More important is the fact that he 'converted', in particular, Ralph Cudworth's proof of 'substantial creation' into a 'deductive form of the argument from design', to make it accord with his earlier reconciliation of the honourable and the useful.[179] He was strongly aware, as I have tried to show, of the importance of conventional judgements about human motivation, knowing that judgement is rooted in the 'Maxims, or Fashions' of a particular place and time.[180] This formed a further part of his discussion of the '*Law of Opinion or Reputation*' that follows from the analysis of divine and civil law in the *Essay*. Updating classical concerns about *fama* or reputation, this was designed to show how virtue and vice would relate to actions 'in their own nature right and wrong' if they were (as they rarely in fact are given the desire to be 'in reputation and in credit') actually 'co-incident with the divine law'.[181]

Despite these important qualifications, Locke essentially followed Cicero in judging virtue in terms of the quality of action, rather than character, detailing this position in an argument that would have considerable impact throughout the course of the eighteenth and nineteenth centuries.[182] He also saw that the Epicurean search for tranquillity or

---

[175] Thomson 2008, pp. 56ff, 117, 164.

[176] Scott 1994, pp. 139–50, esp. pp. 142ff, 147.

[177] Locke 1984, III. ix, p. 490; IV. xix. 13, pp. 703f; IV. xx. 3–4, pp. 707ff.

[178] MS Locke f. 8, p. 264; Locke 1843, esp. pp. 554f, 560, 566–74; discussion in Schuurman 2001, pp. 454f; Johnson 1958, esp. pp. 551, 552ff; Aarsleff 1982, p. 54; McCracken 1983, pp. 146, 148f, 156–79. On Locke and Damaris Masham, see Goldie 2005; Masham 2003, pp. 167–93. Finally, see also Norris 2005, esp. pp. 184–220.

[179] Hutton 1996, pp. xxv, xxii; for the claim about Locke and Cudworth, see Ayers 1996, II, pp. 174ff.

[180] Locke 1984, II. xxviii. 10, p. 353.

[181] Locke 1984, II. xxviii. 10, p. 353; J. Coleman 2005.

[182] Locke 2006c, p. 390; cf. Locke 1954, pp. 156, 214; Cicero 1991, bk. 1, §§ 12–18, pp. 6ff.

ataraxia (αταραχια) that comes from seeking pleasure and avoiding pain had considerable relevance. *Ataraxia* is seen as flowing from justice understood as a principle of association (το δικαιον) that in turn presupposes that we will respect the rights of others to justice when it is in our interest so to do, just as friendship is equally based on self-interest properly understood.[183] Updated, the idea of responsible or rational agency means being held accountable to shared standards of justice motivated by Christian duty and geared towards the good, even though justice is imperfectly realized as human artifice in the worldly *saeculum*.[184] To make sense, finally, of this part of the story and how it relates liberty and propriety, we must try to understand what Locke thought it meant to be a person who is capable of acting at liberty in the first place. In so doing, we will find an answer to the question of why he thought propriety to be the foundation of justice, and thereby freedom.

LIBERTY AND PERSONAL IDENTITY

Locke frames personal identity through consciousness, rather than physical bodily identity or the essence of what it might mean to be human, such as the soul.[185] It was an argument with radical implications.[186] Many of Locke's eighteenth-century interpreters examined such a theory, asked what it could really mean, and came to the conclusion that he took consciousness as a surrogate for memory. They challenged his assessment by suggesting that forgetfulness and memory were too flimsy as foundations for identity, and that instead one should look to the immaterial substance of the soul as providing the core of personhood. This essentially religious view nevertheless misread certain of Locke's provisos, and also underestimated the challenge of the new naturalist accounts of identity that came to 'engulf' the new century.[187] Moreover, Locke's discussion of liberty as a process pertinent to self-reflective creatures buttressed his account of the relationship between selfhood and consciousness, as well as extending it into more obviously political questions about money and appropriation in the *Second Treatise*.[188] Ownership is once again the 'Rule of propriety', because the regulation of civil life in a money economy requires an idea of the self-propriety of individual members in civil society, who

---

[183] Erler and Schofield 1999, pp. 667ff; Long 1974, pp. 69ff.
[184] Locke 1997j, p. 318.
[185] See Marshall 1994, pp. 152ff.
[186] Ayers 1996, II, pp. 315 n. 94, 314 n. 71.
[187] Martin 2000, p. 44; cf. Ayers 1996, II, pp. 220f, 224f, esp. pp. 266ff.
[188] Locke 1988, II, §§ 36–37, 47, pp. 292ff, 300f; also Locke 1954, pp. 168, 206, 212.

make and accept claims based on judgement, experience, and reasonable agreement.[189]

In the *Essay*, Locke argued that consciousness and memory of past actions, combined with a future-oriented interest in rewards and punishments motivated by the search for happiness, constitute awareness of oneself as a person. Through the appropriation of memory or self, as a form of self-consciousness, an individual agent effectively claims ownership of the self and becomes a person. It is an account that once again recalls the Stoic 'cradle' argument for *oikeiōsis*. Put another way, though, the immediate consciousness of a self is simply that, consciousness of a self in time. Yet although this consciousness does not necessarily imply personhood through time, it is consciousness, Locke claimed, which unifies a person both in time and over time when considering his or her particular forms of existence and actions.[190] This idea hinges upon his claim that most people conventionally assume the essence of man lies in outward shape or form, but that this assumption confuses the issue of how we might achieve knowledge about persons. Once again, our knowledge of substance or *propria* is too unclear, even if in practice the 'more probable Opinion is, that this consciousness is annexed to, and the Affection of one individual immaterial Substance', or a man.[191] Consciousness and its natural evolution over time therefore helps to differentiate personhood from selfhood for Locke, but this division is not without its own philosophical problems of social discounting and future identity.[192]

It is crucial to Locke's account of personhood that it involves an evaluative and comparative component. In dealing with thorny questions about whether the soul is immaterial and eternal, or whether it can move between individuals, Locke concluded that 'Nothing but consciousness can unite remote Existences into the same Person, the Identity of Substance will not do it'.[193] The account was not at all incompatible with Socinianism, where 'Any Substance vitally united to the present thinking Being, is a part of that very *same self* which now is: Any thing united to it by a consciousness of former Actions makes also a part of the *same self*, which is the same both then and now'.[194] Immediately following this section, he clarified that '*Person*, as I take it, is the name for this *self*', so crucially the concept of person is a 'Forensick Term appropriating Actions and their

---

[189] Locke 1991, p. 40; see also McClure 1996, pp. 251, 258f, 262ff, 286; cf. pp. 229f, 238.

[190] Locke 1984, II. xxvii. 25, pp. 331f, 346.

[191] Locke 1984, IV. iv. 15–16, pp. 570ff; II. xxvii. 25, p. 345.

[192] Parfit 1984, appendix F.

[193] Locke 1984, II. Xxvii. 23, p. 344.

[194] Locke 1984, II. Xxvii. 25, p. 346.

Merit; and so belongs only to intelligent Agents capable of a Law, and Happiness and Misery'. It extends backwards in time only through consciousness, and in so doing 'owns and imputes to it *self* past actions' just as it does present ones, namely on the grounds of seeking happiness and virtue through pleasure and the avoidance of pain.[195] So too does it move forward, thinking about future rewards and punishments under law.[196] And the idea of law (as protection of property) was 'not so much the Limitation *as the direction of a free and intelligent Agent* to his proper interest'. This meant that '*the end of Law* is not to abolish or restrain, but to *preserve and enlarge Freedom*', most notably, from being 'subject to the arbitrary Will of another'.[197]

Thus, Locke's conceptions of self and person are closely related but terminologically distinct, with the idea of a self presupposing a conscious thinking thing, a substance of whatever kind, whilst a person is that 'thinking, intelligent Being, that has reason and reflection'. This seems to mean that although one could be a self without being a person, one cannot be a person without being a self.[198] There is a process of mental and moral development that combines in the development of a person throughout the course of a life. This comes about through self-consciousness, and indeed the appropriation of one's consciousness to oneself, in and through time. Just as we are not born with innate ideas, but are generally thought of as having moral capacities that can develop and change, our own sense of self also develops in and through time until we become fully-fledged persons. The argument once more ties in with Ciceronian claims about self-appropriation, and is independent of Locke's account of bodily substance.[199] Life itself provides the necessary unity to both the substance of phenomenal identity and its realization in the form of conscious personhood.[200] Persons appropriate their actions and merit through consciousness of the relationship between past and present actions, and the forensic character of personhood means that moral persons are best understood as 'rational selves'. From this, the moral ideas we associate with rational (and free) action represent to us the real essence of what it means to be human. This is also what it means

---

[195] Locke 1984, II. Xxvii. 26, p. 346.

[196] See Sorabji 2006, pp. 105f; cf. Locke 1984, II. xxvii. 17, p. 341, on the self as 'concern'd for it *self* as far as that consciousness extends'.

[197] Locke 1988, II, § 57, pp. 305f; also II, §§ 137, 139, pp. 359f, 361f.

[198] Locke 1984, II. xxvii. 17, p. 241; cf. II. xxvii. 27, 9, p. 335.

[199] Cicero 1927, 3. 5–7, pp. 233–45; see also Nussbaum 1994, pp. 361, 373; on personal identity here, see Ayers 1996, II, pp. 261ff.; Seigel 2005, pp. 95f.

[200] Ayers 1996, II, p. 221.

for Locke's account of 'moral man' to be itself a 'moral proposition', un-affected by complex claims about substance.[201]

There are some powerful and well-known objections to this line of argument, focusing on its natural, rather than ethical presuppositions, and arguing that bodily identity is always a necessary (though not a sufficient) condition of personal identity. But it seems to me that Locke argued for aspects of all of these positions.[202] On Locke's account, one temporarily has proprietorship of one's body and its actions only through internal control of the passions, and external responsibility for those actions that follow rational deliberation. As persons we can be said quite literally to own our selves, even though as persons we can never actually own our body, a fact that has quite significant implications, I think, for those who use Locke to discuss claims about self-ownership.[203] For Lockean liberty presents a particular account of self-ownership, through its connections to natural law, education and the conventional development of both sentiment and approbation.[204] In Locke's view, our understanding of our own personhood is always incomplete, and we can only understand our own conception of ourselves by considering our own consciousness, our relations to others by which they judge us, and our theoretically complete but always practically incomplete knowledge of selfhood in light of the fact of our creation by God.[205]

As Sorabji has recently conjectured, there is evidence to provide a compelling case that Locke was well aware of classical Stoic debates about the nature of appropriation, through consciousness, of memory about one's own actions as a person over time. This too required a simultaneous focus on the body that houses a person.[206] Self-concern as legitimate appropriation, or *oikeiōsis*, seems to be of considerable importance to Locke's analysis. It also seems to remain the case that for Locke, one comes naturally to appropriate this consciousness of personhood in and through time, which is what renders an individual both substantially and consciously unified. With life itself the principle of this unity, we can be held accountable for our actions as natural or moral persons, even though our actions themselves are judged in the artificial context of shared moral conventions. Of course, for Locke, God also judges us. His judgement, however, is ultimately beyond rational comprehension unless we have received the light of revelation. What this means, though, is that Locke is concerned with both private and public criteria of personal

---

[201] Mattern 1980, esp. pp. 25, 29, 35.
[202] Ayers 1996, II, pp. 266ff; Williams 1999, esp. pp. 1, 3, 11.
[203] Cohen 1995, esp. pp. 209ff, 213ff, 230; cf. Ryan 1984, p. 15.
[204] Cohen 1995, pp. 68f and n. 4, 211, 236f.
[205] Seigel 2005, p. 103.
[206] Sorabji 2006, pp. 107f.

identity.[207] This concern makes his work surprisingly consonant with more recent theories of the relationship between personhood and free will, particularly those concerned with whether an individual will is consonant with second-order volitions that are produced by the first-order desires that motivate action. For if they are consonant, we can judge the capacity of agents to be held responsible to the extent that they identify with these desires more or less wholeheartedly.[208]

Clearly this sort of account requires conventional standards of judgement, and the conventionality of morality was a theme that Locke considered at length. Even so, the idea of differentiating between virtue and vice remained simultaneously subject to the laws of reason as well. Morality and opinion, taste and sentiment, fashion and language are all interrelated in a complicated manner with Lockean natural law, for opinion without reason is not knowledge, and if it concerns 'God and religion [it] deserves the name of Enthusiasme'.[209] Ultimately, though, the morality of individual action is reconciled with a theory of political liberty under the framework of propriety as justice. Moral actions are understood to be the actions of free agents, and free agents are those who make choices and are able to be held responsible and accountable for those actions. Morality that motivates obligation requires a foundation given by a lawgiver, and in this case, the supreme lawgiver is God. Therefore, although morality may practically operate in different ways in different times and places (indeed Locke repeatedly emphasized that environmental factors can lead to changes in ideas), in principle the ethics of true morality are limited to those effects of good and evil determined by natural law. The argument holds as much in the state of nature as in civil society.[210] For Locke, the use of reason to determine natural law and hence morality is itself a product of conscious personhood through time, because conscious personhood is the prerequisite to being able to appropriate actions and hence to be held accountable.

Although the recursive and indeed discursive character of responsibility has been of notable import to other contemporary theories of freedom and cultural identification, it seems to have important roots in Locke's political philosophy.[211] His political thought illustrates the beginning in British intellectual history of a mainstream political thinker discussing freedom as a form of appropriate conduct, undertaken by persons able to appropriate, or answer for, their own actions, both in the eyes of

[207] Williams 1999, pp. 13ff, 17; cf. pp. 76–79.
[208] See Frankfurt 1971, esp. pp. 15ff; 2006, esp. pp. 171f, 174ff.
[209] Locke, Letter 687, to Damaris Cudworth, *c.* February 21, 1682, in Locke 1976–89, vol. 2, p. 488; Locke 1984, IV. xix. 10, pp. 700ff.
[210] Locke 1997h, p. 304; also Carey 2004, esp. pp. 264f, 271f; Seigel 2005, p. 106.
[211] Pettit 2001, pp. 102f, 152, 52, 59, 61; Rorty 1994, pp. 152–66.

their peers and before their maker. Such an 'overcoming' of self had clear precedent in English culture with Milton, even though Locke's modification of such ideas seems to have come just as much through his engagement with Pierre Nicole and the French neo-Augustinian revival of the mid-seventeenth century.[212] It also puts Locke at the centre of important new ways of thinking about a radically disengaged self, at once subjectivist but exceptionally self-reflexive.[213] Indeed, this conception of a free agent, characterized by self-propriety and an idea of being one's own man, actually resembles central claims of Leveller politics despite Locke's apparent rejection of such politics. Freedom as independence remained as central to his vision as it did to theirs, as did the combination of theology and common law upon which both rest.[214]

To conclude, freedom for Locke is about governing conduct. Through self-government, we overcome the malign qualities of natural self-interest, and redirect our hedonism towards civil peace. On his account, free agents are those who act responsibly and appropriately towards their position as persons in a political society, the standards of which are set by the demands of justice and law. Thus understood, Locke's contemporary legacy is best sought elsewhere than in theories of self-ownership or Christian equality, and instead in theories of agency and answerability that understand the reactive and emotional roots of our responses to injustice as forms of resentment.[215] His reflections on the 'psychic impact of human socialization' in terms of the harm resulting from injustice to reputation and credit are just as provocative as those assayed by his successors.[216] In any case, Locke presents us with a theory of liberty that is worried about both the nature of personhood and the cultivation of the self towards personhood, as well as being bound up with the idea that personhood requires a public, rather than a private, sense of obligation to others under justice.[217] These were certainly issues with a lengthy post-Lockean afterlife, and it is to Montesquieu, one of the most illustrious proponents of liberty as doing what one should want to do, that my discussion now turns.[218]

---

[212] Scott 2003, pp. 320f, 342f.

[213] Taylor 1996, esp. pp. 161ff, 169–72, 241ff; cf. Macintyre 1994, p. 217.

[214] Skinner 2006, esp. pp. 163ff; Cromartie 2006, pp. 278f.

[215] See Strawson 1968, esp. pp. 84ff, 96; cf. Jay-Wallace 1994, esp. pp. 55f, 62ff, 66f, 69, 208.

[216] Cf. Dunn 1990, p. 34.

[217] Coleman 2004, esp. pp. 128f, 136.

[218] See Frankfurt 2006a, pp. 25, 31, 33, 36f; cf. Mill 1969e, CW, vol. 10, pp. 259, 256; Moreau 2005, esp. pp. 296ff, 301.

CHAPTER TWO

Passionate Liberty and Commercial Selfhood: Montesquieu's Political Theory of Moderation

Charles-Louis de Secondat, Baron de la Brède et de Montesquieu, is central to many histories of modern liberalism. His analysis of the causes, contexts and consequences of human action, however, takes him far beyond conventional liberal claims of freedom as the absence of interference or silence of the laws. Instead, rather like John Locke, Montesquieu considered the propriety or quality of action to be central to its derivation as free. Because of this, he discussed political liberty as a form of regulated conduct, and free agency more generally as appropriate and self-directed regulation of the passions. To act freely we must be aware of, and attempt to balance, the competing passions that move us to act within spheres of action that are nevertheless constrained by numerous forces beyond our direct control. Such constraints, or indeed structures, include the various types of laws that govern action (divine, political and natural), alongside more obviously human relations that spring from physical, intellectual, and passionate causes.

Given this requirement of balance and the reality of multiple and conflicting demands upon us, any form of constitutional engineering must navigate around a problem: although there are immutable natural and physical laws, this fact has no direct analogue in the political or social sphere. For although there are laws, contingency and uncertainty, failures of understanding and interpretation, and a complexity that stands little chance of rational explanation, defines political and social life. There can therefore be no idea of political or individual perfection, because 'perfection does not concern men or things universally'. There are only approximations to it, and then only in particular contexts when cultivated by a wise and prudent legislator.[1] As what might be termed 'composite creatures', we have passions that, for Montesquieu, may be more or less reasoned, but our reasoning capacity is limited, just as Pascal and the Jansenists had suggested.[2] In fact, Montesquieu continues the relative

---

[1] Montesquieu 1989, 5. 24. 7, p. 464; 1964, p. 700: 'car la perfection ne regarde pas l'universalité des hommes ni des choses'.

[2] Pascal 1966, no. 110, p. 58; see too Krailsheimer 1962, chs. 6–7; Krause 2006, pp. 215f.

dethroning of reason in political analysis outlined by writers like Nicole and indeed Locke. When discussing our subjection to these multiple forces, he was quite clear that reason alone 'never produces great effects on the spirits of men'.[3] Passions and their potentially chaotic character needed to be governed, moulded, and regulated for great effects to be produced. But only after beginning with these theoretical premises and their associated intuitions, did Montesquieu turn towards history to support his claims.[4]

In his greatest work, *De L'Esprit des Lois*, first published in 1748, one finds an attempt to reconcile two sets of claims. One is that free actions, which is to say actions that are self-directed and chosen rather than already determined by some other factor, are motivated by passions of the soul. Another is that the framework within which this self-directed agency takes place is inevitably constrained by factors such as climate, laws, religion, politics and so on. In combination, such freedom and determinism constitutes the general 'spirit' of a society, and only its contextual specificity allows us to make general judgements. For example, although he suggested that 'vanity is as good a spring for a government as arrogance is a dangerous one', Montesquieu thought that definite national traits underscored such general conceptions. He could therefore contrast the alleged laziness of the Spaniard with the industriousness of the Frenchman, while concluding that it should be 'unnecessary to say that moral qualities have different effects according to the other qualities united with them'. Roman arrogance, 'joined to a vast ambition, to the greatness of ideas, etc'., had produced results well enough known to render simple-minded social theorems redundant.[5] This chapter aims to take seriously the account of moderation and liberty as responsible and regulated agency offered by Montesquieu, and to investigate how he came to develop such a position. Montesquieu presents a synthetic natural jurisprudence to assess the importance of justice and natural law; uses historical constitutional theory to draw lessons from both the ancient world and the French monarchy for contemporary purposes; and presents an account of human agency as rooted in the passions of the soul, but only properly free if adequately regulated. How such passions motivate particular forms of politics, and how various regimes might extend political liberty whilst maintaining order and decorum, is filtered through Montesquieu's understanding of the legislator. If successful, legislation can combine moderation and freedom in support of natural human de-

---

[3] Montesquieu 1989, 3. 19. 27, p. 327; 1964, p. 648: 'Cette nation, toujours échauffée, pourrait plus aisément être conduite par ses passions que par la raison, qui ne produit jamais de grands effets sur l'esprit des hommes'. Cf. Shklar 1987, pp. 103, 106, 109.

[4] Desgraves 1995, p. 72.

[5] Montesquieu 1989, 3. 19. 9, pp. 312f; 1964, pp. 642f.

sires and the requirements of a modern commercial society. But success is rare in politics, and the argument suggests that political liberty is a form of conduct appropriately regulated both by individuals and by citizens. To put the point another way, this is why political liberty appears to be a form of propriety once more, precisely because it requires moderation and regulation. In order to show how all this fits together, my discussion takes each topic in turn, beginning with Montesquieu's analysis of justice.

JUSTICE

Montesquieu opened *De L'Esprit des Lois* with the general claim that the 'laws of nature' clearly 'derive from the constitution of our being'.[6] In fact, the very first sentence declared that when 'taken in the broadest meaning', laws 'are the necessary relations deriving from the nature of things; and in this sense, all beings [whether divine or secular, human or animal] have their laws'.[7] These laws provide the framing context within which justice can be discussed, and claims of justice will have to find a way of appropriately balancing the demands and values of these different spheres. The problem is not wholly dissimilar to more recent claims about justice and complex equality.[8] For Montesquieu, in fact, this problem interestingly included a scalar conception of taxation and liberty. The more liberty one has, the heavier taxation can be, whereas the fiscal trade-off for living under despotism is that one pays lower taxes.[9] But even here there is to be found a natural balance or appropriate relation between things, a contention that mirrors the earlier and celebrated account of justice expressed in his *Lettres persanes* of 1721. Assuming God exists and is just, it follows that

> Justice is a relation of suitability [*Convenance*] which one actually finds between two things: this relation is always the same, whichever being considers it, whether God, an Angel, or finally a Man.
>
> It is true that men don't always see these relations: often even those which they do see, they turn away from [*s'éloignent*]; & their own interest is always that which they see best. Justice raises its voice; but finds it hard to make itself heard amongst the tumult of the passions.[10]

[6] Montesquieu 1989, I. 1. 2, p. 6; 1964, p. 531; cf. Montesquieu 1989, 5. 26. 6, pp. 498f; 1964, p. 712.

[7] Montesquieu 1989, I. 1. 1, p. 3; 1964, p. 530.

[8] Walzer 1994, esp. pp. 18ff.

[9] Montesquieu 1989, 2. 13. 12, p. 221; 1964, pp. 610f.

[10] Montesquieu 2004, Letter 81, p. 359: 'La Justice est un rapport de Convenance, qui se trouve réellement entre deux choses: ce rapport est toujours le même, quelque Etre qui le

Much scholarly ink has been spilt in trying to determine exact sources and influences of this claim.[11] For my purposes, the interconnection between justice and the passions is crucial. It suggests that justice writ large pertains to a general relationship between things, whatever their nature, independent of human law. Justice under human law, or justice writ small, however, must have its foundations in 'the existence and the sociability of reasonable beings'.[12] When justice is put in these terms, Montesquieu seems to be developing a much broader tradition of natural jurisprudence, out of which he synthesizes at least three positions about justice and natural law. First, he is very close to something like the notorious clause in Grotius's *De Jure Belli et Pacis*, which observed that rational agency, natural law and natural sociability would still have force 'even were we to suppose' (*etiamsi daremus*) that God did not exist.[13] Although the assumption of divine existence presupposed for Montesquieu claims about God's perfection and justness, he nevertheless has Usbek say that even if there were no God, we 'must always love Justice; that is to say to make an effort to resemble this being, of whom we have such a wonderful idea'.[14] His self-proclaimed novelty was to take such natural jurisprudential arguments and to apply them to the realm of civil or positive laws. Thus it was that he saw his text as a creation without a mother, and as creating a 'modern' theory of natural law.[15]

Montesquieu's theory of law and justice as a *rapport de convenance* certainly connotes a relationship grounded in thin theories of sociability and rational action. A second point of synthesis, however, stems from the search for what is *proprium* to human relationships. Montesquieu, like Locke before him, seems to cultivate the Ciceronian account of *oikeiōsis*, which was also important to both Grotius and Pufendorf.[16] As some in-

---

considere, soit que ce soit Dieu, soit que ce soit un Ange, ou enfin que ce soit un homme. Il est vrai que les hommes ne voyent pas toujours ces rapports: souvent même lors qu'ils les voyent, ils s'en éloignent; & leur interêt est toujours ce qu'ils voyent le mieux. La Justice éleve sa voix; mais elle a peine à se faire entendre dans le tumulte des passions'.

[11] Macdonald 2003, pp. 112ff.

[12] Montesquieu 1955f, esp. pp. 159, 161f: 'la Justice n'est pas dépendante des lois humaines, qu'elle fondée sur l'existence & la sociabilité des êtres raissonables'.

[13] Grotius 2005a, vol. 3, p. 1748; cf. Grotius 2005, vol. 1, § XI, p. 89. Grotius's discussions of *mare liberum* and *mare clausum* were equally well known to Montesquieu. See BN N. A. F. 12837, fo. 3ʳ (= Montesquieu, *Collectio Juris*, vol. 1); Lewis 1995, esp. pp. 307, 314.

[14] Montesquieu 2004, Letter 81, p. 360: 'Ainsi quand il n'y auroit pas de Dieu, nous devrions toujours aimer la Justice; c'est à dire faire nos efforts pour ressembler à cet Etre, dont nous avons une si belle idée'. Cf. Montesquieu 2004, Letter 81, p. 359, for the claim that if God were not perfect in his justness, he 'would be the worst and most imperfect of beings [*le plus mauvais & le plus imparfait de tous les Etres*]'.

[15] Courtney 2001, esp. pp. 45f; cf. Ehrard 1963, vol. 2, p. 498; Tuck 1990, pp. 99–22; Montesquieu 1964, p. 874 (*Pensées*, no. 191).

[16] Grotius 2005, vol. 1, esp. pp. 80f; cf. Tuck 2005, p. xxix n. 34; 1999, pp. 172–76.

terpreters of Cicero have noted, the relational conception of the virtues in *De Officiis* might indeed be best understood in French as either *convenance* or *convenables*, and it would be unsurprising if this interpretation was not precisely what Montesquieu had in mind. The language was well known.[17] Indeed, an important transmitter or filter for these ideas was the work of Jean Barbeyrac, and in particular his classic preface to the translation of Pufendorf's *De Jure Naturae*. With the scepticism and Epicureanism of Pierre Bayle as his target, Barbeyrac illustrated how 'a great philosopher', namely Locke, had related morality and freedom of action. Locke had shown, he wrote, that morality was related to agency to the degree that one could try to attain certainty in the course of choosing between different courses of action, based on comparing 'carefully certain *Relations*, which we conceive between *human Actions* and a certain *Rule*'.[18] Moral determinations could be properly assessed through our conventional experience of natural law as persons, where claims of right or justice underpin property, that is to say, under moderate government.[19] This view connected neatly with Montesquieu's use of extant French legal thought, and in some ways his major work seems to be a direct attempt to update *Les Lois civiles dans leur ordre naturel*, published between 1689 and 1694, by the Jansenist Jean Domat. Domat's eleventh chapter considered directly the nature and the 'spirit' of laws, famously dividing the variety of laws into either immutable and natural, or arbitrary and artificial.[20] The purpose of legal study as Domat (and equally Montesquieu) defined it, was therefore 'nothing else but the Art of discerning Justice and Equity'.[21] Given the Jansenist connections, it is unsurprising that Domat had also developed the provocative argument that the 'social ethic' underpinning his age, that of the *honnête homme*, was at root a mask for human corruption.[22] And though Montesquieu did not quite go that far, as later sections will show, his similar awareness of honour as both natural and simultaneously artificial was important.

Nevertheless, the claim about justice and moderation also illustrated the important Platonic and neo-Platonic debts he owed to Gravina, Malebranche, Leibniz and Shaftesbury in particular. These constitute the third

[17] Milton-Valente 1956, esp. pp. 171, 188f; Sonenscher 2008, pp. 214f.

[18] Barbeyrac 1749, p. 3 and n. 9; see the discussion in Hochstrasser 1993, esp. pp. 294ff, 298ff, 303–4 n. 58; Desgraves 1995, p. 71.

[19] Hochstrasser 1993, pp. 307f; 2000, pp. 21ff; cf. Saunders 2003, esp. pp. 479f, 483–85.

[20] See Domat 1722, vol. 1, ch. 11, 'Of the Nature and Spirit of Laws', pp. xxvii–xliv; discussion in Keohane 1980, pp. 303–6.

[21] Domat 1722, p. xliv; Sonenscher 2007, pp. 154ff; cf. Domat 1965, pp. 85f; Goyard-Fabre 1993, esp. pp. 71ff, 75f, 78ff, 82f; Keohane 1980, pp. 416f, 305; see Lewis 1995, pp. 309f, for Montesquieu's use of Domat.

[22] Viner 1972, p. 56; Parrish 2005, esp. pp. 220f, 225–30.

element of his conceptual synthesis. Montesquieu based his terms 'Political State' and 'Civil State' most explicitly on Gravina's authority, where the former is the union of '*all individual strengths*', whilst the latter is the '*union of these wills*'.[23] He did so less for Gravina's Platonism, however, than for his rejection of unitary and indivisible sovereignty, in favour of a conception of political unity where the general will is the expression of the civil law.[24] This seems to have done more work for Montesquieu than the cognate account of general and particular wills he could find in Hobbes's *De Cive*, which seems in fact to have paved the way for Rousseau's later discussion.[25] There, Hobbes had focused on the subjection by each man of 'his *will* to the *will* of a *single* other [*alterius unius*], to the *will*, that is, of one *Man* [*Hominis*] or of one *Assembly* [*Concilium*], in such a way that whatever one *wills* on matters essential to the common peace may be taken as the *will* of all and each [*omnes et singuli*]'.[26] Such a union results in the civil person of the commonwealth or state being formed, since 'the will of each citizen is comprehended in the will of the commonwealth in all matters)'. This makes the individual will 'free whenever it so wishes', for it is 'not obligated by the *civil laws*; for the civil laws are the laws of a commonwealth, and if it were obligated by them, it would be obligated to itself' and no commonwealth can be 'obligated to a citizen'.[27] This was compatible with Montesquieu's defence of honour, though the absolute and unitary sovereignty of the Hobbesian commonwealth had to be rejected.

More obviously Platonic was Malebranche's claim that ideas of just and unjust, of truth and falsity, were all equally the same whether considered by God, man, or the angels, because justice is a relationship of mathematical proportion.[28] Montesquieu added that if God exists, for whom we must once again assume a benign and beneficent universal will, then there are divine origins to the human passions, which although they

---

[23] Montesquieu 1989, I. 1. 3, p. 8; 1964, p. 532, emphasis in original; cf. Locke 1988, I. ix, §§ 98–99, p. 213; Goyard-Fabre 1993, pp. 92, 95f; Montesquieu 1964, pp. 876, 938 (*Pensées*, nos. 209, 598).

[24] Montesquieu 1989, I. 1. 3, p. 8; 1964, pp. 531f, citing Gian Vincenzo Gravina, *Origine Romani juris*, 1739, bk. 2, ch. 18, p. 160, and bk. 3, ch. 7, p. 360n. This text by Gravina is not in the catalogue of Montesquieu's library, though it does contain Montesquieu's copy of Gravina, *Della Ragion poetica*, 1716. See Desgraves 1954, no. 2407, p. 148. For a biographical note concerning Gravina, see Wokler and Goldie 2006, p. 740. See also Volpilhac-Auger 2001, p. 119. For Gravina's Platonic-inspired rejection of Locke and the *Lochisti*, see Israel 2006, pp. 522–26; also Stapelbrook 2008.

[25] Rousseau 2003, bk. 1, ch. 7, pp. 51–53; bk. 4, ch. 1, pp. 121f.

[26] Hobbes 1998, ch. 5, §§ 6, 9, pp. 72f. Emphasis in original.

[27] Hobbes 1998, ch. 5, § 14, p. 84. Emphasis in original.

[28] Malebranche 1962–84, vol. 11, part 1, ch. 1, p. 19, quoted in Montesquieu 2004, p. 359 n. 2.

are common to persons in general, can equally be understood as 'particular causes'. In so arguing, Montesquieu was part of a well-explored linguistic and conceptual transformation of the divine into the civic, even though he rather tempered the mathematical exactitude of Malebranche in favour of the rough proportionality in justice suggested by others like Aristotle.[29] Similarly, in terms of its phrasing, the analysis recalls Locke's old intellectual sparring partner in matters Hobbesian, the third Earl of Shaftesbury.[30]

It has long been known that Montesquieu drew from contemporary travel literature, as had Locke and Shaftesbury, precisely to undermine claims of moral universalism. We also know that he incorporated something of Shaftesbury's neo-Stoic form of innate moral sense, to argue for the possibility of an appropriate balance between virtue and the passions.[31] Montesquieu's awareness of and proximity to Shaftesbury's ideas would be buttressed with a wide variety of concerns, some of which could have been clarified still further during his stay in England from 1729 to 1731. For example, this visit allowed him to develop in private a view of England as the exemplar of a liberty greater than that of Venice or Holland.[32] At this time he was extremely close to the Whig circle of Bolingbroke and the secretive Club d'Entresol, and could engage with the debates between writers like Lévesque de Pouilly (friend of Bolingbroke, theorist of moral sentiments and apparent plagiarist) and Nicolas Fréret.[33] More generally, though, Shaftesbury's language—a 'thousand other Springs, which are counter to *Self-Interest*, have as considerable a part in the Movements of this Machine'—is highly suggestive of the various *ressorts* to which Montesquieu alludes when discussing the passions and actions of the human 'machine'.[34] Added to this view was an idea of suitability that Montesquieu seems to take almost directly from Leibniz's *Théodicée*.[35] There, through a critique of Hobbes's account

[29] Riley 1986, pp. 111, 113f; Nelson 2004, esp. pp. 169–76.

[30] See Klein 1994.

[31] Crisafulli 1943, esp. pp. 372ff, 376–80, 382ff, 386f.

[32] Montesquieu 1964, pp. 331–34 ('Notes sur l'Angleterre'); 1964, pp. 326–31, esp. p. 330 ('Hollande'). For the general connections, see Shackleton 1988, esp. p. 14; Keohane 1980, pp. 376–91. Cf. Montesquieu 1964, pp. 1035ff (*Pensées*, no. 1805); and for Dutch readings of Montesquieu, see Israel 2006, pp. 359f; Velema 1997, pp. 44–63.

[33] On Pouilly's alleged plagiarism, Nadel 1967, esp. pp. 439f, 441ff; more broadly Raskolnikoff 1992, pp. 148ff, 152ff, 419–46, 712; also Pocock 1999, pp. 156f, 226ff; Ehrard 1963, vol. 2, pp. 555f. Cf. Fréret 1758; while Golden 1951, remains the standard Anglophone account of Pouilly. On the Club d'Entresol, see Childs 2000.

[34] Shaftesbury 2001, vol. 1, part 3, § 3, p. 72; also Viner 1972, p. 70.

[35] Desgraves 1954, no. 405, p. 32; no. 1532, p. 112, shows the editions owned in Montesquieu's library catalogue; discussion in Mason 1975, pp. 21, 22 n. 45, 24, 28, 178ff; Crisafulli 1937, esp. pp. 774f, 777.

of freedom and the will, Leibniz described a 'kind of justice which has for its goal neither improvement nor example, nor even redress of the evil. This justice has its foundation only in the fitness of things, which demands a certain satisfaction for the expiation of an evil action'. This punitive and 'avenging justice', which he claimed that 'the Socinians, Hobbes and some others do not admit', was certainly recognized by Montesquieu.[36]

Leibniz's account of the relationship between justice and causality offered to 'defend Aristotle against the cavil of Grotius' (and presumably Hobbes too), by arguing that 'Justice (particular) is a virtue serving the mean in the affections of one man toward another, the affections of enjoying or harming, or those of good will and hate. The role of the mean is to gratify another (or myself) as long as this does not harm a third person (or another)'.[37] Montesquieu could have said much the same without distorting his own theory, even though as a young man he found Leibniz's critique of European politics and republicanism less than satisfactory.[38] He was more sympathetic, one imagines, to Leibniz's Platonist metaphysics. This was structured around an account of cosmic harmony and the equivocal character of causation, and led him to the proposition that justice is the 'charity of the wise', a universal relationship as well as a virtue that structures social interaction.[39] Whilst on its own Leibniz's work could not do everything Montesquieu wanted, in combination and synthesis with the other elements of his work already outlined it created a vast and complex lens through which to see particular problems of justice.[40] It structured the answers to a variety of questions that intrigued him, ranging from probability and contingency, chronology and evidence (in politics and morals as well as natural science), through to the nature of classical history.

Montesquieu continued to suggest that just as there are physical and invariable laws that determine matter and motion, so too are there invariable laws that govern the 'intelligent world'. And although agency as self-determined action could play a part on this stage, once again it is important to note that the intelligent world is 'far from being as well governed'

[36] Leibniz 1952, § 73, p. 161.

[37] Leibniz 1969, pp. 75f; cf. Goyard-Fabre 1993, pp. 86–89, 91.

[38] Montesquieu, Letter no. 352, to Baron von Stein, October 17, 1729, in Montesquieu 1998a, pp. 406–9.

[39] Mercer 2001, pp. 174, 175 n. 5, 176, 178, cf. pp. 209, 361; see also Leibniz 1969, pp. 74f: 'It is very improbable that the term cause expresses an unequivocal concept to cover efficient, material, formal, and final causes'. On Leibniz's political thought more generally, see Riley 1999, esp. pp. 30ff, 37f; Leibniz 1988, esp. pp. 47ff; Leibniz 1988a, esp. p. 71; Leibniz 1988b, esp. p. 171; Hunter 2004, esp. pp. 681–89.

[40] Nelson 2004, esp. pp. 146–54.

as the natural or physical world. This upholds his rather deflationary account of the importance of reason (as rational calculation) in human affairs.[41] The intelligent world, he wrote, 'does not follow its laws consistently' even though such rules or laws are a 'consistently established relation'. This is because 'every diversity is *uniformity*, every change is *constancy*'.[42] As a physical being, man is 'governed by invariable laws like other bodies'. As an intelligent being he is 'limited' by his 'nature', often makes poor use of his reason, and is fallible because he consistently makes bad use of the 'thousand passions' to which he is subject.[43] And in a rhetorical move that subverted standard accounts of the relationship between character and virtue, Montesquieu suggested that the 'man of spirit', that is to say, an individual who is moved by passions, is universal. Given the variety of factors that affect a person's character, however, the 'man of spirit' who is also a man of 'character' is extremely rare.[44] Universalism and particularism here combine to show how complicated moral and political judgements are, and how infinite their variety can be, as infinite in fact as our individual responses to questions of beauty or aesthetics. All judgements are based in our passions and desires, and the variety of our judgements is once again an illustration of the 'weakness of the human condition [*foiblesse de la condition humaine*]'.[45] Because Montesquieu's analysis once more implies an account of inclinations and judgements rooted in our soul, it suggests a rather aesthetic appreciation of politics.[46] That claim rings true in his assessment of Plato, alongside Shaftesbury, Malebranche and Montaigne as the four greatest poets rather than political thinkers.[47]

What unites all of these thinkers into Montesquieu's synthesis, however, is the requirement of moderation in the face of worldly uncertainty and confusion, constancy (a central theme of early-modern politics derived from Tacitean commentary) amidst the turbulence of the passions, and recognition of the complex relations between the worlds of nature

[41] Montesquieu 1989, I. 1. 1, pp. 3f; Montesquieu 1998, p. 7: 'Mais il s'en faut bien que le Monde intelligent soit aussi bien gouverné que le Monde physique'.

[42] Montesquieu 1989, I. 1. 1, p. 4; Montesquieu 1998 (Version imprimée), p. 6: 'Ces régles sont un rapport constamment établi . . . chaque diversité est *uniformité*, chaque changement est *constance*'. Emphasis in original.

[43] Montesquieu 1989, I. 1. 1, p. 5; Montesquieu 1998 (Version imprimée), pp. 8f: 'L'homme, comme Etre physique, est, ainsi que les autres Corps, gouverné par des Loix invariables. Comme Etre intelligent, il viole sans-cesse les Loix que Dieu a établies, & change celles qu'il établit lui-même . . . il devient sujet à mille passions'.

[44] Montesquieu 1955i p. 419. For discussion and translation, see Richter 1976, pp. 132–38; Montesquieu 1976, pp. 139–62.

[45] BN, N. A. F. 717 [*Autographes XV–XIXᵉ Siècles*] fo. 29ʳ.

[46] Thomas 2005, esp. pp. 75, 77f; also Shackleton 1988c, esp. p. 104.

[47] Montesquieu 1964, p. 1073 (*Pensées*, no. 2095); cf. Casabianca 2008.

and politics.[48] Out of this heady concoction of what one might think of as philosophical worldliness, Montesquieu tried to render his account of comparative constitutionalism scientific, in two ways: first, by developing a particular form of constitutional theory, an amalgam memorably designated by Sheldon Wolin as 'a variant of organizational theory and political methodology';[49] second, by promulgating a science of laws, or legal pluralism, that 'struck a mortal blow' against absolutism in France generally, and unitary accounts of political sovereignty in particular.[50] Such an account has political force, but also highlights the problems of both political and moral judgement under conditions of uncertainty.[51] It is at least probable that Montesquieu wished to update the classical theory of justice as correct proportion in light of his thinking about liberty as security on the one hand, and, on the other, the idea of commercial justice as upholding a 'just price' under conditions of economic uncertainty.[52] If he could do so, he would show that wealth and luxury prompt passions that might conflict with justice, and that economic ambition can foster the commodification of 'moral reasoning'.[53] At the level of the polity, luxury is an index measuring inequality, and at the level of the individual a soul corrupted by luxury will eventually turn against those laws that constrain it. This could be dangerous for both republics and monarchies, though the solutions provided by each are different.[54] Both require individual self-propriety, but where the one sought austerity and virtue, the other gloried in self-interest and honour. Because the former was thought by Montesquieu to be inapplicable to the modern age, it meant that he first had to draw a series of appropriate lessons from classical visions of politics, so as to avoid their earlier mistakes.

Lessons in Classics: Politics, Friendship and Despotism

Montesquieu's youthful *Dissertation sur la politique des Romains dans la religion* was read to the Academy of Bordeaux on June 18, 1716.[55] Although he ultimately rejects Machiavelli's attempts to promote Rome as a political model as both impossible and undesirable for modern com-

[48] On the rise of Tacitean commentary, see Momigliano 1949, pp. 190–92; 1947, esp. pp. 97f, 100; also Volpilhac-Auger 1985, esp. pp. 129ff.
[49] Wolin 2004, p. 351, on 'constitutional theory'.
[50] Keohane 1980, pp. 394, 406, on Montesquieu's 'constitutionalism'.
[51] Keohane 1980, p. 394; Wootton 2008, pp. 21–53.
[52] Spector 2005, pp. 217–42, pp. 222, 235f; cf. Montesquieu 1955g, p. 214.
[53] Kingston 1996, p. 211.
[54] Montesquieu 1989, I. 7. 2, p. 98; 1964, p. 565. See too Spector 2006, p. 138.
[55] Shackleton 1988d, esp. pp. 120f; Oake 1953, p. 548.

mercial society, Montesquieu's focus on the importance of religion to the development of Roman law and society offered another synthesis, this time of Machiavellian prudence and contemporary social and political thought.[56] It was then filtered through the lens of a comparison between Greece and Rome as imperial powers.[57] Thinking the Romans more 'tolerant' of other religions than the Greeks (using the treatment of Socrates as an example) but harsher in their educational requirements, Montesquieu first assessed the practical utility of Roman religion. In so doing his presentation mirrored the language of contemporary translations of Machiavelli, and the opening line suggested that neither fear, nor piety, but 'necessity' was the basis of religion in general, but Roman religion particularly.[58] Indeed, just as Machiavelli talked of the founding of a great city and then empire as a matter of great *fortuna*, which *virtù* could only try to maintain, Montesquieu had long thought the founding of Rome was based on the luck of having a Numa in the right place at the right time.[59] Like most of Montesquieu's work, his use of such ideas had both an historical and a contemporary purpose. First, it suggested parity between climate, religion, laws and maxims of government, moeurs and manners as explanatory variables 'mutually related to one another', and which together determine the 'general spirit' or character of a state.[60] Equally, however, just as Machiavelli proceeded by subverting his classical authorities, so too did Montesquieu use the developing and unmasking language of Tacitean political writing to overturn conventional contemporary thoughts about political prudence. This was clearest in his analysis of universal monarchy, which in turn buttressed a still further analysis of Rome.[61]

During 1734, Montesquieu had composed his *Considérations sur les causes de la grandeur des Romains et de leur Décadence* for publication in Holland. This was nearly seventeen years after his initial paper on Rome to the Bordeaux Academy, and he conceived of it as a separate

[56] Myers 1995, p. 47; Bayle 1702, esp. p. 1959, note E.

[57] Montesquieu 1955a, pp. 45, 48; Montesquieu 1964c, p. 41. For Montesquieu's account of Greek imperialism, see Volpilhac-Auger 2002, pp. 49–60, on the folly of conquest; see too Muller 2002, pp. 64ff.

[58] Montesquieu 1964c, p. 39: 'Ce ne fut ni la crainte ni la pieté qui établit la religion chez les Romains; mais la nécessité où sont toutes les sociétés d'en avoir une'. Shackleton 1988d, pp. 120f, notes the similarities with Testard's contemporary translations of Machiavelli.

[59] Machiavelli 1989, bk. 1, chs. 1–3, 9, pp. 192–202, 217–20; Montesquieu 1964c, p. 48.

[60] See Oake 1953, pp. 553f, 557, 549, who notes that for Montesquieu religion is a 'social force which has parity with others'. Quotations from Montesquieu 1964, p. 948 (*Pensées*, no. 645); cf. Montesquieu 1989, 3. 19. 4, p. 310; 1964, p. 641.

[61] Soll 2005, esp. pp. 95ff, 120, and more broadly pp. 59ff; cf. Robertson 1993, esp. pp. 353, 372.

publication.[62] However, it actually followed another essay from 1727 that had been bundled together with papers on the debts and riches of Spain, and which focused on the idea of a universal monarchy in Europe. These *Réflexions sur la monarchie universelle en Europe* were initially planned to form the concluding part of the *Considérations*, making clear their contemporary import through a joint critique of both historical Rome and contemporary imperial politics.[63] If the French were proposing to advance a universal monarchy, they would have to engage in still further stockpiling of public debt; taxation would therefore fail to be 'just and proportional' (*juste & proportionelle*), and its support would require the sort of 'fictional wealth' (*richesses de fiction*) that the Spanish (and the English) had gathered up but which distorted political realities.[64] Many thought Louis was following this sort of Spanish model.[65]

Fictional wealth went along with universal monarchy, and an attack on one was simultaneously an attack on the other. In developing searing criticisms of recent Spanish imperial practice, Montesquieu was therefore also attacking contemporary French politics under the 'grand prince'. The Spanish were corrupted by luxury, as could be seen in their plundering of the Americas and their debasing of 'natural' by 'artificial' credit. Indeed he had long thought the French could and should manage their (rather smaller) empire much more effectively.[66] But the French king had 'lost the heart of his subjects' through the prosecution of 'a vain war' that was a direct result of 'intolerable taxes'.[67] The recent Wars of the Spanish Succession had clarified this loss of allegiance, and had highlighted the failure to tackle those real (rather than fictitious) problems facing a prince, which stemmed from the 'immutability of his condition' (*immutabilité de sa condition*).[68] Instead of appreciating this need to govern, Europe had been ravaged by a general 'rage for conquest'.[69] The begin-

[62] Montesquieu 2000, vol. 2, pp. 89–98; also in Montesquieu 1964e, pp. 435–85. See too Montesquieu, Letter to Lady Hervey, September 28, 1733, and Père Castel, Letter to Montesquieu, April 23, 1734, both in Montesquieu 1955j, pp. 954ff, 962f. See Kingston 1996, pp. 51ff, on Montesquieu and the Academy.

[63] Spector 2006, p. 403.

[64] Montesquieu 1955, esp. p. 25; cf. BN Mss. Fr. 7767, for the wide selection of responses to the question of what to do about the French debt. See too Montesquieu 1989, 3. 19. 27, p. 327; 1964, p. 648.

[65] Spector 2006, p. 444.

[66] Montesquieu 1955e, pp. 142ff, 147ff; cf. Rahe 2005, p. 70 n. 82.

[67] Montesquieu 1964, p. 937 (*Pensées*, no. 596): 'Le Roi avait perdu le Coeur de ses sujets par les tributs intolérables dont il avait chargés, soutien necessaire d'une guerre vaine'.

[68] Montesquieu 2000a, §§ 6–7, 9–10, 16–19, 23–24, pp. 345f, 348f, 355, 358, 360, 362.

[69] Montesquieu 1734; 1734a. The phrasing belongs to Tobias Smollet, who appears to have translated a version of Montesquieu's text. See Montesquieu 1752; discussion in Miller 2004, esp. pp. 175ff.

ning of Montesquieu's thinking about moderation, which would dampen such rage, is to be found in these early texts. It is therefore unsurprising to find him beginning by focusing on the problems faced by Europe as the heir of the Roman Empire.[70] Rome was motivated by a passion for conquest through military honour and glory, and that singular focus (which might well be an exaggeration but which was Montesquieu's view of the general Roman spirit) exemplified why it could not be a model for any society with an awareness of multiple causes and myriad passions, all of which might make some claim to legitimacy. It was 'morally impermissible' (*moralement impossible*) to follow Rome in the modern world, where new modes of warfare based upon the equality of men and states had triumphed over earlier models of aggressive territorial expansion. Indeed, 'today victories confer only sterile laurels' (*lauriers stériles*) as well as being politically and financially problematic.[71]

Similar problems applied to an excessive valorisation of the Greeks. As a nation of warriors and athletes, they too were moved by a singular species of passion, rooted in severity and anger. Modern European societies, subject to contradictory fortunes, to movements of spirits and to a 'variety of passions' that 'continually change circumstances', were clearly unlike Greece and Rome. Yet these monarchies were disadvantaged compared to republics governed by 'views of the public good', because their own turmoil reflected internal favouritism and ambition.[72] Paradoxically, that which was designed to oil the wheels of the monarchical machine was becoming corrupted, both in terms of the pursuit of universal monarchy and in terms of a general decline in respect for the monarch upon which such authority rested. But although one should reject the Roman model, the contrast between monarchies and republics still had contemporary purchase, because both were threatened by luxury.[73] So while Montesquieu rejected Machiavelli's celebration of republican frugality and empires for increase as inapplicable to commercial society, he recognized the truth of the claim about the nature of republics in general and republican virtue in particular.[74] His own analysis suggested 'that in

[70] Montesquieu 2000a, pp. 5, 322. See too Montesquieu 1964, pp. 192–97; Rahe 2005, esp. pp. 59f, 67 n. 70; Kuhfluß 1987, pp. 281, 287f.

[71] Montesquieu 2000a, § 1, pp. 339–40.

[72] Montesquieu 2000a, §§ 2–3, pp. 341, 343f: 'l'inconstance de la fortune, la mobilité des esprits, la varieté des passions, le changement continuel des circonstances, la difference des causes font naître mille obstacles'. Therefore, 'Les Monarchies ont sur-tout ce desavantage qu'on s'y gouverne tantôt par les vües du Bien public, tantôt par des vües particulieres, & qu'on y suit tour à tour les interest des Favoris, des Ministres & des Rois'.

[73] Spector 2006, p. 138; in general see Montesquieu 1989, 2. 11. 6, p. 166; 1964, p. 590; cf. Montesquieu 1989, I. 5. 7, pp. 50f; 1964, p. 547. Cf. Machiavelli 1989, bk. 3, ch. 33, pp. 502f.

[74] Montesquieu 1989, I. 5. 3, pp. 43f; 1964, p. 545; cf. Pocock 2003a, esp. pp. 484,

republics where wealth is equally divided, there can be no luxury', so that 'the less luxury there is in a republic, the more perfect it is'.[75] Luxury was 'always proportionate to the inequality of fortunes', and it was dangerous precisely because it fed on natural ambitions and desires; the close proximity of people to one another in towns and cities makes them 'more vain', and 'the more they feel arisen within them the desire to call attention to themselves by small things'. Luxury 'produces this expectation' and lays a path to ruin.[76] Under monarchy, such problems had also to be watched carefully, but a well-ordered monarchy could use this natural vanity and harness it towards a social ethic of honour, which was both economically advantageous and politically moderate.

Montesquieu's analysis was of a piece with his broader contrast between commercial and military investment, and indeed between the 'political polarity of monarchic instability versus democratic stasis'.[77] As well as being a deluded attempt to ape either Rome or the Spanish, a desire for universal monarchy resembles the illegitimate engrafting onto European political culture of a despotic rule more familiar to the great empires of Asia. For Europe was 'nothing more than one nation composed of many'.[78] Such unity in multiplicity once more showed it to be unlike Rome, even if the attractions of imperium were obvious.[79] And there is something about the grip of the *imperium Romanum* that rendered Montesquieu's attack upon its most recent manifestation as *monarchia universalis* particularly interesting. He remained in thrall to the Romans intellectually whilst rejecting the contemporary relevance of their politics. Ideas of a universal monarchy that drew on them simply presented a 'contradictory compound', backwards looking and bound up with European interstate rivalry. In fact, after the collapse of the Holy Roman Empire, the idea of universal monarchy quickly became a negative form of political association, open to criticism from radicals and moderates alike.[80]

In its place, Montesquieu's post-Machiavellian political economy rejected the positive correlation between warfare and trade in contempo-

---

488–92; also Montesquieu 1989, I. 5. 4, p. 44; 1964, p. 545; Montesquieu 1989, 4. 20. 3, p. 339; 1964, p. 651; cf. Machiavelli 1989, bk. 1, chs. 16–18, 25, 29, 30, 36, pp. 235–44, 252f, 257–61, 272–75; bk. 3, chs. 24–25, pp. 485–88.

[75] Montesquieu 1989, I. 7. 2, p. 98; 1964, p. 565.

[76] See Montesquieu 1989, I. 7. 1, pp. 96f; 1964, pp. 564f; cf. Montesquieu 1989, I. 5. 8, p. 53; 1964, pp. 548f.

[77] Mason 1996, esp. pp. 63f, 69f, 72f.

[78] Montesquieu 2000a, §§ 8, 18, pp. 348, 360; cf. Montesquieu 1964, p. 918 (*Pensées*, nos. 555, 562); Rahe 2005, esp. pp. 65f and n. 64.

[79] Rahe 2005, pp. 62f and n. 58; see too Shklar 1987, pp. 64f.

[80] Bosbach 1986, esp. pp. 123f; cf. Bosbach 1998, esp. pp. 90ff, 95ff; Robertson 1995, pp. 3–36.

rary Europe. That could only foster bankruptcy, decline, or even both, and none were in the interests of a Bordeaux wine seller.[81] In this at least, his was clearly a traditional vision of Enlightenment as progress.[82] Yet on such grounds, Montesquieu suggested that only in 'free nations' could citizens maintain their liberty, because they are prouder (*superbes*) than those who can 'more easily be vain'.[83] There are echoes of Machiavelli here, but it is equally important to note the direction in which Montesquieu pushes the argument, and its implications for his account of monarchy. By reworking early Greek discussions of liberty as requiring something like a combination of equality in property and the rule of the wise, into a modern-sounding compound of economic redistribution under conditions of inequality and rule by elites, he was part of the gradual transformation of the language of republicanism for modern political theory. In turn, this development required an account of the separability of commerce from nobility. For the moderns, 'commerce is the profession of equal people' so that when nobles become merchants, the decline of a republic is imminent. Indeed, Montesquieu clearly thought it 'is against the spirit of commerce for the nobility to engage in it in a monarchy', just as it is 'against the spirit of monarchy for the nobility to engage in commerce'. Thus, the 'usage that permitted commerce to the nobility in England is one of the things that most contributed to weakening monarchical government there'.[84] Against the mercantilism of French monarchical policy, Montesquieu seemed to be suggesting that 'the spring of interest is exclusively the spirit of constraint', so that constraining behaviour for the better pursuit of interest requires moderation or propriety, not overbearing political speculation and aggrandizement.[85]

All of this rendered Montesquieu's critique of universal monarchy doubly intriguing. He first suggested that defeat by the Spanish at the Battle of Blenheim was a blessing in disguise for the French, for if Louis been victorious, the infrastructure required to support and supplement his newfound position as sole European monarch would have been unsustainable. Better now to be *primus inter pares*. Second, there is a schol-

[81] Montesquieu 2000a, § 1, p. 340. See also Hont 2005, esp. chs. 2, 4; Mason 1996, pp. 73ff, 81ff; Montesquieu 1955h, pp. 263–73; Larrère 1997, pp. 103–16; cf. PRO 30/24/47/35, Locke's papers on viticulture, which were collected in Locke 1720. See also Lough 1953a, pp. 54, 58f. Richard Ashcraft made much of this for a decoding of Locke's politics, but see the criticisms in Goldie 1992, esp. pp. 563f; P. Milton 2000, esp. pp. 651f, 656f, 664ff.

[82] Mason 1996, esp. pp. 66ff; Ehrard 1973, vol. 2, p. 493.

[83] Montesquieu 1989, 3. 19. 27, p. 332; 1964, p. 650: 'Les nations libres sont superbes, les autres peuvent plus aisément être vaines'.

[84] Montesquieu 1989, 4. 20. 21, p. 350; 1964, p. 655.

[85] Spector 2006, pp. 204, 206 n. 1, 207; quotation on p. 396: 'le ressort d'intérêt est exclusif de l'ésprit de contrainte'.

arly curiosity here. The *Réflexions* and *Considérations* were considered for publication together in 1734, the draft chapter on England from *De l'Esprit des lois* also stems from around 1734, and both the *Considérations* and the draft chapter are in the hand of the same amanuensis. If we consider the two works together, numerous political analogies become clearer. The comparison between a commercial English government and a rapacious Rome, on the one hand, and between the moderate monarchy of France and a Spanish empire for increase, on the other, provide a compelling lens through which to view the political dynamite of Montesquieu's analysis.[86] Because of its explosive character Montesquieu unsurprisingly chose not publish the two texts together, and he revised his account of the Romans in light of fears about censorship. But the texts demand to be read in combination, and were clearly considered as meditations on the character of expansionism both ancient and modern, with appropriately critical lessons to be drawn from them.[87] Small wonder that the English were so keen to translate his work (which in fact built on English sources for the account of Roman agrarian laws, for example), while in France Montesquieu had to seriously tone it down.[88]

Indeed, Montesquieu's analysis of Rome and religion was pointedly delivered as a broadside against contemporary French historical scholarship. The celebrated Bishop Bossuet, who had argued for the providential character of human history via the divine right of kings, outlined a universal history that was anathema to Montesquieu. For although Montesquieu would willingly talk of general causes such as passions, he would insist on contextually specific instances, always assuming that events could have turned out otherwise.[89] His analysis was also a rejection of the claims of Father Huet, bishop of Avranche, over the comparative utility of understanding ancient history. Huet had written of the *Histoire du commerce et de la navigation des Anciens* in 1716, suggesting that Roman expertise in navigation underscored expansion through a commitment to commerce.[90] Montesquieu rejected the religious and naval narrative in favour of his analysis of Rome as a land-based empire. Moreover, even though Huet's general scepticism was both important and not unconducive, his defence of Rome (and its impact on actual politicians) was something Montesquieu railed against.[91]

---

[86] See Montesquieu 2000a, §§ 16–17, pp. 358f; Rahe 2005, pp. 64f, 80ff.

[87] See Montesquieu 1964, p. 860 (*Pensées*, no. 80).

[88] Nelson 2004, esp. pp. 138 n. 46, 141–45, 159–63.

[89] Bossuet 1990, p. xxviii; cf. Shklar 1987, pp. 52f, 55.

[90] Huet 1727, p. 120.

[91] Popkin 1955, esp. 67–70; cf. Popkin 1979, pp. 65–93; Spector 2006, esp. pp. 411, 413ff, 418; see too Volpilhac-Auger 2001, esp. pp. 261–64, for Montesquieu's desire to

In rejecting both Bossuet and Huet, Montesquieu had more sympathy for Fénelon, even if he was ambiguous about the nature of the *quiétisme* implied by true devotion to the love of Christ, or *pur amour*.[92] And while Fénelon did not go as far as the Jansenists, and Montesquieu in turn did not go as far as Fénelon over questions of religion and grace, the implication that action be either interested or disinterested not only chimed well with contemporary debates about self-interest and selfhood more generally.[93] It also had clear implications for understanding the history of commerce.[94] Because of it, some in England even modified Fénelon in dreadful doggerel for the purposes of defending English liberties over 'partial' Rome.[95] In his own discussion of the Troglodytes, however, Montesquieu had firmly rejected a Fénelonian utopia, where the people 'are entirely free from pride, vanity, deceit, and all desire of extending their territories', as surely as he had rejected Hobbesian sovereignty. In its place, Montesquieu proposed retelling a history of progress from savagery to civility through the growth of private property and monarchy.[96] Only once this history was understood could a reformed Fénelonian Salentum be presented as an allegory for the rule of James II, and this narrative could draw the moral of his story out effectively. It implied that with an appropriate moderation of property relations and constitutional engineering, trade between enemies (France and England) could lead to prosperity and peace.[97] Property was therefore only one element in a stadial history, which focused on problems of honour and monarchy.[98]

Yet the major cited source on which Montesquieu drew for his early account in the essay on Roman religion was Cicero, in particular *De Divinatione*. From it Montesquieu cited well-known justifications for the close interconnection between religious sentiment and patriotic attach-

---

incorporate the discussion of Rome into his '*livre du commerce*'. Cf. Whatmore 2009, esp. pp. 56f, 62–65.

[92] See Montesquieu 1964, p. 988 (*Pensées*, no. 1080); Riley 1986, pp. 63f, 68f, 75 n. 26, 76; Sonenscher 2008, pp. 231–48. Fénelon's defence of 'free quietism', against Bossuet, is visible in his Letters to Bossuet of March 8, 1695, and December 7, 1695, in Fénelon 1976, vol. 4, pp. 15f, 47f.

[93] C. J. Coleman 2005, esp. pp. 304f, 312–15.

[94] Force 2004, pp. 183–200; Holmes 1995, esp. pp. 42–68.

[95] Duke of D——— 1709, p. 3, written 'in allußion to the Archbishop of *Cambray's Telemachus*'.

[96] Fénelon 1994, pp. 113, 110: 'Do they [richer nations] enjoy greater liberty, tranquillity, and contentment? On the contrary, they must be jealous of one another ... since they are enslaved by so many false necessities'. For the context, see Hont 2006, esp. pp. 404ff; Sher 1994, pp. 371–74. On progress, see also Montesquieu 1989, I. 3. 4, p. 25; 1964, pp. 537f; cf. Montesquieu, *Lettres persanes*, Letter 106, in Montesquieu 1964, pp. 117f.

[97] Sonenscher 2007, p. 117; 2008, pp. 207ff.

[98] See Hont 2005, pp. 183f; Meek 1976, pp. 31–33, 131ff, 171ff; Spector 2006, pp. 67ff.

ment to the city. To bolster his argument, he retold stories of Crassus, Lucullus, Tarquin and others in terms of their consultation of the oracles in the hope of extracting religious premonitions of military success, in order show that a new (*nouvel*) feature of Roman politics was the occasional punishing of generals who failed to follow religious protocol. This was done with the aim of showing the people that failure, lost battles, captured cities (*villes prises*) were not due to the effects of a 'bad constitution of the state, or to the feebleness of the republic, but to the impiety of a citizen, against whom the gods had become irritated'.[99] Montesquieu (like Augustine had before him) appreciated that such myths were designed to counter the bad judgement of the citizens, as much as to keep them politically in the dark, and that they were beneficial to the state.[100]

The appeal to Cicero was not only conventional, given the staple diet of early-modern Ciceronian style Stoicism in European moral and political thought. It also reflected a more personal and youthful admiration, and Montesquieu's cognate search for an appropriate balance between the useful and the good, the *utile* and the *honestum*, can be seen in his 'Discourse sur Cicéron'.[101] Dated variously between 1709 and 1717, this paper shows a compelling debt to Cicero's style and rhetoric as well as to his example. The Stoic subordination of the passions to reason and virtue seems to have illustrated an ideal to be followed, though as I have tried to suggest already, Montesquieu's relationship to this aspect of the Stoic tradition was quite complex, and his suspicion of the applicability of virtue to politics extremely deep. Refuting the charge that Cicero was effectively 'feeble and timid' (*faible et timide*), Montesquieu averred that he was in fact a 'great man' who 'always subordinated all of his passions, his fear and his courage, to wisdom and reason'.[102] Importantly, this subordination of the passions was learned through the practical nature of true friendship, and Montesquieu clearly alluded to Cicero's wider discourses as evidence.[103] In his own treatise on friendship, Cicero had

---

[99] Montesquieu 1964c, p. 41: 'On voulait faire voir au people que les mauvais succès, les villes prises, les batailles perdues, n'étaient point l'effet d'une mauvaise constitution de l'État, ou de la faiblesse de la République, mais de l'impiété d'un citoyen, contre lequel les dieux étaient irrités'.

[100] Montesquieu 1964c, p. 41: 'Varron avait découvert par là tout le secret des politiques et des ministres d'État', citing (in French translation) Augustine, *The City of God*, bk. 4, ch. 31. See also Oake 1953, pp. 553f.

[101] Moore, 'Utility and Humanity', esp. p. 385.

[102] Montesquieu 1964b, pp. 34–36, p. 35: 'Ce grand homme subordonna toujours toutes ses passions, sa crainte et son courage, à la sagesse et à la raison'; cf. Montesquieu 2002, p. 735.

[103] Montesquieu 1964b, p. 35: 'Tantôt il nous dévoile les charmes de l'amitié et nous en fait sentir tous les délices; tantôt il nous fait voir les avantages d'un âge que la raison éclaire, et qui nous sauve de la violence des passions'; Montesquieu 2002, p. 734.

presented a dialogue with Laelius over the legacy of their mutual friend, Scipio. After rehearsing various standard presentations of the topic, Cicero concluded that 'the first law of friendship' (*prima lex amicitiae*) is to 'ask of friends only what is honourable', and to 'do for friends only what is honourable'.[104]

The true foundation of friendship is in virtue and honour, not utility or vanity. Thus, as Peter Brunt has noted, Cicero (and Augustine in part after him) clearly thought it was right, indeed a duty, to 'subordinate' claims of friendship to the needs of the state.[105] Developing this line of argument, Montesquieu claims that particular duties or obligations always yield to moral universals such as an attachment to the state.[106] Thus understood, political life might look like an extended form of friendship. In any event, according to Cicero nature has provided for the fact that like will be friends with like, so that the good are always friends with the good.[107] His definitive answer stands in contrast to the more ambiguous Platonic dialogues on the subject.[108] Relationships between friends are based on openness, honesty, and truth.[109]

Misguided ambition is presented as one of those traits inimical to friendship so understood. At the same time, however, Montesquieu recognized ambition as a natural human trait rooted in the very source of human agency, namely the soul. Therefore he tried to separate out in his discussion the political effects of ambition and despotism from their natural role in human motivation. The excessively ambitious and the despotic seem to avoid even the veneer of moderation necessary to both friendship and to political freedom. Conversely, the ideal of the citizen as frank speaker and friend, or *Parrhasiastes*, was updated to make it relevant for Montesquieu.[110] Frank speech is important for the modern man of honour, but this is not because of an interest in truth or even sincerity. Instead, the modern *Parrhasiastes* shines in social situations, appearing daring and manly, an emblem of vigour (and one presumes virility). Montesquieu's occasional connection of virtuous and free action with sincere action, for example, equally recognized that sincerity was often misdirected by self-interest.[111] He therefore examines a form of selfhood that is genuinely rooted in natural sentiments, but which is made appro-

[104] Cicero 1996, 13, pp. 154ff; 44, p. 189.
[105] Brunt 1988, p. 40; cf. Brunt 1988a, esp. pp. 464f; Augustine 1979, pp. 79f, 83, 88.
[106] Riley 1986, pp. 142f, 148f.
[107] Cicero 1996, 5–6, esp. pp. 127, 130f; 14, p. 163.
[108] Plato 1997a, 210c–d, 213, 213b–c, 215a–b, 220e.
[109] Cicero 1996, 24–25, pp. 197–203.
[110] On *parrhasia*, see Monoson 2000, esp. pp. 54–57; updated by Montesquieu 1989, I. 4. 2, pp. 32f; 1964, p. 541, into the monarchical virtue of the *honnête homme*.
[111] Montesquieu 1955c, pp. 63, 65.

priate to the needs of commercial society under a moderate monarchy. Much as Locke had suggested before him, for Montesquieu this vision of the citizen was educative and exemplary. His analysis in fact of the place of education under different regimes serves as a forcible reminder of this connection between politics, persuasion and emotion.[112]

Ambition then served a twin role in the analysis. If unchecked in their ambition, individuals are unlikely to be true friends or trustworthy citizens. In both cases, unchecked ambition can distort judgement and promote hypocrisy, making it a central issue for politics.[113] In distorting judgement, the ambitious might scorn others and laugh at them, thus exemplifying the 'suddaine glory' that threatens civil peace by bursting the boundaries of decorum or magnanimity.[114] Indeed, though Montesquieu thought that 'humour is the passion of the spirit', a gift from God just like food and *amour-propre*, it had always to be appropriate, even (or especially) in the case of parody, a tool Montesquieu wielded frequently and well.[115] Because passionate selfhood was unavoidable, its excesses had to be tempered if moderation was to be achieved. This could best be done under a moderate government that promotes political liberty. Political liberty requires 'human ingenuity in contriving a balance between the political ambitions of various interests'. It therefore becomes, in fact, the 'moral criterion by which any political system is to be judged'.[116] Other forms of rule that fail to defend it were implicitly de-legitimized, in an argument that had an immediate take-up in translation and then a lengthy intellectual afterlife.[117] However, although this view might seem to depend upon hypocrisy, and present self-propriety simply either as a mask or as a front for something like possessive individualism, Montesquieu did not think that it did; and even if it were true, it is not clear that he

---

[112] Aristotle 1984, bk. 3, 4, 1276ᵇ1 (on virtue and the constitution); III, 4, 1276ᵇ1, 1277aI, 1277bI, bk. 6, 1140a, 1142b–1143a (on practical wisdom and deliberation); cf. Monoson 2000, pp. 56, 60f, 174f.

[113] Thompson 2005, pp. 210–14.

[114] Hobbes 1991, ch. 6, p. 43; discussion in Skinner 2002f, esp. pp. 147ff, 151ff, 172, 175f.

[115] Montesquieu 1964, p. 993 (*Pensées*, no. 1165): 'Je disais: "L'humeur est la passion de l'esprit."' Cf. Montesquieu 1964, p. 987 (*Pensées*, no. 1036): 'M. Nicole dit très bien que Dieu a donné l'amour-propre à l'homme comme il a donné le goût aux mets'. See in general Wade 1977 vol. 1, p. 437.

[116] Hampson 1968, p. 116.

[117] Adair 1998; cf. Pettit 2001, esp. ch. 7; on Nugent's translation, see Montesquieu, Letter to Thomas Nugent, Paris, October 18, 1750, in Montesquieu 1955j, p. 1333; also Shackleton 1978, pp. 248–59. Cf. Montesquieu 1750; Montesquieu 1750a; cf. BL Add Mss. 40, 759, vol. 4, esp. fos. 154, 156ᵛ⁻ʳ, and Montesquieu 1989, pp. 214ff, for different translations. Discussion in Sher 1994, esp. pp. 370f; Howard 1959, pp. 44–46; Courtney 2009, esp. pp. 31f, 43.

would have minded. For although many have castigated hypocrisy, this ordinary vice is one that writers from the early modern period recognize as absolutely fundamental to societies where moral or political virtue is a concern secondary to propriety. Its veneer promotes peaceful exchange, and the radical truth-telling frank speaker is transformed into the peaceable citizen who is moderately sociable, free to pursue honour and self-interest, but willing (or forced) to respect the rights of others under the law.[118]

These issues attracted Montesquieu's attention because they had contemporary relevance to his analysis of despotism and tyranny. The principle of fear upon which despotism is based is stationary or static, and for Montesquieu this meant that it was contrary to nature. Despotism cannot cope with diversity, and to the extent that the ancient world could not deal with diversity and faction in its search for political unity, it had to be rejected.[119] Equally, under conditions of *stasis* and uncertainty, political argument could easily become immoderate and radical. The transformation of the political language of virtuous moderation into despicable unmanliness under such conditions, recounted in Thucydides' discussion of Corcyra, was a classical example. Montesquieu needed to steer a path between both extremes.[120] On the one hand, his vision of despotism was contemporary, a term of abuse for the last years of the reign of Louis XIV that had also been investigated by Bayle.[121] Its high political import was obvious. Yet not only could the term both explain and justify the oppression of foreign peoples, it also embodied a linguistic attack upon tyranny that related back to classical arguments from both Plato and Aristotle.[122] In advancing the term *despotisme* Montesquieu was promoting a significant evolution in political language, which allowed him to run together these meanings whilst also rejecting a simple-minded application of classical political theory to contemporary political realities. It permitted a separation of tyranny and despotism, whilst recognizing the threat posed by monarchs as well as merchants.[123]

Thus although notions of despotism or tyranny formed part of a classically Polybian cyclical schema, Montesquieu did not account for tyranny in constitutional terms alone. Tyranny could refer either to the 'violence of the government' (as in Polybius's degenerate democracy) or to 'opinion, which is felt when those who govern establish structures that run

---

[118] Shklar 1984, esp. p. 77; Runciman 2008, pp. 12ff, 37–41, 202f.
[119] Berent 1998, pp. 331–61; Manicas 1982, pp. 673–88; Ehrard 1963, vol. 2, pp. 497f.
[120] Thucydides 1972, III. 82; cf. Fuks 1971, pp. 48–55.
[121] Desgraves 1954, no. 1538, p. 113.
[122] Venturi 1963, esp. pp. 134f, 138; cf. Kassem 1960, pp. 97, 104, 108, on the Aristotelian, as well as Platonic, debts of Montesquieu.
[123] Koebner 1951, esp. pp. 300ff; Boesche 1990, esp. pp. 741ff, 753–57.

counter to a nation's way of thinking'.[124] Despotism, by contrast, creates
uniformity and promotes inequality, and because it is the only regime in
Montesquieu's typology based solely on the passions, it produced a tragic
irony. Its prevalence meant that Montesquieu's preferred and 'moderate'
regime was an exceedingly rare 'masterpiece of legislation that chance
rarely produces and prudence is rarely allowed to produce. By contrast, a
despotic government leaps to view, so to speak. It is uniform throughout,
because only passions are needed to establish it, and everyone is good
enough for that'.[125] His allegiance to Aristotelian argument is important
in understanding this difference too. Aristotle had seen despotic rule as
outside the properly political realm, in its attempt to transform politics
into something akin to household management. Despotism pursued a
process of de-politicization because it gave free rein to the passions. For
although the passions are the source of agency, they need to be controlled
for moderate politics and hence political liberty to flourish.

The tyrant, in Aristotle's account, rules like the head of a household
rather than the head of a state. Montesquieu's tyrant literally transforms
the public realm into an *oikos*, turning citizens into slaves and making
government the expression of an arbitrary power. It all 'comes down to
reconciling political and civil government with domestic government, the
officers of the state with those of the seraglio [*sérail*]'.[126] The subversive
implications were not lost on critics of the French monarchy, and in its re-
making of the state as a seraglio, the tyrannical ruler or the despotic society was both morally corrupt and politically sick. The language, of course,
recalls the celebrated attack on princely self-absorption well known from
Fénelon's *Télémaque*, as well as the powerful parody of a bankrupt and
venal courtly system in the *Lettres Persanes*, which reiterated views about
Louis XIV the 'grand magicien' that were too licentious for the censors in
Rome.[127] The conclusion to that book, with Roxanne's revolt, her claims
of independence from Usbek and for a society of many lovers, as well as
her poisoning of the eunuchs, illustrates a radical (and erotically charged)
response to despotism. And that once again ties Montesquieu back to

[124] Polybius 1922–27, bk. 6, pp. 287ff; Montesquieu 1989, 3. 19. 3, p. 309; 1964, p. 641.
See too Millar 2002, esp. pp. 28–36.

[125] Montesquieu 1989, I. 5. 14, p. 63; 1964, p. 553.

[126] Montesquieu 1989, I. 5. 14, p. 60; 1964, p. 551; see Krause 2001, esp. pp. 240ff,
255ff.

[127] Montesquieu, *Lettres persanes*, Letter 24, in Montesquieu 1964, pp. 74–75; cf. Montesquieu 1964, pp. 936f (*Pensées*, nos. 595–96). See also Riley 1986, pp. 148, 153, for the
argument that bad legislators in the *Lettres Persanes* are similar to Malebranche's pagan
deities. For a reproduction of the text that placed Montesquieu's book on the Index in 1762
see Macé 2005, pp. 57ff, see also p. 49 n. 3.

the ideas of Bayle and Epicureanism.[128] Equally, his claim that society could be despotic, but that legal tyranny or slavery could ensue under the auspices of a nominally 'free' or democratic government, would go on to have significant impact. This was so particularly in terms of the idea of 'self-recognition' in British political thought, and, somewhat ironically, English propaganda aiming to 'raise the resentment' against the French, could also use it successfully.[129]

Crucially, however, for the comparative utility of Montesquieu's typology, this was not just a French symptom.[130] Rather it illustrated the constant 'flux and reflux of empire and liberty'.[131] Thus, although Montesquieu's case for making moral judgements about politics stemmed from the 'legitimate desires' of human beings for security, society and knowledge, connecting despotism and current policy was designed to show the inapplicability of ancient heroic politics to modern, commercial societies. That was an outdated form of 'superhuman transcendence'.[132] Building on his earlier analysis, Montesquieu even claimed that the Roman Empire was the 'head of a body formed by all the people of the world', in the perfect image of a globalized Leviathan.[133] Its fall, at least on this reading, was the result of both corruption and luxury. Even philosophy did not escape, and when the Stoics had advanced *amour-propre* to such a degree that suicide could be justified as the true 'love of our being' (*l'amour de notre être*), the die was well and truly cast.[134] While the Stoics might make good laws, good rules and perhaps good citizens, and even if the ideal Stoic polity was theoretically conceivable, Montesquieu knew its citizens 'would be an unamiable lot', completely out of place in the modern world. This is due to the fact that the 'inherent disharmony' between man and nature makes perfection impossible, and only balance and equanimity can provide (temporary) satisfaction in the face of this misalignment. While he appreciated the Stoic vision, indeed numbering the destruction of Zeno's sect as 'among the misfortunes of human kind', Montesquieu found such virtue inapplicable to modern politics. What he surely wanted to show people was the sort of austere example that virtue

---

[128] Gilbert 1994, p. 58; Hundert and Nelles 1989, esp. pp. 236–42; Schaub 1995; Spector 1997; Mosher 2007, pp. 109ff.

[129] Gunn 1983, esp. pp. 15ff., 35, 38–40, 239; [Anon.] 1756, p. 1.

[130] Fénelon 1994, esp. pp. 332f.

[131] Montesquieu 1964, p. 1011 (*Pensées*, no. 1475): 'Voila, comme il y a toujours en flux et reflux d'êmpire et de liberté'.

[132] Krause 2006, pp. 222f; Starobinski 1953, pp. 54, 28.

[133] Montesquieu 2000, ch. 6, p. 140: 'Ainsi Rome n'étoit pas proprement une Monarchie, ou une République, mais la Tête du Corps formé par tous les Peuples du monde'.

[134] Montesquieu 2000, chs. 11–12, pp. 160, 162f, 181.

required for the making of good men, citizens and emperors, in order not only to prove the power of the example, but also to show how great was the distance between the ancients and the moderns.[135] Certainly, modern commercial society could not proceed according to such criteria, for the 'world of that time was not like our world today', and modern forms of policy and commerce make the grand schemes of the ancients ever more difficult to envisage.[136] Only in England, it seemed, was an appropriate combination of physical, moral, political and intellectual motivation buttressed by a political form germane to the maintenance of commercial liberty, and even English liberty was a contradictory compound. And in any case, the self-same political liberty seen in England had to stem, as I now hope to show, from his much broader account of the fundamental causes and consequences of human action in the passions of the soul. This vision underpinned his entire synthesis, and if the political consequences of natural ambition could result in despotism, he had first to show how this ambition lay at the root of human agency itself, in order then to harness it for different ends.

The Passions of the Soul and the Actions of the Machine

Although Montesquieu did not pursue a direct and extensive dialogue with Descartes, comparing their accounts of the passions of the soul brings Montesquieu's conception of agency into sharper focus.[137] In his work, there is an intimate connection between ambition and the soul as the source of self-directed agency, for the soul directs our passions towards actions we freely choose. In this way Montesquieu opens up a space for thinking about human freedom, in a world governed by a multiplicity of laws, which locates him in wider debates about the passions.[138] Put simply, the soul is the source of Montesquieu's challenge to determinism. Our happiness and the passions of the soul are intertwined. For example, he noted pithily that there are, in general, two sorts of 'unfortunate people [*gens malheureux*]', those who have some 'failure of the soul, which they can do nothing about [*defaillance de l'âme, qui fait rien ne la remue*]', and those who simply 'want what they can't have [*desire ... tout ce qui'ils ne peuvent pas avoir*]'. This second sort of person is destined to be unhappy, being afraid of death but equally scared of life,

---

[135] Shklar 1979, esp. p. 317, provides this memorable assessment of the 'unamiable lot'. See Montesquieu 1989, 5. 24. 10, pp. 465f; 1964, p. 700; though compare the earlier, more cynical criticisms of Stoicism in Montesquieu 1955c, esp. p. 61.

[136] Montesquieu 2000, pp. 263f; discussion in Rahe 2005, pp. 75f.

[137] Montesquieu 1955d, p. 112.

[138] Cf. Sonenscher 2008, p. 228.

while the first is obviously limited. The question for Montesquieu, then, was how to understand the relationship between the passions of the soul and the promotion of happiness.[139]

Happiness requires the capacity to act freely, and is therefore a property of responsible agents. In fact, 'human actions are the subject of needs', needs which we can 'submit to conventional laws'. Similarly, our 'machine' (a Lockean-sounding combination of perceptions, passions and sentiments) 'accustoms our soul to think in a certain way'.[140] With such language, Montesquieu seemed to be developing the classic but highly critical analysis of Descartes's treatise, *Les passions de l'âme*, conceived of in dialogue with Princess Elizabeth and ultimately published in 1645–46.[141] In that work, Descartes had presented a fierce and complex attack on traditional accounts of the soul by the 'ancient' metaphysicians. The force of this Cartesian claim is that the soul is action in the body, yet simultaneously separate from it. The body is moved by 'animal spirits', which are a combination of heat and motion in the form of blood pushed around the system from the heart, and which are therefore nothing but miniature 'material bodies'.

Within the text, from a basic list of six fundamental primitive passions (admiration, love and hate, desire, joy and sadness), an indefinite number of further passions branch out, all of which bring equal benefit to the soul.[142] Actions are understood as desires or volitions, which could be focused in either the soul or the body, while the passions are 'those kinds of perception or forms of knowledge which are found in us, because it is often not our soul which makes them what they are' but our body instead.[143] Our perceptions, then, can be caused either by the soul or by the body, and if they are caused *either* by external objects acting on the body, *or* by internal appetites of the body that mostly depend upon the nerves, then they are properly passions of the soul. Descartes was emphatic that passions of the soul are to be understood as 'the perceptions, feelings [*sentimens*], or emotions of the soul which we relate specifically to it, and which are caused, maintained, and fortified by some movement of the spirits'.[144] Their force was engineered quite precisely in the tiny pineal gland, located at a midpoint between the brain and the heart, which, 'diversely moved by the soul, or by such other cause', then 'thrusts the

---

[139] Montesquieu 1964, pp. 915f (*Pensées*, no. 549): 'Le propriétaire de cette âme est toujours dans la langueur ... il n'aime pas la vie, mais il craint la mort'.

[140] Montesquieu 1964, p. 938 (*Pensées*, no. 597): 'Les actions humaines sont le sujet des devoirs ... qui nous soumettent éternellement aux lois d'habitude'.

[141] On the background to the treatise, see Gaukroger 1997, p. 387.

[142] Levi 1964, pp. 274ff.

[143] Descartes 1967, vol. 2, art. 17, p. 340.

[144] Descartes 1967, vol. 2, art. 27, p. 344; Descartes 1955, art. 27, p. 86.

spirits which surround it towards the pores of the brain, which conduct them by the nerves into the muscles, by which means it causes them to move the limbs'.[145]

Different people feel different passions in different ways, and through experience they learn conventional and appropriate responses that stay with them throughout their lives.[146] 'Our capacity to discriminate' between various feelings is literally 'marked on the body'. This means, for instance, that 'we do not need to make a judgement in order to feel that a situation is frightening; we simply experience it as frightening', a capacity that is both rational and central to our self-interest.[147] It also means, of course, that our judgement about the worth of an object will structure our response to it, which is to say again that our intellectual passions are judgements of value that we cultivate over time. From this it follows that intellectual passions concern judgements about our knowledge of the worth of particular objects; indeed, the usefulness of ethical or moral theory is that it teaches us how experience can come to regulate desire.[148] The movements of these animal spirits can 'represent to the soul the objects which stimulate the senses, or the impressions occurring in the brain', in which case they 'have no influence on the will'. Or they 'cause the passions or the bodily movements which accompany the passions', and therefore directly influence the will.[149] In conclusion, this implies that 'as long as our soul always has the means of happiness within itself, anything external is powerless to harm it'.[150]

Even more pertinent for the development of Montesquieu's account of liberty, however, was Descartes's rhetorical rejection of the classical language of the divided soul split between reason and desire.[151] Instead, the conflicts we feel when reflecting on the passions of the soul are conflicts between soul and body, and not between parts of the soul. The usefulness of the passions is that 'they incite and dispose their soul to desire those things for which they prepare their body'.[152] With these points made, although the passions of the soul are presented as mostly 'passive per-

---

[145] Descartes 1967, vol. 2, art. 34, p. 347.

[146] Gaukroger 1997, p. 402; Levi 1964, p. 270; James 1997, pp. 98f.

[147] James 1997, pp. 103ff, 107; on joy in Descartes, see James 1997, p. 97; Gaukroger 1997, pp. 403f.

[148] Levi 1964, pp. 280ff.

[149] Descartes 1967, vol. 2, art 47, p. 353; see too James 1997, p. 101.

[150] Gaukroger 1997, p. 404. As Levi 1964, p. 272, puts it: 'one is master of one's passions in so far as one can successfully halt the flow of spirits which sustains them, and in so far as one can resist consenting to those actions which are solicited from the soul by the body in passion. In order to be master of one's passions one requires, therefore, strength of soul'.

[151] Descartes 1967, vol. 2, art. 47, pp. 352ff; see too James 1997, p. 258.

[152] Descartes 1967, vol. 2, art. 40, pp. 349f.

ceptions of bodily motions', this reciprocal unity of body and soul is the key.[153] It means there is a cognate relationship between the passions and bodily health.[154] For Descartes, passions are 'good in their nature and we have nothing to avoid but their evil uses or their excesses', so that when we feel moved by them, we should 'abstain from pronouncing any judgement on the spot' until we are becalmed.[155] Such suspension of judgement requires recognition of the fact that an ethic of generosity (*générosité*) underpins the idea that one only acts well to the extent that one does not will what one should not.[156] Indeed, in the third part of his treatise, this discussion of generosity (a seemingly Christian virtue) was offered as both a cure for the 'disturbances of the passions' and the key to all the other virtues. *Générosité* ties our free will to the capacity to choose well, thereby tending to promote virtuous action, or at least actions that it is in our power to control as the only basis for calling them voluntary or free. By so doing, we might achieve a 'general remedy for all the disorders of the passions'.[157] Here, 'the utility of all the passions consists alone in their fortifying and perpetuating in the soul thoughts which it is good it should preserve, and which without that might easily be effaced from it'.[158] The soul is a result of providential design.[159]

In similar sounding terms, Montesquieu suggested that one could 'accustom one's soul to examine things as they are', and that the passions of the soul are neither equivalent nor reducible to those of the body. Man was not something to be worked on 'like the tool of an artisan', nor could everything be reduced to the power of the soul even if liberty and action were unthinkable without it. Instead, 'man is equally composed of the two substances' of body and soul, and each in 'flux and reflux' acts on the substantial union.[160] A relational unity is once again the key. Like the intelligent world more generally, body and soul have their own rules

---

[153] James 1997, pp. 87ff, 94, 106f.

[154] See Levi 1964, pp. 260–63; Shapin 2000, pp. 131–54.

[155] Descartes 1967, vol. 2, art. 211, pp. 425f.

[156] Gaukroger 1997, p. 404.

[157] Descartes 1967, vol. 2, arts. 156, 161, pp. 402f, 406; cf. Rodis-Lewis 1998, pp. 186f; Levi 1964, pp. 282ff.

[158] Descartes 1967, vol. 2, art. 74, p. 364.

[159] Menn 1997, esp. pp. 17f, 29f; see Williams 1978, pp. 167ff, 145–54; 2006a, pp. 236f; Levi 1964, p. 282.

[160] Montesquieu 1964, p. 874 (*Pensées*, no. 183): 'Lorsque les médecins et les auteurs moraux traitent des passions, ils ne parlent jamais la même langue: les moraux trop sur le compte de l'âme; les autres, trop sur celui des corps; les uns regardent plus l'homme comme un esprit; les autres, plus comme la machine d'un artisan. Mais l'homme est également composé des deux substances, qui chacune comme par un flux et reflux, excertent et souffrent l'empire'.

of conduct and engagement.[161] The general 'machine', or unified body and soul, embraces connections between moral, physical and intellectual relations that are part and parcel of the fabric of human existence. And the closest Montesquieu gets to any form of determinism about this machine is to say that 'goodness and badness consist in a certain disposition of organs, favourable or unfavourable'. It is simply accidental that one person is rich and another poor, one person ambitious and another indolent.[162] Our understanding of vice and virtue, however, is determined by how such 'dispositions' depend upon the 'mechanism' of our body and soul.[163] Specifically, 'just as human virtues and vices are ordinarily the effect of the passions, and the passions an effect of a certain state of the machine', Montesquieu himself 'speak[s] of the material of the passions, and not of the forms, which is to talk of the satisfaction felt by the soul in following the movements of its machine'.[164] He noted that 'nearly all the virtues are a particular relation of one specific man with another', using ideas of friendship, patriotism and pity to illustrate this regularity. Most importantly for my own story, he also noted that 'justice is a general relation', and therefore that those apparent 'virtues that destroy this general relation are not really virtues'.[165] In a claim that would have central ramifications for writers like Smith and Mill, Montesquieu noted that, as a word, 'justice is often extremely equivocal'.[166] That lack of specificity simply mirrors the idea that what constitutes the 'majority of contradictions of man is the fact that physical and moral reasons are not always in agreement'.[167] He also claimed that the foundation of justice was a feeling

---

[161] Montesquieu 1964, p. 985 (*Pensées*, no. 996): 'Or, on peut accoutumer son âme à examiner les choses telles qu'elles sont'. Cf. Montesquieu 1989, I. 1. 1, pp. 3f; Montesquieu 1998, p. 7: 'Mais il s'en faut bien que le Monde intelligent soit aussi bien gouverné que le Monde physique'.

[162] Montesquieu 1964, pp. 915f (*Pensées*, no. 594): 'Le bonheur ou le malheur consistent dans une certaine disposition d'organes, favourable ou défavorable'.

[163] Montesquieu 1964, p. 938 (*Pensées*, no. 597): 'C'est ici que la physique pourrait trouver place dans la morale, en nous faisant voir combine les dispositions par les vices et les vertus humaines dépendent du mécanisme'.

[164] Montesquieu 1964, p. 874 (*Pensées*, no. 183): 'Comme les vices et les vertus humaines sont ordinairement l'effet des passions, et les passions l'effet d'un certain état de la machine – je parle du matériel des passions, et non pas du formel, c'est-à-dire de cette complais[s]-ance l'âme sent à suivre les mouvements de sa machine'.

[165] Montesquieu 1964, p. 996 (*Pensées*, no. 1214): 'Presque toutes les vertus sont un rapport particulières d'un certain homme à un autre; par exemple: l'amitié, l'amour de la patrie, la pitié, sont des rapports particulières. Mais la justice est un rapport général. Or, toutes les vertus qui détruirent ce rapport général ne sont pas des vertus'.

[166] Montesquieu 1964, p. 948 (*Pensées*, no. 641): 'Le mot de *justice* est souvent très équivoque'. Emphasis in original.

[167] Montesquieu 1964, pp. 995f (*Pensées*, no. 1208): 'Ce qui fait la plupart des contradic-

of resentment against injustice, or rather a desire for 'vengeance' against those who have offended us, and not always a claim rooted in 'reason'.[168]

Two major implications flow from this argument, one of which has already been noted, namely that perfectionism is irrelevant to the political life of human beings. Instead, something like moderation or propriety is required for happiness, justice and tranquil civic life, for it is an artifice that reason can only explain after the fact. One cannot hope to fully quit the world for the contemplative life, nor can one reasonably expect to dominate others, because both are ultimately despotic solutions to the problem of selfhood. A second and related claim is that it is impossible to understand these relations between physical, moral and intellectual causes if one does not use both history and philosophy to illuminate particular contexts; a wry aside concerning the philosophy of Thales, for instance, illustrates his point.[169] History, for Montesquieu, is the best expression we have of human reason and human freedom acting in time, but those expressions receive their clearest distillation in philosophy. Thus, a better guide to understanding the 'laws and morals of the Greeks' is found in Plato's 'two Republics' and Aristotle's *Politics*. To think that one could find this understanding in the historians would, he said, be 'as if we wanted to find our own in reading about the wars of Louis XIV'.[170] Once more, theory drives the historical explanation, whilst history (as action in time and place) is simultaneously granted autonomy. Such an approach mapped onto his study of the passions, and might be illustrated in his projected, though never completed, history of the idea of jealousy, as distinct from claims about jealousy of trade.[171] The idea was taken up by some later authors in explicitly Montesquieuean fashion, but to a large extent it still remains an unwritten, possibly an unwritable, history.[172] Its most famous claims appear as clichés today, where jealousy is 'necessary in hot countries; liberty in cold climates', a claim to which he

---

tions de l'homme, c'est que la raison physique et la raison morale ne sont presque jamais d'accord'.

[168] Montesquieu 1964, p. 990 (*Pensées*, no. 1102): 'Le but naturel de la vengeance est de réduire un homme a ce sentiment de désirer de ne nous avoir point offensé'.

[169] Montesquieu 1964, p. 1009 (*Pensées*, no. 1463): 'quand un philosophe nous dit que le principe des choses est l'eau, nous voyone bien que nous n'avons qu'un mot, et que nous ignorons le sens'.

[170] Montesquieu 1964, p. 1007 (*Pensées*, no. 1452): 'Il faut réfléchir sur *la Politique* d'Aristote et sur les deux *République* de Platon, si l'on veut avoir une juste idée des lois et des moeurs des Grecs. Les chercher dans leur historiens, c'est comme si nous vouillons trouver les nôtres en lisant les guerres de Louis XIV'.

[171] See Sonenscher 2007, ch. 2; Hont 2005, esp. pp. 267–324; Hont 2007, esp. pp. 261–64, 278; cf. Joseph Addison [?] 1729, pp. 292–96.

[172] Mills 1772, esp. pp. 122f, 126f, 181f; see also Hont 2007a, esp. p. 393 n. 11.

appended a mixture of reasons from physical and sexual maturity to the differential strength of reason. It also bolstered his explanation of why despotism and servility begin with the drowsiness (and jealousy) found in hot climates.[173] For although Montesquieu left only fragmentary notes about how this history might be written, in them he once again justified its interest by claiming that that 'it is not always reason and nature that governs men, but often pure chance'.[174] Only history could show this fact, and though he failed to complete his project, in his myriad illustrations of the passionate causes and consequences of free human action, Montesquieu brought out the implications of his approach for what one might call the politics of soulcraft.

MODERATION AND SOULCRAFT: THE ACTION OF PASSIONATE SELFHOOD

In my account of liberty as propriety, free agency requires two things: First, that one be able to control the passions that motivate action in order to deliberate effectively, and second that one identify with and be responsible for such passionately or affectively grounded actions, because one can be judged according to conventional standards of justice. In order to act with political liberty, the passionate self has to be able to pursue its ends freely, but to desire those ends that are of common benefit. This requires moderation, or propriety. Indeed, because freedom on this account derives principally from persons and their capacities, not just from choices and options, political liberty accords with self-regulation, moral responsibility and appropriate action under the law. For most writers of the early-modern period, the obvious starting point for such arguments was to be found in discussions of the nature of the soul, and Montesquieu was (again like Descartes) no exception. The soul, he reiterated, is a 'combination' of ideas that is separately moved by moral and physical causes, and which 'suffers when it is not occupied', feeling as if something has 'menaced' its very existence.[175] This occupation is the pursuit of agency for our happiness, but in order that this free agency might be made to

---

[173] Montesquieu 1964, p. 989 (*Pensées*, no. 1087): 'La jalousie me semble nécessaire dans les pays chauds; la liberté, dans les climates froids'. Cf. Montesquieu 1989, 3. 14. 13, p. 243; 1964, p. 617: 'Servitude always begins with drowsiness'.

[174] Montesquieu 1964, p. 920 (*Pensées*, no. 579): 'On verra dans *l'Histoire de la Jalousie* que ce n'est pas toujours la Nature et la Raison qui gouvernent les hommes, mais le pur hazard'.

[175] Montesquieu 1964, p. 916 (*Pensées*, no. 551): 'Notre âme est une suite d'idées. Elle souffre quand elle n'est pas occupé, comme si cette suite était interrompue, et qu'on menaçât son existence'. See also Starobinski 1953, p. 32.

accord with political liberty, its ends have to be either forcibly checked or carefully manipulated. For that reason, political liberty is neither democracy nor free choice. It is, instead, doing what one should want to do, the hallmark of which is moderation.

The language is again revealing when this thought is applied to the soul. Like Descartes, Montesquieu considered it important that to be happy the soul 'needs to have an object, because it is a means of giving life to our action'. It 'becomes more important according to the nature of the object' which 'further occupies our soul'.[176] Both in his *Pensées* and in his published works, Montesquieu presented the soul as a form of active, even creative energy and certainly as the source for what my own story thinks of as free agency.[177] In a striking formulation, he laid it down that the 'soul' of the economy matches the souls of the individuals in a particular regime, so that 'the economy of the state, which always follows the frugality of individuals, gives its economic commerce a soul, so to speak'.[178] His language, though qualified by the 'so to speak', is not accidental. Just as he synthesized various Platonic claims in his jurisprudence, the ultimate analogy between the individual soul and the soul of the state is also Platonic, and Montesquieu's soul can search for higher pleasures than those of the body alone. The implications had clear political import. For example, under a moderate government a slave would feel both internally and externally excluded from society. He could have no security, which is the very premise of liberty, and thus while 'his master's soul can expand ... his own soul is constantly constrained to sink'. The soul is 'debased without ceasing'.[179] Politics and soulcraft are closely intertwined in the pursuit of moderation or propriety.

These very specific recommendations were part of Montesquieu's attempt to move beyond the confines of overtly mechanistic explanations. Once again, and just as Locke had been, Montesquieu was uncomfortable with the deterministic (as well as political) implications of what was taken to be Spinozist or Hobbesian materialism. He seems instead to have adopted the Cartesian idea that perceptions (*sentimens*) of the mind are 'almost always a result of all the different movements which are produced in the diverse organs of our body'. On this reading, virtue and vice are 'the effect of the passions', and therefore themselves 'the effect of a certain state of the machine' (*les passions l'effet d'un certain état de la machine*). However, precisely because 'machine' here seemed to mean

---

[176] Montesquieu 1964, p. 916 (*Pensées*, no. 551 [1675]): 'Pour être heureux, il faut avoir un objet, parce-qu'c'est le moyen de donner de la vie à nos actions. Elles deviennent même plus importantes selon la nature de l'objêt, et par là, elles occupent plus notre âme'.

[177] Desgraves 1995, esp. pp. 65, 70.

[178] Montesquieu 1989, 4. 20. 11, p. 345; 1964, p. 653.

[179] Montesquieu 1989, 3. 15. 13, p. 256; 1964, p. 622; cf. Williams 2006, esp. 113ff.

body and soul in combination, his analysis ended up looking strongly materialistic. Indeed his critics argued that Montesquieu's assessment of the laws made the biblical Commandments little more than a particular *modalité* of a particular set of relations, and hence far too close to atheistic materialism.[180] That is why many thought him rather too close to Spinoza for his own good.[181] In his replies, Montesquieu fought hard to rebut the politically loaded charge, polemically accusing Spinoza of falsely treating liberty, and effectively making human beings little more than insects, with no free will to speak of.[182] But Spinoza had similarly claimed that 'the best commonwealth is one in which men live in harmony', that 'citizens are not born, but made', and that 'men's natural passions are the same everywhere' so that their effect on the commonwealth will be relative to the quality of the laws enacted. It is surely possible that Montesquieu's public refutation of the charge was purposefully sceptical (or even ironic).[183]

This was, after all, the same Montesquieu who chose to celebrate contingency whilst noting transhistorical similarities in human nature. Accounting for the rise and fall of Rome, for example, he wrote that men have had 'at all times the same passions'. Therefore, although 'the occasions which produce great changes are different', clearly 'the causes are always the same'.[184] This central distillation forms the backdrop to the famous (but somewhat gnomic) claim that law is an exact relation between things. The particular character of those complex 'relations' (*rapports*) that make up the spirit of laws are mirrored in the particular relationship between body and soul, and together they structure the conditions required for purposeful human agency.[185] Liberty as self-directed and appropriate agency is the action of this 'machine' in history, and while the soul is partly independent of the body, it is somewhat like a faculty that helps to regulate passionate excess.[186] Alongside Descartes, Montesquieu thought the soul was clearly affected by its perception of natural, external objects, but that it also nevertheless acts as a mediator to our initial perceptions and the passions that they provoke. This allows us both to retain

---

[180] See Montesquieu 1964a, pp. 809ff, 814, 821; Goyard-Fabre 1993, p. 127; Oudin 1911, pp. 65, 69; Spector 2001, p. 39; Lynch 1977, pp. 487–500.

[181] Montesquieu 1964, pp. 8744, 915f, 1035 (*Pensées*, nos. 183 [2035], 549 [30], 1798 [943]); see too Krause 2003, esp. pp. 239ff, 244ff, 250ff, an analysis to which I am indebted.

[182] Montesquieu 1964, p. 942 (*Pensées*, no. 617): 'Ce même philosophe veut bien, en ma faveur, détruire en moi la liberté'.

[183] See Spinoza 1958, ch. V, § 2, p. 309; discussion in Balibar 1998, pp. 66f; cf. Israel 2006, pp. 279f, 288ff, 292f, and esp. 824–39. See also Bayle 1702a, pp. 2767–88, esp. 2770, 2786ff; Kristeller 1984, pp. 1–15; James 1993, esp. pp. 296–301, 306–10, 315.

[184] Montesquieu 2000, § 1, p. 91.

[185] See Oudin 1911, esp. pp. 64f, 67, 69, 74ff, 77, 128f, 134, 159.

[186] Brewer 2008, esp. pp. 82, 87.

some independency of judgement through the use of our limited reason, and to allow the soul time to redirect our passions towards those things that are good for us. Such reconciliation and redirection between reason, the passion and the good life was common.[187]

According to Montesquieu, then, the soul is a faculty that allows us to compare phenomena and their effects upon us, beneficial or otherwise, even as we are continually stymied in our actions because of it. Developing medically inspired arguments about the movement of liquids and fibres around the body (in terms of the stimulation by external objects that give the soul sensations it can recall, though not reproduce), Montesquieu suggested that the soul 'in our body is like a spider in its web'.[188] Its capacity is greater when the threads or fibres connecting the organs and senses together are more tautly bound.[189] The naturalistic analogy underscores his reiterated claim that 'passions act with great effect upon us', and that life is really 'only a collection of passions, which are sometimes stronger, sometimes weaker'. Truly 'there is no doubt that the combination of these passions during the whole of a life, combining differently in each man, is responsible for the great variety of their minds [esprits]'. The passions, in what should be recognized as Montesquieu's guiding theme, are various and relational. Some give a 'spring [ressort] to the fibres' whilst others relax them; anger was but one Aristotelian-inspired example. Moreover, this language of springs, fibres and spirits relates obviously to Montesquieu's wider interest in natural science as much as it does to the problems of legislation.[190] Nevertheless, his understanding of the politics of soulcraft had still to show how liberty both requires and simultaneously promotes a moderate or appropriate balance between passionate selfhood and free action.

The passions had to be tamed for the benefit of social and political life because Montesquieu understood human nature in terms of a constant movement of the passions that could easily lead to conflict. Such movement embodied a struggle for power, glory and material gain, but it was also more than that. For although he agreed that the soul clearly does take 'delight in dominating other souls', and that if left alone the political consequences of such will to power were likely to end in tragedy, the solution lay not in the sovereign power of the Leviathan, as Hobbes had supposed, but rather in the moderation of behaviour between the individual and the

[187] James 2006, esp. pp. 205–10.

[188] Montesquieu 1964d, esp. pp. 486f, and the citation from p. 489: 'L'âme est, dans notre corps, comme une araignée dans sa toile'. For a translation, see Montesquieu 1976, pp. 141f, 144; see too Shklar 1979, p. 319.

[189] Descartes 1967, vol. 2, art. 30, p. 345.

[190] Montesquieu 1964d, p. 498; Montesquieu 1976, p. 145; for a discussion of Aristotle on anger see Harris 2001, esp. pp. 94–98.

state. This was premised on a rejection (and misunderstanding in fact) of Hobbes's analysis of the state of nature.[191] Yet Montesquieu transposed a Hobbesian concern with self-interested individuals onto something approaching a comparative historical sociology of the passions, in order to explain why absolute sovereignty was never going to be the right solution all of the time. Context was key, and to promote the solutions he wanted would require something like an enlightened legislator, about which more is said in the following section. In general, though, the supreme difficulty was that 'by a misfortune attached to the human condition, great men who are moderate are rare; and, as it is always easier to follow one's strength than to check it, perhaps, in the class of superior people, it is easier to find extremely virtuous people than extremely wise men'.[192] Too often great men give free rein to their own passions, which leads to despotism and tyranny.

Individuals have to learn how to redirect their passions to things that are useful and appropriate, in order to truly act at liberty according to Montesquieu's analysis. The language and his analogies are exercises in therapy.[193] In claiming to show how a moderate and balanced politics could be a palliative for the extremes of absolutism or despotism, his neo-Hippocratic vocabulary was clearly noticed by contemporaries.[194] Indeed, he contributed to the development of a language of politics that would remain profoundly important to later political and artistic developments through the French Revolution, including perhaps most explicitly the 1792 painting of *Hippocrates Refusing the Gifts of Artaxerxes*, by Anne-Louis Girodet.[195] Pursuing a form of self-therapy, one could also learn techniques through study and concentration, indicating that such redirection is effortful and difficult. For example, Nicole had claimed that work through scholarship and education was one way to cure oneself of the self-interested *ennui* of everyday life.[196] Montesquieu agreed, and found in study the 'sovereign remedy' to all the 'disgusts [*désgouts*] of life'.[197] From this idea of moderated selfhood, the political implications

[191] Tuck 1999, pp. 185, 197–207; Waddicor 1970, pp. 167ff. Goyard-Fabre 1993, p. 101 condenses Montesquieu's well-known criticisms; Malcolm 2002, esp. pp. 436ff, 441ff, 449f.

[192] Montesquieu 1989, 6. 28. 41, p. 595; 1964, p. 747; cf. Montesquieu 1964, p. 996 (*Pensées*, no. 1213): 'Il est bien moins rare d'avoir un esprit sublime qu'une âme grande'.

[193] Frierson 2002, esp. p. 321; Krause 2003, pp. 246ff; Peter 1972, pp. 138–70, and the splendid paper by Shklar 1979, esp. pp. 321f.

[194] See Peter 1972, pp. 138–70; Shklar 1979, esp. pp. 316ff. For an illustration of his thoughts on the scientific personality, see Montesquieu 1955b, esp. p. 52.

[195] Crow 2006, esp. pp. 140–44.

[196] Nicole 1671, part 2, § 23, p. 287; Nicole 1970c, § XII, esp. p. 429. For discussion, James 1972, pp. 109–12.

[197] Shklar 1979, p. 327; Montesquieu 1964, p. 853 (*Pensées*, no. 4): 'L'étude a été pour moi le souverain remedé contre les dégouts de la vie, n'ayant jamais eu de chagrin qu'une heure de lecture ne m'ait ôté'.

of the analysis could be developed to suggest legislative cures for sickly polities. At the level of the individual and the state, it was the general craze for recognition that would have to be tempered or effectively manipulated, and it is here that Montesquieu most obviously reconnected with Pierre Nicole.

Nicole's updated Augustinianism, one should recall, argued that civil life was predicated upon self-interest, so that in the secular realm the ideal of charity and the reality of *amour-propre* were 'exceedingly similar in their effects even if they were different principles' (*conformité d'effets en des principes si différents*). The latter was found in particular when examining such apparently great and powerful passions for admiration, respect, confidence and love.[198] The paradoxical implications of such an argument were not lost on later writers like Mandeville, keen to assert the underlying vice behind apparent virtue. But in Nicole's hands, as Locke had already discovered, the 'best traits of mankind' (*l'honnêteté humaine*) were to be found in the 'suppression' (*suppression*) of such self-love, which was simply 'another love within our heart' (*un autre amour dans notre coeur*).[199] Yet this all just seemed to modify a more foundational problem that Pascal had already outlined, namely that the 'bias towards self is the beginning of all disorder, in war, politics, economics, in man's individual body'.[200] When such self-concern became conventional and viewed as natural, as for example when the rich, through their ancestry and property, deemed themselves naturally to occupy an elevated social position, this outcome was only really a triumph of human artifice, much as Rousseau would later argue.[201] However, unlike Rousseau, Nicole suggested that this was the result of a natural (and not artificial) need. This was the need for recognition, mutual love and respect in the 'commerce of self-interest' (*commerce d'amour-propre*) that forms the basis of human civility (*civilité humaine*).[202] Recognition was not a problem in principle, but its effects in practice had to be closely monitored to avoid the evils of flattery and corruption instead of moderation and probity. Montesquieu concurred.[203]

The *honnête homme* of Nicole's Jansenism was a synthesis of numerous contemporary and Epicurean ideas of 'natural' man and his sociability, which coalesced around the problem of how to overcome the excesses

---

[198] Nicole 1970, pp. 179–206, esp. ch. 1, p. 179; ch. 3, p. 183. See too C. J. Coleman 2005, esp. pp. 304f, 306, 309f.

[199] Nicole 1970, ch. 1, p. 180; van Kley 1987, esp. pp. 72ff; Hulliung 1994, p. 19.

[200] Pascal 1966, no. 421, p. 154; see too Keohane 1980, pp. 294f, 296ff; Kolakowski 1998, pp. 175–81.

[201] Pascal 1965, pp. 67ff; Rousseau 2003, bk. 4, ch. 8, p. 142.

[202] Nicole 1970b, ch. 1, p. 268.

[203] James 1972, p. 139; Montesquieu 1955c, p. 68; Spector 2003, pp. 23–69.

of the passions through reason and self-legislation.[204] As Domat had reiterated, it was a social ethic that masked fundamental human failings. Nicole nonetheless tempered the rigidity of the harshest Jansenist position about moral motivation (which stated that actions not grounded in cupidity are corrupt), offering instead the weaker thesis that the best people can do is try to motivate their will towards appropriate action in a combination of voluntarism and reason.[205] Although God still owes us nothing on his account, the connection between our inner life (or conscience) and the manner in which we interact with people in the real world becomes paramount to governing conduct. In general, this seems to be an attempt to allow reason to triumph over the passions whilst keeping it subservient to faith, whilst recognizing that the very real needs of human beings are not simply expressions of their fallen status.[206] Montesquieu took a similar approach, except in his case reason really does look rather more like a slave to the passions. He agreed with Nicole that it is only by knowing our own faults that we are able to overcome the natural vices to which we are all subject, and that this self-reform is the very foundation of justice and the needs (*devoirs*) of civility.[207] He could therefore also agree with Nicole's conclusions, namely that 'appropriateness of conduct to capacities is the golden rule'.[208] Agency requires propriety, and political liberty is designed to produce it even if it is unnatural. Furthermore, if this is what matters for the individual, it matters at least as much for the legislator. And how the skilful legislator might balance these various passions so as to produce and maintain political liberty under moderate government was the task Montesquieu set out to evaluate.

LEGISLATIVE PASSIONS AND CIVIL RELIGION

'If it is true', wrote Montesquieu, 'that the character of the spirit and the passions of the heart are extremely different in the various climates', then 'laws should be relative to the differences in these passions and to the

---

[204] Keohane 1980, pp. 277f, 283, 286, 288f; Thweatt 1980, pp. 21, 24f, 28f, 31, 38; Levi 1964, ch. 8.

[205] James 1972, esp. pp. 109, 113, 115; cf. Thweatt 1980, p. 71.

[206] For the wider context, see Davies 1990, pp. 4, 22, 26f, 28f; Kolakowski 1998, esp. pp. 94ff.

[207] Nicole 1970a, esp. ch. XIV, p. 237: 'La charité nous obligeant à compâtir à la faiblesse de nos frères et à leur ôter tout sujet de tentation, nous oblige aussi à nous avons marques; mais ce n'est pas la charité seulement, c'est la justice même, et la loi éternelle qui le prescript, comme il est facile de le faire voir, tant au regard des témoignages de gratitude qu'a l'égard des devoirs de civilité'; also ch. XI, p. 265.

[208] James 1972, p. 121.

differences in these characters'.[209] Even his apparently frivolous examples about sexuality and climate serve to illustrate that, for Montesquieu, wise legislators are needed to enact laws that reflect the needs rather than the vices promoted by particular climates.[210] That is what determines the 'degree of liberty the constitution can support'.[211] One of the central aims of Montesquieu's text, which continues to reject the applicability of Machiavellianism to modern politics, is to prove that 'the spirit of moderation should be that of the legislator', because 'the political good, like the moral good, is always found between two limits'.[212] In this effort, he was, he wrote, retreading ground that had been well prepared by some illustrious forebears, whom he couldn't 'even pretend to compare myself with [*je ne pretends pas me comparer à eux*]'. Those figures were Bossuet, Nicole and Pascal.[213] Accordingly, moderation in morals as well as in politics promotes propriety and decorum, and propriety in action is the hallmark of self-directed agency motivated by the passions. Equally, at the level of the legislator, moderation is the best guarantee of political liberty that can allow propriety to develop, which is why it is the medicine for feverish politics.

Moving beyond the therapeutic, Montesquieu's language most obviously recalls Aristotle's doctrine of the mean and of the rough proportionality of justice that requires moderate rule and practical wisdom.[214] The good legislator with the political skill (*politike*) needed to rule, as well as the practical wisdom (*phronesis*) necessary to rule well, can promote the good of the city as a whole.[215] Such Aristotelian sympathies form part of Montesquieu's criticism of Hobbes and Grotius, both of whom rejected the applicability of the mean to questions of morals and justice, even though he retained their account of thin sociability.[216] But his more important point remains general, and relates to mediocrity as

---

[209] Montesquieu 1989, 3. 14. 1, p. 231; 1964, p. 613.

[210] Montesquieu 1989, 3. 14. 2, pp. 233f; 1964, pp. 613f.

[211] Montesquieu 1989, 1. 1. 3, p. 25; 1964, p. 532, where terrain 'doivent se rapporter au degré de liberté que la constitution peut suffrir'.

[212] Montesquieu 1989, 6. 29. 1, p. 602; 1964, p. 749; cf. Montesquieu 1989, I. 1. 4, p. 25 n. 9; 1964, p. 532.

[213] Montesquieu, Letter to Mgr de Fitz James, October 8, 1750, in Montesquieu 1955j, pp. 1327–29, p. 1328.

[214] Aristotle 1998, 1261a31–36, 1273b5–6, 1284a1–3; also Frank 2005, esp. pp. 97ff, 101, 103, 108.

[215] Aristotle 2000, 1141b24; cf. Frank 2005, p. 124.

[216] Hobbes 1998, ch. 3, § 32, pp. 55f; discussion in Skinner 1996, pp. 323f; Grotius 2005, vol. 1, § XLV, pp. 118ff; Grotius 2005a, vol. 3, p. 1749; cf. Grotius 2005, vol. 1, § VIII, pp. 85f: '*This sociability, which we have now described in general, or this Care of maintaining Society in a Manner conformable to the Light of human Understanding, is the Fountain of Right, properly so called*'. Emphasis in original.

Aristotle had presented it, even as it upends Aristotle's suggestion that
virtue is a natural tendency in the perfection of particular regimes. Although virtue is rule for excellence, and although that is the defining
'spring' of republics, according to Montesquieu, there is nothing natural
about it. It is contrary to nature, as in fact all politics is, and that includes
moderate government. To be an adequate spring for action, republican
virtue must depend upon a strict overcoming of the natural ambition of
the soul, whose energies must be redirected towards the *patrie*. Indeed,
all types of free agency that exist under political liberty require this discipline, but his point is that such self-restraint or self-overcoming is never
undertaken without pain. Furthermore, we all want to use our power to
the fullest, and those in power are no different. This makes republics, and
republican virtue, especially tense. Rather like Christian asceticism, virtue
has its limits and requires self-sacrifice, but in so noting Montesquieu
relies on Machiavelli's similar sort of claim.[217] In republics, to continue
his metaphor, the springs are always tightly coiled because the necessary
attachment of citizens to the fatherland is something that can only be
cultivated artificially.[218]

Politics can indeed try to promote policies of self-sacrifice or self-
overcoming, but the best form of government is one where the unnatural
character of such asceticism or virtue is not required, and which allows
the political body to become a less tense, more self-correcting organism.
For this process, a moderate politics based on laws, and which allows
individuals to pursue self-interest and a desire for gain without worry,
is the ideal solution. Moderate monarchy works best for achieving this
self-direction, and in combination with commercial prosperity might just
allow a chance for 'men of state' to concern themselves with doing 'good
things'.[219] So although moderation is almost always as much a matter of
luck rather than good judgement, under monarchy honour might at least
promote it, because it is both favoured by the passions and favours them
in turn.[220] It is, so to speak, the best expression of divine workmanship
that is possible on earth, because it accords with principles and desires
implanted in us by a creator. Equally, because it sets our natural desires
free, it does not require the arduous self-renunciation of virtue.

The extent to which either virtue or moderation might be cultivated
politically, then, depends upon the passions of both the legislator and the
citizen. 'Sometimes', Montesquieu writes, the passions of the citizen 'pass
through and are colored [by the legislator]; sometimes they remain there

---

[217] Machiavelli 1989a, bk. 3, ch. 7, p. 1151; Pocock 2003a, p. 491.

[218] Rahe 2001, esp. pp. 73f; Carrithers 2001, esp. pp. 121f.

[219] Montesquieu 1964, p. 873 (*Pensées*, no. 193): 'C'est dans un siècle des lumières que
les hommes d'État acquièrent le grand talent de faire à propos les choses bonnes'. Cf. Shackleton 1979, esp. pp. 310–13; Mass 1980, esp. pp. 41f, 46.

[220] Montesquieu 1989, I. 4. 5, p. 36; 1964, p. 542.

and are incorporated'.[221] Given his general classification of governments into monarchies, republics, and despotisms, with their cognate *ésprits* of honour, virtue and fear, these characteristics are their 'nature', and the principles that make these political forms move are simply the 'human passions that make it act'.[222] This nature is a form of artifice engrafted upon passionate individuals. However, moderate monarchy looks to be the most promising candidate for political liberty in commercial society precisely because it is governed by laws and because power is checked through the social implications of honour. Its springs are less taught than republics or despotisms, so it has the potential to maintain itself in the absence of austere virtue, or a common enemy, or indeed fear. Good citizens (if not always good men) are plentiful because ambition has 'good effects under a monarchy', though it can be 'repressed' by the sovereign when necessary. Honour thereby takes the place of virtue, and 'makes all of the parts of the body politic move'. It is, once again, artificial because political in conception, but even 'false honour' can uphold moderate monarchical government. And if the principle of honour is to 'demand distinctions', a moderate monarchy is its best constitutional form provided that appropriate intermediary powers are in place.[223] This is Montesquieu's defence of magistracy, as 'nothing gives greater force to the laws than the extreme subordination of the citizens to the magistrates'.[224] His claim could also of course be pressed into both contemporary and historical service. First, it supported a political critique that Sieyes would later make infamous in France apropos the Estates General, arguing that if the 'legislative body were not convened for a considerable time, there would no longer be liberty'.[225] Second, it once again challenged the applicability of republican virtue to modern politics. Addressing those who lauded Italian city-states for their freedom, Montesquieu asks his readers to take their measure by comparing them with the English system of liberty, the curious hybrid of a republic hiding under a monarchy with its mixture of legislative, executive and judicial powers. In Italian city-republics 'where the three powers are united', he claims, 'there is less liberty than in our monarchies'. He continues:

> Observe the possible situation of a citizen in these republics. The body of the magistracy, as executor of the laws, retains all the power it has given itself as legislator. It can plunder the state by using its general

---

[221] Montesquieu 1989, 2. 11. 9, p. 168; 1964, p. 591; 1989, 6. 29. 19, p. 618; 1964, p. 755. See also Krause 2006, esp. pp. 214f.

[222] Montesquieu 1989, I. 3. 1, p. 21; 1964, p. 536.

[223] Montesquieu 1989, 2. 11. 3, p. 155; 1964, p. 586; cf. Montesquieu 1964, p. 538: 'La nature de l'honneur est de demander des preferences et des distinctions'.

[224] Montesquieu 1989, I. 5. 7, pp. 50f; 1964, p. 547.

[225] Montesquieu 1989, 2. 11. 6, pp. 162, 161; 1964, p. 588.

wills [*il peut ravager l'Etat par ses volontés générales*]; and, as it also has the power of judging, it can destroy each citizen by using its particular wills.[226]

Laws, provided they are certain, protect honour even when honour is false. Therefore monarchy best appeals to and supports our natural vanity, but demands less of us in terms of virtue because of the stability provided through security and law. The potentially arbitrary power of the monarch is similarly checked by the principle of honour, which promotes internal excellence or regulation, and external recognition as its validation, and which in practice can support policies like office selling for profit, something of personal importance to Montesquieu.[227] In all of this, Montesquieu certainly presages Adam Smith's account of the paradoxical stability and self-sustaining character of modern commercial society, using honour (an ultimately selfish passion) and a desire for recognition to promote the common good. At the same time, his use of honour seems to update Machiavelli's satirizing of princely *clementia* as the true source of political virtue. Like Machiavellian prudence, honour could dissimulate, could be relative, could be false and artificial, but it was certainly nothing like classical virtue. None of that mattered though so long as the law was constant.[228] The utility of honour therefore lies in its capacity to recalibrate or redirect agency towards governed conduct under laws, because the power of the monarch is checked and regulated by the power of various intermediary bodies. Such a claim also allowed Montesquieu to insert a rhetorical and conservative defence of honour into his wider and circuitous genealogy of the French monarchy.[229] Honour is appropriate to the ideal of a modern monarchy, which has to somehow justify vast inequalities of rank, status and wealth but govern well, and which is incapable of reintroducing (even though it should not even want to do so) an impossibly demanding ideal of ancient virtue to meet its goals.[230]

---

[226] Montesquieu 1989, 2. 11. 6, p. 157; 1964, p. 587; also Sullivan 2006, esp. p. 277, and n. 42.

[227] Rahe 2001, pp. 77–80; cf. Krause 2002a, pp. 42f, 45f, 82, 98f. Montesquieu defends office selling under monarchy *contra* Plato, arguing that chance will produce 'better subjects than the choice of the prince'. See Montesquieu 1989, I. 5. 19, pp. 70f; 1964, p. 555, citing Plato 1997b, bk. 8, 551c. Cf. Hobbes 1998, ch. 5, § 13, p. 112, praising it for clarifying issues of succession and transferral of offices; cf. Goyard-Fabre 1993, pp. 3f, 6, 7–9, 15.

[228] Montesquieu 1989, I. 3. 6–7, pp. 26f; 1964, p. 538; 1989, I. 6. 21, pp. 94f; also Montesquieu 1964, p. 564; cf. Machiavelli 1997, chs. 16, 18, 21; Shackleton 1988d, pp. 116–31. Cf. Mosher 1984. p. 184.

[229] Sonenscher 2007, esp. pp. 137–52.

[230] See Mosher 2001, esp. pp. 200ff; De Dijn 2008, esp. pp. 26–31; Rahe 2001, esp. pp. 91ff.

It is unsurprising therefore to find Montesquieu suggesting that the connections between laws, the constitution of the state and the various passions of the people, all 'meet [in] the passions and prejudices of the legislator'. It was a claim that allowed him to present Aristotle and Plato, Machiavelli, Thomas More, and James Harrington as precursors of his argument.[231] Balance, moderation and propriety structure Montesquieu's political thinking, and he saw the need for it everywhere, whether in terms of balancing property and political power, or in terms of the need to balance our natural self-interest with the demands of political stability. It was equally vital, though, that the 'genius' of the legislator recognize the need for concision and simplicity in style. Laws should be like the Roman Twelve Tables, not the 'Novellae of Justinian' or the overly rhetorical laws of princes in the East. They certainly should not change 'without sufficient reason'.[232] They should also sit well with the mediocrity or generality of the middling sort, as Aristotle had proposed.[233]

When Montesquieu inserted the later 'Avertissement' to the 1757 edition of De l'Esprit des lois, he developed these ideas to relate them to claims about virtue once more. True political virtue, the spring (ressort) for action that unites the good man to the ideal republic, is neither moral, nor Christian, nor indeed classical and heroic virtue.[234] Only political liberty, and hence moderation or propriety, can foster the promotion of political virtue through the artificial manipulation of natural passions, and while monarchy might best achieve this aim, part of the human ingenuity that makes this artifice possible stems from the wisdom of the legislator who knows how to relate religion to politics. Civil religion is another tool, like honour, for promoting a well-ordered polity. Just as intermediary powers help to balance moderate regimes by cultivating good citizens, so too should 'religion and the civil laws' aim 'principally to make good citizens of men'. To the extent that one or the other 'departs from this end', the other force should attempt to counterbalance it. The more repressive religion is, the less repressive the civil law should be, and

---

[231] Montesquieu 1964, p. 1073 (Pensées, no. 2095).

[232] Montesquieu 1989, 6. 29. 16, pp. 612, 614; 1964, p. 753; cf. Montesquieu 1989, 6. 30. 16, p. 614; 1964, p. 754: 'The laws should not be subtle. They are made for people of limited understanding [mediocre entendement]'. Montesquieu was critical of Plato's discussion of Greek laws against suicide undertaken for weakness of the soul. Because the person committing suicide can easily evade such laws, and because their motives can never be fully known, no rational punishment can be handed out. See also Montesquieu 1989, 6. 29. 16, p. 616; 1964, p. 754; cf. Montesquieu 1989, 6. 20. 9, pp. 606f; 1964, p. 653. Finally, see Montesquieu 1964, pp. 879f (Pensées, no. 258).

[233] Montesquieu 1989, 5. 25. 7, p. 486; 1964, p. 707; Aristotle 1998, 1293a40, 1294a15–25, pp. 92, 94.

[234] Montesquieu 1989, 'Author's Foreword', pp. xlif.

vice versa.[235] He added that 'the less we can satisfy our particular passions, the more we give ourselves up to passions for the general order.[236] This claim appears as part of a discussion of patriotism, but is further illustrated with the curious example of a monkish order. The more austere the rules that deprived them of their ordinary passions, Montesquieu noted, the more the monks would redirect their passionate attachment to this law itself.[237] This unnatural form of self-propriety is, once more, precisely what is generally required of the good citizen, namely an artificial overcoming of self, which nevertheless allows for the pursuit of a natural desire for honour and distinction. Taken individually, both Christian and political virtue are excessive, but in combination, they can be moderated and take on the characteristics of honour. That seems to be the best that can be achieved.[238]

The strict conceptual terms of political liberty are outlined in the following section, but it is clear already that political liberty both requires and cultivates propriety or moderation. This is so in the double sense that political liberty is appropriately directed agency under law, whilst appropriate and self-directed agency is (in tautologous fashion) the hallmark of free agency. Because agency requires self-regulation, and because it is at best an artificial and temporary fix for the problems of otherwise unregulated self-interest and ambition, political liberty is a delicate balance between self-interest and political order. Insofar as we are individuals, the passions relate our nature to the question of temporality, or action in time.[239] Insofar as we are citizens, political liberty is the sphere of action open to us under law within which we can act on these passions to achieve our goals. For those reasons political liberty is best fostered by a moderate regime, because moderate regimes (like moderate individuals) are not burdened by an overarching, potentially despotic, and unitary form of sovereignty. They can deal with passionate diversity and difference so long as all are clear about the nature of the laws, because clear laws check and regulate human agency to create a political union of general wills out of this multiplicity of particular wills. Union between passion and action in the individual machine, therefore, is analogous with political union in the body politic. Both are a form of harmony where different parts of the machine (political or individual) balance and check one another appropriately. This explains in part why Montesquieu was

---

[235] Montesquieu 1989, 5. 24. 14, p. 468; 1964, p. 701; see also Montesquieu 1989, 5. 24. 15–16, pp. 470f; 1964, pp. 701f.

[236] Montesquieu 1989, I. 5. 2, p. 43; 1964, p. 544: 'moins nous pouvons satisfaire nos passions particulières, plus nous nous livrons aux générales'.

[237] For discussion, see Krause 2002a, pp. 37ff, 64ff; cf. Crisafulli 1943, esp. pp. 122f.

[238] Cf. Israel 2006, pp. 377–80.

[239] Goldzink 2001, p. 84.

interested in developing a general and secular political theory based on *ésprit générale*, alongside a defence of the plural intermediary powers that monarchy promoted. The history of the French monarchy and its 'fundamental laws' could elucidate and give lustre to Montesquieu's argument, he thought, because rightly understood, honour actually rules according to fundamental laws.[240] Indeed, perhaps the most general expression of this argument is presented in the formulation that honour is found 'only in the disposition of the laws, and especially [*même*] of the fundamental laws, which form liberty in its relation to the constitution'.[241] The concerns seem to have their roots in an argument begun in earnest by Pascal, who had claimed that society is a body of 'thinking members', that a 'multitude which cannot be reduced to unity is confusion', and that unity that is 'not a multitude is tyranny'.[242] For Montesquieu, as for Rousseau after him, only a general will of this sort could transform bare power into legitimate political authority, and only certain political forms would permit it.[243] The implications were clear to both, even if their solutions were opposed, a situation that led Rousseau to offer his famously backhanded compliment that the 'illustrious Montesquieu' had begun the scientific study of politics, but that it remained a 'grand and useless science'.[244] For Montesquieu, however, commercial liberty and human acquisitiveness could flourish in the modern world, and they could best flourish under a moderate monarchy ruled by law and governed by honour. As he wrote, 'in a nation that is in servitude, one works more to preserve than to acquire; in a free nation, one works more to acquire than to preserve'.[245]

Furthermore, just as honour in monarchy served to support the laws, so too was there a spatial dimension to the analysis. If the 'principles of the established government' are dependent upon its size, its 'spirit'

[240] Israel 2006, p. 279; Keohane 1980, pp. 348ff; De Dijn 2008, pp. 24ff; Loy 1977, pp. 183–92. On the history of the French monarchy in Montesquieu's text, see Sonenscher 2007, esp. pp. 48f, 129ff, 137f; Kingston 1996, pp. 35ff, 57, 175; cf. Carcassonne 1927, pp. 67, 92f, 95, 659f; Mosher 2007, pp. 104f.

[241] Montesquieu 1989, 2. 12. 1, p. 187; 1964, p. 598: 'Il n'y a que la disposition des lois, et même des lois fondamentales qui forme la liberté dans son rapport avec la constitution'. On the particular use of fundamental laws in Montesquieu, see Ehrard 2005, pp. 267ff, 272–75. 'Annexe I', pp. 279f, and 'Annexe II', pp. 281–86, who lists the occurrences of the terms *loi(s) fondamentale(s)* and *constitution* in *de l'Esprit des lois*. Cf. Thompson 1986, esp. pp. 1110.

[242] Pascal 1966, nos. 368–73 [473, 474, 480, 483] 604 [871], pp. 135f (on thinking bodies), 231f (on unity and multiplicity); see Riley 1986, esp. p. 19.

[243] See Riley 1986, pp. 63, 101.

[244] Rousseau 1969, p. 836. Thomas Nugent also undertook one of the first English translations of Rousseau's *Émile*. See Rousseau 1763, vol. 1, pp. 365f, for this quotation.

[245] Montesquieu 1989, 4. 20. 4, p. 341; 1964, p. 652.

will change to the 'degree to which its boundaries are narrowed or extended'.[246] Therefore the 'natural tendency' (*propriété naturelle*) of small states is towards government by republic, while despots will rule over vast empires.[247] Therefore, 'it is in the nature of a republic to have only a small territory; otherwise, it can scarcely continue to exist'. Large republics have 'little moderation in spirits', and 'the common good is sacrificed to a thousand considerations'.[248] For the moment, the monarchies of France and Spain were 'precisely the requisite size' to be able to defend their middle-sized territories effectively, and potentially arbitrary power was tempered by both 'ecclesiastics' and strict laws. Similarly, Holland, Germany and the Swiss Leagues were of appropriate size and scale as federal republics.[249] Indeed, in a paragraph that Rousseau would take up almost verbatim (but with a significant disagreement about Rome), Montesquieu thought that all states had a particular object or purpose that drives them.[250] All should nevertheless be wary of growing flabby and potentially despotic, from which point it is but a short step to begin to see why England was so important to Montesquieu.[251] England appeared to be a paradigmatic illustration of a 'moderate' government, and it is only in 'moderate governments' (if not always 'moderate states') that 'political liberty is found'.[252] Montesquieu had therefore also claimed that the English were right to remove the 'intermediate powers that formed their monarchy' in order to maintain their liberty. They would be 'one of the most enslaved peoples on earth' without it.[253] He never did outline what he saw as the principal spring of English government, but he did say that 'political liberty' there has a 'direct purpose', which is to balance the sectional interests of the three different estates in order to maintain the liberty and the power of the state. Yet even if Montesquieu thought the task of politics and legislation was to reconcile all of these potentially

[246] Montesquieu 1989, I. 8. 20, p. 126; 1964, p. 576; cf. Aristotle 1998, 1296a9–11, p. 98, 1296b17–27, p. 99.

[247] Montesquieu 1989, I. 8. 20, p. 126; 1964, p. 576.

[248] Montesquieu 1989, I. 8. 16, pp. 124f; 1964, p. 575. See also Montesquieu 1989, I. 9. 1, p. 131; 1964, p. 577, claiming that small republics are 'destroyed by a foreign force', but 'if it is large, it is destroyed by an internal vice'.

[249] Montesquieu 1989, 2. 9. 1, 3, 6, pp. 131, 133, 135f; 1964, pp. 577ff; also Montesquieu 1989, I. 2. 4, p. 18; 1964, p. 535.

[250] Montesquieu 1989, 2. 11. 5, p. 156; 1964, p. 586; Rousseau 2003, bk. 2, ch. 11, p. 79. See Ehrard 1987, esp. pp. 68ff. Montesquieu also noted in this connection the importance of trade and his contemporary example was that of Marseilles; cf. Montesquieu 1989, 4. 20. 5, p. 341; 1964, p. 652; also Takeda 2006, pp. 707–34; Larrère 2000, esp. pp. 7, 9, 12f.

[251] Montesquieu 1989, I. 8. 17–20, pp. 125f; 1964, pp. 575f; Machiavelli 1989, bk. 2, ch. 6, p. 209.

[252] Montesquieu 1989, 2. 11. 4, p. 155; 1964, p. 586; Spector 2006, pp. 415f.

[253] Montesquieu 1989, I. 2. 4, p. 19; 1964, p. 535; Rousseau 2003, bk. 3, ch. 15, p. 114.

divergent interests in their particular contexts, he also knew that it could not flatten out the commotions and contradictions altogether. Thus if neither republican virtue nor despotism is appropriate or acceptable, then one wants to know how else the limited and artificial arena of politics might cultivate a moderate liberty to pursue the common good. Part of the answer is that it cannot do so directly, and the best hope Montesquieu suggests is the chance cultivation of liberty that comes about accidentally when monarchies allow individuals to pursue their glory and honour under laws. Not reason, but chance, does the job, and yet there is still a central role for politics within this process.

One central issue that Montesquieu continued to focus on therefore concerned the role of the legislator, particularly in terms of the promotion of a civil religion. In general, of course, the laws adumbrated by the legislator need to be relative to the principles of government under consideration; hence the virtue of the republic, the honour of the monarchy, and the fear embodied in despotism would always present themselves in ideal (and hence abstract) form as the appropriate expression of the passions of the legislator in any given context. These 'relations between the laws and the principle tightens all the springs of the government, and the principle in turn receives a new force from the laws'.[254] The legislator must follow the spirit of the nation when doing so is not contrary to the principles of the government, because, much like Adam Smith, who would later outline a system of natural liberty, Montesquieu thought that 'we do nothing better than what we do freely and following our natural genius'.[255] In general, 'laws are conceived so as not to run counter to the nature of things', including relations of 'honour, those of morality, and those of religion'.[256] Moreover, there are 'different orders of law; and the sublimity of human reason consists in knowing well to which of these orders principally relate those things that require statute', and which will not contradict the fact that men are always 'governed by diverse sorts of laws'.[257] This is as close as Montesquieu comes to giving reason a leading role, but the sublimity of human reason here is analogous to the skill of the wise politician who knows that societies have a multiplicity of virtues and vices, but that 'political vices' are not necessarily 'moral vices', nor

[254] Montesquieu 1989, I. 5. 1, p. 42; 1964, p. 544; cf. Machiavelli 1989, bk. 1, chs. 4, 10, pp. 202ff, 220ff; also bk. 1, ch. 58, p. 317; bk. 3, chs. 1–2, 29, pp. 419–24, 493f.

[255] Montesquieu 1989, 3. 19. 5, p. 310; 1964, p. 642.

[256] Montesquieu 1989, 6. 29. 16, p. 616; 1964, p. 754.

[257] Montesquieu 1989, 5. 26. 1, p. 494; 1964, p. 710: 'Les hommes sont gouvernés par diverses sortes de lois. . . . Il y a donc différents ordres des lois; et la sublimité de la raison humaine consiste à savoir bien auquel de ces ordres se rapportent principalement les choses sur lesquelles on doit statuer, et à ne point mettre de confusion dans les principes qui doivent gouverner les hommes'.

moral vices necessarily political ones. Knowing this, the legislator can use religion to cultivate moderation rather than virtue.[258]

In explaining the utility of religion to politics in this way, Montesquieu also wanted to do more than simply note its instrumental value. He directly countered Bayle's provocative thesis about the possibility of a society of virtuous atheists, seeing it as 'sophistry' and faulty moral judgement.[259] Instead, 'religion, even a false one, is the best warrant men can have of the integrity of men'.[260] This of course led to a familiar paradox, because 'men are exceedingly drawn to hope and fear, and a religion that had neither hell nor paradise would scarcely please them'.[261] Correlatively, 'men who believe in the certainty of rewards in the next life will escape the legislator', for you cannot constrain the man 'who believes himself sure that the greatest penalty the magistrates can inflict on him will end in a moment only to begin his happiness'.[262] The legislator, therefore, must be possessed of an appropriate, or moderate, religious sensibility that can be filtered through to the general population. And in this regard, Montesquieu seems to defend something like Machiavellian *virtù*; having separately assailed Machiavelli's own satire on princely clemency and virtue, Montesquieu now claimed that 'a prince who loves and fears religion is a lion who yields to the hand that caresses him'. He knows his appropriate limits. By contrast a prince 'who fears and hates religion' can only be 'like the wild beasts who gnaw the chain that keeps them'. For 'he who has no religion at all is that terrible animal that feels its liberty only when it claws and devours'.[263] It is the duty of the state to impose civil religion in order to promote propriety and decorum by strengthening the laws. By so doing, it will uphold political liberty in pursuing a balance, or mean, between the sometimes contradictory demands of morality, commerce and religion.[264] Christianity was the best illustration of a religion that had not simply tried to 'establish a dogma', but had also directed it

---

[258] Montesquieu 1989, 3. 19. 10–11, pp. 313f; 1964, p. 643; cf. Ehrard 1963, vol. 1, p. 379; Shklar 1979, p. 326; Spector 2006, pp. 112, 144–49.

[259] Montesquieu 1989, 5. 24. 1–2, 6, pp. 459f, 463f; 1964, pp. 698f.

[260] Montesquieu 1989, 5. 24. 8, p. 465; 1964, p. 700; see Israel 2006, pp. 271f.

[261] Montesquieu 1989, 5. 25. 2, p. 480; 1964, p. 705; cf. William Warburton, Letter to Montesquieu, February 9, 1754, in Montesquieu 1955j, pp. 1488–95.

[262] Montesquieu 1989, 5. 24. 14, p. 469; 1964, p. 701; cf. Rousseau 2003, bk. 4, ch. 8, pp. 150f.

[263] Montesquieu 1989, 5. 24. 2, p. 460; 1964, p. 698: 'Un prince qui aime la religion et qui la craint, est un lion qui cède à la main qui le flatte, ou à la voix, qui l'apaise: celui qui craint la religion et qui la hait, et comme les bêtes sauvages qui mordent la chaîne qui les empêche de jeter sur ce qui les passent: celui qui n'a point du tout de religion, est cet animal terrible qui ne sent sa liberté qui lorsqu'il déchire et qu'il dévore'.

[264] Crisafulli 1943, p. 384.

as required.[265] It therefore seemed to Montesquieu that the type of government best suited to a Christian religion is a 'moderate' one, because it 'soften[s] the mores of men' and redirects their honour and ambition towards commonly beneficial purposes. Protestantism, with its rigidities and self-denying ordinances, is best suited to republics, and Catholicism (unsurprisingly) to monarchies. The general direction given by Christianity to dogma concerning the immortality of the soul, in turn, 'makes us hope for a state we believe in' and thereby directs or diverts our actions in ways that Locke could certainly have agreed with.[266]

COMMERCIAL SOCIETY AND POLITICAL LIBERTY

The rise of modern commercial society had prompted Montesquieu's defence of a moderate monarchy, and underscored his rejection of Machiavellian politics based on reason of state. If 'experience itself has made known that only goodness of government brings prosperity', then 'one has begun to be cured of Machiavellianism, and one will continue to be cured of it'. Commerce had similarly demystified the *arcana imperii*, making mysteries of state and esoteric political prudence, of the sort defended even by libertines like Gabriel Naudé, little more than 'imprudences' (*imprudences*) in the modern world.[267] Indeed, monarchies that aimed either at imperialism or universal monarchy following this model would necessarily end in ruin because of it.[268]

Commerce can produce beneficial effects even though it is rooted in self-interested behaviour, particularly if it is governed by a moderate monarchy in which the spring of honour is allowed to flourish alongside the desire for 'exact justice'.[269] This had literally world-historical importance. Commerce, for example, had simultaneously overcome the irrational hostility of barbarous Europeans towards the Jews, once this persecuted people had 'invented letters of exchange'. Thanks to commerce, therefore, the 'theologians were obliged to curb their principles' and instead of criticizing commerce as 'bad faith' (*mauvaise foi*) they returned it 'so to speak, to the bosom of integrity'.[270] Montesquieu then presents an early version of a thesis about the movement from the passions to the interests

[265] Montesquieu 1989, 5. 24. 19, p. 473; 1964, p. 703.

[266] Montesquieu 1989, 5. 24. 4–5, pp. 462f; 1964, p. 699; 1989, 5. 24. 19, p. 473; 1964, p. 703.

[267] Montesquieu 1989, 4. 21. 20, p. 389; 1964, p. 673; Donaldson 1992, esp. pp. 142, 159f, 164, 166; Keohane 1980, pp. 171ff.

[268] Spector 2006, p. 405.

[269] Montesquieu 1989, 4. 20. 1–2, p. 338; 1964, p. 651.

[270] Montesquieu 1989, 4. 21. 20, p. 389; 1964, p. 672.

in modern politics. He claims that 'to the speculations of the schoolmen [*scolastiques*] we owe all the misfortunes that accompanied the destruction of commerce; and to the avarice of princes we owe the establishment of a device that puts it, in a way, out of their power'.[271] The exact justice of commercial society, when buttressed by moderate monarchy and appropriate honour, provided the best possible shell for political liberty. Yet it is important to remind oneself of the strictness of what passed for liberty according to Montesquieu.

Political liberty might allow laws to be strictly and observably applied, but this did not mean that societies were in general more equal. How could it be anything else under a monarchy? Montesquieu actually has a rather complicated view of inequality, suggesting that equality meant little more than it had for the Greeks. That is to say, it meant little more than 'obeying and commanding one's equals'. Thus, the perfect equality and independence (there is, importantly, no liberty here) of a state of nature is lost upon entering society, and only through political liberty and laws can individuals 'become equal again'. This equality, however, is limited to the fact that one has to obey one's equals, which in turn requires a common standard of excellence that relates fitness to rule with social position or hierarchy. It is a model for the preservation of property and rule by elites.[272] It is not a model that supports democracy, for democracy, according to Montesquieu, allows persons to do what they want and not what they should. Democracy is, therefore, immoderate, and also seems to require an overly burdensome conception of virtue and participation in order to uphold it. In fact Montesquieu saw participation as 'one of the great drawbacks [*inconvénients*] of democracy'.[273]

His is instead a model that supports honour, because honour can only exist in a state 'whose constitution is fixed and whose laws are certain'.[274] As he would say in his discussion of aristocracy, although an aristocratic state could not be classified as free, '*moderation* is therefore the soul of such governments'.[275] Having liberty was more important than living in a 'free state'. Indeed, his critique of Venice, the emblematic 'aristocratic

[271] Montesquieu 1989, 4. 21. 20, p. 389; 1964, p. 672; cf. Hirschman 1977, pp. 38ff, 42, 50ff, 70–74, 97; Montesquieu 1964, p. 948 (*Pensées*, nos. 640, 641), on the relationship between princes, corruption and justice.

[272] See della Volpe 1978, esp. pp. 127–30.

[273] Montesquieu 1989, 2. 11. 6, p. 159; 1964, p. 587; also Montesquieu 1989, 3. 19. 27, p. 326; 1964, p. 647, for the idea that the 'great advantage' of modern over 'ancient democracies' is that trusted representatives could 'revise the bad impressions' expressed by the people, and 'calm these emotions'. Cf. Shklar 1985, esp. pp. 184f.

[274] Montesquieu 1989, I. 3. 8, p. 27; 1964, p. 538.

[275] Montesquieu 1989, I. 3. 4, p. 25; 1964, p. 538: 'La *moderation* est donc l'âme de ces gouvernements'. Emphasis in original. cf. Montesquieu 1964, p. 1035 (*Pensées*, no. 1804): 'On ne peut appeler *libre* un État aristocratique'. Emphasis in original.

republic', is typical in this regard. It builds extensively on an unmasking narrative of the Venetian government along the lines of Tacitus, whose scepticism Montesquieu appreciated.[276] This sort of account, provided by various contemporaries like Amelot de la Houssaye, argued that dictatorship and degeneration lay behind the façade of Venetian liberty and constitutional stability.[277] The myth of Venice in fact hid the realities of a more conventional despotism.[278] From this record Montesquieu drew the general conclusion that both extreme liberty and extreme democracy are devalued forms of the true equality of a 'regulated' polity governed by moderation and not excess. Yet there are so many allusions here it can be hard to know where to begin. It sounds practically derivative of Cicero's attempt in the *De Officiis* to reconcile liberty with equality understood as difference (in status, wealth, hierarchy and so forth). But because it equally applies to political, military and economic conduct, the discussion seems to be an expression of Montesquieu's Tacitean fascination with the Germanic roots of liberty, the nature of slavery and questions concerning reason of state.[279] Its emphasis provides the resources needed for a contemporary and updated Tacitean critique of corruption, whether monarchical or republican.[280]

The most general claim seems also to be an Aristotelian-inspired critique of excess. For not only does moderation imply a degree of balance between extremes, but it is possible that Montesquieu's criticisms of extreme political forms are also drawn directly from Aristotle's own claims about the debased character of 'extreme democracy'. This form of government, 'in which not the law, but the multitude, have the supreme power and supersede the law by their decrees', comes about through the rise of demagogues and clearly might lead to tyranny.[281] That was the im-

---

[276] Carrithers 1991, esp. pp. 250f, 252f, 258, 264; Volpilhac-Auger 1993, pp. 25f; cf. Volpilhac-Auger 1985, esp. pp. 129ff; Senaralens 2003, p. 106.

[277] Soll 2005, esp. pp. 18f, 62–66; Wootton 1994, esp. pp. 354ff, 362, 365ff. The French police were certainly aware of the radical implications of Amelot's Tacitean criticism, and watched him closely. See Soll 2003, esp. pp. 313f. Montesquieu also used the work of Didier, 1680.

[278] See Whelan 2001, pp. 619–47.

[279] Montesquieu 1989, I. 8. 3, p. 114; 1964, p. 571; cf. Machiavelli 1997, ch. 10, p. 38; Machiavelli 1989, bk. 1, ch. 55, pp. 306–10; bk. 2, ch. 2, pp. 328–33; see too Waddicor 1970, pp. 150ff, 154, 156f, 163; Volpilhac-Auger 1985, pp. 129ff, 139ff, 178f; Carcassonne 1927, p. 659. Cf. Montesquieu 1964, pp. 884, 860 (*Pensées*, nos. 297, 73).

[280] Desgraves 1954, no. 3084, p. 223; cf. Tuck 1993, esp. pp. 40f, 47, 54, 59, 67f, 71ff, 77, 80f, 85; Malcolm 2007, esp. pp. 35f, 94–97, 100 n. 22, 101–4, 115ff, 119–23; Rahe 2001, pp. 92ff.

[281] Aristotle 1998, 1292a5–8, p. 89. The other four forms of democracy are those based 'strictly on equality', the election of magistrates based on a property qualification, a third where all eligible citizens share in the government but the law remains 'supreme', and a

plication Cicero had drawn, and like Cicero, Montesquieu of course favoured a 'mean' between democracy and oligarchy as the ideal constitution of a state. Only this sort of a state has 'good fortune', and its 'citizens
have a moderate and sufficient property'. A majority of the 'middle class'
of people, without extremes of wealth, poverty and excellence, is 'clearly
best', though for Montesquieu once more moderate monarchy best
achieves this distribution.[282] It was indeed fortunate, he thought, that 'in
most kingdoms (not republics) in Europe, the government is moderate'.[283]

As one might by now expect, his recognition that commerce expressed
natural ambition should not be assumed to allow it completely free rein,
for that would be excessive and immoderate. His discussion of the liberty of commerce maintains that it was 'not a faculty granted to traders
to do what they want', because that again would mean the 'servitude
of commerce'. Montesquieu argues instead that laws hamper trade in
favour of commerce in well-regulated polities.[284] Such was the English
example, 'sovereignly jealous of the commerce that is done there' with
only a few binding treatises and strong laws.[285] Typically, this liberality
was tied to size. As states grow, so do the threats to liberty, but commerce
could keep this danger in check because the 'natural effect of commerce
is to lead to peace'. Moreover, although commerce 'corrupts [*corrompt*]'
pure moeurs, this is not a devastating objection, because commerce also
redirects and polishes them, making them less fierce and curing 'destruc-
tive prejudices' through 'exact justice' and politeness.[286] It was altogether
a paradoxically beneficial enterprise, and one can see here still further
precursors of Adam Smith. Indeed, just as many have tried to fold Smith
into a republican political tradition, given the character of Montesquieu's
reflections, it is perhaps unsurprising that some have attempted to align
him with the recovery of a neo-Roman concern with liberty as freedom
from arbitrary power. It is important to remember, though, that for Montesquieu political liberty is not the same as independence, even though it
depends upon a conception of persons and their capacities for its foundation as a theory of political freedom.[287] In political society, liberty 'can

---

fourth where all eligible citizens are 'admitted to the government, but the law is supreme as
before'. Aristotle 1998, 1291b31–1292a4, pp. 88f.

[282] Aristotle 1998, 1295b40–1296a1–10, p. 98; Montesquieu 1989, I. 4. 2, pp. 32f; 1964,
pp. 540f.

[283] Montesquieu 1989, 2. 11. 6, p. 157; 1964, p. 586: 'Dans la plupart des royaumes de
l'Europe, le gouvernement est modéré'. Cf. Montesquieu 1989, 2. 13. 12, 13 p. 221; 1964,
pp. 610f.

[284] Montesquieu 1989, I. 8. 3–4, pp. 114f; 1964, pp. 571f; also Montesquieu 1989, 4. 20.
12, p. 345; 1964, p. 653.

[285] Montesquieu 1989, 4. 20. 7, pp. 342f; 1964, p. 652.

[286] Montesquieu 1989, 4. 20. 1–2, p. 338; 1964, p. 651.

[287] Pettit 2007, pp. 711, 715.

consist only in having the power to do what one should want to do and in no way being constrained to do what one should not want to do'. Liberty 'is the right to do everything the laws permit'.[288] The resonance with Thomas Hobbes's political language is striking, however, as his earliest translators noted.[289]

Hobbes had famously asserted that civil liberty lies in the silence of the laws, and in his *Leviathan*, that liberty in general is simply the absence of external impediments to motion. In the work of Hobbes that Montesquieu was more familiar with, namely the *De Cive*, which was available in both Latin and French translation, this latter point had not yet been developed.[290] Indeed, in this text Hobbes was much more ambiguous about freedom, and it caused his system several difficult moments. For although political liberty was still regulated by the laws, he suggested more generally that liberty could be restricted both by external and by internal impediments. He equally claimed that internal impediments to action are derived from the will, which led to the conclusion that any impediments to one's freedom are those freely chosen by oneself, because they stem from the individual will (*arbitrium*). They are arbitrary in a classical sense of that term, a point he continued to wrestle with when thinking about the relationship between fear and freedom.[291]

That this caused internal problems for Hobbes's political theory is less interesting for my argument than the claim that Montesquieu attempted to characterize liberty in similar fashion. Liberty according to Montesquieu is the idea of actively doing something that one should do, and being actively constrained from doing that which, if one were properly aware, one should not wish to do in the first place.[292] Thus, if 'political liberty consists in security or, at least, in the opinion that one has security', this then means that the central defence of the liberty of the citizen must come from the 'goodness or quality [*bonté*] of the criminal laws'. We know that commerce prompts a desire for exact justice, so that helps make sense of some of this argument, but it seems also to imply that restrictions on one's liberty might be self-imposed. If what it means to

---

[288] Montesquieu 1989, 2. 11. 3, p. 155; 1964, p. 586.

[289] Nugent 1750, vol. 1, pp. v–vi.

[290] On the publishing history of *De Cive*, see Hobbes 1983, esp. pp. 8–13; also Malcolm 2002, esp. pp. 458–60; Thomas Hobbes, Letter 197, to Anthony Wood, April 20/30, 1674, in Hobbes 1997, vol. 2, pp. 744 (Latin), 746 (English translation). See also Hobbes 1997, vol. 2, pp. 893–99, p. 895; See the other correspondence in Letter 50, to Samuel Sorbière, February 18/28, 1647; Samuel Sorbière, Letter 51, to Thomas Hobbes, February 22/March 4, 1647; Thomas Hobbes, Letter 52, to Samuel Sorbière, March 12/22, 1647, in Hobbes 1997, vol. 1, pp. 152f, 154f, 155–59.

[291] Hobbes 1998, ch. 9, § 8, p. 111; cf. ch. 13, §§ 15–17, pp. 150ff; Hobbes 1991, ch. 21, p. 145. See too Skinner 2008, esp. pp. 127ff.

[292] Cf. Rousseau 2003, bk. 1, ch. 8, pp. 53f.

act freely is simply to allow passions to motivate one to do what one wills, that is anarchy; to act at liberty, or rather to act with political liberty, Montesquieu suggested, is to cultivate one's agency and do what one should. Hence, the account of civil liberty offered in *De Cive* meant that freedom is not 'doing everything of our own freewill', as that would contradict the necessity of government and the seeking of peace. It also means that civil liberty is simply understood as the space in which one has to move freely, to be free from coercion.[293] Constraints upon liberty are therefore those which individuals choose themselves through actions of their own will.[294] Montesquieu offers a similar account.

For Montesquieu too, the relations between individuals under the civil state are 'governed by conventions' (*reglés par des conventions*) that are minimally structured at least in terms of their adherence to the basic precepts of natural law. In his mind, the civil state is indispensable to the procurement of social harmony, but as a 'necessary evil' (*mal nécessaire*) it is 'always menacing' (*toujours menaçant*), and its power counteracts the existence of other, contradictory powers or forces.[295] Laws and politics have to combine effectively to promote such right conduct, and when the two are in rare alignment, if 'liberty can only be founded in this knowledge', a well-ordered state could be the result. Laws cultivate liberty, on this reading, and their absence simply allows excessive individual passions free rein, an argument with profound implications. For example, 'a man against whom proceedings had been brought and who was to be hung the next day would be freer than is a pasha in Turkey'.[296] Punishment is of course important to this claim, and of the four major types of crimes that exist (those counter to religion, moeurs, tranquillity and security), the latter two are those that prompt punishment.[297] Once again, though, the important point to note is that such punishments should be 'derived from the nature of the thing'. So not only does punishment become predominantly retributivist in the sense that it is just if it fits the crime, it must also be proportional and in 'harmony' with the

[293] Hobbes 1998, ch. 9, § 9, p. 111.

[294] Hobbes 1998, ch. 9, §9, p. 111; discussion in Skinner 2008, pp. 110–14. Cf. Hobbes 1969, bk. 1. ch. 12, § 3, p. 62; Hobbes 1991, chs. 6, 21, pp. 44f, 146f.

[295] Ehrard 1973, vol. 2, pp. 500, 504f, alludes to the famous passage in Montesquieu 1989, 2. 11. 4, p. 155; 1964, p. 586, where to prevent its abuse, 'power must arrest power by the arrangement of things [*il faut que, par la disposition des choses, le pouvoir arête le pouvoir*]'.

[296] Montesquieu 1989, 2. 12, 2, p. 188; 1964, p. 599; See too Montesquieu 1964, p. 1035 (*Pensées*, no. 1802), where security from caprice is the 'only advantage that a free people have over another [*Le seul avantage qu'un peuple libre ait sur un autre, c'est la sécurité où chacun est que le caprice d'un seul ne lui ôtera point ses biens ou sa vie*]'.

[297] Montesquieu 1989, 2.12. 4, pp. 189ff; 1964, p. 603.

wider framework of justice and natural law, and hence dissuade others of committing similar crimes.[298]

Punishment properly understood guarantees security and justice, which in turn stems from the law expressed by intermediate powers in a moderate regime. To the extent that politics can provide this justice, then for Montesquieu 'political liberty in a citizen is that tranquillity of spirit which comes from the opinion each one has of his security [*sûreté*], and in order for him to have this liberty the government must be such that one citizen cannot fear [*craindre*] another citizen'.[299] Hobbes of course had no compunction about suggesting the compatibility of both fear and freedom. Indeed, for Hobbes 'citizens have no greater liberty in a popular state than in a Monarchical'. What allows them to falsely think that they do is their participation as part of a 'sovereign *people*'.[300] The claim about the problem of participation was one Montesquieu could agree with, but he could not accept the connection between fear and political liberty. Fear was the principle of despotism and insecurity, and fear was most obvious in Hobbes's work in the state of nature, which is partly why it had to be rejected.

Montesquieu therefore continued to focus on the apparent injustice of Hobbes's state of nature arguments, claiming that 'to say that there is nothing just or unjust but what positive laws ordain or prohibit is to say that before a circle was drawn, all its radii were not equal'.[301] Yet although the account Hobbes gave of the state of nature in *De Cive* was well known and read, it certainly did not say that in this state men are naturally evil or that they could do whatever they liked whenever they wanted. Few contemporary French readers, Montesquieu included, ever really acknowledged this fact when they pilloried Hobbes's position.[302] Despite this fact, however, Montesquieu's account of the constant struggle after power or recognition as an inherent part of human relationships was as Hobbesian as anything else.[303] At the same time, the analysis of

[298] Montesquieu 1989, I. 6. 16, p. 91; 1964, p. 563; for discussion, Carrithers 1998, esp. p. 218ff, 239f.

[299] Montesquieu 1989, 2. 11. 6, p. 157; 1964, p. 586: 'La liberté politique dans un citoyen est cette tranquilité d'esprit qui proivent de l'opinion que chacun a de sa sûreté'.

[300] Hobbes 1998, ch. 10, § 8, pp. 121f; 1998, ch. 7, §§ 3–4, pp. 92ff; cf. Hobbes 1991, ch. 21, p. 149.

[301] Montesquieu 1989, I. 1. 1, p. 4; I. 1. 2, p. 6; 1964, pp. 530f.

[302] Cf. Glaziou 1993, and the sharply critical review by Wokler 1995, pp. 473ff.

[303] This fact makes Rousseau's reaction to the presentation of Hobbes's arguments by Diderot exceptionally interesting, as Hobbes's moral theory of the passions outlined in *Elements of Law* was then largely unknown. See Diderot 1779, esp. pp. 581, 585, 589; Wokler 1975, pp. 55–111. For the text, see Hobbes 1969, bk. 1. ch. 8, §§ 5, 8, ch. 9, § 1, pp. 34ff, 36f.

envy in particular and honour in general as a lubricant of social progress suggests the key conclusion that Adam Smith would take still further.[304] That was the idea that overly austere morals and overly rational political speculation, which try to nullify those egotistical traits of mankind 'inscribed on our souls', are always doomed to fail. It is only when fortune or fate is 'appropriate' (*mediocre*) that we can be happy.[305] Indeed, 'fortune is our mother; adversity, our governor'.[306] Such adversity governs our individual will, and thereby structures even a purely philosophical idea of liberty, which 'consists in the exercise of one's will, or at least (if one must mention all systems) in one's opinion that one is able to exert one's own will'.[307] When removed from this conceptual abstraction, though, the 'word *liberty* in politics does not signify, in many ways, that which the orators and poets thought it did'. Instead, 'properly signified the word is a relation', and should not be used to 'distinguish different states of government'.[308] Political liberty is not about free government or free states, but is instead a relation between passion and right action at the level of the individual and of the legislator, and for that reason it fits well with the idea of liberty as propriety. One can be a free agent if one deliberates rationally, but volitional and responsible freedom for Montesquieu requires either willingly regulating agency (which is always difficult), or having political liberty in a state that allows natural tendencies to flourish, and where free agency becomes the same as doing what one should want to do because the scope of legitimate actions is clearly constrained by law. The combination of prudent management and pure chance thus required lay behind Montesquieu's admiration for the traditional French monarchy, and his account of modern English liberty.

In making these arguments, Montesquieu seemed to be rejecting Locke's general claim about the relationship between liberty and the will. Recall

---

[304] Montesquieu 1964, p. 987 (*Pensées*, no. 1042): 'C'est l'envie de plaire qui donne de la liaison à la société, et tel à été le bonheur du genre humain que cet amour-propre, qui devait dissoudre la société. La fortifie, au contraire, et la rend inébranlable'.

[305] Montesquieu 1964, p. 859 (*Pensées*, nos. 69–70).

[306] Montesquieu 1964, p. 987 (*Pensées*, no. 1022): "Je disais: "La Fortune est notre mère; l'adversité, notre gouverneur.""

[307] Montesquieu 1964, p. 1035 (*Pensées*, no. 1798 [943]); Montesquieu 1989, 2. 12. 2, p. 188; 1964, p. 598: 'La *liberté* philosophique consiste dans l'exercice de sa volonté, ou du moins (s'il faut parler dans tous les systèmes) dans l'opinion où l'on est que l'on exerce sa volonté'. Montesquieu 1964, p. 1035 (*Pensées*, no. 1798 [943]): 'La liberté pure est plutôt un état philosophique qu'un état social'.

[308] Montesquieu 1964, p. 947 (*Pensées*, no. 631): 'ce mot de *liberté* dans la politique ne signifie pas, à beaucoup près, ce que les orateurs et les poètes lui fort signifier. Le mot n'exprime proprement qu'on rapport et ne peut servir à distinguer les différantes sortes de gouvernements'. Emphasis in original.

that for Locke, uneasiness (and hence passion) determines the will, and liberty is the capacity to suspend judgement before acting so as to pursue our true happiness. Both look very much like doing what one should want to do is the *sine qua non* of free action, but despite this appearance, Montesquieu thought that uneasiness, or lack of tranquillity, was contextually specific. Some nations and some peoples suffered from it, whilst others did not, and those whose government was not moderate were the most obvious candidates for such a feeling of what Locke's French translators suggested was *inquiétude*. Such uneasiness seems particularly germane to Montesquieu's understanding of the English character. With their history, character and climate the English have an excellent political system that suits them and which is beneficial for commerce. However, whilst the English political system was admirable, the English themselves were hardly cheered by their condition. They were an unhappy lot, always worried about something, always moved by uneasiness, but even this uneasiness could not be the principal spring behind the system of liberty in a republic presented as a monarchy.[309] It had first to be transformed by something like fear, though not exactly like it. Fear was both the principle of despotism (and England was not despotic), and it provided a central unifying focus to classical republics (and England was not classically republican either). In the English case, unease combined with vigilance in the face of fear over political corruption, in an argument that seems to derive from Montesquieu's sympathy with Bolingbroke's Whig critique of British politics. Maintaining their security in the face of corruption, a necessary prerequisite for their liberty, kept the English uneasy in general, and the strong middle class (those *gens médiocres* upon which stable politics is built) particularly tense. They had something like virtue, but not of any recognizably republican sort. Theirs was instead the virtue of owners, watchful over their property in case someone tried to steal it. Such a commodification of uneasiness meant that although the English were free, they were too restless ever to properly enjoy their condition.[310] English morals were clearly enraged by passions like 'hatred, envy, jealousy and the ardour for enriching and distinguishing oneself', and the nation 'could more easily be led by its passions than by reason'.[311] Overall, then, one would do well to follow good English institutions, rather than live in England.

---

[309] See Rahe 2001, pp. 88f, to whose analysis I am indebted here; also Sonenscher 2008, p. 235 and n. 79. Cf. Montesquieu 1964, p. 1005 (*Pensées* no. 1430).

[310] Rahe 2001, esp. pp. 95ff.

[311] Montesquieu 1989, 3. 19. 27, pp. 325ff; 1964, p. 648; Shklar 1979, esp. pp. 324f. See too Manicas 1981, esp. pp. 323–29; Gilbert 1994, esp. pp. 54ff; Spinoza 1958, ch. 6, § 1, p. 315.

Thus in 1749, a year after the publication of his *De L'Esprit des lois*, Montesquieu wrote to his friend William Domville to assuage his fears about corruption in English politics, claiming that 'in Europe the last sigh of liberty will be heaved by an Englishman'.[312] If the system of English liberty was the best expression of commercial freedom in a European context suffused with Anglophobia, at least two further elements were of profound importance to Montesquieu's explanation. The first of these was the general transformation in the understanding of the relationship between liberty, national identity and reason of state in the English maritime empire up to the Restoration.[313] This clarified the contrast between the English and the Roman example, and in a modified form, Montesquieu presented a version of what has more recently become known as the 'credible commitment' thesis.[314] Rather than comparing their wealth with the Romans, the English would be better advised to examine instead the source of their own riches. This would show why they should worry about their liberty, which is linked to commerce, and which in turn 'is linked in some fashion to your existence'.[315] The commercial character of their corruption needs to be examined.[316]

Second, however, since the regicide, the English nobility had collapsed, and those 'intermediate powers' that buttressed the monarchy had been removed. This paradoxical development meant that in England a modern 'republic hides under the form of a monarchy'.[317] Moreover, if the English somehow lost their precarious constitutional structure, they would in effect revert to something like a monarchical despotism and become 'one of the most enslaved peoples on earth', as recent discussions of habeas corpus illustrated.[318] In trying to prevent France from falling prey to similar dangers, Montesquieu's arguments were designed to show that any form of political or economic hegemony was necessarily fragile and historically conditioned, and that all attempts to mitigate decline (whether containing territorial expansion effectively or by English-style constitutional balance), could only ever be temporary.[319] Given this precarious circumstance, the spirit of liberty defended by the English constitution

[312] Montesquieu, Letter to William Domville, July 22, 1749, in Montesquieu 1955j, pp. 1244–45.

[313] See Acomb 1950; also Pincus 1998, pp. 75–104; 2001, pp. 272–98.

[314] North and Weingast 1989, pp. 803–32.

[315] Montesquieu, Letter to Domville, in Montesquieu 1955j, p. 1245.

[316] See Desserud 1999, esp. pp. 147ff; see too Sonenscher 2007, p. 47; text in Montesquieu 1989, 4. 21. 14, p. 381; 1964, p. 669.

[317] Montesquieu 1989, I. 8. 9, p. 118; 1964, p. 573.

[318] Montesquieu 1989, I. 2, 4, p. 19; 1964, p. 535; cf. Montesquieu 1989, I. 5. 19, p. 70; 1964, p. 555; discussion in Manin 2008, esp. pp. 40ff.

[319] Spector 2006, p. 151, 403, 404ff; Krause 2002, esp. pp. 714–19.

best expressed Montesquieu's wider claim that moderation is the best policy, and that 'men almost always accommodate themselves better to middles than to extremities [*mieux des milieux des extrémités*]'.[320] The worry that he sought to outline was that English liberty was the result of an institutional compound that could easily tip over into a despotism where the legislature could 'examine' but could not 'check' the executive. This is where the passion or virtue of uneasiness, which moved Englishmen to vigorously defend their liberty, came dangerously close to the principle of despotism, namely fear.[321]

If these thoughts make his otherwise generous praise for the English constitution a little more muted both historically and politically, they nevertheless show the importance of propriety and moderation to political liberty in Montesquieu's work. In order to clarify this importance, Montesquieu's narrative involves a series of interpretative steps. The first offers a general outline of his synthetic account of justice, an account that feeds into an awareness of the limitations of classical politics for contemporary ends. From here, one can see how the very idea of liberty itself, according to Montesquieu, requires an account of the passions of the soul, whilst his analysis of political liberty also requires an account of those passions that set politics in motion. Writ small, freedom is simply human action in particular contexts. Writ large, political freedom is responsible action governed by laws and justice appropriate to a particular polity. The spirit of the laws thus becomes a theory of embodied political freedom, and a measure of the success of commercial society is how far it is able to balance self-interest with the need to regulate conduct. The difficulty of coming to terms with such questions must in part explain the terrifically complex lineage and apparently sprawling character of the work.[322] Yet because Montesquieu's reflections on the nature of modern politics, the passions, judgement, and on liberty, all cohere around the central themes of moderation, appropriateness, measured happiness and self-development, his was a gargantuan synthesis that many could draw upon. Its synthetic unity results from his attempt to marry an historical sociology of liberty with claims about passions and actions, in order to explore how the passions that set politics in motion have to navigate between divine, physical, intellectual and moral causes, that is to say, between justice and the natural order of things. Only then can

---

[320] Montesquieu 1989, 2. 11. 6, p. 166; 1964, p. 590.

[321] Montesquieu 1989, 2. 11. 5, p. 156; 1964, p. 586; Montesquieu 1989, 2. 11. 6, pp. 160, 162; 1964, p. 588; Rahe 2001, pp. 96f.

[322] Cf. Volpilhac-Auger 2005, esp. pp. 152–84, 'Genèse de *L'Esprit des lois*', and 'Annexe III. Les secretaries de Montesquieu après 1748', pp. 200–212; Benrekassa 2004; also Shackleton 1988a, pp. 49–63; 1988d, pp. 65–72.

one understand the spirit of the laws.[323] His political thought itself represents something of a middle way between the extremes of enthusiasm and imagination in the aftermath of the political rejection of Jansenism in France.[324] In fact, through an awareness of the Jansenist heritage he acknowledged the importance of the passions in explaining human action, and recognized that even apparently selfish passions can be necessarily and positively related to social unity and political moderation. From this point he was led to certain conclusions about the limits of human rationality and the fragility of political order.

The impact of his work in Britain, even on an elite fully versed in Francophone culture, was profound. For critics like Domville, Montesquieu's analysis was grist to the mill concerning the potentially disastrous effects of corruption.[325] Conversely, the Reverend David Williams took up Montesquieu's method of analysis even as he thought he was criticizing it. He did so in order to comment upon and critically evaluate the idea of a balanced constitution, an idea which in no way implied the idea of a passive entity that was simply acted upon. Instead he noted (as had Montesquieu, in fact) that balance was an active principle of the movement of powers in concert.[326] Understanding this balance was necessary to fully appreciate the true and just order of the relationships between things.[327] And in thinking through the historical and philosophical implications of both his and John Locke's political theories in particular, British political thought would in the following century come to develop an abiding concern with the paradoxical character of liberty both had outlined, particularly its relation to that equivocal word, 'justice', which Montesquieu had thought to be buttressed by our feelings of resentment and the desire for 'vengeance'.[328] His considerations were actively taken up by many of the most perspicuous of eighteenth-century political thinkers, but my hope in the following chapter is to show that in this regard few were more perceptive than Adam Smith.

[323] Volpilhac-Auger 2004, esp. pp. 173–76.

[324] Goldstein 1998, p. 32; cf. La Vopa 1988, pp. 103f; see also Dedieu 1928, pp. 161–214.

[325] Fletcher 1939, pp. 157, 159f.

[326] Cf. Montesquieu 1989, 2. 11. 6, p. 164: 1964, p. 589: 'The form of these three powers [legislative, executive, judiciary] should be rest or inaction. But as they are constrained to move by the necessary motion of things, they will be forced to move in concert'. For general discussion, Gunn 1983, pp. 67f, 199, 203, 210; Holmes 1995, p. 166; cf. Courtney 2001a, esp. pp. 278f, 281. See too Montesquieu 1964, pp. 1005f (*Pensées*, nos. 1428–33).

[327] Williams 1782, pp. 3f, 7 (citing Montesquieu on the 'unnecessary' distinction between civil and political liberty), pp. 9f (on 'balance'), and p. 53 (organisation of the people).

[328] Montesquieu 1964, p. 990 (*Pensées*, no. 1102): 'Le but naturel de la vengeance est de réduire un homme a ce sentiment de désirer de ne nous avoir point offensé'.

CHAPTER THREE

'The True Propriety of Language':
Persuasive Mediocrity, Imaginative Delusion
and Adam Smith's Political Theory

The moral and political philosophy of Adam Smith famously states that natural ambition and self-interest, a 'desire of bettering our condition', lies at the heart of human motivation.[1] However, this desire masks a more fundamental 'love of domination and authority', made manifest in the pleasure we have in getting others to carry out our will. This can be even more strongly expressed as the natural 'love of domination and tyrannizing'.[2] What seems to have interested Smith the most, however, was how this natural desire for superiority comes to be tempered by countervailing social tendencies, and in particular by the peculiar and unnatural configuration of modern commercial society. In tandam with Montesquieu's account of honour, commercial society, according to Smith, utilizes our naturally avaricious tendencies, and counterbalances ambition and a love of domination with an equally deep-seated need for social acceptance and recognition. A fear of shame, a reflex of the 'natural right' to preserve our 'reputation', underscores the tension and results in politeness or decorum as the norm.[3] Commerce alone, however, seems able to reconcile these conflicting demands without the explicit use of force and through the division of labour instead. It therefore avoids a more 'natural' state of slavery and domination.[4] It is a symbol of progress.

The progress of opulence that the division of labour promotes, while it works with our natural sentiments also threatens our psychic development. It makes us value trinkets and baubles, ephemera over substance, and this in turn suggests a day when the 'nobler parts of the human character may be, in a great measure, obliterated and extinguished in the great body of the people'.[5] Like Montesquieu, Smith thought that under an increasingly complex division of labour the 'minds of men are con-

---

[1] Smith 1976, *WN*, II. iii. 28, pp. 341f.

[2] Smith 1975, *LJ (A)*, iii. 114, p. 186.

[3] Smith 1975, *LJ (B)*, 8, 192, pp. 399, 480f.

[4] Smith 1976, *WN*, III. ii. 10, p. 388; III. iv. 11, p. 420; cf. Smith 1975, *LJ (B)*, 333, p. 541; discussion in Luban 2008, esp. pp. 4, 25–30, 33f, 38ff; Rasmussen 2008, p. 149.

[5] Smith 1976, *WN*, V. i. f. 51, pp. 783f; 1975, *LJ (B)*, vi. 6, p. 333.

tracted' and easily become incapable of elevation.[6] He has therefore been understood as theorizing the emergence of a new social imaginary, based on a self-consciously modern disenchantment of the human condition, where freedom is constantly subject to entrapment.[7] Clearly the idea of something like an alienated self is central to understanding Smith's political and moral theory, and coexists with his critical assessment of the political economy of commercial society. His account of the mental harm done to the worker in the pin factory is an argument about the internal effects of external drudgery.[8] At the same time, a lowly English labourer was, despite high levels of inequality, incomparably more prosperous than any tribal chief in a savage society. This highlighted for Smith the comparative advantages of commerce.[9] Yet according to Smith, both of these processes, that is to say, the elevation as well as the corruption of our sentiments, are always possible. Which one will triumph depends upon the path we choose in order to gain the 'respect and admiration of mankind' that we seek. We can either be virtuous, noble and of 'proud ambition', or be taken in (as most are) and worship at the 'gaudy and glittering' altar of 'wealth and greatness'.[10] The deep irony of Smith's discussion, in line with a theme that has been prominent in the previous two chapters, is that the practical effects of both possibilities actually end up being very similar.

Our natural state is to feel 'love and admiration' for those whose 'character we approve of'. Indeed, the source of our drive to better our condition stems from 'emulation, the anxious desire that we ourselves should excel' and which 'is originally founded in our admiration of the excellence of others'. Nevertheless, 'in order to attain the satisfaction this brings, we must become the impartial spectators of our own character and conduct. We must endeavour to view them with the eyes of other people, or as other people are likely to view them'.[11] As Smith wrote, 'rendering ourselves the *proper* objects of esteem and approbation, cannot with any propriety be called vanity'. And the proper approval of appropriate agency moves beyond 'even the love of well-grounded fame and reputation'.[12] Only here will we find 'the principle and foundation of all

---

[6] Lamb 1973, esp. p. 278; Berry 1997, pp. 144ff.

[7] Taylor 2004, esp. pp. 49ff, 62ff, 79, 167; cf. Chowers 2004, esp. pp. 188, 193ff.

[8] See Waldron 1988, pp. 229ff.

[9] Smith, 'Introduction and Plan of the Work', in Smith 1976, WN, pp. 10f; cf. Locke 1988, II. v, § 40, p. 296; Hont 2005, pp. 258–66, 301ff, 439; also Waldron 1988, esp. pp. 224f.

[10] Smith 1976, TMS, I. iii. 3. 2, p. 62.

[11] Smith 1976, TMS, III. 2. 3, p. 114.

[12] Smith 1976, TMS, VII. ii. 4. 8, p. 309, emphasis added. Cf. Fleischacker 2004, pp. 104–18.

real and satisfactory enjoyment', what Smith calls 'tranquillity'. We must therefore learn to balance the 'frivolous pleasures of vanity and superiority', and see social life as an exercise in persuasion of a very particular sort, where others approve of the claims we make on them and judge the actions we undertake on the basis of how persuasive our claim to their approval or sympathy might be. To be persuasive requires a standard of judgement, and that standard of judgement in Smith is propriety. This relates to the demands of intersubjective recognition, which in turn are governed by claims of justice and sympathy.[13]

To suggest some persuasive reasons why these claims fit together in Smith's work is the aim of this chapter, which traces his accounts of persuasion, sympathy and propriety, of justice and political theory, and of the origins of government, in order to illustrate the interconnections. It tries to do so by using the example of empire as a continual theme within the narrative, and hopes to show that Smith's analysis requires a form of persuasive mediocrity in order to meet our needs and structure our politics in a commercial society. All too often, he suggests, the objects we pursue are inappropriate to our real needs, and our vanity deludes us. To try to get around this possibility, Smith defends commercial society for its strict enforcement of the rules of justice, as had Montesquieu before him. For we can only pursue appropriate approbation, he suggests, if we are able to act at liberty in society, because only with the guarantee of political liberty can our agency be recognized as worthy of praise (assuming such praise is in fact truly owed to us), and our passions consistently and appropriate restrained. This requires politics to be reconciled with what he called the natural system of liberty, which expresses our natural desires and whose standard is propriety. Neither virtue nor excess, but once again something like moderation, is the key.

Persuasive Agency

In his early lectures on jurisprudence Smith commented that the 'disposition' towards 'trucking' and exchange is found in the 'natural inclination every one has to persuade'. In fact, individuals 'always endeavour to persuade others to be of their opinion even when the matter is of no consequence to them'.[14] Moreover, it is most likely that this 'propensity to truck, barter and exchange one thing for another' developed from our 'faculties of reason and speech'.[15] Our natural sociability embodies

---

[13] Smith 1976, *TMS*, III. 3. 31, p. 150; cf. Kalyvas and Katznelson 2008, pp. 24f, 28, 30ff.
[14] Smith 1975, *LJ (A)*, iv. 56, p. 352.
[15] Smith 1976, *WN*, I. ii. 1, pp. 25, 27.

a 'principle to perswade which so much prevailes in human nature', it forces us 'mainly to cultivate the power of perswasion', and means that 'since a whole life is spent in the exercise of it, a ready method of bargaining with each other must undoubtedly be attained'.[16] In order to successfully persuade others to sympathize with our actions and hence of our claims to their sympathy, we must, however, act with an appropriate degree of propriety, or mediocrity. Consider Smith's point that 'the propriety of every passion excited by objects peculiarly related to ourselves, the pitch which the spectator can go along with, must lie, it is evident, in a certain mediocrity. If the passion is too high, or if it is too low, he cannot enter into it'. He argues that 'this mediocrity, however, in which the point of propriety consists, is different in some passions'. So 'if we consider all the different passions of human nature, we shall find that they are regarded as decent, or indecent, just in proportion as mankind are more or less disposed to sympathize with them'.[17]

Persuading others of the appropriateness (and hence of the mediocrity) of our claims is the hallmark of action governed by propriety and in accordance with justice. Without propriety our actions will fail to generate sympathy, and if they are unjust, they will generate resentment towards us. Without sympathy we cannot persuade others of the validity and the merit or demerit of our actions and claims, nor then feel the satisfaction of thinking something done appropriately, because that is how we would have done it. Finally, without political liberty we can neither act freely in the pursuit of our desires, nor be held responsible for them at the bar of a shared and strictly enforced standard of justice. The chain of reasoning is important, and its rhetorical elements are purposeful. What Smith recognized as the 'true propriety of language' and speech is absolutely necessary for legitimate persuasion to occur.[18] Indeed, because the 'desire to be believed, the desire of persuading, of leading and directing other people, seems to be one of the strongest of all our natural desires', it is 'the instinct upon which is founded the faculty of speech'. From this analysis, he deduces that 'speech is the great instrument of ambition, of real superiority, of leading and directing the judgements and conduct of other people'. It is, he writes, 'always mortifying not to be believed, and it is doubly so when we are supposed to be unworthy of belief'.[19] The 'delightful harmony' or 'certain correspondence of sentiments and opinions' illustrative of sympathy can therefore only occur when 'there is a free

---

[16] Smith 1975, *LJ (B)*, 221, pp. 493f.

[17] Smith 1976, *TMS*, I. ii. Introduction. 1–2, p. 27.

[18] Smith 1983, *LRBL*, Lecture 11. 137, p. 56; McKenna 2006, pp. 36, 134; Lewis 2000.

[19] Smith 1976, *TMS*, VII. iv. 25–26, p. 336.

communication' between persons based on 'frankness and openness'.[20] In what follows, therefore, Smith emerges as a thinker deeply concerned with the idea of freedom as appropriate conduct, or propriety. It is conduct that develops over time and according to the extent to which an agent can 'view his situation in a candid and impartial light', learning to see things as others see them and to act accordingly.[21] These ideas have been important to the development of some recent political philosophy concerning impartiality, exchange, and even market-led development. My concern, however, is to account for the nature and extent of these ideas about propriety in light of the idea of persuasive mediocrity.[22]

Given the need for approbation, persuasion and propriety, it is unsurprising that in beginning his discussion of moral sentiments Smith felt compelled to reject what has been termed the 'selfish' hypothesis, particularly the 'licentious' system associated with Bernard Mandeville in particular. Against the claim that virtuous action is only veiled self-interest, Smith countered that even the 'greatest ruffian' is not without 'some principles in his nature, which interest him in the fortune of others, and render their happiness necessary to him, though he derives nothing from it except the pleasure of seeing it'.[23] Pity was an illustration of this general sentiment, although in making this claim Smith was also rejecting the account given by Rousseau in his discussion of sociability and natural man.[24] Smith thought pity was always itself indicative of interdependence and sociability, whereas he read Rousseau as suggesting that pity was a natural sentiment only of uncorrupted man. Indeed, as Dugald Stewart emphasized, according to Smith 'pity arises from the fiction not of *future*, but of *present* calamity to ourselves'.[25] It is related to our views of action, which concern propriety, approbation and sympathy, and these ideas already assume the interaction of actor and spectator. That is to say that the very kind of self-splitting (perhaps even 'self-annihilation') and theatrical model of agency that Rousseau so vehemently rejected as artificial masking is precisely what Smith assumed to be the reality of human sociability.[26]

The theme of masking and unmasking was therefore as critical to Smith's theory as it was Rousseau (and indeed Mandeville), but Smith's

---

[20] Smith 1976, *TMS*, VII. iv. 28, p. 337.

[21] Smith 1976, *TMS*, I. i. 4. 8, p. 22.

[22] Cf. Sen 2002, esp. pp. 446f, 449ff, 455f; Sen 1999.

[23] Smith 1976, *TMS*, I. i. 1. 1, p. 9.

[24] Smith 1980b, *EPS*, pp. 243, 250; Rousseau 2002, pp. 127, 152; cf. Rousseau 2002a, pp. 267f, 273f, 282; Rousseau 2002, Preface, § 9, pp. 137f; Sonenscher 2008, p. 210, on pity and conscience in Rousseau.

[25] Stewart 1855, vol. 6, p. 195.

[26] See Marshall 1988, esp. pp. 143ff.

assessment was more obviously positive.[27] Both agreed that dependence upon others is a harm, and Smith even claimed that only in the absence of dependence on traditional and arbitrary political power can someone be 'really free in our present sense of the word Freedom', a view with which Rousseau could surely have concurred. It is, however, interdependence itself which Smith takes to be as natural as the self-love that moves us.[28] In fact, interdependence is the root of a hugely beneficial social shortcut in terms of persuasive agency. Because we cannot fawn over people all of the time to make certain we get what we want, this natural condition of interdependence means that the individual 'stands at all times in need of the cooperation and assistance of great multitudes, [even] while his whole life is scarce sufficient to gain the friendship of a few persons'.[29] So where Rousseau saw real problems of imitation and opacity in a world of representations, Smith thought one could transcend the opposition by appealing to the self-interest of those we rely on, like butchers and bakers.[30]

Persuasion therefore takes place in an interdependent world and is expressed through speech, which in turn is the faculty whose origins lie in our natural desire to persuade and dominate. In this conclusion, Smith's analysis bore a closer resemblance both to Rousseau's account of the origin of language and to the philosophical history of inequality, morals and manners that one might draw out of it if only one assumed natural sociability instead of natural independence, and propriety instead of some sort of innate moral sense.[31] The development of speech and language is, according to Smith, dependent upon the openness and moral sophistication of the society in which it operates, and is used to the extent that it is useful in achieving our ends.[32] Rhetoric, for example, remains central, but its focus or use is contextually specific. Smith claimed the cultivated rhetorician (or simply the sophisticated language user) understands that language only persuades if it pleases, and it only pleases the listener if used with propriety, which in itself is actually a classical claim. The language of modern commercial societies, then, works best when it cultivates the 'plain stile'. For just as politics in the modern world is not about heroic

---

[27] Dickey 1990, pp. 387–431; Hundert 1994, pp. 149ff, 221f, 224f; cf. Wahrman 2004, pp. 166f, 169, 171–74.

[28] Smith 1976, *WN*, III. iii. 5, p. 400.

[29] Smith, 'Early Draft of Part of the *Wealth of Nations*, ch. 2', in Smith 1975, *LJ (B)*, 22, p. 571.

[30] Smith 1976, *WN*, I. ii. 2, pp. 26f; see also Tribe 2008, pp. 514–25.

[31] Rousseau 2002, part 1, §§ 15, 17, pp. 140f; cf. part 1, §§ 27, 30, pp. 146ff; Phillipson 2001, p. 77.

[32] Otteson 2003, pp. 259–74.

leadership, neither is modern rhetoric any longer understood as a public form of warfare by other means. Ornate figures and tropes are unnecessary, and a language of political prudence could and should be similarly updated for the modern age.[33] Institutionally, this opinion chimed with developments in the teaching of civil law in Scotland that moved away from Latin instruction towards the vernacular.[34] Historically, it connected well with Smith's general analysis of how moral needs are to be satisfied through a combination of linguistic and commercial advance, because language too has its own rules and division of labour.[35] Overall, though, Smith simply claimed that when language expresses our meaning with propriety, then it is as perspicuous as it can be.[36] This is the sound of persuasive mediocrity, so to speak, which is as important as the 'harmony and coincidence' that results from the 'perfect concords' of an original passion approved of by a spectator.[37] For Rousseau, this was simply artifice once more, and he attacked it as such; for Smith, however, such artifice becomes important in explaining how it is that commercial society unnaturally allows the peaceful pursuit of natural passions that otherwise tend towards domination.[38] For both Rousseau and Smith, though, only when justice governs men is improvement or adaptability (*perfectibilité*) likely.[39] This requires both individual self-control and external regulation through legislation and perhaps even civil religion; the Stoic legacy the two writers drew upon suggested both internal and external constraints were needed.[40] However, Smith reframes the problem to focus instead on the mechanisms involved in really sympathizing with the actions of other agents. That is the true demand of 'bringing your case home to myself', which is what sympathy requires, and it is as far from being a 'selfish principle' as it can be.[41] By seeing things through the eyes of another, our sympathy can be transmitted through a process of envisioning and re-visioning.[42] The optical metaphor itself is illuminating, because the vi-

---

[33] Smith 1983, *LRBL*, Lecture 25, ii. 139, esp. pp. 148f; cf. Howell 1971, pp. 565–71; Skinner 1996, p. 47; Phillipson 1993, pp. 317ff.

[34] Cairns 1991, esp. pp. 34, 47f.

[35] Smith 1976, *TMS*, VII. ii. i. 10, pp. 269f; also Smith 1983a, *LRBL*, p. 223.

[36] Smith 1983, *LRBL*, Lecture 6, i. v. iv, p. 26.

[37] Smith, Letter (40) to Gilbert Elliot, October 10, 1759, in Smith 1987, pp. 48–57, p. 51.

[38] Rousseau 2002a, ch. 20, p. 299; cf. ch. 7, p. 265; also Rousseau 2002, part 1, §§ 36–38, pp. 152ff; Rousseau 2002a, ch. 2, p. 253; Brooke 2001, pp. 94–123.

[39] Rousseau 2002, part 2, §§ 20, 32, 56, pp. 168, 173, 185f.

[40] Shklar 1985, pp. 166, 184; cf. Wokler 1995, pp. 66ff. See also Schwartzberg 2003, pp. 387–403; Rorty 1996, p. 351; cf. Rousseau 2002, part 2, §§ 11, 16, 18, pp. 164, 166f; Shklar 1966, pp. 25–51.

[41] Smith 1976, *TMS*, VII. iii. 1. 4, p. 317.

[42] See also Gordon 1995, esp. pp. 741f.

sual quality of sympathy was not only crucial to his argument, but also develops aspects of John Locke's earlier analysis.

Locke's account of vision had led to a debate about the relative importance of sight in producing sensations, and therefore about knowledge and sociability in general. Rousseau, for example, when comparing natural and social man, had considered the case of the feral child Victor de l'Aveyron, recently reintroduced into society, as illustrating his claims.[43] For his own part, Smith's understanding of society as a mirror of the individual prompted similar reflections on the question of how one learns to be an agent in the absence of conventional social experience. As well as the examples given by Locke and Rousseau, he would have been familiar with the related case of Peter the Wild Boy, examined by Lord Monboddo.[44] His thoughts about such questions, however, suggested that immediately upon entering society one would always learn to act appropriately, because of the convergence between natural sociability and the idea of society as a 'mirror'. This natural capacity is geared towards self-preservation and allows us to cultivate our natural desire to persuade. Thus although 'our first moral criticisms are exercised upon the characters and conduct of other people', unsurprisingly 'we soon learn that others are equally frank with regard to our own'.[45] The capacity for sympathy is thus practically innate, possibly even conceivable as an internal humour or vital fluid.[46] It certainly highlights both natural sociability and a capacity to self-identify with the figure of a spectator.[47] It also relates to vision.

In fact, Smith's early essay 'On the External Senses' explores directly the importance of vision for awareness of physical sensation, and draws explicitly on Locke's *Essay*. One reason for this focus was his interest in developments since William Molyneux's early challenge to Locke's position. Molyneux had asked how, if a person was born blind but then somehow regained their sight, they would be able to distinguish between physical objects such as tables and chairs, and other solid objects requiring extension, if their brains had never received the initial sensations afforded by vision that were fundamental to Lockean psychology. Smith gave his own answer to Molyneux's question with recourse to the Berkeley's more recent *New Theory of Vision*, by distinguishing 'objects of sight' (colour) and 'objects of touch' (solidity).[48] He also referred to another contemporary illustration, this time of the practical treatments

[43] Yousef 2001, pp. 245–63.
[44] Raphael 2007, pp. 130ff.
[45] Smith 1976, *TMS*, III. i. 3–5, pp. 111–12.
[46] Schabas 2003, p. 272.
[47] Smith 1976, *TMS*, III. iii. 28, p. 148; cf. Campbell 1971, esp. pp. 95, 150f.
[48] Smith 1980a, *EPS*, pp. 135–68, p. 149.

undertaken by the surgeon William Cheselden upon a young man with cataracts, whose vision he helped to restore.[49] According to Smith, and here the similarity to earlier accounts of the passions is intriguing, the senses were part of nature's design, not because they tell us about 'the actual situation of our bodies', but because they alert us to the situation of external bodies, which may sooner or later affect our situation 'and eventually either benefit or hurt us'.[50] The senses and self-preservation are intertwined, and vision is only one sense.

Combining the claims led Smith to present vision as being derived from representational computation filtered through the medium of imagination. He illustrated the resultant combination of imagination (as both perception and as moral judgement) in a discussion of painting.[51] Put simply, what we actually see is not everything that is visible, and what is visible has been designed in a particular way for us to see it thus. So we are required to use our senses in combination with our imagination, rather like the way in which someone like Richard Wollheim famously discussed the idea of 'seeing-in' a picture.[52] It is just the same in moral judgement, where we are required to imagine the situation of another and to judge the context in which the person acts, as well as the action itself, both in terms of our own immediate sense of it and also in terms of our own perception or judgement of ourselves as the judge of actions. This split between imagination and perception is central, because the analogy of visual perception and moral calibration allows us to consider distance, and therefore gauge appropriate levels of sympathy. For example, 'in the same manner, to the selfish and original passions of human nature, the loss or gain of a very small interest of our own, appears to be of vastly more importance' than the 'greatest concern of another with whom we have no particular connexion'.[53] Yet equally because of the progress of human societies through language and sociability, we are able to learn over time to cultivate the more general value of sympathy and approbation towards strangers as well as friends and compatriots. Indeed, our continual development as a species actually requires that we conform to this 'constitution of human nature', and thereby begin to identify personal situations and actions in the same way that an 'ideal man within

---

[49] Smith 1980a, *EPS*, pp. 135f, 153–61; cf. Jay 1994, esp. pp. 97–102, for an account of Diderot's contemporary 'dethroning' of vision in his 1749 pamphlet *Letter on the Blind for the Use of Those Who See*.

[50] Smith 1980a, *EPS*, p. 168.

[51] Smith 1980a, *EPS*, pp. 152f; Smith 1976, *TMS*, III. 3. 2, pp. 134f.

[52] Wollheim 1996, esp. pp. 205–26.

[53] Smith 1976, *TMS*, III. 3. 3, p. 135; cf. Smith 1976, *TMS*, VI. ii. 1. 13, p. 223, for the way in which commercial society promotes this distancing from earlier, more communal forms of interaction.

the breast' would do—in other words, to see ourselves as strangers see us. In cultivating this capacity, we come to internalize a certain way of thinking about moral judgement as embodying our own conscience, so that we can, in an abstract sense, imagine ourselves in the place of another.[54] This then allows an agent to become the 'impartial spectator of his own situation'.[55] And even if this theory of self-development and self-regulation through conscience is only 'another fiction generated by language, rhetoric and the imagination', or a genetic account of conscience, the general account is both plausible and attractive as the spectatorial requirements of moral and political action become real through the demands of persuasive agency.[56]

Indeed, the connections between sensual and moral judgement were obvious to Smith, and the quest for propriety traverses both spheres. It meant, of course, that vision alone is insufficient. On the one hand, we learn (and it is important to remember that this is a process) how to see 'neither with our own eyes nor yet with his, but from the place and with the eyes of a third person' who can 'judge impartially between us'.[57] On the other hand, however, any attempt at impartiality requires in the first place an effort of sympathetic interpretation of the situation, which is governed by considerations of proximity and which is always necessarily partial.[58] In general, this ideal or 'impartial spectator is the personification of that which is permanent, universal, rational, natural in the phenomena of sympathy'.[59] It is a clear updating of Hutcheson's view of distributive justice as benevolence, combined with a view of self-interest as something like Stoic *oikeiōsis*, identifying with and caring about that which properly concerns us.[60]

There is a problem, though. For we cannot literally see ourselves as others see us, nor see others in all their complexity, without an imaginative and sympathetic effort in the first place. Literal envisioning is therefore insufficient as a theory of judgement, and to that extent one could see why Rousseau and Smith would still disagree over the sort of split between actor and spectator that Smith's moral judgement presupposes. Yet Smith has more to offer than just the focus on vision in response to

---

[54] Smith 1976, *TMS*, VII. iii. i. 4; cf. Smith 1976, *TMS*, VI. iii. 25; Phillipson 2001, pp. 78–82.

[55] Smith 1976, *TMS*, III. 3. 29–31, pp. 148f.

[56] Phillipson 2001, p. 82; Raphael 2007, esp. pp. 7, 128f; Otteson 2003, pp. 66–80, for contrasting interpretations. Cf. Smith 1976, *TMS*, III. ii. pp. 129–31n.

[57] Smith 1976, *TMS*, III. 3. 3, p. 135.

[58] Smith 1976, *TMS*, III. 3. 4, p. 136.

[59] Morrow 1923, p. 72.

[60] Griswold 1999, p. 137; cf. Vivenza 2001, pp. 200 and n. 36, 204 and n. 62, 206; Tuck 1990, pp. 107ff. See too Dickey 2004, esp. 296f, 300, 316.

such possible objections, because of the centrality of both language and imagination to the determination of propriety. In determining the ways in which Smith says that he has to 'divide myself, as it were, into two persons' to 'examine my own conduct', this 'I, the examiner and judge, represent[s] a different character from that other I, the person whose conduct is examined into and judged of'. Put in the terms of his general argument, the first person is the 'spectator, whose sentiments with regard to my own conduct I endeavour to enter into, by placing myself in his situation', whilst the 'second is the agent, the person whom I properly call myself, and of whose conduct, under the character of a spectator, I was endeavouring to form some opinion'. In different terms, the first person is the judge, the second, the 'person judged of'.[61]

This seems to suggest that Smith recognized the partiality of sympathy through vision, and that even if visual persuasion is necessary it is insufficient, because we always assess the propriety of agency in a variety of other ways. By calling attention to the imagination, Smith sets up his worry that we might easily be deluded about what we see and hear, and thus about what we deem appropriate in the first place. In fact, not only are we often deluded about the actions of others, we are equally often deluded about what is truly in our interest. Following the gaudy attractions of wealth rather than our own tranquillity might be one pertinent illustration of this pattern. But despite the delusional possibilities, it is always through the filter of our imagination that we come to sympathize with others, and on the basis of this imperfect information that we come to live peacefully alongside them in commercial society. Irrespective of whether one accepts that claim, for Smith it remains the case that although we might be deceived about questions of reasonableness or rationality, for example, such deception might also turn out to be consequentially beneficial, whether because of providence or benign yet unintended consequences.[62] In general it seems right to say that for Smith, sub-optimal behaviour becomes increasingly irrational and problematic the further it travels from our natural sentiments.[63] In context, moreover, Smith quite literally toyed with conventional eighteenth-century and Addisonian concerns over the relationship between proximity and imagination, and its consequent effects on politics and sociability.[64] This model of a society of spectators surely relates in part to the 'Fraternity of Spectators' adumbrated in the early numbers of *The Spec-*

[61] Smith 1976, *TMS*, III. 1. 6, p. 113.

[62] Smith 1976, *TMS*, III. 4. 3, p. 157; Morrow 1923, p. 73.

[63] Viner 1972, pp. 78–83, 66ff.

[64] See Garsten 2005, esp. pp. 124–29, 160f, 170f, 177ff, 188–92; also Sheehan 2005, pp. 164ff.

tator, and which became a defence for the 'Pleasures of the Imagination' that were neither 'so gross as those of Sense, nor so refined as those of the Understanding'.[65]

Questions of trust (through proximity) and judgement (through spectatorial propriety and justice) remained at the heart of his analysis, and Smith therefore continued to rebut claims that right, justice and morality were little more than masks for self-deception and self-interest. The question of how one could motivate approval, or how one might sympathize with propriety, was his response to the potentially cacophonous display of masking and unmasking in developed societies.[66] Concomitantly, political liberty seems to be both a spur towards and a consequence of a more natural desire for approbation and emulation.[67] It helps to structure and limit the rational ordering of preferences under law.[68] That is, through the cultivation of our natural disposition to truck and barter, political liberty helps to make our desires 'useful' by underpinning the division of labour and the progress of opulence within the state.[69] Whether a street-porter or a philosopher, he suggests, we all fulfil our needs and wants based on the four primary distinctions of colour, form, variety or rarity and imitation, in a general process whose benefits appear to be universal even if unintended.[70] This is because of the structuring relationship of sympathy and propriety.

SYMPATHY AND PROPRIETY

In Smith's hands our imaginative capacity for sympathetic judgement or moral approbation is capable of being generalized. Imaginative projection into the sphere of other agents, or metaphorically seeing things their way, is something that is always undertaken by an individual when acting and judging. But it can be generalized to think about how any individual within a society could and should offer or refuse approbation. Actual judgements about sympathy that are grounded in propriety are always publicly motivated because they always take place in specific contexts, but Smith also wants to show how it is that we come to internalize a

---

[65] Addison 1902, *The Spectator*, no. 10 (March 12, 1711); no. 411 (June 21, 1712), pp. 19, 593; also the more general letters, 'The Pleasures of the Imagination', *The Spectator*, nos. 411–21; Brewer 1997.

[66] Hanley 2008, pp. 137–58; 2006, pp. 177–202.

[67] Force 2004, pp. 14–17.

[68] Cf. Hundert 1995, esp. pp. 588f, 591f; also Hundert 1987–88, esp. pp. 188f.

[69] See Rothschild 2001, p. 97; Smith 1976, *TMS*, III. ii. 8, 29, pp. 117, 127.

[70] Smith 1975, *LJ (A)*, vi. 16, pp. 336–37; vi. 48, 50, pp. 348–49; vi. 52, p. 350.

more general point of view about morality itself, through the development of independence and conscience over time. That is, he wants to show how the actual external spectator we rely upon and from whom we learn as children, for example, eventually becomes the abstract man within our breast, forcing us to consider our judgements in the light of what we know about morality and sympathy. The cultivation of conscience (the 'great demigod within the breast') that provokes us into this austere self-judgement is, he thinks, our secular imitation of the 'work of a divine artist', meaning that conscience is both the will or voice of God and a natural effect of the spectatorial theory of sympathy.[71]

Smith's account of conscience and approbation developed in responses to criticism and questioning from various sources. Sir Gilbert Elliot posed questions to Smith similar to those from Hume, concerning pleasure and approbation. But Smith's account clearly requires more than a Humean focus on passionate contiguity.[72] For although Smith recalls his friend's account of passion and experience as differentiated from one another through sense impressions, he does not follow Hume's assertion of the 'conversion' of an idea into an impression when discussing the nature of 'sympathy'.[73] Nor does he follow Hutcheson, for whom our '*Sympathy* with others' brought about a '*Conjunction of Interest*' between individuals, so that the happiness of others 'becomes the means of private Pleasure to the Observer'.[74] However, as Dugald Stewart's critical assessment shows, Hutcheson understood benevolence to be the only motivation that 'could bestow upon any action the character of virtue'. Once that account is modified, however, what one is left with is the idea that '*Self-government*' alone could pursue the 'abstract conception' of justice as the actions of 'rational beings'; self-love and benevolence could be reconciled as the twin motivations of human action, and our moral faculty would be the 'power by which we approve or disapprove of the conduct of others'.[75] For Stewart, this tying together of propriety, property and sympathy provided the structure 'adopted by Mr. Smith in his Lectures on Jurisprudence', which was first derived from Hutchesonian beginnings even if it moved beyond them.[76] Our natural desire for approbation is both a cause and a result of sympathy and spectato-

[71] Smith 1976, *TMS*, VI. iii. 25, pp. 247f; cf. III. 5. 12–13, p. 170.

[72] Smith, Letter (40) to Gilbert Elliot, October 10, 1759, in Smith 1987, pp. 48–57, esp. p. 51; discussion too in Raphael 2007, esp. pp. 36–42.

[73] Hume 1981, *THN*, pp. 320, 319.

[74] Hutcheson 1728, p. 10.

[75] Stewart 1855, vol. 7, pp. 229f, 234f, 243f, 247. See too Darwall 1995, p. 241.

[76] Stewart 1855, vol. 7, p. 263, emphasis in original; cf. Darwall 1995, p. 297, on Hume's distinction between justice and benevolence.

rial judgement. Those judgements, moreover, derive from an assessment of propriety.[77]

Judgements of propriety are judgements of right and wrong, or of the fittingness or impropriety of action. They are themselves the culmination of an ever more refined awareness of the general rules of society that have developed over time. The appropriate understanding of these general rules is consequently 'of great use in correcting the misrepresentations of self-love'.[78] As an updated model of *oikeiōsis*, negative forms of self-love are redirected towards the public good and conventional morality when we appropriately understand the circles of sympathy that envelop us. The 'humbler department' to which man is 'allotted' first requires him to make arrangements for the 'care of his own happiness, of that of his family, his friends, his country'.[79] Like the illustration of a painting, propriety thus understood is both an ethical and an aesthetic category. It is a form of social grammar, though not as strict as justice, and amenable to aesthetic and contextual transformations over time. Yet it is precisely this situated propriety (as the judgement of appropriateness in context) that motivates sympathy, and which in turn upholds the strict standards of justice and decorum.[80] Thus, the individual who acts unjustly fails to exhibit propriety in something like the same way that parents who feel nothing for their children lack an appropriate capacity; they have in fact an 'extraordinary sensibility'.[81]

Propriety might then seem at first glance to be a rather weak and relative standard upon which to base a moral and political theory, but Smith seems to be claiming that without propriety, there could be neither moral progress nor any way of assessing the basic validity of claims to sympathy and the demands of justice it brings about. Propriety or impropriety consists in the 'suitableness or unsuitableness, in the proportion or disproportion, which the affection seems to bear to the cause or object which excites it'.[82] To this extent, it is an expressive judgement about the rightness or wrongness of an action, and also a standard of judgement concerning the motivation behind the action. Some have suggested that this approach unnecessarily separates the standard of judgement from the capacity to sympathize with it.[83] However, because propriety first makes proper sense in context, and because sympathy is derivative from

---

[77] Darwall 1999, esp. pp. 142, 144; Ignatieff 1986, p. 122; cf. Fleischacker 1999, p. 157.

[78] Smith 1976, *TMS*, III. iv. 12, p. 160.

[79] Smith 1976, *TMS*, VI. ii. 3. 6, p. 237 cf. Griswold 1999, pp. 141ff; Vivenza 2001, pp. 192ff.

[80] Griswold 1999, pp. 183ff, notes the ethical and aesthetic connections.

[81] Smith 1976, *TMS*, III. 3. 14, pp. 142f.

[82] Smith 1976, *TMS*, I. i. 3. 6, p. 18.

[83] Raphael 2007, esp. pp. 12–26.

propriety, both are bound up with Smith's wider theory of spectatorial moral judgement. Indeed, there are perhaps two provocative points to note here. First, through sympathy, derived from propriety, general rules of justice and common standards of judgement develop over time. In making such a claim, Smith was once more elaborating upon certain Humean connections. Hume's analysis understood approbation to be based on stable judgements made according to the contingent fixity of accepted or conventional general rules. For him, 'the approbation of moral qualities most certainly is not deriv'd from reason, or any comparison of ideas; but proceeds entirely from a moral taste, and from certain sentiments of pleasure or disgust'. So, to 'arrive at a more *stable* judgment of things, we fix on some *steady* and *general* points of view'.[84] This general point of view was equally central to Smith, but his account of sympathy and propriety remained distinctive. In the terms of modern moral philosophy, Smith's account is agent-relative.[85]

Moreover, imagination (without which we cannot act with sympathy for another) might not always recognize propriety, because we are easily deceived. Indeed, self-deception is a 'fatal weakness of mankind' and 'the source of half the disorders of human life'.[86] Failing to see ourselves as others see us, we suffer from 'self-delusion'.[87] To try to minimize this tendency, an appropriate distance is necessary for the impartial judgement of oneself and others. This distance is clearly difficult to obtain, though, and Smith suggested that the solution was to be sought in the messiness of ordinary life and interactions. Acknowledging that certain facts of our nature (our desire for approval, authority and reputation) lead us towards the 'general rules or morality', he claimed that our judgements are 'ultimately founded upon experience of what, in particular instances, our moral faculties, our natural sense of merit and propriety, approve, or disapprove of'. The original approval or condemnation of actions does not relate to whether 'they appear to be agreeable or inconsistent with a certain general rule'. Instead, the general rule 'is formed, by finding from experience, that all actions of a certain kind, or circumstanced in a certain manner, are approved or disapproved of'.[88]

Through socially acceptable action, therefore, we cultivate our own capacity for independent moral judgement through the development of conscience and the vision of the impartial (ideal) spectator. That is to say, we come to be able to make judgements about morality in general,

[84] Hume 1981, *THN*, pp. 581f, emphasis in original; cf. Smith 1976, *TMS*, III. 5. 5, pp. 164f; VII. iii. 2. 7, p. 320.

[85] Darwall 1998, pp. 261–82.

[86] Smith 1976, *TMS*, III. 4. 6, p. 158; cf. Forman-Barzilai 2005, esp. pp. 193, 200–204.

[87] Smith 1976, *TMS*, III. 4. 4, 6, pp. 157ff.

[88] Smith 1976, *TMS*, III. 4. 8, p. 159.

separable from social or conventional morality. We move, as Haakonssen has suggested, from being actual spectators ruled by conventional propriety, to thinking as impartial spectators and judging ourselves in terms of an absolute or a general propriety for each particular situation. Our subsequent agency is simply our best effort to reconcile the real and the ideal in these senses, and in any event our judgements of propriety always come before judgements of merit or demerit.[89] As Smith expressed the point, 'in the beneficial or hurtful nature of the effects which the affection aims at, or tends to produce, consists the merit or demerit of the action, the qualities by which it is entitled to reward, or is deserving of punishment'.[90] The second and related point is, therefore, that it is precisely this continual search for the general point of view, which (although unceasing and always incomplete) actually makes social life possible and progressive. Because society is a mirror, we learn to temper our actions appropriately if we want to get the approval and sympathy we crave. We hone this capacity over the course of a lifetime, seeking out what is appropriate and rooting out the inappropriate. We come, through experience therefore, towards knowledge of the general rules of society, rather than knowing first a set of general rules that should govern our actions. As a mechanism of selection, therefore, propriety roots out inadequate or unpersuasive agency, because our natural desire for emulation and approbation means that we simply cannot do without recognition and approbation.[91] All social action (including property acquisition) is filtered through these mechanisms of mutual sympathy, and Smith would argue, as had Montesquieu, that laws, morals and manners are typically those that are the most suitable or appropriate to the particular situation of a nation. They express a form of 'situational propriety'.[92]

Because we are able, as rational agents, to cultivate this situational propriety alongside a more general assessment of morality, it seems that we can also successfully (rather than problematically) separate intention from consequence in making judgements. Related to this point is the interesting problem that our actions take place in contexts over which we do not have complete control; they are subject to that 'Fortune, which governs the world'.[93] And as writers from Herodotus to Montesquieu had outlined, this idea of a wheel of fortune was itself governed by something like divine jealousy, which is one reason why we lack control of it.[94] Even if it is possible, therefore, that our intentions can be judged separately

[89] Haakonssen 1989, esp. pp. 54–57.
[90] Smith 1976, TMS, I. i. 3. 7, p. 18.
[91] Haakonssen 1989, esp. pp. 106f; Smith 1976, WN, I. x. c, p. 138.
[92] Haakonssen 1989, pp. 58ff, 62.
[93] Smith 1976, TMS, II. 3. 3. 1, p. 104.
[94] Salingar 1976, ch. 4, esp. pp. 133ff.

from our acts, if we are both deluded about our intentions and lack direct control over the consequences of our actions, then whether our actions are approved of or sympathized with can in fact be separated from whatever our initial intentions were. Most of us act without any specific concern for the public good most of the time, but so too did those merchants whose self-interested actions unintentionally advanced the progress of opulence. Therefore, just as actions have consequences beyond our control, commercial progress occurs independently of the fact that there are very few men of excellence and virtue.[95] There is a triple move here that underscores the implications of the development of moral reasoning Smith outlines. First, he offers a consequentialist ethics where an action is judged according to its propriety, and then its merit or demerit, on its own terms. Second, however, because the ethics of intention behind the action is at least conceptually separable in terms of thinking about its propriety, the consequences of our agency can also be judged in light of those intentions. Third, because our good intentions can go badly wrong, or lead to unintended consequences, those consequences will inevitably inform how people look back on our intentions in the first place. Smith's is a theory of situated or embodied judgement that runs these three elements together for the purposes of explaining appropriate or responsible agency under conditions of uncertainty. In these terms, Smith comes close to the claims about an ethics of conviction and of responsibility in the political thought of Max Weber. Indeed, the well-intentioned agent whose actions unintentionally produce bad consequences 'strives to regard himself, not in the light in which he at present appears, but in that which he ought to appear, in which he would have appeared had his generous designs been crowned with success'. This requires 'his whole magnanimity and firmness of soul'.[96]

At the margins, Smith adds a further level of complexity to this agent-to-agent relationship, by inquiring into the sympathy or approval we feel towards the actions of another agent who is acting upon a third party. Whether we sympathize or approve constitutes a judgement either of our gratitude and approbation or of our disapproval and possibly resentment. Thus, when 'to the hurtfulness of the action is joined the impropriety of the affection from whence it proceeds, when our heart rejects with abhorrence all fellow-feeling with the motives of the agent, we then heartily and entirely sympathize with the resentment of the sufferer'.[97] The resentment that follows unjust action is a result of the real 'injury', and is caused by

[95] Griswold 1999, pp. 268ff, 372–76, discusses the Platonic and Socratic connections.

[96] Smith 1976, *TMS*, II. iii. 3. 6, p. 108; discussion in Haakonssen 1989, pp. 65f, whose excellent analysis informs my account here.

[97] Smith 1976, *TMS*, II. i. 4. 4, p. 74.

violating the strict grammar of the negative virtue of justice. It offends both literally and metaphorically, affecting our real judgements as well as our sense of justice and its clearly laid down requirements and standards of interpretation.[98] We know this because injustice prompts a universal reaction amongst spectators of resentment. This means, as Smith prosaically expresses the point, that 'resentment seems to have been given us by nature for defence, and for defence only. It is the safeguard of justice and the security of innocence'.[99] Justice is necessity, while resentment, in an updated rendering, is 'a reaction to injury or indifference'.[100] Propriety is its handmaiden.

If before approving of resentment we 'must disapprove of the motives of the agent', it is the converse with gratitude.[101] This stems instead from our judgement of the 'beneficent tendency of the action' and the cognate 'propriety of the affection from whence it proceeds'. It occurs 'when we entirely sympathize and go along with the motives of the agent' so that the 'love which we conceive for him, upon his own account, enhances and enlivens our fellow-feeling with the gratitude of those who owe their prosperity to his good conduct'.[102] As he had earlier expressed the same point, both 'gratitude and resentment, therefore, are the sentiments which most immediately and directly prompt to reward and to punish'. They are 'proper and are approved of, when the heart of every impartial spectator entirely sympathizes with them, when every indifferent by-stander entirely enters into, and goes along with them'.[103] Because sympathy requires more than propriety, Smith illustrates its essence through the medium of the imagination once more. He asks us to imagine our feelings in certain highly unusual situations; seeing our brother on the rack, or imagining our sympathy for the happiness of the man who is ignorant of the fact that he has lost his mind. He also asks us to consider our sympathy with the dead, deprived as they are of all the beauty of nature. All require at least a trick of our imagination, and although these situations are perhaps as unnatural as the commercial order itself, Smith seems to imply that some form of imagination (and possibly imaginative delusion) is required to understand both these situations and that order.[104]

Underpinning all of this remains the idea that sympathy applies to actions undertaken according to the rules of justice and with propriety,

[98] Smith 1976, *TMS*, III. 6. 11, p. 175.
[99] Smith 1976, *TMS*, II. ii. I. 4, p. 79.
[100] Strawson 1968, p. 84.
[101] Smith 1976, *TMS*, II. i. 4. 3, p. 74.
[102] Smith 1976, *TMS*, II. i. 4. 2, p. 73.
[103] Smith 1976, *TMS*, II. i. I. 7, p. 69; II. i. 2. 2, p. 69.
[104] Force 2004, pp. 223f, 243ff; Hirschman 1977, pp. 110ff, 120f; Holmes 1995, esp. pp. 61ff; Berry 1992, pp. 69–88; also Smith 1976, *WN*, IV. ii. 9, p. 456.

and it is here that the value of mediocrity becomes apparent, because the justice-driven requirements of a polite and commercial society require a basic level of civility. For social interaction that goes beyond merely 'sitting still', it is necessary that there be 'persuasive mediocrity' in order to bridge the gap between propriety (judgement of appropriateness or justness) and sympathy (as an evaluation of the merit or demerit if an action). With this model of persuasive agency, through vision, speech, action or imagination, individual agency is judged both in terms of intentions and in terms of consequences. Yet Smith also argues that the person of good or just character will have to have 'habitual reverence' for the rules of justice, and the religious tenor of his language is indeed striking.[105] The threat of exact justice in the next world still seems to be one of the final causes of human motivation, and certainly in this at least Smith's view resembles Locke's political theory. Locke argued that religious sentiments constrain the rationality of individual action, while Smith appears at first glance to offer a secular version of the argument about the inviolability of individual freedom based on observing strict rules of justice. Yet the rhetoric of providentialism seems to justify his stance in ways that may well constitute his most serious response to problems earlier raised by Bayle.[106] He directly contrasted the rule of nature (to 'love ourselves only as we love our neighbour') that is presumed by his view of spectatorial judgement, with the Christian ethos that we 'love our neighbour as we love ourselves'. Exemplary standards of judgement could indeed help to motivate individual actions and to militate against the parochialism of partial and misguided self-interest. As Smith expresses it, these concerns remain internal to the individual, and rooted in processes of social reproduction that are assumed in 'the love of what is honourable'.[107] Between the ideal of impartiality and the reality of situated propriety is where we act, and recognizing both spheres clearly affects our practical reasoning.[108] Nevertheless, by suggesting that we still structure our actions in the light of assumptions about divine providence, his account of final causes seems to Christianize the otherwise classical roots of the impartial spectator, which in other ways bears more than a passing resemblance to the Aristotelian *phronimos*, the Polybian 'witness' or the Epictetan 'neighbour'.[109]

For Locke, the resolution of this problem was to be found in the civil authority of the sovereign as judge in trust, in structuring political inter-

---

[105] Griswold 1999, pp. 237ff.

[106] See Dunn 1985, esp. p. 119; cf. Harris 2003, esp. pp. 240f.

[107] Dunn 1985, pp. 119–22; Smith 1976, *TMS*, III. 3, p. 137.

[108] Campbell 1971, pp. 160, 162, 166f; Jay-Wallace 1994, esp. pp. 56ff.

[109] Vivenza 2001, p. 83.

actions between citizens who are otherwise best governed by the requirements of natural law. Smith, whose theological position has long been
the subject of debate, certainly did not structure the limitations of government around any concern with divine origins or posit anything other
than 'natural' inclinations towards society. He also thought rather weak
Locke's attempt to get around the absolutist reality of sovereign power
by an appeal to heaven.[110] Yet the fact that he could not defray the sense
(as well as the language) of providential foundations in various places in
his work makes the idea of a sharp break between Locke and the Scottish
Enlightenment less than completely convincing.[111] The theological reading of final causes in Smith is still a powerful one.[112] For alongside Locke
and Nicole (and indeed Shaftesbury), Smith perceived the importance of
religion for buttressing a natural sense of duty.[113] Nevertheless, and just
as Locke had suggested, Smith also saw how easily contemporary religion could be misdirected towards 'enthusiasm'. But he could not travel
completely along the Lockean path. Where Locke argued for the necessity of toleration and the impropriety of imposing belief on the part of
the magistrate unless civil peace was threatened, Smith recalibrated the
argument in favour of an account of open impartiality that could also
apply to religion. Impartiality and propriety would combine to produce
a multiplication of sects, all of which could be sympathized with only by
those who are imaginatively connected to them. The likely result would
be similar to Locke's, namely a society based on the toleration of diverse
viewpoints if everyone thinks and acts according to the requirements of
the impartial spectator, but for Smith there is no necessary right or revealed religion. Rather, for him, religious sects would have to compete, as
it were, for potential converts in a competitive struggle for their flock.[114]
The irony is palpable, even if we agree that Smith remained a theist.[115] In

[110] Haakonssen 1989, esp. pp. 127–33.

[111] See Locke 1936, pp. 121ff, 123–25 (transcriptions of Ms. Locke, f. 6, 'On the Immortality of the Soul', February 20, 1682, pp. 25–44; Ms. Locke, f. 6, 'On Knowledge of God',
February 21, 1682, pp. 33–38); also Marshall 1994, pp. 152ff; cf. Smith 1976, TMS, III.
2. 33, p. 132, on the 'exact justice' applied in the 'world to come'; Smith 1976, TMS, III. 3.
6, p. 138, on the need to overcome self-preference; Smith 1976, TMS, III. iv. 12, p. 160, on
general rules of appropriate behaviour that 'are of great use in correcting the misrepresentations of self-love'; Smith 1976, TMS, III. 5. 12–13, pp. 170, where 'religion reinforces the
natural sense of duty', and God is 'the great avenger of injustice' and 'Great Superior'. Cf.
Dunn 1985, pp. 119–35.

[112] Kleer 1995, esp. pp. 278f, 295ff; Raphael 2007, pp. 2, 104ff.

[113] Viner 1972, ch. 3; cf. Griswold 1999, pp. 272ff, and his discussion of Smith 1976,
TMS, III. 5. 3–4, 13, pp. 163f, 170; cf. Smith 1976, TMS, III. 6. 1, p. 171.

[114] Griswold 1999, pp. 278ff.

[115] See also Otteson 2003, esp. pp. 239–52, for an overview of the debate about final
causes in Smith.

fact, the combination of Stoic self-command and the Christian virtue of love remained crucial to appropriate agency in his analysis. Both require a vision of providential order, but in the Christian form we must love our neighbor as we love ourselves, not think too much of our own interest in the face of the misfortune of others, and develop self-command as the 'great discipline that Nature has established for the acquisition of this and of every other virtue; a regard to the sentiments of the real or supposed spectator of our conduct'.[116] The combination would be equally important for Mill after him.

Although he rejected Locke's appeal to heaven, conscience as the voice of God has binding force, and for Smith the 'greater interest of the state or sovereignty' must be tempered with a cosmological recognition that 'universal happiness' is not the concern of men. That 'is the business of God'.[117] Indeed, an awareness of the very real limits to human reason and capacities underpins Smith's critique of perfectionism, particularly as it applies to politics. It is a philosophy of the unintended consequences of efficient causes, an assessment that connects the desires, rules and forums of exchange with a resulting 'system' that governs both moral agency and the system of natural liberty.[118] Perfection is impossible, but balance or mediocrity is available to all through justice and propriety, and this applies at the level of the state itself. The tasks of the legislator are difficult in practice, even if definitionally simple, and require that laws, legislation and justice be enacted and public education be undertaken. Political speculation and system building are to be avoided at all costs.

Just as with the individual who sympathizes with social rather than antisocial passions in terms of their approximation to the mean, there is a major issue here about both judgement and the relationship between commercial progress and corruption or delusion at the level of the state.[119] Smith's analysis provides yet another account of the 'mean principle of national prejudice', a principle that upends the 'noble' condition of proper patriotism and has relatively predictable effects on international relations that are not always beneficial for trade or commodious living.[120] The Hobbesian understanding of 'national prejudice' that Smith discerned in formal adherence to the 'laws of nations' showed that be-

---

[116] Smith 1976, *TMS*, I. i. 5. 5, p. 25; III. 3. 5, pp. 137ff; III. 3. 21, p. 145; discussion in Raphael 2007, pp. 34, 40; cf. Phillipson 1993, pp. 308f, 317ff; Haakonssen 1989, pp. 74–77.

[117] Smith 1976, *TMS*, VI. ii. 3, pp. 235ff; cf. 1976, *WN*, V. i. f. 27–30; discussion in Griswold 1999, pp. 280 nn. 40, 281–86.

[118] Haakonssen 1989, pp. 79ff, 83, 88; Otteson 2003, esp. pp. 124ff, 286–89.

[119] Smith 1976, *TMS*, I. ii, p. 27; Aristotle 2000, II. 6, 1106a–1107a; Hont 2006, pp. 379–418.

[120] Smith 1976, *TMS*, VI. ii. 2. 3, p. 228.

cause states exist without a 'common superior to decide their disputes, all live in continual dread and suspicion of one another'. Sovereigns therefore act according to 'pretence and profession' and treat their neighbours with the minimum of justice. This reality can nevertheless have malign consequences, when the distorted patriotism of our misdirected attachments persuades us to view the 'prosperity and aggrandizement of any other neighbouring nation' with 'malignant jealousy and envy'.[121]

In such contexts, when our spectatorial vision is directed against an entire nation, a new question emerges of how another nation is to be held responsible for actions that only a sovereign can undertake.[122] It was a clear example of Smith's wider analysis, that noble and honourable sentiments were debased when viewed solely according to the dictates of an inward-looking national policy. Indeed, once 'mercantile jealousy' is unleashed, commercial trade quickly becomes debased in the search for monopolies, and the 'sneaking arts of underling tradesmen are thus erected into political maxims for the conduct of a greate empire'.[123] It equally illustrates the social fawning that Smith understood to be necessary but which he ultimately decried, because it exemplified the corruption of our moral sentiments by a slavish aping and desire 'almost to worship, the rich and powerful', whilst despising or neglecting those of 'poor and mean condition'.[124] Given these claims, it is perhaps unsurprising that Smith's arguments in his own day were thought of as radical and practically seditious.[125]

As the theme of delusion is so central to Smith's moral, political and economic thinking, it applies to high politics as much as to those everyday individuals who dream of winning the lottery as a solution to the psychic problems of modern life. Empires, for instance, are fictive projects, financial speculators and 'projectors' are subject to 'golden dreams' of money-making, the Atlantic empire is the 'golden dream' of British politicians, and the projects of gold and good fortune in the New World were as 'absurd' as the search for the philosopher's stone.[126] Empire is an instance of impropriety, based on the illusory construction of a distorted vision of political economy and a misunderstanding of the question of

---

[121] Smith 1976, *TMS*, VI. ii. 2. 3, p. 228; discussion in Haakonssen 1989, pp. 133f.

[122] Smith 1975, *LJ (B)*, 342–45, pp. 546ff; cf. Walzer 1977.

[123] Smith 1976, *WN*, IV. iii. c. 13, p. 496; IV. iii. c. 8–9, p. 493.

[124] Smith 1976, *TMS*, I. iii. 3. 1, p. 61.

[125] Rothschild 2001, pp. 55, 58, 66, 68–72.

[126] Smith 1976, *WN*, II. ii. 69, p. 310; VI. vii. a. 18–19, p. 563; cf. Smith 1976, *WN*, IV. vii. a. 19, p. 563, where 'the dream of Sir Walter Raleigh' concerning Eldorado illustrates his succumbing to 'such strange delusions'. See also 'Appendix C: Jeremy Bentham's "Letters" to Adam Smith (1787, 1790)', in Smith 1987, pp. 386–404, p. 399.

distance.[127] Smith's recognition of the limitations of human wisdom is mirrored clearly here in his account of a politics of imperfection applied to contemporary issues.[128] To manage the politics of imperfection requires ordinary prudence under commercial society, which naturally is less burdensome than the 'superior prudence' required for virtuous politics. Even ordinary prudence, however, had been distorted in the politics of the British Empire. For a start, Smith suggested that what there was was a 'splendid and showy equipage' that reflected the project, not the ideal, of an empire. To think otherwise, as various politicians clearly did, was nothing more than political hubris tinged with misdirected sentiments. For over a century, Smith claimed, British political leaders had 'amused the people with the imagination that they possessed a great empire on the west side of the Atlantic. This empire, however, has hitherto existed in imagination only'.[129] This idea of imagination as fancy, a classically eighteenth-century trope and in more conventional terms a play on the distinction between appearance and reality, could then be judged according to both the strict standards of justice, and the contextual grammars of propriety and approbation. Against these standards, imperial policy fell well short, and neither authority nor utility, the twin poles of Smith's historical and conceptual political theory, could justify it. 'Superior prudence' in the ideal (if not the reality) of the statesman or military general requires self-command, benevolence and 'just and clear discernment', not delusions of grandeur.[130]

In order to counteract these delusions, Smith certainly did not think that extra oversight by a society of more impartial spectators, or a society of impartially observing citizens, was possible or desirable. He did nevertheless think that institutional safeguards (the separation of powers, for example) should be able to mitigate outright stupidity and corruption on the part of politicians because of the extra transparency and balance they offer.[131] The impartial spectator nevertheless remains as central for assessing the actions of statesmen as for those of citizens, and although individuals often fail to act or to sympathize as the impartial spectator demands, we should all be able to act with basic propriety. Indeed, Smith's analysis is precisely designed not to be overly morally demanding, for it is only 'the wise and virtuous man [who] directs his principal attention' to what Smith terms the 'idea of exact propriety and perfection'.

[127] Stewart 1991, esp. pp. 289ff, 293, 294 n. 25.
[128] Griswold 1999, p. 309.
[129] Smith 1976, *WN*, V. iii, p. 946.
[130] Smith 1975, *LJ (A)*, v. 129, p. 321; 1976, *TMS*, VI. i. 15, p. 216; VII. ii. 1. 6, p. 268.
[131] Haakonssen 1989, pp. 130f; cf. Fleischacker 2002, pp. 913f.

Such a sage is not only highly unusual but actually abnormal. Everyone, however, is capable of acting according to less 'exact' forms of appropriate conduct.[132] This requires an understanding of propriety as it relates to the passions, and in this context Smith outlines the differences between the passions of the body and those of the mind. Bodily passions require temperance for propriety, whereas the passions of the mind are governed by our imagination.[133] That our imaginations can be transformed by uncommon knowledge is seen in his treatment of the history of science and language. Unlike technical knowledge, however, Smith argues (like Hume) that to receive assent, moral philosophy must present itself as being in line with common opinion.[134] This applies to everyone, because even though philosophy does quite literally begin with wonder, actual philosophers are motivated by natural human inclinations and a desire to seek after the approbation of others, just like everybody else.[135] Therefore, imagination becomes central to the construction and the evaluation of different intellectual as well as social systems, and when allied to the natural competition fostered by intellectual rivalry, excellence in learning becomes possible. This learning can be allowed to follow its own path internally in specific contexts. For example, Smith claims that in the most stringent of the natural sciences, public opinion counts for little once the internal community of science has set its own standards of evaluation; in a culture with myriad clubs, societies, associations and so forth, this was not a strange idea.[136] But in more general subjects, avoiding public opinion is more difficult.[137] Civil and political discourse, for example, can therefore be analytically separated from philosophic and scientific language. For although both make claims about their relationship to knowledge, only one is in principle always open to all.

This requirement of conventionality or artifice relates to the issue of distance once more, and can equally be applied to the problem of empire. Just as Smith had noted some of the problems and pathologies of distance in terms of judgement, he also saw the great political benefits of appropriate distance, whether literal or imaginative. Applying this to the context of empire, Smith wrote suggestively that the 'great scramble of faction and ambition' that is the 'spirit of party' is something that has weaker effects upon those provinces that exist at some 'distance' from the 'centre of the empire'. By entering 'less into the views of any of the contending

---

[132] Smith 1976, *TMS*, VI. iii. 23, p. 247; I. ii. I. 4, p. 28.

[133] Vivenza 2001, p. 198.

[134] Smith 1980, *EPS*, pp. 33–105, IV. 33, p. 75; see too Schliesser 2005, esp. pp. 709ff; cf. Ross 2003, pp. 412f, for the claim about Hume.

[135] Smith 1980, *EPS*, III. 3, pp. 50f.

[136] Smith 1980b, *EPS*, p. 246; discussion in Lomonaco 2002, pp. 663ff, 668–71.

[137] Smith 1976, *TMS*, III. 2. 18–21, pp. 123f.

parties', the provinces are actually 'more indifferent and impartial spectators of the conduct of all'. This appropriate indifference seems to suggest
that a lack of proximity or direct involvement with imperial politics is,
in fact, a necessary requirement of good and impartial judgement. This
is because those involved in it are literally blind to the nature of their
actions. Provocatively, and one presumes self-referentially, Smith made
this argument into a plug for the Scottish Enlightenment and its enlightened responses to the demands of an Atlantic empire, which suffused the
political debates he and Hume were concerned with.[138] By noting that
the 'spirit of party prevails less in Scotland than in England', if union
with Ireland were to be achieved, then the 'colonies would probably soon
enjoy a degree of concord and unanimity at present unknown in any part
of the British empire'.[139] He had in fact spent some four years in London
during which time he published his 'very violent attack' upon the 'whole
commercial system of Great Britain', in a text that struck a blow at the
very heart of the British Empire. Smith suggested that rather than paying
for defence of the realm in times of peace and war, Great Britain should
'endeavour to accommodate her future views and designs to the real mediocrity of her circumstances'.[140] And that language of mediocrity takes
us once more back to the question of justice, and right back to the heart
of Smith's political theory.

A PASSION FOR JUSTICE: SMITH'S POLITICAL THEORY

In Smith's general political theory, authority and utility are the twin
principles that explain the nature of sovereign political power. Authority
underpins a natural deference to superiority, whether in terms of qualifications, age, fortune or birth.[141] This argument leads into a discussion
of the major principles of political allegiance, namely the principles of
authority and the common or general interest, which in turn mirror a
distinction between Tories (representing authority) and Whigs (representing utility).[142] In related fashion, these twin principles underwrite Smith's
theory of obligation. Authority relates to non-rational, and utility to ra-

---

[138] Rothschild 2005, esp. pp. 17–21, 29ff; 2004, esp. pp. 8f, 12f. For his direct engagement with imperial concerns, see Hume's diary of his voyage with the military to Port Louis,
in BL. Add. Mss. 36638, 'D[avid] Hume. Diary, Sept 18–2 Oct 1746'.

[139] Smith 1976, *WN*, V. iii. 90, p. 945; cf. Smith 1975, *LJ (A)*, vi. 4–7, pp. 332–33.

[140] Adam Ferguson, Letter (138) to Adam Smith, September 2, 1773, in Smith 1987, p.
169, n. 2; see too Ross 2003, p. 248; Adam Smith, Letter (208) to Andreas Holt, October
26, 1780, in Smith 1987, pp. 249–53, p. 251; cf. Smith 1976, *WN*, V. iii. 92, p. 947.

[141] Smith 1975, *LJ (A)*, v. 123, pp. 318f.

[142] Smith 1975, *LJ (A)*, v. 123–24, pp. 319f; cf. 1976, *TMS*, VI. ii. 2. 16, p. 233, and n. 7.

tional, forms of obedience. In direct contrast to Locke, Smith writes that all sense of 'morall duty' stems from that which persons are explicitly 'conscious of', namely utility and authority.[143] He rejected completely Locke's contortions over questions of sovereignty, tacit consent, and indeed the very idea of the social contract. We obey kings not because we are convinced of their divine legitimacy or conceive of them philosophically as only servants of the people, but because we are persuaded of their authority through nature.[144] Indeed more generally we sympathize eagerly with the powerful in our pursuit of riches, and defer to those we perceive to hold a higher station or to be more fashionable.[145] Yet despite the Humean-inspired rhetorical rejections of Locke, it is quite clear that key aspects of Smith's history of government were designed to offer a reading of the history of authority (for utility could be set aside here) that was a credible alternative to Locke.[146]

Like Montesquieu in his account of monarchical corruption, Smith argued that practical issues of 'lunacy, nonnage, or ideotism' would 'entirely destroy the authority of a prince'. Although resistance to authority is only justified when it is couched in the language of the 'common good', 'absurdity and impropriety of conduct and great perverseness destroy[s] obedience, whether it be due from authority or the sense of the common good'.[147] The conclusion drawn by Smith from this 'imprecise' discussion was the bald statement that 'the sovereign power is in all governments absolute, and as soon as the govt. is firmly established becomes liable to be controuled by no regular force'. Though it was 'far otherwise' for the early shepherds who had unintentionally invented government, today 'we must always end in some body who have a power liable to no controul from a regular power. The whole is trusted to them without any restriction'. This arrangement is no guarantee that such power 'will always be exercised with the greatest propriety', and it cannot be said 'how far the sovereign power may go with safety'.[148]

Smith's defence of sovereign political power is therefore premised upon something approaching Montesquieu's distinction between political regimes. Thus, because everyone has a natural disposition to respect established authority and perceived superiority, the principle of authority applies most clearly to monarchies. By contrast, republican governments are more typically obeyed because of their 'utility', but in long-standing

---

[143] Dunn 1985, p. 133, glossing Smith 1975, *LJ (A)*, v. 127–29, p. 321.

[144] Smith 1976, *TMS*, I. iii. 2. 3–4, pp. 52ff; on Smith's misunderstandings of Locke, see Dunn 1985, p. 129; cf. Hont 2009, pp. 139ff, 143ff.

[145] See Smith 1976, *TMS*, I. iii. 2–3, p. 173; Smith 1976, *WN*, I. ii, pp. 25–30.

[146] Hont 2009, esp. pp. 149–55.

[147] Smith 1975, *LJ (A)*, v. 126–27, pp. 320f, 311–30.

[148] Smith 1975, *LJ (A)*, v. 140–42, p. 326.

republican states that utility has force because it is buttressed by deference to the authority of particular ideas or institutions (of democracy, the people, or office for instance). In Britain, with its curious mixture and balance of power between king, Commons and people, 'there is also the principle of utility in it'.[149] Utility, then, is a central principle of evaluation, though it can never be the foundation of justice or moral agency generally, because justice requires putting propriety first. And for that there has to be a concrete relationship between individuals. We want to do things that are worthy of being praised, not just in ways that we benefit from.[150] So although we might well seek after pleasure and hope to avoid pain, the utility of an action is 'irrelevant to what first recommends an action to our moral approbation'.[151] For that we need propriety, followed by sympathy, and because of the immediacy of passions and the reactions they invoke in us, 'pleasure and pain are always felt so instantaneously' that they cannot be *post facto* justifications of behaviour. Indeed, Smith is here reiterating his provocative claim about the way the self is engaged in constituting the social world.[152] This is again something that underpinned his rejection of imperial politics. Prominent Scots in general, from Hutcheson and Hume onwards, had found the idea of 'first possession' intellectually troubling yet impossible fully to do without in explaining the right and utility of property rights.[153] But it was Smith who proposed outwardly that there was little sense that colonies had at their inauguration any 'utility' at all that could justify an argument from first possession. It was instead more reasonably rooted in conventional explanations such as avarice and cruelty, 'folly and injustice'.[154]

Because of these problems, justice requires clear and rigidly enforced laws. Its demands are as strict as the rules of grammar, but applied to society. Yet as a negative virtue, justice seems to require nothing more than mere propriety to uphold it. This is because reactions to injustice are universal, and the consequence of injustice is the unsocial passion of resentment. Everyone can sympathize with resentment as the face of injustice, but because it is a universal reaction, resentment can very quickly lead to social and political breakdown. In this way, the accounts of resent-

[149] Smith 1975, *LJ (A)*, v. 123, pp. 318f.

[150] Smith 1976, *TMS*, VII. ii. 2. 7, 11–14, pp. 308f, 311–14; II. i. 5 7–10, pp. 76ff; cf. Griswold 1999, pp. 126ff.

[151] Otteson 2003, p. 36; see also Rosen 2000, pp. 79–103.

[152] Smith 1976, *TMS*, I. i. 2. I, pp. 13f; III. i. 3, pp. 71ff; cf. Berry 2004, esp. pp. 455f, 458; Smith 1976, *TMS*, VII. iii. 2. 27, and the gloss in Griswold 1999, pp. 362, 105–8; also Hulliung 1994, pp. 25, 28; Robertson 2005, p. 396; Dickey 1986, esp. pp. 590–97.

[153] See Moore 1994, esp. pp. 47–51; Fleischacker 2004, pp. 180–92; see also ch. 1, n. 171.

[154] Smith 1976, *WN*, IV. vii, pp. 558, 588; Miller 1994, esp. pp. 218f, 402ff.

ment offered by Hume and Smith have certain similarities.[155] To counter the disruptive force of resentment, however, justice had to be rigidly enforced, and Smith therefore saw it as the central organizing framework of society. His well-known contrast between the necessity of justice and desirability of beneficence shows this conception of its role. Although beneficence (a clearly Ciceronian compound) and dutiful actions are the ends of honourable patriotism and an attachment to public service, Smith claims that they are still insufficient to form the bedrock of a society.[156] Justice, by contrast, is 'the last and greatest of the four cardinal virtues' and 'the foundation which supports the whole building'.[157] As the following, quite well known quotation clearly shows:

> Society ... cannot subsist among those who are at all times ready to hurt and injure one another. The moment that injury begins, the moment that mutual resentment and animosity take place, all the bands of it are broken asunder, and the different members of which it consisted are, as it were, dissipated and scattered abroad by the violence and opposition of their discordant affections. If there is any society among robbers and murderers, they must at least, according to the trite observation, abstain from robbing and murdering one another. Beneficence, therefore, is less essential to the existence of society than justice. Society may subsist, though not in the most comfortable state, without beneficence; but the prevalence of injustice must utterly destroy it.[158]

Put simply, the absence of justice causes resentment, whereas the development of beneficence is a positive phenomenon that can be cultivated but whose removal does not threaten society as a whole. This is slightly different from Hume's argument about justice as the type of artificial relationship appropriate for property owners.[159] Instead, for Smith, justice and property are related as part of the history of liberty through the rise of independence and regular law that can check the power of judges; gaining 'perfect security to liberty and property' requires an independent judiciary, executive, and regular laws enacted by an independent legislative. Justice is not just an expression of interest and utility, but also an historical evolution of spectator behaviour over time.[160] Even if the origins of government were invented, so to speak, as a revolutionary response to

---

[155] See Baier 1980, esp. pp. 145f; Haakonssen 1985, pp. 242, 245ff; Vivenza 2001, pp. 102f.

[156] Vivenza 2001, p. 66, discussing Smith 1976, *TMS*, VI. ii. 2. 11–12; see too Cicero 1991, bk. 2, § 72, p. 92.

[157] Smith 1976, *TMS*, VII. ii. i. 9–10, pp. 269f; II. ii. 3. 4, p. 86; III. 6. 10–11, pp. 175f.

[158] Smith 1976, *TMS*, II. ii. 3. 3, p. 86.

[159] Moore 1976, esp. pp. 111ff; see too Phillipson 1993, esp. pp. 314 and n. 36, 319. Hume 1982, *EPM*, III. i. 149, p. 188.

[160] Smith 1975, *LJ (A)*, v. 108–11, pp. 313f; *LJ (B)*, 92–93, pp. 433f.

political illegitimacy, Smith paraphrases Rousseau in suggesting that that 'civil government, so far as it is instituted for the security of property, is in reality instituted for the defence of the rich against the poor, or of those who have some property against those who have none at all'.[161] Or, in an earlier variant, he writes that 'laws and government may be considered in this [he is particularly referring to the origins of government] and indeed in every case as a combination of the rich to oppress the poor, and preserve to themselves the inequality of the goods which would otherwise be soon destroyed by the attacks of the poor'.[162] The origins of money, trade and commerce would require a modification to this norm.[163]

In general, though, as one account has it, for Smith 'the rules of justice arise from spectator disapproval of injustice'.[164] To begin with, it is not enough for societies to claim to be civilized if their citizens simply leave one another alone, yet that seems to be all that is required for a society to be just. In earlier editions of Smith's work on moral sentiments, the man who 'barely abstains from violating either the person, or estate, or reputation of his neighbour, fulfils all the rules of what is peculiarly called justice', which may be achieved simply by 'sitting still and doing nothing'.[165] The last edition of his text reads similarly, but instead of fulfilling 'all the rules of what is peculiarly called justice', the man who simply acts with 'propriety in the practice of justice' nevertheless 'has surely very little positive merit'.[166] Merit or demerit, of course, relates to the actions undertaken by an agent, and sympathy relates to our fellow feeling with those actions, which is to say, that actions are judged by the extent to which they relate to justice and resentment, to right and wrong, and hence propriety. From that basis, the observer might be persuaded into sympathy.[167] Although bare adherence to justice therefore requires little more than negative obedience to the rules of propriety, failure to obey these strict rules of justice is in fact an evil. It really is the negative virtue. The 'violator of the laws of justice ought to be made to feel himself that evil which he has done to another; and since no regard to the sufferings of his brethren is capable of restraining him, he ought to be over-awed by the fear of his own'.[168] We internalize this rule through our conscience, and through it we might come to behave in ways that move beyond the

---

[161] Smith 1976, *WN*, V. i. b, p. 715.

[162] Smith 1975, *LJ (A)*, iv. 22f, p. 208; Vivenza 2001, p. 101.

[163] Smith 1975, *LJ (A)*, vi. 137, p. 381; 1975, *LJ (B)*, 254, 261, pp. 508, 511; cf. Smith 1976, *WN*, II. iv, pp. 353ff; IV. i. pp. 430–35.

[164] Haakonssen 1989, p. 86; cf. Vivenza 2001, pp. 99f; Hume 1982, *EPM*, III. i, § 145, pp. 183f; Pack and Schliesser 2006, pp. 47–63.

[165] Smith 1804, *TMS*, vol. 1, p. 165, cited in Moore 1976, p. 118.

[166] Smith 1976, *TMS*, II. ii. I. 9, p. 82.

[167] Smith 1976, *TMS*, I. i. 3. 7, p. 18.

[168] Smith 1976, *TMS*, II. ii. I. 10, p. 82.

juridical minimalism of formal reciprocity. As a basic minimum, though, bare adherence to laws is enough for justice, and propriety is how we must begin to think about appropriateness in the context of strict rules of justice. Here, crucially, the real lives and experiences of concrete individuals determine Smith's account, and this theme was in fact been taken up (without explicit acknowledgement) in one of the most celebrated twentieth-century discussions of freedom and resentment, when Strawson presented his claim for the necessity of conventional standards of interpretation in order to judge the passion of resentment.[169]

Given its place as the cardinal but negative virtue, upholding justice is clearly the foundational task of government. When it upholds those laws that 'give the inhabitants of the country liberty and security', then 'their benign influence gives room and opportunity for the improvement of all the various arts and sciences'.[170] It is how the system of 'natural liberty' develops in parallel to the progress of society towards opulence, and his account of the science of the legislator and the conventional tasks of police that it assumes are most profitably considered under a system of commercial society.[171] 'Police' here simply refers to the traditional understanding of 'policy, politicks, or the regulation of government in general', a simple standard that allowed Smith to attack Physiocracy in France for its rationalist, overly demanding vision of the legislator on the one hand, whilst focusing on the ordinary operations of government on the other.[172] In Britain, police focused on the 'attention paid by the public to the cleanlyness of the roads, streets, etc', to security, and 'thirdly, cheapness or plenty, which is the constant source' of security.[173] Then, just as Montesquieu had also suggested, Smith writes that to guarantee this justice and popular security, 'in generall the best means of bringing about this desirable end is the rigorous, severe, and exemplary execution of laws properly formd for the prevention of crimes and establishing the peace of the state'.[174]

This process could be explored historically, through the ways in which morals, manners and sentiments have driven transformations in politics, and which in turn have cultivated particular developments in these aspects of human relations. For there to be freedom, laws must provide justice, whose commerce, Smith writes, 'is one great preventive' of the

[169] Strawson 1968.

[170] Smith 1975, *LJ (A)*, vi. 18–19, pp. 337f.

[171] On the background to police science, see Tribe 1995, ch. 1; Maier 1980, esp. pp. 24–27, 29–32.

[172] Smith 1975, *LJ (A)*, i. 2, p. 5, vi. 1, p. 331; also Bell 2001, pp. 26, 36f; Berry 1994, esp. pp. 152–73.

[173] Smith 1975, *LJ (A)*, vi. 1, p. 331.

[174] Smith 1975, *LJ (A)*, vi. 2, p. 331.

customary slide towards dependence and domination. For just as 'nothing tends so much to corrupt and enervate and debase the mind as dependency', equally 'nothing gives such noble and generous notions of probity as freedom and independency'.[175] Commerce and civilization is a story of the rise of opulence, the arts and commerce, and 'in order to consider the means proper to produce opulence it will be proper to consider what opulence and plenty consist in, or what are those things which ought to abound in a nation'.[176] The science of the legislator and the science of political economy go together, so that when political economy is 'considered as a branch of the science of a statesman or legislator', it must firstly 'provide a plentiful revenue or subsistence for the people'. That is, it must 'enable them to provide such a revenue or subsistence for themselves; and secondly, to supply the state or commonwealth with a revenue sufficient for the publick services. It proposes to enrich both the people and the sovereign', to cultivate the moral and political education of a population, and to regulate the sphere of politics effectively. Indeed, his critique of 'the ignorance and stupidity' that tends to 'benumb the understanding' of the majority under commercial societies underscores his rage against the failure to educate to minimal standards the majority of the population.[177] Different systems of political economy, therefore, represent particular approaches to a science of the legislator, and hence to a science of politics, even though for Smith the premier function of all government was defence and justice. This is because the principal purpose of defence is to allow 'the chief design of every system of government' to be pursued, and that is the maintenance of justice. Third in this order of lexical priority is the noted concern with education and improvement as a function of government, for example, through legislation to ameliorate the condition of the poorest in society, which was justified on the simple basis of an appeal to human decency.[178]

In turn, the historical development of justice as the 'separation of the judicial from the executive power', in Smith's formulation, 'seems originally to have arisen from the increasing business of the society, in consequence of its increasing improvement'.[179] Like Montesquieu, Smith attacked universal monarchy, because where 'the judicial is united to the executive power, it is scarce possible that justice should not frequently be sacrificed to, what is vulgarly called, politics'. Individual liberty de-

---

[175] Smith 1975, *LJ (A)*, vi. 4–7, pp. 332–33; see too Fleischacker 1999, pp. 151f.

[176] Smith 1975, *LJ (A)*, vi, 8, p. 333.

[177] Smith 1976, *WN*, V. i. f–g. 61, p. 788; cf. Smith 1976, *WN*, IV. 'Introduction', p. 428; Haakonssen 1989, pp. 122, 131, on the importance of education to Smith's argument.

[178] Smith 1975, *LJ (A)*, i. I, p. 5; also Haakonssen 1989, esp. pp. 94f; Rothschild 2001, pp. 37ff.

[179] Smith 1976, *WN*, V. i. b, pp. 715–23, esp. pp. 718, 722.

pends in contrast on the 'impartial administration of justice', for only that can provide security for 'commerce and manufactures'.[180] Therefore, even when pressed at a quite abstract level, justice cannot be founded on predetermined conceptions of the good. Nor is it enough to focus on its utility in maintaining peace and security. Instead, the foundations of justice as a negative virtue are to be sought in the relationships between individuals, who are simply the only bodies capable of feeling resentment about the absence of justice.[181] Much like Montesquieu, Smith embedded his account of justice in debates concerning civil philosophy and natural jurisprudence, particularly the work of Grotius, Pufendorf and Locke. Here his use of these debates presented the system of natural liberty as the best resolution to the problems of inequality under market society.[182] My account in what follows assumes its centrality, which has been extensively discussed in the scholarly literature, but leaves further assessment of the importance of such historical jurisprudence to the end of this chapter. What I want primarily to note here is that commutative justice (principally punishment) is the most important aspect of Smith's analysis because it is involuntary, and must be specified carefully and defended strongly by state power. It is exact, but relational.[183] In cognate fashion, Smith's image of the self-interested individual who fulfils the minimal requirements of justice by straining every nerve and sinew in the pursuit of his own advantage, but who is explicitly barred from actively wresting goods from his neighbour, also builds on a Stoic heritage.[184] Distributive justice, on the other hand, cannot be so 'exact', and inequalities will remain, necessarily so one might say in the case of Smith's thoughts about the distinctions of rank and status between persons.[185]

If the principal task of government therefore sounded mundane, it had profound consequences. States uphold justice through defending rights, because 'the first and chief design of all civill governments is', according to Smith, 'to preserve justice amongst the members of the state and prevent all incroachments on the individuals in it, from others of the same

---

[180] Smith 1976, *WN*, V. i. b, pp. 722f; V. iii. 7, p. 910.

[181] Smith 1976, *TMS*, VII. ii. i. 10, pp. 269f.

[182] Salter 1999, p. 222.

[183] Vivenza 2001, pp. 92, 198 and n. 28, 199; cf. Brett 2002, esp. p. 44, on the amending of traditional derivations of political justice from Aristotelian doctrines particularly by Grotius. He discussed justice in terms of 'what is repugnant to the society of rationals', reworking Aristotle's distributive justice as a form of particular justice. See also Tuck 1999, p. 88.

[184] Vivenza 2001, pp. 4ff, 70, 90f.

[185] Smith 1976, *WN*, IV. ix. 51, pp. 687f; V. i. b. 1, pp. 708f; V. i. c. 2, p. 723; cf. Griswold 1999, pp. 249–56. On Grotius and his impact on strands of British political thought, see van Gelderen 2006, esp. pp. 160ff, 167ff; cf. Haakonssen 1985, pp. 246, n. 48, 260; Trevor-Roper 1992, pp. 47–82. In general, see Locke 1988, II, §§ 30, 36, pp. 289f, 292f; Tuck 1999, pp. 106, 174.

society.—{That is, to maintain each individual in his perfect rights.}'[186] This reflection of the ethics of his teacher, Frances Hutcheson, assumes that breaches of perfect rights can lead to social breakdown (because we all sympathize with reactions to injustice), and claims that sympathy is the 'effect of our nature'.[187] Smith was once again in agreement with Montesquieu's work as well, given the way that his account of justice and its relation to the passions depends on a rather loose understanding of the Aristotelian mean, characterized by an individual reluctance to accept unjust distributions.[188] With justice thus understood, Smith could rethink what unjust distributions or actions might be in the light of his own theory. For him, justice may be 'violated', which is another way of saying that a man may be 'injured', if he is 'injured as a man', or, 'as a member of a family', or finally, 'as a citizen or member of a state'. When justice is aligned with Smith's traditional view of jurisprudence as the 'theory of rules by which civil governments ought to be directed' and whose aim is to establish how far 'different systems of government' are 'grounded in reason', the importance of justice to his political science of the state is abundantly clear.[189]

The system of natural liberty that justice should uphold requires a strong, yet clearly limited political authority. Smith's political antennae were not directed at powerful statesmen in general, because for Smith a powerful legislator is needed to guarantee realistic (as opposed to utopian) forms of economic and political freedom. Only such power could legislate effectively against those 'little hells of vexation' like trades unions and apprenticeships; indeed, anything that could be generally understood as being subject to arbitrary or non-standard law was to be rejected.[190] He directs his attacks, therefore, on those who try to use their sovereign power to transform political society along some pre-determined pursuit of perfection, or of a rational 'system'. John Law's financial 'system' in France was surely very much in his mind here, illustrating that such 'projectors' and 'men of system' can be delusional, and showing that this sort of statesman is one who seeks 'to erect his own judgment into the supreme standard of right and wrong'. This claim is profoundly important, because of all 'political speculators, sovereign princes are by far the most dangerous' in their 'arrogance', and they consider 'the state as made for themselves'. Such vanity and hubris are to be rejected, but there is also

---

[186] Smith 1975, *LJ (A)*, i. 9, p. 7.

[187] Hutcheson 1747, pp. 122f; 1728, pp. 10f.

[188] Williams 1981, esp. pp. 90f.

[189] Smith 1975, *LJ (A)*, i. I, p. 7; i. I, p. 6; cf. 1975, *LJ (A)*, iv. I, p. 200, where the point is repeated.

[190] Rothschild 2001, esp. pp. 28ff, 33f, 90–112, citation on p. 33; also Jones 2006, pp. 61–73; cf. Rothschild 2001, pp. 87–90.

a positive side to the story. Just as self-interested merchants unintentionally brought about commercial benefits for everyone, so too did the self-deception of new and political rulers mark a pivotal moment in the rise of the modern state, separating power from the traditional 'authority of the nobility'.[191] The history of government shows that a gradual move away from such arbitrary power towards an institutional separation of powers that can check each another is the logical outcome of Smith's discussion of natural liberty. It is the only system that needs to be upheld.

As already noted, the national prejudice that went along with this history could lead to rather sub-optimal outcomes.[192] Neighbouring states such as France and England should really be partners for mutual advantage in terms of commercial trade, for example, no matter that the wealth of a neighbour is always 'dangerous in war and politicks'. Indeed, Smith rejected attempts to defend 'with all the passionate confidence of interested falsehood' the idea that an 'unfavourable balance of trade' was the natural result of open competition.[193] Openness and competition leads to commercial enrichment in all spheres, even if the progress of commercial society itself was a temporal anomaly and potentially corrosive. Its corrosion was seen most clearly again in the responses of the British state to problems of empire and finance. Disguising public bankruptcy through a 'raising of the denomination of the coin' had been the common way of dishonourably disguising the event, but was a 'pernicious' and transparent 'juggling trick' that had no real virtue.[194] In fact, this 'simple augmentation' is worse than the 'injustice of open violence'. As 'adulteration', it 'is an injustice of treacherous fraud' that rightly incites 'indignation'.[195] Locke of course had had similar concerns whilst at the Board of Trade.[196] In the case of the relationship between the British Empire and its colonies, however, such currency manipulation would be doubly problematic, because unusually in this case the metropolis lacked 'a footing of equality with the colonies'.[197] Pointing to a concern John Stuart Mill would reiterate in the following century, Smith was wary of the political authority granted to profit-making bodies like the East India Company, whose

[191] Smith 1976, *TMS*, VI. ii. 2. 18, p. 234; cf. Skinner 2002d, pp. 368–413; Sonenscher 2008, p. 261.

[192] Smith 1976, *WN*, IV. iii. c. 13, p. 496; IV. iii. c. 8–9, p. 493; Fleischacker 2004, pp. 250–57.

[193] Smith 1976, *WN*, IV. iii. c. 13–14, p. 496; cf. 1975, *LJ (B)*, 342, pp. 546f.

[194] Smith 1976, *WN*, V. iii. 59–60, pp. 929f; cf. Smith 1976, *WN*, II. ii, pp. 308–12 (on paper money and credit).

[195] Smith 1976, *WN*, V. iii. 64, p. 932.

[196] Laslett 1957, p. 379, n. 21; see MS Locke c. 36 for his minutes; also Locke 1823a, vol. 5, pp. 13, 42ff; cf. Child 1740, pp, 2–8, 39, 48ff, 52–55, 209ff, 235ff, 255f. See too Cranston 1985, pp. 118f, 350–54.

[197] Smith 1976, *WN*, V. iii. 64, p. 932; cf. Hall 2002, pp. 12, and 'Prologue'.

influence was another illustration of arbitrary and irregular interest in politics.[198] What was needed instead was a natural system of free trade between colony and metropole.[199] For while the 'effects' of colony trade are 'always and necessarily beneficial', the 'monopoly of that trade' is 'always and necessarily hurtful'.[200] Great Britain currently 'derives nothing but loss from the dominion which she assumes over her colonies', which relied on a defence of monopoly trade that contradicts the natural order of things.[201]

Smith's resolution of this problem of empire in British political thought was novel, rejecting the interest of companies as well as the standard Tacitean critique of empire that many others had outlined. Instead, he seemed to favour a neo-Grecian solution, offering imperial federation through representation.[202] This would be more appropriate to the needs of commercial society, even if the scale of the finances involved made it a quite terrifying proposition.[203] Moreover, although Smith discussed the problem of universal monarchy less explicitly than either Montesquieu or Hume, his discussion of debt and national belligerence in terms of a Franco-British antipathy, whose contours were suffused with worries about the relationship between public debt, credit, and liberty, was just as engaged.[204] He even offered a direct comparison of the decline of the Roman republic with the possibility of defeat in the American War of Independence, by strongly disavowing the 'piddling for little prizes' that is 'found in what may be called the paltry raffle of colony faction'.[205]

In numerous places, then, Smith was explicit that once 'all systems of either preference or restraint' were removed, the 'obvious and simple system of natural liberty establishes itself of its own accord'.[206] This was the only 'system' that the statesman or legislator should properly attempt to balance, and the origins and implications of such a system of natural

[198] Smith 1976, WN, IV. vii. c, pp. 636f; V. i. e. 26, pp. 746–53; V. ii. a. 7, p. 819; V. ii. d, pp. 838ff; see too Rothschild 2004, esp. pp. 18ff; Muthu 2008, esp. pp. 187ff 191f 200, 205f.

[199] Miller 2004, pp. 410ff.

[200] Smith 1976, WN, IV. vii. c, pp. 608, 607.

[201] Smith 1976, WN, IV. vii. c, p. 616.

[202] Soll 2003, pp. 305f, 309; cf. Hume 1985, pp. 18f; Pocock 2003, pp. 377f. See also Smith 1976, WN, III. iii, p. 406; IV. vii. a, pp. 556ff; IV. vii. c, pp. 593f; cf. Smith 1976, WN, IV. vii. c, pp. 620ff.

[203] Smith 1976, WN, V. iii, pp. 946f; cf. Smith 1976, WN, IV. vii. c, p. 621; also Benians 1925, esp. pp. 251ff, cf. p. 273.

[204] Smith 1976, WN, V. iii. 10, p. 911; cf. Hont 2005, esp. pp. 326ff; Pocock 2003, pp. 372–75, 382, 386f, 391; Robertson 1993, esp. pp. 355f, 357–61, 371; Pincus 1995, esp. pp. 52–62.

[205] Smith 1976, WN, IV. vii. c, p. 621; also Smith 1976, WN, V. ii. v, p. 830.

[206] Smith 1976, WN, IV. ix. 51, p. 687.

liberty was that which Smith's conjectural history sought to explain.[207] This system of natural liberty entails that 'every man, as long as he does not violate the laws of justice, is left perfectly free to pursue his own interest his own way'. Moreover, when this situation arises, 'the sovereign is completely discharged from the duty' of 'superintending the industry of private people, and of directing it towards the employments most suitable to the interest of the society'.[208] Thus, 'according to the system of natural liberty, the sovereign has only three duties to attend to; three duties of great importance, indeed, but plain and intelligible to common understandings'. These are the 'duty of protecting the society from the violence and invasion of other independent societies', followed by 'the duty of protecting, as far as possible, every member of the society from the injustice of oppression of every other member of it, or the duty of establishing an exact administration of justice', and finally 'the duty of erecting and maintaining certain publick works and certain publick institutions, which it can never be for the interest of any individual, or small number of individuals, to erect and maintain'. Protection, justice, and the provision of public goods structured the remit of the legislator, whose sovereign power stemmed from the historically contingent development of moderate and balanced government, our obligations to which are underpinned by the principles of authority and utility.[209]

However, the idea that the pure system of natural liberty could ever be realized was a Utopia (or Oceana) according to Smith, in an obvious allusion to Plato, More and Harrington. Clearly, commercial society had not (and could not) solve all the problems of needs and justice, even if his more pessimistic conjectures about the relationship between the 'complement of riches' available to a country and the level of wages have been shown to be inaccurate, at least in the English case.[210] More generally, relationships of perfect propriety in the sphere of politics and the economy, a completely just distribution of economic goods, for example, were all impossible. This is once again because of Smith's general rejection of rationalism and utopianism, something it is important to remember in relating Smith's politics to his role in the French Revolution.[211] For the natural desire to better one's condition, which is promoted and

---

[207] Stewart 1980, p. 293, on Smith's 'conjectural history'.

[208] Smith 1976, WN, IV. ix. 51, p. 687.

[209] Smith 1976, WN, IV. Introduction, p. 428; IV. ix. 51, pp. 687f; cf. I. x. c. 59, p. 157.

[210] Smith 1976, WN, I. ix, § 14, p. 111; IV. ii. 43, p. 471; discussion in Wrigley 2000, esp. p. 127.

[211] Smith 1976, TMS, VI. ii. 2. 17, 18, pp. 233f; cf. Winch 1996, pp. 90ff, 135; for a note about revisions to the final edition of TMS during 1789, see Adam Smith, Letter (287) to Thomas Cadell, March 31, 1789, in Smith 1987, pp. 319f; Whatmore 2002, p. 72. The language goes as far forward as Carlyle 1868, p. 113, at least.

fostered by the political liberty of a commercial government, is at the same time counterbalanced by an active self-delusion occasioned by the imagination.[212] Our happiness and our freedom are both real and yet distorted. Therefore, for politics and natural liberty to flourish, one needs the prudence of a statesman who can utilize, where appropriate, a definite 'political wisdom' that will avoid the extreme inequalities promoted by the man of system. It must counter excess and promote moderation. Though difficult in times of 'public discontent, faction, and disorder', Smith's analysis clearly resembles Montesquieu's hope for moderation and prudence under conditions of uncertainty by passionate individuals, overseen by (the science of) the legislator.[213] For it is the presence of 'hostile factions, whether civil or ecclesiastical', that prevents the 'real, revered, and impartial spectator' from emerging.[214] Faction can only aid the 'publick morals of a free people' to the extent that they remain of 'good temper and moderation'.[215] To promote this end, the legislator needs persuasive agency just as much as anyone else.

Precisely because of his awareness of delusion and imagination, Smith's historical narrative of commercial society is replete with paradoxes. For example, the ever-stricter ideas of justice and punishment that accompany social progress clearly help make people richer and guarantee the property rights without which political liberty cannot develop. Yet although we think that we're happier because of it, such processes also bind us to accepting contemporary political and economic arrangements as natural, given our deference to authority. In similar fashion, our natural fear of the consequences of acting unjustly can delude us, for if we are free simply to chase after 'golden dreams', mere trinkets and baubles, then what possible use can freedom be?[216] This is where Smith's variation on Hume's account of glory and natural fame as potentially conformist seems to develop, but he once more adds a radical twist with the idea of the impartial spectator. Not only do the external institutions of justice constrain our actions for fear of punishment, individuals also internalize conformity through conscience. This is the cause of progress, as already noted. But the darker side of the story in this history of morality, which resembles Nietzsche quite remarkably on the effects of an 'internalization of man', is that social progress can create individuals who are their own harshest judges and who will delude themselves into thinking that they are truly free. Smith even traced the roots of this possibility to the divi-

[212] Smith 1976, *WN*, IV. ii. 43; V. iii. 68, also Griswold 1999, p. 302; cf. Mitchell 1987, pp. 405–21.

[213] Smith 1976, *TMS*, VI. ii. 2. 12, pp. 231f; cf. VI. ii. 2. 15–17, pp. 232ff.

[214] Smith 1976, *TMS*, III. 3. 43, pp. 155f.

[215] Smith 1976, *WN*, V. i. f. 40, p. 775.

[216] Rasmussen 2006, pp. 309–18.

sion of philosophy in the ancient universities, which had subordinated
the 'duties of human life' to 'the happiness of a life to come'. Salvation
was available to the 'austerities and abasement[s] of a monk', while 'ca-
suistry and ascetic morality made up, in the most cases, the greater part
of the moral philosophy of the schools', a clear case of the 'corruption'
of philosophy.[217] Smith therefore proposed a rejection of 'false notions of
religion' that corrupt the natural sentiments, and which might mistake
one hour of 'futile mortifications' in a monastery with a lifetime's service
in the 'ennobling hardships and hazards of war'. To think like that was to
mistake the requirements laid down by the 'great Judge of the world'.[218]
The rise of conscience and the impartial spectator as a demigod is a ju-
dicially severe formulation of our own divided self that is a prerequisite
of progress, but which can also be terrifically restrictive. To succeed, we
shall have to learn to judge well.

However, if we can never fully comprehend the passions of others, but
instead only hope to judge them according to the criterion of propriety
and sympathize with them on the basis of merit and fellow-feeling, then
we shall want to know what sorts of passions might elicit what sort of
sympathy. Thought about in these terms, the Stoic resonance of Smith's
ethics seems clearest, but we must not be blind to the irony and omissions
of his argument.[219] The pursuit of virtue is the preserve of the few (the
Stoic sage), and it is practical excellence, but even as an ideal it seems
completely improbable. Propriety, by contrast, is simply 'that degree of
approximation to this idea which is commonly attained in the world' by
the majority of persons'.[220] More than anything, perhaps, Smith seems
sceptical of all forms or systems of moral philosophy that attempt to base
their analysis of propriety in general accounts of morality, whether concerning virtue, prudence or self-love, for example. Although what Smith
thinks important in the 'propriety of conduct' is equivalent 'in every respect' with what Plato considered virtue, none of the various systems
of moral philosophy 'either give or even pretend to give, any precise or
distinct measure by which this fitness of propriety of affection can be
ascertained or judged of'. This is crucial, because it highlights the intersubjective and developmental account of propriety offered by Smith,
where 'that precise and distinct measure can be found nowhere but in
the sympathetic feelings of the impartial and well-informed spectator'.[221]

---

[217] Smith 1976, *WN*, V. i. f. 30, pp. 771f.

[218] Smith 1976, *TMS*, III. 6. 12, pp. 176f; III. 2. 35, p. 134.

[219] See Smith 1976, *TMS*, I. i. 5. 7, p. 25; I. i. 5, pp. 48f; Campbell 1971, pp. 167ff; cf.
Waszeck 1984, esp. pp. 601–5.

[220] Smith 1976, *TMS*, VI. iii. 23–26, pp. 247f.

[221] Smith 1976, *TMS*, VI. ii. I. 11, p. 270; VII. ii. 1. 49, p. 294.

Propriety is necessary for virtue, but not sufficient for it, so although Platonic virtue might equate with Smithian propriety, Smithian virtue is not Platonic virtue.

The tone of his presentation suggests a scepticism towards all forms of moral philosophy in general, just as there is a scepticism towards all theories of politics as well; one cannot determine in advance the expression of something that is only determined contextually. Even if such scepticism is warranted, it is unsurprising that Smith would be reluctant to say so explicitly in print; he would only have to look at the treatment of his sceptical friend Hume to see the reputational and the political costs as well as the intellectual difficulties of such a position.[222] Indeed, Smith would surely have found it easier to castigate the Stoics as unnatural, rather than use them to outline his broader scepticism about the power of reason alongside his desire to relocate philosophy in the realm of ordinary life.[223] Hume's rather more explicit attack on Jansenism is also submerged in Smith's own analysis.[224] This is why, just as with some of the earlier arguments outlined in this book, scholarship, hard-thinking and intellectual integrity are presented by Smith as one way of soothing frustration in the real world. His early essay on the history of astronomy, an essay about which he retained considerable pride and which some see as the 'door into his thought', might be one self-referential clue to the therapy intellectual labour can provide.[225] In that essay, the transformation of scientific systems of thought depends upon their capacity to explain and make sensible complex phenomena, but also upon their capacity to make individuals feel better and to calm fevered minds through work and knowledge acquisition. Tranquillity of mind, as well as the capacity to act on rational desires, is a necessary prerequisite of happiness, and as he had already noted, a mixture of self-command and stoical fortitude was important to this tranquillity.[226] Smith talked positively of Socrates and of pride in the face of grief to illustrate the claim.

If we ask again, however, what sorts of passions might best elicit sympathy if our relevant actions are viewed with propriety, Smith assures us that there are differences between passions of the body (for example, those of hunger, sexual desire and appetite) and passions of the imagination. They require different types of propriety, and the temperance re-

[222] Griswold 1999, pp. 155–73, esp. pp. 169ff; cf. Burnyeat 1983, pp. 117–48; cf. Norton 1994, pp. 119–39; Schliesser 2005, pp. 697f, n. 3.

[223] Smith 1976, *TMS*, esp. VII. ii. I. 34, p. 287; cf. Griffin 1986, esp. pp. 68, 71; 1986a, pp. 195, 198ff.

[224] Macintyre 1994a, pp. 83–100.

[225] Schliesser 2005, esp. pp. 701–7; Buchan 2003, p. 125.

[226] Smith 1976, *TMS*, III. 3. 30–33, pp. 149–52.

quired to express bodily passions is much harder to sympathize with. Indeed, one of the typically striking examples he gives is of the starving man, suggesting that we can sympathize with the distress caused by hunger but not with the feeling of hunger itself. Correlatively, in controlling 'appetites of the body consists that virtue which is properly called temperance'.[227] Other examples include pain, which, unless it is accompanied by danger, we will have no sympathy for. If we have never experienced the same symptom, how we feel towards bodily afflictions cannot be imaginatively sympathized with in the normal way. Passions of the imagination can be equally problematic, even if one refers to apparently natural passions like love or infatuation. We are apt to sympathize with the feeling of love, but with someone who is blinded by love (a complex emotion in Smith's vocabulary), or who doesn't exercise the appropriate reserve when talking about love or work (think of the office bore or the deluded personality explaining how marvellous is his wit or skill) then we can have no sympathy. The friend whose love for a new partner is so intense to her is quite simply 'ridiculous' to us.[228]

For passions to be deemed appropriate by others, their pitch must have what seems to me to be a form of persuasive mediocrity. For instance, we are apt to have greater degrees of fellow feeling with non-bodily passions. It is 'fellow feeling', the situation that excites the passion and the reaction that flows from it in the form of an action, rather than the passion or the idea itself, which is primarily important. So 'a disappointment in love, or ambition' for example, will 'call forth more sympathy than the greatest bodily evil'.[229] Yet there is still a capacity for self-deception and inappropriate action, and if the pitch of our passions is too high or too low, the spectator cannot go along with them.[230] Only persuasively mediocre expressions of the passions will lead to actions that meet with the standards of propriety (and justice), and only actions meeting those standards can be sympathized with. This intersubjective 'commerce of sympathy' between passions and actions gives us pleasure, and once again develops (internally) our awareness of the general and stable rules of justice.[231] We should not be excessive, therefore, because in general 'it is always miserable to complain, even when we are oppressed by the most dreadful calamities'. In related fashion, 'the triumph of victory is not always ungraceful, while prudence would often advise us to bear our prosperity with more moderation. It would teach us how to avoid

[227] Smith 1976, *TMS*, I. ii. I. 4, p. 28.
[228] Smith 1976, *TMS*, I. ii. 2. 1–6, pp. 30–34.
[229] Smith 1976, *TMS*, I. ii. 6, p. 29.
[230] Smith 1976, *TMS*, I. ii. intro. 1, p. 27.
[231] Smith 1995, esp. pp. 449, 452–56.

producing that envy which, more than anything, such a triumph is apt to excite'.[232]

In Smith's account there are still further subdivisions between social and unsocial passions. What unites anger and resentment as the principal unsocial passions is that they divide our sympathy, and in the case of resentment this strengthens our resolve for justice. They do so because we must consider first the propriety of the passion (for instance, how much resentment is expressed by someone and whether it is the right or wrong amount) in light of our own experience. Then we must also divide our sympathy between the person expressing resentment and the person towards whom the resentment is directed. To use Smith's own illustration, we can hate Iago as much as we admire Hamlet, though our sympathies in the matter are divided.[233] Common standards of interpretation or general rules of conduct should still govern our actions and sympathies in these contexts, but it remains possible for us to be uninformed, if not outright wrong, if we are inappropriately indifferent to an action. Appropriate indifference, on the other hand, which is to say the passionate indifference of the 'impartial spectator' properly understood, represents Smith's best attempt to account for the difficulties of sympathizing with unsocial passions in particular. That this is natural in Smith's mind is indicated by the fact that 'the word sympathy, in its most proper and primitive signification, denotes our fellow-feeling with the sufferings, not that with the enjoyments, of others'.[234] However, he also writes that where there is no envy, then our propensity to sympathize with joy over sorrow is much stronger.

Just as the bodily passions require temperance for sympathy, the unsocial passions must also be similarly well controlled, for they are the basis of claims about justice writ large and writ small. Recall that resentment is the reflex against injustice. Therefore we must express anger, hate, and love with magnanimity, and in public wear an appropriate mask in dealing with these unsocial passions. We may find it difficult, but the mask of magnanimity is itself just another regulative ideal with beneficial consequences.[235] This is similar, of course, to earlier discussions by Hobbes and Locke as well as Montesquieu on the propriety of magnanimity over vainglory and scornful laughter.[236] Indeed, because the social passions of generosity, esteem, humanity, kindness, mutual

---

[232] Smith 1976, *TMS*, I. iii. 1. 10, p. 47; cf. Smith 1976, *TMS*, VI. iii. 19, p. 245, on the need for balance in response to injury or praise; also Smith 1976, *TMS*, III. 2. 18, p. 123, on the complaints of artists about the reception of their work.

[233] Smith 1976, *TMS*, I. ii. 3. 2, p. 34.

[234] Smith 1976, *TMS*, I. iii. 1. 1, p. 43.

[235] Valihora 2001, esp. pp. 142, 147f, 149f.

[236] Hobbes 1991, ch. 6, p. 43; cf. Skinner 2002f, esp. p. 172; also Fleischacker 2004, pp. 101ff.

friendship and so forth, equally contend for our sympathy, magnanimity becomes particularly important to a commercial polity largely built on the fragmented attachments to strangers upon whom one relies. It seems very much like an updating of classical models of political friendship as relationships of exchange.[237] In contrast with selfish passions, moreover, the social passions redouble rather than divide our sympathy. For we have every instinct to sympathize with benevolent affections and to sympathize with both the 'actor' and the person being acted upon in this context.

Finally, selfish passions appear to stand at the midpoint between social and unsocial passions and do not seem to be passions of the body at all. They are the roots of our desire to better our own condition and to seek after our self-interest rightly understood as a form of prudential reasoning towards actions that the impartial spectator could sympathize with.[238] Given that selfishness and emulation are not necessarily simply facts of our nature, Smith locates the selfish passions at the mean between the extremes of social and unsocial affect, and in so doing brings them into line with his analysis of agency as taking place at the point of propriety between impartiality and simple-minded spectatorship. These natural traits make us ambitiously pursue our reputation, even while constrained by the demands of spectatorial justice and propriety. The conclusion is, again, strikingly contemporary in its desire to return philosophy to the real world. In terms of a phenomenology, Smith presents ordinary life as the guide from which we construct our theoretical account of nature and the world, and from which we then judge our own conduct and that of others. It is certainly at one level an attempt to naturalize the 'metaphysical sophisms' of traditional Stoicism, and similar reasoning applies to his theory of politics and his rejection of system.[239] He suggests something like a morality without principles, although in not quite so 'pagan' a form as Hume.[240] However, if his analysis is designed to show the results of a system of natural liberty run free, the major question remaining for Smith concerns how the system had come to be, and why it might now be retarded or distorted. Commercial society was, after all, what he termed unnatural and retrograde.[241] Smith's history of the origins of government and jurisprudence was designed to provide an answer to this question.

---

[237] Smith 1976, *TMS*, I. ii. 4, pp. 38ff; cf. Hill and McCarthy 2004, esp. pp. 3, 5ff, 9ff; Den Uyl and Griswold Jr. 1996, pp. 609–37; Schofield 1998, pp. 37–51.

[238] Griswold 1999, pp. 118f; Force 2004.

[239] See Smith 1976, *TMS*, II. 3. 1. 5, pp. 96f; III. 3. 14–16, pp. 142f, and the excellent discussion in Griswold 1999, pp. 319ff, 323.

[240] Cf. Dancy 2004; Phillipson 1993, p. 311.

[241] Winch 1996, pp. 106, 108.

THE ORIGINS OF GOVERNMENT AND THE PARADOXES OF POLITICAL LIBERTY

Smith saw commercial society as anomalous in historical time. The 'order of things' imposed by the 'natural inclinations of man' means that 'subsistence' is 'prior to conveniency and luxury'. Therefore, the 'cultivation and improvement of the country' that provides such subsistence must 'be prior to the increase of the town'.[242] Such natural progression, however, 'in all the modern states of Europe, [has] been, in many respects, entirely inverted'. City-based commerce and 'finer manufactures' have 'given birth to the principal improvements in agriculture', and not the other way around, as one would think. The 'manners and customs which the nature of their original government introduced' have 'forced them into this unnatural and retrograde order'.[243] Nevertheless, 'order' and 'good government' in Smith's political theory provide the 'liberty and security of individuals', and this development was only fully introduced with the rise of 'commerce and manufactures' in his four-stage historical narrative.[244] Indeed, 'how servile soever may have been' the original condition of those in towns, they 'arrived at liberty and independency much earlier than the occupiers of land in the country'.[245] With the further revocation of 'villanage and slavery' they 'became really free in our present sense of the word Freedom'.[246]

The history of different forms of government thus developed according to the natural inclinations of man, not from any form of contract, and it happened in discernible stages. Society moved from hunter-gatherers, for whom there was 'nothing which could deserve the name of government', through the 'imperfect and rude sort which takes place amongst shepherds', towards the rise of aristocratic and latterly democratic republics, which could be divided according to whether they were slave societies or not. If they were slave societies, moreover, they tended to last longer.[247] The 'age of shepherds is that where government properly first commences', which was in line with the rise of human interdependence and the distinctions that develop out of property relations.[248] Smith repeats this point in other discussions, where shepherding, the 'second period of society', points to where 'inequality of fortune first begins to take place',

---

[242] Smith 1976, *WN*, III. i, p. 377.
[243] Smith 1976, *WN*, III. i, p. 380; cf. Smith 1976, *WN*, III. iv, p. 418.
[244] Smith 1976, *WN*, III. iv, p. 412; cf. pp. 405, 414.
[245] Smith 1976, *WN*, III. iii, p. 398.
[246] Smith 1976, *WN*, III. iii, p. 400.
[247] Smith 1975, *LJ (A)*, iv. 19, p. 207; iv. 114, pp. 244, 243.
[248] Smith 1975, *LJ (A)*, iv. 7–8, p. 202.

by introducing 'some degree of that civil government which is indispens-
ably necessary' for the preservation of the authority and subordination
that emerged from this point onwards.[249] The Germanic shepherding societies that had ravaged the Roman Empire but had transformed European history unintentionally were an obvious illustration of his point
about the paradoxical character of progress and decline.[250]

The movement towards a regular administration of justice was crucial
to the story, and under an agricultural stage of development the beginnings of that security needed for both good government and civil liberty
began to be provided.[251] To a 'rude people', of course, the establishment
of courts of justice seemed to 'have an authority altogether insufferable',
but rules of conduct soon developed to legislate legal activity. At first,
when there are no laws, 'every one trusts to the naturall feeling of justice
he has in his own breast and expects to find in others'. This means that
were laws to be established prior to the establishment of judges, 'they
would then be a great restraint upon liberty, but when established after
them they extent [i.e., extend] and secure' such freedom.[252] The contrast
between ancient and modern was thereby well illustrated in the change
in position and perception of the judge, a figure that to an 'early nation'
will 'appear very terrible', but who is 'now rather a comfortable than a
terrible sight as he is the source of our liberty, our independence, and
our security'.[253] And because Smith was keen to show the importance
of the development of legal regularity to the rise of commercial society,
his account of early government necessarily illustrates their very different systems of justice, where unusual punishments like trials by boiling
water, by ordeal and so forth, are 'all signs of the weak authority of the
court, which could not oblige those who came before it to stand to its
judgement'.[254] The true origins of government were thus irregular, and
although found in the hunter-gatherer stage, only arbitrary and not 'regular' government existed there. Such peoples lived, as both Hobbes and
Locke had said, 'according to the laws of nature'.[255] Correlatively, the necessity of a non-arbitrary, common judge to counter misunderstandings
of the general laws of nature was Smith's rather Lockean solution to this
problem.[256] In fact, Locke had suggested that the 'first and fundamental

[249] Smith 1976, *WN*, V. i. b, p. 715.

[250] Smith 1976, *WN*, IV. vii. c, p. 624; see too Vivenza 2001, pp. 106–9; cf. Mann 1986, vol. 1, pp. 283–95.

[251] Smith 1975, *LJ (A)*, v. 121, p. 318.

[252] Smith 1975, *LJ (A)*, v. 110f, p. 314.

[253] Smith 1975, *LJ (A)*, v. 108–11, pp. 313–14.

[254] Smith 1975, *LJ (A)*, iv. 28–29, pp. 210–11.

[255] Smith 1975, *LJ (B)*, 19f, p. 404.

[256] Locke 1988, II. ix, §§ 123–31, pp. 350–53; II. xi, §§ 134–36, pp. 355–59.

positive Law of all Commonwealths, is the establishing of the Legislative Power', which for him was a relationship of trust rooted in natural law.[257] In a slightly different iteration, when Smith came to distinguish between the major forms of government (monarchical and republican, with the latter including both democracy and aristocracy), he observed that in order to understand the veracity of such a classification one needed to understand the first forms of government. Moreover, the origins of liberty were to be sought rather further back than the Germanic and Gothic origins that Montesquieu had suggested.[258]

Developing his argument, Smith claimed that the initial supreme political power was a 'federative' power, which formed the basis for decisions about peace and war, and was therefore precarious in its foundations. Judicial power was next established, and although its origins were precarious, in time it too, as well as the legislative power, came to be absolute.[259] The development of political power and the origins of government were traced not in terms of a (hypothetical) social-contract tradition, but 'from the natural progress that men make in society'. Nevertheless, the rise of commerce and manufactures at the expense of agriculture led to a 'revolution of the greatest importance to the publick happiness' even though it simultaneously remained 'contrary to the natural course of things'.[260] Feudal lords had given up their authority for little more than a 'pair of diamond buckles'.[261] With the abolition of feudalism and the decline of lordly tenure, commerce between nations became possible. This was an early paraphrase of Smith's later account of the 'silent and invisible operation of foreign commerce'.[262] Monarchical government, previously a threat to individual liberty, was therefore shown to be central to the full and proper development of civil liberty. The increased power of both the state and centralized institutions of political control (more simply, princely absolutism) helped to curb the irregular and potentially despotic power of older feudal regimes. In returning to the English example, Smith suggested that the 'liberty of the subjects was secured in England by the great accuracy and precision of the law'.[263]

[257] Locke 1988, II. xi, §§ 134, 142, pp. 355ff, 363.
[258] Cf. [Anon.] 1758, pp. 17f 19, on the difference between ancient and modern republics and the characteristics of 'Gothic' governments.
[259] Smith 1975, *LJ (A)*, v. 104–8, pp. 312–13; also Smith 1975, *LJ (A)*, iv. 2–3, p. 200. Emphasis in original.
[260] Smith 1976, *WN*, III. iv, p. 422.
[261] Smith 1976, *WN*, III. iv, 10, pp. 418f.
[262] Smith 1976, *WN*, III. iv, 10, pp. 418f.
[263] Smith 1975, *LJ (A)*, v. 12, p. 274, v. 31, p. 282; cf. v. 15, p. 275. Smith 1975, *LJ (A)*, v. 21, p. 278, v. 26–32, pp. 280ff, discussed the rise in power of the Chancellor of the Exchequer, for example, after 'Edward [I] had ... broke judiciall power', suggesting that although the chancellor was 'certainly as arbitrary a judge as most ... neither is he very dangerous to

Under a system of feudalism tempered by monarchy, a general or universal form of civil liberty could never properly evolve. It could not properly develop until the power of nobles 'fell to ruin'. This happened 'as soon as arts and luxury were introduced'. Indeed, the 'nobility are the greatest opposers and oppressors of liberty that we can imagine. They hurt the liberty of the people even more than an absolute monarch', so that 'the people . . . never can have security in person or estate till the nobility have been greatly crushed'.[264] Arts, commerce and moeurs in combination are the best account Smith gives of the nature and extent of the commercial revolution, showing how the essentially private self-interest that seems to form the heart of his account of human motivation was thereby transformed. The mutually reinforcing reciprocity between commerce, manners and government therefore forms the lynchpin of Smith's account of the development of political liberty, which itself marks a transformation in the historical approach to the question of political authority.

Alongside this narrative of noble displacement, distinctions between persons in terms of authority and rank were also of general importance to the argument. In earlier societies the distinction between the lowest freeman and a slave was not so great, so Smith could argue that 'Liberalitas, ελευθερια, species liberalis, signify no more than the behaviour and appearance of a gentleman. For the distinction betwixt free and slaves made the same as betwixt the vulgare and the people of fashion or gentlemen'.[265] It therefore makes no sense on Smith's terms to talk of the paradoxes of political liberty in ancient society, in the same way that it clearly does make sense to talk of the paradoxes of modern commercial societies that are based on justice yet also explicitly and hugely unequal.[266] The liberty of the ancients was based on slavery, whilst in modern republics 'every person is free, and the poorer sort are all employed in some necessary occupation'.[267] Here Smith recapped the central assumptions of his analysis, noting the origins of government amongst a 'nation of shepherds' such as had arisen in Athens and Sparta, for 'the age of shepherd is that where government properly first commences. And it is at this time too that men become in any considerable degree dependent on others'.[268] These societies, moreover, became the 'originall form' of small

---

the liberty of the subject, as he can not try any causes besides those which have no remedy at common law'. For discussion of the medieval origins of the *cancellarius saccarii*, see Vincent 1993, pp. 105–21.

[264] Smith 1975, *LJ (A)*, iv. 165–66, p. 264.

[265] Smith 1975, *LJ (A)*, iv. 69, p. 226.

[266] Hont 2005, pp. 442f.

[267] Smith 1975, *LJ (A)*, iv. 69, p. 226; Finley 1981, ch. 6.

[268] Smith 1975, *LJ (A)*, iv. 7, p. 202: See also 1975, *LJ (A)*, iv. 23, p. 209: 'Settled laws therefore, or agreements concerning property, will soon be made after the commencement of the age of shepherds'.

republics, from which governmental form could take two conjectural trajectories. Either the 'state' continued as a large city in a small republic, or it must 'extend its territory and conquer some of the adjacent states' in order to prevent its 'totall ruin'.[269] Those which attempt to maintain their small size through the diminution of the number of 'fighting men' prompt an increase in the 'arts and sciences' and a 'great declension in the force and power of the republick in all cases'. The process was uneven and depended upon the existence or otherwise of slavery.[270] In the case of Greece and Rome, both developed through imperial expansion, while the security provided by their jealous guardianship permitted the arts and sciences to flourish.[271] Smaller republics were thereby threatened by the general 'improvement of the military art', exemplified by a 'conquering state' like Rome or Carthage, whilst conquering states were also threatened, but this time from the natural process of introducing arts and luxuries into the state.[272] 'Liberty' was put 'in danger by its own subjects', whether this took the form of moral corruption through luxury or military corruption through the particular ties that the lowest soldiers felt to their generals over and above the republic.[273] To put the point another way, while improvements in the arts and cultivation lessened the capacity of defensive republics for war, republics for increase (Sparta and Rome were classic examples) achieved peace at home whilst their armies conquered abroad. This allowed wealth and industry to flourish for a time, but 'the wealth this introduces, joined to that which is brought in by the conquest of other nations, naturally occasions the same diminution of strength as in a defensive republick'.[274]

With something of a deflationary conclusion, however, Smith could only note that the field of historical jurisprudence and public law was such that greater precision than presented in his account was nearly impossible.[275] It is perhaps unsurprising, therefore, that Smith's historical jurisprudence is best viewed as providing a novel and exceptionally broad-ranging agglomeration of republican and jurisprudential themes, because his chief focus was to illustrate the appropriateness of his theory of propriety and spectatorial sympathy to questions of justice and the historical progress of natural liberty. Political freedom, on this reading, is about being able to 'breathe the free air of liberty and independency', which derives from our attempts to subdue the 'private, partial

---

[269] Smith 1975, *LJ (A)*, iv. 75, pp. 228–29.

[270] Smith 1975, *LJ (A)*, iv. 77, p. 229; iv. 81–82, p. 231; cf. iii. 103, p. 181: 'The authority of the masters over the slaves is therefore unbounded in all republican governments'.

[271] Smith 1975, *LJ (A)*, iv. 61–65, pp. 223ff; iv. 75, p. 228; 1975, *LJ (B)*, 31, pp. 408f.

[272] Smith 1975, *LJ (A)*, iv. 86, 88, pp. 232f.

[273] Smith 1975, *LJ (A)*, iv. 88, p. 233; 91–92, pp. 234f.

[274] Smith 1975, *LJ (A)*, iv. 93, p. 235.

[275] Smith 1975, *LJ (A)*, v. 102, p. 311; see too *LJ (A)*, v. 86, p. 304, v. 91, p. 306.

and selfish passions' where appropriate.[276] Recognizing the centrality of self-interest properly understood, however, means that for Smith the end of government is certainly not virtue or perfection, but rather simply the safeguarding of the interest and opinion of citizens. Slavery, for example, was abolished due to interest and the rise of commerce, certainly not as the necessary result of moral progress. Nevertheless, an increase in freedom makes fear of slavery even more pronounced, and Smith presented a moral and a politico-economic case against slavery that was radical both in its implications and its attack on vested interests and influence.[277] His explanation for its longevity was, partly like that offered by Montesquieu, that it was rooted in the 'pride of man', which 'makes him love to domineer'.[278] In related fashion, his analysis of its decline was a result of the paradoxical history of modern political liberty derived from immediate predecessors like Carmichael and Hutcheson.[279] Their discussions of Pufendorf, slavery and imperialism in part lay behind Smith's defence of a regular administration of justice.[280] And 'having considered the original principles of government, and its progress in the first ages of society, [and] having found it in general to be democratical', Smith's discussion went on to contrast the liberty of 'barbarous nations' with the rise of civil liberty in the classical republics of the ancient world.[281] Ultimately, however, as later commentators would more polemically assert, the decline of austere virtue through decadence and degeneration ruined the classical republics, and the liberty of the ancients was forever lost.[282]

The natural jurisprudential origins of his four-stage narrative, first premiered in his lectures on the topic to undergraduates in Glasgow, is clearly central to this account.[283] A focus on subsistence, (legal) evolution

[276] Smith 1976, *TMS*, VII. ii. I. 40, p. 290; the 'love of independency' was also, of course, what Smith saw as the root of Hume's 'great and necessary frugality' and 'happily balanced' temper. See Adam Smith, Letter (178) to William Strahan, November 9, 1776, in Smith 1987, pp. 217–21, p. 221.

[277] Pitts 2005, p. 31, discussing the relevant sections of Smith 1975, *LJ (A)*, iii, p. 111; cf. Griswold 1999, pp. 198–202; Haakonssen 1989, pp. 141, 177.

[278] Smith 1976, *WN*, III. ii. 10, p. 388; Montesquieu 1989, 6. 28. 41, p. 595; 1964, p. 747.

[279] See Carmichael 2002, pp. 140, 165f; cf. Moore and Silverthorne 1984, esp. pp. 8ff; Robertson 2005, pp. 141ff.

[280] Hutcheson 1747, p. ix; Scott 1937, pp. 112, 294; Hutcheson 1749, pp. 3–13; for the wider debates about punishment and slavery, see Tuck 1999, pp. 144f, 170–77; Locke 1988, II. iii, § 19, pp. 280f; II. viii, §§ 100–101, pp. 333f; II. xviii, § 207, pp. 403f; Scott 1992, esp. p. 582; Hont 2005, pp. 425–30; Thompson 1988, esp. pp. 280, n. 16, 293. See also Hutcheson 1755, pp. 308f; Adam Smith is listed as a subscriber to this edition.

[281] Smith 1975, *LJ (B)*, pp. 408ff.

[282] See Constant 1999, esp. pp. 314f; Fontana 1997, pp. 385–90; Rosenblatt 2008, pp. 162ff.

[283] Scott 1937, pp. 56, 111, 319, 327, 341; also Cairns 1991, pp. 31–58; Clark 1992, pp. 76, 81f, 98f; cf. Pocock 1999a, pp. 315ff.

and debates about sociability were important spurs to the argument.[284] Smith's engagement with the 'socialism' of Pufendorf, the rights-based historicist jurisprudence of Hugo Grotius, the civil political theory of John Locke, and of course the historical illustration of Roman law underpinned his account of natural sociability.[285] Equally, Smith's general argument recalled Locke's discussion of the community as a common 'Umpire', out of which an impartial earthly judge could provide a right of appeal to citizens of the Commonwealth.[286] In particular, however, Smith took over Pufendorf's general critique of Hobbes, to argue that natural man is driven by need towards society because of his sociability, rather than his fear.[287] Reason or mind (*cultura animi*) thus expressed was the defining characteristic of human development, and it gave the state its character as a compound moral person.[288] Pufendorf equally explained the desire for society by self-interested individuals in terms of reconciling divine Providence, interest and need, as well as a constant desire for recognition and intersubjective credit; he explicitly related ideas about the esteem of persons to the way one compares the price of things, and his thesis was rooted in an idea of 'unsocial sociability' that Kant would later make famous.[289]

All of this seems to have been of more direct use to Smith than Locke's similar work, whose account of the origins of government and political society he updated.[290] He rejected Locke's analysis of tacit consent, allegiance, and the origins of private property.[291] Yet the same Locke had

---

[284] Meek 1976, esp. pp. 2f, 15ff, 32ff, 35, 68ff, 72f, 91, 99–104, 107–29 (on Smith particularly and the idea of a 'predisposition' towards this claim), 239; cf. Stein 1980, pp. 39f, 42f, 45f, 48; Vivenza 2001, pp. 100, 137.

[285] Haakonssen 1985, esp. pp. 240ff; on the intellectual origins of Grotian natural sociability, see Winkel, esp. pp. 395–98. Winkel (p. 401 n. 51) also refers to the important argument of Palladini 1996, pp. 61–69; cf. Straumann 2006, esp. pp. 341ff.

[286] Locke 1988, II, §§ 8–15, pp. 272–78; §§ 19–21, pp. 280ff; §§ 87–90, pp. 323–26; § 133, p. 355.

[287] Palladini 2004, esp. p. 250; for more general thoughts, see too Wokler 1994, esp. pp. 383ff, 390ff; Black 1993, pp. 57–76.

[288] Hont 2005, pp. 163, 171ff; 180f; Hochstrasser 2000, pp. 97, 101. Pufendorf 1749, bk. 1, ch. 1, pp. 7f; bk. 7, ch. 3, pp. 650–56; see also Carr and Seidler 1996; Tuck 1999, pp. 142f, 144f, 148ff. As Miller 1994, pp. 246f, notes, Blackstone's account was identical.

[289] Pufendorf 1749, bk. 8, ch. 4, pp. 800f, 803, 805–10; see also Skinner 2002d, esp. pp. 407f. Cf. Smith 1976, TMS, VI. ii. I. 1, p. 212; Hont 2005, pp. 175f, from which this draws; Nussbaum 1997, esp. pp. 15–22; Reich 1939, esp. pp. 353f; 1939a, esp. pp. 450f, 457ff, 462.

[290] Locke 1988, II. viii, §§ 95–99, pp. 330–34; cf. Dunn 1969, p. 116; Pocock 1990, esp. pp. 235–38; on the origin of government, see Locke 1988, II. viii, §§ 105–7, 112, pp. 336–39, 343; cf. Dunn 1969, pp. 115f.

[291] Locke 1988, II. viii, §§ 114–22, pp. 344–49; also Locke 1988, II. ii, §§ 14–15, pp. 276ff; ix, §§ 123–31, pp. 350–53. Cf. Locke 1988, II. viii, §§ 116–18, pp. 345ff, and Dunn

noted that that it was 'God, who is the author and Giver of Life', and that writers like Filmer were so 'dazled with thoughts of Monarchy' and paternal authority that they forgot this origin at their peril.[292] His attack had shown that historical precedent was no guarantee of normativity, and although Smith (and Hume) agreed, the temporal reproduction of existing social arrangements was not presumed in Locke in quite the same way it was by the Scots.[293] Smith's analysis advocated a similar awareness of the importance of God, particularly in terms of the effect that assumptions of an afterlife made on the conduct of the living in this world. Indeed, this was the place where 'exact justice' for temporal conduct would be meted out.[294] Perhaps what Smith found more telling in Locke was his recognition of the 'vain ambition' of concupiscence and the 'fantastical uneasiness' we feel when literally itching after honour and riches.[295]

If all political forms fail, though, the question is in what manner and style failure should be staved off. That this was a traditional political question was obvious to Smith, and had already received pictorial expression and interpretation that Smith could well have been aware of. For example, as Erwin Panofsky's classic analysis of Poussin's canvas *Et in Arcadia Ego* suggests, death is even present in paradise, a theme whose subversive implications and complex translations were clearly understood (if only 'precariously') in England through Reynolds and others in Smith's own time. One would like to think that he had some such image in mind when expressing his argument.[296] In any case, the issue had clear implications for his account of English liberty especially. Smith wanted to show why the much later medieval Italian republics (with their scholastic and humanistic foundations) seemed to develop similarly to the early Greek model, with security, trade and prosperity, but then failed because of luxury and a reliance on mercenary armies. If that account held up, he could then present a sharp counterblast to long-standing assessments of English exceptionalism and offer a new historical argument. Claiming that there was little to support the idea that English 'liberty' was a deep-rooted product of the Norman Conquest and ancient constitution, Smith countered instead that English liberty had been lost early, but was

---

1985, pp. 129ff. On the property argument, see Dunn 1969, pp. 67f; Tuck 1999, p. 155; Haakonssen 1989, pp. 106f, 142f.

[292] Locke 1988, I, § 52, p. 178.

[293] Dunn 1969, esp. pp. 105ff; cf. Smith 1975, *LJ (A)*, v. 114–15, p. 316; also Smith 1975, *LJ (A)*, v. 118, p. 317. Cf. Locke 1988, II. viii, § 119, pp. 347f; Simmons 2000; Pack and Schliesser 2006, pp. 52ff; Dunn 1985, pp. 133f; Robertson 2005, pp. 394ff.

[294] Smith 1976, *TMS*, III. 2. 33, p. 132.

[295] See Locke 1984, II. xxi, § 45; 1988, II. viii, § 111, pp. 342f.

[296] Panofsky 1970, esp. pp. 352f, 364; cf. Hume 1982, *EPM*, III. i. 151, p. 189.

restored as modern liberty during the English civil wars. He ran parallel historical and conceptual arguments together about the rise and fall of both ancient and modern liberty in a panoramic sweep. Thus, if European political development had been 'unnatural and retrograde', the rise and decline of the Italian republics could be presented in a fashion similar to the rise and decline of the ancient city-states. To explain his curious claim about the restoration of English freedom, however, Smith compared the subjugation of the powerful republic by Dyonysius, with the reduction in power of the British republic by Cromwell, who had in fact turned it into a 'military monarchy'. Subsequent union with Scotland allowed the English to have 'recovered their liberty' after having lost it.[297] This was clearly a suggestive spin on Montesquieu's analysis of an English republic lying underneath the façade of English monarchy after the Interregnum, but it was also a clear rejection of the Tacitean idea that the roots of liberty were to be found in the German forests. Smith posited a much earlier origin to political liberty in general, whilst his joined-up parallel histories of ancient and modern liberty pointed more sharply to the very specific character of English liberty in particular. This analysis both added another layer to his history of government and offered a polemically crucial point about the character of freedom. It could be lost, and then found again, but in circumstances not always of one's own choosing.[298]

Conclusions

Smith explained political liberty as the supplement to regularity and security (the seedbed of civil liberty); the 'happy mixture' of the two resulted in an institutional defence against arbitrary and unchecked political power. Political sovereignty was confusingly understood to be both absolute and simultaneously divided.[299] With this apparent paradox Smith once more approached something like Montesquieu's analysis.[300] Moreover, it was in England that this achievement had been most profound, because although 'the absolute power of the sovereigns has continu'd ever since its establishment in France, Spain, etc. In England alone a different government has been established from the naturall course of things'. The reasons for this history (union with Scotland, island status, the dissipation of monarchical revenue and the power of the Commons)

---

[297] Smith 1975, *LJ (A)*, iv. 105, p. 240; iv. 168, p. 265.

[298] For discussion of this history, see Hont 2009, pp. 155–69.

[299] Smith 1975, *LJ (A)*, iv. 19, p. 207; on the paradoxical quality of Smithian sovereignty see Haakonssen 1989, pp. 132f.

[300] See Castiglione 2000, pp. 60, 64f.

eventually made 'keeping up a standing army' less important, given the unlikelihood of invasion.[301] Smith's prize, though, was to show the connections between justice and the origins and development of human societies, whose progress and opulence could then be critically evaluated.[302] This allowed him to reject attempts to engraft ancient moeurs onto commercial society, as would Hume, for 'when a country arrives at a certain degree of refinement it becomes less fit for war'.[303] The plan of his major work of political economy expressed this conclusion clearly, for he thought he had resolved the classical republican dilemma (of empire and liberty) by explicating anew the complex relationship between economic and political transformations. His analysis of the 'slow and uncertain' progression of an unnatural history developed from the collapse of the Roman Empire onwards, and explored how a 'revolution of the greatest importance to publick happiness' was 'brought about by two different orders of people', the 'great proprietors' and 'merchants and artificers'. These people 'had not the least intention to serve the publick', but had done so inadvertently.[304]

If in order to understand the implications of this temporal anomaly of modern commercial society a detailed historical political theory was required, a further implication of Smith's analysis was normatively more profound, but can be more quickly stated. This has to do with the redirection of our natural concern with self-interest, pride, reputation and ambition towards the particular ends of commercial society. To put the point strongly, Smith thinks that people too often pursue their natural ambition for remarkably trivial ends. Although their purposes are natural (given our 'original desire to please'), the majority of people seek to emulate persons of wealth and polish, but this is problematic when social norms dictate the calibre of what is deemed praiseworthy, in ways that are detrimental both to virtue and to duty and justice.[305] It is through our 'disposition to admire, and consequently to imitate, the rich and the great, that they are enabled to set, or to lead what is called the fashion'.[306] But in seeking to find self-worth or affirmation in those

---

[301] Smith 1975, *LJ (A)*, iv. 168, p. 265; also Smith 1975, *LJ (A)*, v. 2–3, pp. 270–71.

[302] Harpham 1999, esp. p. 450.

[303] Smith 1975, *LJ (B)*, p. 411; cf. Ferguson 1995, pp. 132, 149, 204, 211, 213, 220; cf. Kalyvas and Katznelson 2008, pp. 51–87; Skinner 2002e, esp. pp. 365f. For Hume, particularly on the American crisis and the limits of imperial politics, see David Hume, Letter (509) to William Strahan, October 26, 1775, in Hume 1932, vol. 2, p. 300. See also Clark 1992, pp. 98f, 113, 116, 125ff, 138, 297; Armitage 2002, esp. pp. 48f, 52ff, 56, who stresses the importance of Vattel to his discussion, on whom, see in general Whelan 1988, pp. 59–90.

[304] Smith 1976, *WN*, III. iv, p. 422; see also Robertson 2005, p. 391.

[305] Smith 1976, *TMS*, III. 2. 6–7, pp. 116f.

[306] Smith 1976, *TMS*, I. iii. 3. 7, p. 64.

trinkets and baubles that are valued as luxuries in commercial polities, individuals deceive themselves and misdirect their natural energies towards meaningless ends. This activity might still have public benefits, but by mistaking and 'over-rating the difference between one permanent situation and another', a process in which 'avarice over-rates the difference between poverty and riches', any person 'under the influence of any of those extravagant passions, is not only miserable in his actual situation, he is often disposed to disturb the peace of society'.[307] At the level of the individual, imaginative delusion could be easily felt. For although the 'love of just fame, of true glory, even for its own sake, and independent of any advantage' is 'not unworthy even of a wise man', most people simply fail to see its value . The search for fame and reputation instead often leads to stultifying social conformism, even though that is not without its utility.[308] Worse still, as Smith also noted, was that this search can also affect political leaders. Smith's critique of statesmanship in the imperial context shows that he thought the natural rules of justice and prudence had been relinquished by politicians, and that national policy was too often presented as pursuing the delusional ends of imperial glory merely for the sake of keeping up appearances in the eyes of Europe.[309] In his attacks on the British Empire, Smith was at one with Hume's suggestion that he was 'an American in his principles', but quite possibly also a Ciceronian in his virtues, hoping to redirect the generous fame of those few individuals who possess true virtue, and to make that passion safe for society against the dangers of overzealous seeking after reputation.[310]

Smith went still further, however, suggesting that for the ideal and well-ordered man, such fame is unnecessary (a Stoic-sounding 'indifferent' concern). Indeed, the well-governed individual 'even despises it', because 'he has the most perfect assurance of the perfect propriety of every part of his own conduct'. Under such idealized circumstances, there is no perceptual or imagined need for the external validation of one's actions by 'other men', for 'self-approbation' prompted by conscience is enough.[311] The norm lies in the mean, however, because if we really are self-contained enough not to feel the need for external recognition, then we have become godlike, anti-social, or sage, none of which Smith thinks of

[307] Smith 1976, *TMS*, III. 3. 31, p. 149.
[308] Stewart 1991, p. 281; cf. Sabl 2006, esp. pp. 546ff.
[309] See also Smith 1976, *WN*, IV. vii. c, pp. 590f.
[310] Adam Smith, 'Smith's Thoughts on the State of the Contest with America, February 1778', in Smith 1987, pp. 377–85, at p. 383; cf. David Hume, Letter (510) to Baron Mure of Caldwell, October 27, 1775, in Hume 1932, vol. 2, p. 303; also Letter (511) to William Strahan, November 13, 1775, in Hume 1932, vol. 2, pp. 304f; Conway 2000, esp. pp. 325–45. Cf. Hume 1982, *EPM*, IX. I. 276, § 225, p. 276; Sabl 2006, pp. 547–54.
[311] Smith 1976, *TMS*, III. 2. 7, p. 117.

as plausible or desirable. So although self-reliance and self-command are important means of circumnavigating some of the negative effects of conformism, standing aloof from society is undesirable. The best that those with superior prudence can do is to act as exemplars, which is the role (at least in part) of the ideal statesman. For with an appropriate degree of self-command, someone who seeks only the 'well-weighed approbation of a single wise man' finds 'more heartfelt satisfaction than all the noisy applauses of ten thousand ignorant though enthusiastic admirers'.[312] Nevertheless, although Smith thought that the ideal of autonomy as freedom from context was an imaginative delusion, he reckoned hard with the force of the claim that 'great success in the world, great authority over the sentiments and opinions of mankind, have very seldom been acquired without some degree of this excessive self-admiration'. Even if the 'religion and manners of modern times give our great men little encouragement to fancy themselves either Gods or even Prophets', they still think themselves greater than they are. Statesmen are particularly prone to this sort of delusion, and Smith referred to the lack of 'temperate coolness and self-command' of men of system when viewed against the 'great Duke of Marlborough' or even the greatest of enlightened reformers, including Frederick the Great and Gustavus Adolphus.[313] When not deceived by the 'excessive self-estimation' of appropriately 'splendid characters', the impartial spectator can sympathize with them as 'spirited, magnanimous and high-minded'. But where no such standard of judgement exists, there can be neither sympathetic attachment nor perfect propriety.[314]

Properly understood, propriety militates against political speculation by the statesman as much as it does inappropriate or unjust action by the citizen. It is also tied to an idea of civility, and while recent philosophical accounts of the relationship between freedom, civility and practical judgement have built upon Kantian foundations, similar arguments could just as well be inspired by Smith.[315] For both authors, arguments about the necessity of perceptual as well as social recognition for a minimally decent civil life meet with philosophical arguments about the rational character of human freedom. They similarly merge with long-standing questions about how one might judge the quality of agency within a civil association, a question whose intellectual history highlights the complexity of many possible answers.[316] If the answer provided by this chapter has been at all correct, Smith's historical jurisprudence aims to highlight

[312] Smith 1976, *TMS*, VI. iii. 31, p. 253.
[313] Smith 1976, *TMS*, VI. iii. 28, pp. 250ff.
[314] Smith 1976, *TMS*, VI. iii. 33, p. 255; cf. VI. iii. 30, pp. 253f.
[315] Pippin 2004, esp. pp. 235ff.
[316] Fleischacker 1999, pp. 127, 130.

the transformations wrought by the system of natural liberty over time towards the strict justice of modern society. That system of natural liberty expresses our natural desire for superiority, which is rooted in our need to persuade others of the validity of our claims. And in order to be persuasive as agents, we have to be able to act with propriety. Failure to do so might leave us without the approbation we seek, and at worst, it might provoke resentment. Moderation is therefore the hallmark of a well-ordered commercial society, which is why Smith rejects a Machiavellian view of politics and the economy, and why he also rejects the delusional politics of empire.[317] Discussing the 'real futility of all distant dominions' as the subject 'upon which the public prejudices of Europe require most to be set right', Smith explained that there was always 'ruin' in a nation, and empire simply made this danger worse. He avidly hoped for the 'dismemberment of the empire', and playing with a celebrated theme, he noted that England bred 'men of great professional abilities in all different ways', but not statesmen fit to deal with the 'awkward' problems of empire. His 'Memorandum to Lord Wedderburn' was simply the most extensive of his recollections on the problems of a 'nation whose government is influenced by shopkeepers'.[318]

Yet whilst Smith was engaged in this high political critique of empire, a distinctive theoretical foundation underpinned it all. For the bulk of his account of political and moral judgement was geared towards an explanation of agency in ordinary life. Because of this purpose, Smith argued that the propriety of liberty or persuasive agency requires that one's actions be undertaken in such a way as to persuade both the real and the impartial spectator of his mediocrity. The propriety of liberty, however, can coexist with the realities (and psychological traumas) of self-deception and imaginative delusion that commercial society promotes because of the particular ways it works with our natural sentiments. In combination, Smith's ideas were a powerful synthesis, and the legacy of his arguments would be profound. Although most have, of course, focused their attention on his role as a figure in the development of the discipline of political economy, which is a story with its own very particular afterlife, my concern has been with the need for persuasion and

---

[317] Cf. Pocock 1982, esp. pp. 335, 347; Bourke 2000, esp. pp. 467ff.

[318] Adam Smith, Letter (221) to John Sinclair of Ulbster, October 14, 1782, in Smith 1987, p. 262, and n. 3 about the natural 'ruin' in any nation; Adam Smith, Letter (231) to William Strahan, October 6, 1783, in Smith 1987, p. 269, hoping for the 'dismemberment of the empire'; also Adam Smith, Letter (158) to William Strahan, June 3, 1776, in Smith 1987, pp. 196f, on the English breeding of professionals; and finally 'Smith's Thoughts', in Smith 1987, pp. 380–85. Cf. Alexander Wedderburn, Letter (159) to Adam Smith, June 6, 1776, in Smith 1987, pp. 197f; Smith 1976, WN, IV. vii. c. 63, p. 613 (for the claim about a nation of shopkeepers). See also Mossner 1948, no. 259, pp. 517f, for Hume's position.

agency to combine in their propriety in order to approach Smith's spectator theory of political life on its own terms. From this sort of concern, some have attempted to tell the story of a general shift from the active and engaged actor of the eighteenth to the silent and passive spectator of the nineteenth century.[319] That claim, though, is probably too general to capture the nuances of the transition. For in turning to the writings of John Stuart Mill we can see Smith's conception of persuasive mediocrity taken a stage further. Not only did Mill admire the synthetic vision of persuasive agency that Smith provided, he also shared Smith's focus on the centrality of justice and propriety. At the same time, Mill substantially added to Smith's concerns about self-limitation, delusion and the tyranny of opinion, and pursued still further the darker side of the propriety of liberty and the threats to the twin requirements of self-government and justice that the modern citizen might have to face.

[319] Sennett 1976, pp. 205–18.

CHAPTER FOUR

Taking Things as They Are:
John Stuart Mill on the Judgement of Character
and the Cultivation of Civilization

Taking 'things as they are' was an ironic phrase of the philosophic radicals. Though alluding most probably to William Godwin's novel *Caleb Williams*, it naturally also bears some resemblance to Rousseau's vision of taking men as they are, and laws as they might be. Yet although Rousseau's legacy was only minimally important to the development of John Stuart Mill's political thinking, other French writers from Montesquieu to Guizot, Tocqueville and Comte played a more obvious role. Thus, many standard accounts of Mill's political thought tell us how he tried to transform a strict utilitarianism in ethics (grounded in seeking pleasure for the end of happiness), into an awareness of the incommensurable character of the values and goods that individuals cherish. That is to say, they discuss Mill's movement away from a concern with liberty as one form of self-interest, to liberty understood as both an internal and an external (or social) orientation, where the sociological quality of French debates about the *état social*, among other things, seems to have helped foster this development. These standard accounts do not usually tell us, however, that in response to a question concerning the nature of statesmanship and the practicalities of upholding laws either as they are, or indeed as they might be, Mill replied that apart from Bentham 'there are few writers better worth studying to an European thinker than Adam Smith, Montesquieu, [and] Tocqueville'.[1] Smith indeed was early on recognized by Mill as 'a great philosopher and practical judge of human nature', both for his analysis of the corrosive effects of despotism on individual character and for understanding that an excess veneration for titles, ranks and riches could 'warp the judgements of the people in favour of their rulers'.[2] This set of connections will be particularly important to my discussion. For although it assesses some of the major developments in Mill's political

---

[1] John Stuart Mill, Letter to Frederick J. Furnivall, March 30, 1871, in Mill 1972c, *CW*, vol. 17, pp. 1812f, at p. 1812.

[2] Mill 1984, *CW*, vol. 21, pp. 25, 13; also Harling 2001, pp. 107–34.

thought over time, this chapter aims to provide a synthetic interpretation that brings my account of liberty and propriety into the nineteenth century, and continues discussion about the importance of the post-Lockean political theory so far traced both for Mill in particular, and Victorian political thought in general.[3]

By 1861 and in light of many serious critiques of utilitarianism, Mill had formally recognized that even as he defended a modified utilitarianism, 'questions of ultimate ends do not admit of proof'.[4] This recognition has of course been hugely influential theoretically.[5] His *Autobiography* therefore laid down in some detail his own reasons for this conclusion, claiming his own ultimate ends involved seeking happiness indirectly, finding meaning in working for the benefit of others, and relating 'human well being, to the internal culture of the individual'.[6] This focus on internal culture is evident in Mill's sense of self. A moving letter to his friend John Sterling in 1832 found Mill asking for personal information about Sterling, instead of the wider intellectual gossip that could be found elsewhere, because such 'knowledge is the most proper object of letters, between friends'.[7] It is a poignant reminder of Mill's intellectual and emotional fragility, because his loneliness, and the lack of 'individual sympathy' he felt in the absence of a 'common object' to pursue with others, had for some years had a profound impact upon him.[8] Indeed, the youthful essays on Bentham and on Coleridge illuminate the polarities of his thought, ranging from self-realization to the utilitarian calculus, even though he was never really one of what '"the people called utilitarians"'. In fact he held 'scarcely any one of my secondary premises in common with them'.[9]

Mill's fragmentary notes on Kant similarly betrayed his awareness that universalizable maxims based on a moral law were insufficient to prompt good actions in the here and now. This point holds even though Mill's knowledge of Kant was quite generally refracted through the complex

[3] Cf. Chitnis 1986, esp. ch. 3; Burrow 1985, p. 85; Jones 2000, pp. 7ff, 14, 39, for general assessments.

[4] Mill 1969e, CW, vol. 10, p. 234.

[5] For example Berlin 1991, pp. 131–61.

[6] Mill 1981, CW, vol. 1, pp. 145ff; cf. Mill 1969e, CW, vol. 10, pp. 224f. See too Heydt 2006, esp. pp. 286–300.

[7] Mill, Letter to John Sterling, May 24, 1832, in Mill 1963, vol. 1, CW, vol. 12, pp. 98ff; cf. John Stuart Mill, Letter to John Sterling, May 29, 1844, in Mill 1963, vol. 2, CW, vol. 13, pp. 628ff, p. 629: 'Even by your existence you do more good than many by their laborious exertions'.

[8] Mill, Letter to John Sterling, April 15, 1829, Mill 1963, vol. 1, CW, vol. 12, pp. 28ff, p. 30.

[9] Mill, Letter to Thomas Carlyle, January 12, 1834, in Mill 1963, vol. 1, CW, vol. 12, p. 207.

and often distorting lens of English translations.[10] More generally, Mill's essays that most clearly show him to be the 'active and autonomous propagandist of the Benthamite doctrine' simultaneously also highlight the wider political attempts of philosophic radicalism to move beyond 'sectarian Benthamism'.[11] This was the backdrop to his wider thinking about the relationship and transition between eighteenth- and nineteenth-century thought.[12] It is not surprising, then, to find that Mill's political thinking is a project aimed at reconciling utility, autonomy and human flourishing within civilized political communities; in the view of one recent commentator, he stands between Aristotle and Bentham.[13] Only such a project, he thought, could give space both to passion and to efficiency, and this synthetic vision makes Mill's work particularly germane to understanding the contours of liberty as propriety.[14] His focus on the agency of individuals at liberty not only turns on their capacity to act upon their desires. It also shows how those desires and preferences could be ranked and judged according to the criteria of justice and value in a public forum where, ultimately, there is progress towards increasingly rational forms of political life. If that was the hope, at least, it would require a series of exemplary individuals or political theories to show the way, and this focus on the exemplary figure gives some clues to the ways in which Mill tried to defend his reconciling project and how it developed over time.

LIBERTY BY EXAMPLE

Mill's early account of Bentham's philosophy was not wholly charitable, and polemically contrasted a focus on interest with the exemplary moralism embodied by Socrates and Jesus. His concern with the cultivation of character through moral education by example was present throughout his political philosophy, and the exemplary moralism and knowledge drawn from these figures could, he argued, be brought to bear on considerations of the nature of a human life worth living. This was in part a riposte to both the felicific calculus and the predominance of representation amongst 'separate sinister interests'.[15] It was also a theme that was equally brought to bear on discussions of the need for toleration of diverse viewpoints in *On Liberty*.[16]

---

[10] Wellek 1931.

[11] Rosen 2007, esp. pp. 126, 128ff; cf. Thomas 1979; Halévy 1972, pp. 480f.

[12] Mill 1969d, *CW*, vol. 10, p. 170.

[13] Nussbaum 2004, pp. 60–68.

[14] Ryan 2007, p. 165.

[15] Mill 1977a, *CW*, vol. 18, p. 45.

[16] Mill 1977f, *CW*, vol. 18, esp. pp. 235ff, 261f, 272f.

The need for both passion and efficiency (or rationality) also under-scored Mill's critique of priestly superstition and political despotism. Such irrational and closed forms of reasoning could only be countered with the growth and development of knowledge alongside freedom of expression. He used the claim to withering effect in early debates, rhetori-cally lampooning those who rejected the need to reform representation in the British constitution and Parliament and to expand civic education.[17] Recognizing the motivating force of self-interest that drove even mem-bers of the clergy, Mill suggested that even in this 'enlightened country' the 'evils of feudal despotism and superstition' remained present in the political system. The theme was reiterated in Mill's presentation of his candidacy at Westminster, which pushed against both Tory and Burkean paeans to heritage and convention.[18] Indeed, his language was often se-vere in its castigation of the 'monster misgovernment'.[19] The current con-stitution was 'at best a shattered fragment of the feudal system', where 'religious intolerance' and the 'domination of a despotic aristocracy' were so powerful that Mill found it 'astonishing that mankind should ever have emancipated themselves' from their clutches. It was here too that he rejected the 'ascetic sophistry of the fanatic Rousseau' as a solution.[20] The idea of a general will sits uneasily with Mill's preference for developmen-tal and managed progress that allows for self-cultivation. His concomi-tant rhetorical attacks on the despotism of British political life opened up many opportunities. In particular, it helped to provide justification for one of Mill's celebrated arguments about the iniquity of denying women the vote, something he saw as contrary to both 'the general principles of justice' and to the 'particular principles of the British Constitution'.[21]

More broadly, of course, Mill's analysis of despotism in both the pri-vate and the public realms structured his attack on the subjection of women and gave it a crucial polemical edge. Marriage, like political so-ciety, should be a 'voluntary association'. Thus, just as the worry with political despotism was its creeping attack on the critical faculties, so too did the insidious idea that certain aspects of women's characters were fixed make subjection a norm, rather than a recognizably despotic form of authority.[22] Despotism restricts the potential inherent in all reasonable citizens to develop their individuality and to be judged as being in full

[17] Mill 1977, CW, vol. 18, p. 13; cf. Carlisle 1991, p. 161.

[18] Mill 1969, CW, vol. 10, esp. pp. 15f; also Mill 1988, pp. 257–61; cf. Mill 1988a, CW, vol. 26, esp. pp. 264ff; Mill 1988d, CW, vol. 26, esp. pp. 362ff, 369ff; Mill 1988i, CW, vol. 28, esp. pp. 22f.

[19] Mill 1988d, CW, vol. 26, p. 371.

[20] Mill 1988, CW, vol. 26, pp. 261, 260, 257.

[21] Mill 1988l, CW, vol. 28, esp. pp. 152f, 155.

[22] Mill 1984e, CW, vol. 21, esp. pp. 290, 283ff, 329.

possession of their freedom. In similar fashion, his analysis of the perils of a feudal political economy was as provocative as those that Smith had presented; for 'not only is no one safe from the arbitrary will of a master; even that master cannot afford him protection against other despots and slaves'.[23] His proximity to contemporary republican political theory is most obvious here. Yet, when examining Mill's discussion of political liberty, most historical discussions have tended to focus on his later years, after the publication of his major political texts, *On Liberty* and *Considerations on Representative Government*. This gives us Mill the public moralist, the Member of Parliament proposing a radical extension of rights and liberties under a modern representative government.[24] Indeed, his time in the House of Commons is typically judged favourably when seen in the light of his account of reform as a combination of art, science and persuasion.[25] But the concerns of this later period are equally to be found in much earlier work, which one can see by working progressively backwards in time.

Although the attempted synthesis of various opposing elements into a coherent and persuasive compound, central to Mill's reconciliatory political project, remained in the background during the election campaign of 1865, he nevertheless clearly outlined the three elements of his 'political creed'. The first was a recognition that 'perfect government' lay in the future, so that what was required was the 'emancipation of the dependent classes—more freedom, more equality, and more responsibility of each person for himself'. Second, in acknowledging the ideas of Comte that contemporary institutions were, 'or ought to be, in a state of advance', the time was ripe for the presentation of certain truths, 'although the time may not yet have arrived for carrying them into effect. That is what I mean by advanced Liberalism'. The allusion surely referred to his involvement with women's suffrage, parliamentary reform in Britain and Ireland, and the Governor Eyre controversy. Finally, a third element was his recognition of the need for 'reasonable compromise', not just at Westminster, but also in politics more generally.[26] Compromise was justified either for its utility or as a process towards a desired end. It was contingent upon ideas being expressed at culturally apposite moments.[27] This was important to his debate with Gustav d'Eichtal about Saint-Simonism, where he suggested that 'if that doctrine were true', then its adoption 'will be the natural result and effect of a high state of moral and intellectual culture'. It

---

[23] Mill 1988, CW, vol. 26, p. 259.
[24] Collini 1991, ch. 3; 1990, pp. 307–22. See also Carlisle 1998, pp. 143–67.
[25] Kinzer, Robson and Robson 1992, pp. 18f, 21, 22–66.
[26] Mill 1988i CW, vol. 28, p. 23.
[27] Thompson 2007, esp. pp. 175ff.

should not, however, be forced upon peoples not yet ready for it. Liberty was a work in progress.[28] Therefore the systems of the Fourierists and Saint-Simonians looked to a better future without doing 'violence to any of the general laws by which human action, even in the present imperfect state of moral and intellectual cultivation, is influenced'.[29]

In terms of progress and perfectibility, Coleridge's attempt to reconcile the forces of progression with those of permanence in the form of the landed aristocracy and commercial interest had a profound attraction.[30] Mill thought figures like Coleridge and Condorcet were 'perfectibilian' in their concern with the capacity for human excellence.[31] Moreover, the religious and political perfectibilism they enunciated was mirrored in Mill's discussion of the necessary combination of systematically opposed positions even within the British political system. An 'established clergy' teaching only one doctrine, for example, is 'the bitter enemy' because there never is one best way of acting for all time and without fail, and sometimes even barbarians are good for society. Indeed, the idea that the state itself might be an embodiment of superior knowledge is simply a misnomer. Those who think in that way will have to answer the question why 'our perfect government finds it very difficult to prevent half our population from dying of hunger and our perfect religion has not yet found the means of preventing our jails from being constantly full'.[32] Perfect government might be unrealizable, but it was, like individual happiness, the end of political life and required specific guides to action for both individuals and nations. This was a standard position (in fact rather like that of de Staël), and it was, in part, what his analysis of civilization was designed to elucidate.[33] It was a theme of balance, compromise and moderation.

[28] John Stuart Mill, Letter to Gustave d'Eichtal, February 9, 1830, in Mill 1963, CW, vol. 12, pp. 44–49, at p. 49; cf. John Stuart Mill, Letter to Gustave d'Eichtal and Charles Duveyrier, May 30, 1832, in Mill 1963, CW, vol. 12, pp. 107ff, esp. p. 109: 'I suppose that a St Simonian can learn only from his own thoughts or those of other St Simonians; but I who am not a St Simonian, though I greately admire the St Simonians, & think that they are in many respects far ahead of all Europe, am yet firmly convinced that you have yet much to learn, in political economy from the English economists (inferior as they are to you in many points) and in the philosophy of history, literature and the arts, from the Germans'.

[29] Mill 1965, CW, vol. 2, bks. 1–2, bk. 2, ch. 1, § 4, p. 213.

[30] See Capaldi 2003, pp. 98, 120; Edwards 2004, esp. pp. 98ff.

[31] Mill 1988g, CW, vol. 26, p. 430.

[32] Mill 1988f, CW, vol. 26, p. 425.

[33] Mill 1969e, CW, vol. 10, pp. 224f; cf. Brougham 1835, esp. p. 70: 'Constitutional improvements and law improvements are of admirable merit; but the main end of all laws and of every constitution is the solid happiness of the people—and for this end, the people must now have cheap government, and a limited monarchy, on the scale for and sufficing to a limited monarchy, which the English people love, not a haughty and extravagant aristocracy, which they detest'. Cf. Staël 1813, p. 10; cf. pp. 45, 52ff.

Thus, in *On Liberty*, he moved from a discussion of perfectibility to notice that 'in politics, again, it is almost a commonplace, that a party of order or stability, and a party of progress or reform, are both necessary elements of a healthy political life'.[34] There was nothing necessarily radical in this position, as ultra-Tories like de Quincey held exactly the same view.[35] But his creed built on the foundations laid by the analysis of freedom in *On Liberty* in other important ways, particularly where Mill had earlier attempted to demarcate the political from the economic realm. Economic liberty is a matter of political economy, a discipline with its own laws and procedures, and governmental intervention on economic grounds is taken to have nothing to do with political or civil liberty.[36] Political liberty is the sphere within which the 'self-government' of the individual cannot be violated, and is the foundation for those later considerations of responsibility, compromise and progress. Much of the rest of *On Liberty* is taken up with defending this claim about self-government, but defending it in terms of the virtues its defence promotes. Self-government leads towards freedom of opinion and of expression, the freedom to criticize custom and seek after higher pleasures, as well as the maintenance of religious freedom. The related benefits of what might otherwise look like a charivari of moral pluralism, or even of moral distress and non-conformity, all stem from this bedrock of political liberty.[37] This way of expressing the point puts Mill as close to Lockean liberty as propriety, as it does to some more recent political philosophy that moves away from Rawls-inspired discussions of justice.[38]

To be successful, ideas had to be timely, and the limitations of self-government in an age that was not ready for them, and whose citizens were not politically self-aware enough for them, was a constant worry for Mill. This is why the contrast between the ancients and the moderns, particularly between the Greeks and the moderns, held such importance. The moderns certainly lacked anything like 'classical' public virtue, which had now become a 'mere rhetorical ornament'.[39] Equally, though, without self-awareness, the restraints imposed upon themselves by individuals who conform to the dictates of custom can actually rob them of their freedom in two ways. First, their sphere of action is restricted through lack of critical awareness, so that their very desires cease to be

[34] Mill 1977f, CW, vol. 19, pp. 253f.
[35] Lindop 1993, pp. 285f.
[36] Mill 1977, CW, vol. 18, pp. 293, 306; Stimson and Milgate 2001, esp. pp. 233ff; Baum 1999, esp. pp. 500–506.
[37] Waldron 1993, pp. 115–33.
[38] Ashcraft 1989, esp. p. 123; claims repeated in Ashcraft 1998, p. 187.
[39] Mill 1978e, CW, vol. 11, p. 314.

truly their own.[40] The self-censorship that exists in contemporary society, buttressed by industrialization, exploitation of labour, colonial administration and the despotism of custom, is inimical to liberty understood as the full flowering of individuality.[41] Second, although individual freedom may be constrained by material factors, the example of the Greeks (obviously inflected through Humboldt's Germanized Hellenism) showed the centrality of happiness underpinning Mill's vision of liberty.[42] In this, he was part of a wider set of debates that raged about the utility of the classical past for the contemporary world in Victorian England, where philosophers agonized over interpretations of Plato or the Roman Empire, and into which he had been thrust at the tender age of six and a half, when writing on the decline and fall of Rome![43] Two further points are worth noting in this context.

First, Mill's criticism of religious doctrine, and more specifically of an intolerant Calvinism, also provided important background for his account of the prudery and prurience that accompanies many contemporary societies. In the British case especially, Calvinist rigidity in particular, but Puritanism more generally, had distorted national awareness of the social power of the arts and the dynamic force of ideas in history, in favour of self-denial and commercial reward. Reacting against the Puritan legacy of his father seems likely to have had something to do with this as well.[44] In fact Mill's was a reaction against those militant expressions of Protestantism as 'inward warfare' or radical self-denial, even though both he and his opponents thought that rational religion could only flourish in advanced states of civilization. This might mean that England held the key to universal peace and prosperity.[45] Mill would explore these connections between education and commerce in detail in a lengthy inaugural address at St. Andrews, suggesting that the profit motive was detrimental to those seeking cultivation through education. His purpose was obviously to rail against those Englishmen 'whose ambition is self-regarding' and who simply wanted to get rich quickly.[46] It was a pedagogically minded critique of an apparent 'trade morality' or conventional morality

[40] Mill 1977f, CW, vol. 18, p. 241.

[41] Mill 1977f, CW, vol. 18, pp. 264ff.

[42] See Urbinati 2002, esp. pp. 141, 147, 151ff; Williams 1996, esp. pp. 9ff, 13.

[43] Irwin 1992, pp. 279–310; cf. Turner 1986, pp. 577–99; Vance 1997. See also John Stuart Mill, 'The History of Rome', written at the age six and a half. Harriet J. Mill presented the tract to the British Library in a small folio on April 29, 1887. See BL Add. Mss. 33, 230, fos. 10–20. More broadly, Bell 2006, esp. pp. 740ff.

[44] Capaldi 2003, p. 276; Reeve 2007, pp. 18ff; cf. [Anon.] 1844, pp. 477f; Chalmers 1820, esp. pp. 31, 35, 238f, 272f.

[45] Alison 1852, pp. 49f 206f; for later academic reflections, see Pollock 1882, pp. 209–25, pp. 376–91, 453–67; see too Burrow 1984.

[46] Mill 1984d, CW, vol. 21, esp. p. 253.

that he also assailed in the *Principles of Political Economy* (as had Adam Smith) and which could best be countered by education.[47] Fellow travellers like John Pringle Nichol advocated the same thing. By utilizing his expert knowledge of astronomy and the nebular hypothesis especially, Nichol was able to facilitate both popular and scholarly knowledge by promoting the cultivation of character through education.[48] Indeed, expertise and contemporary scientific discussion affected the languages of politics often as much as direct political events, with their focus on character, corruption and degeneration, transformism and the superiority of certain types (often medical) of knowledge.[49]

However, the detrimental effects of religious intolerance were in any case profound, and if 'character' were to be rescued by cultivation, then something more than another form of religious inspiration would be needed. This is, at least in part, what pushed Mill towards his unfinished project of ethology.[50] He submitted that much more than 'Christian ethics' alone would be required for the 'moral regeneration of man', and both Pagan self-assertion and Christian self-denial were complementary to this (never-to-be completed) science of character. In part, this project updated classical historiographical battles over notions of self-fashioning or self-cultivation familiar from interpretations of the Renaissance, though the terminology was specifically drawn from his friend Sterling.[51] In other places, the ideal of good character and therefore of hedonistic utilitarianism seemed to require a synthesis of Epicurean pleasure, Stoic self-control, and Christian self-denial, a claim that perhaps speaks most obviously to its force as an ideal, rather than a possible reality.[52] Yet if the claims in *On Liberty* are to be taken seriously, Mill's ideal-type personality who expressed the synthesis of these divergent elements was Pericles. A modern-day equivalent might be Turgot.[53] The claim about Christian religion, however, clearly struck against those who uncritically viewed scripture as the basis of political power and histori-

[47] Mill 1967b, CW, vol. 5, p. 625; cf. Mill 1965, CW, vol. 2, bk. 2, ch. 1, § 4, p. 210; also Mill 1967, p. 130.

[48] Nichol 1852, esp. pp. 217, 220, 225f; cf. Nichol 1837, esp. Letter VII, 'The Nebular Hypothesis', pp. 145ff. For discussion, Schaffer, esp. pp. 132, 134ff, 143ff, 147f, 152.

[49] See Desmond 1989, esp. pp. 99f, 107, 118, 121; cf. Hilton 2001, esp. pp. 182f, 185ff, 193ff, 197.

[50] Eisenach 1998, esp. pp. 222ff, 226ff; cf. Mill 1974, CW, vol. 8, bk. 6, ch. 5, § 4, pp. 861–74.

[51] Mill 1977f, CW, vol. 18, pp. 246–49, 264–67; also Sterling 1848, vol. 1, p. 190; discussed in Rosen 2004, pp. 181–94. Cf. Bullen, esp. pp. 119f.

[52] Mill 1969e, CW, vol. 10, pp. 210f.

[53] Mill 1967, CW, vol. 4, p. 139: 'With the exception of Turgot, the history of the world does not, perhaps, afford another example of a minister steadfastly adhering to general principles in defiance of the clamours of the timid and interested of all parties'.

cal chronology, to say nothing of its function as exemplary literature. It was precisely this theme that the geological revolution would come to challenge in necessitating revisions to extant notions of time, which then aligned with newly focused appreciations of both cultural difference and the idea of progress.[54] Moreover, in his writings on religion Mill had recognized the autonomy of worldly glory (as exemplified by Achilles) from a belief in Heaven, and even mooted the possibility of the cultivation of humankind through the triumph of 'supernatural religion' over the 'religion of humanity'. But he was also aware of the potentially evil results of attributing supernatural causes to morality, as well as the problematic use of faith to justify politics; as Frederic Harrison would later suggest, do that and 'you might as well give men loaded revolvers and send them to a stormy meeting with orders to convince their opponents'.[55] In fact, Mill seems to have reacted strongly against earlier reformulations of natural religion towards the idea that virtue could coincide with self-interest, and that revelation could be ignored.[56] Combining a focus on political imagination as a particular form of art with a claim that conventional justice was insufficient fully to promote human agency in terms of moral excellence and cultivation, Mill seems to have hoped for a reformation of reformed religion in Victorian society.[57]

His updating of Coleridge's idea of a national clerisy was crucial in grounding the twin ideals of competence and cultivation through the spiritual invigoration of a nation. That project required the use of advanced knowledge by an elite to ensure the progressive development of character. 'Few people' he wrote, 'have exercised more influence over my thoughts and character' than Coleridge. And even with the relatively sparse amount of published material there was to go on, Mill hailed him as 'the most systematic thinker of our time, without excepting even Bentham'.[58] His clerisy was not a body designed to simply impose religious doctrine on the people, but instead to focus on 'the highest per-

[54] See S. R. Bosanquet 1866, esp. pp. 16, 19, 52; cf. Buckland 1836, vol. 1, pp. 6, 8f, 11, and esp. 13f, asserting no discrepancy between the Mosaic narrative and 'our interpretation of the phenomena of Nature'. Cf. Burrow 2000, esp. pp. 210ff; Hilton 2008, esp. pp. 333ff.

[55] Mill 1969g, CW, vol. 10, esp. 'Utility of Religion', pp. 403–28, quotations from pp. 427, 419, 417; Harrison 1885, p. 12.

[56] Mill 1969c, CW, vol. 10, esp. pp. 144f; see too Heydt 2006a, pp. 99–115.

[57] Mill 1974, CW, vol. 8, pp. 943f; see too Devigne 2006, esp. pp. 16ff, 21, 23.

[58] Mill, Letter to John Pringle Nichol, April 15, 1834, in Mill 1963, CW, vol. 12, pp. 220–23, at p. 221; also Knights 1978. See too Mill, Letter to John Sterling, September 28, 1839, in Mill 1963, CW, vol. 13, pp. 405ff, at p. 406. In his manuscripts, Coleridge also elaborated a scheme for the 'total man', derived from Spinoza amongst others. See his discussion in BL. Edgerton Mss. 2801, esp. fos. 2, 3 (on Bayle's 'collectaneous Learning and vain Multiscience' and Spinoza's biography), 4–5, 7 (on his 'vindiciolae Spinozae'), 10–11 (on Spinoza's project), and especially fo. 77 on his 'Schema of the total man as a whole'.

fection of their mental and spiritual nature'.[59] This required still further synthesis, however, as both Protestant and New Testament Christianity were insufficient for the purposes of moral regeneration. Their 'negative' ideals were rooted in asceticism, whilst the pronouncements of the Old Testament were 'intended only for a barbarous people'.[60]

Therefore, the second major point to note is Mill's recognition that merely adhering to the requirements of justice is insufficient to develop liberty as individuality. It is enough to maintain formal freedom as justice, despite the fact that most people take justice and right simply to be 'conformity to custom'.[61] But, for Mill, justice rightly understood is a necessary condition for the potential development of a concern for the claims of others. In turn, this is a further precondition for cultivating an *atmosphere* of freedom'. Only under this atmosphere can genius and conflicts of opinion truly flourish.[62] He knew of the existentially malign effects of conformity, as well as the 'despotism of custom' that promoted 'collective mediocrity', and he drew the political conclusions. Government should always try to prevent itself, in the 'government of mediocrity', from becoming 'mediocre government'.[63] Thereafter, the 'propriety or impropriety of government interference is customarily tested', and people decide best for themselves if they are able to recognize the importance of rule by the 'better Few'.[64]

Mill saw this particular vision of rule as part of a wider project, and focused on the implications of contemporary utilitarian doctrines concerned with the 'greatest happiness principle', particularly their development of Epicurean themes about the importance of justice and intellectual pleasure. This had to be made more appealing, both rhetorically and emotionally, to a new audience in a new age.[65] Equally, although Mill thought the Stoic view of virtue was predicated upon a 'paradoxical misuse of language', he knew his own defence of the worldliness of experience and self-cultivation had clear affinities with Stoicism.[66] Indeed, both endorsing the view that Smith among others had earlier presented and presaging the analysis in *On Liberty*, Mill suggested that multiple in-

[59] Mill 1967a, CW, vol. 4, p. 220; cf. John Stuart Mill, Letter to John Sterling, October 20, 1831, in Mill 1963, CW, vol. 12, pp. 74–88, esp. p. 76.

[60] Mill 1977f, CW, vol. 18, p. 255; cf. John Stuart Mill, Letter to Henry Franks, July 21, 1865, in Mill 1972a, CW, vol. 15, p. 1080, on the logical commensurability between Christian persecution and the 'providential government of human affairs'. Cf. Hales 1794, pp. 26f.

[61] Mill 1977f, CW, vol. 18, p. 272; cf. Smith 1991, esp. pp. 254f.

[62] Mill 1977f, CW, vol. 18, pp. 266ff, emphasis in original.

[63] Mill 1977f, CW, vol. 18, pp. 269, 272f.

[64] Mill 1977f, CW, vol. 18, pp. 223, 269.

[65] Mill 1969e, CW, vol. 10, pp. 210f; cf. Rosen 2003, p. 83.

[66] Mill 1969e, CW, vol. 10, pp. 221, 218.

gredients, more than simple hedonism of an Epicurean cast, were needed
to promote human flourishing. Given his awareness of the multiplicity of
pleasures, Mill laid it down that the right conduct of an agent requires
a focus on the community as a whole. Thus, 'utilitarianism requires him
to be as strictly impartial as a disinterested and benevolent spectator'.[67]
Something similar to a Christian ethic minimally underpins this argument, although just as Smith seemed to use the language of loving one's
neighbour in a slightly ironic way, Mill also seemed to reconcile utilitarian and Christian morality for the purposes of political persuasion more
than anything. To reiterate the point, taken alone, Christian ethics are
not enough. Rather, the broader intersubjective connections that promote
sympathy, even in the 'comparatively early state of human advancement
in which we now live', had to take precedence.[68]

This concern with sympathy remained a long-standing commitment.
When defending his *Logic*, Mill restated the claim that this 'normal
form of moral feeling' is a 'natural outgrowth from the social nature
of man'. On it, when 'combined with a human creature's capacity of
fellow-feeling, the feelings of morality properly so called seem to me to be
grounded, & their main constituent to be the idea of punishment'. Mill's
Smithian sounding use of the benevolent spectator, and his contrast between justice and beneficence, had already been extensively documented
in occasional pieces as well as in his discussion of utilitarianism, which he
thought the 'nearest approach I am able to make to a theory of our moral
feelings'.[69] Whether his synthetic compound remains coherent, given the
claims about causal determinism and compatibilism he also defends, is
a difficult point, as critics noted. In his *Logic*, the idea of dispositional
freedom is elaborated, such that our 'feeling, of being able to modify our
own character *if we wish*, is itself the feeling of moral freedom which we
are conscious of'.[70] The idea of choosing to amend our character seems
to imply unfreedom if the choice is neither acted upon nor open to us,
in what contemporary philosophy would see as a rather atomistic view
of autonomy. But such dispositional freedom cannot be the whole story,
for we must actually have the capacity to succeed in amending our character, and our character is shaped by our context. Indeed, in the last editions of the *Logic* he saw through the press in 1872, Mill added a final
moralizing sentence to his claim about freedom, suggesting that freedom

[67] Mill 1969e, CW, vol. 10, p. 218; cf. Jeffrey 1808, esp. p. 276, who attacked Hume for
promoting Epicurean 'luxury' over liberty; Fontana 1985, pp. 89f.

[68] Mill 1969e, CW, vol. 10, pp. 218, 233; cf. Mill 1977f, CW, vol. 18, pp. 248f, 266.

[69] John Stuart Mill, Letter to William George Ward, November 28, 1859, in Mill 1972a,
CW, vol. 15, pp. 646–50, pp. 649f. Emphasis in original.

[70] Mill 1974, CW, vol. 8, p. 841; cf. Tuck 2008, esp. pp. 138f.

requires a person to be 'confirmed in virtue'.[71] This view is pervasive in his work, even if it is textually problematic, though perhaps some sense can be made of it by focusing on the idea of (social or political) freedom as propriety.[72]

Indeed, Mill elsewhere acknowledged that claims of right are rooted in justice, and that there are no rights or demands that others can claim concerning our beneficence. Thus, claims of justice are those that prompt a 'desire to punish' a 'definite individual' who has done harm to another, and they are rooted in our natural 'instincts', namely the 'impulse of self-defence, and the feeling of sympathy'.[73] Sympathy is a distinctively human trait, but it is not innately moral; it develops as a corollary of the 'essence of conscience', which is to say the properly 'disinterested' development of the 'internal sanction of duty'.[74] Its relevance here lies in Mill's claim that 'the sentiment of justice appears to me to be, the animal desire to repel or retaliate a hurt or damage to oneself, or to those with whom one sympathizes; widened so as to include all persons, by the human capacity for enlarged sympathy, and the human conception of intelligent self-interest'.[75] Mill the liberal utilitarian could hardly have sounded more like Adam Smith, and could therefore hardly be closer to the analysis of liberty as propriety. Equally, it is this 'sense of justice' and reciprocity that John Rawls saw Mill as developing, almost in spite of his self-professed liberal utilitarianism.[76] In his account of why it is necessary to provide justificatory reasons for the defence of what one might term relative virtues like temperance, rather than simply allowing moral judgements to be grounded in public opinion writ large, Mill shows that liberty as propriety is a goal to be worked towards. It requires a certain developmental progress to have been made before it can properly begin to work.[77] Rawls was certainly an astute reader of Mill on this point.

Put slightly differently, justice is rooted in the 'natural feeling of resentment', which is 'moralized' to give it social purchase because the need for security and protection from harm places it 'above the simply Expedient'.[78] Justice therefore is artifice, as are moral feelings, and justice is in fact a 'sentiment which sanctions the rule[s]' of conduct that are universal in terms of being both for the good of all individuals, and which

[71] Mill 1974, CW, vol. 8, p. 841; excellent discussion in Smith 1980, esp. pp. 245f, 249ff.
[72] Smith 1980a, esp. pp. 434ff, 443, 448f.
[73] Mill 1969e, CW, vol. 10, pp. 248f, 247f; see too Mill 1984a, CW, vol. 21, pp. 77–79.
[74] Mill 1969e, CW, vol. 10, pp. 248, 250, 228.
[75] Mill 1969e, CW, vol. 10, p. 250.
[76] Rawls 1973, pp. 501f; cf. pp. 46–50.
[77] Mill 1969d, CW, vol. 10, esp. pp. 194f.
[78] Mill 1969e, CW, vol. 10, pp. 259, 256; cf. Mill 1969e, CW, vol. 10, p. 223.

express a desire to punish those who break these general rules.[79] So the duty of man is to 'amend it' (justice) by his nature, a nature governed by self-interest or a 'kind of selfishness' that only experience can turn into self-control.[80] Justice requires both external rules of conduct and internal sentiments that will sanction and track such rules. To put it in his terms, justice is 'a right residing in an individual', and a 'name for certain classes of moral rules, which concern the essentials of human well-being more nearly, and are therefore of more absolute obligation, than any other rules to the guidance of life'.[81] In this sense, Mill's account of utilitarianism and the relationship of justice to free agency and political liberty appears congruent with Smith's earlier analysis.[82] It focuses on the problem of how to overcome the partiality of self-interest and the lack of mental cultivation that promotes harm, under conditions of limited sociability.[83] Because natural sociability was clearly weaker than various unsocial instincts, only the 'rightly brought-up human being' could adequately counter them.[84] As he would reiterate, those acts injurious to the rights of others 'are fit objects of moral reprobation, and, in grave cases, of moral retribution and punishment'.[85] He knew full well that resentment stemmed from 'wrongful aggression' as well as unjust impediments to freedom, and he found plenty of resources in the work of the ancient Greeks to prove it.[86]

GREEK LEGACIES

Something of the Greek cast of Mill's political theory was integrated into his discussion of moral sentiments. He argued that the 'most anti-social and odious of all passions, envy; dissimulation and insincerity; irascibility on insufficient cause, and resentment disproportioned to the provocation; the love of domineering over others; the desire to engross more than one's share of advantages (the πλεονεχια of the Greeks)' were the staple features of bad character, if not 'properly immoralities'. But such passions are 'only a subject of moral reprobation where they involve a breach of duty to others, for whose sake the individual is bound to have care for him-

[79] Mill 1969e, CW, vol. 10, pp. 249f.
[80] Mill 1969g, CW, vol. 10, 'Nature', pp. 373–402, esp. pp. 396f, 394; Mill 1969e, CW, vol. 10, p. 230.
[81] Mill 1969e, CW, vol. 10, p. 255.
[82] Mill 1969e, CW, vol. 10, p. 249.
[83] Mill 1969e, CW, vol. 10, pp. 215ff. 231, 228, 232.
[84] Mill 1969, CW, vol. 10, pp. 263–368, p. 310; cf. Mill 1969e, CW, vol. 10, p. 231.
[85] Mill 1977f, CW, vol. 18, p. 279.
[86] Mill 1969e, CW, vol. 10, pp. 255f.

self'. Duty is equable with 'self-respect or self-development', and on Mill's terms, was to be extracted from individuals just like a debt, in a variation on the Platonic theme of just individuals as those who pay their debts and who act in ways that promote both psychic and political harmony.[87] This is the way of overcoming the negative consequences of both a desire for more, and a desire for more than others have, indicative of *pleonexia*.[88] Nevertheless, the true expression of morally cultivated character and the mark of a civilized society is that duty and responsible moral action (the *honestum* and the *utile*) coincide without coercion, even though external sanctions are still required to promote care for others.[89] Just as Smith had inferred, in Mill's eyes as well those agents who show rashness or self-deceit 'must expect to be lowered in the opinion of others, and to have a less share of their favourable sentiments'. They must also know that they have no right to complain about such treatment.[90] The important role for moral sentiments here was clearly compatible with Mill's earlier accounts of how those who cultivate both their mental faculties and their 'fellow-feeling' with others are liable, on the evidence of any 'competent judges', to live a more worthwhile life than those who do not.[91] Indeed, recognizing the effects others have on our lives provides one of the foundation stones of morality according to Mill, for it requires us to focus on the 'regulation of outward actions'. The other element, as has already been implied and as is well known, is that of 'self-education'.[92]

The more general contrast often drawn by Mill between Jesus and Socrates in another obvious way helps to illustrate the Greek legacies behind his intellectual position. Not only were they moral exemplars, crushed by the conformity of law and opinion prevalent in their own time.[93] They also had contemporary political relevance. This was particularly true in the case of Socrates, though in the so-called Golden Rule of Jesus of Nazareth one could equally read 'the complete ethics of utility'.[94] Mill admired the translation by Connop Thirlwall in *The Philological Museum* of Schleiermacher's essay 'On the Worth of Socrates as a Philosopher'.[95] He also used Thirlwall's translation of Schleierma-

---

[87] Mill 1977f, *CW*, vol. 18, p. 279.

[88] Plato 1997b, 442E–443A; Schofield 2006, pp. 306f, 278f, n. 38.

[89] Mill 1969e, *CW*, vol. 10, pp. 246, 232.

[90] Mill 1977f, *CW*, vol. 18, p. 278.

[91] Mill 1969e, *CW*, vol. 10, pp. 215, 213.

[92] Mill 1969b, *CW*, vol. 10, p. 98.

[93] See John Stuart Mill, Letter to John Allen, May 27, 1867, in Mill 1972b, *CW*, vol. 16, part 3, pp. 1273f: 'I do not undervalue "what teachers of religion can affect". I rate it most highly, but what they *do* effect I rate very low'. Emphasis in original.

[94] Mill 1969e, *CW*, vol. 10, p. 218.

[95] See Mill 1978f, *CW*, vol. 11, pp. 241ff; Schleiermacher 1833, pp. 538–55; 1833a, pp. 556–61; Mill 1978c, *CW*, vol. 11, pp. 151–74. See too Demetriou 2002, esp. pp. 55–58.

cher's introduction to the 'Apology of Socrates', when presenting that speech to an English audience. In his early notices of several of Plato's dialogues, Mill would typically convey some note of current import into his discussion. For example, he argued that the intellectual origins of Anglo-European logical philosophical analysis were rooted in Platonic thought.[96] More obviously political was the question, outlined when citing from *Protagoras*, of whether virtue could be taught. Already in 1831 Mill suggested that Socrates upholds 'as emphatically' as it was ever presented by Epicurus or Bentham the 'principle of utility', even if the more general tenor of Plato's dialogues seemed to suggest that 'certain qualities of mind are good and evil in themselves', irrespective of questions of pain and pleasure.[97] If virtue could be taught, there was a naturally a special role for political leadership and competence.

In these discussions, Mill entered the battle over this classical heritage that was informing contemporary politics. As he put it, 'interest in Grecian history is unexhausted and inexhaustible', and within that field, 'all others are eclipsed by Athens'.[98] It was a 'source of light and civilization' to the world.[99] Writers like Francis Mitford and the ecclesiastical and Tory authors in the *Quarterly Review* 'exaggerated grossly the mischievous tendency [and influence] of what the Sophists taught', with the 'base purpose of discrediting free institutions and freedom of inquiry', he suggested.[100] This was a long-standing ideological refrain in Mill's work, and he claimed that the current contempt towards the Sophists 'would be better bestowed on the tuition of Eton or Westminster'.[101] The Tory view of Greece was offered as a clear example of the dangers of democratic institutions. But it was not properly until George Grote's account of Plato particularly, and of Greece in general, that a sustained defence of Greece began to matter to debates about the British constitution, and which could counter the Tory preference for Sparta.[102] Mill would himself call the Spartans 'those hereditary Tories and Conservatives of Greece'.[103] He was both a friend and critic of Grote, but as radical reformers both were

[96] Mill 1978a, CW, vol. 11, esp. pp. 93ff.

[97] Mill 1978, CW, vol. 11, esp. p. 61.

[98] Mill 1978d, CW, vol. 11, p 273; Mill 1978e, CW, vol. 11, p. 315.

[99] Mill 1986, CW, vol. 22, esp. p. 253; also Freeman 1873, pp. 107–48.

[100] Mill 1978, CW, vol. 11, p. 43; cf. Mill 1981, CW, vol. 1, p. 15; Grote 1826, pp. 269–311; Momigliano 1952.

[101] Mill 1981b, CW, vol. 1, pp. 335f.

[102] Turner 1981, pp. 228f, 237, 448f; Mill 1978e, p. 329, for Grote on Plato's one-sided view of the Sophists; see too Mill 1988d, CW, vol. 26, p. 367, *contra* Mitford. In general, Demetriou 1996, pp. 280–97; 2009, pp. 35–61.

[103] Mill, 1978d, CW, vol. 11, p. 303.

keen, as Mill put it, to learn all that they could from those intelligent partisans with whom they disagreed.[104] And they often also disagreed amongst themselves. Grote's analysis directly criticized aristocratic or conservative dominance within democratic constitutions, features Mill took care to emphasize in the British context as he saw the need for competent, indeed 'scientific' governors, a theme he would reiterate in numerous places, particularly in discussions of colonial rule.[105] Grote, on the other hand, was clearly more disposed to the indeterminacy of 'democracy', as his critical engagement with Thucydides showed.[106] Mill sided instead with Montesquieu, who thought representation a valuable good precisely because the public were not well placed to deliberate upon political business. Both, however, desired what Mill termed a form of 'deference to mental superiority'.[107]

Similarly, Mill's anti-hedonistic reading of Socrates was important. He ignored Grote's obvious worry that Socrates looked rather like a utility-maximizing individual, in a vision of self-interest that Mill thought Grote (and indeed Plato) saw everywhere.[108] He also ignored Grote's pointed criticism that Socrates wouldn't be allowed to be himself, at least as the character we think we know, if he ever happened to find himself in Plato's ideal Republic.[109] He cut a frustrated and frustrating figure.[110] So instead Mill utilized his discussion of Plato, and Grote on Plato, to bring out the importance for his own views of the problem of social conformity, even as he upheld the ideal that something like a Socratic and questioning standard could really be the best way normatively to organize political life.[111] That is to say, Mill welcomed Plato's belief that rulers had to be inured against the malignant effects of customary despotism in order to be able to do their job, whilst still praising the virtues of Athenian democracy. In his mind, these two things were not at all contradictory. This

---

[104] Grote, BL Add. Mss. 29, 519, fos. 11–12, with Mill's marginal annotations on Grote's style, particularly the friendly but chiding: 'I think it is a very frequent practice with you to join together two verbs where one would suffice: this gives a degree of heaviness to the style'. See too Mill 1969c, CW, vol. 10, p. 163.

[105] Mill 1977g, CW, vol. 19, esp. pp. 567ff, 573.

[106] Mill 1978g, CW, vol. 11, p. 439; Mill 1978e, CW, vol. 11, pp. 322, 329.

[107] Mill 1977g, CW, vol. 19, p. 510; cf. Montesquieu 1989, 2. 11. 6, p. 159; 1964, p. 587; Urbinati 2002, pp. 67ff; Manin 1997, pp. 70–74.

[108] Mill 1978g, CW, vol. 11, pp. 438f, writes that it is 'continually visible in Mr. Grote's book, as well as in the works themselves, how strong a hold the idea of the Division of Labour had taken on Plato's mind. He propounds it as explicitly as Adam Smith'.

[109] Irwin 1998, esp. pp. 424f, 426–31, 437ff.

[110] See Grote, BL Add. Mss. 29, 522, esp. fos. 161–167ᵛ.

[111] Burnyeat 1998, esp. pp. 360ff, on the contrasting interpretations of Socrates by Grote and Mill; cf. Urbinati 2002, esp. pp. 129f, 132–38, 141f.

was so despite the fact that promoting certain forms of civic sentiment might well conflict with the idea of toleration for diverse viewpoints, and despite Mill's reticence to explicitly acknowledge the similarities between his aims and objectives and those of his classical forebears.[112] As an argument for leadership by experts, the claim was certainly powerful and keenly felt in Victorian intellectual circles, but if conformity to received opinion was the central problem, it could affect political leaders as much as ordinary citizens.[113]

In his presentation of the *Gorgias*, Mill lamented the fact that 'civilization, with its *laissez-aller* and its *laissez-faire* which it calls tolerance', had rendered individuals safe. Now at least there was no likelihood of having to drink hemlock like Socrates, or being put on the cross, like Christ, but equally there was little in the way of obvious reward for the 'moral hero'.[114] This ambivalent feature of civilization would be continually refined in his work, particularly that expressed in periodical writing. The text of his celebrated essay on 'Civilization' was itself first published in a journal he edited, and editors and contributors to such publications played a huge role in shaping nineteenth-century British political discourse.[115] Mill was no exception to this pattern, save in his finding the shifting valence of anonymity in many of the reviews 'one of the evils of modern periodical writing'.[116] He echoed too his father's views on the *Edinburgh Review*, suggesting it 'exhibited the vices which are described as likely to characterize a periodical publication of the Opposition party'. For this reason, the elder Mill's axioms about the capacity of good government to trump claims about advancing liberty were taken as a yardstick for evaluating attitudes to political events.[117] Many ideologically motivated opponents held similar views about the *Edinburgh*, though for different reasons.[118] When writing to Tocqueville apropos his forthcoming review of the second volume of *Democracy in America* for that journal, Mill reminded his correspondent that the *Edinburgh* had failed to review the first part because it was 'the most perfect representative of the 18th century to be found in our day'. This might have been one of the reasons why Mill found the review 'tough work', while he would surely have appreciated the Greek elements of Tocqueville's account of

[112] See Irwin 1998, esp. pp. 433f, 442ff, 452–56.
[113] Mill 1978g, CW, vol. 11, p. 403; cf. Schofield 2006, pp. 138ff; Demetriou 1996a, esp. pp. 17ff, 32ff.
[114] Mill 1978b, CW, vol. 11, p. 149.
[115] Milne 1984, p. 92.
[116] Mill 1981c, CW, vol. 1, p. 370.
[117] Mill 1981a, CW, vol. 1, pp. 293, 295.
[118] See [Anon.] 1817, esp. pp. 17, 20; [Anon.] 1810.

rule as well.[119] However, in this world of periodical publication he supplemented these eighteenth-century legacies with not only Tocqueville, but also the political thought of the French *Doctrinaires*. In general, these writers (particularly Guizot) had highlighted an irony: as civilization has progressed, 'power and fitness for power, have altogether ceased to correspond'.[120] This central paradox of the 'spirit of the age' so-called was that although history might be divided into eras of progress and regress, to say so was simply to highlight the chasm between the ancients and the moderns.[121] What societies that progress share is a capacity to synthesize the best in previous belief systems and to update them according to the needs of the contemporary moment. This was a theoretical as well as an historical point for Mill, expressed in his account of the role of religion, alongside 'critical philosophy' in the development of society.[122] It highlighted a still more general thesis about the primacy of ideas in societal and civilisational advance.[123] Progress was the gradual overcoming of bad ideas or of ideas unfit for their times, so that the 'entire history of social improvement has been a series of transitions, by which one custom or institution after another, far from being supposed a primary necessity of social existence, has passed into the rank of a universally stigmatised injustice and tyranny'.[124]

As Mill expressed the by now common thought, the ancients thought that 'worldly power' was 'habitually exercised by the fittest men'. By contrast, the moderns in general, and the Americans in particular, assumed that 'possession of power itself calls forth the qualifications for its exercise' given the general lack of political judgement by the majority.[125] This transformation was as important to early nineteenth-century British political thought as it had been to writers from Montesquieu onwards. It certainly informed Mill's view of the liberty-enhancing effects of ancient Athenian institutions and the rule of the most able.[126] His neo-Grecian homage, however, was filtered through a critical engagement with writers

---

[119] John Stuart Mill, Letter to Alexis de Tocqueville, May 11, 1840, in Mill 1963, *CW*, vol. 13, pp. 433ff, p. 435. On finding the review 'tough work', see John Stuart Mill, Letter to Robert Barclay Fox, August 3, 1840, in Mill 1963, *CW*, vol. 13, pp. 440ff, p. 441. For suggestive remarks on Tocqueville here, see Nelson 2004, pp. 234–51.

[120] Mill 1986, *CW*, vol. 22, p. 255.

[121] Mill 1977e, *CW*, vol. 18, esp. p. 197, citing Guizot.

[122] Mill 1974, *CW*, vol. 8, p. 682.

[123] Mill 1974, *CW*, vol. 8, pp. 926f.

[124] Mill 1969e, *CW*, vol. 10, p. 259; cf. Mill 1969f, *CW*, vol. 10, esp. pp. 309–27.

[125] Mill, 1986, *CW*, vol. 22, pp. 253f; cf. Mill 1977a, *CW*, vol. 18, p. 24, on the need for recognition by the majority of their imperfect judgement about most political questions. Cf. [Various] 1878, pp. 797–822.

[126] Forbes 1952, esp. pp. 63, 66; Mill 1978e, *CW*, vol. 11, pp. 324ff.

like Guizot and Tocqueville, which led him to claim that 'underneath all political philosophy, there must be a social philosophy—a study of agencies lying deeper than forms of government'.[127] Moreover, his account of the requirements of an open society for the promotion of human flourishing and the maximizing of a sphere of self-government was predicated upon a certain definition: 'I understand by Sociology not a particular *class* of subjects included *within* Politics, but a vast field *including* it—the whole field of enquiry & speculation respecting human society & its arrangements, of which the forms of government, & the principles of the conduct of governments are but a part'.[128]

In spite of this stance, it has been suggested that Mill had an 'unchanging' notion of human nature, one incompatible with broader Liberal Anglican discussions of a cyclical theory of historical progression, based on ideas of an adaptable human nature and a theory of history derived from Vico.[129] The first part of this claim surely cannot stand. If it were true, Mill's account of an educable populace capable of taking responsibility for their development would be meaningless, and his statement in the *Logic*, that 'mankind have not one universal character', incomprehensible.[130] Mill's hostility to the Benthamite assumption that 'mankind are alike in all times and all places' was clear, and he noted (rather like Montesquieu) that 'the same institutions will no more suit two nations in different stages of civilization, than the same lessons will suit children of different ages'.[131] As to the second claim, Vico was not at all unknown in English political thought (and in fact the previous century had been 'full of "Vichian" thoughts'). This, however, was also a result of the influence of French historians like Michelet, whose history of France in the Middle Ages Mill would explore in the *Edinburgh Review* of 1844.[132] Discussing the review with his editor, Mill claimed his views on the topic were 'Guelphic', in that he typically sided 'with the popes against the Kings'; moreover, 'the principles it involves lie at the heart of all my opinions on politics and history'.[133] In saying this, he was updating an analysis of the relationship between civilization, progress, and religion, where progress could even be determined in the throes of barbarism. Vico's work had

[127] Mill 1985a, *CW*, vol. 20, pp. 183f; cf. John Stuart Mill, Letter to Alexis de Tocqueville, December 15, 1856, in Mill 1972a, *CW*, vol. 15, pp. 517f, esp. p. 518.

[128] John Stuart Mill, Letter to John Chapman, June 9, 1851, in Mill 1972, *CW*, vol. 11V, part 1, pp. 67ff, p. 68. Emphasis in original.

[129] Forbes 1952, pp. 127, 29.

[130] Mill 1974, *CW*, vol. 8, p. 864; cf. Mill 1969e, *CW*, vol. 10, p. 224.

[131] Mill 1969, *CW*, vol. 10, p. 16.

[132] Forbes 1953–54, p. 658.

[133] John Stuart Mill, Letter to Macvey Napier, March 3, 1842, in Mill 1963, *CW*, vol. 13, pp. 504–5.

also received extended tribute in *The Philological Miscellany*, the same journal that published Schleiermacher, alongside Savigny, Arnold, and many more.[134] So although the connection between Vico and Mill is indirect, the idea that Mill outlined a static or naturalistic view of human nature immune to context fails to convince, and sounds rather more like the claims of his father. James Mill recognized the 'accidental, but in several respects unavoidable connexion between the interests of the community, and the interests of the governing classes', a connexion to which 'the nations of the world owe almost all that is excellent in the actual system of their laws'.[135] Though he was well aware of the Scottish legacy, his science of politics depended upon an account of human nature as universally grounded in associationist psychology that could be related to a utilitarian theory of value.[136] His son once more found his father's account too rigid, and while John Mill thought Bentham much less inflexible, he too was inadequate as an analyst of the moral interaction between individuals in context.[137] It was in properly Smithian terms that Mill discussed such interactions, as experiences that develop first through the attempt to put oneself in the position of another, and which then mature to allow conscience to act as both guide and judge.[138]

In related fashion such claims fail to appreciate how important Montesquieu was to Mill's thinking. Indeed, in his early account of Montesquieu, Mill took issue with his great friend and intellectual opponent John Sterling, who had failed to recognize the non-determinist character of *De l'Esprit des lois*. Mill's brief discussion of Montesquieu's political thought (most of the speech is a rather tedious retort to Sterling) is a defence of the idea of a 'universal science of politics'. According to Sterling's presentation, which was itself supposed to be a defence of Montesquieu against Bentham, the former was to be preferred to the latter because he recognized the need for a nationally specific and 'separate science of politics'. Mill's retort was that although Montesquieu was 'confused' about the 'metaphysics of law', which is to say those ideas that are understood to be 'involved in the very conception of law', he was 'guiltless of the absurdities' that Sterling thought he was defending. Instead, Montesquieu had a *pro tanto* universal science of politics, in that he applied common standards of judgement to questions concerning the differences between desirable and actual forms of government in specific contexts. Rather than

---

[134] See M. C. Y. and I. K. 1832, esp. p. 630; Savigny 1832, pp. 150–73; [Anon.] 1832, pp. 196–202.

[135] James Mill 1809, pp. 89, 88; cf. Forbes 1951–52, pp 19–33; Young 2000, esp. pp. 109f.

[136] Haakonssen 1996, p. 308; Berry 1997, pp. 65ff.

[137] Pitts 2005, pp. 135–38.

[138] Phillipson 2000, esp. pp. 78–82; Fontana 1985, p. 77.

looking to Montesquieu for a defence of the metaphysics of law (which was 'a branch of science which we owe entirely to Mr. Bentham and to those who have followed in his footsteps'), Mill defended instead something like a contextualist method in intellectual history.[139] This would help him in his project of ethology too, as a deductive science of character applicable to both the individual and the nation.[140] When applied to the broad and general idea of national character, it would allow him to focus on elemental ideas (akin to Braudel's appreciation of historical time), and upon moral psychology (whether from Combe's phrenology, Hartley's associationism, or Smith's moral sentiments).[141] There were the passions, too, such as those that Fourier delineated in his 'passional tree', in which passions were classed 'in the same way according to the degrees of a generative scale', all stemming from the same root (the trunk of the tree, or 'unityism'). All were 'good conditionally', especially in the case of 'associative development'.[142] But in general, this broader awareness of the relationship between ideas and interests, sentiments or passions, and context, was what gave Mill's account of sociology its particular piquancy. He recapitulated claims made in his *Autobiography* when he wrote that theories and philosophies of politics rely upon 'a previous theory of human progress', just like a 'philosophy of history'.[143] But where Bentham failed to adequately investigate national character, Mill could still find plenty in his predecessors to relate questions of freedom and individuality to debates about civilization and civility.[144]

CIVILIZATION, CIVILITY, COOPERATION

Once we have noted the important function of educated journals in Victorian intellectual life, there is little doubting the connection between Mill's private concerns with cultivating opinion through education, and his public editorship of the *London*, then the radical *London and Westminster Magazine*. This began between 1834 and 1835; he took full con-

---

[139] Mill 1988h, CW, vol. 26, pp. 443–53, p. 451; see the discussions of English philosophy in John Stuart Mill, Letter to Hippolyte Taine, March 15, 1861, in Mill 1972a, CW, vol. 15, pp. 722f; also John Stuart Mill, Letter to Auguste Comte, October 5, 1844, in Mill 1963, CW, vol. 13, pp. 636–39, esp. pp. 638f.

[140] Mill 1974, CW, vol. 8, esp. pp. 868, 872f, 875–78.

[141] See Mill, Letter to Alexander Bain, November 14, 1859, in Mill 1972a, CW, vol. 15, pp. 645f; cf. Combe 1828, pp. viii–ix, 15f, 33, 39f, 43.

[142] Fourier 1851, pp. 1f, 5, 10.

[143] Mill 1981, CW, vol. 1, p. 169; Spadafora 1990, esp. pp. 212, 302.

[144] Mill 1974, CW, vol. 8, p. 869; Smith 1993, pp. 70–86.

trol only in 1838, but the connection was 'terminated' in April 1840.[145] Mill wanted a broad-based journal that would help to cement radical opinion, and we must assume that by this point he was no longer as 'sick of politics' as he had been just a few years earlier.[146] This did not mean that he was any more astute a political operator, however, despite his obvious analytical skills.[147] And against his father's own input, Mill asserted that the 'spirit of the review will be democratic'.[148] The topics covered a broad array of themes, even if it was a constant effort to actually get copy from writers he wanted.[149] Nevertheless, the general focus of his concern is neatly encapsulated in the major essay he contributed to the journal on the character of civilization, particularly in the relationship he outlined between civilization and political civility or appropriateness.

When he came to write 'Civilization', he built upon a discussion already undertaken in a review of Guizot's 'Lectures on European Civilization'. Mill's French connections were increasingly explicit by 1836, and he even suggested elsewhere that the continuing movement for progressive reform that had begun in England in 1832 was 'our taking of the Bastille'.[150] For although he saw contemporary problems for France, the country remained his lodestone, one to which 'in tastes and predilections I am more attached' in life, as he would literally be in his grave.[151] On Guizot's account there was a stark contrast between the tremendous 'unity' of ancient civilization and the more deeply fractured nature of the contemporary age. The modern world was a 'picture of stormy chaos', and Britain was prone to exceptionally heavy weather.[152] Modern civilization, moreover, rendered it difficult to safeguard liberty even, or perhaps especially, in Britain.

Many European observers of Britain in the early nineteenth century also noted this chaos. Jean-Baptiste Say, with whom Mill was in close contact, offered a vision of the development of British political economy

[145] Capaldi 2003, pp. 128, 124; John Stuart Mill, Letter to Macvey Napier, April 22, 1840, CW, vol. 13, in Mill 1963, pp. 428f; for the wider context, see Turner 2001, pp. 18–40; Ashton 2006.

[146] John Stuart Mill, Letter to Thomas Carlyle, April 11/12, 1833, CW, vol. 12, in Mill 1963, pp. 148–52, at p. 151; see Thomas 1985, pp. 44–50.

[147] Thomas 1979, esp. p. 200.

[148] Robson and Robson 1985, pp. 240f, 237.

[149] Robson and Robson 1985, p. 241.

[150] Mill 1982, CW, vol. 6, p. 321.

[151] Mill, Letter to Alexis de Tocqueville, August 9, 1842, CW, vol. 13, in Mill 1963, pp. 535ff, p. 536.

[152] Mill 1985b, CW, vol. 20, p. 381. Earlier (pp. 374ff), Mill took up Guizot's account of French civilization as being far in advance of Germany and Italy, and compared the situation to that of England. For generous discussion, see Varouxakis 2002, pp. 35–43.

underscored with a now classic account of how public debt was outstripping the 'fruits' of 'English industry'. The English were 'compelled to perpetual labour', and Say's fear was that 'this state of things produces a deplorable effect on the mind'.[153] One way, therefore, in which civility could be re-aligned was to look to what Guizot had termed the sovereignty of reason, which he saw as the unifying principle for modern representative government. Mill clearly found the focus on civilization as progress, on pluralism as freedom, and on the paradoxical effects of modern equality (something he shared with Tocqueville) an appealing synthesis.[154] Recognition of 'reason, truth and virtue' as the guiding principles of a just social order, which themselves cannot be represented, provided Mill with a framework for interpretation.[155] It also allowed him to re-confirm his focus on exemplary moralists, marking out free thinkers and those who had died for their beliefs as responsible for 'no small share in the honour of the ultimate emancipation of the human mind'.[156] Upholding truth and challenging conventional opinion is crucial to self-government in general, and to an understanding of the particular power of ideas as agents of historical and social change.[157] Such a view lies behind the message of *On Liberty*, after all, that the state cannot interfere to compel belief. At the same time, and as he had suggested when reviewing Grote's work, what constitutes virtuous conduct today simply indicates the distance between contemporary civilization and classical heroism.[158]

As Guizot had also argued, civilization could be seen as a movement from aristocratic republics and Asian societies towards the early Middle Ages, combining individual liberty with vast inequality. The fourth stage was the contemporary world, a world of individual liberty underpinned by equality of conditions. This was precisely the problematic relationship between equality and liberty that Guizot and Tocqueville focused upon, and which had such an impact on Mill's writings.[159] Guizot's historical account of these four stages itself bears close connection to Adam Smith's analysis, but neatly also dovetails with Mill's understanding of the social significance of modern politics. The politics of commercial society no longer requires, as Smith and Montesquieu had reiterated, heroic personalities or statesmen, nor in fact noble individuals more generally. Mill concurred. In 'ordinary times' the 'government of an already well-

[153] Say 1816, pp. 11, 14, 25, 26f; also Stedman Jones 2002, esp. pp. 70f, 82–85, 89ff.
[154] Langford 1989.
[155] See Craiutu 2003, pp. 32–47, 59–70, 93–100, 110, 130; cf. pp. 144f.
[156] Mill 1985b, *CW*, vol. 20, p. 393.
[157] Semmel 1998, esp. pp. 75f.
[158] Mill 1978e, *CW*, vol. 11, p. 314.
[159] Craiutu 2003, p. 100.

ordered society' has no need for such 'great talents'.[160] All that is required is free government. On the other hand, in adapting Tocqueville's account of democracy and its preconditions, Mill understood democracy first as an *état social*, then as a social and political formation, and finally as a political state underpinned by participation, political liberty and 'systematic antagonism'.[161]

Civilization held open the promise of outlining the development of properly constituted representative government where competence and capability, rather than that 'master fallacy', class-representation, could take priority.[162] Yet because of its 'double meaning', civilization 'sometimes stands for human improvement in general, and sometimes for certain kinds of improvement in particular'. Therefore, we typically 'call a country more civilized if we think it more improved, more eminent in the best characteristics of Man and Society; farther advanced in the road to perfection; happier, nobler, wiser'. However, this is only one meaning of the word. Another suggests that civilization 'stands for that kind of improvement only, which distinguishes a wealthy and powerful nation from savages or barbarians'.[163] This latter point would highlight Mill's general focus, and the contrast between civilized and savage peoples was well known to him from Scots such as Smith, Millar and Stewart, as well as from his father and Jeremy Bentham.[164] The intellectual baggage that underpins the claim is clearly recognizable from what remains of Mill's library catalogues at Somerville College, Oxford. They present a striking collection of authors and texts, many of which have been discussed in this book, including Amelot de la Houssaye and Machiavelli's *Opere*, and works by Hume, Hutcheson and Smith, particularly Smith's *Essays on Philosophical Subjects*, which contains the essay on astronomy that Mill often quoted. Alongside Mandeville were Montesquieu's *Considérations*, two volumes of Leibniz and translations of Fichte, as well as Barbeyrac's editions of Pufendorf and earlier original copies of Grotius—something like the European republic of letters was very much at his disposal. And while none of this is to present anything like a claim about influence, just

[160] Mill 1977b, CW, vol. 18, pp. 47–90, p. 76; cf. Mill 1977g, CW, vol. 19, pp. 437ff; Mill 1978d, CW, vol. 11, pp. 302f.

[161] Richter 2004, esp. pp. 69–73; cf. Varouxakis 1999, esp. pp. 301f. On the personal and intellectual connections between Mill and Tocqueville, see Brogan 2006, esp. pp. 290f, 303f, 370f, 388, 664 n. 52.

[162] Mill 1977e, CW, vol. 18, pp. 155–204, p. 196; Mill 1977a, CW, vol. 18, p. 43, on class-representation.

[163] Mill 1977d, CW, vol. 18, p. 119.

[164] On Millar's debts to Smith, see Jeffrey 1803a, pp. 155f, 158f, 176; cf. Fontana 1985, pp. 24f, 28ff.

noting the availability of and interest in these texts might add something further to the usual array of suspects presented as background for understanding Mill. For when this background is realigned with the largely Francophone discussions of civilization that affected Mill, one sees why he was keen to grasp hold of the paradoxical character of a progressive transformation in modern culture, whose public debt and industrialization its representative politics found difficult to manage. It was quite natural, therefore, to wonder how the term 'civilization' came quickly to connote politeness and civility, given that Mill well understood how a veneer of civility might conceal as much as it revealed about progress and barbarism. That is to say, Mill worried about how civilization could promote self-deception at the same time as it advanced commercial progress and liberty, and that is a story with a very lengthy history, some of which has already been told earlier on in this book.[165]

However, one of the more surprising elements of Mill's intellectual advance is that he chose not to work through the full implications of his critique of Bentham, towards a sophisticated analysis of cultural differences. Instead, he pressed a binary opposition between civilization and barbarism into political service in rather unsubtle fashion. Most recent interpreters of his political thought have used this fact to locate him in the foundational movement of British liberalism towards a hard-headed defence of empire.[166] Put another way, it seems that it was in earlier writers like James Dunbar, who attacked the binary opposition between civilization and barbarism as both overplayed and problematic, that the more open-ended legacy of Adam Smith's visions were played out. In fact, Dunbar had wondered whether terms of censure and approbation should more particularly be addressed to specific cases, rather than trying to move along a scale from rudeness to polish, or barbarism to civility. This would counter the presupposition or 'opinion of their own superiority over other nations which Europeans are prone to entertain'.[167] But Mill also wanted to keep a view of human diversity as 'incredible', alongside an awareness of context for understanding custom and standards of justice in diverse settings. He also reckoned, as did Dunbar and indeed most authors with whom this book has been concerned, on the character-shaping effects of commerce and the different standards of 'genius' and 'civility' between nations and forms of government.[168] As part of the later nineteenth-century updating of these

[165] Starobinski 1993, esp. pp. 4f, 11–17.

[166] Pitts 2005, ch. 5; cf. Ryan 2007, pp. 150–53; Schultz 2007, esp. pp. 110–19; Mehta 1999, pp. 49, 88f, 97–106, 214.

[167] Dunbar 1780, pp. 146f; see also Pitts 2007, esp. pp. 76ff.

[168] Dunbar 1780, esp. pp. 158, 168, 405ff; Berry 1997, esp. pp. 87f; see too Wahrman 2004, pp. 139, 145, 254.

arguments, Mill only went so far; other critics concluded that 'civilization amongst any people in what state it may be', actually 'produces no effect upon that inequality of condition, and rank, and power, and property, which also exists everywhere, amongst every people, and under all systems of government or polity, rude or refined'. Providence, however, lay behind that sort of assertion about the gradual enhancements of civility and refinement, and Mill could not countenance much optimism on that score.[169]

Given his focus on civilization as opposed to barbarism, one of the principal defences of civilization he affirmed was that it increases social co-operation for common purpose.[170] In this instance, although the claim was general, its application was particularly directed towards Britain. If anything, his analysis was a quirky take on Montesquieu's dictum that the English are free and commercially prosperous (civilized), but morose and gloomy (lacking civility). Both Montesquieu and Mill tied civilization and civility to accounts of what is normally referred to as civil history, and these concerns were further developed in a second review of Tocqueville, where Mill noted that the 'habitual dissatisfaction of each with the position he occupies' is a recognizably English characteristic.[171] The irony of Tocqueville's popularity in England, a nation the 'most suspicious of general reasonings', was widely noted, as Tocqueville seemed to place 'himself in the highest elevations of transcendental ratiocination'.[172] Mill's more general point was, however, expressed in the proposition that a by-product of civilisational advance is that the individual becomes lost in the crowd, and power passes from individuals to masses. Yet in England this 'equalization of conditions has made least progress' and the 'extremes of wealth and poverty are wider apart'.[173] Two factors accounted for this inequality, namely property and the 'acquirements of mind'. But the growth and development of co-operation was perhaps the crucial catalyst in the process, for co-operation requires combination, which necessarily effects compromise, and this is what distinguishes civilized from 'savage communities', which are 'poor and feeble' in this respect. For just as 'lions and tigers' were unable to overcome early humans by their lack of capacity and co-operation, so too did 'incapacity of co-operation' denote the savage and the slave.[174]

---

[169] Doubleday 1852, pp. 38, 110.

[170] Mill 1977d, *CW*, vol. 18, p. 120.

[171] Mill 1977e, *CW*, vol. 18, p. 193.

[172] [Anon.] 1840, esp. pp. 391, cols. 1, 2; cf. [Anon.] 1840a, esp. pp. 415, col. 1 on the late invention of self-government by the Greeks, and p. 416, col. 1, on Tocqueville's reliance on a philosophy of history.

[173] Mill 1977e, *CW*, vol. 18, p. 193.

[174] Mill 1977d, *CW*, vol. 18, pp. 121, 122.

The notion of cooperation as a practical activity (although not as a generic principle of social organisation), had affected Mill's earlier portrayal of various 'utopian' and Christian socialists as well as cooperative theorists.[175] In these earlier discussions Mill had developed a critique of the methods of the cooperative system as advocated by Robert Owen, stating that he 'should be sorry if it were thought that I am an enemy to Mr. Owen's system', for he was 'an enemy to no system which has for its object the amelioration of mankind'. However, what Owen and his followers failed to realize was that the true source of human motivation was self-love. 'There is a principle in man, far more constant and far more universal than his love for his fellows—I mean his love for himself: and without excluding the former principle, I rest my hopes chiefly on the latter'.[176] Expanding the point rhetorically, he claimed not to be 'one of those, who set up liberty as an idol to be worshipped'. In fact, 'I am even willing to go farther than most people in regulating and controlling when there is a special advantage to be obtained by regulation and control'. For although 'perfect freedom of action' is hugely enjoyable, sacrifices must be made because modern man, just like the 'savage in the forest', cannot be the happiest of creatures without sacrificing some independence for the 'comforts of civilized life'.[177] To understand differences in various laws and polities, therefore, one needed to have an understanding of different national characters. Yet if he thought neither Bentham nor Montesquieu adequate guides to this field, Montesquieu's analysis of despotism, especially in Russian and Chinese guise, nevertheless formed the foundation for his attack on pedantocracy. It was associated with the malignant effects of stationariness that accompany 'unmitigated despotism', leading to a narrowness of mind and spirit, and a foreclosing of political conflict.[178] Thus, just as Montesquieu had argued that 'power must arrest power by the arrangement of things' in order to prevent despotism, so too did Mill by arguing that security means both 'protection *by* the government, and protection *against* the government'.[179] This focus on security relates back to the analysis of justice, liberty and to the propriety or quality of agency.

[175] John Stuart Mill, Letter to an Unidentified Correspondent, June 9, 1851, in Mill 1972, CW, vol. 14, p. 70; cf. John Stuart Mill, Letter to John Wilson, January 31, 1863, in Mill 1972a, CW, vol. 15, pp. 832f.

[176] Mill 1988c, CW, vol. 26, esp. pp. 323f; cf. Maurice 1851, esp. p. 22; Capaldi 2003, pp. 76f, 338–52.

[177] Mill 1988c, CW, vol. 26, p. 321.

[178] See Mill 1977f, CW, vol. 18, pp. 273ff; Mill 1977g, CW, vol. 19, p. 384; cf. Kurfurst 1996, pp. 73–87.

[179] Mill 1965, CW, vol. 2, bks. 1–2, bk. 1, ch. 7, § 6, p. 112, emphasis in original; cf. Montesquieu 1989, 2. 11. 4, p. 155; 1964, p. 586; Varouxakis 1999, pp. 303f.

Bentham's arguments failed because he did not recognize the complexity lying behind the claims, or so Mill suggested.[180] To Mill's mind, 'a philosophy of laws and institutions, not founded on national character, is an absurdity'. And according to Mill, Bentham thought only of the 'moral' view of agency (that is to say, whether something is right or wrong). This ignored the other two principal forces of 'aesthetic' and 'sympathetic' determination, when in fact all three were necessary to understand properly 'the morality of an action'. Indeed, agency 'depends upon its foreseeable consequences; its beauty, and its loveliness, or the reverse'.[181] This was not an isolated refrain. For example, in *Utilitarianism* the observance of moral rules that 'forbid mankind to hurt one another (in which we must never forget to include wrongful interference with each other's freedom) are more vital to human well-being than any maxims'.[182] Although a moral faculty may not be part of our nature, it is nevertheless a 'natural outgrowth from it'.[183] The specifically Smithian resonance of the claim was noted elsewhere by Mill, when discussing Smith's account of sympathy as a theory 'respecting the nature and origins of our feelings of morality'.[184] His father had glossed this theme, but only really as it related to associationist psychology. And though James Mill alluded to Adam Smith, in the younger Mill's revision of his father's analysis the Smithian connections are rather more pronounced. There, the 'idea of *deserving* praise is but a more complex form of the association between our own or another person's acts of character, and the idea of praise'.[185] This view of ethics is counter to the consequentialist motivations of the legislator, whose laws prohibit certain actions irrespective of their 'moral excellence'. Moreover, the internal dimension of self-education and development requires a set of concerns that 'government house utilitarianism' simply cannot provide.[186] Correlatively, what associationist psychology (properly understood) actually highlighted was that the only constant uniformity in human nature and ideas was diversity.[187] However, in developing his theory of the internal and external sanctions required for moral and political freedom, Mill suggested that only a truly enlightened legislator could properly constrain the realms of action in accordance

---

[180] Mill 1977a, CW, vol. 18, esp. pp. 18f; see too Burns 1969, pp. 291ff.
[181] Mill 1969b, CW, vol. 10, esp. pp. 99, 91, 112.
[182] Mill 1969e, CW, vol. 10, p. 255.
[183] Mill 1969e, CW, vol. 10, p. 230.
[184] Mill 1969a, CW, vol. 10, p. 26.
[185] Mill 1989, CW, vol. 21, pp. 230f. Emphasis in original. Cf. James Mill 2002, vol. 2, esp. pp. 223–32.
[186] Mill 1969, CW, vol. 10, pp. 7ff; cf. Williams 1995, p. 166, for the remark about utilitarianism.
[187] Hartley 1749, vol. 1, p. 442.

with the common good, and that people would recognize this fact when their development (in terms of civility and civilization) had reached an appropriate point. Only then would they choose legislators as they chose physicians, in order to heal themselves and their polities.[188] In Mill's eyes, Gladstone was a possible candidate for this role in the British case, even while Turgot remained the modern ideal.[189] Gladstone was one of the 'very few political men whose public conduct appears to me to be invariably conscientious, and in whom desire of the public good is an active principle, instead of at most, a passive restraint'.[190] Small wonder that Gladstone was prompted in return to write a doggerel ditty entitled 'A Triple Hurrah for Mill'.

I

Come, lads and lasses behold here
One better than laces and gold,
Than cakes and wine or your speeches fine,
A man that's as true as he's bold—
The people's soldier in woe and weal,
So shout, brave lads, to your fill—
Hurrah for WORTH and the BRAINS, lads,
And a triple hurrah for MILL!!!

II

The silks and fans, will all fade lads,
And the feathers, be blown away,
And with the first shower of rain, lads,
Our ribbons will quickly decay,
But a man both honest and true, lads,
Shall endure, and always will.
Then, hurrah for WORTH and the BRAINS, lads,
And a triple hurrah for MILL!!!

In honour of JOHN STUART MILL Esq.,
Candidate for Westminster, 1868.[191]

Clearly there were already hints in Mill's analysis of civilization of the glaring psychic implications of modern life for the individual, which would become famous in *On Liberty* some twenty-three years later.[192] If civilization could only be achieved through practical co-operation, the fruits of which could now be seen all over England with its clubs and

[188] Burns 1967, esp. p. 20.
[189] Reeve 2007, pp. 410f.
[190] John Stuart Mill, Letter to William E. Gladstone, August 6, 1859, in Mill 1972a, CW, vol. 15, p. 632.
[191] BL Add. Mss. 44, 756, fo. 55.
[192] Capaldi 2003, p. 252.

associations, then the 'greatest novelty of all is the spirit of combination which has grown up among the working classes'. The problem was that whilst this type of power had increased, there had been no correlate increase in 'mental' powers.[193] Mill grappled with this issue in different fashion in his writings on political economy, where he suggested that with increased co-operation, conflict between workers would decrease and the economy would move towards its optimal 'stationary state' of balanced equilibrium with a recognition of shared interests.[194] The deductive principles of political economy as much as civilization and progress were pressed into work in an evaluation of contemporary society.

It was central to Mill's account that increased co-operation between individuals, in particular between members of the working class, would permit them to see how their preferences are formed in a process of mutual recognition and deliberation. Furthermore, this process itself (an educative one) would have the subsequent effect of allowing people to see that there are some pleasures and goals which are more important than others, and that they should live their lives accordingly. Religion of course had a role to play in this process, but the economic benefits were the most immediately pressing, and here once more there appears to be a distinction between economic and political liberty. However, if the relationship between common sympathy and economic development is in fact reciprocal, then the economic and political dimensions of liberty might be reconciled for mutual benefit.[195] Thus, if a balance of classes is necessary to a functioning system of representative government, then the relationship between workers and owners of the means of production had to be addressed, which is partly what the chapters on socialism in Mill's discussion of political economy provide. They show Mill to have been favourably disposed to applying the idea of co-operation to this sphere as much as anywhere else.[196] Co-operation prevents despotism, broadly understood as the 'preponderance' of any class whatsoever (even a democratic one) that could pursue its own interests against others at will. But the rise of the middle class in England, alongside the American 'many', illuminated the modern danger that accrues 'whenever any variety of human nature becomes preponderant in a community, [namely that] it imposes upon all the rest of society its own type; forcing all, either to submit to it or to imitate it'.[197]

In turn, this mirrored Tocqueville's sentiments. As Richter has suggested, an unpublished draft of the first volume of Tocqueville's study of

---

[193] Mill 1977d, CW, vol. 18, p. 125.
[194] Riley 1999, pp. 295, 297, 311ff.
[195] Stimson and Milgate 2001, esp. pp. 233ff, 241.
[196] See Claeys 1987, pp. 122–47.
[197] Mill 1977e, CW, vol. 18, p. 196; cf. Burns 1969, p. 325.

democracy shows he did not believe it possible to organize government 'for the benefit of the middle classes. Even if I did believe that, I should oppose it'.[198] Mill should surely have agreed, and he tried to defend individual particularity against despotic conformism within the workplace as well as without. In much the same way that Locke worried about drudgery and Smith about alienation, Mill was keenly aware of the effect of mindless work on the moral sentiments, and pushed to enlarge the sphere of sympathy wherever possible.[199] He was equally aware in later years of the importance of the relationship between capital and labour in structuring political debates.[200] Indeed, he delineated the relative unfreedom and exploitation of workers under a system of private property in ways that have clear affinities to Marx.[201] Given that Marx's early political analyses of capitalism and exploitation in England were drawn from sources that were easily available to both, this commonality is less surprising than it otherwise might be.[202] Moreover, a critical attitude towards the overbearing character of commercialism drives much of Mill's critique, and at points his work would seem to be well attuned to the radical development of republican arguments about the necessity for representation in the well-ordered modern republic. So the 'success of cooperation on any large scale, will establish a practical minimum of wages', and this 'will strike at the root of the opposition of apparent interest between employers and labourers'.[203] Such connections to English radicalism are conceptually important, but do not fit easily within the standard historiographical narratives given his cognate focus on political rule by the fittest.[204] However, recent attempts to rethink the nature of republicanism as a political tradition suggest some alternative lines of inquiry.

Excursus: Republicanism, Radicalism and Representation

Although Mill was certainly keen to support those engaged in Chartist politics, for he despised 'class legislation' both 'on principle' and 'in the

[198] Tocqueville 1992, vol. 2, p. 1179; discussion in Richter 2004, pp. 73f.

[199] Mill 1977, CW, vol. 19, p. 411.

[200] John Stuart Mill, Letter to Charles Loring Brace, September 23, 1871, in Mill 1972c, CW, vol. 17, pp. 1837f, and Ashcraft 1998, pp. 178f.

[201] Mill 1965, CW, vol. 5, p. 714.

[202] Miles Taylor 1996, esp. pp. 234f, 241, 244f.

[203] John Stuart Mill, Letter to Henry Fawcett, May 17, 1863, in Mill 1972a, CW, vol. 15, pp. 859f, p. 859; Chadwick 1975, pp. 46f, classically saw this move as the beginning of a more collectivist strain of liberalism.

[204] Ashcraft 1993, pp. 249–72, is one attempt to illustrate the connections; cf. Burns 1969, esp. pp. 283, 289f; Vincent 1966, pp. 189ff, offers a tart assessment. See too Semmel 2000, pp. 140–75.

present state of civilization', he was not prepared to join them.[205] His antipathy towards explicitly republican politics in his own time was clear. Yet comparison between republican radicalism and Mill's political theory is not futile, because the focus on representation as a common bulwark against despotism in nineteenth-century thought unites them both. Because of this connexion, some recent writers have tried to fold Mill into a broadly neo-Roman, republican, or even a civically minded liberal political theory.[206] Yet this is neither necessary nor necessarily desirable. Even the *Edinburgh Review* thought that 'oppressive governments must always be insecure; and that after nations have attained a certain measure of intelligence, the liberty of the people is necessary to the stability of the throne'.[207] Of more interest are the conceptual connections to recent discussions of liberty and republicanism and Mill's synthetic project. For Mill, the idea of liberty requires both external sanctions provided by just laws and internal sentiments directed to upholding such laws in the first place. It is once more both an exercise and an opportunity concept, but opportunity is here also bounded by a distinct ordering of preferences and a claim about rationality and freedom.[208] Constraints can increase freedom, because they allow individuals to cultivate their capacities. Nevertheless, and in the language of republican political theory, one may possess all one's liberties, whilst not necessarily being a self at liberty if these constraints fail to adequately or appropriately track one's real interests.[209] Mill's attack on feudalism and arbitrary power showed his understanding of the nature of the problem, and his assessment was no less acute than that provided by Locke, Montesquieu and Smith before him.[210] Self-limiting, self-censoring, and servile individuals cannot act freely. They regulate their own conduct according to convention and defer to authority. At the same time, however, regulated conduct is indispensable to freedom of choice in the tradition outlined in this book. It is fundamental to the idea of liberty as propriety that both internal self-appropriation and external actions governed by justice are reciprocally related, so that propriety is itself both a cause and a consequence of free agency. Locke understood this relationship, as did Montesquieu and Smith. So too did Mill. Its ramifications extend throughout his work, and his project might indeed be thought of as a defence of liberty for its cultivation in particu-

---

[205] John Stuart Mill, Letter to William Lovett, July 27, 1842, in Mill 1963, CW, vol. 13, pp. 533f; see too Stedman-Jones 1982, esp. p. 51.

[206] See Biagini 2003, pp. 55–72.

[207] Jeffrey 1814, p. 25; cf. Jeffrey 1803, p. 1.

[208] Taylor 1979, pp. 175–91.

[209] Skinner 1997, pp. 22, 54ff; cf. Pincus 1998a, p. 710. See too Skinner 2002a, esp. pp. 19–26; Glover 1999, 47–80; Pettit 2002a, pp. 339–56; cf. Skinner 2002, pp. 237–68.

[210] Markell 2008, esp. pp. 21ff.

lar of good judgement in the face of confusion and conformity.[211] Taking him at his word, as some early commentators did, implies that Mill thought tranquillity, 'coolness of judgement', and a body of electors and representatives who are 'enlightened', are all necessary components for the cultivation of character and thus for the promotion of liberty.[212]

This shows, furthermore, just how deep are the resources for thinking about freedom as responsibility between persons, implied in much contemporary republican political thought. For both republican writers and those whom I have been considering in this book, the relationship between freedom and the quality of agency is paramount. Therefore, one important historical and conceptual move that I would like to question is the idea that towards the end of the eighteenth and through the nineteenth centuries arguments about freedom in terms of the status of persons, or the quality of their agency, were largely eclipsed by utilitarian assessments of negative liberty until in fact they were largely absent from political discourse.[213] In a variation on the so-called Gothic bequest, this move assumes that an updated Hobbesian idea of liberty as the absence of impediment, given renewed force by Bentham, gained near total prominence over other theories of freedom.[214] Indeed, one might then say that this is still the predominant conception of liberty operative in modern political philosophy.

Yet although there seems little reason to doubt that most contemporary political philosophy works within the framework of negative liberty, nor that some of the language of neo-Roman argumentation died out in the later eighteenth century, two points are worth making. First, the extent of its apparent linguistic and political collapse is hardly clear.[215] For example, it might be that republicanism understood as non-domination was simply not that prevalent to begin with, and therefore that its decline was not as marked as might first appear. In fact as many have noted, an increasingly thinned language of republicanism could accommodate 'a wide range of potentially divergent political and philosophical positions', whilst remaining rooted in issues of political liberty and constitutional security.[216] Second, if the central claim of this book is right, that conventional understandings of freedom referred to the capacity of agents both to act responsibly under their own power internally (even if they suffer

---

[211] Berkowitz 1999, esp. pp. 146–50.

[212] Quotations are from [Anon.] 1835, pp. 329, 227.

[213] Skinner 2002b, esp. pp. 177–85; cf. Kelly 2001, pp. 13–31; Patten 1996, pp. 25–44; Larmore 2001, pp. 230–43.

[214] Smith 1987.

[215] Vernon 1997; see too Epstein 1994, chs. 1, 3.

[216] Philp 1998, esp. p. 244; cf. Rosen 1992; 1997, pp. 177–88; Eastwood 1993, pp. 197–212.

from self-deception), and to be capable of being held responsible according to standards of justice in the public realm, then there would seem to be a great deal of continuity in terms of *these* central premises from the seventeenth through to the nineteenth centuries. This holds irrespective of the rise or the decline of specifically neo-Roman theories of liberty. A general challenge remains, though, for those interested in either of these ways of thinking about political liberty, of how to locate them within discussions of republicanism in the nineteenth century. This is because the predominant historiography tends to focus on radicalism and social history or, typically and simultaneously, to abstract claims of liberty from their context whilst suggesting that nineteenth-century political thought is too different from what has gone before to share any meaningful relation to earlier languages of politics.[217]

Political languages of constitutionalism and constitutional security were of course transformed with developments in the concept of representation attendant upon the American and French Revolutions. Mill thought the distinction drawn by Tocqueville, between delegation and representation, in this regard was 'capital'. His political theorizing in general was designed to underpin indirect representative government, so representatives clearly could not simply be delegates.[218] Equally, though such events and arguments had certainly inspired republican conceptual innovation, the transformation in political language towards this thinner vision of republicanism made it at once both more capacious and harder to pin down. That flexibility was central to Mill.[219] For neither Kant's discussion of a republican constitution, nor the claims of Sieyes about constituent power and the contrast between an ancient *démocratie brute* and a modern (or Jacobin) liberty, nor indeed Paine's attempt to graft representation onto democracy, quite capture what Mill derived from these changes in general, and theoretically most obviously from Guizot and Tocqueville.[220] Even when certain continental messages about representation and reform were mediated through bodies like the Society for the Friends of the People, or the London Corresponding Society, such neo-republicanism was only part of a wider story.[221] Indeed, Mill filtered these changes into the more general discussions that were of interest to his

---

[217] Gossman 1962, pp. 47–60; Belchem 1981, pp. 1–32. Cf. Taylor 1999; Prochaska 2000; Weinstein 1965, pp. 145–62.

[218] Mill, Letter to Alexis de Tocqueville, December 11, 1835, in Mill 1963, CW, vol. 12, pp. 287ff, p. 288.

[219] Armitage 2002, esp. pp. 43ff, 58ff; cf. Sheps 1975, pp. 3–28; Pole 1971; Alexander 1997, pp. 29ff.

[220] Stedman-Jones 1994, esp. pp. 155–58; Pasquino 1999; Hont 2005, esp. pp. 474–508; Whatmore 2001, esp. pp. 148, 136, 153f.

[221] Hampsher-Monk 1979, pp. 70–89; also Turner 1990, esp. pp. 85, 99, 112.

reconciliatory project, hoovering up everything that might persuade or cajole in the service of appropriate reform.[222] This is surely also one reason why claims about the novelty of nineteenth-century political thought can easily be misleading.[223] In Mill's hands, for example, a modern focus on representation led away from virtue and slavery towards interest and opinion, but an older concern with corruption of character and of office remained just as important.[224]

Though the idea that liberty mattered only to the free citizen of a free state ceased to predominate in John Bull's England, Mill's political vision updated this view to turn a spotlight on executive preponderance within British government as an instance of class domination. Such domination made a mockery of the homespun homily that the constitution was virtuously balanced.[225] Mill curtly dismissed the rhetorical commonplace that the lower house was the 'bulwark of liberty, and the glory of our constitution' with roots in Magna Carta.[226] His criticisms were developed further through engagement with Thomas Hare's radical work on parliamentary representation.[227] Hare's account of the use of 'political machinery', the need for a 'love of fairness and justice' amongst MPs, and the importance of 'responsibility' were all themes that Mill developed and tried to augment.[228] It is also interesting to note that Hare cited Guizot's discussion of the origins of representative government, specifically when Guizot praised Pascal's claim that unity without multiplicity was tyranny, and took it as 'the happiest expression and the most exact definition of representative government'.[229] Through his work, as well as that of Tocqueville and Montesquieu beforehand, the French Jansenist legacy so important to the development of liberty as propriety retained (an albeit less direct) presence in thinking about reform in nineteenth-century England. It had an explicit impact upon Mill, alongside more conventional and domestic arguments about patriotism and loyalism.[230] Popery and radicalism were similarly live issues.[231]

---

[222] Madison, Hamilton and Jay 1987, esp. nos. 10, 51, pp. 122–28, 318–22; cf. Manin 1994, pp. 27–62.

[223] Morrow and Francis 1994, pp. 3–7; cf. Bevir 1996, esp. p. 115.

[224] Hampsher-Monk 1979, pp. 81ff; Armitage 2002a, vol. 2, pp. 29–46.

[225] Mill 1988e, CW, vol. 26, p. 377; Taylor 1992, pp. 93–128.

[226] See [Anon.] 1810a, p. 37; Atkinson 1841, esp. pp. 17–21, 29, 64; also Atkinson 1838.

[227] Mill 1988j, CW, vol. 28, pp. 62f, 65; cf. Mill 1988j, CW, vol. 28, pp. 74f.

[228] Hare 1857, pp. 31, 33, 109; also Eastwood 1997, pp. 106f, 110.

[229] Guizot 2002, pp. 52f and n. 2; Hare 1857, pp. 37f; connections suggested in Sonenscher 2007, p. 153 n. 162.

[230] Harling 1996, pp. 1159–81; Finn 1992, pp. 637–59; Cunningham 1984, pp. 8–33. See also Quinault 1988, pp, 831–51.

[231] Williams 1828, is typical; so too [Anon.] 1828; cf. Jeffrey 1807, esp. p. 131. See in general Colley 1992; Eastwood 1989, pp. 308–31; Philp 1995, pp. 42–69; Gilmartin 2002, pp. 291–328.

Some contemporary radical republican claims even asserted the importance of a national convention to uphold the sovereignty of the nation and general equality between 'ranks'.[232] There was often a religious element to this emphasis, brought out well in Thomas Paine's engagement with Edmund Burke, but amplified in many other Tory responses to such calls for equality. One baroque example presented equality as a sorceress, a 'sly, artful, insinuating strumpet, who deceives the people with her wiles, tempts them to her embraces, and then robs them of their reason and common sense together', something altogether hyperbolic.[233] The serious point about equality, however, surely illustrated an implicit critique of the veneration given to martial valour in some earlier (and republican-inspired) civil histories.[234] Moreover, if the republicanism of the period after the American Constitution and the French Revolution was concerned with the question of representation, the import of these discussions was quickly operationalized in the debates over the Reform Act of 1832. This in turn provided an intellectual focus to radicals and liberals alike, taken up in short-lived publications like James Lorymer's journal *The Republican*.[235] Yet although its themes bore a strong family resemblance to his political vision in places, the radical style was more outré than anything Mill committed to print. In fact, although Mill had been engaged intensively with the reform movement and its progress over representation, the general point of his concern is perhaps best brought out in a letter to Sterling from shortly after the Reform Act. In it he pondered whether the British people would revolt if representation remained unreformed, and his answer was negative. However, he continued, 'the case of the evil is one which I foresaw and predicted long before—the anomaly of a democratic constitution in a plutocratically constituted society'.[236] He clearly savoured the impetus towards reform that French radicalism provided, but he sought to marry it with traditions of thought that were deemed appropriate for British politics.[237]

One important lesson that flows from this brief consideration of republicanism in nineteenth-century British political thought is the centrality of a concern with *character*. The 'adaptation' of notions of traditional claims about independence towards a focus on the idea of 'character' meant a renewed focus on society and public opinion, and a claim that the principal threat to liberty could not just be framed in terms of jus-

---

[232] Parssinen 1973, pp. 504–33; cf. Whatmore 2001, pp. 153f.

[233] Harris 1993, pp. 34–62; cf. [Anon.] 1792, pp. 8f.

[234] For example Ferguson 1995, esp. pp. 24–28, 58–60, 132, 138f; cf. Millar 1812, vol. 4, pp. 189, 200; Berry 1997, pp. 146–49.

[235] Prochaska 2000, p. 62; Kelly 2005, pp. 41–52.

[236] John Stuart Mill, Letter to John Sterling, July 10, 1833, in Mill 1963, CW, vol. 12, pp. 164–67, p. 166.

[237] Mill 1981, CW, vol. 1, p. 179.

tice and constitutional security, but had also to deal with the threat of 'stagnation, [and] submission to the inertia of mediocrity'.[238] These were indeed renderings of classically eighteenth-century debates about virtue, commerce and history, highlighting a revised analysis of the cycle of corruption and hubris that eighteenth-century authors had discussed. It thereby also signalled a newer focus on the nemesis of stagnation and the foregoing of an independent character, which seemed such a threat to nineteenth-century authors.[239] In Mill's hands the outcome of this twin focus could be quite paradoxical for thinking about free agency and the politics of civilization.

THE POLITICS OF CIVILIZATION

Mill's writings, with their focus on exemplary individuals, civility and corruption, traverse a vast spectrum, ranging from interpretations of the classics through to political engagement with currents of radicalism. He took on aspects of both the classical and the radical in his account of the necessary requirements of character for civilized liberty. Similarly, he thought that although the 'mental capacities' of the working class in advanced civilizations made something like his plural voting schema a necessity, the masses were at least thought capable of 'improvement' by government. Savage, rude or barbarous and despotic governments, on the other hand, those who stifle autonomy and use military power to achieve their ends, were incapable of undertaking such programmes of reconstruction. As already implied, however, this type of analysis fed into Mill's particular justifications of imperial politics, which sometimes involved him in rather hackneyed ranking of different cultures and their levels of civilization. To reiterate a point made already, despite his criticisms of Bentham, national character for Mill seems rather less amenable to the 'riot of eccentricity and individual singularity' that otherwise supports his account of individual freedom.[240] This lies in part behind John Vincent's memorable assessment of Mill's patrician opinions, which, he says, seem to 'have all the rude health of the retired Indian administrator'.[241] For in a similar fashion, Mill used these civilisational criteria to discuss those situations in which it might be defensible for one country to intervene in the affairs of another.

[238] Burrow 1985, p. 89; cf. Claeys 1994, esp. p. 285.
[239] Collini 1991, pp. 108ff.
[240] See Pitts 2003, esp. pp. 222f.
[241] Vincent 1966, p. 188.

Representative government was the best possible solution to the problem of despotism and pedantocracy, because fitness for office stems not from social position but from competition and competence. This was an attempt to resolve a key paradox of modern politics, where individual responsibility is displaced into the hands of a paternalistic cadre of bureaucratic experts.[242] Equally, differentiating between democracy and government allowed Mill to suggest styles of despotism, from the obvious and traditional, through to the idea that it might even be an expedient designed to be temporarily paternalistic in order to promote the gains of civilization in broadly non-liberal countries—something like emergency powers to recast unenlightened states.[243] Importantly, this expedient need not necessarily provide a justification for imperialism, or make the principle of nationality anything other than a means to an end. In fact, Mill was reluctant to allow direct political control over colonists by colonial powers, and indigenous forms of government were always to be preferred, so that only their governance was to be monitored by intermediary bodies like the East India Company. What these different forms of despotism seem to share, however, is the fact that those who are subject to despotic rule are prevented from utilizing their intellectual faculties to the full, and their energy is usually either sapped or misdirected.[244] It was a wholly and unsurprisingly Montesquieuean refrain.

If despotism was always a possibility, Mill nevertheless remained sanguine about the positive moral effects of civilization itself. As civilization progresses, individuals become increasingly interdependent and the spectacle of pain is progressively hidden from view, to be replaced with an emphasis on politeness and sociability.[245] Agreement and civility become the norm, not the exception, and Mill saw the move from 'force' to 'politics', from personal power to rational administration, as indicative almost of modernity itself. Just as others had shown, one sign of this advance was that sober reflection on the requirements of political order under advanced civilizations required less individual talent, and more bureaucratic and rational co-ordination.[246] It was yet another mark of progress that the gulf between the ancients and the moderns rested on this relative routinization of political ability and choice.[247] One pos-

---

[242] Mill 1977g, CW, vol. 19, pp. 421, 429f; Thompson 1976, pp. 65ff; cf. Arneson 1980, pp. 470–89.

[243] Mill 1977g, CW, vol. 19, pp. 424, 432; Urbinati 2007, p. 77; cf. Mill 1977g, CW, vol. 19, pp. 573, 577; Burns 1969, p. 327; Varouxakis 2007, esp. pp. 280, 294.

[244] Mill 1977g, CW, vol. 19, p. 410; [1859] 1977f, CW, vol. 18, pp. 306ff.

[245] Mill 1977d, CW, vol. 18, pp. 130f.

[246] Mill 1977b, CW, vol. 18, p. 76.

[247] Mill 1977g, CW, vol. 19, p. 438.

sible worry, however, was that despotism itself might become routinized into a bureaucratic pedantocracy, which is a political corollary of social conformity. This is why democratic participation remains necessary as an antidote, and underscores his suggestion that it is constantly necessary to challenge opinions and test truths.[248]

Within this framework, it nevertheless remains unclear how Mill's preferred individuals of genius were to come forward to monitor and to advance public opinion accordingly. It should be recalled that Mill thought that the genius was not the only person who lives the exemplary (and possibly experimental) life. He added, unsurprisingly perhaps given his own circumstances, that a London newspaper editor, or even an MP, might be able to change people's minds just as satisfactorily. As such a figure, could Mill as 'genius' try to synthesize extant ideas and recast them according to the needs of the time?[249] With this thought we confront Mill's idea that his own period would be both a reaction against, and a synthesis of what was best in, the previous century. Updating his previous review of Tocqueville, Mill once more noted that today 'the individual is lost and becomes impotent in the crowd', and that 'individual character itself becomes relaxed and enervated'. To respond to the 'first evil, the remedy is, greater and more perfect combination among individuals; for the second, national institutions of education, and forms of polity, calculated to invigorate the individual character'.[250] Only government intervention could help, but in Mill's mind this could justify projects of colonization that are not necessary to the idea of liberty as propriety, but which he clearly thought were complementary to it.[251]

With attitudes like this, Mill seemed to be remoulding eighteenth-century concerns in the light of his conception of liberty as freedom from stagnation and dependence, building on the general conceptual shift from corruption to stagnation, and from virtue to character, indicative of this period of transition, although it is a transition that remains incompletely understood.[252] The danger of civilization and civility thus understood, however, was that it might be little more than a simulacrum. As S. W. Burgess suggested, the 'legislative code of very polished people' in fact hides a 'frightful view of human depravity', such that natural human ferocity can only be 'reduced by means of civilization, and by the culture of virtue'. Curbing our natural inclinations permits the opportunity of facing 'all worldly incident with tranquillity'.[253] And this sort of mixture of tran-

---

[248] Burns 1969, p. 322.
[249] Mill 1977d, CW, vol. 18, p. 135.
[250] Mill 1977d, CW, vol. 18, p. 136.
[251] Mill 1965, CW, vol. 3, p. 963.
[252] See Burns 1969, esp. pp. 300ff.
[253] Burgess 1825, vol. 1, pp. 255f, 260, 507.

quillity, self-command and practical worldliness seems in line with Mill's ethological concern with character. That, it seems to me, is his synthetic amalgamation of Roman and Stoic, Christian and Pagan, Hellenistic and aesthetic elements, whose very instability in combination could be seen as analogous to the tense and nervy ideal of Mill's free citizen.[254]

Mill's aversion to corruption and political manipulation also under-pinned his charge that 'the British government is an aristocracy'. Attempts to justify balance were often chimerical, because 'every govern-ment which has ever been called a balance', he wrote, 'has really been an aristocracy'. This led Mill to the conclusion that if he really had to live under a system of 'uncontrouled power', then he would rather live under a despotism with 'one master, who may be wise and honest, not a body of masters [i.e. the House of Commons] who cannot'.[255] Indeed, he would even defend the rotten borough if the current system were to be retained, on the principle that with enough money one can win such a seat and remain independent, 'but I defy anyone who is not a slave, to be returned for a nobleman's pocket burgh, or for a county'.[256] What makes good government and what promotes liberty and security is a 'properly constituted representative organ', but the current system of administra-tion was 'more worthy of the barbarous age which gave it birth, than of the civilized age which is now called upon to gaze and worship without inquiry'.[257] His attachment to the development of character nevertheless remained paramount in the face of this fact.[258] Moreover, the cultiva-tion of individual excellence lay in holding true to such perfectibilian themes. Yet Mill countered those who wished to resurrect something akin to a Stoic doctrine and extirpate the passions as the root of all vice. This would be an error, 'because it is they [the passions] which furnish the active principle, the moving force; the passions are the spring, the moral principle only the regulator of human life'.[259] The passions were of course fundamental to Mill's project of ethology, and their character meant that certain forms of analysis were appropriate to the tasks of a science of politics as discussed in the *Logic*.[260] The best that could be done, given the multifaceted nature of the problem, was to try to discern something like a 'national' character, those 'distinctive characteristics' based on the groups of individuals who inhabit or who are citizens of a particular place. Such a 'political ethology' refers to the 'formation of the features of a people

[254] Cf. Burrow 1985, pp. 89, 92f.
[255] Mill 1988a, *CW*, vol. 26, esp. pp. 264ff; Mill 1988b, *CW*, vol. 26, p. 283.
[256] Mill 1988b, *CW*, vol. 26, p. 275.
[257] Mill 1988b, *CW*, vol. 26, pp. 281, 285; cf. [Anon.] 1824, pp. 292, 296.
[258] Carlisle 1991, ch. 3.
[259] Mill 1988g, *CW*, vol. 26, p. 432.
[260] Burns 1976, pp. 4ff, 9.

in a given age or nation'.[261] But the types of generalization permissible from such arguments are linked to explanations of the stability of civil societies, which in turn require at least three components; a system of education that contains the means of restraining individual conduct, a feeling of loyalty or allegiance, and those common sympathies that stem from the principle of nationality.[262]

Mill used the concepts of civilization and culture as moral categories. In so doing, his judgements of character and cultivation become questions of both art (or imagination) and science. Put more simply, this was about means and ends, and these means and ends had to combine with an account of human nature.[263] Individual freedom in this sense can only be acquired and developed through time, given the reciprocal relationship between character and civilization. Thus, individuality is expressed ethically through sympathy and cooperation, and legally through the defence of rights and social equality. The relational character of citizenship is what provides its legitimacy.[264] If this is an audacious combination, it certainly rings true for most understandings of Mill's liberalism, particularly its radical political implications for justifying intervention. His discussion of intervention defended the commercial expansion of the British state against charges of colonialism, and also defended the way that civilization and commerce give 'encouragement to intercourse'. Indeed, he noted that the interconnected world (here he is discussing the issue of what to do about the Suez Canal) gives 'easy access to commerce [which] is the main source of that material civilization'.[265]

In his account, Mill differentiated between laws of international morality that govern warfare between nations of 'the same, or something like the same, degree of civilization'. This is because 'to suppose that the same international customs, and the same rules of international morality, can obtain between one civilized nation and another, and between civilized nations and barbarians, is a grave error, and one which no statesman can fall into'. International morality requires reciprocity, and 'barbarians will not reciprocate'. Ultimately 'the only moral laws for the relation between a civilized and a barbarous government, are the universal rules of morality between man and man'.[266] Yet in the wider context of his vindication

---

[261] Carlisle 1991, pp. 137f; cf. Mandler 2006, esp. pp. 47–57.

[262] Burns 1969, p. 303; see too Mill 1974, CW, vol. 8, p. 923.

[263] See Robson 1999, esp. pp. 338f, 345f.

[264] Urbinati 2002, esp. pp. 123f.

[265] Mill 1984b, CW, vol. 21, p. 116.

[266] Mill 1984b, CW, vol. 21, pp. 118f; cf. Varouxakis 1997, esp. pp. 61–67, 71. See also Miller 1961, pp. 510f. Cf. Mill 1977g, CW, vol. 19, esp. pp. 547ff, for the hyperbolic claim that free institutions can only exist in countries with a small number of different nationalities.

of the February 1848 revolution in France written a decade earlier, Mill had contended that not only was international law subject to development in any given progressive context, but also that 'the circumstances of Europe have so altered during the last century, that the constitutions, the laws, the arrangements of property, the distinctions of ranks, the modes of education, the opinions, the manner—everything which affects the European nations separately and within themselves, has changed so much, and is likely to change so much more, than in no great lapse of time they will be scarcely recognisable'. Therefore, 'what is called the law of nations is as open to alteration, as properly and even necessarily subject to it when circumstances change or opinions alter, as any other thing of human institution'.[267] The question was raised, then, of how to differentiate between laws of morality under conditions of uncertainty and thereby how to apply them. And he seemed to think that contemporary political discussion was no help in answering that question. For just as he had denigrated some of the original French revolutionaries in *On Liberty*, in 1848 he thought it 'wretched to see the cause of legitimate Socialism thrown so far back by the spirit of reaction against that most unhappy outbreak at Paris in June'.[268]

The best he seemed able to suggest in the end was that there are some universal laws of morality, which dictate relations between civilization and barbarism, and they seem therefore to render certain forms of intervention acceptable. He noted that 'a civilized government cannot help having barbarous neighbours', and that 'when it has, it cannot always content itself with a defensive position'. This is in fact 'the history of the relations of the British Government with the native States of India'. The British 'had reduced the military power of those States to a nullity. But a despotic government only exists by its military power. When we had taken away theirs, we were forced, by the necessity of the case, to offer them ours instead of it'.[269] Once again, there is here an attempt to show the unity of 'civilized peoples' amongst the 'equal community of nations, like Christian Europe', and the differential standards of progress that demarcate civilized and barbarous nations.[270] It is still quite a common

[267] Mill 1985c, *CW*, vol. 20, esp. p. 345.

[268] John Stuart Mill, Letter to John Pringle Nichol, September 30, 1848, in Mill 1963, *CW*, vol. 13, pp. 738ff, p. 739. The discussion comes as part of a response to Auguste Comte, *Discours sur l'ensemble du Positivisme*, Paris, 1848, which Nichol had thought a 'strange book'; cf. Tocqueville 1971, p. 297, who noted that after the February Revolution the French 'were left with nothing but the sterile goodwill of the English'.

[269] Mill 1984b, *CW*, vol. 21, p. 119. His discussion of British policy in Oudh is critically assessed by Richard J. Moore 1991, pp. 95f, on governmental failure to honour treaty obligations. See too Kohn and O'Neill 2006, esp. pp. 209–13.

[270] See Mehta 1999, esp. pp. 88f, 97ff, 101ff, esp. 103ff.

argument.[271] Mill had also long sanctioned differential administrative and governmental relations with different types of colonies. In fact both he and Sterling were early members of the Colonization Society, engaged principally with the predominantly white settler colonies and the ideas of people like Goldwin Smith.[272]

But most famously his *Considerations on Representative Government* presented certain territories and peoples as 'capable and ripe for representative government', namely America and Australia, whilst India was 'still at a great distance from that state'.[273] Consonant with his views about the economic benefits of colonization, and even when contemplating independence, Mill wanted to retain pacific relations between countries. This was always the prerequisite for co-operation and universal peace, and only with it could the relationship between colony and metropole be one of mutual advantage, where either or both parties could (allegedly voluntarily) consent to separation if and when required.[274] Recalling Adam Smith's analysis of the fateful projects of the British Empire seems to be at least one reason for Mill's concern in presenting such an argument. But Ireland was the great anomaly here. Mill recognized the nefarious consequences of British imperial policy, though he claimed that this state, apparently in a lower stage of civilization, would have to be enabled if it were to govern itself adequately.[275] The end goal was, of course, that the form of government that did the enabling should facilitate a 'transition to a higher stage of improvement' from a lower one, because civilized states should be able to supply such forms of government and political rule consistently. Though he felt it would benefit from a 'stout despotism', as he told his friend John Pringle Nichol, democracy had gained enough of a foothold in Ireland to disallow such a reading off of an appropriate form of government for a particular stage of development; but clearly problems remained that he could not resolve.[276] By proposing something like an analogy between the 'individualities of nations' and the 'individualities of persons', whose mutual imperfections were a 'beneficial arrangement' for considering 'general improvement', Mill attempted to negotiate potentially thorny conceptual problems raised by his otherwise binary model of civilization or barbarism.[277] In fact, his scalar vision

[271] Rawls 1999, esp. pp. 23f.

[272] Mill, Letter to John Sterling, October 20, 1831, in Mill 1963, CW, vol. 12, p. 87 and n. 35; Bell 2007; Hall 2002, p. 438.

[273] Mill 1977g, CW, vol. 19, p. 562.

[274] Mill 1977g, CW, vol. 19, p. 565.

[275] Mill, Letter to John Pringle Nichol, December 21, 1837, in Mill 1963, CW, vol. 12, pp. 363–66, p. 365; see Kinzer 2001, esp. pp. 34f.

[276] Mill 1977g, CW, vol. 19, pp. 567ff.

[277] Mill 1977c, CW, vol. 18, p. 91f.

of progress that worked alongside his binary model also explains why
Mill should want to see international treaties and obligations as akin
to commercial relationships. This correspondence had, in fact, become
an important part of evangelical social theory in nineteenth-century England, and one author went so far as to claim that if unjust wars could
be fought by nations who could then be held responsible according to
the laws of Moses, so too could public companies.[278] Such commercial
and international connections came together in Mill's views on India in
particular, although in later accounts the classic contrast between reason
of state and the 'inviolability of treaties' gained renewed importance.[279]

Given what has already been said, it is unsurprising to find considerable overlap between Mill's public analyses of civilization and the internal private politics of the East India Company. Debates between 'Orien-
talists' such as H. H. Wilson and Anglicists like Charles Trevelyan (who
had the support of Macaulay) were profoundly important to Mill's development, and he rejected the proposed policy for the 'engraftment' of
both positions upon India.[280] Mill found it 'altogether chimerical to expect that the main portion of the mental cultivation of a people can ever
take place through the medium of a foreign language', further arguing
that 'revitalising traditional centres of learning' was the educational and
political solution.[281] The Anglicists won the argument when the governor
general, William Bentwick, decided in their favour in 1835. On behalf of
the Board of Directors, Mill's attempt to reverse the defeat was rejected
by John Cam Hobhouse, president of the Board of Control.[282] Even this
very brief outline, though, shows that Mill's position on India is (at least
on occasion) more complex than some discussions of his 'liberal imperialism' might otherwise suggest.[283] In fact, the defence of native traditions
of property, literature and historical myths was something that Mill saw
as universal, even while he simultaneously promoted colonization. The
urgency of the situation arose because the English 'have done, and are
still doing, irreparable mischief, by blindly introducing the English idea
of property in land into a country where it did not exist and never had
existed'. This was a naked 'injustice' undertaken by the 'English rulers of

---

[278] [Anon.] 1846, pp. 8f, 14f, 29, 56. See too Hilton 1988, pp. 137ff.

[279] Mill 1984f, CW, vol. 21, esp. pp. 343f, 346.

[280] Zastoupil 1994, pp. 39, 5.

[281] Mill [c. July–December 1836] 1999, §§ 15–16, pp. 232f; see also Richard J. Moore
1991, p. 104, on the policy of 'engraftment'; and Zastoupil 1994, p. 43.

[282] Zastoupil 1994, pp. 40, 44, 46.

[283] Sullivan 1983, pp. 607–13, who discusses his economic, cultural, and political justifications of empire; cf. Zastoupil 1994, pp. 184ff, 176, who claims that Mill's work 'cannot
be reduced to participation in the discourse of imperialism'. Mehta 1999, ch. 5, outlines
Burke's concerns about imperial rule, though cf. Armitage 2000a, pp. 617–34.

India, for the most part innocently, from sheer inability to understand institutions and customs almost identical with those which prevailed in their own country a few centuries ago'.[284] Indeed although he lost the debate, and even when, after 1857, Parliament planned to take over control from the company, Mill still defended a strict separation between national parliamentary democracy and rule over external territories that should be 'administered by some intermediate body, constituted expressly for the purpose'.[285] Parliament was a 'body so ignorant and incompetent on Indian (to say nothing of other) subjects' that rational government, a key issue for domestic politics as well, would be 'an impossibility'.[286] Only 'double' government would remain, and 'if the cry of Double Government is to prevail, none of the free institutions of this country, except perhaps the House of Commons, are safe; and we may be thankful if the principle is not applied to Parliament too'.[287]

PROPRIETY IN TIME

Mill's focus on the cultivation of character, on the need for education to overcome the potential yoke of custom and public opinion, and the outlining of a broadly qualitative hedonism underpinning individual self-interest, are clear to most interpreters.[288] Some early critics, however, thought he had discounted the obligations of individuals to society, and that contemporary civilization was really much better than he gave it credit for.[289] Yet, as Mill operated with a philosophy of history that differentiated between 'critical' and 'organic' movements, movements that seem to imply a pattern of general progress affected by continual rupture, disunity, and possible contention, there is no fixed position from which to know how civilization and character will in fact develop. It is dependent upon time and context.

This flexibility allowed Mill to recognize that forms of government will have an effect on human nature, but that the choice of particular forms of government will always be a matter for rational debate. Political institutions are of moral and educational concern. In turn, this means that any

[284] Mill 1990a, CW, vol. 30, p. 222; cf. Burrow 1974, pp. 255–84; Zastoupil 1994, pp. 186–89.

[285] Mill 1977g, CW, vol. 19, p. 573; cf. Mill 1990, CW, vol. 30, p. 99; for the quotation, see Mill 1990, CW, vol. 30, p. 175.

[286] John Stuart Mill, Letter to Henry Samuel Chapman, July 8, 1858, CW, vol. 15, in Mill 1972a, pp. 557–60, p. 560; Mandler 1990, pp. 99f.

[287] Mill 1990, CW, vol. 30, p. 178.

[288] Riley 2003, pp. 410–18.

[289] See [George Vasey?] 1867, pp. 23, 25.

action or policy is to be judged in terms of its moral, aesthetic and sympathetic aspects, and it is this latter, sympathetic element, which concerns our relationships with our fellow citizens and certainly impacts upon the qualitatively hedonistic sentiment of justice present in Mill's thought. Here, common sympathy and a project of, broadly speaking, education for sociability and morality is something that links Mill back to earlier (particularly Scottish) attempts to shed the 'light of reason' upon human affairs. This means, I think, that whilst it is certainly true to see Mill's analysis as more obviously in tune with a form of imperial liberalism than the writings of Montesquieu and Smith, there remains a great deal that they share. Thus, just as to posit too sharp a break between Locke and the Scottish Enlightenment bends the twig too much in one direction, to see yet another wholesale rupture between the Scots and Mill makes a similar error.

For example, Adam Smith's *Lectures on Jurisprudence* provided a wealth of material for understanding his notions of sympathy, benevolence and historical progress, but they were unknown to Mill. It was only later in the nineteenth century, in 1896, that these texts became available. Mill did, however, read and assess Smith's discussions in *Wealth of Nations* and *Theory of Moral Sentiments* as well as other central texts. Furthermore, as the third book of the *Wealth of Nations* concerning the progress of opulence and commerce is, writ large, a summation of the themes present in the earlier lectures, the absence of these specific early texts matters less to my argument, which in any case suggests that Mill was developing themes visible in Smith's major published works.[290] In correlate fashion, Mill's analysis of political economy and its philosophical roots is grounded in the epistemological discussions central to the Scots, and outlined by Smith's early biographer, Dugald Stewart. That framework helped to underpin Mill's position, both in arguments with the Oxford Noetics and with his father.[291]

Although his account of savagery and barbarism relates less to specific social structures than that of earlier stadial theorists, Mill's focus on individual interaction, justice and conscience tempers these differences in ways that clearly recall Adam Smith.[292] The theory of self-development he offers, in fact, most obviously resembles Smith's discussion of the impartial spectator and the grammar of justice it provides, which the previous chapter outlined in some detail. For Mill, writing about civilization over savagery, the relationship was equally and provocatively clear. Just as Smith's commercial stage of human society opened up discussion of

---

[290] Harpham 1999, esp. pp. 447–54.
[291] Corsi 1987, esp. pp. 134ff.
[292] Cf. Mantena 2007, pp. 304ff, 309ff; Holmes 2007, esp. pp. 322–25, 334ff.

artificial sociability in an historical period that was 'unnatural and retrograde' (partly because it managed to artificially restrain the natural
libido dominandi), perhaps Mill's arguments might be similarly understood. The cognate form of constitutional morality or sentiment that Mill
seems to be proposing also goes to the heart of his awkward discussions
of the relationship between political competence and participation over
time. And when, in the *Considerations on Representative Government*,
Mill made the case that the only 'government which can fully satisfy all
the exigencies of the social state is one in which the whole people par-
ticipate', we can see the precursors of his position in the review essay on
representation some two decades earlier. There, he had noted that 'any
person capable of an independent will' should not be excluded from the
franchise, even if plural voting was hardly an overwhelmingly egalitarian proposal.[293] Mill's focus on the dual character of equality grounds
his theoretical distinction 'between the normative (political sovereignty)
and the prudential (decisionmaking capacity)' levels.[294] This principle of
competence is in turn symbiotically related to participation.[295] It helps to
explain why Mill supported a national clerisy, rather than a utilitarian or
'identity' theory of interest and representation.[296]

Mill's analysis of liberty as propriety also reveals itself in his assessment
of the deeply ponderous but highly popular essays collected by Archibald
Alison on the French Revolution. In his review, Mill suggested that history is 'interesting under a two-fold aspect; it has a *scientific* interest,
and a *moral* or *biographic* interest'.[297] The biographical interest in figures
from history and their impact in synthesizing and moving forward debates about social and political organisation was a major strand of Mill's
thinking. But it was principally with the scientific element, where 'general
laws of the moral universe' are enacted, which he thought necessarily
entailed a presuppositional inquiry as to what those laws might be.[298]
This led to a focus on the 'principle of systematic antagonism' derived
from Guizot and Tocqueville; the principle recognized both the need for
active participation to maintain liberty and the contradictory character
of historical change that could stymie such activity. Thus, if the 'governing body' becomes 'so numerous' that the 'large majority of it do not and
cannot make the practice of government the main occupation of their
lives, it is utterly impossible that there should be wisdom, foresight, and
caution in the governing body itself'. Furthermore, if this is the case, then

---

[293] Mill 1977g, CW, vol. 19, p. 412; Mill 1977a, CW, vol. 18, p. 29.
[294] Urbinati 2002, p. 97; cf. pp. 48–54, 89–95.
[295] Miller 2003, pp. 651ff, 657; cf. Thompson 1976, esp. pp. 80ff, 84f, 89ff.
[296] Burns 1969, pp. 303f; cf. Pitkin 1967, esp. p. 144.
[297] Mill 1985, CW, vol. 20, p. 117; Capaldi 2003, p. 136.
[298] Mill 1985, CW, vol. 20, p. 118.

such qualities 'must be found, if found at all, not in the body, but in those whom the body trust'.[299] The quality of responsible agency is once again at the forefront of Mill's political vision.

He thought that competence, alongside the wisdom associated with indirect representation, was required for reasonable and rational government. This was said to be both the cause and the consequence of the natural progression of civilization. Yet the general principles of such forward or progressive movement have nevertheless to be reconciled with a 'critical' recognition of the presence of countervailing and antagonistic forces. Indeed, the negative effects of civilization had to be counterbalanced, and the simple lust for commercial advance and increased wealth controlled. In fact, a fear that the advances of civilization might be forever lost pervades his writing.[300] However, what I have tried to suggest is not only that the idea of civilization as progress is central to Mill's politics, but that it should be seen as an extension of both French and Scottish debates about sympathy and the progress of natural liberty. From this standpoint, Mill promotes a particular type of constitutional sentiment in his defence of representative government, which in turn upholds political and individual liberty under conditions of general equality. By underscoring the importance of liberty and the quality of the freedom that it promotes, Mill hoped to help make sense both of the origin and development of modern freedom, and also of its possible implications. It was akin to an ethology of modern civilization.

The propriety of liberty retains a sharp focus in Mill's analysis given his almost existential awareness of the self-limiting character of individual actions when governed by the despotic rule of custom. This self-limitation is both part and parcel of the experience of commercial society in much the same way it had been for Montesquieu and Adam Smith, and has severe implications both for the internal moral sentiments and for freedom as self-development. Remember that Mill defined justice as an external duty underscored by legal authority, whose legitimacy stems from the internal sentiments of citizens. His is therefore a vision of freedom as enlightened self-government through cultivation, education, and publicly responsible agency governed by justice. Perhaps this is why he fails to fit neatly into any of the paradigmatic traditions of thinking about the concept of freedom in mainstream scholarship, even if he is quite conventional in relating liberty and propriety. To be at liberty, one must act, and to act requires both capacity and opportunity, which means that 'modern nations will have to learn the lesson that the well-being of a people must exist by means of justice and self-government, *dikaiosúne* and

[299] Mill 1977b, *CW*, vol. 18, p. 79.
[300] Varouxakis 1999, pp. 298f, 301f, 304; cf. Mill 1977b, *CW*, vol. 18, p. 50.

sophrosúne, of the individual citizen'.[301] His was a provocative vision, and tracing part of Mill's legacy further and into the work of Thomas Hill Green is the subject of the next chapter because Green, like Mill, thought that 'England has been ruled by class-representation ever since the revolution'. It is to his search for the intellectual and practical origins of real freedom in the history of that revolution that my discussion now turns.[302]

[301] Mill 1965, *CW*, vol. 3, bks. 3–5, bk. 4, ch. 7, § 2, p. 763.
[302] Mill 1977a, *CW*, vol. 18, p. 44.

CHAPTER FIVE

Idealism and the Historical Judgement of Freedom: T. H. Green and the Legacy of the English Revolution

In January 1867, T. H. Green, who for the past seven years had been a fellow and tutor in moral philosophy at Balliol College, Oxford, took the floor at the Edinburgh Philosophical Institution to deliver a series of 'Four Lectures on the English Revolution'.[1] Green's family history practically ensured an interest in the history of Puritanism generally and the figure of Oliver Cromwell in particular. Indeed, he was thoroughly immersed in many of the political and religious controversies of the later quarter of the nineteenth century, whose language and tone typically derived from comparison with this period of British history. Nevertheless, his assessment of the English Commonwealth as a fruit of the Reformation, rather than as a discrete transformation in political culture, has received relatively little sustained attention. This chapter assesses those lectures, in order to show their importance for understanding his analysis of freedom. I argue that without a grasp of his account of the origins of modern legal freedom, beginning with the English Revolution, analysis of his theory of freedom remains partial and incomplete. Both in content and form, the combination of political philosophy, German theology, and English exceptionalism that buttresses Green's arguments makes his claim among the last major embodiments of the tradition of the propriety of liberty. Yet his work clearly also built on Mill here, for just as Mill thought that various of the malignant effects of social conformity could be traced to the evils of a class representation whose origins were found in the English Revolution, so too did Green's similarly 'advanced liberalism' claim to uncover the historical roots of these limits to real or true freedom.

On this most contested of terrain, Green's tone was rather uninspiring for the beginning of a popular lecture series. Noting that rather unlike

---

[1] Nettleship 1997, in Green 1997, CW, vol. 3, pp. lviiiff. Green lectured on January 8, 11, 15 and 18, 1867, receiving subsequent local press attention in the *Edinburgh Evening Courant* on January 9, 1867, p. 4; January 12, 1867, p. 5; January 16, 1867, p. 4; January 19, 1867, p. 4. For details, see the editorial checklist in Green 1997, CW, vol. 5, p. 405.

the interest one might have in the French Revolution as a 'movement still in progress', an Englishman's interest in the period of the English Commonwealth in particular could only be 'purely historical'. Indeed, in a supremely deflationary opening, Green suggested that the 'cycle' of the English Revolution 'was limited, and belonged essentially to another world than that in which we live'.[2] But its pertinence for locating Green's arguments within a wider set of debates about the character of English liberty, and hence of English exceptionalism in comparison with an apparently absolutist Europe, became quite clear as his argument unfurled. Earlier chapters have illustrated various interrelationships between ideas of liberty and propriety in the development of modern political thought, and in Green's case the two themes coalesce around an idealist conception of freedom that is married to an historicist reading of the origins of liberty and rights in the modern world. His argument highlights the longevity of the propriety of liberty in the nineteenth century, and certainly helped to inform his views of contemporary politics.[3]

Some indication of Green's general judgement of the turbulent world of contemporary English political life can be seen in a letter he wrote to James Bryce in March 1866, concerning the Tests Abolition Bill. He thought that 'Dizzy [Disraeli] and Stanley discouraged their followers from voting with a view to facilitating alliance with the super-intellectual liberals', and he believed 'the Government may carry the Reform Bill yet, if they show enough fight, but few people agree with me'.[4] His speech on the Reform Bill a year later, in March 1867, amplified this point, drawing parallels between anti-democratic reform in England and the American Civil War; Green was an early supporter of the North, as Mill had been before him.[5] The radicalism of Green's position on electoral reform within the advanced liberalism surrounding the Second Reform Bill has often been underplayed in interpretation, as has the importance of John Bright to his political views, over and above those of Mill and Gladstone, for example.[6] Correlatively, however, the connection between Green's idealism and his concrete engagement with practical political issues has largely centred on his most famous lecture, 'Liberal Legislation and Freedom of Contract', delivered in 1881. This illustrated, amongst other things, a concern for political education as the foundation of a

---

[2] Green 1997r, CW, vol. 3, p. 277.

[3] Harvie 1976, pp. 257f.

[4] Green, Letter to James Bryce, March 23, 1866, in Green 1997, CW, vol. 5, pp. 419ff, at pp. 420f.

[5] Green 1997y, CW, vol. 5, p. 229; see also de Sanctis 2005, p. 82; cf. Harvie 1976, pp. 105–15; Gerlach 2001, ch. 1. See too Mill 1984, CW, vol. 21, esp. pp. 135ff, 139; Williams 1989, pp. 102–11.

[6] Tyler 2003, esp. pp. 441–46, 453ff.

morally decent democracy.[7] Yet at the same time, many see Green as intensely paradoxical. His apparently 'indolent' character prevented him from writing on bribery for the seminal *Essays on Reform* of 1867, to take just one example, while he was clearly active enough to write a great amount and to be a central figure in the temperance movement and on commissions for school reform.[8]

In sum, Green is well known to historians of political ideas for his mixture of idealism and social reform in the late Victorian period, and known to political theorists for his development of a 'positive' conception of freedom.[9] Indeed, various studies have offered penetrating readings of themes in general and in some relation to these lectures.[10] The relative lack of sustained attention afforded them in particular is nevertheless surprising, both because of the pertinence of the subject matter to Green's biography, and because of the well-known Victorian interest in the Stuart heritage. This chapter suggests that Green's historically informed writings do in fact lay the foundations for his wider theory of politics and freedom, without which they are incomplete. Moreover, Green's account of the Interregnum highlights the philosophical and religious character of his historical thought. It shows his idealist account of political liberty, as real (moral) freedom, is necessarily dependent upon a prior negative or juristic conception of freedom, whose historical origins he traced to this period. Once again, this is a conception of liberty that requires both freedom of the will and responsible agency; it therefore explores the social or public context within which agency is judged and understood according to shared norms or standards of justice and decorum. It builds on accounts of character, cultivation, and sympathy that have been central to the previous chapters and once again shows clear connections with contemporary theories of agency. For example, when Green talks about desire as the 'consciousness of opposition between a man's self and the real world', he claims that our will is the expression in action of our resolute desires that we most identify with, and that the cultivation of

[7] Vincent and Plant 1984, p. 80.

[8] [Various] 1867. Green was on the 'Taunton Commission' examining the status of endowed public schools, and wrote on the character of English state schools, at a time when educational reform was being much discussed in Oxford. See Harvie 1997, p. 705; Harvie 1976, p. 130; cf. de Sanctis 2005, pp. 65ff; Green 1997t, Green 1997u, *CW*, vol. 3, pp. 387–455; On Green's character, see Collini 1991, esp. pp. 82f, 247f; Vincent 2004; and Harvie 1976, p. 200, who discuss Green's representation as Professor Grey in Mrs. Humphry Ward's *Robert Elsmere*. See also Erb 2001, pp. 158–72; Richter 1964, p. 79; Schultz 2004, esp. pp. 339–48.

[9] See Berlin 1988, pp. 123–54; cf. MacCallum 1972; Baldwin 1984; Nelson 2005, esp. pp. 60–63, 74f n. 17; Bevir 1993, pp. 639–61.

[10] Richter 1964; Green 1986; Green 1997e, *CW*, vol. 3, pp. 335–53; Vincent 1986, pp. 48–61; see too de Sanctis 2005, esp. pp. 68–74, and Leighton 2004, esp. pp. 172–76.

our character over time is a result of making particularly appropriate 'habit[s] of will' normal or conventional. Our self has a history and is the principal actor in the drama of our life, whilst our will, which appears often to oppose our desire, simply *is* our action, in time.[11] In a fashion similar to the analysis of second-order volitions in contemporary political philosophy, for Green one must identify consistently and wholeheartedly with particular desires to have desires, so that our reasons for action must be self-conscious and in line with the appropriate cultivation of our character. Only then can the ensuing action based on this cultivation be said to be truly that of our own will.[12] Society is necessary to enable the development of character, but the necessity of both (negative) legal frameworks and (positive) social enablement gives Green's theory of freedom and action a clear connection back to Mill and indeed Kant, as well as a forward-looking glance towards what he also thought of as an advanced liberalism. As an illustration of how these elements cohere into an historical, as well as a normative theory, his account of the English Revolution is central.

CHARACTER AND ACTION

Green's immediate concerns were clear in his focus on the 'character' of the period. In his understanding, it was the character neither of 'partisans' nor 'judicious historians', nor even the 'reaction from the latter' as outlined by 'Mr. Carlyle'. Indeed, Carlyle's account 'puts personal character in the boldest relief, but overlooks the strength of circumstance, the organic life of custom and institution'.[13] Green instead wished to focus on the 'tragedy' of the human condition, whereby the tensions between 'the historic hero, strong to make the world new, and exulting in his strength, has his inspiration from a past which he knows not, and is constructing a future which is not that of his own will or imagination'. This focus showed that 'the providence which he serves works by longer and more ambiguous methods than suit his enthusiasm or impatience'. Therefore 'it is as such a tragic conflict between the creative will of man and the hidden wisdom of the world, which seems to thwart it, that the "Great Rebellion" has its interest. The party spirit of the present day is ill-spent on it'.[14]

This vision of tense value conflicts and the critique of party spirit was a fairly standard trope of contemporary political discourse, and Samuel

---

[11] Green 1969, esp, §§ 101, 131, 136, 153.
[12] Weinstein 2007, esp. pp. 33, 37–40, 48f, 97f, 101 n. 31, 104f, 130.
[13] Green 1997r, CW, vol. 3, p. 277.
[14] Green 1997r, CW, vol. 3, p. 278.

Bosanquet was a typically hyperbolic exponent. He claimed that any politics without theological foundations was illegitimate, and that 'every form of secular government, upon secular and worldly principles, must be tried, and deposed, for mal-administration'.[15] Meanwhile, the spirit of party was applied with almost fanatical prejudice by the 'conservatism', 'liberalism', and the 'oligarchic' and '"levelling" [radical] zeal' that Green discerned in his own time.[16] Yet he was clear that such partisan positions could make little sense of a conflict he saw as bounded by the struggle for divine-right monarchy on the one hand, and freedom through grace on the other.[17] In order to understand the religious character of the civil wars and the establishment of the Commonwealth (a prominent theme in much more recent writing on the period) one had to interpret it with a proper appreciation of the godly character of human action. Of course, this all went rather well with the corresponding focus in Green's wider political and social thought, which emphasized the importance of the cultivation of individual character and whose nineteenth-century development built on the general 'court' and 'country' narratives of independence from the previous century, just as Mill had done.[18] Indeed, rather than seeing the period as in some sense inferior to the contemporary age because it was moved by different passions and sentiments, Green suggested that we must recognize the nobility of purpose in all properly rational, or responsible, action.

He told his audience that 'we do but dishonour God and the rationality of his operation in the world, if, by way of cheap honour to our hero, we depreciate the purposes no less noble than his own which crossed his path'. To do so would be to imply that there was 'nothing but unreason in that necessity of things which was too strong for his control', and that certainly could not be true.[19] Although conflicts between values always exist, there is an order to such antagonism that illustrates what he would call the force of circumstances.[20] Hence, in his account of the 'short life of English republicanism' Green would 'treat it as the last act in a conflict beginning with the Reformation', where opposing forces had their own basis in reason. This was a prelude to understanding the 'reconciliation of the forces at issue of another kind than could to an actor in the conflict be apparent'. It was a theme closely bound up with his wider teaching and

---

[15] Bosanquet 1843, Essay XI, 'False Principles of Politics—Party', esp. p. 197.

[16] Green 1997r, CW, vol. 3, p. 278. See also Donnelly 1988, pp. 261–69; de Sanctis 2005, esp. pp. 76–82.

[17] See Dzelzainis 2002, vol. 2, pp. 27–42; cf. Skinner 2002c, pp. 245–63.

[18] Burrow 1985, p. 89; Collini 1991, pp. 91–118; de Sanctis 2005, pp. 51–53.

[19] Green 1997r, CW, vol. 3, p. 278.

[20] Green 1997f, CW, vol. 3, pp. 3–10; cf. Green 2005, pp. 41f, 44, 46.

thinking.[21] In his lectures on 'Moral and Political Philosophy' given at Oxford in 1867, he laid it down that there are two great divisions in the history of thought. 'One starts from materialism and ends in a contract and a state machine'. The other is Hegel's 'antithesis of conception and idea, i.e. externalized, realized conception. Thus, the state is a realized idea of which morality is the conception'.[22] This idealist conception of the state as the highest contemporary embodiment of rationality and morality both inspired Green's assessment of the Reformation and its legacy and presaged later arguments about freedom as rationally willed action.[23]

Green argued that prior to the Reformation the authority of the church was based on ordinances, having not yet 'been questioned by ... reason'. This meant that 'the obedience rendered to them [church authorities] was that of the servant rather than of the son'. Medieval political life was ordered along the lines of a dual sovereignty between the temporal and spiritual realms of church and state (similar in focus to later accounts of ascending and descending political authority and issues of political theology), and 'together they built up the firmament of custom and ordinance, which the boundless spirit had not yet learned to feel as a limitation'.[24] It was the attempt to rationalize individual behaviour and to 'reconcile to the spirit the dogmas of the church' which not only prompted Luther's 'spiritual revolt' but which also meant that 'the very effort of the reason to break its shell had complicated its confinement'.[25] For Green, Luther was an exemplary figure who embodied the 'force of circumstances'. In these terms he was akin to the 'hero' in the works of Hegel and Kant, as well as Carlyle, whose actions go beyond their own context to shape a new period of world history and to rethink notions of obligation.[26] The connections to ideas of genius as previously elaborated in Mill's political theory were equally clear, as was the aesthetic character of the analysis.[27] Therefore, to understand the Reformation adequately one

[21] Green 1997r, CW, vol. 3, p. 278.

[22] Green 1997w, CW, vol. 5, esp. pp. 110f, 176–79, 181. The lecture notes are reproduced from the papers of F. H. Bradley, on which see Peter Nicholson, 'Editor's Note', in Green 1997, CW, vol. 5, pp. 105ff; Tyler 2005, vol. 1, pp. 2, 6ff, a prelude to Green 1997i, CW, vol. 3, pp. 46–91. See also Weil 1998, esp. pp. 18–55.

[23] Nelson 2005, p. 61.

[24] Green 1997r, CW, vol. 3, p. 279, cf. p. 285; Vincent 1986, pp. 54, 56, 60. Cf. Ullmann 1975, pp. 30ff; Kantorowicz 1985.

[25] Green 1997r, CW, vol. 3, p. 280.

[26] See Green 1997f, CW, vol. 3, pp. 3–10; de Sanctis 2005, pp. 132–35, 137 n. 36; cf. Weil 1998, esp. pp. 86–90.

[27] Green 1997a, CW, vol. 3, esp. p. 12; cf. Green 1997g, CW, vol. 3, 11–19; Green 1997h, CW, vol. 3, pp. 20–45. As Nettleship 1997, in Green 1997, CW, vol. 3, p. xxx, suggests, this was premised on the idea that 'the world in its truth is a unity, governed by a single law, animated by an undivided life, a whole in every part'.

needed to account for the tense new relationship between the belief of the individual and the continued spiritual dominion of the godly spirit within the walls of the church, now an institution 'which only honoured him [God] with the lips'. Furthermore, 'only by considering the modes in which the spiritual forces brought into play in the reformation had their relations adjusted elsewhere', can we 'appreciate the nature of their collision and reconciliation in England'. There were three such modes; 'jesuitry, the divorce of the secular from the religious, and the complete assimilation of the religious to the political life of states'.[28] Jesuitry, the first of these modes, was the Catholic response to this new emergency, which demanded individual spiritual satisfaction and which often sought such satisfaction in political obedience.[29]

Green was incredibly hostile to this mode. He claimed that Protestant ideas about 'an inward light, to whatever extravagances it might be open, stimulated the sense of a universal law which the inward light revealed'. Jesuitry, by contrast, was 'the ruin of all public spirit'. Its reconciliation of the individual to the church was based on 'casuistical devices', and 'in saving the soul it ruins nations' because it makes salvation a 'process of self-seeking no other than the satisfaction of the hunger of sense'. He deemed Jesuitism 'antagonistic to rational freedom' because it misunderstood the true nature of the will.[30] One might also note here Green's cognate hostility to certain elements within his own philosophical heritage. He thought most forms of intuitionism misunderstood the nature of the will, by focusing on common sense and learned experiences as the basis for knowledge of virtue and duty, instead of reconciling religious concerns with rational action. Nevertheless, elements from William Whewell's attempts to render systematic the ethical implications of scientific endeavour, culminating in the idea of progressive revelation and which Green knew just as much about as did Mill, had a more positive reception in his thought. The case of Julius Hare is illustrative. For Hare, morality 'properly studied reveals a progressive development toward a harmonious and coherent religious and spiritual standpoint; and the fact that it does is evidence of the spiritual structure of the universe'.[31] Similarly, certain other strains of intuitionism developed by Hare and his student, F. D. Maurice (focusing in Maurice's case on the 'knowability of God', and in Hare's on the 'perfect renewal of God's image in man'), were received more favourably.[32] This was the promise of philosophy, the history of which could illumi-

---

[28] Green 1997r, CW, vol. 3, p. 281.
[29] Cf. Höpfl 2002, esp. pp. 231f.
[30] Green 1997r, CW, vol. 3, p. 282; cf. Green 1997k, CW, vol. 3, esp. pp. 178ff.
[31] Schneewind 1977, pp. 101, 98.
[32] Schneewind 1977, pp. 97f; also Schultz 2004, pp. 52f; de Sanctis 2005, p. 15 and n. 20.

nate a path towards realising 'the idea of humanity'. But Green's general schema also had a regional dimension, and this brings out the hitherto implicit contrast between the rational development of English national character, in contrast to the rest of Europe.

Catholic countries in general and the 'Romance nations' in particular, Green argued, remained content with the unreconciled character of religion and morality as 'principles of action', principles which stood in contradistinction to the spiritual completeness craved by the Teuton. Jesuitry 'derationalised' the state from its position as the 'passionless expression of general right', rendering it instead the 'engine of individual caprice under alternating fits of appetite and fear'. At the level of the individual subject, Green thought Jesuitry 'gave him over to private interests'.[33] This again reflected both personal and intellectual concerns. One can see the former in Green's attacks on the Jesuitism of his pupil, Gerard Manley Hopkins.[34] One sees the latter in the context of debates about divine morality. Writers like Maurice had worried about the failures of conscience underpinning modern selfishness and caprice, and Green's attempt to understand knowledge of God as the foundation of ethics stood opposed to the arguments of Henry Mansel's celebrated 1858 Bampton Lectures. Those lectures, as Hilton suggests, 'tried to counter moral objections to sacrifice, whether Christ's or Isaac's, on the Butlerian grounds that divine morals are different from and unknowable by humans'.[35] It was an argument whose epistemology was widely rejected, and whose implications then filtered through to Mill and George Grote, in part through the work of a little-known Matthew Boulton.[36] Jesuit religion was regulated in Catholic states, but quickly became 'mere ceremonial' to the now passive citizen, while women and the devout were left as the only elements in society for whom religion was a permanent influence. This theme was of considerable contemporary import in building a contrast between European (Catholic) confusion and a strong, English and Protestant constitutionalism that was exceptionally durable.

This sharp assessment led Green into a general theory of the origins and outcome of both the French Revolution and the Reformation, which exemplified the second mode earlier identified; namely, the general divorce of the secular from the sacred. Here he suggested that 'Wherever in catholic countries, under the influence of the revolutionary revival of the last century, the reorganisation of society has been achieved; it has only

[33] Green 1997r, CW, vol. 3, p. 282.

[34] Green 1997r, CW, vol. 3, p. 283. Cf. Boucher and Vincent 2000, p. 34; Clark 2000, esp. pp. 251, 260ff, 274f.

[35] Green 1997r, CW, vol. 3, p. 283. See Maurice 1853, p. 300; cf. Maurice 1865, p. 35; see Hilton 1988, p. 290, for discussion of Mansel.

[36] Kinzer 2009, p. 15.

been under the condition of this confinement and passivity of religion'. France exemplified this tendency, and its recent history was 'the natural sequel, indeed, of the compromise of interests effected by Henry IV'.[37] In similar fashion, Green's analysis of the Reformation offered a complex theorem by which the character of English republicanism could be explained:

> The opposition between the inward and outward, between reason and authority, between the spirit and the flesh, between the individual and the world of settled right, no longer a mere antithesis of schools, was being wrought into the political life of Christendom. It gives the true formula for expressing the nature of the conflict which issued in the English commonwealth.[38]

In Germany, which represented the third mode identified by Green, northern Protestantism had so closely aligned itself with extant state institutions, that it had been able to avoid internal fissures during the wars of religion at least until the Thirty Years' War. From then onwards, however, survival was predicated upon 'the sword of Gustavus and the diplomacy of Richelieu'. Yet Germany emerged in such a 'state of wretchedness' that organized religion was in no position to compete with the 'constituted anarchy' of the Peace of Westphalia.[39]

To explain its survival, the wider issue of German character was adduced. The 'German, with his speculative grasp, has no difficulty regarding church and state as two sides of the same spiritual organism', even though this might lead to a combination of 'intellectual fusion' and 'moral acquiescence'.[40] England's exceptionalism in this regard was clear to Green, because the impact of the Reformation on national character, its focus on individual knowledge of God and a personalized relationship with the Bible, were themes that had concerned him since his undergraduate days.[41] In order to read the word of God, individuals had first to be able to read, and once religion could be 'internalised and individualised, preaching, as the action of soul on soul, becomes the natural channel of communication'. For the expanding English Protestant nation, as Green well knew, 'a people's bible, a reading bible, and a preaching ministry, were the three conditions of protestant life'.[42] Puritanism was the most immediate and extreme embodiment of this rupture between the old system and the new, and it instantiated a new system by estab-

---

[37] Green 1997r, CW, vol. 3, p. 283.
[38] Green 1997r, CW, vol. 3, p. 281, see also p. 285.
[39] Green 1997r, CW, vol. 3, p. 284.
[40] Green 1997r, CW, vol. 3, p. 284.
[41] See Green 2005a, esp. p. 190.
[42] Green 1997r, CW, vol. 3, p. 285; cf. Hastings 1997; Scribner 1998.

lishing the distinctiveness of such doctrines as predestination.[43] It also clearly aided in the development of a distinctively English sense of national identity, bolstering the idea of freedom as independence (whether from irrational or ungodly action, the tyranny of rulers, or simply a being one's own man) in the seventeenth century that was important to nineteenth-century reinterpretations of the moral character of freedom and independence.[44]

However, Green argued that 'such a system soon builds again the bondage which it began with destroying', for the Reformation effectively shackled the spiritual elevation of the individual with '"secular chains"'. The important domestication of the Puritans by the Victorians, coupled with Green's awareness of Hume's political critique of Puritan enthusiasm, combine here in an interesting synthesis.[45] The Reformation achieved supremacy in Presbyterian form in Scotland, and was much more fully developed there than was English Puritanism because, 'happily' for the English, no one who looked to scripture for 'moral impulse and principle' could sympathize with such a doctrine.[46] The 'reforming impulse' was with the Puritans, and their critique of traditional religion was mirrored in an attack on contemporary politics. Thus, whereas Elizabeth had ruled a 'nation', 'James and Charles never rose beyond the conception of developing a royal interest'. Green certainly did not see them as contributing to the reformulation of traditionally territorial *raison d'état* arguments by other means, as some more recent scholars have done.[47] He did argue, however, 'there arose that combination, by which the catholic reaction had everywhere worked, of a court party and a church party, each using the other for the purpose of silencing the demand for a "reason why" in politics and religion. Charles and Laud alike represented that jesuitical conscience (if I may be allowed the expression) which is fatal to true loyalty'.[48] Green then discussed the policy of religious discrimination in the fifteen years prior to the establishment of the Long Parliament, alongside the development of various resistance theories.[49] But the pivotal moment in the lecture arrives when Green gives his sympathetic portrayal

[43] Collinson 1988, pp. 24ff.

[44] Kumar 2002, p. 214.

[45] Green 1997r, CW, vol. 3, p. 286; Lang 1996, p. 11. Green was an editor of Hume's collected works in 1874–75; see his major (and polemical) introductions to Hume in Green 1997a, CW, vol. 1, pp. 1–371, esp. pp. 336, 369, 371, for the claim that Hume 'de-rationalizes respectability' thus removing any place for 'higher morality'. Cf. Green 2005d, vol. 1, pp. 43–47; Walsh 1986, esp. pp. 31, 33; Green 1997b, CW, vol. 2, pp. 83–97; Thomas 1987, pp. 59ff.

[46] Green 1997r, CW, vol. 3, p. 286.

[47] Pincus 1998, pp. 75–104; Pincus 2001, pp. 272–98.

[48] Green 1997r, CW, vol. 3, p. 287.

[49] Green 1997r, CW, vol. 3, p. 289; Green 1997r, CW, vol. 3, pp. 350ff; cf. de Sanctis 2005, pp. 71–74.

of the 'young Sir Harry Vane' as a 'representative of independency' in the Long Parliament, which returns us once again the historical and conceptual foundations of Green's political thinking.[50]

In his support for a form of freedom as independence, something illustrated by Vane (and also Cromwell), Green once more disagreed with Thomas Carlyle's account of character. His support for Vane indeed runs counter to Carlyle's scathing portrayal in his bestselling 1845 edition of the *Letters and Speeches of Oliver Cromwell*, the source for Green's quotations in the later lectures.[51] According to Green, Vane's 'ideas are worth studying, for they are the best expression of the spirit which struggles into brief and imperfect realisation during the commonwealth'. In his works are found a 'strange intensity of intellectual aspiration, which, if his secondary gifts had been those of a poet instead of a politician, might have made him the rival of Milton', who in turn also admired him.[52] With his overarching 'zeal for liberty of conscience', and a 'nurturing of righteousness', Vane was presented as an upright defender of liberty who refused the oath of supremacy at Oxford because he was a 'man above ordinances' (and who might also have been influenced by the philosophy of Jacob Boehme).[53] Vane's example, however, illustrated the 'tragedy of the commonwealth', because it 'exhibits in little the forces whose strife, [were] tempered but not governed by the practical and stern genius of Cromwell'.[54] Vane was often critical of Cromwell (another reason, perhaps, for the divergent responses of Green and Carlyle to the period), but Green developed Vane's general account of politics. Thus, it 'proceeds within biblical and theological frames of reference', and its 'project was to defer theocracy', avoid degeneration or 'unregeneracy', and promote a form of spiritual and political regeneration.[55] In fact, Green suggested that in England (a society based on the 'unity of opinion') the creation of a republic by a minority in the presence of 'ancient interests' could only cause friction of the highest order. Green therefore looked to Vane as someone independent of both positions. He used him to show the character of the movement towards a republic in England, and through his example, Green illustrated the religious character of individual and rational action.

He did so by using Vane's theory of the twofold nature of creation, one side of which is spiritual and represented by heaven, while the other,

---

[50] Green 1997r, *CW*, vol. 3, p. 290.

[51] See Lang 1996, p. 117; Morrow 1993, p. 218; cf. Morrow 1997, pp. 97–110.

[52] Green 1997r, *CW*, vol. 3, p. 291; see also Coffey 1998, p. 969.

[53] Green 1997r, *CW*, vol. 3, p. 291; Green 1997r, *CW*, vol. 3, pp. 292, 295, citing George Sikes, *The Life and Death of Sir Henry Vane*, London, 1662 ed., p. 8. See Parnham 2003, pp. 1–34.

[54] Green 1997r, *CW*, vol. 3, p. 294.

[55] Parnham 2001, esp. pp. 58, 62, 64; cf. Hill 1990.

material side, is represented by the earth. Man, 'made of dust in the image of God, includes both'. Development, therefore, is a result of the 'gift of rational will', or a gradual process towards pure spirituality. This was an argument of some contemporary as well as historical concern to Green, who was well aware of cognate debates in British political and theological circles.[56] Moreover, in the conscience of man this 'spiritual sublimation', according to Vane, had three stages. The first was a natural conscience, which was 'the light of those who, having not the law, were by nature a law unto themselves'. Second, legal conscience 'was the source of the ordinances and dogmas of the christian'. Finally, a third, evangelical conscience appears when the human spirit is advanced to such a stage, in accordance with Christ's death and resurrection, that it holds 'intercourse ... with the divine'.[57] Although such 'theosophy' was derided by many, including later commentators like Hume, Green suggested that it was through these theological foundations that Vane derived 'certain practical principles' as a statesman, which are 'now of recognised value', even though they would eventually come into conflict with Cromwell.[58] Indeed, such principles concerning the rational character of moral or godly action seem to have a clear resonance with Green's wider theory of true or moral freedom.

Reformation and Revolution

Green began his second lecture by suggesting that in Vane's writings could be found the first 'doctrine of natural law and government by consent, which, however open to criticism in the crude form of popular statement, has yet been the moving principle of the modern reconstruction of Europe'.[59] This period, typically drawn up in most histories of political thought as the birth of toleration based on religious autonomy, was not, for Vane, based upon 'indifference of all religious beliefs'. Rather, Green found Vane's position grounded on 'the conviction of the sacredness of the reason, however deluded, in every man, which may be constrained by nothing less divine than itself'.[60] This account of natural law was premised upon the religious character of legitimate public power, suggesting that government must be based on the outward man and that it remained separate from the 'proper concerns of Christ's inward

[56] Green 1997r, CW, vol. 3, p. 294.
[57] Green 1997r, CW, vol. 3, p. 295.
[58] Green 1997r, CW, vol. 3, p. 296; cf. Green 1997r, CW, vol. 3, pp. 344f.
[59] Green 1997r, CW, vol. 3, p. 296. See Cromartie 1999, esp. pp. 84, 88, 97, 119; cf. Skinner 2002g, esp. pp. 204–8; 2002a, pp. 9–28.
[60] Green 1997r, CW, vol. 3, p. 297.

government'.[61] Scriptures could not be turned to for eternal truths. Instead, one should wait and seek out the true meaning of scripture 'by the gradual manifestation in the believer of the spirit which also spoke in them'. From this quasi-Lockean sounding argument, Green then made an important set of connections between reason, character and moral action in Cromwell, seeing in him 'the application of this waiting spirit to practical life'. He simultaneously recognized that such a view would eventually come into conflict both with 'the spirit of presbyterianism on the one hand and the wisdom of the world on the other', concluding that the history of this tension is actually 'the history of the rise and fall of the English commonwealth'.[62]

During the Long Parliament, Vane stood opposed to both episcopacy and Presbyterianism, though finding the latter less offensive than the former. Overall, however, the 'worldly wisdom' of the Parliament was essentially Erastian. The 'spirit of Presbyterianism' advanced with the calling of the Assembly of Divines in 1643, and culminated in the adoption of the Solemn League and Covenant with the Scots. This afforded numerous opportunities for inserting biblical parallels into interpretations of national histories, and to explain religious covenants as sources of authorized actions.[63] Equally, it 'gave spirit and strength to their [the London Presbyterians'] disciplinarian humour, and in a few months, men who had come to the assembly anxious only for some restraint on episcopal tyranny, were clamouring for the establishment of presbyterianism as *jure divino*'.[64] Vane, as one of the English negotiators with the Scots, was keen to keep the relationship rooted in civil law rather than theological doctrine. Yet Green documents how quickly the Presbyterian cause strengthened, noting that 'nearly every military success of importance that had been won for the parliament had been won by these soldiers of conscience, and unhappily their conscience was not of a kind that would brook presbyterian uniformity'.[65] Possibly taking another swipe at Carlyle, Green also suggested that the idea of Cromwell as the sole moving force of the New Model Army was false. He was instead a 'genuine enthusiast' undertaking God's work, in a theme that would later underscore as many negative as positive interpretations.[66] Green thought that 'the prevalent conception of our time, that the great men of history have not

---

[61] Green 1997r, *CW*, vol. 3, p. 297.

[62] Green 1997r, *CW*, vol. 3, p. 297.

[63] Vallance 2000, esp. p. 67.

[64] Green 1997r, *CW*, vol. 3, p. 299.

[65] Green 1997r, *CW*, vol. 3, pp. 300, 304.

[66] Green 1997r, *CW*, vol. 3, p. 309. See Pocock 1998 esp. pp. 10–14; cf. Green 2005b, in de Sanctis 2005, pp. 193–96.

created popular ideas or events, but merely expressed or realised them with special effect, excludes such a view'.[67]

Green quoted again from Carlyle's edition of Cromwell's letters and speeches. He used the early letters in particular to highlight Cromwell's infectious enthusiasm and his choice of godly men as a rational solution to fractious English politics both on and off the battlefield. Indeed, attempting to strengthen the covenant was anathema to the 'sectarian soldiers, who had been fighting, not for a theory of parliamentary right, but for a spiritual freedom which the sacerdotal establishment had not allowed'.[68] Alongside this narrative, Green had noted the vacillations of Charles I, who was unwilling to align himself with one camp over another, having 'not enough breadth of view even to play his own game with advantage'.[69] Thus, Cromwell had watched until 1647 from a position of strength, with Vane a strategic supporter given his interest 'in freedom of opinion on deep religious grounds'. But Vane was no revolutionary leader, having 'none of the rough geniality which gives personal influence at such times', and was indeed thought of as a coward physically. Cromwell could not control him though.[70] And unlike the 'high republicans', Cromwell had 'the fatalism about him without which nothing great is achieved in times of political crisis; the consciousness of a divine work that must be done through him, though personal peace and honour were wrecked in the doing. They [Vane and the army] were men of theory and principle'.[71]

Green nevertheless fulsomely discussed the army's demands, portraying with sympathy their claims for regular pay and liberty, and chronicling the peaceful character of their march to London. He argued, though, that the 'army was becoming rapidly republican', and this was a republicanism whose 'mode' was the '"levelling spirit"', the spirit of resentment against "gentry, ministry, and magistracy"'. The '"levelling" zeal' of his own day, recall, was one that he was more than a little uncomfortable with.[72] Green also portrayed Cromwell's persistent negotiations with the King as part of his wider character, one that exemplified a desire for 'such a reconciliation of parties as would at once prevent government by faction and secure the "godly interest."'[73] Again, the theme of reconciling divergent positions in the interests of a godly ethics also had contempo-

---

[67] Green 1997r, CW, vol. 3, pp. 305f.

[68] Green 1997r, CW, vol. 3, p. 315.

[69] Green 1997r, CW, vol. 3, p. 315.

[70] Green 1997r, CW, vol. 3, p. 316.

[71] Green 1997r, CW, vol. 3, p. 348, cf. p. 347; Richter 1964, pp. 246ff.

[72] Green 1997r, CW, vol. 3, p. 321; cf. Green 1997r, CW, vol. 3, p. 324; Green 1997r, CW, vol. 3, pp. 277f. See also Barber 1998, ch. 2.

[73] Green 1997r, CW, vol. 3, p. 321. See also Somerville 1990, esp. pp. 249–54.

rary relevance. The legacy of writers like Coleridge for Victorian ethics (through Hare and Maurice, and latterly Whewell and Mill) supported the view that 'truth' may be found in combining the deepest religious thoughts of particular thinkers. In fact, Green lectured extensively on Mill's logic concerning precisely these questions of validity in reasoning.[74] Politics trumps logic on occasion, however, and when Charles I signed with the Scots as the last roll of the dice, the positions were finally clear. 'Either the new royalist rising would prevail and restore a short-lived tyranny of presbyters to end in a longer one of priests, or it would fail, and on its wreck be established a military republic'.[75]

At the end of his broadly chronological narrative to this point, culminating in the regicide, Green outlined the determinist thesis behind his account. The death of Charles I was a logical necessity for the establishment of the Commonwealth, but the Commonwealth itself was the 'result of the strife of forces, or more properly, the conflict of ideas, which the civil war involved'. Lest this be thought to be based simply around a 'confused web of personal relations', beyond it 'may be seen the conflict of those religious ideas which I have spoken of as resulting from the action of the Reformation on the spirit of christendom'. That is to say, the Reformation was both a necessary and a sufficient cause of the English Commonwealth, and the Commonwealth itself contained numerous contradictions between authority and conscience, virtue and liberty, opinion and reason, tradition and progress.[76] Indeed, Green noted that the majority of the people retained a reverence for 'familiar names, and resentment against virtues which profess to be other than customary and commonplace'.[77] Yet the boundaries of republican disdain for monarchy (as tyranny or idolatry) were also shaped by Milton's critique of the 'sensual degradation' of a populace who could not understand government based on reason. For Green, Milton became the 'the true exponent of the higher spirit of the republic'.[78] His *Tenure of Kings and Magistrates* was the 'best illustration of the real feeling of the republican clique in London towards the preaching presbyterian royalists'.[79] What this meant was that the English Commonwealth was a 'democracy without a demos' and 'rested on an assertion of the supremacy of reason, which from its very exclusiveness gave the reason no work to do'.[80] Green's point here concerned the relationship between rationality and its institutionaliza-

---

[74] Schneewind 1977, p. 99; Green 1997c, CW, vol. 2, esp. pp. 195–306.
[75] Green 1997r, CW, vol. 3 p. 323.
[76] Green 1997r, CW, vol. 3, p. 327, see also p. 325.
[77] Green 1997r, CW, vol. 3, p. 329.
[78] Green 1997r, CW, vol. 3, p. 329.
[79] Green 1997r, CW, vol. 3, p. 333.
[80] Green 1997r, CW, vol. 3, p. 330.

tion. As he suggested, 'the reason of the case is obvious. It is the true nemesis of human life that any spiritual impulse, not accompanied by clear comprehensive thought, is enslaved by its own realisation'.[81] By examining the Civil War and the foundation of the Commonwealth as the working through of spiritual and religious controversies that began with the Reformation, Green not only presaged many later discussions of the English Civil War as a war of religion.[82] He also allowed his account to be dominated by the tensions between struggles over individual freedom of conscience on the one hand, and the claims of government based on 'reason' on the other. These were tensions that went to the heart of his concern with the relationship between freedom and moral progress.[83] In trying to resolve them, Green's focus on the propriety of liberty is updated to suggest that freedom is rational will, understood as action in time, and appropriately grounded in both reason and revelation.

The practical tensions between politics and religion were made more obviously palpable in British politics in 1867, with crisis in Ireland concerning the status of the National Church, alongside the stumbling towards electoral reform first under the Liberals, and then the Conservative government under Derby.[84] Gladstone's near contemporary struggles to resolve the Irish problem peacefully might well help to account for the relatively minor role Green accorded to Cromwell's earlier hated policies in Ireland at this point in his talk.[85] For although he could not ignore the Irish question, he certainly did not grant it the major status that recent historians of the civil wars have accorded it, nor did he seem to give it the recognition that it clearly had in mid-Victorian politics. Indeed, he discusses it in much less detail than did Mill, then Member of Parliament for Westminster.[86] This is perhaps because his concerns were more general.

Green explored the general hostility to the new government not only from the gentry and the clergy, but also from the 'commercial class', a class 'which never loves experiments in government' and for whom the 'financial necessities' of a military republic 'aggravated the offence of its moral and spiritual innovation'.[87] Taking a 'superficial view' might sug-

---

[81] Green 1997r, *CW*, vol. 3, p. 332.

[82] See Burgess 2000, pp. 180f, 185ff, 196–99; also Morrill 2002, esp. pp. 16f, 19.

[83] Vincent and Plant 1984, p. 15.

[84] Parry 1994, pp. 195–98, 207–17.

[85] Gladstone's numerous drafts of speeches pertaining to this issue in 1868 can be found in the 'Gladstone Papers', vol. DCLXXI, BL Add Mss. 44, 756, fos. 134–37; see also Shannon 2000, p. 30.

[86] Kinzer 2001, esp. pp. 128f (on Maynooth), 27–33 (on civilization and progress). More generally, see Hoppen 1998, esp. pp. 572–90.

[87] Green 1997r, pp. 334.

gest that the Reformation, which gave rise to the Commonwealth, had simply continued 'the plutocracy under feudal forms which has governed England since the death of William III'.[88] The contemporary demands made by those disgruntled commercial elements in British society over free trade, for example, would surely not have missed the pertinence of Green's argument. He repeated it in a speech some two months later to the Oxford Reform League.[89] In other words, Green reiterated Mill's analysis almost verbatim. Because the 'restoration' of free trade in Britain after the repeal of the Corn Laws was so closely 'intertwined with a dominant narrative of political democracy', that is, the importance of political economy as a language of politics and general welfare in British life distinct from the post-Napoleonic protectionism of Europe, these implications would have been quite clear to his audience.[90] British 'exceptionalism' underpinned Green's discussion, and intermingled with wider debates about evangelicalism and social reform.[91]

But there were still wider concerns parallel to the main thrust of his lectures that Green was developing. The position of the republic, he thought, depended upon an uneasy, and somewhat unwilling 'temporary coalition between three sets of men … between whom there was no real love; the genuine commonwealth's men, a section of the "grandees of the parliament", and the leaders of the army'.[92] Furthermore, the English republic contained only one member whose actions and intent could be said to have 'some touch of the modern French republican about him', and this was another regicide, Henry Marten, whom Green had first discussed in the second lecture alongside Vane.[93] The republicans must, says Green, have felt the uneasiness of their position.[94] Edmund Ludlow (another regicide) and Marten had 'too much of the ancient Roman in them, Marten, perhaps, rather of the ancient Greek' to sympathize with the army, who were the 'real constituency of the republican parliament'.[95] One might profitably note here the divergent readings of the history of republicanism in both Greek and Roman guises, offered by Green's Victorian assessment of the English Commonwealth. This is particularly pertinent, given the predominantly Roman reading of the republican heritage in most recent discussions of the subject. Green was just as aware as Mill had been of the importance of the Greek republican heritage to nineteenth-century

---

[88] Green 1997r, CW, vol. 3, p. 364.
[89] Tyler 2003, esp. p. 447.
[90] Howe 2002, pp. 210f; Trentmann 2009.
[91] Hilton 1988, pp. 262ff, 276–80.
[92] Green 1997r, CW, vol. 3, p. 335.
[93] Green 1997r, CW, vol. 3, p. 316. See also Barber 2000, esp. chs. 2–3.
[94] Green 1997r, CW, vol. 3, p. 336.
[95] Green 1997r, CW, vol. 3, pp. 337. On Ludlow, see Worden 2001, chs. 1–4.

Britain. The Aristotelian conception of virtue that his teachings often recommend has already been noted, while the key role he assigns to the state to promote equality can equally be traced to Greek beginnings.[96] Updating the analogy of the modern state as either machine or contract, Green broadened the contrast between Greece and Rome. 'Greece is intense individuality recognized in few men. In Greece, morality is aesthetic; in Rome the state has an abstract end and you can only attain individuality if you merge your will in the state end'.[97] He would nevertheless surely have agreed with James Bryce's contemporary claim, that 'If the history of Greece and Rome teaches anything, it teaches us that it is not democracy but the interested government of an upper class which naturally and inevitably produces the worst type of demagogue'. This demagogue 'is the legitimate consequence of a system which abandons the idea of an undivided Commonwealth, in whose prosperity all citizens are to share, and which substitutes for this conception that of a State composed of different classes with discordant interests'.[98]

In this regard, perhaps the most obvious political point made by Green concerned reform. Assessing the Leveller's petitions as essentially a 'continuation of the agreements and remonstrances issued by the council of the army during the agitation of 1648', Green actually (and with some rhetorical irony) suggested that many of those desired reforms were 'for the most part stood over for nearly another two hundred years, till they began to be carried out by the "purged parliament" of 1832'.[99] The distinct connection between the English past and contemporary parliamentary reform once again mirrored the assessment Mill had earlier outlined concerning class representation in British political life. So the fact that the contemporary reform movement (and the interconnections between participation and state-led policies designed to promote individual responsibility) was thought of as announcing a 'New Reformation' would again not have been lost on Green. The term alluded both to contemporary accounts of Irish policy in the 1820s and to seventeenth-century views of the Glorious Revolution.[100] Green was sympathetic to the Levellers and the Diggers, viewing the latter as exemplary of that 'sectarian enthusiasm, seeking wildly to withdraw itself from secular, as it had already done

[96] Turner 1981, esp. pp. 359–65, focuses on the posthumously published work in Green 1969. This consolidated some of the earlier 1867 lectures on moral and political philosophy, which were of more immediate relevance to Green's lectures on the English Revolution. See also Turner 1986, esp. pp. 592f; Irwin 1992, pp. 279–310; Nelson 2004.

[97] Green 1997w, CW, vol. 5, p. 181.

[98] Bryce 1867, p. 270.

[99] Green 1997r, CW, vol. 3, p. 338.

[100] Burns 2004, esp. pp. 155f; see too Beales 1999, esp. pp. 161, 165; Mandler 1990, p. 38.

from religious ordinance'.[101] However, they were prolegomena to the substantial problem. In the two years following the execution of Charles I, that is, up to the autumn of 1651, the 'republican oligarchy was able to shut its eyes to the real situation', while its military were engaged in battle on the Celtic fringes. Again, though, the war in Ireland is relegated to a secondary act in a much broader drama. The only chance for success and a degree of permanence was if the republic should 'avail itself of this interval to establish itself on a more popular basis, and initiate practical reforms' geared towards constituency representation. But this was not to be.[102] This was because the army, as the basis of the republic, temperamentally could not leave the republic to find its own way. In conclusion, the paradoxical but 'essential difficulty of the situation was aggravated by the oligarchical temper which it bred in the republican leaders'.[103]

ENTHUSIASM AND REFORM

Green cast Cromwell in the role of the tortured leader with heavy responsibilities, the godly moralist of historical commonplace, as well as the enthusiast recognized by all from Locke and Montesquieu to Smith and Mill. He continued to note Cromwell's reluctance to sever all connections with monarchical government, and this reluctance continued to play an important part in later nineteenth-century debates over Cromwell's reputation.[104] After summarizing and recapitulating some of the key political developments after 1647, Green therefore went on to make yet another contemporary political point that would not have been lost on his audience. He suggested that had Cromwell's plan come to fruition, 'in completeness it would have given England at once a genuine parliamentary government and a free national church'. The result would have been that 'two centuries of government by borough-mongering and corruption, of church-statesmanship and state-churchmanship would have been saved'.[105] The analysis clearly suggests that Green found the first

[101] Green, CW, vol. 3, p. 341; see also Peacey 2000, pp. 625–45.

[102] Green 1997r, CW, vol. 3, pp. 342f.

[103] Green 1997r, CW, vol. 3, pp. 343f.

[104] Green 1997r, CW, vol. 3, p. 347; cf. Smith 1968, pp. 17–39; Worden 2001, chs. 8–11. The 'Cromwell in the Nineteenth Century' archive at the Bodleian Library, MS Eng. C. 6759, fo. 68, illustrates the importance of reputation to debates about the erection of a statue of Cromwell in Manchester. Clyde Binfield (fo. 84) argues, quite rightly, that if Cromwell 'belonged to anybody in the 19th Century England, he belonged to the Dissenters, and particularly to those in the Independent tradition'. See also Richter 1964, pp. 40f, 46–51.

[105] Green 1997r, CW, vol. 3, p. 346; Gardiner 1958, § 71. 'The Heads of the Proposals Offered by the Army' (August 1, 1647), pp. 316–26. See also Morrill 2002, p. 29; Croft 1996, pp. 163–74.

Reform Act wanting, both in terms of its move towards the ten-pound franchise, and in its failure to reform adequately the relationship between church and state.

Such relations would have been a keen topic of contemporary interest, given Green's awareness of Coleridge's discussion of the 'ideas' underpinning any discussion of the constitution of church and state, which had also already been taken up by the younger Gladstone. Gladstone was of course the author of *The State in its Relations with the Church*, in which he modified Coleridge's arguments to suggest both that the state clearly was a moral personality and that its extent was the only thing that should be the subject of debate. It was a position he retained until 1865, when, like Green, he wrote of a providential order of history and freedom from the Greeks onwards.[106] Aristotelianism mixed with a Protestant-inspired message in Gladstone's writings as much as Green's, and a similar vision clearly helped inform Green's account of human association in the modern state. Contemporary worries about reform, both its semantic as well as its political instability given the association with moral improvement it assumed, all coalesced for Green around the 1867 Reform Bill.[107]

Cromwell's attempt to reconcile 'godly' with 'worldly' interests illustrated for Green a wider and more general tension between the spiritual and the secular. His assessment of Cromwell suggested that in the end, a complete reconciliation was impossible. It nevertheless seems to me that the attempt, if not the reality, of reconciliation is a critical component of Green's political thought. So despite his other criticisms of Carlyle's interpretation of Cromwell, Green still made a case for his exemplary status, arguing that 'in these days of playing at heroes among the "inferior races", such men, perhaps, receive less credit than is their due'. He went further, suggesting that it was not his 'purpose to measure the man of principle against the "man of destiny", who may be a political gambler, but merely to indicate their inevitable collision'.[108] While he was keen to show Cromwell's ambivalence towards the republican triumph, Cromwell's military endeavours (and here Ireland is mentioned) were now likened to biblical struggles, in line with the providentialism both Green and

---

[106] Gladstone 1838, pp. 17, 83, 236; 1868, pp. 14f 19. Cf. Gladstone 1865, esp. pp. 19, 33, 56: 'I submit to you, that the true *Praeparatio Evangelica*, or the rearing and training of mankind for the Gospel, was not confined to that eminent and conspicuous part of it ... but extends likewise to other fields of human history and experience; among which, in modes and degrees, varyingly perceptible to us, the Almighty distributed the operations preliminary and introductory to His one great, surpassing and central design for the recovery and happiness of mankind'. See too Parry 1994, pp. 248–73.

[107] Innes 2004, pp. 71–97.

[108] Green 1997r, *CW*, vol. 3, pp. 348f.

Cromwell saw in his actions more generally.[109] This interpretation added zealousness to political action in ways that Green's audience would have easily identified with, in terms of wider debates in the British Parliament about Catholic emancipation and the Irish church. With rhetorical force, Cromwell was now cast as being possessed with the 'fire of enthusiasm' as he 'led his army into Ireland, as Joshua unto Canaan'.[110] The central conflict nevertheless remained between the Parliament and the army, the 'antique republicanism' of the former contrasting with the 'interests' of the latter, the 'military saints'. In fact, the 'theoretical republicans of the Rump were in favour of constituting themselves a permanent body on the Venetian model, only filling up vacancies as they should occur'.[111] The eventual dissolution of the Rump in 1653 was the decisive step, but, as one might suspect, this could do nothing to alter the irreconcilable contradictions between the religious and secular spheres upon which the conflict was ultimately premised. Reconciliation was impossible.[112]

In the transition from Commonwealth to Protectorate, the mismatch was so sharply illustrated because the 'three points of the Cromwellian programme', namely restoration of the old constitution, law reform, and liberty of conscience, were inconsistent with one another. The constitution could not be restored without the restoration of royalism, and that in turn would mean the 'subjection of the godly'.[113] As Austin Woolrych has suggested, this tension between 'radical millenarian Puritanism and moderate constitutionalism' structured the whole transformation.[114] Green's overall assessment was nevertheless positive. The real result of the Puritan revolution, as opposed to the 'superficial' account of the Commonwealth he had earlier noted, was to save England from Catholic reaction, to create '"dissenting bodies"' and to implement 'fifteen years of vigorous growth which Cromwell's sword secured for the church of the sectaries, [which] gave it a permanent force which no reaction could suppress, and which has since been the great spring of political life in England'. Offering a wider context for the importance of the concept of 'enthusiasm' and its religious connotations, Green argued that such enthusiasm 'was not

---

[109] Green 1997r, CW, vol. 3, pp. 350ff; and see Oliver Cromwell, Letter 85, 'Letter to Colonel Robert Hammond', November 25, 1648, in Carlyle 1845, pp. 90–101, esp. pp. 91–94.

[110] Green 1997r, CW, vol. 3, pp. 353f; Oliver Cromwell, Letter 105, 'For the Honourable William Lenthall, Esq. Speaker of the Parliament of England', September 17, 1649, in Carlyle 1845, pp. 166–74, esp. p. 171.

[111] Green 1997r, CW, vol. 3, pp. 356f; Glover 1999.

[112] Green 1997r, CW, vol. 3, p. 360.

[113] Green 1997r, CW, vol. 3, p. 361.

[114] Woolrych 2000, pp. 4, 395ff.

puritanic or English merely'. In fact, he wrote that 'it belonged to the *universal spiritual force* which as ecstasy, mysticism, quietism, philosophy, *is in permanent collision with the carnal interests of the world*, and which, if it conquers them for a moment, yet again sinks under them, that it may transmute them more thoroughly to its service'. Vane's 'enthusiasm' therefore 'died that it might rise again. It was sown in the weakness of feeling, that it might be raised in the intellectual comprehension which is power'.[115] Propriety here is transformed into rational providence.

Such in outline is the substance and style of Green's lectures, analysis of which reveals him to have had a clear awareness of the meaning of the term 'revolution' as an illustration of both divine providence and the secular progression of human affairs.[116] As well as bringing these wide-ranging lectures more clearly into view, my other major concern is to show how this account of the English republican moment affects Green's general theory of freedom as the rational and moral action of free citizens as agents. This highlights not only the theoretical import of his analysis of agency and will, but also that his celebrated diagnosis of negative freedom, as a prerequisite to the development of true or moral freedom, has in fact an historical origin. For although a spiritual impulse lies behind Green's theory of true freedom, this argument depends upon a prior realization of the negative or juristic freedom of individuals, which was precisely the type of freedom that Green thought had originated with the English Commonwealth.

REAL FREEDOM

Because the conflict between the secular and the sacred underpins Green's intellectual history of the Commonwealth, it helped him try to reconcile a theory of English exceptionalism with his awareness of the tensions between a moral view of politics and the 'carnal interests of the world'.[117] His theory of freedom is in fact designed specifically to show how an adequate reconciliation of these conflicting interests in a plural society might at least be possible, whilst his analysis of the English Commonwealth explains why he thought the potential for reconciliation was central to this period. The theory itself has a tripartite structure, whose most basic element is the 'formal' freedom of the individual will, without which we could not talk about freedom at all. Second, he builds in the 'juristic' or 'legal' freedom of individuals. Third comes the idea of 'real' freedom, and

---

[115] Green 1997r, *CW*, vol. 3, p. 364. Emphasis added.
[116] See Rachum 1995, esp. pp. 199–202; also Sonenscher 2007, ch. 1.
[117] Green 1997r, *CW*, vol. 3, p. 364.

this is the overarching concept of which the commonly referred to idea of 'positive freedom' is a subset.[118]

Freedom of the will is codified juristically as negative freedom, in terms of the prevailing social relations between individuals. If legally one is then free to do what one wills within the limits laid down within a civil association, 'real' freedom consists in the willing, for its own sake, of an object or end that an individual thinks of as a good itself. Legal freedom is the recognition of formal freedom under law (a traditionally understood 'negative' freedom), while 'real' freedom is something rather different. It builds upon negative freedom to suggest that individuals can only be free in a society of formal equality, which means that formal freedom has predominantly instrumental value, as a means to the end of real freedom. Such freedom, which can only be achieved in a social context, is therefore best 'expressed in terms of the power or capacity to do what one ought, which does not necessarily imply that the power is exercised'.[119] This is as much a claim about the rationality of freedom as of its actualization, and although this type of freedom is usually thought of as 'positive', thus understood it expresses the tradition of liberty as a form of propriety that has been the principal subject of this book. In saying this, it seems quite clearly to flow from the standard discussions found in Locke, Montesquieu, Smith and Mill, in requiring both internal self-regulation and publicly governed conduct. Green's focus is similarly on the quality of the agency undertaken, and he also finds a moral content to the exercise of real freedom that is dependent first upon the realisation of juristic freedom. Both the style and presentation of Green's reflections on the nature of freedom lend themselves well to the two principal components of the propriety of liberty that I have been concerned to delineate, namely, internal self-government and external action that one is responsible for according to the public criteria of justice.

Where Green is more explicit than his predecessors is in his claim that the state has the capacity to rationally, or knowingly, effect this transformation. It is well known that Green's account of real freedom requires a distinctively proactive role for the state, for as an institution that not only creates and sustains the conditions that make the development of real freedom possible, the state can also actively realize it. To this extent real freedom belongs in the sphere of morality. Its logical precursor, juristic freedom, can be created by the state, and hence belongs in the sphere of the political.[120] His account suggests that 'a man gains his sense idea of

---

[118] Nicholson 1990, p. 116, and in general pp. 116–31, is fundamental.

[119] Nicholson 1990, pp. 121f, also 125ff.

[120] See Green 1997s, CW, vol. 3, pp. 365–86. Cf. Dimova-Cookson 2003, esp. pp. 509, 525; Baldwin 1984, pp. 136–41, esp. p. 141; Nesbitt 2001, pp. 423–37.

how to be free, his ideal of what he ought to be, from his society'. Indeed, 'Green's very important point is that a man cannot be free except in a society, and that the degree of his freedom depends upon the level of his society'.[121] This also means that his conception of freedom is distinctively related to the power, or capacity, of an individual and not just to the absence of constraint, which is one reason why claims about positive liberty as self-realization have come in for such strong criticism.[122] Nevertheless, my contention is that the rise of a modern, juristic freedom as the basic requirement for the realising of true freedom is precisely the type of freedom that he associates with the individual freedom and citizenship emerging from the English Commonwealth. If my interpretation is correct, then the importance of Green's recognition of the conflict between the sacred and the secular that underpins the English Commonwealth has more than just historical interest.

His account of true freedom depends upon an account of moral action, and this account is itself underpinned by a religious metaphysics. This religiously inspired vision of freedom more obviously returns us to the seventeenth century, and in particular to Locke's conception of responsible agency. Such circularity illustrates one reason why Green stands at this particular culmination of the tradition of liberty as propriety explored in this book. In fact, when discussing the ideal of the common good, Green presupposes a metaphysical conception of the inherently religious or godly character of 'real' freedom, which is an attempt to overcome the limitations of juristic freedom but in a language that draws explicitly upon his analysis of social conflict and social action in the English Revolution. By so doing, Green both argues for a greater role for the state than others in the tradition outlined earlier, and also moves the claim about the rationality of moral action onto the plane of something like a political theology that is more overt than anything Locke would countenance. In a seminal statement on the freedom of the will written over a decade after his lectures, Green made the connection clear, and this lengthy quotation is worth taking seriously:

> In modern Christendom, with the extension of citizenship, the security of family life to all men (so far as law and police can secure it), the establishment in various forms of Christian fellowship of which the moralising functions grow as those of the magistrate diminish, the number of individuals whom society awakens to interests in objects contributory to human perfection tends to increase. So far the modern state, in that full sense in which Hegel uses the term (as including all the agencies for common good of a law-abiding people), does contribute to the

---

[121] Nicholson 1990, p. 130.
[122] Nelson 2005, pp. 62ff. 66f.

realisation of freedom, if by freedom we understand the autonomy of the will or its determination by rational objects, objects which help to satisfy the demand of reason, the effort after self-perfection.[123]

His account of moral activity, then, seems predicated on an attempt to reconcile the 'contrast between the possible self and the actual self', and to outline a theory of moral progress between the two.[124] Therefore there can be no simple definition of freedom that does not take account of the fact of moral progress, because freedom is the 'liberation of the powers of all men equally for contributions to a common good'.[125] In fact, his lecture on the freedom of the will simply spells out (in quite Kantian philosophical language) the implications of his account of the potential development of rational and moral action during the English Commonwealth. Both involve the codifying of individual legal freedoms by the state, whilst the necessary conceptual precursor to the full expression of real freedom required some sort of historical genealogy to account for its development. In the lectures on the English Commonwealth Green provided it, even if in later life he extended this claim even further back to the Stoics.

In the most general sense, however, the attempted reconciliation between the sacred and the secular through the twin spheres of juristic and real freedom is a classically Aristotelian endeavour. It relates in intimate fashion the progressive development of society with the progressive development of freedom, as people in effect learn how to be good.[126] From this premise, the desire for 'real' freedom can only be attained through the performance of moral actions, or rather, actions that are morally valuable, for which people have good reasons, and which are predicated upon a wider theory of historical progress. As he elsewhere wrote concerning the relationship between life and popular philosophy exemplified in the reaction to the American Civil War, although modern 'European society stands apparently square and strong on a basis of decent actual equity', there is in fact no 'adequate rationale' for this basis. Thus, the 'hedonism of Hume has been turned into utilitarianism, the Jacobinism of Rousseau into a gentle liberalism', but furthermore, 'neither *ism* could save the "culture" of England, in the great struggle between wilfulness and social right across the Atlantic, from taking sides with the wilfulness'. The reason for this was rooted in a misunderstanding of freedom, for 'whatever might be the case practically, it had not learnt speculatively that freedom

---

[123] Green 1997d, CW, vol. 2, esp. pp. 313f; cf. Buchwalter 1992, esp. pp. 572f.

[124] Vincent and Plant 1984, p. 15; Harris 1988–89, pp. 538–62.

[125] Green 1997s, CW, vol. 3, p. 372; Nicholson 1990, pp. 117–22, also 131: 'Thus Green's perspective extends beyond negative freedom in two directions. It includes the internal as well as the external side of a person, and it sets the person in the context of his society'.

[126] See Burnyeat 1980, esp. pp. 82f, 86ff.

means something else than doing what one likes. A philosophy based on feeling was still playing the anarch in its thoughts'.[127] Moreover, Green argued that only when understood as part of the gradual unfolding of reason and progress in civilization could the true nature of the debates about freedom, religion and toleration during the English Revolution be fully explained.[128]

Numerous political philosophers have seen in the general struggle for individual freedom of conscience associated with the English Revolution part of the legacy of the wars of religion to the birth of modern liberalism.[129] That, of course, is both an ideological construct and an anachronism. Most accounts of Green's writings, in building on this view, have led him to be located within the actual historical development of a social or new liberalism, a movement that he himself recognized and was part of. This liberalism was more concerned with relating a political theory of welfarism to a focus on individual character in the social context of later Victorian and Edwardian Britain, challenging the effects of an unequal distribution of wealth and resources. It also proposed that those capable of acting in the interests of the common good should do so, providing a joint focus on both the beneficiaries of reform and the reformers themselves.[130] Freedom thus understood relates not just to self-perfection but also to the perfection of society. Legal freedom provides a defence of individual rights by the rational political state, but is only the first stage in the development of a society moved by ideas of the common good, providing the foundation for the development of real freedom through societal progress. It is at the second stage that the relationship to Green's lectures on the English Commonwealth is most clear, because it was in the struggle to achieve individual rights and juristic freedom that the possibility (if not the reality) of moving towards real freedom and the common good was most clearly achieved. And the fact that these struggles were precisely to do with the conflict between religious freedom and worldly powers was no accident. For Green's ideal of the common good seems precisely dependent upon an idea of the perfectibility of mankind, a vision of God as the moving spirit in the world. That is to say, Green's vision of the real freedom of man is not where man is a potential representation of the historical figure of Christ, but where the individual becomes quite literally a 'Christed self', an individual capable of rational self-perfection.[131] This vision, present both in Green's account of the different senses of freedom,

---

[127] Green 1997j, CW, vol. 3, esp. p. 117. See also Lang 1996, pp. 17ff. See also Green 1997v, CW, vol. 5, pp. 267ff on the limitations of hedonism.

[128] Green 1997r, CW, vol. 3, p. 296.

[129] Rawls 2000, p. 5.

[130] See Harris 1992, pp. 116–41; Clarke 1978, esp. pp. 14–17; also Freeden 2005, esp. pp. 60–77.

[131] Boucher and Vincent 2000, p. 50; cf. Green 1997p, CW, vol. 3, pp. 230–52.

and in his historical evaluation of English republicanism, relied for its broad principles upon those native debates about intuitionism and non-conformism that were a large part of his own intellectual inheritance. Those discussions, however, were also coupled with an engagement with largely German Protestant theological sources, especially those outlined by Hegel and Ferdinand Christian Baur.[132]

POLITICAL THEOLOGY

The impact of Hegel on Green's writings has often been alluded to, even though he was far from an uncritical admirer.[133] Nevertheless, the idea behind Green's argument that the Teutonic spirit of the Reformation proposed a spiritual unity of church and state, and which rendered it immune to the Jesuit schismatics of the Romance nations, is something already found in Hegel's work. For example, in the third section of the *Enzyklopädie der philosophischen Wissenschaften*, Hegel outlined the 'reciprocal relations between the state and religion'. He explained that the 'moral life is the state retracted into its inner heart and substance, while the state is the organization and actualization of moral life; and ... religion is the very substance of the moral life itself and of the state'.[134] Such an attempted reconciliation between the state and religion for the promotion of the common good was similarly central to Green's assessment of both the Commonwealth and the history of philosophy. His account closely resembled Hegel's discussion of the interconnectedness between ethical life and the principle of religion in the Protestant conscience (*sittlichen Gewissens*) in both 'the constitution and the code in their interactions [*Betätigungen*]'. This embodies 'the principle and the development of the moral life, which proceeds and can only proceed from the truth of religion, when reinstated in its original principle and in that way as such first become actual'. Hegel concludes by saying that 'the moral life of the state and the religious spirituality of the state are thus reciprocal guarantees of strength'.[135]

There is an important and similar chain of reasoning in Green's account of freedom that leads to his Protestant reconciliation between reli-

---

[132] See Helmstadter 1988, p. 82.

[133] See Nicholson 1995, pp. 61–72.

[134] Hegel 1986, Bd. 10, p. 355: 'die Sittlichkeit der auf sein substantielles Inneres zurück-geführte Staat, dieser die Entwicklung und Verwirklichung derselben, die Substantialität aber der Sittlichkeit selbst und des Staats die Religion ist'. English translation in Hegel 1990, § 552, p. 283.

[135] Hegel 1986, Bd. 10, p. 365: 'Die Verfassung und Gesetzgebung wie deren Betätigun-gen haben zu ihrem Inhalt das Prinzip und die Entwicklung der Sittlichkeit, welche aus der zu ihrem ursprünglichen Prinzip hergestellten und damit erst als solches wirklichen

gion and the state, and it depends, as I have already suggested, upon the structure of his analysis of freedom. First, the will is the process by which a self-conscious subject attempts to satisfy his or her desire; second, practical reason refers to the consciousness of this possibility of perfection within the subject. In God, these two spheres are united, 'but in men, the self-realising principle, which is the manifestation of God in the world of becoming, in the form which it takes as will at best only *tends* to reconciliation with itself in the form which it takes as reason. Self-satisfaction, the pursuit of which is will, is sought elsewhere than in the realisation of that consciousness of possible perfection, which is reason'.[136] It is the role of the state, underpinned by religion and a sense of duty, to help to realize this latent tendency towards perfection. In so far as this is possible, Green relies upon a view that Christ-like perfectibility is at least a latent possibility within each and every individual.

This understanding took practical form in his position within the wider temperance movement in Victorian Britain, including his famous plea for rigorous liquor legislation.[137] Yet he needed to reconcile the idea of state control with his promotion of voluntary associations, as worthy by-products of a more reasoned understanding of one's place in society. His support for such associations is well known, and was certainly a prominent feature of the English intellectual landscape thanks to the efforts of moralists like Maurice.[138] There was also, of course, a religious metaphysics underpinning this quasi-republican idea of using law and the state to cultivate patriotism, and thereby increasing juristic freedom by motivating the common good.[139] Reiterating his central theme, in 'historical man' reason and will 'tend' towards perfection, but 'in God, or rather in the ideal human person as he really exists in God, they are actually one ... the perfection of the human person'.[140] Thus, 'a certain action of the self-realising principle' produces 'conventional morality', and from this foundation (with the assumption of progress) questions of the good of society can be posed. The 'moral progress of the individual' under this conventional morality of rules and regulations requires first that the

---

Wahrheit der Religion hervorgeht und daraus allein hervorgehen kann. Die Sittlichkeit des Staates und religiöse Geistigkeit des Staates sind sich so die gegenseitigen festen garantien'. English translation in Hegel 1986, § 552, p. 291. For the long-standing Protestant-informed character of Hegel's political thought, see Dickey 1989.

[136] Green 1997d, *CW*, vol. 2, pp. 326f. Emphasis in original.

[137] Harrison 1993, is a classic discussion. See also Nicholson 1985, pp. 517–50; Anderson 1991, pp. 671–93; Vincent 2004; cf. Tyler 2003, p. 457.

[138] Maurice 1851, pp. 22, 26; Davies 1996, pp. 283–315, and Richter 1964, p. 49. Cf. Biagini 2003, p. 65; Hoffman 2003, esp. pp. 291ff.

[139] Tyler 2006, pp. 262–91; Richter 1964, p. 87.

[140] Green 1997d, *CW*, vol. 2, p. 329; cf. Berlin 1988, p. 133n, 150.

'modes in which he seeks self-satisfaction are regulated by the sense of what is expected of him'. This focus on liberty, progress and propriety certainly resembles Smith's *Theory of Moral Sentiments*, and Smith was in fact one of the eighteenth-century 'ethicists' on whom Green also lectured. He nevertheless rendered the argument idealist in both content and form.[141]

Not only does Green's account require a process of education through which the will of the individuals is reconciled to the 'universal or rational human will'. It also requires a process of self-reflection, whereby 'this feeling in the individual of what is expected of him becomes a conception (under whatever name) of something desirable, of a single end or object of life'.[142] This does seem to require rather more than a Smithian desire to undertake praiseworthy actions, even if all action is for Green rooted in passionate desire. As he wrote: 'The moral progress of mankind has no reality except as resulting in the formation of more reflective individual characters; but on the other hand every progress towards perfection on the part of the individual character presupposes some embodiment or expression of itself by the self-realising principle in what may be called (to speak most generally) the organisation of life'.[143]

Turning to the writings of Ferdinand Christian Baur, associated with the Tübingen school of theology in the nineteenth century, provides a further and related perspective for understanding Green's assessment of Christianity and revelation in historical perspective.[144] They seem to have helped inform Green's account of the Reformation and Revolution as wars of religion, though the impact can more easily be seen as Green develops an account of the Christ-like motivation of the self. Indeed, Green was so taken with Baur's writings that he began (though never finished) a translation of the first volume of the third edition of Baur's five-volume *Geschichte der Christlichen Kirche* as early as 1863, planning to go to Heidelberg to undertake further research.[145] For Baur, the conflict between Pauline and Petrine doctrine was critical in demonstrating the fundamental character of the Christian religion. Baur assumed that Pauline

[141] See Green 2005d, vol. 1, esp. pp. 50f.

[142] Green 1997d, *CW*, vol. 2, p. 330.

[143] Boucher and Vincent 2000, pp. 41ff.

[144] Vincent and Plant 1984, pp. 12f; Vincent 1986, pp. 50f, 53f; Reardon 1986, esp. pp. 41ff.

[145] An English translation was undertaken by Menzies 1878–79. See de Sanctis 2005, pp. 57–61; Peter Nicholson, 'Editors Footnote', in Green 1997, *CW*, vol. 5, p. 432n; Richter 1964, pp. 87–91, esp. p. 90 where Green is cited as saying of Baur that he is 'nearly the most instructive writer I ever met with'. See also de Sanctis 2005, pp. 53–60, esp. pp. 58f nn. 116, 117, 118 and p. 68. For Green's plans to go to Tübingen that year, see his Letter to Donald Crawford, May 30, 1863, in Green 1997, *CW*, vol. 5, pp. 417ff; cf. Thomas 1987, pp. 58f.

religion was true Christianity and universal in its reach, whilst Petrine religion was particularistic and associated with Judaism. Furthermore, Baur's writings asserted that the majority of Paul's letters in the New Testament were historically inaccurate. He thought only Corinthians 1, 2, Romans and Galatians legitimately Pauline, with the other letters attributed to Paul providing evidence of a split between Judaism and Christianity. Baur therefore suggested that the Pastoral Epistles could not have been written by Paul, but were emendations pertinent to the direction in which the Christian church was moving at that time. Thus, the four principal letters were Paul's, and the other collections of letters had doubtful or dubious authenticity.[146]

Baur's was an essentially historical approach to the study of the New Testament, for which Schleiermacher had laid the foundations. Schleiermacher resolved the theological problem of how to explain the historical Jesus by asserting, in his work on the Christian faith, that Christianity was a spirit present in everyone. His pantheism, indeed, had no truck with supernatural explanations of miracles, and he chose instead to equate the idea of God with something like the Kantian moral law.[147] According to this reading, 'Christ was not the divine Son of God in the traditional sense, but rather an Idea—the most perfect Idea of the highest God—which represented a particular stage in the development of the religious consciousness', a consciousness which had to be developed and nurtured by the state itself.[148] Baur's critical engagement with this argument centred on whether evidence suggested the historical Jesus could be said to possess the characteristics that Schleiermacher had imputed to him. The problem of whether miracles were possible was absolutely crucial to this argument. Equally important for political reasons, Baur had to differentiate himself from the claims of his former student David Strauss, particularly Strauss's *Life of Jesus*, which had been published in 1835 and famously discussed and translated into English by George Eliot in 1846. He wanted to maintain that he did in fact believe in several of the revelatory aspects of the Bible, so as not to attract unnecessary criticism whilst seeking academic promotion.[149] But his attempts were often perceived to be unsuccessful, and cost him offers of chairs at various universities, even

---

[146] Harris 1978, esp. 182f, and on p. 184. Baur used a classificatory scheme in his work on Paul to the effect that the thirteen letters were divided into *homologoumena* or acknowledged writings, *antilegomena* or disputed writings, and *notha* or unauthentic writings. The *Pastoral Epistles* were deemed *notha*, the remaining six letters *antilogomena*. See Harris 1978, p. 197.

[147] Dilthey 1976, p. 46.

[148] Harris 1978, p. 150. See also Schleiermacher 1955, pp. 185, 195f, 198–201.

[149] Harris 1978, pp. 30–36; Ashton 1980, pp. 147–55 on Strauss specifically; also Altholz 1988, esp. pp. 163ff; Vincent and Plant 1984, pp. 12–15.

while he was insisting publicly that Strauss simply offered a 'negative critical' approach to his subject.[150] In his work between 1833 and 1847, Baur was most clearly 'under the Hegelian flag', disagreeing only on 'the Christological question', where in fact 'Baur sided with Strauss, who had declared that the unity of God and man is expressed not in a single individual but in humanity as a whole'. The 'deviation' permitted Baur to hold to a modified Hegelianism.[151] By 1853, however, and with the publication of his *Church History*, the work that Green would endeavour to translate, 'all trace of his former Hegelianism has vanished and what remains to Christianity is of purely ethical value'. Baur's de-Hegelianized argument seems wholly germane to Green's analysis:

> The absolute content of the Christian principle expresses itself in the moral consciousness. What confers on man his highest moral value is alone the purity of a truly moral disposition which rises above all that is finite, particular, or merely subjective. But this moral content in the disposition is also the determining standard of man's relation to God. That which gives man his highest moral value also sets him in the new relationship to God which corresponds to the idea of God.[152]

Whilst he agreed that the historical and the transcendental Jesus needed to be reconciled, Baur thought Hegel's account had not gone far enough. He therefore made the extra move of saying that it was the consciousness of the believers that balanced the secular and the spiritual elements of the equation. Thus, although he was willing to challenge the authenticity of the Pauline letters, the disjuncture between the historical and the literal Jesus of the Gospels could be explained, according to Baur, if one understood Christianity as an ethical idea where all persons contain a Christ-like capacity within themselves. This is certainly what Green seems to have taken from his works. Reconciling Hegel and Baur, along with a Kantian insistence on freedom as rational and moral action, Green suggested that 'Protestant theology, in its proper form' tries to bring about the reconciliation of reason and belief. This was a project made concrete in the struggles of the English Commonwealth, which was not therefore a study in empirical action only.[153] Hence the problem of the historical Jesus and the transcendental person had to be modified. Christian dogma 'must be transformed into a philosophy' because to the 'modern

---

[150] See Brown 1995, esp. pp. 191, 199f, 211.

[151] Harris 1978, p. 156; Brown 1995, pp. 205, 208f, 215.

[152] F. C. Baur, *Das Christenthum*, p. 31, quoted in Harris 1978, p. 158.

[153] Green 1997k, *CW*, vol. 3, p. 181; Richter 1964, pp. 91f; O'Neill 2000, pp. 42ff. Cf. Ashton 1980, p. 152, quoting Strauss 1846, vol. 3, p. 396: 'Thus at the conclusion of the criticism of the history of Jesus, there presents itself this problem: to re-establish dogmatically that which has been destroyed critically'.

philosopher', not the individual (i.e., Jesus) but 'the idea itself is the reality. To him, Christ is the necessary determination of the eternal subject, the objectification by this subject of himself in the world of nature and humanity'.[154] In effect, Christian dogma as philosophy should try to bring out the Christ-like character of every individual, and Green's immersion in these Anglo-German theological ethics paved the way for such a conclusion.[155] His account of 'The Conversion of Paul' equally proposed a deliverance from the law understood as an external imposition, towards a view of law as the internal consciousness of God.[156] Furthermore, the unfinished fragment written by Green as commentary on the meaning of the phrase 'The word is nigh thee' from Romans and Deuteronomy suggested in grand fashion that

> To say then that God is the final cause of the moral life, the ideal self which no one, as a moral agent, is, but which everyone, as such an agent, is, however blindly, seeking to become, is not to make him unreal. It *is*, however (and this may seem at once more presumptuous and less reasonable) in a certain sense to identify him with man, and that not with an abstract of collective humanity but with the individual man.[157]

Succinctly expressing his claims in the strongest possible terms, Green averred that 'our formula then is that God is identical with the self'.[158] This way of putting the point shows, I think, why Green seems to be one of the last in the line of writers I have discussed to elaborate an understanding of liberty as propriety. Both self-government and publicly responsible conduct are the hallmarks of freedom properly understood, but the metaphysical components of his theory of true freedom and the idea that cultivating character might ultimately be a form of divine mimesis, as opposed to conventional propriety, stands at the limit of my story. Historically, of course, given his fascination with Baur's analysis of the Christian church, it is improbable that Green would have been unaffected by Baur's seminal earlier account of Paul's position as Christ's apostle, or even from his earlier assessment of the atonement. Equally, of course, those debates about intuitionism in British philosophy and ethics turned on similar conflicts between reason and the revelation of God's will as noted earlier. But Baur's work had a profound impact, and not only on Green. Its reverberations had already been felt nearby at Cambridge, where J. B. Lightfoot had criticized both the Tübingen school in

---

[154] Green 1997k, CW, vol. 3, pp. 182–83; cf. Green 1997i, CW, vol. 3, pp. 48, 51f.

[155] See Nettleship 1997, in Green 1997, CW, vol. 3, p. xxxix.

[156] Green 1997l, CW, vol. 3, esp. p. 188.

[157] Green 1997o, CW, vol. 3, p. 225.

[158] Green 1997o, CW, vol. 3, p. 227. For discussion, Vincent 1986, esp. pp. 56, 60. This was apparently the biblical text that Green, on his deathbed, asked to be read to him. See Nettleship 1997, in Green 1997, CW, vol. 3, pp. clix–clx; Tyler 2005, vol. 1, p. 70, n. 207.

general and Baur's assessment of Galatians in particular. In fact, a good deal was in fact known in theological circles of German biblical scholarship (about both the Old and New Testament), knowledge that gives the lie to the common view of an absence of engagement with German biblical criticism in Victorian intellectual life.[159] Indeed, some time later, in 1895, Lightfoot was one of those who proved, to the satisfaction of many scholars still, the actual authenticity (*pace* Baur) of the Ignatian Letters, a proof which left a gaping hole in Baur's overall system that could not be sutured.[160]

Given these facts, it is interesting if unsurprising that all the commentaries on biblical texts that are conserved in Green's writings are commentaries in one way or another on Paul. These include fragments on Galatians, the Epistle to the Romans, on the incarnation and the witness of God. In the lecture on Romans, we find explicit use being made of the Pauline doctrine of justification by faith and the nature of death, to make the claim that '"moral life" is a process in which we become less and less mere parts of the world, determined by natural influences, but not thereby less related to the world. That relation to it which consists in understanding, and love determined by understanding, gradually takes the place of that which consists in animal affection'.[161]

THE REVOLUTIONARY INHERITANCE

An idea of the religious character of rational, moral action underpins Green's notion of real freedom. This metaphysical claim can, however, be explored historically and contextually through Green's engagement with historical biblical criticism and modern German philosophy, through his awareness of debates over intuitionism in particular, and through his assumption that rational societies progress historically towards a stage whereby the prerequisite of real freedom, legal freedom, can develop. The struggle for such legal freedoms engendered, according to Green,

[159] See Rogerson 1984, esp. chs. 12 and 13; Parsons 1988, pp. 240ff; also Sheehan 2005, ch. 9.

[160] Harris 1978, pp. 262, 213–16.

[161] Green 1997m, *CW*, vol. 3, pp. 205f. See also Green 2005e, vol. 1, p. 96: 'The individual is no more real without the universal, than the universal without the individual'. Cf. Green 2005e, vol. 1, p. 92: 'Thus the change in the relation between man and God, which St. Paul calls justification, is not a change in God, which is impossible, but a change in the consciousness of man'. Cf. Green 1997n, *CW*, vol. 3, p. 217, Green continued this argument, stressing the impossibility of actually seeing God in any corporeal sense, so that the phrase 'he that hath seen Christ has seen the Father' can only mean the following: 'The seeing of Christ, then, must mean a spiritual sight, an intellectual apprehension of him, which is not merely speculative, but also moral, *i.e.* leading to action'. See also Green 1997q, *CW*, vol. 3, pp. 253–76.

the major boundary positions in the English Civil War and Common-wealth.[162] However, although this would seem to make Green something of a revisionist *avant la lettre* in his account of the period, his wider po-litical metaphysics explained why the distinction between the sacred and the secular continued to stymie Puritan reform and hinder the realization of true freedom.

That a Protestant political philosopher, interested as much in religion as in philosophy itself, should have embarked upon such a course of lec-tures in the climate of mid-1860s Britain is also unsurprising. As part of what John Wolffe has aptly termed the Protestant crusade, Victorian Britain was saturated with anti-Catholic sentiments, some of which ap-pear in thinly veiled form through Green's attacks on Jesuitism as well as in his exploration of the exceptional character of English political de-velopment.[163] He had carried such concerns with him since his time as a student.[164] And his arguments certainly can be interpreted as offering a particular illustration of this common trope of English historiography after the Restoration, as well as developing an interpretation of the Stu-art heritage.[165] Further, with a rising interest in republicanism after the period of Chartism allied to the clearly social aspect of Green's own 'lib-eralism', the context of his own period could not have failed to have an impact on his sense of English exceptionalism.[166] Yet although there is little that is exceptional in Green's status in this regard, the timing of his account effectively complicates the idea that the defence of a Protestant constitutionalism in England effectively imploded around the time of the 1832 Reform Act.[167] Its peculiarly religious underpinning seems in fact to challenge such an argument on its own terms, equally highlighting the lengthy promulgation of a non-conformist defence of Protestant consti-tutionalism well into the later nineteenth century.[168] It is the sophistica-tion of the synthesis, however, which marks out Green's account of the propriety of liberty.

The idea of seventeenth-century Puritanism as a benchmark against which to judge contemporary representative government, and the pro-

---

[162] Morrill 2002, p. 27.

[163] See Wolffe 1991; Wolffe 1998, esp. p. 299.

[164] Nettleship 1997, in Green 1997, CW, vol. 3, pp. xxiv, discusses Green's undergradu-ate politics, and in particular his distinction between the 'anti-Gallican feeling, of which the *Times* was making itself the exponent', and the anti-Napoleonic sentiment current in many areas of British political culture. Cf. Parry 2001, esp. pp. 160, 169–70.

[165] See Adamson 1990, esp. p. 649; cf. Strong 1978; Quinault 1992, pp. 79–104; Morrow 1991, esp. pp. 646–49, 659f.

[166] See Taylor 2000, pp. 25–34; cf. Craig 2003, esp. pp. 179–81.

[167] Biagini 2003, esp. pp. 59–62; cf. Nettleship 1997, in Green 1997, CW, vol. 3, p. xliii, who discusses Green's Oxford Union discussion 'in vindication of Mazzini'; Harvie 1976, p. 104; see too Chadwick 1979, esp. pp. 254f; Conlin 2003, pp. 341–74.

[168] Clark 2002; cf. Dicey 1967, esp. p. 77.

motion of a vision of the political hero who could transcend mere 'dry as dust' historical analysis, were compelling narratives. They could easily be aligned with moralizing visions of the classical past and contemporary reinterpretations of evangelicalism and social thought.[169] Equally, they could also be related to new forms of eschatology that developed alongside schemes for social improvement during the second half of the nineteenth century, and which militated against traditional Christian explanations of social position in terms of free will and individual sin.[170] Green's political and historical account of the English Commonwealth used this connexion, folding it into an idealist vision of history, and combined it with a political philosophy requiring both metaphysics and practical legal-political rules for the cultivation of morally decent, truly free citizens. Clearly, the 'real' freedom Green wished to promote was dependent upon the sustained development of what we commonly refer to as negative freedom, and he focused on the period of the English Commonwealth because it was during this time that such negative or juristic freedom came most clearly to be constitutionalized through the state. From this basis, his interpretation of rational action as necessarily religious in character not only helps to explain the paradoxical political nature of the Commonwealth, and perhaps why neither Vane nor Cromwell was able to illustrate 'real' freedom as they nevertheless pointed the way towards it. It also provided the basis from which he could discuss the more general character of moral action. If my explanation is in any way correct, it suggests that intellectual historians and political theorists might find in these lectures important clues that can help us to better understand both Green's historical vision and his political philosophy. It might also show why we can think of Green's political theory as one legitimate culmination of this tradition of the propriety of liberty.

Green thought of agency as constitutive of human freedom over time, worried about the effect of commerce upon character in time, and located the nature of freedom itself in terms of what it means to be a per-

---

[169] See Lang 1996, pp. 117–38; Morrow 1993, esp. pp. 212, 216; Worden 2000, pp. 138ff, 144, 147, 155, n. 156, 158, 162f, 165, 168.

[170] Hilton 1988, p. 270, also pp. 272–80, 319–39, on the rise of incarnational theology, especially at Oxford with Jowett (Green's undergraduate tutor), Pattison and Matthew Arnold; cf. Hilton 1988, p. 337; Richter 1964, ch. 3. The idea of a 'true' spirit of commerce was deemed by the undergraduate Green to have 'more than counterbalanced' private selfishness (which had been the ruin of the Venetian republics) as 'an indispensable condition of any national cultivation of the intellect'. See Green 1997x, CW, vol. 5, p. 3, also Nettleship 1997, in Green 1997, CW, vol. 3, esp. pp. xviff. The essay was first read to the 'Old Mortality Society', on which see Harvie 1976, esp. pp. 64–67; Brock and Curthoys 1997, p. xxv (a note to the corresponding plate showing members of Old Mortality in 1860); and esp. Monsman 1970, pp. 359–89; Monsman 1998; Richter 1964, pp. 80–83. For an attractive recent overview that explores Green's Oxford context, see Nicholson 1998, pp. 15–22; also Prest 1998, pp. 23–26.

son who judges the actions of others. His theological commitments and his profound concern with the religious crisis of the English Revolution therefore quite neatly closes the circle of this book, by returning it to its beginning and to the similar concerns of John Locke. However, where Locke could not see a way out of what seemed to him paradoxical, that God had created everything but that man was equally and completely free, Green seems to have done rather more than just shift the goalposts in his provocative reconciliation of God with the self. He nevertheless remains recognizably within the same terrain as Locke and those others studied here in focusing on the quality of responsible, rational and free agency. Perhaps it is from this concern with the quality of agency that the legacy of these thinkers might find purchase in some of the contemporary work of philosophers of action.

For the lessons one can find in Green's work in particular, and in the work undertaken by those studied in this book more generally, is that there is not an absolute, complete or philosophically closed theory of freedom to be found. Judged by the standards of contemporary analytical and moral philosophy, the propriety of liberty is not in any obvious senses negative, positive, or republican. What the propriety of liberty does suggest, though, is that the pre-eminent concerns of much contemporary writing about agency and moral responsibility actually have a detailed history that is all but occluded in current preoccupations with the philosophical coherence of epistemic analyses of emotional states, of responsibility, and of the rationality of reasons given as justification for action. All the writers discussed in this book thought of agency as a synthesis of these elements, and something has clearly gone awry if the technical scholasticism of much recent academic work on agency and freedom fails to see in its own intellectual history resources for its future development. That this often seems to be the case is pointedly illustrated in the typically sterile attempts to sharply demarcate liberal from republican political theories on the part of some current protagonists. If this book has shown anything of the sophistication and the centrality of thinking about liberty and its relationship to an idea of propriety in modern political thought, then perhaps it might also have done enough to show the necessity (as well as the utility) of intellectual history to the study of political theory.

CHAPTER SIX

Coda: Liberty as Propriety

A history of the idea of liberty is a project of such enormity that it evaded even Lord Acton, and though this book has only attempted to tell one small part of that story, even then the narrative has threatened continually to burst the bounds of decorum. What I have tried to show is that a distinctive part of modern political theory is concerned with a conception of liberty that requires both individual and public governing of conduct, and that within this framework the relationship between personhood, the passions, and political judgement is central. I have also suggested that there is more to this idea than the claim that liberty is a 'police' concept, and that it is by no means necessarily unappealing as an ideal when compared with, for example, republican conceptions of freedom and responsibility. This history does seem to contain more resources than it has often been given credit for, particularly in terms of its relationship to current thinking about agency.[1] A concern with planning, the limitations of purely instrumental (as opposed to facilitative) views of rationality, the priority of practical deliberation and an interest in an agent's history and motivation, as well as questions concerning possible weakness of will and self-deception, are all central to the philosophy of action in contemporary philosophy.[2] They are also, as this book has tried to show, central to the history of modern political and moral philosophy. Putting the two issues together might allow us to see new ways in which a history of normativity and rational agency could be written. And perhaps this would show another, different version of the example provided by the lectures on the history of moral and political philosophy by John Rawls.[3] For they are often instructive precisely for the way in which they illuminate Rawls's vision as much as they tell us about the figures he is explaining. Properly doing something like this would require another book, however, and in the following coda I would simply like to restate the central argument of this book, and present a case for some of the broader implications of its principal claims.

[1] Pettit 2001, ch. 4; Bratman 2006; Watson 2004, esp. part 3.
[2] Bratman 2000, pp. 35–61; Nozick 1993, ch. 5; Raz 1999, chs. 11–13; Jay-Wallace 2001, pp. 1–26; 2002, pp. 429–70; cf. Scanlon 1998, pp. 73f; Mele 2009, pp. 161–81; Mele 2001; Knobe 2003, pp. 309–24.
[3] Rawls 2000; 2007.

Stating things baldly, I have suggested that one strand of the historiography of liberty in modern political thought has provided us with at best what amounts to only a partial reconstruction of its own intellectual history. What the various chapters have tried to show is that the development of a particular history of liberalism in modern western political theory, might in fact be better understood and assessed when looked at through the lens of propriety. As I have continually reiterated, this has two main implications. The first is that the propriety of liberty refers to the capacity of agents to act freely to the extent that they are capable of owning their actions, or identifying with the desires that motivate them, and therefore being held responsible for them. In the terms of most interest to the writers I have been discussing, you are free if you self-consciously choose particular courses of action, but in so doing, you are able to actively govern and direct the passions towards the end of achieving your happiness. Indeed, your happiness (correctly understood) is thought precisely to be the outcome of responsible agency, and responsible agency towards this end is necessarily regulated agency. Related to this claim is the argument that only those who are publicly recognized as persons can be held responsible for their actions. Though this might sound exclusionary, persons in this sense are simply those agents capable of choosing freely, or acting voluntarily, so that a sense of personhood is actually a prerequisite to the very idea of responsibly appropriating particular passions and judgements about particular courses of action. This first understanding of liberty as propriety refers to the relationship between personhood and the passions, which is to say, it refers to the type and quality of agency undertaken by persons acting at liberty. It is therefore bound up with traditional arguments about agency, willing and freedom.

A second implication, however, looks outward towards the relationships that pertain between members of a civil association. Put simply, those writers who discuss the propriety of liberty typically engraft a theory of politics and political liberty onto their analysis of agency. Thus understood, the idea of liberty as a form of propriety also refers to the extent to which the free actions of particular sorts of agents are judged by others to be appropriate and responsible and to meet the demands of justice. Notice that this is not simply an argument that says that civil or political liberty is encapsulated in types of laws that constrain certain types of actions and by their silence permit others. This is a necessary, though not a sufficient, condition. Taken alone it fails to take account of the passionate underpinning of the idea of justice that is motivationally important.[4] There are two further aspects worth noting within this double framework. One is that the notion of responsibility reflects an

[4] See Krause 2008, pp. 85–89.

assumption that certain forms of conduct are just, and others unjust, which is simply to say that conceptions of justice are rooted in the moral sentiments of individuals within a polity. A second aspect, and a corollary of the first, is the idea that justice considers the quality of the particular agency involved in the interactions between persons, according to shared standards of appropriateness and decorum. This is why the second major implication of the argument concerns specifically intersubjective judgements about agency.

I have tried to show that much of the modern tradition of political theory conceived of liberty in precisely these terms, and in such terms what becomes particularly interesting is not whether or not we might consider these accounts of liberty as variously negative, positive, neo-Roman or republican. Indeed, it strikes me that in the end these labels are simply unhelpful. The content and the context of agency-freedom is what matters, and what the historical trajectory of the propriety of liberty theorists shows is a sustained agreement over the reciprocal relationship between individual and political aspects of freedom both in and through time. Liberty here is clearly a politically and socially constructed value.[5] Or to put the point another way, liberty as propriety concerns the quality of responsible agency, and this focus on the quality of agency fills in the space between what have traditionally been seen as different and competing conceptions of freedom. Recognizing particular persons, particular impediments, and particular forms of behaviour as appropriate to free agents is the interesting content of the general theoretical proposition. In this way it stands in some contrast to recent attempts to gauge the quality of freedom by focusing simply on the relationship between the liberty of an agent and that person's power to act, or on the relative number of conjunctive action possibilities open to an agent at a particular time.[6] At the same time, however, the account seems to suggest certain broad implications for particular contemporary theories of freedom.[7]

Problems of Self-Ownership

One aspect of the historical genealogy offered in the previous chapters concerns the idea of self-interest or self-love as a determinant of human action. It is indeed a theme with fantastically interesting and complicated

[5] Nelson 2005, pp. 73f.

[6] Kramer 2001, pp. 204–16, esp. p. 207: 'Under my theory of negative liberty, then, some person P who lacks the power-to-act must ipso facto lack the liberty-to-act'; cf. Berlin 1988, p. 121.

[7] Pettit 2001, esp. pp. 52, 59, 61; cf. Pettit 2007, pp. 171–201; Miller 2004, esp. pp. 243, 246ff, 254f, 262ff.

conceptual history that clearly goes far beyond what often passes for rational self-interest in much contemporary political science.[8] A related area of concern to this field, however, has not yet been subject to similar intellectual archaeology, namely the idea of self-ownership.

According to various recent interpreters, the idea of self-ownership in Locke refers principally to his argument that individuals have a property in their own person, and is central to debates between left and right libertarians.[9] Individuals in effect 'own' themselves and have property rights to the extent that they are permitted to do so, whilst they exist as God's workmanship.[10] Correlatively, this conception of self-ownership becomes the fundamental basis for Locke's theory of the transformative power of labour, which allows individuals to 'mix' their labour with an object, perhaps a piece of land, and come to own it as property. Provided they then abide by the so-called Lockean proviso to leave 'enough and as good' for others according to natural law, we find a formulation of property rights in Locke amenable to certain left-libertarian philosophers.[11] Parts of this were explored historically in the first chapter, where the relationship between such a conception and the duty of care attendant upon others that Locke's analysis provides, was said to be intertwined with his conception of charity and traditional religious doctrine.[12] However, although the labour theory of appropriation, so central to left-libertarian argument, has been subject to various apparently fatal criticisms, two are particularly pertinent here. These hold both that Locke's focus on labour as the sole source of value is technically incorrect, and that his justification of private property in the *Second Treatise* fails to hold once one has entered a world governed by money and unequal exchange. If true, the argument runs, it becomes logically impossible ever to meet the Lockean proviso, because acquisition for personal use is now incapable of increasing the common stock of mankind. There is simply no longer enough and as good left over for others, even if one were capable of improving one's property to the absolute fullest by labouring.[13] Therefore, left-libertarianism becomes incoherent, and instead it is claimed that for Locke's argument to work, the analysis of someone like Robert Nozick would have to be brought to bear on the conclusions. If that is done, private property could only be upheld according to the justness of its acquisition. But if Nozick's arguments, which are predicated on a theory of self-ownership as absolute

---

[8] Holmes 1995, pp. 42–68; Ivison 1997, pp. 125–46; Tuck 2008, esp. part 2.

[9] Otsuka 2003, ch. 6; cf. Carter 1999, esp. pp. 153–56, 163f.

[10] Waldron 1988, esp. pp. 177–80.

[11] Waldron 1988, esp. pp. 142–47.

[12] See Coleman 2004, esp. pp. 134ff; Waldron 2002, esp. pp. 177–87.

[13] See Cohen 1995, esp. pp. 175f, 180f, 183f; Waldron 1988, pp. 143–47.

bodily integrity and the right not to be forced to undertake service for anyone else, should themselves fail, then Locke's arguments will also fail once again.[14]

According to Gerry Cohen, Nozick's arguments do indeed fail. They do so because although they legitimately update the Lockean proviso to compensate others for losses through property acquisitions, they illegitimately weaken it by asking what would have happened to the provision if the world had remained the same. But of course the world does not remain static, so the revised question has to be whether the appropriation of an unowned object actually worsens the situation of others.[15] For Cohen, the *concept* of self-ownership must therefore be a reflexive one, so that 'to say that *A* enjoys self-ownership is just to say that *A* owns *A*'. The *thesis* of self-ownership, however, runs counter to egalitarian claims and should therefore be rejected. Thus, even if one cannot demolish the concept of self-ownership, the thesis must be rejected in part because it contradicts such staples of 'other assisting' policies as redistributive taxation that even modest egalitarians might want to defend.[16] To reiterate, according to these claims, Locke's justification for the appropriation of private property only succeeds if Nozick-style claims to self-ownership also succeed, but both fail. Therefore Locke's justification for private property is deemed unsustainable. In similar fashion, Jeremy Waldron has outlined parallel conceptual criticisms of a Lockean theory of self-ownership. Highlighting the apparent binary opposition between self-ownership and slavery, Waldron argues for the importance of context, suggesting that there is no 'normal course of events' such that we should always expect absences of self-ownership to be *pro tanto* arguments about slavery. In this he concurs with Cohen.[17] But Waldron extends the argument to consider the thesis of self-ownership as a problem between having the *right* and having the *opportunity* to own private property in terms of Locke's conception of a person. Put briefly, he argues that the explicit definition of a person in Locke's *Essay*, about which I made significant claims in earlier discussion, is not capable of justifying an argument about the temporality of rights either to liberty or of self-ownership as outlined in the *Second Treatise*. If, for Locke, man has mastery over his person but not his body (which remains the property of the creator)

---

[14] Cohen 1995, esp. pp. 187f, 213, 215.

[15] Cohen 1995, pp. 75, 83ff, 89.

[16] Cohen 1995, pp. 211, 222, n. 29, 223; cf. pp. 209, 213f, 216f, on the concept and its possible determinacy through the allocation of universal rights of self-ownership; cf. Otsuka 2003, esp. pp. 34f.

[17] See Nozick 1974, pp. 206f; Waldron 1988, pp. 400, 405, 408; Cohen 1995, p. 233.

then this is a position that renders his analysis of self-ownership at best problematic.[18]

There are perhaps two points worth making in reply. One could of course reject the language of rights altogether, in favour of arguments about political justification more generally.[19] Alternatively, one might say that the notion of agents who have a property in their person means several and perhaps several different things for Locke, not all of which are consistent. Moreover, although Waldron cites extensively from Locke's account of a person in the *Essay*, the claim is still more complex. The notion of an internal property within a body is one that Locke himself thinks we can never have complete and secure epistemological knowledge of. Indeed, ideas of the *propria* or property of bodies and substances require us to make certain assumptions in the face of our imperfect knowledge. Thus, the concept of a person that Locke is working with is inherently unstable. This is part of the reason, surely, why after his long, difficult, but often funny disquisitions about talking parrots, princes and cobblers, or the possible permutations of Socrates as man and person, Locke concludes that really it is through the body that we come to think of persons as persons in an everyday manner. Second, however, he does wish to maintain that persons are capable of owning things other than particular goods even while they cannot own their bodies in a similar fashion, and this ownership refers to their own actions and characters. Expressed still more strongly, it appears that for Locke although we only have temporary jurisdiction over our bodies whilst on earth, if we are truly persons, we can be held responsible for bodily actions according to the criteria of natural law. With this temporary jurisdiction over our bodies, our spheres of action are nevertheless constrained by the requirements of justice, which seems to mean that persons must have something like ownership of their own selves if they are to be held responsible for the quality of their agency. The idea of being held responsible for actions both past and present is as problematic for Locke as it is for Waldron, but to be held responsible for your actions as a person clearly requires an account of agency that can accommodate this problem. And it is here that the relationship between agency and judgement, or between liberty and propriety, permits a different, non-libertarian reading of this (apparently Lockean) idea of self-ownership. For if the concept of self-ownership is at least reflexive in the sense Cohen suggests, surely there is nothing to prevent it also being literally *self*-reflexive.

---

[18] Waldron 1988, pp. 178–83, 392ff, 397f, 401; cf. Garnsey 2008, esp. pp. 142ff; J. W. Harris 1996, ch. 11.

[19] See Bedi 2009.

By contrast, Cohen states that the idea that 'what is owned, according to the thesis of self-ownership, is not a self, where "self" is used to denote some particularly intimate, or essential, part of the person'. In similar fashion, Waldron rejects the adequacy of Locke's account of personhood to do the work required by his concept of liberty as self-mastery.[20] However, in place of these two strands of argument, one implication of the historical genealogy I have traced is that for Locke something like self-ownership is precisely concerned with the ownership of a self as a particularly intimate and essential part of the person.[21] This might not be adequate to justify a peculiar conception of property rights in terms of ownership of goods, if the body of a person is a thing that cannot be properly owned let alone adequately conceptualized as an idea because of makers' rights.[22] It certainly seems to be enough, though, to constitute temporary ownership of one's own self by a person, and that I think is precisely what Locke was trying to suggest. It is the temporary right of ownership over oneself as a conscious, thinking thing embodied in the form of a person which constitutes the locus of Lockean self-ownership. In part, this reflects the theological premises of his outlook, where personhood is constrained by responsibility under natural law. Equally this position avoids the horns of Nozick's dilemma, because the absence of self-ownership thus understood does not lead to *pro tanto* arguments about slavery. This is because personhood is an active or developmental process of cultivation that requires a particular form of free agency at the level of the individual. The free person in this sense can deliberate upon passionate choices and act in ways geared towards achieving their true happiness, both in private and then in public, because the quality of his or her agency can be judged by legislators and citizens alike.

This argument neither suggests that all claims about self-ownership need recourse to Locke, nor judges whether such arguments are worth pursuing. As Brian Barry once sardonically suggested, you might simply have to be crazy to believe in the idea at all.[23] My claim is the related one that you might have to be crazy to believe that Locke provides you with clear-cut answers to the question of self-ownership. Those who seek authority in Locke for this position should reconsider the Lockean theory of personhood upon which their claims are based. If my argument is at all correct, there are at least two incommensurable readings of Lockean

---

[20] See Cohen 1995, pp. 68f and n. 4, 211, 236f; Waldron 1988, pp. 180–83 2002, pp. 162ff.

[21] Fisher 2002, p. 166.

[22] Waldron 2002, p. 172.

[23] Barry 1996.

self-ownership, and the one that I have taken to be most important to Locke is precisely the claim that what persons own, or have special rights over, is their own self. To this extent, I find myself in agreement with those who suggest that contemporary and general claims about the intuitive appeal of some sort of conception of self-ownership have failed to get to grips with the importance of the idea of property in the person, in their focus on issues of exploitation.[24] Indeed, what I have tried to highlight in these brief remarks, and in the book more generally, is that if we take seriously Locke's conception of what it means to be a person and what implications it has for the idea of a person being 'Master of himself', then it is both to the public judgement of agency and to the moral sentiments that underpin our actions that we should look in order to understand it.[25]

If conventions of justice that govern property rights in things as well as relationships between persons are understood to be temporal and artificial rather than eternal, then when the natural law elements in Locke were secularized or reconfigured by his successors, what came to the fore was an account of property and social relations rooted in the passions that could be explained historically, or at least conjecturally, in terms of convention, artifice and public justification. In the tradition of political theory this book has delineated, therefore, personhood and liberty as responsible agency continued to live on long after the temporary body over which Locke granted men no ownership rights had passed away.

Related to this general argument are the metaphorical implications of Locke's argument and its legacy. This is the idea of responsible agency by persons governed by 'Esteem and Discredit, Vertue and Vice', or more generally the reputation they possess. This is grounded by the 'Law of God', which unites persons even when their happiness is 'placed in different things'.[26] The relationship between morality and politics in the international sphere provides an obvious analogue to such concerns, and a focus on state jealousy, public credit and war, as well as physiocracy and cameralism, clearly also structured much of the development of post-Lockean political theory.[27] That is only one side of the story, however, and it is with the implications of such accounts for the related idea of liberty as a form of propriety between individuals and within states that I have been most concerned. Thus, one part of what this book has been trying to do is to trace the legacy of an apparently Augustinian argument

[24] See Pateman 2002, esp. pp. 22ff; 26ff, 33; cf. Arneson 1992, pp. 201–30; Tully 1993 esp. pp. 81, 86ff.
[25] Locke 1988, II, §§ 44, 123, 190, pp. 298f, 350, 393f.
[26] Locke 1984, II. 28, § 12, p. 356; II. 21, § 54, p. 268; cf. Thomas 2009, p. 266.
[27] Sonenscher 2007, esp. chs. 1–2; Hont 2005.

about the nature of fallen man and the consequences of pride's tyranny over charity and the necessity of grace. That, in part, is what is provided by Wierix's powerful image of the fall of man reproduced on the dust jacket. About this image Knipping remarks that the fall of worldly man into the vault, where a scantily clad figure of Sin waits to mortally wound him, and the devil to place the net of death over him, is averted only through God's grace. This alone can prevent the ultimate tragedy of death in a state of sin.[28] Now in Locke's case, his engagement with the neo-Augustinian vision of Pierre Nicole over the need to seek peace, and concerning the existence of God, informed his argument that mankind errs through the partiality of self-interest. The political implications of this fact drove men to seek a government they could trust and in which they themselves would have constituent power. Here legislators become impartial judges who act as umpires between competing claims, and this is part of the meaning of Locke's dictum that through faith, which requires trust, we find both the roots of, and a justification for the defence of, our desire for society. That the partiality of pride was a natural attribute of man, but that its operation could be tempered for the common good with appropriately governed conduct that would in practice, if not design, imitate the obligations of charity, was fundamental to Locke. It had been fundamental to Nicole, and it would be an argument with profound implications for the development of political ethics.[29] Montesquieu developed the idea that human interactions in commercial states capable of moderate government could transform this veritable commerce of self-interest. At the same time he showed that this was a fragile, if potentially lucrative, institutional arrangement for the promotion of civil liberty. In building explicitly on the Jansenist legacy, he both illuminated the natural qualities of self-interest that men possessed, and highlighted the positive but unintended consequences of such self-interested agency.

This was of course further developed in Smith's account of the commercial system as unnatural and retrograde, capable of advancing formal freedoms out of its proper historical time whilst corrupting moral sentiments within it. The implications for the individual within society as well as the statesman ruling over it were profound, and profoundly disquieting. Yet Smith also seemed to offer a variant on providential determinism that remains deeply provocative and cloudy, and which ties him to Locke in ways that remain important, if not always clear. He attempts to reconcile duty with conscience internally, while focusing on external obligation to the extent that one must act justly in order to avoid provoking resentment. In related fashion, religious belief or doctrine is squared with our

---

[28] Discussion in Knipping 1974, vol. 1, esp. pp. 78f.
[29] See Parrish 2007; Keohane 1980.

already natural sense of propriety, in that it helps reinforce our sense of the rightness of an action, rather than providing a freestanding justification for it. In general this chimes well with contemporary formulations of agency in the Kantian tradition as well.[30] Nevertheless, for Smith, to the extent that our natural sense of propriety errs, we naturally look to God and his providential design (a design that necessarily includes an afterlife), to explain and justify our actions.[31] Such a belief provides hope and consolation for those who have been badly treated, whilst also providing a further rationale for why one should act appropriately in this life. If the possibility of reward in the next world continues to exist in the minds of men, then it will remain a factor that constrains the scope of responsible agency-freedom, as was noted in chapter 3 especially.[32] The problem of preferring one's own self to others, a trait castigated by Nicole and Locke, therefore remained central to Smith. Yet in the final edition of *Theory of Moral Sentiments* he removed the most explicitly religious passages of the book, where in his discussion of merit and demerit he had connected the 'holiness of God' and divine revelation with the plan of nature. Nevertheless, he retained the Humean-sounding note that with every religious Elysium there is also a Tartarus, or place of punishment for the wicked.[33] Smith's recognition that any connection with Hume's mitigated scepticism was dangerous is clearly important to this comment, but their differences seem to me once again a good enough reason for having focused much more attention on Smith than on Hume in this book.[34]

Furthermore, the natural jurisprudential tradition in general was keen to talk of the relations between persons in terms of their credit, debt and reputation, whose value and trustworthiness could be gauged and measured as if it were a tradable commodity. The self-interest of these persons would structure a constant and unending desire both for the goods of society and for personal credit and gain in terms of reputation, recognition and reward. How to be a good man and a good citizen therefore became the sort of paradox that would exercise Rousseau perhaps most famously, although the claim of unsocial sociability would leave its mark upon Kant, and henceforward into mainstream contemporary liberal and

[30] O'Neill 2000, esp. pp. 40, 42–45; Fleischacker 1999.

[31] Harris 2003, pp. 237ff, 244f.

[32] See ch. 3, n. 111.

[33] Smith 1976, *TMS*, II. ii. 3. 12, p. 91; for the context of the changes, as well as a reprinting of the manuscript fragment on justice, see Smith 1976, *TMS*, Appendix II, pp. 383–401, esp. pp. 388–92, for the fragment and the passages suppressed in the final edition. See also Kleer 1995, pp. 278f, 295ff, 299; Raphael 2007, pp. 2, 102ff.

[34] Rivers 2000, esp. pp. 303–7, on Smith's attempt to counter Hume in print; see too Adam Smith, Letter (208) to Andreas Holt, October 26, 1780, in Smith 1987, pp. 249–53.

radical thought.[35] The general framework, though, is part of the background to Smith's explanation of the twin principles of authority and utility, and the natural desire of persons prompted by ambition and envy, as the motors of social progress. I have tried to show the legacy of such ideas for John Stuart Mill, particularly through the interconnection in his writings between internal sanctions grounded in moral sentiments, and the external and political system of sanctions that uphold justice. When combined with opinion, Mill's analysis of the relationship between action, approbation and liberty points to the potentially malign effects of relying upon self-interest alone. If distorted by the yoke of custom, for example, the faculty of judgement is weakened. This debilitation can have deeply problematic existential implications for understanding the propriety of liberty. One solution could be to seek a natural end state of self-realization where talk of individual agency could be said to embody real or true freedom. The prime exponent of such a position, Thomas Hill Green, manifests all the tensions inherent in such claims in his own work. Green's vision of liberty seems clearly to express the requirements of internal self-regulation and externally appropriate action governed by the dictates of justice, which once more is close to the formulations of some contemporary Kantian philosophy of autonomy. At the same time, his determination to provide freedom with an explicit essence while rooting it in a specific conception of personhood that developed at a particular moment in European history, seems to me to constitute one appropriate end point of the particular genealogy with which I have been concerned, where historicism and idealism combine.

RESPONSIBLE AGENCY

Agency-freedom requires a detailed account of personhood, in order to make sense of agency beyond the limits of empiricist theories of action. A conception of personhood aids in the adjudication between competing claims of justice, because those claims are rooted in natural feelings that Hume called noble resentment. Although Hume, for example, controverted Locke to argue that uneasiness was not the principal cause of our motivation, the unease with which we face injustice seems very much to prompt those feelings of resentment towards inappropriate and unjust conduct. And those feelings will, *in extremis*, legitimate punishment. This way of putting the point once again seems to capture something central about the propriety of liberty, and it is certainly a summary version of Smith's argument. Our 'darker passions', in Humean terms, under-

[35] Honneth 2007, esp. pp. 168f, 173, 178.

score the intrinsically moral dimension of our feelings about justice, even though justice itself is at least in part an artificial construction.[36] This is why an important aspect of the relationship between liberty and propriety explored here has to do with the cultivation of character, or a sense of personhood, capable of being morally responsible and politically free throughout the process of a life lived in particular contexts.[37]

One reason, then, why liberty might be thought of as a form of propriety is that there is a recognizable unity to the conception of the person or agent undertaking particular forms of action. In related fashion, the quality of agency, that is to say its public or intersubjective propriety, depends for its motivation in being grounded in something all such persons share. For the writers in this book, it seems to be a general concern with justice and liberty that reconciles persons, passions and judgement, and I have suggested that there are interesting ways in which this historical genealogy might map onto contemporary philosophy.[38] Another of those areas is the relationship between agency and desires.

At a personal or individual level, what we particularly care about, to take the illustration of Harry Frankfurt's philosophy, or indeed what we love, might well provide us with reasons for acting. This is because it provides for 'volitional rationality'. For example, if what we all care about is not being subject to injustice, understood as actions or inferences that lead to resentment and hence either to punishment or to social disorder, then our actions as persons can be judged according to particular standards. What we care about is itself founded on a recognition of what is required for individuals to appropriate to themselves what it is properly theirs to have; it is something like a modified form of Stoic *oikeiōsis* as care for the self. This is then moralized to give it social purchase, as John Stuart Mill suggested, in external sanctions that are rooted in human judgement.[39] In keeping with this sort of analysis, the Lockean legacy of bodily unity giving rise to a conception of personhood that is constructed and cultivated throughout the living of a life could also be developed to show that the basic fact of our shared existence together as persons gives rise to our desire to make plans and to construct projects for ourselves. Put another way, it is not our capacity to have projects and make plans that gives rise to our speaking of a life properly understood expressed in personhood and character, but personhood, character and indeed life that permits us to develop certain projects and plans.[40] Smith had earlier said

---

[36] Livingstone 1998, pp. 182f.

[37] M. Clark 1992, esp. pp. 22f, 27.

[38] Cf. Otteson 2006, ch. 2; Milgram 2005; Sen 1999.

[39] Frankfurt 2004, pp. 25, 31, 33; Mill 1969e CW, vol. 10, pp. 259, 256.

[40] Frankfurt 2006a, pp. 36f; cf. Williams 1981, esp. pp. 12–14.

as much. An agent has to take responsibility for his or her own character by identifying with 'certain of his own attitudes or dispositions, whether or not it was he that caused himself to have them'. Moreover, 'in identifying with them, he incorporates those attitudes and dispositions into himself and makes them his own'.[41]

Certain difficulties might arise in this account of holding an agent responsible if one fails to identify with the volitional necessity (or intention) that motivated an action, and it might not be capable of strengthening arguments for autonomy. A defence lawyer might claim something like temporary insanity, for example, if claims about volitional determinism and identification are paramount. Many other Frankfurt-style hard cases abound, but this is a matter that the imperfect judgement of persons simply has to deal with, as Smith again had suggested, whether in the form of a trial by jury or simply in everyday human interactions governed by justice.[42] In sum, it is the overall equation of responsible agency with a conception of personhood that permits this reconciliation of liberty and propriety. In the terms that structured Locke's argument, for example, propriety connotes both dignity and right, and these twin elements would remain critical for the tradition I have tried to delineate. For writers concerned with the propriety of liberty, agents are responsible for their own character through a process of identification with their desires or passions, when they act upon them by appropriating them to themselves and indeed through making their own judgements about them. Such actions, once undertaken, are then assessed in a public context and, if the agent is recognized as a person, he or she will be held responsible for them. If the argument is put in these terms, it is unsurprising that there was such an intimate connection between conceptions of character and the nature of constitutions and constitutional government in the period with which this book has been concerned.[43]

Such an account also seems to me to strike the right balance between the appropriation of individual action through practical deliberation and self-government over time, and the constitutive aspects of character formation that stem from the external social or public sphere in which we act. There is, as always, a little more to be said philosophically. To think of responsibility in these terms is to tie it to our moral sentiments, and to adjudicate between claims of responsibility and free agency requires a shared commitment to a common criterion or standard of judgement. Might there really be such a shared standard? If it is, in fact, impossible

[41] Frankfurt 2006a, p. 7.
[42] Dan-Cohen 1992, pp. 959–1003; 2001, pp. 404–34; 2006, esp. pp. 95ff, 100; cf. Watson 2004, ch. 8; O'Neill 2000, pp. 35f, 38.
[43] Kidd 2003, pp. 40–61.

to hold people to account for something they have done if they cannot be said to properly care about their actions or identify with their desires in the same way that others do, or to deal adequately with the *akratic* personality, then we shall want to know more. Indeed, we shall want to know whether there are any sets of characteristics or qualities that all members of a civil association could in fact share. In related language, one might ask whether there is anything they could all reasonably reject.[44] This is, of course, one of the central problems of contemporary political and moral philosophy, and much turns on how one answers the question.[45] The way in which those authors I have chosen to concentrate upon answered the question was by recognizing that public actions must be undertaken with a minimal standard of appropriateness, if they are to be judged as the type of action one could sympathize with, or that one wouldn't reasonably resent. So as well as offering potentially fruitful revisions to the concept and the thesis of self-ownership, perhaps the history of the idea of liberty as propriety might also provide intellectual foundations for contemporary political and moral philosophy concerned with personhood, permissibility and responsible agency.[46] These are themes which many have begun to link to debates about freedom and human rights, by focusing on the value of autonomy and respect for persons.[47]

All such claims are based on reactive attitudes, where our passions are both judgements on and expressions of particular forms of human action. They are equally rooted in the fact that we can legitimately hold persons responsible in terms of our expectations of them, as much as we can by their direct actions, because of the shared context of claims about justice. The analysis of liberty as propriety therefore traverses the boundary that seems to exist between holding someone morally responsible in terms of expectation, and the 'economy of threats' that affect personal autonomy through punishment.[48] This is because it recognizes both the 'attitudinal' element of responsibility and the threat of sanctions that normally results from pursuing certain courses of action. It is therefore not an exclusively expressivist account of the relationship between passion and action, in the sense that our practices do not simply express our passions. Instead it concerns judgements about actions informed by backward-looking and reactive passions. Actions on this reading are therefore *post facto* judgements rather than obvious and unmediated expressions of our feelings.[49]

[44] Scanlon 1988, pp. 149–216; 1998, *passim*.

[45] See Rorty 1994, pp. 152–66.

[46] Scanlon 2008, pp. 188ff.

[47] Copp 2002, esp. pp. 390, 371, 382; cf. Griffin 2001, esp. pp. 319ff, 322, 311–12; Miller 2002, esp. p. 182.

[48] Hart 1968, pp. 43f.

[49] Strawson 1968, esp. pp. 84ff, 96; cf. Jay-Wallace 1994, esp. pp. 55f, 62ff, 66f, 69.

Responsibility in this context therefore requires 'not just the general powers of reflective self-control, but also the opportunity to exercise those powers on a specific occasion'.[50] It challenges us to think about and judge why it might be that we disagree with the actions of others, and whether or not we should take those disagreements seriously, something that certain conceptions of freedom ignore.[51] In the thinkers and arguments I have discussed, this set of moral expectations is provided by the common and passionate underpinning of a shared sense of justice and the cultivation of situational propriety. The fact that Smith's account seems to show this most clearly, illustrates just how wrong his early readers were when they dismissed his account of moral sentiments as a mere compendium of good manners. He was precisely concerned with ethical questions or right and wrong and how we can hold people responsible for what they do.

STATE PROPRIETY

A final implication of this book moves outwards to the realm of the state itself. If this at first appears seems like an unexpected leap from my previous arguments about liberty and propriety, it might be because the broader implications of the relationships between commerce, morality and politics that have structured recent discussions of these topics are rather more in the background than at the forefront of my narrative. They were given a supporting role in the text, in order to concentrate on the relationship between persons, passions and political judgement as the other side of this interpretative issue. But the relationship between personhood and liberty at the individual level has often been seen as analogous to the case of the state, and many have explicitly considered the state to be a person in its own right, both historically and conceptually, and a person in possession of the liberty to act as a responsible agent.[52]

The movement towards Hobbes's famous illustration of the state as the artificial man of the Commonwealth, literally the body politic made one through the unity of the body representing it, was the culmination of an extraordinarily rich debate about the nature of sovereign power in early modern Europe.[53] In Hobbes, of course, this idea has multiple meanings given the fact that almost anything in his terms is capable of being some kind of person. The crucial question here becomes what type of person

[50] Jay-Wallace 1994, p. 208.
[51] Williams 2001, esp. pp. 15–23.
[52] Cf. Tuck 1999, pp. 226–34.
[53] Hobbes 1991, ch. 16, pp. 111ff, 120f; Skinner 2002d, esp. pp. 390–413; cf. Runciman 2000, pp. 268–78.

something like a state might be, whether it is natural and can be said to own its own actions, or whether it is artificial and capable of being represented. If it is the latter, can it be represented truly, or by fiction? As an artificial person, its actions must be secondary, or rather attributed to it by some other body, and in Hobbes's terms the sovereign represents the 'person' that is the state, which is formed when the multitude are made one through covenanting and representation. The analysis had profound implications for European political thought.[54]

One aspect of what Hobbes had radicalized with this idea of the state as a person nevertheless soon became commonplace through the development of the law of nations.[55] In particular, the thought that there might be a clear analogy between the individual person and the state offered tremendous potential for building on classical Roman sources.[56] It still has contemporary purchase too.[57] For Hobbes, as for Kant later, it had to mean that states as persons existed in an international state of nature, even though this did not mean a state of anarchy in the way that contemporary realist theories of international relations have often assumed.[58] Instead of such anarchy, moreover, what several later writers attempted to show was that not only could states be persons, but also that collections of states in their relations with one another could share something like a sense of personhood. This rather organic image of a community of nations conceived of as one political entity was most pertinently applied to the idea of Europe, a territory with an apparently shared sense of culture and values rooted in Christianity, and within which common standards of decorum pertained.[59] Indeed, such an assumption was part of the reason behind the widespread critique of the French Revolution by those who adhered to such a shared vision.

This was exemplified in the changing justifications for intervention in French affairs provided by Edmund Burke, who came to assail the revolutionary legacy for its challenge to the shared sense of civilization, propriety and liberty within Europe as a whole. Importantly in Burke's case, the idea that Europe was a shared political entity, or commonwealth, meant that a justification for intervention did not have to be sought in the realm of the law of nations. Instead such justification could be located within domestic law. This conceptual reversal of the idea of Europe as a separate international system of states, to be replaced with the idea of

[54] Hobbes 1991, pp. 10, 14; Copp 1980, esp. pp. 583, 589–93, 595; see too Kelly 2004, pp. 113–34.

[55] Dickinson 1917, pp. 564–91.

[56] See Nussbaum 1952, esp. pp. 682–85; cf. Tuck 1979; Malcolm 2002, ch. 13.

[57] Wendt 2004, pp. 289–316; Pettit 2002, pp. 443–70; Erskine 2001, pp. 67–85.

[58] Tuck 1999, esp. pp. 207–14, 216–25; Malcolm 2002, ch. 13.

[59] Hay 1957, pp. 118–25; cf. Pocock 2002, pp. 55–71.

Europe as a territorial entity whose population was broadly united by shared manners, customs and civilization, was a sophisticated move.[60] The implication of the argument, of course, is that a political entity with shared culture and values can have trust in the judgement of its various component parts. If such trust is broken, then, like Locke's citizens who can legitimately resist tyrannical rule, those sanctions appropriate to domestic political arrangements will come into force. Burke here seems to propose a radically Lockean shift in a post-Lockean world of international relations that would remain central at least as far forward as the Anglospheric vision of the British imperial federalists.[61] Once considered in these terms, the idea of the state as a legal and cultural personality would have implications both for modern intellectual history and for discussions about the nature of liberty within and between states. It is obviously also related to the rise of the state as an information-gathering, lexically ordering enterprise of domination.

Such developments equally combined with more recent discussions of the intellectual origins of revolutionary documents like the *Déclaration des droits de l'homme*.[62] Background assumptions about the shared cultural and legal heritage of European state forms based on the idea of personality became hugely important in later nineteenth- and early twentieth-century political and legal theory. In the work of Georg Jellinek, for example, this search for intellectual antecedents bore considerable fruit given his account of the two-sided character of the state. That theory presupposed the claim that a state exists both as a legal and as a political entity, which can be analytically separated for the purposes of differentiating between facts and norms, but which can also be understood historically as the literal embodiment of the predominant will of the people. In this vision, politics really is the state, but it is both a real and a fictitious legal person.[63] In German juridical discussion, these conceptions of personality achieved a level of detail and technical scholasticism sufficient to be considered now quite arcane, even though the political implications of the arguments, largely structured around a liberal or conservative nationalism, were never far from the surface. Each version tried to conceive itself as the legitimate heir to an expansive notion of freedom under the *Rechtsstaat*.[64]

Jellinek's overall account had suggested that the intellectual origins of the French declaration were simply a radical product of a shared Euro-

[60] See Hampsher-Monk 2005, pp. 65–100.
[61] Bell 2007.
[62] Baker 1990; Pasquino 1999; van Kley 1994.
[63] Kelly 2004a, pp. 493–529; for a critique, see Ghosh 2008, pp. 299–347. More broadly, see Jennings 1992, pp. 839–59.
[64] Hewitson 2000, esp. pp. 44ff.

pean legal and political culture, a heritage that recognized, as had Montesquieu, the Teutonic origins of liberty. It also showed that what appeared novel in revolutionary language had in fact more to do with the outcome of struggles that began with the Reformation. The originality of Locke was therefore downplayed in Jellinek's account, but in outlining the importance of the Reformation for modern liberty his argument was similarly in tune with the general tenor of writers like Green. Their shared (somewhat Kantian) idealism might account for such similarity, but British political thought more broadly developed rather different visions of the state as a personality, which were filtered through the growth of political pluralism.[65] In this broad tradition, rather than being the very stuff of politics, the princely place of state was gradually eroded. It was a development that many in both England and Germany rejected, and as these traditions rapidly fell out of favour, the theory of liberty as propriety seems equally to have been relegated to a minor role. My hope in this book is simply to have opened up for consideration one dimension of our intellectual history that might remind us of the background to these developments, by showing the interdependence between passion and reason in our thinking about liberty and agency. If it shows any of the benefits that can come from historically informed study of such topics, it will have served another, equally important purpose.

[65] Runciman 1997.

Bibliography

MANUSCRIPT SOURCES

British Library, London

BL Add. Ms. 4281. Jean Barbeyrac. Letters to Pierre Desmaizeaux.
BL Add. Ms. 15,462. *Memorandum Book of J. Locke. 1679.*
BL Add. Mss. 29,519. George Grote. *History of Greece, Colonies.* Fos. 11–12.
BL Add. Mss. 29,522. George Grote. 'Digest of the Dialogues of Plato' and 'The Character of Sokrates'. Fos. 161–167ᵛ.
BL Add. Mss. 33,230. J. S. Mill. 'The History of Rome'. Fos. 10–20.
BL. Add. Mss. 36,638. 'D[avid] Hume. Diary, 18 Sept–2 Oct 1746'.
BL Add Mss. 40,759. Francis Papers. Vol. 4, fos. 153ᵛ–170ʳ.
BL Add. Mss. 44,756. Gladstone Papers. 'A Triple Hurrah for Mill'. Fo. 55.
BL. Edgerton Mss. 2801. 'Coleridge. Autograph. Philosophical Remains'.

Bodleian Library, Oxford

MS Eng. C. 6759. 'Cromwell in the Nineteenth Century'.
MS. Locke c. 29, f. 27. Papers relating to medicine.
MS Locke c. 34. 'Critical Notes'. Fos. 158–60.
MS Locke c. 36. Minutes of the Council of Trade and Plantations, 1699–1700.
MS Locke d. 10. Lemmata Ethica . . . 1659.
MS Locke f. 1. Locke's Journal, 1675–76.
MS Locke f. 2. 'Notebook'.
MS Locke f. 5. 'On Reason, Passion, Superstition'. May 16, 1681, p. 59.
MS Locke f. 8.

Archives National and Bibliothèque National, Paris

BN N. A. F. 12837. Montesquieu's *Collectio Juris.*
BN N. A. F. 717. *Autographes XV–XIXᵉ Siècles.*
BN Mss. Fr. 7767.

Public Records Office, Kew

PRO 30/24/47. Shaftesbury Papers.

PRINTED PRIMARY SOURCES

Addison Joseph [?]. 1729. 'State Jealousy'. *The Freeholder: or, Political Essays.* No. 52, Monday June 18. 4th edn. London: D. Midwinter, pp. 292–96.
———. 1902. *The Spectator: A New Edition Reproducing the Original Text, both as first issued and as Corrected by its Authors.* Ed. Henry Morley. London: Routledge & Sons.

Alison, Alexander. 1852. *The Future, or, the Science of Politics*. London:J. Roswell.

[Anon.]. 1677. *Moral Essays, Contain'd in several Treatises on Many Important Duties. Written in* French, *by* Messieurs de Port Royal. *Faithfully Rendered into* English, *by A Person of Quality*. London: J. Magnes and R. Bentley, vol. 1.

[Anon.]. 1756. *The Progress of the French, in their Views of Universal Monarchy*. London: W. Owen.

[Anon.]. 1758. *National Spirit, Considered; As a True Source of Political Liberty*. London: M. Cooper.

[Anon.] Philo-Patrie. 1792. *A Letter to a Friend, concerning the effects of the French Revolution upon the People of England*. London: Richard Edwards.

[Anon.]. 1810. *A Reply to the Calumnies of The Edinburgh Review against Oxford. Containing an Account of Studies pursued in that University*. 2nd edn. Oxford: J. Mackinlay.

[Anon.]. 1810a. *Considerations on the Power and Privileges of the Lower House of Parliament*. London: James Ridgway (by W. Flint).

[Anon.]. 1817. *Remarks on the Principles of the Eclectic Review, with reference to Civil and Ecclesiastical Subject; illustrated by extracts from that publication*. London: F. C. and J. Rivington.

[Anon.]. 1824. 'Of Arbitrary Governments'. *ER*, vol. 39, no. 78, pp. 281–99.

[Anon.]. 1828. *Thoughts on the Roman Catholic Question. By a Peelite*. London: C. J. G. & F. Rivington.

[Anon.]. 1832. 'Savigny and the *Edinburgh Review*'. *TPM*, vol. 1, pp. 196–202.

[Anon.]. 1835. *The Rationale of Representation, by the Author of Essays on the Formation of Opinions, &c, &c*. London: R. Hunter.

[Anon.]. 1840. 'Review of *Democracy in America*, Part II, by Alexis de Tocqueville'. *The Athenaeum*, no. 655, Saturday, May 16, p. 391, cols. 1, 2.

[Anon.]. 1840a. 'Review of *Democracy in America*, Part II, by Alexis de Tocqueville'. *The Athenaeum*, Saturday, May 23, pp. 415–18.

[Anon.]. 1844. *Remedies suggested for some of the evils which constitute "The Perils of the Nation"*. 2nd rev. edn. London: Seeley Burnside and Seeley.

[Anon.] William Gilbart [?]. 1846. *The Moral and Religious Duties of Public Companies*. London: Waterlow and Sons.

Aristotle. 1984. *On Rhetoric*. In J. Barnes ed., *The Complete Works of Aristotle*. 2 vols. Princeton NJ: Princeton University Press, vol. 2.

———. 1998. *The Politics*. Ed. S. Everson. Cambridge: Cambridge University Press.

———. 2000. *Nicomachean Ethics*. Ed. Roger Crisp. Cambridge: Cambridge University Press.

Atkinson, W. M. 1838. *The State of the Science of Political Economy Investigated*. London: Whittaker & Co.

———. 1841. *The Spirit of Magna Charta; or Universal Representation the Genius of the British Constitution*. London: Pelham Richardson.

Augustine. 1979. *Confessions*. Trans. R. S. Pine-Coffin. London: Penguin.

Bagshaw, Edward. 1660. *The Great Question Concerning Things Indifferent*. Oxford, n.p.

———. 1660a. *The Great Question Concerning Things Indifferent in Religious Worship*. 3rd edn. London.

Barbeyrac, Jean. 1749. 'An Historical and Critical Account of the Science of Morality'. Trans. Mr. Carew. In Samuel Pufendorf, *Of the Law of Nature and Nations*, done into English by Basil Kennett. 5th edn. London: J. Watthoe et al.

Bayle, Pierre. 1702. 'Machiavel'. *Dictionaire historique et critique*. 2nd edn. Vol. 2. Rotterdam: Reinier Leers, pp. 1958–63.

———. 1702a. 'Spinoza'. *Dictionaire historique et critique*. 2nd edn. Vol. 3. Rotterdam: Reinier Leers, pp. 2767–88.

———. 2004. *Correspondance de Pierre Bayle*. Ed. Elizabeth Labrousse et al. Vol. 3. Oxford: Voltaire Foundation.

Bosanquet, S. R. 1843. *Principia: A Series of Essays on the Principles of Evil Manifesting Themselves in these last Times in Religion, Philosophy and Politics*. London: James Burns.

———. 1866. *The Bible: Its Superiority in Character, Composition, Information and Authority to all Uninspired Literature: A Lecture*. London: Hatchard.

Benigne-Bossuet, Jacques. 1990. *Politics drawn from the Very Words of Holy Scripture*. Ed. and trans. Patrick Riley. Cambridge: Cambridge University Press.

Brougham, Henry. 1835. 'Thoughts upon the Aristocracy of England'. *ER*, vol. 61, pp. 64–70.

Bryce, James. 1867. 'The Historical Aspect of Democracy'. In [Various] *Essays on Reform*. London: Macmillan, pp. 239–78.

Buckland, William. 1836. *Geology and Mineralogy Considered with Reference to Natural Theology*. Bridgewater Treatises, vol. 1. London: William Pickering.

Burgess, S. W. 1825. *Illustrations of the Origin and Progress of the Passions*. London: Longman, Hurst, Rees, Orme, Brown & Green.

Carlyle, Thomas. 1845. *Letters and Speeches of Oliver Cromwell*. London.

———. 1868. *The French Revolution*. London: Chapman and Hall.

Carmichael, Gerschom. 2002. *Natural Rights on the Threshold of the Enlightenment*. Ed. J. Moore and M. Silverthorne. Indianapolis IN: Liberty Fund.

Chalmers, Thomas. 1820. *The Application of Christianity to the Commercial and Ordinary Affairs of Life, in a Series of Discourses*. 2nd edn. Glasgow: Chalmers & Collins.

Child, Josiah. 1740. *A New Discourse of Trade* [1698]. 4th edn. London: J. Hodges.

Cicero. 1927. *Tusculan Disputations*. Cambridge MA: Harvard University Press/ Loeb Classical Library.

———. 1967. *De Finibus Bonorum et Malorum*. Ed. H. Rackham. London: Heinemann/Loeb Classical Library.

———. 1991. *On Duties*. Ed. and trans. M. Griffin. Cambridge: Cambridge University Press.

———. 1996. *De amicitia*. Trans. W. A. Falconer. Cambridge MA: Harvard University Press/Loeb Classical Library.

Combe, George. 1828. *The Constitution of Man, Considered in Relation to External Objects*. Edinburgh: John Anderson Jun/London: Longman.

Constant, Benjamin. 1999. 'The Liberty of the Ancients Compared with that of the Moderns' [1819]. In B. Fontana ed. and trans, *Constant: PW*. Cambridge: Cambridge University Press, pp. 309–28.

Descartes, René. 1955. *Les Passions de l'âme*. Ed. G. Rodis-Lewis. Paris.

Descartes, René. 1996. *Meditations on First Philosophy* [1630]. Ed. and trans. John Cottingham. Cambridge: Cambridge University Press.

———. 1967. *The Passions of the Soul.* In J. Cottingham et al., eds., *Descartes: Philosophical Writings.* 3 vols. Cambridge: Cambridge University Press, vol. 1, pp. 329–427.

Desgraves, L. 1954. *Catalogue de la bibliothèque de Montesquieu.* Geneva: Droz.

Dicey, Albert Venn. 1867. 'The Balance of Classes'. *Essays on Reform.* London: Macmillan, pp. 67–84.

Diderot, Denis. 1779. 'HOBBISME, OU PHILOSOPHIE DE HOBBES'. In Denis Diderot and J. R. D'Alembert, eds., *Encyclopédie, ou Dictionnaire Raisonné des Arts et des Métiers.* Lausanne: Sociétés Typographiques, vol. 17, pp. 574–90.

Didier, Alexandre. 1680. *La ville et la république de Venise.* Paris.

Dilthey, Wilhelm. 1976. *Life of Schleiermacher.* In *Selected Writings.* Ed. and trans. H. P. Rickman. Cambridge: Cambridge University Press, pp. 35–77.

Domat, Jean-Louis. 1722. *The Civil Law in its Natural Order: Together with the Public Law.* 2 vols. Trans. W. Strahan. London: J. Bettenham.

———. 1965. 'Les "fondements naturels" des sociétés'. *Les loix civiles dans leur ordre naturel. Traité des loix.* 2nd edn. Paris, 1695, p. xli. Repr. in R. Taveneaux, ed., *Jansénisme et Politique.* Paris: Armand Colin, pp. 85f.

Doubleday, Thomas. 1852. *Essay on Mundane Moral Government: Demonstrating its analogy with the System of Material Government.* Edinburgh: William Blackwood and Sons.

Duke of D———. 1709. *The Charms of Liberty a Poem.* London: n.p.

Dunbar, James. 1780. *Essays on the History of Mankind in Rude and Cultivated Ages.* London: W. Strahan/Edinburgh: J. Balfour.

Fénelon, François de Salignac. 1976. *Correspondance de Fénelon.* Ed. J. Orcibal. Paris: Klincksieck.

———. 1994. *Telemachus, son of Ulysses.* Ed. and trans. P. Riley. Cambridge: Cambridge University Press.

Ferguson, Adam. 1995. *An Essay on the History of Civil Society.* Ed. Fania Oz-Salzberger. Cambridge: Cambridge University Press.

Filmer, Robert. 1991. *Patriarcha or the Natural Power of Kings.* In *Filmer: Patriarcha and other Writings.* Ed. J. Somerville. Cambridge: Cambridge University Press.

Foucault, Michel. 1986. *The History of Sexuality*, vol. 3: *The Care of the Self.* Trans. R. Hurley. London: Penguin.

———. 2005. *The Hermeneutics of the Subject: Lectures at the Collège de France 1981–1982.* Ed. F. Gros. Trans. G. Burchell. Basingstoke: Palgrave.

Fourier, Charles. 1851. *The Passions of the Human Soul.* Trans. Rev. John Reynell Morrell. Intro. Hugh Doherty. Vol. 1. London: Hippolyte Baillliere.

Fréret, N. 1758. *Défense de la Chronologie fondée sur les monumens de l'histoire Ancienne, contre le Systême Chronologique de M. Newton.* Paris: Durand.

Freeman, E. A. 1873. 'The Athenian Democracy' [1856]. *Historical Essays.* 2nd series. London: Macmillan, pp. 107–48.

Gardiner, S. R., ed. 1958. *Constitutional Documents of the Puritan Revolution, 1625–1660.* 3rd edn. Oxford: Oxford University Press.

Gladstone, W. E. 1838. *The State in its Relations with the Church*. London: John Murray.

———. 1865. *Address on the Place of Ancient Greece in the Providential Order of the World*. Edinburgh: Oliver & Boyd.

———. 1868. *A Chapter of Autobiography*. London: John Murray.

Green, T. H. 1969. *Prolegomena to Ethics* [1884[1]]. Ed. A. Bradley. New York: Krause Reprint.

———.1986. *T. H. Green: Lectures on the Principles of Political Obligation and other Writings*. Ed. Paul Harris and John Morrow. Cambridge: Cambridge University Press.

———. 1997. *CW*. Ed. R. L. Nettleship and P. Nicholson. 5 vols. Bristol: Thoemmes.

———. 1997a. 'Introductions to Hume's "Treatise of Human Nature"' [1874]. *CW*, vol. 1: *PhW*. Ed. R. L. Nettleship and P. Nicholson. Bristol: Thoemmes, pp. 1–371.

———. 1997b. 'The Metaphysics of Ethics'. *CW*, vol. 2: *PhW*. Ed. R. L. Nettleship Bristol: Thoemmes, pp. 83–97.

———. 1997c. 'Lectures on Logic'. *CW*, vol. 2: *PhW*. Ed. R. L. Nettleship. Bristol: Thoemmes, pp. 158–306.

———. 1997d. 'On the Different Senses of "Freedom" as Applied to Will and to the Moral Progress of Man' [1879]. *CW*, vol. 2: *PhW*. Ed. R. L. Nettleship. Bristol: Thoemmes, pp. 307–33.

———. 1997e. 'Lectures on the Principles of Political Obligation' [1879–80]. *CW*, vol. 2: *PhW*. Ed. R. L. Nettleship Bristol: Thoemmes, pp. 335–553.

———. 1997f. 'The Force of Circumstance' [1858]. *CW*, vol. 3: *Miscellanies and Memoir with Appendix*. Ed. R. L. Nettleship Bristol: Thoemmes, pp. 3–10.

———. 1997g. 'The Influence of Civilization on Genius'. *CW*, vol. 3: *Miscellanies and Memoir with Appendix*. Ed. R. L. Nettleship. Bristol: Thoemmes, pp. 11–19.

———. 1997h. 'An Estimate of the Value and Influence of Works of Fiction in Modern Times'. *CW*, vol. 3: *Miscellanies and Memoir with Appendix*. Ed. R. L. Nettleship. Bristol: Thoemmes, pp. 20–45.

———. 1997i. 'The Philosophy of Aristotle' [1866]. *CW*, vol. 3: *Miscellanies and Memoir with Appendix*. Ed. R. L. Nettleship. Bristol: Thoemmes, pp. 46–91.

———. 1997j. 'Popular Philosophy in its Relation to Life'. *CW*, vol. 3: *Miscellanies and Memoir with Appendix*. Ed. R. L. Nettleship. Bristol: Thoemmes, pp. 92–125.

———. 1997k. 'Essay on Christian Dogma' [1858]. *CW*, vol. 3: *Miscellanies and Memoir with Appendix*. Ed. R. L. Nettleship. Bristol: Thoemmes, pp. 161–85.

———. 1997l. 'The Conversion of Paul'. *CW*, vol. 3: *Miscellanies and Memoir with Appendix*. Ed. R. L. Nettleship. Bristol: Thoemmes, pp. 186–89.

———. 1997m. 'The Epistle to the Romans'. *CW*, vol. 3: *Miscellanies and Memoir with Appendix*. Ed. R. L. Nettleship. Bristol: Thoemmes, pp. 190–206.

———. 1997n. 'The Incarnation'. *CW*, vol. 3: *Miscellanies and Memoir with Appendix*. Ed. R. L. Nettleship. Bristol: Thoemmes, pp. 207–20.

Gladstone, W. E. 1997o. 'Fragment of an Address on the Text "The Word is Nigh Thee": (ROM. x. 8; DEUT. xxx. 14)'. *CW*, vol. 3: *Miscellanies and Memoir with Appendix*. Ed. R. L. Nettleship. Bristol: Thoemmes, pp. 221–29.

———. 1997p. 'Witness of God'. *CW*, vol. 3: *Miscellanies and Memoir with Appendix*. Ed. R. L. Nettleship. Bristol: Thoemmes, pp. 230–52.

———. 1997q. 'Faith'. *CW*, vol. 3: *Miscellanies and Memoir with Appendix*. Ed. R. L. Nettleship. Bristol: Thoemmes, pp. 253–76.

———. 1997r. 'Four Lectures on the English Revolution' [1867]. *CW*, vol. 3: *Miscellanies and Memoir with Appendix*. Ed. R. L. Nettleship. Bristol: Thoemmes, pp. 277–364.

———. 1997s. 'Lecture on Liberal Legislation and Freedom of Contract' [1881]. *CW*, vol. 3: *Miscellanies and Memoir with Appendix*. Ed. R. L. Nettleship. Bristol: Thoemmes, pp. 365–86.

———. 1997t. 'Lecture on the Grading of Secondary Schools' [1877]. *CW*, vol. 3: *Miscellanies and Memoir with Appendix*. Ed. R. L. Nettleship. Bristol: Thoemmes, pp. 387–412.

———. 1997u. 'Two Lectures on the Elementary Schools System in Britain' [1878]. *CW*, vol. 3: *Miscellanies and Memoir with Appendix*. Ed. R. L. Nettleship. Bristol: Thoemmes, pp. 413–55.

———. 1997v. 'Hedonism and the Ultimate Good' [1877]. *CW*, vol. 4: *Prolegomena to Ethics with Appendices*. Ed. R. L. Nettleship and P. Nicholson. Bristol: Thoemmes, pp. 266–69.

———. 1997w. 'Lectures on Moral and Political Philosophy' [1867]. *CW*, vol. 5: *Additional Writings*. Ed. P. Nicholson. Bristol: Thoemmes, pp. 108–82.

———. 1997x. 'The Effect of Commerce on the Mind of a Nation'. *CW*, vol. 5: *Additional Writings*. Ed. P. Nicholson. Bristol: Thoemmes, pp. 3–6.

———. 1997y. 'Speech on the Reform Bill'. March 25, 1867. *CW*, vol. 5: *Additional Writings*. Ed. P. Nicholson. Bristol: Thoemmes, pp. 226–32.

———. 2005. 'The Spirit of Poetry'. Repr. in Alberto de Sanctis, *The 'Puritan' Democracy of T. H. Green*. Exeter: Imprint Academic, p. 174.

———. 2005a. 'The English National Character Compared with that of the Germans'. Repr. in Alberto de Sanctis, *The 'Puritan' Democracy of T. H. Green*. Exeter: Imprint Academic, pp. 188–91.

———. 2005b. 'Enthusiasm'. Repr. in Alberto de Sanctis, *The 'Puritan' Democracy of T. H. Green*. Exeter: Imprint Academic, pp. 193–96.

———. 2005c. 'Rudiments of "The Philosophy of Aristotle" and Related Texts [*c.* 1866–67]'. In Colin Tyler, ed., *Unpublished Manuscripts in British Idealism: Political Philosophy, Theology and Social Thought*. 2 vols. Bristol: Thoemmes, vol. 1, pp. 1–13.

———. 2005d. 'Metaphysic of Ethics, Moral Psychology, Sociology or Science of Sittlichkeit' [*c.* late 1860s–early 1870s]. In Colin Tyler, ed., *Unpublished Manuscripts in British Idealism: Political Philosophy, Theology and Social Thought*. 2 vols. Bristol: Thoemmes, vol. 1, pp. 14–71.

———. 2005e. 'Notes of Lectures on the Epistle to the Romans [*c.* 1871]. Ed. Henry Nettleship and Colin Tyler. In C. Tyler, ed., *Unpublished Manuscripts in British Idealism: Political Philosophy, Theology and Social Thought*. 2 vols. Bristol: Thoemmes, vol. 1, pp. 88–110.

Grote, George. 1826. 'The Institutions of the Ancient Greeks'. *Westminster Review*, vol. 5, pp. 269–311.

Grotius, Hugo. 2004. *The Free Sea*. Ed. D. Armitage, Indianapolis IN: Liberty Fund.

———. 2005. *The Rights of War and Peace* [1738 Jean Barbeyrac edn.]. Ed. Richard Tuck. 3 vols. Indianapolis IN: Liberty Fund.

———. 2005a. 'Prolegomena to the First Edition of *De Jure Belli ac Pacis*' [1625]. Trans. Richard Tuck. In *The Rights of War and Peace* [1738 Jean Barbeyrac edn.]. ed. Richard Tuck. 3 vols. Indianapolis IN: Liberty Fund, vol. 3, pp. 1745–62.

Guizot, François. 2002. *The History of the Origins of Representative Government in Europe* [1851]. Ed. Aurelian Craiutu. Trans. A. R. Scoble. Indianapolis IN: Liberty Fund.

Hales, William D. D. 1794. *The Scripture Doctrine of Political Government and Political Liberty*. Dublin: George Grierson.

Hare, Thomas. 1857. *The Machinery of Representation*. 2nd edn. London: W. Maxwell.

Harrison, Frederic. 1885. *Politics and a Human Religion*. London: E. W. Allen.

Hartley, David. 1749. *Observations on Man, His Frame, His Duty, and His Expectations*. 2 vols. London: S. Richardson.

Hegel, G.W.F. 1986. *Enzyklopädie der philosophischen Wissenschaften im Grundrisse 1830: Dritter Teil: Die Philosophie des Geistes. Werke in 20 Bänden*. Frankfurt am Main: Suhrkamp, vol. 10.

———. 1990. *Hegel's Philosophy of Mind*. Pt. 3 of *The Encyclopaedia of the Philosophical Sciences* [1830]. Trans. William Wallace. Oxford: Oxford University Press.

Hickes, George. 1692. *A Vindication of Some among our selves Against the False Principles of Dr. Sherlock*. London: n.p.

Hobbes, Thomas. 1969. *The Elements of Law Natural and Politic*. Ed. F. Tönnies. 2nd edn. London: Frank Cass.

———. 1983. *De Cive: The Latin Version*. Ed. Howard Warrender. Oxford: Oxford University Press.

———. 1991. *Leviathan*. Ed. Richard Tuck. Cambridge: Cambridge University Press.

———. 1997. *The Correspondence of Thomas Hobbes*. Ed. N. Malcolm. 2 vols. Oxford: Oxford University Press.

———. 1998. *De Cive*. Ed. Richard Tuck. Trans. M. Silverthorne. Cambridge: Cambridge University Press.

Huet, Pierre Daniel. 1727. *Histoire du commerce et de la navigation des Anciens*. 3rd edn. Paris: Antoine Urbain-Coustelier.

Hume, David. 1932. *Letters of David Hume*. Ed. D. Grieg. 2 vols. Oxford: Oxford University Press.

———. 1981. *A Treatise of Human Nature*. Ed. L. A. Selby-Bigge and P. H. Nidditch. Oxford: Clarendon.

Hume, David. 1982. *Enquiries concerning Human Understanding and concerning the Principles of Morals*. Ed. L. A. Selby-Bigge and P. H. Nidditch. Oxford: Clarendon.

Hume, David. 1985. 'That Politics may be Reduced to a Science'. In *Essays Moral, Political and Literary*. Ed. Eugene F. Miller. Indianapolis IN: Liberty Fund, pp. 14–31.

Hutcheson, Francis. 1728. *An Essay on the Nature and Conduct of the Passions and Affections. With Illustrations on the Moral Sense*. London: P. Crampton.

———. 1747. *A Short Introduction to Moral Philosophy, in Three Books; containing the Elements of Ethicks and the Law of Nature*. Trans. from the Latin. Glasgow: Robert Foulis, Printer to the University.

———. 1749. 'Exercitatio de Animi Cultura'. In *Varorium Opuscula ad Cultiorm Jurisprudentiam Adsequendam Pertinentia*. Vol. 1. Aug. Pizzorno: Pisis, 1749, pp. 3–13.

———. 1755. *A System of Moral Philosophy. In Three Books*. Glasgow: R. and A. Foulis: London: A. Millar/T. Longman.

James, William. 1983. 'What is an Emotion'. In *CW of William James: Essays in Psychology*. Cambridge MA: Harvard University Press, pp. 168–87.

Jeffrey, Francis. 1803. 'The State of Europe'. *ER*, vol. 2, no. 3, pp. 1–30.

———. 1803a. 'Millar's View of the English Government'. *ER*, vol. 3, no. 5, pp. 154–81.

———. 1807. 'Pamphlets on the Catholic Question'. *ER*, vol. 11, no. 21, pp. 116–44.

———. 1808. 'Fox's History of James II'. *ER*, vol. 12, pp. 217–306.

———. 1814. 'State and Prospects of Europe'. *ER*, vol. 23, no. 45, pp. 1–40.

Johnson, Samuel. 1755. *A Dictionary of the English Language: In which The Words are deduced from their Originals, and Illustrated in their Different Significations, by Examples from the best Writers, to which are Prefixed A History of the Language and An English Grammar*. 2 vols. London: W. Strahan.

Lawson, George. 1992. *Politica sacra et civilis*. Ed. Conal Condren. Cambridge: Cambridge University Press.

Le Clerc, Jean. 1699. *Parrhasiana, ou Pensées Diverses sur des Matiéres de Critique, D'Histoire, De Morale et de Politique. Avec la Défense de divers Ouvrages de Mr. L. C., par Theodore Parrhase*. Amsterdam: D'Antoine Schelte.

———. 1706. *The Life and Character of Mr. John Locke, author of the Essay concerning Humane Understanding, written in French by Mr. Le Clerc*. London: n.p.

Leibniz, G. W. 1952. *Theodicy: Essays on the Goodness of God the Freedom of Man and the Origin of Evil*. Ed. A. Farrer. Trans. E. M. Huggard. London: Routledge and Kegan Paul.

———. 1969. *Philosophical Papers and Letters*. Selected, trans. and ed. Leroy E. Loemker. 2nd edn. Dordrecht: D. Reidel.

———. 1988. 'The Common Concept of Justice'. In *PW*. Ed. P. Riley. Cambridge: Cambridge University Press, pp. 45–64.

———. 1988a. 'Opinion on the Principles of Pufendorf'. In *PW*. Ed. P. Riley. Cambridge: Cambridge University Press, pp. 64–75.

———. 1988b. '*Codex Iuris Gentium (Praefatio)*'. In *PW*. Ed. P. Riley. Cambridge: Cambridge University Press, pp. 165–76.

Locke, John. 1686. 'Methode nouvelle de dresser des Recueuils' [July]. *Bibliothèque Universelle*, vol. 2, pp. 315–40.

———. 1688. 'Abregé d'un ouvrage intitulé Essai philosophique touchant l'entendement'. Trans. Jean Le Clerc. *Bibliothèque Universelle et Historique*, vol. 8, art. 2, pp. 49–142.

———. 1690. 'Two Treatises'. *Bibliothèque Universelle et Historique*, vol. 19, art. 8, pp. 559–91.

———. 1720. *A Collection of Several Pieces of Mr. John Locke, Never Before Printed, nor note extant in his Works*. Ed. Pierre Des Maizeaux. London.

———. 1755. *Du Gouvernement Civil, par Mr. Locke*. 5th edn. Éxactement revûë & corrigée fur la 5. Edition de Londres & augmentée de quelques notes, par L. C. [Jean Le Clerc], R. D. M. [David Mazel?], A. D. P. Amsterdam: J. Schreuder & Pierre Mortier le Jeune.

———. 1823. *The Works of John Locke*. New corr. edn. 10 vols. London: Thomas Tegg et al.

———. 1823a. 'Some Considerations of the Consequences of lowering the Interest and raising the Value of Money. In a Letter sent to a Member of Parliament in the year 1691'. In *The Works of John Locke*. New corr. edn. 10 vols. London: Thomas Tegg et al., vol. 5, pp. 1–116.

———. 1843. 'An Examination of P. Malebranche's Opinion of Seeing all Things in God; with Remarks upon some of Mr. Norris's Books'. *The PhW of John Locke*. With a Preliminary Discourse and notes by J. A. St. John, Esq.. London: George Virtue, pp. 551–85.

———. 1936. *An Early Draft of Locke's Essay: Together with Excerpts from His Journals*. Ed. R. I. Aaron and J. Gibb. Oxford: Clarendon.

———. 1954. *Essays on the Law of Nature*. Ed. Wolfgang von Leyden. Oxford: Clarendon.

———. 1954a. 'Censor's Valedictory Speech' [1664]. In *Essays on the Law of Nature*. Ed. Wolfgang von Leyden. Oxford: Clarendon, pp. 220–43.

———. 1967. *John Locke: Two Tracts on Government*. Ed. P. Abrams. Cambridge: Cambridge University Press.

———. 1968. *Epistola de Torelantia/Letter on Toleration*. Ed. R. Klibansky and J. W. Gough. Oxford: Clarendon.

———. 1976–89. *The Correspondence of John Locke*. Ed. E. S. de Beer. 8 vols. Oxford: Clarendon.

———. 1983. *A Letter Concerning Toleration*. Ed. J. Tully. Indianapolis: Hackett.

———. 1984. *An Essay concerning Human Understanding* [1690]. Ed. Peter H. Nidditch. Oxford: Clarendon.

———. 1988. *Two Treatises of Government* [1690]. Ed. Peter Laslett. Cambridge: Cambridge University Press.

———. 1989. *Some Thoughts Concerning Education*. Ed. John W. and Jean S. Yolton. Oxford: Clarendon.

Locke, John. 1990. *Drafts for the Essay concerning Human Understanding and other Philosophical Writings*. Ed. P. H. Nidditch and G. A. J. Rogers. 3 vols. Oxford: Clarendon, vol. 1.

———. 1991. *Locke on Money*. Ed. P. H. Kelly. 2 vols. Oxford: Clarendon.

———. 1997. 'First Tract on Government' [1660]. In *PW*. Ed. Mark Goldie. Cambridge: Cambridge University Press, 1997, pp. 3–53.

Locke, John. 1997a. 'Second Tract on Government' [1660]. In *PW*. Ed. Mark Goldie. Cambridge: Cambridge University Press, pp. 54–78.

———. 1997b. 'Infallibility' [*c*. 1661–62]. In *PW*. Ed. Mark Goldie. Cambridge: Cambridge University Press, pp. 204–9.

———. 1997c. 'Adversaria A' [*c*. 1670?]. In *PW*. Ed. Mark Goldie. Cambridge: Cambridge University Press, p. 215.

———. 1997d. 'On Civil and Ecclesiastical Power' [1674]. In *PW*. Ed. Mark Goldie. Cambridge: Cambridge University Press, pp. 216–21.

———. 1997e. 'Pleasure, Pain, the Passions' [1676]. In *PW*. Ed. Mark Goldie. Cambridge: Cambridge University Press, pp. 237–45.

———. 1997f. 'Atheism' [July 29, 1676]. In *PW*. Ed. Mark Goldie. Cambridge: Cambridge University Press, pp. 245f.

———. 1997g. 'Morality' [1677–78]. In *PW*. Ed. Mark Goldie. Cambridge: Cambridge University Press, pp. 267ff.

———. 1997h. 'Of Ethick in General' [1686–8?]. In *PW*. Ed. Mark Goldie. Cambridge: Cambridge University Press, pp. 297–304.

———. 1997i. 'On William Sherlock' [*c*. 1690–91]. In *PW*. Ed. Mark Goldie. Cambridge: Cambridge University Press, pp. 313–17.

———. 1997j. 'Ethica A' [1692]. In *PW*. Ed. Mark Goldie. Cambridge: Cambridge University Press, pp. 318f.

———. 1997k. 'Ethica (B)' [1693]. In *PW*. Ed. Mark Goldie. Cambridge: Cambridge University Press, pp. 319–20.

———. 1997l. 'Homo ante et post lapsum' [1693]. In *PW*. Ed. Mark Goldie. Cambridge: Cambridge University Press, pp. 320–21.

———. 1997m. 'Voluntas' [1693]. In *PW*. Ed. Mark Goldie. Cambridge: Cambridge University Press, p. 321.

———. 1997n. 'Law' [c. 1693]. In *PW*. Ed. Mark Goldie. Cambridge: Cambridge University Press, pp. 328–29.

———. 2000. *John Locke as Translator: Three of the 'Essais' of Pierre Nicole in French and English*. Ed. Jean. S. Yolton [= *SVEC*, no. 7]. Oxford: Voltaire Foundation.

———. 2000a. 'Discourse concerning in short the natural proof of the Existence of God, & the immortality of the Soule'. In *John Locke as Translator: Three of the 'Essais' of Pierre Nicole in French and English*. Ed. Jean. S. Yolton [= *SVEC*, no. 7]. Oxford: Voltaire Foundation, pp. 15–41.

———. 2000b. 'Discourse of the Weaknesse of Man'. In *John Locke as Translator: Three of the 'Essais' of Pierre Nicole in French and English*. Ed. Jean. S. Yolton [= *SVEC*, no. 7]. Oxford: Voltaire Foundation, pp. 43–113.

———. 2000c. 'Treatise concerneing the way of preserving peace with men'. *John Locke as Translator: Three of the 'Essais' of Pierre Nicole in French and English*. Ed. Jean. S. Yolton [= *SVEC*, no. 7]. Oxford: Voltaire Foundation, pp. 115–259.

———. 2002. *John Locke: Selected Correspondence*. Ed. Mark Goldie. Oxford: Oxford University Press.

———. 2002a. *John Locke: Writings on Religion*. Ed. Victor Nuovo. Oxford: Clarendon.

———. 2006. 'An Essay concerning Toleration' [1667]. In *ECT*. Ed. J. R. Milton and Philip Milton. Oxford: Clarendon, pp. 269–302.

———. 2006a. 'A Letter from a Person of Quality to his Friend in the Country' [1675]. In *ECT*. Ed. J. R. Milton and Philip Milton. Oxford: Clarendon, pp. 337–76.

———. 2006b. 'Iustitia' [1679]. In *ECT*. Ed. J. R. Milton and Philip Milton. Oxford: Clarendon, pp. 387f.

———. 2006c. 'Virtus'. In *ECT*. Ed. J. R. Milton and Philip Milton. Oxford: Clarendon, pp. 390f.

Madison, James, Alexander Hamilton and John Jay. 1987. *The Federalist Papers*. Ed. Isaac Kramnick. London: Penguin.

Malebranche, Nicolas. 1962–84. *Traité de morale*. In *OC*. Paris: Vrin, vol. 11.

Machiavelli, Niccolò. 1989. *The Discourses*. In *The Chief Work and Others*. Ed. Allan Gilbert. 3 vols. Durham NC: Duke University Press, vol. 1, pp. 175–529.

———. 1989a. *Florentine Histories*. In *The Chief Work and Others*. Ed. Allan Gilbert. 3 vols. Durham NC: Duke University Press, vol. 3, pp. 1025–1435.

———. 1997. *The Prince*. Ed. Russell Price and Quentin Skinner. Cambridge: Cambridge University Press.

Masham, Damaris. 2003. 'Lady Masham's Account of Locke'. Ed. Roger Woolhouse. *Locke Studies*, vol. 3, pp. 167–93.

Maurice, F. D. 1851. *On the Reformation of Society and How all classes may Contribute to it*. Southampton: Forbes and Knibb.

———. 1853. *Theological Essays*. London.

———. 1865. *The Conflict of Good and Evil in Our Day, Twelve Letters to a Missionary*. London: Smith, Elder and Co.

Menzies, Allan. 1878–79. *The Church History of the First Three Centuries*. 2 vols. London: Williams and Norgate.

Mill, James. 1809. 'Scipion Bexon—*Code de la Legislation penale*'. *ER*, vol. 15, no. 29, pp. 88–109.

———. 2002. *Analysis of the Phenomena of the Human Mind* [1829]. 2 vols. London: Routledge/Thoemmes.

Mill, John Stuart. 1963. CW 12/13, *The Earlier Letters of John Stuart Mill 1812–1848*, 2 vols. Ed. F. E Mineka. Toronto: University of Toronto Press/Routledge & Kegan Paul.

———. 1963–. *CW of John Stuart Mill*. Ed. J. M. Robson. Toronto: University of Toronto Press/Routledge & Kegan Paul.

———. 1965. *Principles of Political Economy* [1848]. In *CW*, vols. 2–3: *Principles of Political Economy, with Some of their Applications to Social Philosophy*. Ed. V. W. Bladen. Toronto: University of Toronto Press/Routledge & Kegan Paul.

Mill, John Stuart. 1967. 'The Silk Trade' [1826]. In *CW*, vol. 4: *Essays on Economics and Society*, Part I. Ed. Lord Robbins. Toronto: University of Toronto Press/Routledge & Kegan Paul, pp. 127–39.

———. 1967a. 'Corporation and Church Property' [1833]. In *CW*, vol. 4: *Essays on Economics and Society*. Ed. J. M. Robson. Toronto: University of Toronto Press/Routledge & Kegan Paul, pp. 193–228.

Mill, John. 1967b. 'Endowments' [1869]. In *CW*, vol. 5: *Essays on Economics and Society*, Part II. Ed. Lord Robbins. Toronto: University of Toronto Press/ Routledge & Kegan Paul, pp. 615–29.

———. 1969. 'Remarks on Bentham's Philosophy' [1833]. In *CW*, vol. 10: *Essays on Ethics, Religion and Society*. Ed. J. M. Robson. Toronto: University of Toronto Press/Routledge & Kegan Paul, pp. 3–18.

———. 1969a. 'Blakey's *History of Moral Science*' [1833]. In *CW*, vol. 10: *Essays on Ethics, Religion and Society*. Ed. J. M. Robson. Toronto: Routledge, pp. 19–29.

———. 1969b. 'Bentham' [1838]. In *CW*, vol. 10: *Essays on Ethics, Religion and Society*. Ed. J. M. Robson. Toronto: Routledge, pp. 75–116.

———. 1969c. 'Coleridge' [1840]. In *CW*, vol. 10: *Essays on Ethics, Religion and Society*. Ed. J. M. Robson. Toronto: Routledge, pp. 117–64.

———. 1969d. 'Whewell on Moral Philosophy' [1852]. In *CW*, vol. 10: *Essays on Ethics, Religion and Society*. Ed. J. M. Robson. Toronto: Routledge, pp. 165–201.

———. 1969e. *Utilitarianism* [1861]. In *CW*, vol. 10: *Essays on Ethics, Religion and Society*. Ed. J. M. Robson. Toronto: Routledge, pp. 203–59.

———. 1969f. 'Auguste Comte and Positivism' [1865]. In *CW*, vol. 10: *Essays on Ethics, Religion and Society*. Ed. J. M. Robson. Toronto: Routledge, 1969, pp. 263–368.

———. 1969g. *Three Essays on Religion* [1874]. In *CW*, vol. 10: *Essays on Ethics, Religion and Society*. Ed. J. M. Robson. Toronto: Routledge, pp. 371–489.

———. 1972. *CW*, vol. 14: *Later Letters*. Ed. F. E. Mineka and D. N. Lindley. Toronto: University of Toronto Press/Routledge & Kegan Paul.

———. 1972a. *CW*, vol. 15: *The Later Letters of John Stuart Mill 1856–1864*. Ed. F. E. Mineka and D. N. Lindley. Toronto: University of Toronto Press/ Routledge & Kegan Paul.

———. 1972b. *CW*, vol. 16: *The Later Letters of John Stuart Mill 1849–1873*. Ed. F. E. Mineka and D. N. Lindley. Toronto: University of Toronto Press/ Routledge & Kegan Paul.

———. 1972c. *CW*, vol. 17: *The Later Letters of John Stuart Mill 1849–1873*. Ed. F. E. Mineka and D. N. Lindley. Toronto: University of Toronto Press/ Routledge & Kegan Paul.

———. 1974. *CW*, vol. 8. *A System of Logic, Ratiocinative and Inductive* [1843]. Ed. J. M. Robson. Toronto: University of Toronto Press/Routledge & Kegan Paul.

———. 1977. 'The Use and Abuse of Political Terms' [1832]. In *CW*, vol. 18: *Essays on Politics and Society*. Ed. J. M. Robson. Toronto: University of Toronto Press/Routledge & Kegan Paul, pp. 3–13.

———. 1977a. 'Rationale of Representation' [1835]. In *CW*, vol. 18: *Essays on Politics and Society*. Ed. J. M. Robson. Toronto: University of Toronto Press/ Routledge & Kegan Paul, pp. 15–46.

———. 1977b. 'De Tocqueville on *Democracy in America* [I]' [1835]. In *CW*, vol. 18: *Essays on Politics and Society*. Ed. J. M. Robson. Toronto: University of Toronto Press/Routledge & Kegan Paul, pp. 47–90.

———. 1977c. 'State of Society in America' [1836]. In *CW*, vol. 18: *Essays on Politics and Society*. Ed. J. M. Robson. Toronto: University of Toronto Press/ Routledge & Kegan Paul, pp. 91–115.

———. 1977d. 'Civilization' [1836]. In *CW*, vol. 18: *Essays on Politics and Society*. Ed. J. M. Robson. Toronto: University of Toronto Press/Routledge & Kegan Paul, pp. 117–47.

———. 1977e. 'De Tocqueville on Democracy in America [II]' [1840]. In *CW*, vol. 18: *Essays on Politics and Society*. Ed. J. M. Robson. Toronto: University of Toronto Press/Routledge & Kegan Paul, pp. 153–204.

———. 1977f. *On Liberty* [1859]. In *CW*, vol. 18: *Essays on Politics and Society*. Ed. J. M. Robson. Toronto: University of Toronto Press/Routledge & Kegan Paul, pp. 217–310.

———. 1977g. *Considerations on Representative Government* [1861]. In *CW*, vol. 19: *Essays on Politics and Society*. Ed. J. M. Robson. Toronto: University of Toronto Press/Routledge & Kegan Paul, pp. 373–577.

———. 1978. 'The Protagoras' [1834]. In *CW*, vol. 11: *Essays on Philosophy and the Classics*. Ed. F. E. Sparshott. Toronto: University of Toronto Press/ Routledge and Kegan Paul, pp. 39–61.

———. 1978a. 'The Phaedrus' [1834]. In *CW*, vol. 11: *Essays on Philosophy and the Classics*. Ed. F. E. Sparshott. Toronto: University of Toronto Press/ Routledge and Kegan Paul, pp. 62–96.

———. 1978b. 'The Gorgias' [1834]. In *CW*, vol. 11: *Essays on Philosophy and the Classics*. Ed. F. E. Sparshott. Toronto: University of Toronto Press/ Routledge and Kegan Paul, pp. 97–150.

———. 1978c. 'The Apology of Socrates' [1835]. In *CW*, vol. 11: *Essays on Philosophy and the Classics*. Ed. F. E. Sparshott. Toronto: University of Toronto Press/Routledge and Kegan Paul, pp. 151–74.

———. 1978d. 'Grote's History of Greece [I]' [1867]. In *CW*, vol. 11: *Essays on Philosophy and the Classics*. Ed. F. E. Sparshott. Toronto: University of Toronto Press/Routledge and Kegan Paul, pp. 273–305.

———. 1978e. 'Grote's History of Greece [II]' [1853]. In *CW*, vol. 11: *Essays on Philosophy and the Classics*. Ed. F. E. Sparshott. Toronto: University of Toronto Press/Routledge and Kegan Paul, pp. 309–37.

———. 1978f. 'Two Publications on Plato' [1840]. In *CW*, vol. 11: *Essays on Philosophy and the Classics*. Ed. F. E. Sparshott. Toronto: University of Toronto Press/Routledge and Kegan Paul, pp. 239–43.

———. 1978g. 'Grote's Plato' [1866]. In *CW*, vol. 11: *Essays on Philosophy and the Classics*. Ed. F. E. Sparshott. Toronto: University of Toronto Press/Routledge and Kegan Paul, pp. 377–440.

Mill, John Stuart. 1981. *Autobiography*. In *CW*, vol. 1: *Autobiography and Literary Essays*. Ed. J. Robson and J. Stillinger. Toronto: University of Toronto Press/ Routledge & Kegan Paul, 1981.

———. 1981a. 'Periodical Literature' [1824]. In *CW*, vol. 1: *Autobiography and Literary Essays*. Ed. J. Robson and J. Stillinger. Toronto: University of Toronto Press/Routledge & Kegan Paul, pp. 293–325.

Mill, John Stuart. 1981b. 'On Genius' [1832]. In *CW*, vol. 1: *Autobiography and Literary Essays*. Ed. J. Robson and J. Stillinger. Toronto: University of Toronto Press/Routledge & Kegan Paul, 1981, pp. 329–39.

———. 1981c. 'Writings of Junius Redivivus [I]' [1837]. In *CW*, vol. 1: *Autobiography and Literary Essays*. Ed. J. Robson and J. Stillinger. Toronto: University of Toronto Press/Routledge & Kegan Paul, 1981, pp. 369–77.

———. 1982. 'The State of Politics in 1836' [1836]. In *CW*, vol. 6: *Essays on England, Ireland and the Empire*. Ed. J. M. Robson. Toronto: University of Toronto Press/Routledge & Kegan Paul, pp. 319–28.

———. 1984. 'Law of Libel and Liberty of the Press' [1825]. In *CW*, vol. 21: *Essays on Equality, Law and Education*. Ed. J. M. Robson. Toronto: University of Toronto Press/Routledge and Kegan Paul, pp. 1–34.

———. 1984a. 'On Punishment' [1834]. In *CW*, vol. 21: *Essays on Equality, Law and Education*. Ed. J. M. Robson. Toronto: University of Toronto Press/Routledge & Kegan Paul, pp. 77–79.

———. 1984b. 'A Few Words on Non-Intervention' [1859]. In *CW*, vol. 21: *Essays on Equality, Law and Education*. Ed. J. M. Robson. Toronto: University of Toronto Press/Routledge & Kegan Paul, 1984, pp. 111–24.

———. 1984c. 'The Contest in America' [1862]. In *CW*, vol. 21: *Essays on Equality, Law and Education*. Ed. J. M. Robson. Toronto: University of Toronto Press/Routledge & Kegan Paul, pp. 127–42.

———. 1984d. 'Inaugural Address Delivered to the University of St. Andrews' [1867]. In *CW*, vol. 21: *Essays on Equality, Law and Education*. Ed. J. M. Robson. Toronto: University of Toronto Press/Routledge & Kegan Paul, 1984, pp. 215–58.

———. 1984e. *The Subjection of Women* [1869]. In *CW*, vol. 21: *Essays on Equality, Law and Education*. Ed. J. M. Robson. Toronto: University of Toronto Press/Routledge and Kegan Paul, pp. 259–340.

———. 1984f. 'Treaty Obligations' [1870]. In *CW*, vol. 21: *Essays on Equality, Law and Education*. Ed. J. M. Robson. Toronto: University of Toronto Press/Routledge and Kegan Paul, pp. 343–48.

———. 1985. 'Alison's History of the French Revolution' [1833]. In *CW*, vol. 20: *Essays on French History and Historians*. Ed. J. Robson. Toronto: University of Toronto Press/Routledge and Kegan Paul, pp. 111–22.

———. 1985a. 'Armand Carrel' [1837]. In *CW*, vol. 20: *Essays on French History and Historians*. Ed. J. Robson. Toronto: University of Toronto Press/Routledge and Kegan Paul, pp. 167–215.

———. 1985b. 'Guizot's Lectures on European Civilization' [1836]. In *CW*, vol. 20: *Essays on French History and Historians*. Ed. J. Robson. Toronto: University of Toronto Press/Routledge and Kegan Paul, pp. 367–93.

———. 1985c. 'Vindication of the French Revolution of February 1848' [1849]. In *CW*, vol. 20: *Essays on French History and Historians*. Ed. J. Robson. Toronto: University of Toronto Press/Routledge and Kegan Paul, pp. 319–63.

———. 1986. 'Spirit of the Age III [I]' [1831]. In *CW*, vol. 22: *Newspaper Writings December 1827–July 1831*. Ed. A. P. Robson and J. M. Robson. Toronto: University of Toronto Press/Routledge and Kegan Paul, pp. 252–58.

———. 1988. 'The Utility of Knowledge' [1823]. In *CW*, vol. 26: *Journals and Debating Speeches*. Ed. J. Robson. Toronto: University of Toronto Press/ Routledge and Kegan Paul, pp. 257–61.

———. 1988a. 'Parliamentary Reform [1] [1824]. In *CW*, vol. 26: *Journals and Debating Speeches*. Ed. J. Robson. Toronto: University of Toronto Press/ Routledge and Kegan Paul, pp. 261–71.

———. 1988b. 'Parliamentary Reform [II]' [1824]. In *CW*, vol. 26: *Journals and Debating Speeches*. Ed. J. Robson. Toronto: University of Toronto Press/ Routledge and Kegan Paul, pp. 271–85.

———. 1988c. 'Cooperation: Closing Speech' [1825]. In *CW*, vol. 26: *Journals and Debating Speeches*. Ed. J. Robson. Toronto: University of Toronto Press/ Routledge and Kegan Paul, pp. 308–26.

———. 1988d. 'The British Constitution [1]' [1826]. In *CW*, vol. 26: *Journals and Debating Speeches*. Ed. J. Robson. Toronto: University of Toronto Press/ Routledge and Kegan Paul, pp. 358–71.

———. 1988e. 'The British Constitution [2]' [1826]. In *CW*, vol. 26: *Journals and Debating Speeches*. Ed. J. Robson. Toronto: University of Toronto Press/ Routledge and Kegan Paul, pp. 371–85.

———. 1988f. 'The Church' [1828]. In *CW*, vol. 26: *Journals and Debating Speeches*. Ed. J. Robson. Toronto: University of Toronto Press/Routledge and Kegan Paul, pp. 418–27.

———. 1988g. 'Perfectibility' [1828]. In *CW*, vol. 26: *Journals and Debating Speeches*. Ed. J. Robson. Toronto: University of Toronto Press/Routledge and Kegan Paul, pp. 428–33.

———. 1988h. 'Montesquieu' [1829]. In *CW*, vol. 26: *Journals and Debating Speeches*. Ed. J. Robson. Toronto: University of Toronto Press/Routledge and Kegan Paul, pp. 443–53.

———. 1988i. 'Westminster Election [2]' [1865]. In *CW*, vol. 28: *Public and Parliamentary Speeches*, November 1850–November 1868. Ed. J. Robson and B. Kinzer. Toronto: University of Toronto Press/Routledge & Kegan Paul, pp. 18–28.

———. 1988j. 'Representation of the People [2]' [1866]. In *CW*, vol. 28: *Public and Parliamentary Speeches*, November 1850–November 1868. Ed. J. Robson and B. Kinzer. Toronto: University of Toronto Press/Routledge & Kegan Paul, pp. 58–68.

———. 1988k. 'Representation of the People [4]' [1866]. In *CW*, vol. 28: *Public and Parliamentary Speeches*, November 1850–November 1868. Ed. J. Robson and B. Kinzer. Toronto: University of Toronto Press/Routledge & Kegan Paul, pp. 74f.

———. 1988l. 'The Admission of Women to the Electoral Franchise' [1867]. In *CW*, vol. 28: *Public and Parliamentary Speeches*, November 1850–November 1868. Ed. J. Robson and B. Kinzer. Toronto: University of Toronto Press/ Routledge & Kegan Paul, pp. 151–62.

———. 1989. 'James Mill's *Analysis of the Human Mind*' [1869]. In *CW*, vol. 31: *Miscellaneous Writings*. Ed. J. M. Robson. Toronto: University of Toronto Press/Routledge & Kegan Paul, pp. 95–253.

Mill, John Stuart. 1990. 'A Constitutional View of the India Question' [1858]. In *CW*, vol. 30: *Writings on India*. Ed. J. Robson. M. Moir and Z. Moir. Toronto: University of Toronto Press/Routledge & Kegan Paul, pp. 175–83.

———. 1990a. 'Maine on Village Communities' [1871]. In *CW*, vol. 30: *Writings on India*. Ed. J. Robson. M. Moir and Z. Moir. Toronto: University of Toronto Press/Routledge & Kegan Paul, pp. 215–28.

———. 1990b. 'Memorandum of the Improvements in the Administration of India during the Last Thirty Years' [1858]. In *CW*, vol. 30: *Writings on India*. Ed. J. Robson. M. Moir and Z. Moir. Toronto: University of Toronto Press/ Routledge & Kegan Paul, pp. 91–160.

———. 1999. 'First Draft of a Court of Directors' Public Department dispatch to India (Previous Communication 1828) prepared by John Stuart Mill, assistant to the examiner of Indian correspondence, with marginal comments by the president of the Board of Control, Sir John Cam Hobhouse, *c*. July–December 1836'. In L. Zastoupil and M. Moir, eds., *The Great Indian Education Debate: Documents Relating to the Orientalist-Anglicist Controversy, 1781–1843*. Surrey: Curzon, 1999, pp. 225–43.

Millar, John. 1812. *An Historical View of the English Government* [1803]. 4 vols. London.

Mills, John. 1772. 'Of Love and Jealousy'. In *Essays Moral, Philosophical and Political*. London: n.p., pp. 113–90.

Montesquieu, Charles de Secondat, baron de. 1734. *Considérations sur les causes de la grandeur des Romains et de leur decadence*. Amsterdam: Jean Desbordes.

———. 1734a. *Considerations on the Grandeur and Declension of the Romans, by the author of the Persian Letters*. Dublin/London.

———. 1750. *The Spirit of Laws*. Trans. T. Nugent. 2nd edn. 2 vols. London: J. Nourse and P. Vaillant.

———. 1750a. 'Two Chapters of a celebrated French work, intitled, *De l'esprit des loix*'. Edinburgh: Hamilton & Balfour.

———. 1752. *Reflections on the Causes of the Rise and Fall of the Roman Empire*. Trans. from the French of M. de Secondat, Baron de Montesquieu. 3rd edn. Glasgow: Robert Urie.

———. 1955. 'Memoires sur les dettes de l'Etat'. In *OC de Montesquieu*, vol. 3: *Oeuvres Diverses*. Ed. A. Masson. Paris: Nagel, pp. 24–31.

———. 1955a. 'Dissertation sur la politique des Romains dans la religion'. In *OC de Montesquieu*, vol. 3: *Oeuvres Diverses*. Ed. A. Masson. Paris: Nagel, pp. 37–50.

———. 1955b. 'Discours prononcé à la rentrée de l'Académie de Bordeaux le 15 novembre 1717'. In *OC de Montesquieu*, vol. 3: *Oeuvres Diverses*. Ed. A. Masson. Paris: Nagel, pp. 51–57.

———. 1955c. 'Éloge de la sincérité' [1717]. In *OC de Montesquieu*, vol. 3: *Oeuvres Diverses*. Ed. A. Masson. Paris: Nagel, pp. 59–68.

———. 1955d. 'Essai d'observations sur l'histoire naturelle' [1719/1720]. In *OC de Montesquieu*, vol. 3: *Oeuvres Diverses*. Ed. A. Masson. Paris: Nagel, pp. 99–118.

———. 1955e. 'Considérations sur les richesses de l'Espagne'. In *OC de Montesquieu*, vol. 3: *Oeuvres Diverses*. Ed. A. Masson. Paris: Nagel, pp. 137–55.

———. 1955f. 'Traité des devoirs' [1725]. In *OC de Montesquieu*, vol. 3: *Oeuvres Diverses*. Ed. A. Masson. Paris: Nagel, pp. 157–63.

———. 1955g. 'Discours sur l'Équité qui doit régler les jugemens et l'exécution des loix' [1725]. In *OC de Montesquieu*, vol. 3: *Oeuvres Diverses*. Ed. A. Masson. Paris: Nagel, pp. 209–19.

———. 1955h. 'Memoire contre l'arrêt du conseil du 27 février 1725 portant defense de faire des plantations nouvelles en vignes dans la généralité de Guyenne'. In *OC de Montesquieu*, vol. 3: *Oeuvres Diverses*. Ed. A. Masson. Paris: Nagel, pp. 263–73.

———. 1955i. 'Essai sur les causes qui peuvent affecter les esprits & leur caractères'. In *OC de Montesquieu*, vol. 3: *Oeuvres Diverses*. Ed. A. Masson. Paris: Nagel, pp. 397–430.

———. 1955j. *OC de Montesquieu*, vol. 3: *Oeuvres Diverses*. Ed. A. Masson. Paris: Nagel.

———. 1964. *OC*. Ed. D. Oster. Paris: Editions du Seuil.

———. 1964a. *Défense de l'Esprit des lois*. In *OC*. Ed. D. Oster. Paris: Editions du Seuil, pp. 808–22.

———. 1964b. 'Discours sur Cicéron'. In *OC*. Ed. D. Oster. Paris: Editions du Seuil, pp. 34–36.

———. 1964c. 'Dissertation sur la politique des Romains dans la religion'. In *OC*. Ed. D. Oster. Paris: Editions du Seuil, pp. 39–43.

———. 1964d. 'Essai sur les causes qui peuvent affecter les esprits & leur caractères'. In *OC*. Ed. D. Oster. Paris: Editions du Seuil, pp. 485–96.

———. 1964e. *Considérations sur les causes de la grandeur des Romains et de leur decadence*. In *OC*. Ed. D. Oster. Paris: Editions du Seuil, pp. 435–85.

———. 1976. 'An Essay on the Causes That May Affect Men's Minds and Characters'. *PT*, vol. 4, no. 2, pp. 139–62.

———. 1989. *The Spirit of the Laws*. Ed. A. Cohler, B. Miller and H. Stone. Cambridge: Cambridge University Press.

———. 1998. *De l'Esprit des lois*. Livres I et XIII (imprimé et manuscript). Ed. A. Postiglolia (Version imprimée) and G. Benrekassa (Version manuscrite), bk. 1 (Version imprimée). Oxford: Voltaire Foundation.

———. 1998a. *Correspondance*. Ed. Louis Desgraves and Edgar Mass et al. In *OC de Montesquieu*. Oxford: Voltaire Foundation, vol. 18.

———. 2000. *Considérations sur les causes de la grandeur des Romains et de leur Décadence*. Ed. F. Weil and C. Courtney. In *OC de Montesquieu*. Oxford: Voltaire Foundation, vol. 2, pp. 89–98.

———. 2000a. *Réflexions sur la Monarchie Universelle en Europe*. Ed. F. Weil and C. Courteney. In *OC de Montesquieu*. Oxford: Voltaire Foundation, vol. 2.

———. 2002. 'Discourse on Cicero'. Trans. David Fott. *PT*, vol. 30, no. 5 pp. 733–37.

Montesquieu, Charles de Secondat, baron de. 2004. *Lettres persanes*. Ed. E. Mass et al. In *OC de Montesquieu*. Oxford: Voltaire Foundation, vol. 1.

Mossner, E. C. 1948. 'Hume's Early Memoranda'. *JHI*, vol. 9, no. 4, pp. 492–518.

Naudé, Gabriel. 1662. *Bibliographie Politique dv Sr. Navde: Contenant les liures & la methode necessaries à estudier la Politique*. Paris: Gvillavme Pele.

———. 1679. *Considerations politiques sur les Coups d'Estat* [Rome, 1639[1]]. Paris: n.p.

Nettleship, R. L. 1997. 'Memoir' [1888]. In T. H. Green, *CW*. Ed. R. L. Nettleship. Bristol: Thoemmes, vol. 3, pp. xi–clxi.

Nichol, John Pringle. 1837. *Views of the Architecture of the Heavens, in a Series of Letters to a Lady*. Edinburgh: William Tait.

———. 1852. *The Importance of Literature to Men of Business: A Series of Addresses Delivered at Various Popular Institutions*. Rev. and corrected by authors. London: John J. Griffin & Co., pp. 212–52.

Nicole, Pierre. 1671. *De l'Education d'un Prince, Divisée en trois Parties, Dont la derniere contient Divers Traittez Utile à tout le monde*. Paris: Charles Savreeaux.

———. 1677. *Moral Essays, Contain'd in several Treatises on Many Important Duties. Written in French, by Messieurs de Port Royal. Faithfully Rendered into English, by A Person of Quality*. London: J. Magnes and R. Bentley, vol. 1.

———. 1970. 'De la charité et de l'amour propre'. In *OPM*. Ed. C.M.G.B. Jourdain. Hildesheim: Georg Olms Verlag, pp. 179–206.

———. 1970a. 'Des moyens de conserver la paix avec les hommes'. In *OPM*. Ed. C.M.G.B. Jourdain. Hildesheim: Georg Olms Verlag, pp. 207–66.

———. 1970b. 'De la civilité chrétienne'. In *OPM*. Ed. C.M.G.B. Jourdain. Hildesheim: Georg Olms Verlag, pp. 267–79.

———. 1970c. 'De la manière d'étudier chrétiennement'. In *OPM*. Ed. C.M.G.B. Jourdain. Hildesheim: Georg Olms Verlag, pp. 424–35.

Nietzsche, Friedrich. 1968. *Jenseits von Gut und Böse*. In *Nietzsche Werke: Kritische Gesamtausgabe*. Berlin: Walter de Gruyter, vol. 6, part 2.

Norris, John. 2005. *Cursory Reflections upon a Book call'd, 'An Essay concerning Human Understanding'* [1690] and *A Brief Consideration of the Remarques made upon the foregoing Reflections by the Gentlemen of the Athenian Society* [1692]. In E. D. Taylor and M. New, eds., *Mary Astell and John Norris: Letters Concerning the Love of God*. Aldershot: Ashgate, pp. 184–220.

Nugent, Thomas. 1750. 'The Translator to the Reader'. In Montesquieu, *The Spirit of Laws*. 2nd edn. 2 vols. London: J. Nourse and P. Vaillant, vol. 1.

Pascal, Blaise. 1965. 'La Propriété'. In *OC*. Ed. J. Chevalier. Paris: Bibliothèque de la Pléiade, 1962, pp. 616–17. Repr. in R. Taveneaux, ed., *Jansénisme et Politique*. Paris: Armand Colin, pp. 67ff.

———. 1966. *Pensées*. Ed. A. Krailsheimer. London: Penguin.

Petty, William. 1690. *Political Arithmetick*. London: Robert Clavel.

Philodemius, Eutactus [pseud.]. 1649. *The Original & End of Civil Power: Or, A discourse; Wherein is set forth and cleared, What the People are; Their Natural Bent to Sociability and Government* . . . London: n.p.

Plato. 1997. *Cratylus*. In *Complete Works*. Ed. John M. Cooper. Indianapolis IN: Hackett.

———. 1997a. *Lysis*. In *Complete Works*. Ed. John M. Cooper. Indianapolis IN: Hackett.

———. 1977b. *Republic*. In *Complete Works*. Ed. John M. Cooper. Indianapolis IN: Hackett.

Pollock, F. E. 1882. 'The History of the Science of Politics'. Parts I–III. *Fortnightly Review*, vol. 32, pp. 209–25, 376–91, 453–67.

Polybius. 1922–27. *The Histories*. Trans. W. Pater. 6 vols. London: Heinneman.

Pouilly, Levesque de. 1766. *Traité des sentimens agréables, The Theory of Agreeable Sensations*. Trans. [anon]. Edinburgh: J. Dickson.

Price, Richard. 1769. *A Review of the Principal Questions and Difficulties in Morals*. 2nd edn. London: T. Cadell.

———. 1991. *PW*. Ed. D. O. Thomas. Cambridge: Cambridge University Press.

Pufendorf, Samuel. 1749. *Of the Law of Nature and Nations*. Trans. Basil Kennett. 5th edn. 8 books. London: J. and J. Bonwicke et al.

Rousseau, Jean-Jacques. 1763. *Emilius, or, An Essay on Education*. By John James Rousseau, Citizen of Geneva. Translated from the French by Mr. Nugent. 2 vols. London: J. Nourse and P. Vaillant.

———. 1969. *OC de Rousseau*. Vol. 4. Ed. B. Gangebin and M. Raymond. Paris: Gallimard.

———. 2002. *Discourse on the Origin and Foundation of Inequality Among Men*. In *Rousseau: The Social Contract and Other Later Political Writings*. Ed. V. Gourevitch. Cambridge: Cambridge University Press, pp. 111–222.

———. 2002a. *Essay on the Origin of Languages*. In *Rousseau: The Social Contract and Other Later Political Writings*. Ed. V. Gourevitch. Cambridge: Cambridge University Press, pp. 247–99.

———. 2003. *Of the Social Contract*. In *Rousseau: The Discourses and Other Early Political Writings*. Ed. V. Gourevitch. Cambridge: Cambridge University Press, pp. 39–152.

Savigny, Friedrich. 1832. 'On the Origin and Growth of the *Latini* as a Peculiar Class in the Roman State' and 'On the *Jus Italicum*'. From the German of Savigny. *TPM*, vol. 1, pp. 150–73.

Say, Jean Baptiste. 1816. *England and the English People*. Trans. John Richter. 2nd edn. London: Sherwood, Neely and Jones.

Schleiermacher, F. 1833. 'On the Worth of Socrates as a Philosopher'. Trans. C[onnop] T[hirlwall], *TPM*, vol. 2, no. 6, pp. 538–55.

———. 1833a. 'Schleiermacher's Introduction to his Translation of Plato's Apology of Socrates'. Trans. C[onnop] T[hirlwall], *TPM*, vol. 2, no. 6, pp. 556–61.

Seneca. 1928. 'De Otio'. *Moral Essays*. Trans. J. W. Basore. Loeb Classical Library.

Shaftesbury, Anthony Ashley Cooper, third earl of. 2001. *Characteristicks of Men, Manners, Opinions and Times* [1737]. Ed. D. Den Uyl. 3 vols. Indianapolis IN: Liberty Fund.

Sherlock, William. 1691. *The Case of Allegiance*. London: n.p.

Schleiermacher, Friedrich. 1955. 'On the Concepts of Different forms of the State' [1814]. In H. S. Reiss, ed., *The Political Thought of the German Romantics*. Oxford: Oxford University Press, pp. 173–202.

Smith, Adam. 1975. *Lectures on Jurisprudence*. Ed. R. L. Meek, D. D. Raphael and P. G. Stein. Indianapolis IN: Liberty Fund.

———. 1976. *Theory of Moral Sentiments* [1759]. Ed. D. D. Raphael and A. L. Macfie. Indianapolis IN: Liberty Fund.

Smith, Adam. 1976a. *An Inquiry into the Nature and Causes of the Wealth of Nations* [1776]. Ed. R. H. Campbell and A. Skinner. 2 vols. Indianapolis IN: Liberty Fund.

———. 1980. 'The History of Astronomy'. In *Essays on Philosophical Subjects*. Ed. D. D. Raphael. Indianapolis IN: Liberty Fund, pp. 33–105.

———. 1980a. 'Of the External Senses'. In *Essays on Philosophical Subjects*. Ed. D. D. Raphael. Indianapolis IN: Liberty Fund, pp. 135–68.

———. 1980b. 'Letter to the Authors of the *Edinburgh Review*' [1756]. In *Essays on Philosophical Subjects*. Ed. D. D. Raphael. Indianapolis IN: Liberty Fund, pp. 242–56.

———. 1983. 'Lectures on Rhetoric and Belles Lettres' [1762–63]. In *Lectures on Rhetoric and Belles Lettres*. Ed. J. C. Bryce. Indianapolis IN: Liberty Fund.

———. 1983a. 'Considerations Concerning the First Formation of Languages, and the Different Genius of Original and Compounded Languages'. In *Lectures on Rhetoric and Belles Lettres*. Ed. J. C. Bryce. Indianapolis IN: Liberty Fund, pp. 203–26.

———. 1987. *Correspondence of Adam Smith*. Ed. E. C. Mossner and I. S. Ross. Indianapolis IN: Liberty Fund.

Spinoza, Benedictus de. 1958. *Tractatus Politicus*. In *The Political Works*. Ed. A. G. Wernham. Oxford: Oxford University Press.

Staël, Germaine de. 1813. *The Influence of the Passions upon the Happiness of Individuals and of Nations*. Trans. from the French. London: Henry Colburn.

Sterling, John. 1848. *Essays and Tales by John Sterling*. Ed. J. C. Hare. 2 vols. London.

Stewart, D. 1855. *The CW of Dugald Stewart*. Ed. Sir William Hamilton. Vols. 6–7. Edinburgh: Thomas Constable & Co.,

———. 1980. 'Account of the Life and Writings of Adam Smith LD.D'. In Adam Smith, *Essays on Philosophical Subjects*. Ed. W.P.D. Wightman, J. C. Bryce and I. S. Ross. Oxford, pp. 269–351.

Stillingfleet, Edward. 1689. *A Discourse Concerning the Unreasonableness of a New Separation, on account of the Oaths. With an Answer to the History of Passive Obedience, so far as relates to Them*. Licens'd, October 25th. London: Richard Chiswell.

Strauss, David. 1846. *Life of Jesus*. Trans. George Eliot. 3 vols. London.

Sydenham, Thomas. 1991. *Observationes Medicae* (London, 1676) *and his Medical Observations* (MS 527 of the Royal College of Physicians). Ed. G. G. Meynell. Folkestone: Winterdown Books.

Tocqueville, Alexis de. 1971. *Recollections*. Ed. J. P. Mayer and A. P. Kerr. Trans. G. Lawrence. New York: Doubleday.

———. 1992. *De la Démocratie en Amérique*. In OC. Paris: Gallimard, vol. 2.

Thucydides. 1972. *History of the Peloponnesian War*. Ed. M. I. Finley. London: Penguin.

Toland, John. 1751. *Pantheisticon: Or, the Form of Celebrating the Socratic-Society*. London: Sam Paterson.

Tyler, Colin, ed. 2005. *Unpublished Manuscripts in British Idealism: Political Philosophy, Theology and Social Thought*. 2 vols. Bristol: Thoemmes.

[Various.]. 1867. *Essays on Reform*. London: Macmillan.

[Various.]. 1878. 'A Modern "Symposium": Is the Popular Judgement in Politics more just than that of the Higher Orders'. *The Nineteenth Century*, no. 15, pp. 797–822.

[George Vasey?]. 1867. *Individual Liberty, Legal, Moral and Licentious; in which the Political Fallacies of J. S. Mill's Essay 'On Liberty' are pointed out*. London: George Vasey.

Volpilhac-Auger, Cathérine, ed. 2001. *L'Atelier de Montesquieu: Manuscrits inédits de La Brède*. Naples: Voltaire Foundation.

Weber, Max. 1994. 'The Profession and Vocation of Politics'. In *PW*. Ed. P. Lassman and R. Spiers. Cambridge: Cambridge University Press, pp. 309–69.

Williams, David. 1782. *Letters on Political Liberty Addressed to a Member of the English House of Commons on his being Chosen into the Committee of an Associating County*. London: T. Evans.

Williams, Thomas. 1828. *Popery Unmasked: Being a Fair Representation of the Chief Errors of the Church of Rome*. New edn. London: Printed by the Author.

Y. M. C., and I. K. 1832. 'Vico'. *TPM*, vol. 2, no. 6, pp. 626–44.

Yolton, Jean, ed. 2000. *John Locke as Translator: Three of the 'Essais' of Pierre Nicole in French and English* [= *SVEC*, no. 7]. Oxford: Voltaire Foundation.

PRINTED SECONDARY SOURCES

Aarsleff, Hans. 1982. *From Locke to Saussure*. London: Athlone Press.

Acomb, Dorothy. 1950. *Anglophobia in France, 1763–1789: An Essay in the History of Constitutionalism and Nationalism*. Durham NC: Duke University Press.

Adair, Douglas. 1998. *Fame and the Founding Fathers*. Indianapolis IN: Liberty Fund.

Adamson, J. S. A. 1990. 'Eminent Victorians: S. R. Gardiner and the Liberal as Hero'. *HJ*, vol. 33, no. 3, pp. 641–57.

Alexander, Gregory S. 1997. *Commodity and Propriety: Competing Visions of Property in American Legal Thought 1776–1970*. Chicago: University of Chicago Press.

Alexandrowicz, C. H. 1967. *An Introduction to the History of the Law of Nations in the East Indies (16th, 17th and 18th Centuries)*. Oxford: Clarendon.

Altholz, Josef. 1988. 'The Warfare of Conscience with Theology'. In Gerald Parsons, ed., *Religion in Victorian Britain*, vol. 4, *Interpretations*. Manchester: Manchester University Press, pp. 150–69.

Anderson, Olive. 1991. 'The Feminism of T. H. Green: A Late-Victorian Success Story?' *HPT*, vol. 12, no. 4, pp. 671–93.

Annas, Julia. 1994. *The Morality of Happiness*. Oxford: Oxford University Press.

Arena, Valentina. 2007. 'Invocation to Liberty and Invective of *Dominatus* at the End of the Roman Republic'. *Bulletin of the Institute of Classical Studies*, vol. 50, pp. 49–73.

———. 2007a. *Libertas* and *Virtus* of the Citizen in Cicero's *De Republica*'. *Scripta Classica Israelica*, vol. 26, pp. 39–66.

Armitage, David. 2000. *The Ideological Origins of the British Empire*. Cambridge: Cambridge University Press.

———. 2000a. 'Edmund Burke and Reason of State'. *JHI*, vol. 61, pp. 617–34.

———. 2002. 'The Declaration of Independence and International Law'. *WMQ*, vol. 59, no. 1, pp. 39–64.

———. 2002a. 'Empire and Liberty: The Republican Dilemma'. In M. van Gelderen and Q. Skinner, eds., *Republicanism—A Shared European Heritage*. 2 vols. Cambridge: Cambridge University Press, vol. 2, pp. 29–46.

———. 2004. 'John Locke, Carolina and the *Two Treatises of Government*'. *PT*, vol. 32, no. 5, pp. 602–27.

Arneil, Barbara. 1996. 'The Wild Indian's Venison: Locke's Theory of Property and English Colonialism in America'. *PS*, vol. 64, no. 1, pp. 60–74.

Arneson, Richard J. 1980. 'Mill versus Paternalism'. *Ethics*, vol. 90, pp. 470–89.

———. 1992. 'Property Rights in Persons'. *Social Philosophy and Policy*, no. 9, pp. 201–30.

Ashcraft, Richard. 1986. *Revolutionary Politics and Locke's 'Two Treatises of Government'*. Berkeley CA: University of California Press.

———. 1989. 'Class Conflict and Constitutionalism in J. S. Mill's Thought'. In N. Rosenblum, ed., *Liberalism and the Moral Life*. Cambridge MA: Harvard University Press, pp. 105–26.

———. 1993. 'Liberal Political Theory and Working-Class Radicalism in Nineteenth-Century England'. *PT*, vol. 21, no. 2, pp. 249–72.

———. 1998. 'John Stuart Mill and the Theoretical Foundations of Democratic Socialism'. In Eldon Eisenach, ed., *Mill and the Moral Character of Liberalism*. University Park PA: Pennsylvania State University Press, pp. 169–89.

Ashton, Rosemary. 1980. *The German Idea: Four English Writers and the Reception of German Thought, 1800–1860*. Cambridge: Cambridge University Press.

———. 2006. *142 Strand: A Radical Address in Victorian London*. London: Chatto & Windus.

Atkins, E. M. 1990. '"*Domina et Regina Virtutum*": Justice and *Societas* in *De Officiis*'. *Phronesis*, vol. 35, no. 3, pp. 258–89.

Ayers, Michael. 1981. 'Mechanism, Superaddition and the Proof of God's Existence in Locke's *Essay*'. *Philosophical Review*, vol. 40, no. 2, pp. 210–51.

———. 1996. *Locke: Epistemology and Ontology*. London: Routledge.

Baier, Annette. 1980. 'Hume on Resentment'. *Hume Studies*, vol. 6, no. 2, pp. 133–49.

Baker, Keith-Michael. 1990. *Inventing the French Revolution*. Cambridge: Cambridge University Press.

Baldwin, Tom. 1984. 'MacCallum and the Two Concepts of Freedom'. *Ratio*, vol. 16, pp. 125–42.

Balibar, Etienne. 1998. *Spinoza and Politics*. Trans. Peter Snowdon. London: Verso.

Barber, Sarah. 1998. *Regicide and Republicanism*. Edinburgh: Edinburgh University Press.

———. 2000. *A Revolutionary Rogue: Henry Marten and the English Republic*. Stroud: Sutton.

Barry, Brian. 1996. 'You have to be crazy to believe it'. *Times Literary Supplement*, October 25.

Baum, Bruce. 1999. 'J. S. Mill's Conception of Economic Freedom'. *HPT*, vol. 20, no. 3, pp. 494–530.

Baume, Sandrine, and Biancamaria Fontana, eds. 2008. *Les usages de la separation des pouvoirs*. Paris: Michel Houdiard Éditeur.

Beales, Derek. 1999. 'The Idea of Reform in British Politics, 1829–1850'. *PBA*, vol. 100, pp. 159–74.

Beauchamp, Tom. 2008. 'Who Deserves Autonomy, and Whose Autonomy Deserves Respect?' In J. S. Taylor, ed., *Personal Autonomy*. Cambridge: Cambridge University Press, pp. 310–29.

Bedi, Sonu. 2009. *Rejecting Rights*. Cambridge: Cambridge University Press.

Beiner, Ronald. 1983. *Political Judgment*. London: Methuen.

Belchem, J. 1981. 'Republicanism, Popular Constitutionalism and the Radical Platform in Early Nineteenth-Century England'. *Social History*, vol. 6, no. 1, pp. 1–32.

Bell, David A. 2001. *The Cult of the Nation in France: Inventing Nationalism, 1680–1800*. Cambridge MA: Harvard University Press.

Bell, Duncan. 2006. 'From Ancient to Modern in Victorian Imperial Thought'. *HJ*, vol. 49, no. 3, pp. 735–59.

———. 2007. *The Idea of a Greater Britain* Princeton NJ: Princeton University Press.

Benians, E. A. 1925. 'Adam Smith's Project of an Empire'. *Cambridge Historical Journal*, vol. 1, no. 3, pp. 249–83.

Benrekassa, George. 2004. *Les Manuscrits de Montesquieu: Secretaires, Ecritures, Datations* [= *Cahiers Montesquieu*, no. 8]. Oxford: Voltaire Foundation.

Berent, Moishe. 1998. '*Stasis* and the Greek Invention of Politics'. *HPT*, vol. 19, no. 3, pp. 331–61.

Berkowitz, Peter. 1999. *Virtue and the Making of Modern Liberalism*. Princeton NJ: Princeton University Press.

Berlin, Isaiah. 1988. 'Two Concepts of Liberty'. In *Four Essays on Liberty*. Oxford: Clarendon, pp. 118–72.

———. 1991. 'John Stuart Mill and the Ends of Life'. In J. Gray, ed., *J. S. Mill, On Liberty in Focus*. London: Routledge, pp. 131–61.

———. 2001. *The Roots of Romanticism*. London: Chatto & Windus.

Berry, Chris. 1992. 'Adam Smith and the Virtues of Commerce'. In J. W. Chapman and W. Galston, eds., *Virtue* [= *Nomos*, vol. 34]. New York: New York University Press, pp. 69–88.

———. 1994. *The Idea of Luxury*. Cambridge: Cambridge University Press.

———. 1997. *Social Theory of the Scottish Enlightenment*. Edinburgh: Edinburgh University Press.

———. 2004. 'Smith under Strain'. *EJPT*, vol. 3, no. 4, pp. 455–63.

Bevir, Mark. 1996. 'Review Article: English Political Thought in the Nineteenth Century'. *HPT*, vol. 17, no. 1, pp. 114–27.

———. 1993. 'Welfarism, Socialism and Religion: On T. H. Green and Others'. *Review of Politics*, vol. 55, no. 4, pp. 639–61.

Biagini, Eugenio. 2003. 'Neo-Roman Liberalism: "Republican" Values and British Liberalism, ca. 1860–1875'. *HEI*, vol. 29, pp. 55–72.

Black, Antony. 1993. 'The Juristic Origins of Social Contract Theory'. *HPT*, vol. 14, no. 1, pp. 57–76.

Blom, H., C. Laursen and L. Simonutti, eds. 2007. *Monarchies in the Age of Enlightenment*. Toronto: University of Toronto Press.

Boesche, Roger. 1990. 'Fearing Monarchs and Merchants: Montesquieu's Two Theories of Despotism'. *Western Political Quarterly*, vol. 43, no. 4, pp. 741–61.

Bolton, Martha Brandt,. 1983. 'Locke and Pyrrhonism'. In M. Burnyeat. ed.. *The Sceptical Tradition*. Berkeley CA: University of California Press, pp. 353–75.

Bosbach, Franz. 1986. *Monarchia Universalis*. Göttingen: Vandenhoeck & Ruprecht.

———. 1998. 'The European Debate on Universal Monarchy'. In D. Armitage, ed., *Theories of Monarchy 1450–1800*. Aldershot: Edward Elgar, pp. 81–98.

Boucher, D. and A. Vincent. 2000. *British Idealism and Political Theory*. Edinburgh: Edinburgh University Press.

Bourke, Richard. 2000. 'Liberty, Authority and Trust in Burke's Idea of Empire'. *JHI*, vol. 61, no. 3, pp. 453–71.

Boyd, Richard. 2002. 'The Calvinist Origins of Locke's Political Economy'. *HPT*, vol. 23, no. 1, pp. 30–60.

Bratman, Michael E. 2000. 'Reflection, Planning and Temporally Extended Agency'. *Philosophical Review*, no. 109, pp. 35–61.

———. 2006. *Structures of Agency*. Oxford: Oxford University Press.

Brett, Annabel. 2002. 'Natural Right and Civil Community: The Civil Philosophy of Hugo Grotius'. *HJ*, vol. 45, no. 1, pp. 31–51.

Brewer, David. 2008. *The Enlightenment Past*. Cambridge: Cambridge University Press.

Brewer, John. 1997. *The Pleasures of the Imagination*. London: Fontana.

Brito-Viera, Monica. 2003. '*Mare Liberum* vs. *Mare Clausum*: Grotius, Freitas, and Selden's Debate on Dominion over the Seas'. *JHI*, vol. 64, no. 3, pp. 361–77.

Brock, M. G., and M. C. Curthoys, eds. 1997. *The History of the University of Oxford in the Nineteenth Century*. Vol. 6, part 1. Oxford: Oxford University Press.

Brogan, Hugh. 2006. *Alexis de Tocqueville: Prophet of Democracy in the Age of Revolution*. London: Profile Books.

Brooke, Chistopher. 2001. 'Stoicism and Augustinianism in Rousseau's Political Philosophy'. In P. Riley, ed., *The Cambridge Companion to Rousseau*. Cambridge: Cambridge University Press, pp. 94–123.

———. 2006. 'How the Stoics Became Atheists'. *HJ*, vol. no. 2, pp. 1–16.

Brown, Colin. 1995. *Jesus in European Protestant Thought 1778–1860*. Durham NC: Labyrinth.

Brown, Vivienne. 1999. 'The "Figure" of God and the Limits to Liberalism: A Rereading of Locke's *Essay* and *Two Treatises*'. *JHI*, vol. 60, no. 1, pp. 83–100.

Brunt, P. A. 1988. 'The Fall of the Roman Republic'. In *The Fall of the Roman Republic and Related Essays*. Oxford: Clarendon, pp. 1–92.

———. 1988a. 'Factions'. In *The Fall of the Roman Republic and Related Essays*. Oxford: Clarendon, pp. 443–502.

Buchan, James. 2003. *Capital of the Mind: How Edinburgh Changed the World*. London: John Murray.

Buchwalter, Andrew. 1992. 'Hegel's Concept of Virtue'. *PT*, vol. 20, no. 4, pp. 548–83.

Buckle, Stephen. 1991. *Natural Law and the Theory of Property: Grotius to Hume*. Oxford: Clarendon.

Bullen, J. B. 1994. *The Myth of the Renaissance in Nineteenth-Century Writing*. Oxford: Clarendon.

Burgess, Glenn. 1998. 'Was the English Civil War a War of Religion?' *Huntington Library Quarterly*, vol. 61, no. 1, pp. 173–201.

Burke, Peter. 1991. 'Tacitism, Scepticism, and Reason of State'. In M. Goldie and J. Burns, eds., *The Cambridge History of Political Thought 1450–1700*. Cambridge: Cambridge University Press, pp. 479–98.

Burns, Arthur. 2004. 'English "Church Reform" Revisited, 1780–1840'. In A. Burns and J. Innes, eds., *Rethinking the Age of Reform: Britain 1780–1840*. Cambridge: Cambridge University Press, pp. 136–62.

Burns, J. H. 1967. *The Fabric of Felicity: The Legislator and the Human Condition*. Inaugural Lecture, University College, London, March 2. London: H. K. Lewis & Co Ltd.

———. 1969. 'J. S. Mill and Democracy, 1829–1861'. In J. Schneewind, ed., *J. S. Mill: A Collection of Critical Essays*. London: Doubleday, pp. 281–328.

———. 1976. 'The Light of Reason: Philosophical History in the Two Mills'. In J. Robson, ed., *James and John Stuart Mill: Papers from the Centenary Conference*. Toronto: University of Toronto Press, pp. 3–20.

Burnyeat, Myles. 1980. 'Aristotle on Learning to be Good'. In A. O. Rorty, ed., *Essays on Aristotle's Ethics*. Berkeley CA: University of California Press, pp. 69–91.

———. 1983. 'Can the Sceptic live his Scepticism?' In M. Burnyeat, ed., *The Sceptical Tradition*. Berkeley CA: University of California Press, pp. 117–48.

———. 1998. 'Plato as Educator of Nineteenth-Century Britain'. In A. Oksenberg-Rorty, ed., *Philosophers on Education*. London: Routledge, pp. 353–73.

Burrow, John. 1974. '"The Village Community" and the Uses of History in Late Nineteenth-Century England'. In N. McKendrick, ed., *Historical Perspectives: Studies in English Thought and Society in Honour of J. H. Plumb*. London: Europa Publications, pp. 255–84.

———. 1984. *A Liberal Descent*. Cambridge: Cambridge University Press.

———. 1985. *Whigs and Liberals*. Oxford: Clarendon.

———. 2000. 'Images of Time: from Carlylean Vulcanism to Sedimentary Gradualism'. In S. Collini, R. Whatmore, and B. Young, eds., *History, Religion and Culture: British Intellectual History 1750–1950*. Cambridge: Cambridge University Press, pp. 198–223.

Cairns, John W. 1991. 'Rhetoric, Language, and Roman Law: Legal Education and Improvement in Eighteenth-Century Scotland'. *Law and History Review*, vol. 9, no. 1, pp. 31–58.

Campbell, Tom. 1971. *Adam Smith's Science of Morals*. London: George Allen & Unwin.

Capaldi, Nicholas. 2003. *John Stuart Mill*. Cambridge: Cambridge University Press.

Carcassonne, E. 1927. *Montesquieu et la problème de la constitution française au XVIIIe siècle*. Paris: PUF.

Carey, Daniel. 1997. 'Locke as Moral Sceptic: Innateness, Diversity, and the Reply to Stoicism'. *Archiv für Geschichte der Philosophie*, vol. 79, pp. 292–309.

———. 2004. 'Locke's Anthropology: Travel, Innateness, and the Exercise of Reason'. *The Seventeenth Century*, vol. 19, no. 2, pp. 260–85.

———. 2006. *Locke, Shaftesbury and Hutcheson*. Cambridge: Cambridge University Press.

Carlisle, Janice. 1991. *John Stuart Mill and the Writing of Character*. Athens GA: University of Georgia Press.

———. 1998. 'Mr. J. Stuart Mill, M.P., and the Character of the Working Classes'. In E. Eisenach, ed., *Mill and the Moral Character of Liberalism*. University Park PA: Pennsylvania State University Press, pp. 143–67.

Carr, Craig, and Michael Seidler. 1996. 'Pufendorf, Sociality and the Modern State'. *HPT*, vol. 27, no. 3, pp. 354–78.

Carrithers, David W. 1991. 'Not so Virtuous Republics: Montesquieu, Venice, and the Theory of Aristocratic Republicanism'. *JHI*, vol. 52, no. 2, pp. 245–68.

———. 1998. 'Montesquieu's Philosophy of Punishment'. *HPT*, vol. 19, no. 2, pp. 213–40.

———. 2001. 'Democratic and Aristocratic Republics'. In D. W. Carrithers, M. A. Mosher and P. A. Rahe, eds., *Montesquieu's Science of Politics: Essays on the 'Spirit of Laws'*. Lanham MD: Rowman and Littlefield, pp. 109–58.

Carter, Ian. 1999. *A Measure of Freedom*. Oxford: Oxford University Press.

Casabianca, D. de. 2008. *De l'étude des sciences à l'esprit des lois*. Paris: Champion.

Castiglione, Dario. 2000. 'Meanings of Liberty in the System of the North'. In S. Collini, R. Whatmore and B. Young, eds., *Economy, Polity and Society: British Intellectual History 1750–1950*. Cambridge: Cambridge University Press, pp. 48–69.

Chadwick, Owen. 1975. *The Secularization of the European Mind in the Nineteenth Century*. Cambridge: Cambridge University Press.

———. 1979. 'Young Gladstone and Italy'. *Journal of Ecclesiastical History*, vol. 30, no. 2, pp. 231–59.

Chappell, Vere. 1994. 'Locke on Freedom of the Will'. In G.A.J. Rogers, ed., *Locke's Philosophy: Content and Context*. Oxford: Clarendon, pp. 101–21.

Childs, Nicholas. 2000. *A Political Academy in Paris, 1724–1731: The Entresol and Its Members*. Oxford: Voltaire Foundation.

Chitnis, Anand C. 1986. *The Scottish Enlightenment and Early Victorian English Society*. London: Croom Helm.

Chowers, Eyal. 2004. *The Modern Self in the Labyrinth*. Cambridge MA: Harvard University Press.

Claeys, Gregory. 1987. 'Justice, Independence, and Industrial Democracy: The Development of John Stuart Mill's Views on Socialism'. *Journal of Politics*, vol. 49, no. 1, pp. 122–47.

———. 1994. 'The Origins of the Rights of Labor: Republicanism, Commerce, and the Construction of Modern Social Theory in Britain, 1796–1805'. *JMH*, vol. 66, pp. 249–90.

Clark, J. C. D. 1992. *The Language of Liberty*. Cambridge: Cambridge University Press.

———. 2000. 'Protestantism, Nationalism and National Identity, 1660–1832'. *HJ*, vol. 43, no. 1, pp. 249–76.

———. 2002. *English Society 1660–1832*. Rev. ed. Cambridge: Cambridge University Press.

Clark, Mary T. 1992. 'An Inquiry into Personhood'. *Review of Metaphysics*, vol. 46, no. 1, pp. 3–28.

Clarke, Peter. 1978. *Liberals and Social Democrats*. Cambridge: Cambridge University Press.

Coffey, John. 1998. 'Puritanism and Liberty Revisited: The Case for Toleration in the English Revolution'. *HJ*, vol. 41, no. 4, pp. 961–85.

Cohen, G. A. 1995. *Self-Ownership, Freedom and Equality*. Cambridge: Cambridge University Press.

Colclough, David. 2005. *Freedom of Speech in Early Stuart England*. Cambridge: Cambridge University Press.

Coleman, Charly J. 2005. 'The Value of Dispossession: Rethinking Discourses of Selfhood in Eighteenth-Century France'. *MIH*, vol. 2, no. 3, pp. 299–326.

Coleman, Janet. 2004. 'Pre-Modern Property and Self-Ownership Before and After Locke'. *EJPT*, vol. 4, no. 2, pp. 125–45.

———. 2005. 'Scholastic Treatments of Maintaining One's *Fama* (Reputation/Good Name) and the Correction of "Private Passions" for the Public Good and Public Legitimacy'. *Social and Cultural History*, vol. 2, no. 1, pp. 23–48.

Colley, Linda. 1992. *Britons: Forging the Nation, 1707–1837*. New Haven CT: Yale University Press.

Collini, Stefan. 1990. 'The Member for Westminster: Doctrinaire Philosopher, Party Hack, or Public Moralist?' *Utilitas*, vol. 2, no. 2, pp. 307–22.

———. 1991. *Public Moralists*. Oxford: Clarendon.

Collinson, Patrick. 1979. 'If Constantine, then also Theodosius: St. Ambrose and the Integrity of the Elizabethan *ecclesia anglicana*'. *Journal of Ecclesiastical History*, vol. 30, no. 2, pp. 205–29.

———. 1988. *The Birthpangs of Protestant England*. London: St. Martins, 1988.

Conlin, Jonathan. 2003. 'Gladstone and Christian Art'. *HJ*, vol. 46, no. 2, pp. 341–74.

Conway, Stephen. 2000. *The British Isles and the American War of Independence*. Oxford: Oxford University Press.

Copp, David. 1980. 'Hobbes on Artificial Persons and Collective Actions'. *TPR*, vol. 89, pp. 579–606.

Copp, David. 2002. 'Social Unity and the Identity of Persons'. *JPP*, vol. 10, no. 4, pp. 365–91.

Dan-Cohen, Meir. 1992. 'Responsibility and the Boundaries of the Self'. *Harvard Law Review*, no. 105, pp. 959–1003.

———. 2001. 'The Value of Ownership'. *JPP*, vol. 9, no. 4, pp. 404–34.

Dan-Cohen, Meir. 2006. 'Socializing Harry'. In H. Frankfurt, *Taking Ourselves Seriously and Getting it Right*. Ed. D. Satz. Stanford CA: University of Stanford Press, pp. 91–104.

Cooper, John M. 2004. 'Reason, Moral Virtue, and Moral Value'. *Reason and Emotion*. Princeton NJ: Princeton University Press, pp. 253–80.

Corsi, Pietro. 1987. 'The Heritage of Dugald Stewart: Oxford Philosophy and the Method of Political Economy'. *Nuncius. Annali di Storia della Scienza*, vol. 2, no. 2, pp. 89–144.

Courtney, Cecil P. 2001. 'Montesquieu and Natural Law'. In D. W. Carrithers, M. A. Mosher and P. A. Rahe, eds., *Montesquieu's Science of Politics: Essays on the 'Spirit of Laws'*. Lanham MD: Rowman and Littlefield, pp. 41–68.

———. 2001a. 'Montesquieu and English Liberty'. In D. W. Carrithers, M. A. Mosher and P. A. Rahe, eds., *Montesquieu's Science of Politics: Essays on the 'Spirit of Laws'*. Lanham MD: Rowman and Littlefield, pp. 273–90.

———. 2009. 'Morals and Manners in Montesquieu's Analysis of the British System of Liberty'. In R. Kingston, ed., *Montesquieu and his Legacy*. New York: SUNY Press, pp. 31–48.

Craig, David M. 2003. 'The Crowned Republic? Monarchy and Anti-Monarchy in Britain, 1760–1901'. *HJ*, vol. 46, no. 1, pp. 167–85.

Craiutu, Aurelian. 2003. *Liberalism under Siege: The Political Thought of the French Doctrinaires*. Lanham MD: Lexington.

Cranston, Maurice. 1985. *John Locke*. Oxford: Oxford University Press.

Crisafulli, Allesandro S. 1937. 'Parallels to Ideas in the *Lettres Persanes*'. *PMLA*, vol. 52, no. 3, pp. 773–77.

———. 1943. 'Montesquieu's Story of the Troglodytes: Its Background, Meaning and Significance'. *PMLA*, vol. 58, no. 2, pp. 372–92.

Croft, Pauline. 1996. 'The Debate over Annual Parliaments in the early Seventeenth Century'. *Parliaments, Estates and Representation*, vol. 16, pp. 163–74.

Cromartie, Alan. 1999. 'The Constitutionalist Revolution: The Transformation of Political Culture in Early Stuart England'. *P&P*, no. 163, pp. 76–120.

———. 2000. 'Theology and Politics in Richard Hooker's Political Thought'. *HPT*, vol. 21, no. 1, pp. 41–66.

———. 2006. *The Constitutionalist Revolution: An Essay on the History of England, 1450–1642*. Cambridge: Cambridge University Press.

Crow, Thomas. 2006. *Emulation: David, Drouais, and Girodet in the Art of Revolutionary France*. New Haven CT: Yale University Press.

Cunningham, Hugh. 1984. 'The Language of Patriotism, 1750–1914'. *HWJ*, vol. 12, pp. 8–33.

Dacome, Lucia. 2004. 'Noting the Mind: Commonplace Books and the Pursuit of the Self in Eighteenth-Century Britain'. *JHI*, vol. 65, no. 4, pp. 603–25.

Dancy, Jonathan. 2004. *Ethics without Principles*. Oxford: Clarendon.

Darwall, Stephen. 1995. *The British Moralists and the Internal 'Ought': 1640–1740*. Cambridge: Cambridge University Press.

———. 1998. 'Empathy, Sympathy and Care'. *PhilSt*, vol. 89, nos. 2–3, pp. 261–82.

———. 1999. 'Sympathetic Liberalism'. *PPA*, vol. 28, no. 2, pp. 139–64.

———. 2002. *Welfare and Rational Care*. Princeton NJ: Princeton University Press.

Davies, Catherine Glyn. 1990. *Conscience and Consciousness: The Idea of Self-Awareness in French Philosophical Writing from Descartes to Diderot* [= *SVEC*, no. 272]. Oxford: Voltaire Foundation.

Davies, Horton. 1996. *Worship and Theology in England*, vol. 3: *From Watts and Wesley to Maurice, 1690–1850*. Repr. in *Worship and Theology in England from Watts and Wesley to Martineau, 1690–1900*. Ann Arbor MI: University of Michigan Press.

Dawson, Hannah. 2005. 'Locke on Language in (Civil) Society.' *HPT*, vol. 26, no. 3, pp. 397–425.

———. 2007. *Locke, Language and Seventeenth-Century Philosophy*. Cambridge: Cambridge University Press.

De Dijn, Annelien. 2008. *French Political Thought from Montesquieu to Tocqueville: Liberty in a Levelled Society?* Cambridge: Cambridge University Press.

de Sanctis, Alberto. 2005. *The 'Puritan' Democracy of T. H. Green*. Exeter: Imprint Academic.

Dedieu, Joseph. 1928. 'L'Agonie du jansénisme (1715–1790)'. *Revue d'histoire de l'église de France*, vol. 14, pp. 161–214.

della Volpe, Galvano. 1978. 'Montesquieu's and Voltaire's Humanitarianism—and Rousseau's'. In *Rousseau and Marx*. Trans. John Fraser. London: Lawrence and Wishart, pp. 126–37.

Demetriou, Kyriakos. 1996. 'In Defence of the British Constitution: Theoretical Implications of the Debate over Athenian Democracy in Britain, 1770–1850'. *HPT*, vol. 17, no. 2, pp. 280–97.

———. 1996a. 'The Development of Platonic Studies in Britain and the Role of the Utilitarians'. *Utilitas*, vol. 8, no. 1, pp. 15–37.

———. 2002. 'Bishop Connop Thirlwall: Historian of Ancient Greece'. *QdS*, vol. 56, pp. 49–90.

———. 2009. 'Socratic Dialectic and the Exaltation of Individuality: J. S. Mill's Influence on Grote's Platonic Interpretation'. *QdS*, vol. 69, pp. 35–61.

Den Uyl Douglas, and Charles L. Griswold Jr. 1996. 'Adam Smith on Friendship and Love'. *Review of Metaphysics*, vol. 49, no. 4, pp. 609–37.

Desgraves, Louis. 1995. *Montesquieu: L'oeuvre et la vie*. Mayenne: L'ésprit du temps.

Desmond, Adrian. 1989. 'Lamarckism and Democracy: Corporations, Corruption and Comparative Anatomy in the 1830s'. In J. R. Moore, ed., *History, Humanity and Evolution: Essays for John C. Greene*. Cambridge: Cambridge University Press, pp. 99–130.

Desserud, Donald. 1999. 'Commerce and Political Participation in Montesquieu's Letter to Domville'. *HEI*, vol. 21, no. 3, pp. 135–51.

Devigne, Robert. 2006. 'Reforming Reformed Religion: J. S. Mill's Critique of the Enlightenment's Natural Religion'. *APSR*, vol. 100, no. 1, pp. 15–27.

Dewhurst, Kenneth. 1963. *John Locke (1632–1704): Physician and Philosopher. A Medical Biography*. London: Wellcome Historical Medical Gallery.

Dickey, Laurence. 1986. 'Historicizing the "Adam Smith Problem": Conceptual, Historiographical, and Textual Issues'. *JMH*, vol. 58, pp. 579–609.

———. 1989. *Hegel: Religion, Economics and the Politics of Spirit, 1770–1807*. Cambridge: Cambridge University Press.

———. 1990. 'Pride, Hypocrisy and Civility in Mandeville's Social and Historical Theory'. *Critical Review*, vol. 4, no. 3, pp. 387–431.

———. 2004. 'Doux-commerce and humanitarian values'. In Hans W. Blom and Laurens C. Winkel, eds., *Grotius and the Stoa*. Van Corum: Assen, pp. 271–317.

Dickinson, Edwin DeWitt. 1917. 'The Analogy between Natural Persons and International Persons in the Law of Nations'. *Yale Law Journal*, vol. 26, no. 7, pp. 564–91.

Dimova-Cookson, Maria. 2003. 'A New Scheme of Positive Freedom: Reconstructing T. H. Green on Freedom'. *PT*, vol. 31, no. 4, pp. 508–32.

Donaldson, Peter S. 1992. *Machiavelli and Mystery of State*. Cambridge: Cambridge University Press.

Dodds, E. R. 1963. *The Greeks and the Irrational*. Berkeley CA: University of California Press.

Dodge, Guy Howard. 1947. *The Political Theory of the Huguenots of the Dispersion*. New York NY: Columbia University Press.

Donnelly, F. K. 1988. 'Levellerism in Eighteenth and Early Nineteenth-Century Britain'. *Albion*, vol. 20, no. 2, pp. 261–69.

Doyle, William. 2000. *Jansenism*. Basingstoke: Palgrave Macmillan.

Dunn, John. 1969. *The Political Thought of John Locke*. Cambridge: Cambridge University Press.

———. 1969a. 'The Politics of Locke in England and America in the Eighteenth Century'. In J. Yolton, ed., *John Locke: Problems and Perspectives. A Collection of New Essays*. Cambridge: Cambridge University Press, pp. 45–80.

———. 1985. 'From Applied Theology to Social Analysis: The Break between John Locke and the Scottish Enlightenment'. In I. Hont and M. Ignatieff, eds., *Wealth and Virtue*. Cambridge: Cambridge University Press, pp. 119–35.

———. 1989. '"Bright Enough for all our Purposes": John Locke's Conception of a Civilized Society'. *Notes and Records of the Royal Society of London*, vol. 43, no. 2, pp. 133–53.

———. 1990. *Interpreting Political Responsibility*. Oxford: Polity.

———. 1991. 'The Claim to Freedom of Conscience: Freedom of Speech, Freedom of Thought, Freedom of Worship?' In O. P. Grell, J. Israel and N. Tyacke, eds., *From Persecution to Toleration: The Glorious Revolution and Religion in England*. Oxford: Clarendon, pp. 171–93.

Dzelzainis, Martin. 2002. 'Anti-Monarchism in English Republicanism'. In M. van Gelderen and Q. Skinner, eds., *Republicanism—A Shared European Heritage*. 2 vols. Cambridge: Cambridge University Press, vol. 2, pp. 27–42.

Eastwood, David. 1989. 'Robert Southey and the Intellectual Origins of Romantic Conservatism'. *EHR*, no. 104, pp. 308–31.

———. 1993. 'John Reeves and the Contested Idea of the Constitution'. *British Journal for Eighteenth-Century Studies*, vol. 16, pp. 197–212.

———. 1997. *Government and Community in the English Provinces, 1700–1870*. Basingstoke: Macmillan.

Edwards, Pamela. 2004. *The Statesman's Science: History, Nature, and Law in the Political Thought of Samuel Taylor Coleridge*. New York NY: Columbia University Press.

Eisenach, Eldon. 1998. 'Mill and Liberal Christianity'. In E. Eisenach, ed., *Mill and the Moral Character of Liberalism*. University Park PA: Pennsylvania State University Press, pp. 191–229.

Ehrard, Jean. 1963. *L'idée de nature en France dans la première moitié du XVIIIᵉ siècle*. 2 vols. Paris: S. E. V. P. E. N.

———. 1987. 'Rousseau et Montesquieu: Le Mauvais Fils Réconcilié'. *Annales de la Société de Jean-Jacques Rousseau*, vol. 41, pp. 56–77.

———. 2005. 'La notion de "loi(s) fondamentale(s) dans l'oeuvre et la pensée de Montesquieu'. In Cathérine Volpilhac-Auger, ed., *Montesquieu en 2005* [= *SVEC* 2005:05]. Oxford: Voltaire Foundation, pp. 267–86.

Epstein, James A. 1994. *Radical Expression*. Oxford: Oxford University Press.

Erb, P. C. 2001. 'Politics and Theological Liberalism: William Gladstone and Mrs Humphry Ward'. *Journal of Religious History*, vol. 25, no. 2, pp. 158–72.

Erler, Michael, and Malcolm Schofield. 1999. 'Epicurean Ethics'. In K. Algra et al., eds., *The Cambridge History of Hellenistic Philosophy*. Cambridge: Cambridge University Press, pp. 642–74.

Erskine, Toni. 2001. 'Assigning Responsibilities to Institutional Moral Agents: The Case of States and Quasi-States'. *Ethics and International Affairs*, vol. 15, no. 1, pp. 67–85.

Farr, J. 1986. '"So Vile and Miserable an Estate": The Problem of Slavery in Locke's Political Thought'. *PT*, vol. 14, no. 2, pp. 263–90.

Farr, J., and C. Roberts. 1985. 'John Locke on the Glorious Revolution: A Rediscovered Document'. *HJ*, vol. 28, no. 2, pp. 385–98.

Finley, Moses. 1981. *Economy and Society in Ancient Greece*. London: Chatto & Windus.

Finn, Margot. 1992. '"A Vent Which Has Conveyed Our Principles": English Radical Patriotism in the Aftermath of 1848'. *JMH*, vol. 64, pp. 637–59.

Fisher, Philip. 2002. *The Vehement Passions*. Princeton NJ: Princeton University Press.

Fitzmaurice, Andrew. 2003. *Humanism and America*. Cambridge: Cambridge University Press.

Fleischacker, Samuel J. 1999. *A Third Concept of Liberty: Judgment and Freedom in Adam Smith and Immanuel Kant*. Princeton NJ: Princeton University Press.

———. 2002. 'Adam Smith's Reception among the American Founders, 1776–1790'. *WMQ*, vol. 59, pp. 897–924.

———. 2004. *On Adam Smith's Wealth of Nations*. Princeton NJ: Princeton University Press.

Fletcher, F. T. H. 1939. *Montesquieu and English Politics, 1750–1800*. London: Edward Arnold.

Fontana, Bianca. 1985. *Rethinking the Politics of Commercial Society*. Cambridge: Cambridge University Press.

———. 1997. 'Benjamin Constant, la méthodologie historique et *l'Esprit des Lois*'. In M. Porret and C. Volpilhac-Auger, eds., *Le Temps de Montesquieu*. Geneva: Droz, pp. 385–90.

Forbes, Duncan. 1951–52. 'James Mill and India'. *Cambridge Journal*, vol. 5, pp, 19–33.

———. 1952. *The Liberal Anglican Idea of History*. Cambridge: Cambridge University Press.

———. 1953–54. 'Scientific Whiggism: Adam Smith and John Millar'. *Cambridge Journal*, vol. 7, pp. 643–70.

Force, Pierre. 2004. *Self-Interest before Adam Smith*. Cambridge: Cambridge University Press.

Forman-Barzilai, Fonna. 2005. 'Sympathy in Spaces: Adam Smith on Proximity'. *PT*, vol. 33, no. 2, pp. 189–217.

Frank, Jill. 2005. *A Democracy of Distinction: Aristotle and the Work of Politics*. Chicago: University of Chicago Press.

Frank, R. G. 1980. *Harvey and the Oxford Physiologists*. Berkeley CA: University of California Press.

Frankfurt, Harry G. 1971. 'Freedom of the Will and the Concept of a Person'. *JoPh*, vol. 68, no. 1, pp. 5–20.

———. 2004. *The Reasons of Love*. Princeton NJ: Princeton University Press, 2004.

———. 2006. 'Identification and Wholeheartedness'. In *The Importance of What we Care About*. Cambridge: Cambridge University Press, pp. 159–77.

———. 2006a. *Taking Ourselves Seriously and Getting it Right*. Stanford CA: University of Stanford Press.

Franklin, Julian. 1968. *John Locke and the Theory of Sovereignty*. Cambridge: Cambridge University Press.

Frede, Michael. 1986. 'The Stoic Doctrine of the Affections of the Soul'. In M. Schofield and G. Striker, eds., *The Norms of Nature*. Cambridge: Cambridge University Press, pp. 93–110.

———. 2008. 'A Notion of a Person in Epictetus'. In T. Scaltas and A. Mason, eds., *The Philosophy of Epictetus*. Oxford: Oxford University Press, pp. 153–68.

Freeden, Michael. 2005. *Liberal Languages: Ideological Imaginations and Twentieth-Century Progressive Thought*. Princeton NJ: Princeton University Press.

Friedeburg, Robert von. 2002. '"Self-Defence" and Sovereignty: The Reception and Application of German Political Thought in England and Scotland, 1628–1629'. *HPT*, vol. 23, no. 2, pp. 238–65.

Frierson, Patrick, R. 2002. 'Learning to Love: From Egoism to Generosity in Descartes'. *JHP*, vol. 40, no. 3, pp. 313–38.

Fuks, Alexander. 1971. 'Thucydides and the *Stasis* in Corcycra'. *American Journal of Philology*, pp. 48–55.

Garnsey, Peter. 2008. *Thinking about Property*. Cambridge: Cambridge University Press.

Garsten, Bryan. 2005. *Saving Persuasion*. Cambridge MA: Harvard University Press.

Garver, Margaret. 2006. *Stoicism and the Emotions*. Chicago: University of Chicago Press.

Gaukroger, Stephen. 1997. *Descartes: An Intellectual Biography*. Oxford: Oxford University Press.

van Gelderen, Martin. 2006. '"*So meerly humane*": Theories of Resistance in Early-Modern Europe'. In A. Brett and J. Tully, eds., *Rethinking the Foundations of Modern Political Thought*. Cambridge: Cambridge University Press, pp. 149–70.

Gerlach, Murney. 2001. *British Liberalism and the United States*. Basingstoke: Palgrave.

Geuss, Raymond. 2001. *Public Goods, Private Goods*. Princeton NJ: Princeton University Press, 2001.

———. 2005. *Outside Ethics*. Princeton NJ: Princeton University Press.

Ghosh, Peter. 2008. 'Max Weber and Georg Jellinek: Two Divergent Conceptions of Law'. *Saeculum: Jahrbuch für Universalgeschichte*, vol. 59, no. 2, pp. 299–347.

Gilbert, Alan. 1994. '"Internal Restlessness": Individuality and Community in Montesquieu'. *PT*, vol. 22, no. 1, pp. 45–70.

Gill, Christopher. 1988. 'Personhood and Personality: The Four Personae Theory in Cicero, *De Officiis* I'. *Oxford Studies in Ancient Philosophy*, vol. 6, pp. 169–99.

Gilmartin, Kevin. 2002. 'In the Theater of Counterrevolution: Loyalist Association and Conservative Opinion in the 1790s'. *JBS*, vol. 41, no. 2, pp. 291–328.

Glaziou, Yves. 1993. *Hobbes en France au XVIIIᵉ siècle*. Paris: PUF.

Glover, S. D. 1999. 'The Putney Debates: Popular versus Elite Republicanism'. *P&P*, no. 164, 47–80.

Goffman, Erving. 1959. *The Presentation of Self in Everyday Life*. London: Pelican.

Golden, Herbert Hershel. 1951. 'Louis-Jean Levesque de Pouilly, 1691–1750'. PhD diss., Harvard University.

Goldgar, Annette. 1995. *Impolite Learning*. New Haven CT: Yale University Press.

Goldie, Mark. 1980. 'The Revolution of 1689 and the Structure of Political Argument: An Essay and an Annotated Bibliography of Pamphlets on the Allegiance Controversy'. *Bulletin of Research in the Humanities*, vol. 83, no. 4, pp. 473–564.

———. 1980a.'The Roots of True Whiggism 1688–94'. *HPT*, vol. 1, no. 2, pp. 195–236.

———. 1983.'John Locke and Anglican Royalism'. *PS*, vol. 31, no. 1, pp. 61–85.

———. 1991. 'The Theory of Religious Intolerance in Restoration England'. In O. P. Grell, J. Israel and N. Tyacke, eds., *From Persecution to Toleration: The Glorious Revolution and Religion in England*. Oxford: Clarendon, pp. 331–68.

———. 1992. 'John Locke's Circle and James II'. *HJ*, vol. 35, no. 3, pp. 557–86.

Goldie, Mark. 1993. 'Priestcraft and the Birth of Whiggism'. In N. Phillipson and Q. Skinner, eds., *Political Discourse in Early-Modern Britain*. Cambridge: Cambridge University Press, pp. 209–231.

———. 1993a. 'John Locke, Jonas Proast and Religious Toleration, 1688–1692'. In C. Haydon, S. Taylor and J. Walsh, eds., *The Church of England*, c. 1689-c. 1833: From Toleration to Tractarianism. Cambridge: Cambridge University Press, pp. 143–71.

Goldie, Mark. 2005. *John Locke and the Mashams at Oates*. Cambridge: Churchill College.

Goldie, Peter. 2000. *The Emotions: A Philosophical Exploration*. Oxford: Oxford University Press.

Goldstein, Jan. 1998. 'Enthusiasm or Imagination: Eighteenth-Century Smear Words in Comparative National Contexts'. In L. E. Klein and A. J. La Vopa, eds., *Enthusiasm and Enlightenment in Europe, 1650–1850*, San Marino CA: Huntington Library, pp. 29–49.

Goldzink, Jean. 2001. *Montesquieu et les passions*. Paris: PUF.

Gordon, Robert M. 1995. 'Sympathy, Simulation and the Impartial Spectator'. *Ethics*, vol. 105, no. 4, pp. 727–42.

Gossman, N. J. 1962. 'Republicanism in Nineteenth Century England'. *International Review of Social History*, vol. 7, no. 1, pp. 47–60.

Gough, John. 1976. 'James Tyrell, Whig Historian and Friend of John Locke'. *HJ*, vol. 19, no. 3, pp. 581–610.

Goyard-Fabre, Simone. 1993. *Montesquieu: La nature, les lois, la liberté*. Paris: PUF.

Grafton, Anthony. 2007. *What was History?* Cambridge: Cambridge University Press.

Gray, John. 2000. *Two Faces of Liberalism*. Oxford: Polity.

Griffin, James. 1986. *Well-Being*. Oxford: Clarendon.

———. 2001. 'First Steps in an Account of Human Rights'. *EJP*, vol. 9, no. 3, pp. 306–27.

Griffin, Miriam. 1986. 'Philosophy, Cato, and Roman Suicide: I'. *Greece and Rome*, vol. 33, no. 1, pp. 64–77.

———. 1986a. 'Philosophy, Cato, and Roman Suicide: II'. *Greece and Rome*, vol. 33, no. 2, pp. 192–202.

Griswold, Charles L, Jr. 1999. *Adam Smith and the Virtues of Enlightenment*. Cambridge: Cambridge University Press.

Gunn, J. A. W. 1983. *Beyond Liberty and Property: The Process of Self-Recognition in Eighteenth-Century Political Thought*. Kingston, Montreal: McGill-Queen's University Press.

Haakonssen, Knud. 1985. 'Hugo Grotius and the History of Political Thought'. *PT*, vol. 13, no. 2, pp. 239–65.

———. 1989. *The Science of a Legislator*. Cambridge: Cambridge University Press.

———. 1996. *Natural Law and Moral Philosophy: From Grotius to the Scottish Enlightenment*. Cambridge: Cambridge University Press.

Hall, Catherine. 2002. *Civilising Subjects*. Oxford: Polity.

Halldenius, Lena. 2003. 'Locke and the Non-Arbitrary'. *EJPT*, vol. 2, no. 3, pp. 261–79.

Halévy, Elie. 1972. *The Growth of Philosophical Radicalism*. Trans. M. Morris. London: Faber and Faber.

Hampsher-Monk, Iain. 1977. 'The Political Theory of the Levellers: Putney, Property and Professor MacPherson'. *PS*, vol. 24, no. 4, pp. 397–422.

———. 1979. 'Civic Humanism and Parliamentary Reform: The Case of the Society of the Friends of the People'. *JBS*, vol. 18, no. 2, pp. 70–89.

———. 2005. 'Edmund Burke's Changing Justification for Intervention'. *HJ*, vol. 48, no. 1, pp. 65–100.

Hampson, Norman. 1968. *The Enlightenment*. London: Pelican.

Hanley, Ryan. 2006. 'From Geneva to Glasgow: Rousseau and Smith on the Theatre and Commercial Society'. *Studies in Eighteenth-Century Culture*, vol. 35, pp. 177–202.

———. 2008. 'Rousseau's Diagnosis and Smith's Cure'. *EJPT*, vol. 7, no. 2, pp. 137–58.

Harling, Philip. 1996. 'Leigh Hunt's *Examiner* and the Language of Patriotism'. *EHR*, no. 61, pp. 1159–81.

———. 2001. 'The Law of Libel and the Limits of Repression, 1790–1832'. *HJ*, vol. 44, no. 1, pp. 107–34.

Harpham, E. J. 1999. 'Economics and History: Books II and III of the *Wealth of Nations*'. *HPT*, vol. 20, no. 3, pp. 438–55.

Harris, H. 1978. *The Tübingen School*. Oxford: Oxford University Press.

Harris, Ian. 1993. 'Paine and Burke: God, Nature and Politics'. In M. Bentley, ed., *Public and Private Doctrine: Essays in British History Presented to Maurice Cowling*. Cambridge: Cambridge University Press, pp. 34–62.

———. 1994. *The Mind of John Locke*. Cambridge: Cambridge University Press.

———. 2000. 'Locke on Justice'. In M. A. Stewart, ed., *English Philosophy in the Age of Locke*. Oxford: Clarendon, pp. 49–85.

———. 2007. 'The Legacy of "*Two Treatises of Government*"'. *Eighteenth-Century Thought*, vol. 3, pp. 143–67.

Harris, James. 2003. 'Answering Bayle's Question: Religious Belief in the Moral Philosophy of the Scottish Enlightenment'. In D. Garber and S. Nadler, eds., *Oxford Studies in Early-Modern Philosophy*. Oxford: Oxford University Press, vol. 1, pp. 229–53.

———. 2005. *Of Liberty and Necessity*. Oxford: Oxford University Press.

Harris, Jose. 1992. 'Political Thought and the Welfare State 1870–1912: An Intellectual Framework for British Social Policy'. *P&P*, no. 135, pp. 116–41.

Harris, J. W. 1996. *Property and Justice*. Oxford: Oxford University Press.

Harris, P. 1988–89. 'Moral Progress and Politics: The Theory of T. H. Green'. *Polity*, vol. 21, pp. 538–62.

Harris, William V. 2001. *Restraining Rage: The Ideology of Anger Control in Classical Antiquity*. Cambridge MA: Harvard University Press.

Harrison, Brian. 1993. *Drink and the Victorians*. Rev. edn. Keele: Keele University Press.

Harrison, John and Peter Laslett. 1971. *The Library of John Locke*. 2nd edn. Oxford: Clarendon.

Hart, H. L. A. 1968. 'Legal Responsibility and Excuses'. In *Punishment and Responsibility*. Oxford: Clarendon, pp. 28–53.

Harvie, Christopher. 1976. *The Lights of Liberalism*. London: Allen Lane.

———. 1997. 'Reform and Expansion, 1854–1871'. In M. G. Brock and M. C. Curthoys, eds., *The History of the University of Oxford in the Nineteenth Century*. Oxford: Oxford University Press, vol. 6, part 1, pp. 697–730.

Hastings, Adrian. 1997. *The Construction of Nationhood*. Cambridge: Cambridge University Press.

Hay, Denys. 1957. *Europe: The Emergence of an Idea*. Edinburgh: Edinburgh University Press.

Helmstadter, Richard J. 1988. 'The Nonconformist Conscience'. In Gerald Parsons, ed., *Religion in Victorian Britain*, vol. 4: *Interpretations*. Manchester: Manchester University Press, pp. 61–95.

Hewitson, Mark. 2000. *National Identity and Political Thought in Germany: Wilhelmine Depictions of the French Third Republic 1890–1914*. Oxford: Clarendon.

Heydt, Colin. 2006. 'Mill, Bentham and "Internal Culture"'. *BJHP*, vol. 14, no. 2, pp. 275–301.

———. 2006a. 'Narrative, Imagination, and the Religion of Humanity in Mill's Ethics'. *JHP*, vol. 44, no. 1, pp. 99–115.

Hill, Christopher. 1990. *Antichrist in Seventeenth-Century England*. London: Verso.

Hill, Lisa. 2001. 'The Hidden Theology of Adam Smith.' *European Journal of the History of Economic Thought*, vol. 8, no. 1, pp. 1–29.

Hill Lisa, and Peter McCarthy. 2004. 'On Friendship and *necessitudo* in Adam Smith'. *History of the Human Sciences*, vol. 17, no. 4, pp. 1–16.

Hilton, Boyd. 1988. *The Age of Atonement*. Oxford: Clarendon.

———. 2001. 'The Politics of Anatomy and an Anatomy of Politics'. In S. Collini, R. Whatmore, and B. Young, eds., *History, Religion and Culture: British Intellectual History 1750–1950*. Cambridge: Cambridge University Press, pp. 179–97.

———. 2008. *A Mad, Bad, & Dangerous People? England 1783–1846*. Oxford: Oxford University Press.

Hirschman, Albert. 1977. *The Passions and the Interests*. Princeton NJ: Princeton University Press.

Hochstrasser, T. J. 1993. 'Conscience and Reason: The Natural Law Theory of Jean Barbeyrac'. *HJ*, vol. 36, no. 2, pp. 289–308.

———. 2000. *Natural Law Theories in the Early Enlightenment*. Cambridge: Cambridge University Press.

Hoekstra, Kinch. 2004. 'The *de facto* Turn in Hobbes's Political Philosophy'. In T. Sorrell and L. Foisneau, eds., *Leviathan after 350 Years*. Oxford: Oxford University Press, pp. 33–73.

Hoffman, Stefan-Ludwig. 2003. 'Democracy and Associations in the Long Nineteenth Century: Toward a Transnational Perspective'. *JMH*, vol. 75, pp. 269–99.

Hollis, Martin. 1998. *Trust Within Reason*. Cambridge: Cambridge University Press.

Holmes, Stephen. 1995. *Passions and Constraint*. Chicago: University of Chicago Press.

———. 2007. 'Making Sense of Liberal Imperialism'. In A. Zakaras and N. Urbinati, eds., *J. S. Mill's Political Thought*. Cambridge: Cambridge University Press, pp. 319–46.

Honneth, Axel. 2007. *Disrespect*. Oxford: Polity.

Hont, Istvan. 2005. *Jealousy of Trade*. Cambridge MA: Harvard University Press.

———. 2006. 'The Early Enlightenment Debate on Commerce and Luxury'. In R. Wokler and M. Goldie, eds., *Cambridge History of Eighteenth-Century Political Thought*. Cambridge: Cambridge University Press, pp. 379–418.

———. 2007. 'The Rich Country–Poor Country Debate Revisited: The Irish Origins and French Reception of Hume's Paradox'. In M. Schabas and C. Wennerlind, eds., *Hume's Political Economy*. London: Routledge, pp. 222–342.

———. 2007a. 'Correcting Europe's Political Economy: The Virtuous Eclecticism of Georg Ludwig Schmid'. *HEI*, vol. 33, pp. 390–410.

———. 2009. 'Adam Smith's History of Law and Government as Political Theory'. In R. Bourke and R. Geuss, eds., *Political Judgement*. Cambridge: Cambridge University Press, pp. 131–71.

Höpfl, Harro. 2002. 'Orthodoxy and Reason of State'. *HPT*, vol. 22, no. 2, pp. 211–37.

Hoppen, K. T. 1998. *The Mid-Victorian Generation, 1846–1886*. Oxford: Clarendon.

Howard, Alison. 1959. 'Montesquieu, Voltaire and Rousseau in Eighteenth-Century Scotland'. *The Bibliotheck*, vol. 2, pp. 44–46.

Howe, Anthony. 2002. 'Restoring Free-Trade: The British Experience, 1776–1873'. In D. Winch and P. K. O'Brien, eds., *The Political Economy of British Historical Experience*. Oxford: British Academy/Oxford University Press, pp. 193–214.

Howell, S. W. 1971. *Eighteenth-Century British Logic and Rhetoric*. Princeton NJ: Princeton University Press.

Hulliung, Mark. 1994. *The Autocritique of the Enlightenment: Rousseau and the Philosophes*. Cambridge MA: Harvard University Press.

Hundert, E. J. 1987–88. 'The Thread of Language and the Web of Dominion: Mandeville to Rousseau and Back'. *Eighteenth-Century Studies*, vol. 21, no. 2, pp. 169–91.

———. 1994. *The Enlightenment's Fable*. Cambridge: Cambridge University Press.

———. 1995. 'Bernard Mandeville and the Enlightenment's Maxims of Modernity'. *JHI*, vol. 56, no. 4, pp. 577–93.

———. 2000. 'Sociability and Self-Love in the Theatre of Moral Sentiments'. In S. Collini, R. Whatmore and B. Young, eds., *Economy, Polity and Society: British Intellectual History 1750–1950*. Cambridge: Cambridge University Press, pp. 31–47.

Hundert, E. J., and P. Nelles. 1989. 'Liberty and Theatrical Space in Montesquieu's Political Theory: The Poetics of Public Life in the *Persian Letters*'. *Political Theory*, vol. 17, no. 2, pp. 223–46.

Hunter, Ian. 2004. 'Conflicting Obligations: Pufendorf, Leibniz and Barbeyrac on Civil Authority'. *HPT*, vol. 25, no. 4, pp. 670–99.

Hutchinson, Ross. 1991. *Locke in France 1688–1734* [= *SVEC*, no. 290]. Oxford: Voltaire Foundation.

Hutton, Sarah. 1996. 'Introduction'. In Ralph Cudworth, *A Treatise Concerning Eternal and Immutable Morality*. Ed. Sarah Hutton. Cambridge: Cambridge University Press, pp. ix–xxx.

314   •   Bibliography

Ignatieff, Michael. 1986. *The Needs of Strangers: An Essay on Privacy, Solidarity and the Politics of being Human*. New York: Penguin.

Innes, Joanna. 2004. '"Reform" in English Public Life: The Fortunes of a Word'. In A. Burns and J. Innes, eds., *Rethinking the Age of Reform: Britain 1780–1840*. Cambridge: Cambridge University Press, pp. 71–97.

Irwin, T. 1992. 'Eminent Victorians and Greek Ethics'. In B. Schultz, ed., *Essays on Henry Sidgwick*. Cambridge: Cambridge University Press, pp. 279–310.

———. 1998. 'Mill and the Classical World'. In J. Skorupski, ed., *The Cambridge Companion to Mill*. Cambridge: Cambridge University Press, pp. 423–63.

Israel, Jonathan. 2002. *Radical Enlightenment*. Oxford: Oxford University Press.

———. 2006. *Enlightenment Contested*. Oxford: Oxford University Press.

Ivison, Duncan. 1997. 'The Secret History of Public Reason'. *HPT*, vol. 18, no. 1, pp. 125–46.

———. 1997a. *The Self at Liberty*. Ithaca NY: Cornell University Press.

Jacovides, Michael. 2007. 'Locke on the *Propria* of the Body'. *BJHP*, vol. 15, no. 3, pp. 485–511.

James, E. D. 1972. *Pierre Nicole, Jansenist and Humanist: A Study of his Thought*. The Hague: Martinus Nijhoff.

James, Susan. 1993. 'Spinoza the Stoic'. In T. Sorell, ed., *The Rise of Modern Philosophy*. Oxford: Clarendon, pp. 289–316, esp. pp. 296–301.

———. 1997. *Passion and Action: The Emotions in Seventeenth-Century Philosophy*. Oxford: Oxford University Press.

———. 2006. 'The Passions and the Good Life'. In D. Rutherford, ed., *Cambridge Companion to Early-Modern Philosophy*. Cambridge: Cambridge University Press, pp. 198–220.

Jay, Martin. 1994. *Downcast Eyes: The Denigration of Vision in Twentieth-Century French Thought*. Berkeley CA: University of California Press.

Jay-Wallace, R. 1994. *Responsibility and the Moral Sentiments*. Cambridge MA: Harvard University Press.

———. 2001. 'Normativity, Commitment and Instrumental Reason'. *Philosophers Imprint*, vol. 1, no. 3, pp. 1–26.

———. 2002. 'Scanlon's Contractualism'. *Ethics*, no. 112, pp. 429–70.

———. 2006. *Normativity and the Will*. Oxford: Oxford University Press.

———. 2007. 'The Argument from Resentment'. *PAS*, vol. 57, no. 3, pp. 295–318.

Jennings, Jeremy. 1992. 'The *Déclaration des droits de l'homme*: Reaction and *Idéologie*'. *HJ*, vol. 35, no. 4, pp. 839–59.

Johnson, Charlotte. 1958. 'Locke's Examination of Malebranche and John Norris'. *JHI*, vol. 19, no. 4, pp. 551–58.

Jones, Colin. 2006. *The Great Nation*. London: Penguin.

Jones, Howard. 1989. *The Epicurean Tradition*. London: Routledge.

Jones, H. S. 2000. *Victorian Political Thought*. Basingstoke: Macmillan.

Joy, Lynn Sumida. 1987. *Gassendi the Atomist*. Cambridge: Cambridge University Press.

Kalyvas, Andreas, and Ira Katznelson. 2008. *Liberal Beginnings: Making a Republic for the Moderns*. Cambridge: Cambridge University Press.

Kantorowicz, Ernst. 1985. *The King's Two Bodies*. Princeton NJ: Princeton University Press.

Kassem, Badreddine. 1960. *Décadence et absolutisme dans l'oeuvre de Montesquieu*. Geneva: Droz.

Kidd, Colin. 2003. 'Constitutions and Character in the Eighteenth-Century World'. In P. M. Kitromilides, ed., *From Republican Polity to National Community: Reconsiderations of Enlightenment Political Thought* [= SVEC 2003:09]. Oxford: Voltaire Foundation, pp. 40–61.

Kinzer, Bruce L. 2001. *England's Disgrace? J. S. Mill and the Irish Question*. Toronto: University of Toronto Press.

———. 2009. 'Flying under the Radar: The Strange Case of Matthew Piers Watt Boulton'. *Times Literary Supplement*, May 1, pp. 14–15.

Kelly, Duncan. 2002. 'The Political Thought of Isaiah Berlin'. *British Journal of Politics and International Relations*, vol. 4, no. 1, pp. 29–45.

———. 2003. *The State of the Political: Conceptions of Politics and the State in the Thought of Max Weber, Carl Schmitt and Franz Neumann*. Oxford: Oxford University Press/The British Academy.

———. 2004. 'Carl Schmitt's Political Theory of Representation'. *JHI*, vol. 65, no. 1, pp. 113–34.

———. 2004a. 'Revisiting the Rights of Man: Georg Jellinek on Rights and the State'. *Law and History Review*, vol. 22, no. 3, pp. 493–529.

———. 2005. 'Reforming Republicanism in Nineteenth-Century Britain: James Lorymer's *The Republican* in Context'. In J. Jennings and I. Honohan, eds., *Republicanism in Theory and Practice*. London: Routledge, pp. 41–52.

Kelly, Paul. 2001. 'Classical Utilitarianism and the Concept of Freedom: A Response to the Republican Critique'. *Journal of Political Ideologies*, vol. 6, no. 1, pp. 13–31.

Keohane, Nannerl. 1980. *Philosophy and the State in France*. Princeton NJ: Princeton University Press.

Kilcullen, John. 1988. *Sincerity and Truth*. Oxford: Clarendon.

Kingston, Rebecca. 1996. *Montesquieu and the Parlement of Bordeaux*. Geneva: Droz.

Kingston, Rebecca. ed. 2009. *Montesquieu and His Legacy*. New York: SUNY Press.

Kinzer, Bruce L., Ann P. Robson and John M. Robson. 1992. *A Moralist in and Out of Parliament: John Stuart Mill at Westminster 1865–1868*. Toronto: University of Toronto Press.

Klein, Lawrence E. 1994. *Shaftesbury and the Culture of Politeness: Moral Discourse and Cultural Politics in Early Eighteenth-Century England*. Cambridge: Cambridge University Press.

Kleer, Richard A. 1995. 'Final Causes in Adam Smith's *Theory of Moral Sentiments*'. *JHP*, vol. 33, no. 3, pp. 275–300.

van Kley, Dale. 1987. 'Pierre Nicole, Jansenism and the Morality of Enlightened Self-Interest'. In Alan Charles Kors and Paul J. Korshin, eds., *Anticipations of the Enlightenment in England, France, and Germany*. Philadelphia PA: University of Pennsylvania Press, pp. 69–85.

van Kley, Dale. ed. 1994. *The French Idea of Freedom*. Stanford CA: Stanford University Press.

Knights, Ben. 1978. *The Idea of the Clerisy in the Nineteenth Century*. Cambridge: Cambridge University Press.

Knipping, John B. 1976. *Iconography of the Counter-Reformation in the Netherlands: Heaven on Earth*. 2 vols. Leiden: A. W. Sijthoff.

Knobe, Joshua. 2003. 'Intentional Action in Folk Psychology: An Experimental Investigation'. *Philosophical Psychology*, vol. 16, pp. 309–24.

Koebner, Robert. 1951. 'Despot and Despotism: Vicissitudes of a Political Term'. *Journal of the Warburg and Courtauld Institutes*, vol. 14, nos. 3–4, pp. 275–302.

Kohn, Margaret, and Daniel I. O'Neill. 2006. 'A Tale of Two Indias: Burke and Mill on Empire and Slavery in the West Indies and America'. *PT*, vol. 34, no. 2, pp. 192–228.

Kolakowski, Leszek. 1998. *God Owes us Nothing*. Chicago: University of Chicago Press.

Kott, Stanislas. 1957. *Socinianism in Poland: The Social and Political Ideas of the Polish Antitrinitarians in the Sixteenth and Seventeenth Centuries*. Trans. Earl Morse Wilbur, Boston MA: Starr King Press.

Krailsheimer, A. 1962. *Studies in Self-Interest from Descartes to La Bruyère*. Oxford: Oxford University Press.

Kramer, Matthew. 2001. *The Quality of Freedom*. Oxford: Oxford University Press.

Krause, Sharon. 2001. 'Despotism in the *Spirit of the Laws*'. In D. W. Carrithers, M. A. Mosher and P. A. Rahe, eds. *Montesquieu's Science of Politics: Essays on the 'Spirit of Laws'*. Lanham MD: Rowman and Littlefield, pp. 231–71.

———. 2002. 'The Uncertain Inevitability of Decline in Montesquieu'. *PT*, vol. 30, no. 5, pp. 702–27.

———. 2002a. *Liberalism with Honor*. Cambridge MA: Harvard University Press.

———. 2003. 'History and the Human Soul in Montesquieu'. *HPT*, vol. 24, no. 2, pp. 235–61.

———. 2006. 'Laws, Passion and the Attraction of Right Action in Montesquieu'. *Philosophy and Social Criticism*, vol. 32, no. 2, pp. 211–30.

———. 2008. *Civil Passions*. Princeton NJ: Princeton University Press.

Kristeller, Paul Oskar. 1984. 'Stoic and Neoplatonic Sources of Spinoza's *Ethics*'. *HEI*, vol. 5, no. 1, pp. 1–15.

Kroll, Richard W. F. 1984. 'The Question of Locke's Relation to Gassendi'. *JHI*, vol. 45, pp. 339–59.

Kuhfluß, W. 1987. 'La notion de moderation dans les *Considérations* de Montesquieu'. In A. Postigliola, ed., *Storia e ragione*. Naples: Liguori Editore, pp. 277–92.

Kumar, Krishnan. 2002. *The Making of English National Identity*. Cambridge: Cambridge University Press.

Kurfurst, Robert. 1996. 'J. S. Mill on Oriental Despotism, including its British Variant'. *Utilitas*, vol. 8, no. 1, pp. 73–87.

La Vopa, Anthony. 1998. 'The Philosopher and the *Schwärmer*: On the Career of a German Epithet from Luther to Kant'. In L. E. Klein and A. J. La Vopa, eds., *Enthusiasm and Enlightenment in Europe, 1650–1850*. San Marino CA: Huntington Library, pp. 85–115.

Labrousse, Elizabeth. 1982. 'The Political Ideas of the Huguenot Diaspora (Bayle and Jurieu)'. Trans. M. Gerrard-Davis. In R. M. Golden, ed., *Church, State and Society under the Bourbon Kings*. Lawrence KA: Coronado Press, pp. 222–83.

———. 1983. *Bayle*. Trans. D. Potts. Oxford: Oxford University Press.

Lamb, Robert. 1973. 'Adam Smith's Concept of Alienation'. *Oxford Economic Papers*, n.s. vol. 25, no. 2, pp. 275–85.

Lamb, Robert, and Benjamin Thompson. 2009. 'The Meaning of Charity in Locke's Political Thought'. *EJPT*, vol. 8, no. 2, pp. 229–52.

Lang, Timothy. 1996. *The Victorians and the Stuart Heritage*. Cambridge: Cambridge University Press.

Langford, Paul. 1989. *A Polite and Commercial People: England 1727–1783*. Oxford: Oxford University Press.

Larmore, Charles. 2001. 'A Critique of Philip Pettit's Republicanism'. *Philosophical Issues*, vol. 11, pp. 230–43.

Larrère, Cathérine. 1997. 'Bordeaux, le vin et les Anglais, commerce ou passion?' *Dix-huitième siècle*, vol. 29, pp. 103–16.

———. 2000. 'Isaac de Bacalan: Bordeaux et la liberté de commerce'. In Jean Medot and Cathérine Larrère, eds., *Lumières et Commerce: L'exemple bordelaise*. Frankfurt am Main: Peter Lang, pp. 3–16.

Laslett, Peter. 1957. 'John Locke, the Great Recoinage, and the Origins of the Board of Trade'. *WMQ*, 3rd series, vol. 14, no. 3, pp. 370–402.

———. 1988. 'Introduction'. In John Locke, *Two Treatises of Government*. Ed. Peter Laslett. Cambridge: Cambridge University Press, pp. 3–126.

Leighton, Denys P. 2004. *The Greenian Moment*. Exeter: Imprint Academic.

Lennon, Thomas M. 1997. 'Bayle, Locke and the Metaphysics of Toleration'. In M. A. Stewart, ed., *Studies in Seventeenth-Century Philosophy*. Oxford: Oxford University Press, pp. 173–95.

Levi, Antony. 1964. *French Moralists: The Theory of the Passions 1585–1649*. Oxford: Oxford University Press.

Lewis, A. D. E. 1995. 'Montesquieu's *Collectio Juris*'. *JLH*, vol. 16, no. 3, pp. 304–17.

Lewis, T. J. 2000. 'Persuasion, Domination and Exchange: Adam Smith on the Political Consequences of Markets'. *Canadian Review of Political Science*, vol. 33, no. 2, pp. 273–89.

von Leyden, Wolfgang. 1954. 'Introduction'. In Wolfgang von Leyden, ed., *John Locke: Essays on the Law of Nature*. Oxford: Clarendon, pp. 1–92.

———. 1971. 'Locke and Nicole'. *Sophia*, vol. 16, no. 1, pp. 41–55.

Lindop, Grevel. 1993. *The Opium Eater*. London: Weidenfeld.

Livingstone, Donald. 1998. *Philosophical Melancholy and Delirium: Hume's Pathology of Philosophy*. Chicago: University of Chicago Press.

Lomonaco, Jeffrey. 2002. 'Adam Smith's "Letter to the Authors of the *Edinburgh Review*"'. *JHI*, vol. 63, no. 4, pp. 659–76.

Long, A. A. 1974. *Hellenistic Philosophy*. London: Duckworth.

———. 1996. 'Hierocles on *oikeiōsis* and Self-Perception'. In *Stoic Studies*. Berkeley CA: University of California Press, pp. 250–63.

Long, A. A. 2006. 'Cicero's Politics in *De officiis*'. In *From Epicurus to Epictetus*. Cambridge: Cambridge University Press, pp. 307–34.

———. 2006a. 'Stoic Philosophers on Persons, Property-Ownership and Community'. In *From Epicurus to Epictetus*. Cambridge: Cambridge University Press, pp. 335–59.

Losonsky, Michael. 2001. *Enlightenment and Action from Descartes to Kant: Passionate Thought*. Cambridge: Cambridge University Press.

Lough, John. 1953. 'Locke's Reading during His Stay in France'. *The Library*, series 5, vol. 8, no. 4, pp. 229–58.

———. 1953a. *Locke's Travels in France 1675–1679*. Cambridge: Cambridge University Press.

Loy, J. Robert. 1977. '*L'Esprit général* and *la volonté générale*: Theory and Practice in Eighteenth-Century France'. In J. Macary, ed., *Essays on the Age of Enlightenment in Honor of Ira O. Wade*. Geneva: Librairie Droz, pp. 183–92.

Luban, Daniel. 2008. 'Slavery and Self Interest in Adam Smith'. MPhil thesis, University of Cambridge.

Lynch, Andrew J. 1977. 'Montesquieu and the Ecclesiastical Critics of *l'Esprit des lois*'. *JHI*, vol. 38, no. 3, pp. 487–500.

MacCallum, Gerald. 1972. 'Negative and Positive Freedom'. In P. Lasslett, W. G. Runciman and Q. Skinner, eds., *Philosophy, Politics and Society*. Oxford: Blackwell, pp. 174–93.

Macintyre, Alasdair. 1994. *After Virtue: A Study in Moral Theory*. 2nd edn. London: Duckworth.

———. 1994a. 'Hume, Testimony to Miracles, the Order of Nature, and Jansenism'. In J. J. Macintosh and H. A. Meynell, eds., *Faith, Scepticism and Personal Identity*. Calgary: University of Calgary Press, pp. 83–100.

McClure, Kirsty M. 1996. *Judging Rights*. Ithaca NY: Cornell University Press.

McCracken, C. 1983. *Malebranche and British Philosophy*. Oxford: Oxford University Press, 1983.

Macdonald, Sara. 2003. 'Problems with Principles: Montesquieu's Theory of Natural Justice'. *HPT*, vol. 24, no. 1, pp. 109–30.

McKenna, Antony. 1999. *Entre Descartes et Gassendi*. Oxford: Alden Press for the Voltaire Foundation.

McKenna, Michael. 2008. 'The Relationship between Autonomous and Morally Responsible Agency'. In J. S. Taylor, ed., *Personal Autonomy*. Cambridge: Cambridge University Press, pp. 205–34.

McKenna, Stephen J. 2006. *Adam Smith: The Rhetoric of Propriety*. New York: SUNY Press.

Macé, Lawrence. 2005. 'Les "Lettres persanes" devant l'Index: Une censure "posthum"'. In C. Volpilhac-Auger, ed., *Montesquieu en 2005* [= *SVEC* 2005:05]. Oxford: Voltaire Foundation, pp. 48–59.

Maier, Hans. 1980. *Die ältere deutsche Staats- und Verwaltungslehre*. 2nd edn. Munich: C. H. Beck.

Malcolm, Noel. 2002. *Aspects of Hobbes*. Oxford: Oxford University Press.

———. 2007. *Reason of State, Propaganda and the Thirty Years War: An Unknown Translation by Thomas Hobbes*. Oxford: Oxford University Press.

Mandler, Peter. 1990. *Aristocratic Government in the Age of Reform*. Oxford: Clarendon.

———. 2006. *The English National Character: The History of an Idea from Edmund Burke to Tony Blair*. New Haven CT: Yale University Press.

Manicas, Peter T. 1981. 'Montesquieu and the Eighteenth Century Vision of the State'. *HPT*, vol. 2, no. 2, pp. 313–47.

———. 1982. 'War, *Stasis* and Greek Political Thought'. *CSSH*, vol. 24, no. 4, pp. 673–88.

Manin, Bernard. 1994. 'Checks, Balances and Boundaries: The Separation of Powers in the Constitutional Debate of 1787'. In B. Fontana, ed., *The Invention of the Modern Republic*. Cambridge: Cambridge University Press, pp. 27–62.

———. 1997. *The Principles of Representative Government*. Cambridge: Cambridge University Press.

———. 2008. 'The Emergency Paradigm and the New Terrorism'. In S. Baume and B. Fontana, eds., *Les usages de la separation des pouvoirs*. Paris: Michel Houdiard Éditeur, pp. 136–71.

Mann, Michael. 1986. *The Sources of Social Power*. Vol. 1. Cambridge: Cambridge University Press.

Mantena, Karuna. 2007. 'Mill and the Imperial Predicament'. In A. Zakaras and N. Urbinati, eds., *J. S. Mill's Political Thought*. Cambridge: Cambridge University Press, pp. 298–318.

Markell, Patchen. 2008. 'The Insufficiency of Non-Domination'. *PT*, vol. 36, no. 1, pp. 9–36.

Marshall, David. 1988. *The Surprising Effects of Sympathy*. Chicago: University of Chicago Press.

Marshall, John. 1994. *John Locke: Resistance, Religion and Responsibility*. Cambridge: Cambridge University Press.

———. 2000. 'Locke, Socinianism, "Socinianism", and Unitarianism'. In M. A. Stewart, ed., *English Philosophy in the Age of Locke*. Oxford: Clarendon, pp. 111–82.

———. 2006. *John Locke, Toleration and Early Enlightenment Culture*. Cambridge: Cambridge University Press.

Martin, Raymond. 2000. 'Locke's Psychology of Personal Identity'. *JHP*, vol. 38, no. 1, pp. 41–61.

Martin, Raymond, and John Barresi. 2000. *Naturalization of the Soul: Self and Personal Identity in the Eighteenth Century*. London: Routledge.

———. 2005. *The Rise and Fall of Soul and Self*. New York NY: University of Columbia Press.

Mason, Sheila Mary. 1975. *Montesquieu's Idea of Justice*. The Hague: Martinus Nijhoff.

———. 1996. 'Montesquieu's Vision of Europe and its European Context' [= *SVEC*, no. 341]. Oxford: Voltaire Foundation, pp. 61–87.

Mass, Edgar. 1980. 'L'image de Montesquieu dans le "Journal Encyclopédique"'. In D. Droixhe et al., eds., *Livres et Lumières au Pays de Li'ege*. Liège: Desoer Éditions, pp. 33–49.

Mattern, Ruth. 1980. 'Moral Science and the Concept of Persons in Locke'. *TPR*, vol. 89, no. 1, pp. 24–45.

Maynor, John, and Cécile Laborde, eds. 2008. *Republicanism and Modern Political Theory*. Oxford: Blackwell.

Meek, Ronald. 1976. *Social Science and the Ignoble Savage*. Cambridge: Cambridge University Press.

Mehta, Uday. 1999. *Liberalism and Empire*. Chicago: University of Chicago Press.

Mele, Alfred. 2001. *Self Deception Unmasked*. Princeton NJ: Princeton University Press.

———. 2009. 'Moral Responsibility and Agent's Histories'. *PhilSt*, vol. 142, no. 2, pp. 161–81.

Mendus, Susan. 1999. 'The Importance of Love in Rawls's Theory of Justice'. *British Journal of Political Science*, vol. 29, no. 1, pp. 57–75.

Menn, Stephen. 1997. 'Descartes, Augustine and the Status of Faith'. In M. A. Stewart, ed., *Studies in Seventeenth-Century European Philosophy*. Oxford: Clarendon, pp. 1–31.

Mercer, Christia. 2001. *Leibniz's Metaphysics*. Cambridge: Cambridge University Press.

Meynell, G. G. 1993. 'Sydenham, Locke, and Sydenham's *De Peste Sive Febre Pestilentiali*'. *Medical History*, vol. 37, pp. 330–32.

———. 1993a. 'John Locke's Method of Commonplacing, as seen in his Drafts and his Medical Notebooks, Bodleian MSS. Locke d.9, f. 21 and f. 23'. *The Seventeenth Century*, vol. 8, no. 2, pp. 245–67.

———. 1994. 'Locke as the Author of the *Anatomia* and *De Arte Medica*'. *Locke Newsletter*, vol. 25, pp. 65–73.

———. 1995. 'Locke, Boyle and Peter Stahl'. *Notes and Records of the Royal Society of London*, vol. 49, no. 2, pp. 185–92.

———. 1996. 'Locke's Collaboration with Sydenham: The Significance of Locke's Indexes'. *The Locke Newsletter*, vol. 27, pp. 65–74.

———. 1997. 'A Database for John Locke's Medical Notebooks and Medical Reading'. *Medical History*, vol. 42, pp. 473–86.

———. 2006. 'John Locke and the Preface to Thomas Sydenham's *Observationes Medicae*'. *Medical History*, vol. 50, pp. 93–110.

Michael, Fred S., and Emily Michael. 1990. 'The Theory of Ideas in Gassendi and Locke'. *JHI*, vol. 51, no. 3, pp. 379–99.

Miel, Jan. 1969. *Pascal and Theology*. Baltimore MD: Johns Hopkins University Press.

Milgram, E. 2005. *Ethics Done Right*. Cambridge: Cambridge University Press.

Miller, David. 2002. 'Group Rights, Human Rights and Citizenship'. *EJP*, vol. 10, no. 2, pp. 178–95.

———. 2004. 'Holding Nations Responsible'. *Ethics*, no. 114, pp. 240–68.

Millar, Fergus. 2002. *The Roman Republic in Political Thought*. London: Brandeis University Press.

Miller, J. J. 2003. 'J. S. Mill on Plural Voting, Competence and Participation'. *HPT*, vol. 24, no. 4, pp. 647–67.

Miller, Kenneth E. 1961. 'John Stuart Mill's Theory of International Relations'. *JHI*, vol. 22, no. 4, pp. 493–514.

Miller, Peter N. 1994. *Defining the Common Good*. Cambridge: Cambridge University Press.

———. 2000. *Peiresc's Europe*. New Haven CT: Yale University Press.

Milne, Maurice. 1984. 'The "Veiled Editor" Unveiled: William Blackwood and his Magazine'. *Publishing History*, vol. 16, pp. 87–103.

Milton, J. R. 1984. 'The Scholastic Background to Locke's Thought'. *Locke Newsletter*, no. 15, pp. 25–34.

———. 1988. 'The Date and Significance of Two of Locke's Early Manuscripts'. *Locke Newsletter*, vol. 19, pp. 47–90.

———. 1994. 'Locke at Oxford'. In G. A. J. Rogers, ed., *Locke's Philosophy: Content and Context*. Oxford: Clarendon, pp. 29–47.

———. 1995. 'Dating Locke's *Second Treatise*'. *HPT*, vol. 16, no. 3, pp. 356–90.

———. 1998. 'The Dating of "Adversaria 1661"'. *Locke Newsletter*, vol. 29, pp. 105–17.

———. 2000. 'Locke and Gassendi'. In M. A. Stewart, ed., *English Philosophy in the Age of Locke*. Oxford: Clarendon, pp. 87–109.

———. 2001. 'Locke, Medicine and the Mechanical Philosophy'. *BJHP*, vol. 9, no. 2, pp. 221–43.

———. 2004. s. v. 'John Locke'. *ODNB*. Oxford: Oxford University Press.

Milton, J. R., and P. Milton. 1997. 'Selecting the Grand Jury: A Tract by John Locke'. *HJ*, vol. 40, no. 2, pp. 185–94.

Milton, Philip. 2000. 'John Locke and the Rye House Plot'. *HJ*, vol. 43, no. 3, pp. 647–68.

Milton-Valente, P. 1956. *L'éthique stoïcienne chez Ciceron*. Paris: Librairie Saint-Paul.

Mitchell, Harvey. 1987. 'The Mysterious Veil of Self-Delusion in Adam Smith's *Theory of Moral Sentiments*'. *Eighteenth-Century Studies*, vol. 20, pp. 405–21.

Mitsis, Phillip. 2003. 'Locke's Offices'. In J. Miller and B. Inwood, eds., *Hellenistic and Early-Modern Philosophy*. Cambridge: Cambridge University Press, pp. 45–61.

Momigliano, Arnaldo. 1947. 'The First Political Commentary on Tacitus'. *Journal of Roman Studies*, vol. 37, nos. 1–2, pp. 91–101.

———. 1949. 'Juste Lipse et les Annales de Tacite. Une Methode de Critique Textuelle au XVIᵉ Siècle'. *Journal of Roman Studies*, vol. 39, nos. 1–2, pp. 190–92.

———. 1952. *George Grote and the Study of Greek History*. Inaugural Lecture delivered at University College London, February 19, 1952. London: H. K. Lewis.

Monoson, Sara. 2000. *Plato's Democratic Entanglements*. Princeton NJ: Princeton University Press.

Monsman, Gerald C. 1970. 'Old Mortality at Oxford'. *Studies in Philology*, vol. 67, pp. 359–89.

———. 1998. *Oxford University's Old Mortality Society*. Lewiston NY: Edwin Mellen.

Moore, James, and Michael Silverthorne. 1984. 'Natural Sociability and Natural Rights in the Moral Philosophy of Gerschom Carmichael'. In V. Hope, ed., *Philosophers of the Scottish Enlightenment*. Edinburgh: Edinburgh University Press, pp. 1–12.

Moore, James. 1976. 'Hume's Theory of Justice and Property'. *PS*, vol. 24, no. 2, pp. 103–19.

——. 1991. 'Theological Politics: A Study of the Reception of Locke's *Two Treatises of Government* in England and Scotland in the Early Eighteenth Century'. In M. Thompson, ed., *John Locke and Immanuel Kant*. Berlin: Walter de Gruyter, pp. 62–82.

——. 1994. 'Hume and Hutcheson'. In M. A. Stewart, ed., *Hume and Hume's Connexions*. Edinburgh: Edinburgh University Press, pp. 23–57.

——. 2002. 'Utility and Humanity: The Quest for the *Honestum* in Cicero, Hutcheson and Hume'. *Utilitas*, vol. 14, no. 3, pp. 365–86.

Moore, Richard J. 1991. 'John Stuart Mill and Royal India'. *Utilitas*, vol. 3, no. 1, pp. 85–106.

Moreau, Sophia R. 2005. 'Reasons and Character'. *Ethics*, no. 115, pp. 272–305.

Mori, Gianluca. 1999. *Bayle: Philosophe*. Paris. Honoré Champion.

Morrill, John. 2002. 'The Causes and Consequences of the British Civil Wars'. In N. H. Keeble, ed., *The Cambridge Companion to the Writing of the English Revolution*. Cambridge: Cambridge University Press, pp. 13–31.

Morrow, Glenn. 1923. 'The Significance of the Doctrine of Sympathy in Hume and Adam Smith'. *TPR*, vol. 32, no. 1, pp. 60–78.

Morrow, John. 1991. 'William Godwin's *History of the English Commonwealth*'. *HJ*, vol. 34, no. 3, pp. 645–64.

——. 1993. 'Heroes and Constitutionalists: The Ideological Significance of Thomas Carlyle's Treatment of the English Revolution'. *HPT*, vol. 14, no. 2, pp. 205–23.

——. 1997. 'The Paradox of Peel as Carlylean Hero'. *HJ*, vol. 40, no. 1, pp. 97–110.

Morrow, John and Mark Francis. 1994. *A History of English Political Thought in the Nineteenth Century*. London: Duckworth.

Mosher, Michael. 1984. 'The Particulars of a Universal Republic: Hegel's Adaptation of Montesquieu's Typology'. *American Political Science Review*, vol. 78, no. 1, pp. 179–88.

——. 2001. 'Monarchy's Paradox'. In D. W. Carrithers, M. A. Mosher and P. A. Rahe, eds., *Montesquieu's Science of Politics: Essays on the 'Spirit of Laws'*. Lanham MD: Rowman and Littlefield, pp. 159–229.

——. 2007. 'Free Trade, Free Speech and Free Love: Monarchy from the Liberal Prospect in Mid-Eighteenth Century France'. In H. Blom, C. Laursen and L. Simonutti, eds., *Monarchies in the Age of Enlightenment*. Toronto: University of Toronto Press, pp. 100–118.

Mortimer, Sarah. 2009. 'Human Nature and Human Liberty in the Works of Faustus Socinus and his Followers'. *JHI*, vol. 70, no. 2, pp. 191–211.

Muller, James W. 2002. 'The Political Economy of Republicanism'. In D. W. Carrithers and P. Coleman, eds., *Montesquieu and the Spirit of Modernity* [= *SVEC*, 2002:09]. Oxford: Voltaire Foundation, pp. 61–76.

Muthu, Sankar. 2008. 'Adam Smith's Critique of International Trading Companies: Theorizing "Globalization" in the Age of Enlightenment'. *PT*, vol. 36, no. 2, pp. 185–212.

Myers, Richard. 1995. 'Montesquieu on the Causes of Roman Greatness'. *HPT*, vol. 16, no. 1, pp. 37–47.

Nadel, George H. 1967. 'Pouilly's Plagiarism'. *Journal of the Warburg and Courtauld Institutes*, vol. 30, pp. 438–44.

Nadler, Steven. 1989. *Arnauld and the Cartesian Philosophy of Ideas*. Manchester: Manchester University Press.

———. 1998. 'Doctrines of Explanation in Late Scholasticism and in Mechanical Philosophy'. In M. Ayers, ed., *Cambridge History of Seventeenth-Century Philosophy*. Cambridge: Cambridge University Press, pp. 513–52.

Nelson, Eric. 2004. *The Greek Tradition in Republican Thought*. Cambridge: Cambridge University Press.

———. 2005. 'Liberty: One Concept Too Many?' *PT*, vol. 33, no. 1, pp. 55–78.

Nesbitt, Darrin. 2001. 'Recognizing Rights: Social Recognition in T. H. Green's System of Rights'. *Polity*, vol. 33, pp. 423–37.

Nicholson, Peter. 1985. 'T. H. Green and State Action: The Case of Liquor Legislation'. *HPT*, vol. 6, no. 4, pp. 517–50.

———. 1990. *The Political Philosophy of the British Idealists*. Cambridge: Cambridge University Press.

———. 1995. 'T. H. Green's Doubts about Hegel's Political Philosophy'. *Bulletin of the Hegel Society of Great Britain*, no. 31, pp. 61–72.

———. 1998. 'T. H. Green and the Burden of Christian Citizenship'. *Balliol College Record*, pp. 15–22.

North, Douglass, and Barry Weingast. 1989. 'Constitutions and Commitment: The Evolution of Institutions Governing Public Choice in Seventeenth-Century England'. *Journal of Economic History*, vol. 49, pp. 803–32.

Norton, David Fate. 1994. 'How a Sceptic May Live Scepticism'. In J. J. Macintosh and H. A. Meynell, eds., *Faith, Scepticism and Personal Identity*. Calgary: University of Calgary Press, pp. 119–39.

Nozick, Robert. 1974. *Anarchy, State and Utopia*. Oxford: Blackwell.

———. 1993. *The Nature of Rationality*. Cambridge MA: Harvard University Press.

Nuovo, Victor. 2000. 'Locke's Theology, 1694–1704'. In M. A. Stewart, ed., *English Philosophy in the Age of Locke*. Oxford: Clarendon, pp. 183–215.

Nussbaum, Arthur. 1952. 'The Significance of Roman Law in the History of International Law'. *University of Pennsylvania Law Review*, vol. 100, no. 5, pp. 678–87.

Nussbaum, Martha. 1994. *The Therapy of Desire*. Princeton NJ: Princeton University Press.

———. 1997. 'Kant and Stoic Cosmopolitanism'. *JPP*, vol. 5, no. 1, pp. 1–25.

———. 2001. *The Fragility of Goodness*. Cambridge: Cambridge University Press.

———. 2000. *Upheavals of Thought*. Cambridge: Cambridge University Press.

———. 2004. 'Mill between Aristotle & Bentham'. *Daedalus*, vol. 133, no. 2, pp. 60–68.

O'Neill, O. 2000. *Bounds of Justice*. Cambridge: Cambridge University Press.

Orcibal, Jean. 1954. 'Thèmes platoniciens dans l'"Augustinus" de Jansénius'. *Augustinus Magister, Congrès International Augustinien, Paris, 21–24 Septembre 1954*. Etudes Augustiniennes. Paris, pp. 1077–85.

———. 1989. *Jansénius d'Ypres (1585–1638)*. Études Augustiniennes. Paris.

Oake, Roger B. 1953. 'Montesquieu's Religious Ideas'. *JHI*, vol. 14, no. 4, pp. 548–60.

Oshana, Marina, A. L. 2008. 'Autonomy and Free Agency'. In J. S. Taylor, ed., *Personal Autonomy*. Cambridge: Cambridge University Press, pp. 183–204.

Osler, Margaret. 1994. *Divine Will and the Mechanical Philosophy*. Cambridge: Cambridge University Press.

Otsuka, Michael. 2003. *Libertarianism without Inequality*. Oxford: Oxford University Press.

Otteson, James. 2003. *Adam Smith's Marketplace of Life*. Cambridge: Cambridge University Press.

———. 2006. *Actual Ethics*. Cambridge: Cambridge University Press.

Oudin, Charles. 1911. *Le Spinozisme de Montesquieu*. Paris: Librarie Générale de Jurisprudence.

Pack Spencer J., and Eric Schliesser. 2006. 'Smith's Humean Criticism of Hume's Account of the Origin of Justice'. *JHP*, vol. 44, no. 1, pp. 47–63.

Palladini, Fiametta. 1996. '"Appetitus societatis" in Grozio e "socialitas" in Pufendorf'. *Filosofia politica*, vol. 10, pp. 61–69.

———. 2004. 'Pufendorf and Stoicism'. In Hans W. Blom and Laurens C. Winkel, eds., *Grotius and the Stoa*. Assen: Van Corum, pp. 245–55.

Panofsky, Erwin. 1970. '*Et in Arcadia Ego*: Poussin and the Elegiac Tradition'. In *Meaning in the Visual Arts*. London: Penguin, pp. 340–67.

Parfit, Derek. 1984. *Reasons and Persons*. Oxford: Oxford University Press.

Parnham, David. 2001. 'Politics Spun out of Theology and Prophecy: Sir Henry Vane on the Spiritual Environment of Public Power'. *HPT*, vol. 22, no. 1, pp. 53–83.

———. 2003. 'The Nurturing of Righteousness: Sir Henry Vane on Freedom and Discipline'. *JBS*, vol. 42, no. 1, pp. 1–34.

Parrish, John. 2005. 'Two Cities and Two Loves: Imitation in Augustine's Moral Psychology and Political Theory'. *HPT*, vol. 26, no. 2, pp. 209–35.

———. 2007. *Paradoxes of Political Ethics*. Cambridge: Cambridge University Press.

Parry, J. 1994. *The Rise and Fall of Liberal Government in Victorian Britain*. New Haven CT: Yale University Press.

———. 2001. 'The Impact of Napoleon III on British Politics, 1851–1880'. *TRHS*, 6th series, vol. 2, pp. 147–75.

Parssinen T. M. 1973. 'Association, Convention and Anti-Parliament in British Radical Politics, 1771–1848'. *EHR*, no. 88, pp. 504–33.

Parsons, Gerald. 1988. 'Biblical Criticism in Victorian Britain: From Controversy to Acceptance?' In G. Parsons, ed., *Religion in Victorian Britain*, vol. 2: *Controversies*. Manchester: Manchester University Press, pp. 238–57.

Pasquino, Pasquale. 1987. 'Emmanuel Sieyes, Benjamin Constant et le "gouvernement des modernes". Contribution à l'histoire du concept de représentation politique'. *Revue française de science politique*, vol. 37, pp. 214–29.

———. 1999. *Sieyes et l'invention de la constitution Française*. Paris: Éditions Odile Jacob.

Pateman, Carole. 2002. 'Self-Ownership and Property in the Person: Democratization and a Tale of Two Concepts'. *JPP*, vol. 10, no. 1, pp. 20–53.

Engberg-Pedersen, Troels. 1990. 'Stoic Philosophy and the Concept of the Person'. In C. Gill, ed., *The Person and the Human Mind*. Oxford: Oxford University Press, pp. 109–35.

Patten, Alan. 1996. 'The Republican Critique of Liberalism'. *British Journal of Political Science*, vol. 26, no. 1, pp. 25–44.

Peacey, J. T. 2000. 'John Lilburne and the Long Parliament'. *HJ*, vol. 43, no. 3, pp. 625–45.

Peltonen, Markuu. 2005. 'Politeness and Whiggism'. *HJ*, vol. 48, no. 2, pp. 391–414.

Peter, Jean-Pierre. 1972. 'Malades et maladies à la fin du XVIII siècle'. In J. P. Desaive. Ed. *Medécins, climat et épidémies aux XVIII siècle*. Paris, pp. 138–70.

Pettit, Philip. 1997. *Republicanism: A Theory of Freedom and Government*. Oxford: Oxford University Press.

———. 2001. *A Theory of Freedom: From the Psychology to the Politics of Agency*. Oxford: Polity.

———. 2002. 'Collective Persons and Powers'. *Legal Theory*, no. 8, pp. 443–70.

———. 2002a. 'Keeping Republican Freedom Simple: On a Disagreement with Quentin Skinner'. *PT*, vol. 30, no. 3, pp. 339–56.

———. 2007. 'Responsibility Incorporated'. *Ethics*, no. 117, pp. 171–201.

———. 2007a. 'Free Reasons and Free Choices'. *HPT*, vol. 28, no. 4, pp. 709–18.

Phillipson, Nicholas. 1993. 'Propriety, Property and Prudence: David Hume and the Defence of the Revolution'. In N. Phillipson and Q. Skinner, eds., *Political Discourse in Early-Modern Britain*. Cambridge: Cambridge University Press, pp. 302–20.

———. 2001. 'Language, Sociability and History: Some Reflections on the Foundations of Adam Smith's Science of Man'. In S. Collini, R. Whatmore and B. Young, eds., *Economy, Polity and Society*. Cambridge: Cambridge University Press, pp. 70–84.

Philp, Mark. 1995. 'Vulgar Conservatism'. *EHR*, no. 110, pp. 42–69.

———. 1998. 'English Republicanism in the 1790s'. *JPP*, vol. 6, no. 2, pp. 235–62.

———. 2007. *Political Conduct*. Cambridge MA: Harvard University Press.

Pincus, Steve. 1995. 'The English Debate over Universal Monarchy'. In J. Robertson, ed., *A Union for Empire: Political Thought and the British Union of 1707*. Cambridge: Cambridge University Press/The Folger Institute, pp. 37–62.

———. 1998. '"To Protect English Liberties": The English Nationalist Revolution of 1688–89'. In T. Claydon and I. McBride, eds., *Protestantism and National Identity*. Cambridge: Cambridge University Press, pp. 75–104.

———. 1998a. '"Neither Machiavellian Moment nor Possessive Individualism": Commercial Society and the Defenders of the English Commonwealth'. *AHR*, no. 103, pp. 705–36.

———. 2001. 'From Holy Cause to Economic Interest: The Study of Population and the Invention of the State'. In A. Houston and S. Pincus, eds., *A Nation*

Transformed: England after the Restoration. Cambridge: Cambridge University Press, pp. 272–98.

Pippin, Robert. 2004. 'The Ethical Status of Civility'. In *The Persistence of Subjectivity: On the Kantian Aftermath*. Cambridge: Cambridge University Press, pp. 223–38.

Pitkin, Hanna F. 1967. *The Concept of Representation*. Berkeley CA: University of California Press.

———. 1988. 'Are Freedom and Liberty Twins?' *PT*, vol. 16, no. 4, pp. 523–52.

Pitts, Jennifer. 2003. 'Legislator of the World? A Rereading of Bentham on Colonies'. *PT*, vol. 31, no. 2, pp. 200–234.

———. 2005. *A Turn to Empire?* Princeton NJ: Princeton University Press.

———. 2007. 'Boundaries of Victorian International Law'. In Duncan Bell, ed., *Victorian Visions of Global Order*. Cambridge: Cambridge University Press, pp. 67–88.

Pocock, J. G. A. 1982. 'The Political Economy of Burke's Analysis of the French Revolution'. *HJ*, vol. 25, no. 2, pp. 331–49.

———. 1990. *The Ancient Constitution and the Feudal Law*. Cambridge: Cambridge University Press.

———. 1998. 'Enthusiasm: The Antiself of Enlightenment'. In. L. E. Klein and A. J. La Vopa, eds., *Enthusiasm and Enlightenment in Europe, 1650–1850*. San Marino CA: Huntington Library, pp. 7–28.

———. 2002. 'Some Europe's in Their History'. In Antony Pagden, ed., *The Idea of Europe: From Antiquity to the European Union*. Cambridge: Cambridge University Press, pp. 55–71.

———. 1999. *Barbarism and Religion*.Vol. 1. Cambridge: Cambridge University Press.

———. 1999a. *Barbarism and Religion*. Vol. 2. Cambridge: Cambridge University Press.

———. 2003. *Barbarism and Religion*. Vol. 3. *Narratives of Civil Government*. Cambridge: Cambridge University Press.

———. 2003a. *The Machiavellian Moment*. Rev. edn. Princeton NJ: Princeton University Press.

Pole, J. R. 1971. *Political Representation in England and the Origins of the American Republic*. Berkeley CA: University of California Press.

Popkin, Richard. 1955. 'The Skeptical Precursors of David Hume'. *Philosophy and Phenomenological Research*, vol. 16, no. 1, pp. 61–71.

———. 1979. 'Hume and Spinoza'. *Hume Studies*, vol. 5, no. 2, pp. 65–93.

Prest, John. 1998. 'The Death and Funeral of T. H. Green: Charlotte Green's Record of T. H. Green's Illness'. *Balliol College Record*, pp. 23–26.

Prior, Charles, W. A. 2005. 'Ecclesiology and Political Thought in England, 1580–c.1630'. *HJ*, vol. 48, no. 4, pp. 855–84.

Prochaska, Frank. 2000. *The Republic of Britain, 1760–2000*. London: Penguin.

Questier, Michael. 1997. 'Loyalty, Religion and State Power in Early-Modern England: English Romanism and the Jacobean Oath of Allegiance'. *HJ*, vol. 40, no. 2, pp. 311–29.

Quinault, Roland. 1988. '1848 and Parliamentary Reform'. *HJ*, vol. 31, no. 4, pp, 831–51.

———. 1992. 'Westminster and the Victorian Constitution'. *TRHS*, 6th series, vol. 2, no. 2, pp. 79–104.

Raaflaub, Kurt A. 2004. *The Discovery of Freedom in Ancient Greece*. Chicago: University of Chicago Press.

Rachum, Ilan. 1995. 'The Meaning of "Revolution" in the English Revolution, 1648–1660'. *JHI*, vol. 56, no. 2, pp. 195–215.

Rahe, Paul A. 2001. 'Forms of Government'. In D. W. Carrithers, M. A. Mosher and P. A. Rahe, eds., *Montesquieu's Science of Politics: Essays on the 'Spirit of Laws'*. Lanham MD: Rowman and Littlefield, pp. 69–107.

———. 2005. 'The Book that Never Was: Montesquieu's *Considerations on the Romans* in Historical Context'. *HPT*, vol. 26, no. 1, pp. 43–89.

———. 2008. *Against Throne and Altar: Machiavelli and Political Theory under the English Republic*. Cambridge: Cambridge University Press.

Raphael, D. D. 2007. *The Impartial Spectator: Adam Smith's Moral Philosophy*. Oxford: Oxford University Press.

Raskolnikoff, Mouza. 1992. *Histoire Romaine et Critique historique dans l'Europe des lumières*. École française de Rome: Palais Farnèse.

Rasmussen, Dennis C. 2006. 'Does "Bettering our Condition" Really Make us Better off? Adam Smith on Progress and Happiness'. *APSR*, vol. 100, no. 3, pp. 309–18.

———. 2008. *The Problems and Promise of Commercial Society: Adam Smith's Response to Rousseau*. University Park PA: Pennsylvania State UniversityPress.

Rawls, John. 1973. *A Theory of Justice*. Oxford: Oxford University Press.

———. 1999. *The Law of Peoples*. Cambridge MA: Harvard University Press.

———. 2000. *Lectures on the History of Moral Philosophy*. Cambridge MA: Harvard University Press, 2000.

———. 2007. *Lectures on the History of Political Philosophy*. Ed. S. Freeman. Cambridge MA: Harvard University Press.

Raz, Joseph. 1999. *Engaging Reason*. Oxford: Oxford University Press.

———. 2005. 'The Myth of Instrumental Rationality'. *Journal of Ethics and Social Policy*, vol. 1, no. 1, pp. 2–28.

Reardon, Bernard M. G. 1986. 'T. H. Green as Theologian'. In A. Vincent, ed., *The Philosophy of T. H. Green*. Aldershot: Ashgate, pp. 36–47.

Reich, Klaus. 1939. 'Kant and Greek Ethics (I.)'. *Mind*, n.s. vol. 48, no. 191, pp. 338–54.

———. 1939a. 'Kant and Greek Ethics (II.)'. *Mind*, n.s. vol. 48, no. 192, pp. 446–63.

Reeve, Richard. 2007. *John Stuart Mill: Victorian Firebrand*. London: Atlantic.

Rehfeld, Andrew. 2008. 'Jephtha, The Hebrew Bible and John Locke's "Second Treatise on Government"'. *Hebraic Political Studies*, vol. 3, no. 1, pp. 60–93.

Richter, Melvin. 1964. *The Politics of Conscience: T. H. Green and his Age*. London: Weidenfeld and Nicolson.

———. 1976. 'An Introduction to Montesquieu's "An Essay on the Causes That May Affect Men's Minds and Characters"'. *PT*, vol. 4, no. 2, pp. 132–38.

———. 2004. 'Tocqueville and Guizot on Democracy: From a Type of Society to a Political Regime'. *HEI*, vol. 30, no. 1, pp. 61–82.

Riley, Jonathan. 2001. 'Interpreting Berlin's Liberalism'. *APSR*, vol. 95, no. 2, pp. 283–95.

———. 1999. 'Mill's Political Economy: Ricardian Science and Liberal Utilitarian Art'. In J. Skorupski, ed., *The Cambridge Companion to Mill*. Cambridge: Cambridge University Press, pp. 293–337.

———. 2003. 'Interpreting Mill's Qualitative Hedonism'. *Philosophical Quarterly*, vol. 53, no. 212, pp. 410–18.

Riley, Patrick. 1986. *The General Will Before Rousseau: The Transformation of the Divine into the Civic*. Princeton NJ: Princeton University Press.

———. 1999. *Leibniz's Universal Jurisprudence*. Cambridge MA: Harvard University Press, 1999.

Rivers, Isabel. 2000. *Reason, Grace and Sentiment*, vol. 2: *Shaftesbury to Hume*. Cambridge: Cambridge University Press.

Robertson, John. 1993. 'Universal Monarchy and the Liberties of Europe: David Hume's Critique of an English Whig Doctrine'. In N. Phillipson and Q. Skinner, eds., *Political Discourse in Early-Modern Britain*. Cambridge: Cambridge University Press, pp. 349–73.

———. 1995. 'Empire and Union: Two Concepts of the Early-Modern European Political Order'. In J. Robertson, ed., *A Union for Empire: Political Thought and the British Union of 1707*. Cambridge: Cambridge University Press/The Folger Institute, pp. 3–36.

———. 2004. s. v. 'David Hume'. *ODNB*. Oxford: Oxford University Press.

———. 2005. *The Case for the Enlightenment*. Cambridge: Cambridge University Press.

Robson Ann P., and John M. Robson. 1985. 'Private and Public Goals: John Stuart Mill and the *London and Westminster*'. In Joel. H. Wiener, ed., *Innovators and Preachers: The Role of the Editor in Victorian England*. Westport CT: Greenwood Press, pp. 231–57.

Robson, John. 1999. 'Civilization and Culture as Moral Concepts'. In J. Skorupski, ed., *The Cambridge Companion to Mill*. Cambridge: Cambridge University Press, pp. 338–71.

Rodis-Lewis, Geneviève. 1998. *Descartes: His Life and Thought*. Trans. Jane Marie Todd. Ithaca NY: Cornell University Press.

Rogerson, John. 1984. *Old Testament Criticism in the Nineteenth Century: England and Germany*. London: SPCK.

Rorty, Amélie Oksenberg. 1990. 'Persons and Personae'. In C. Gill, ed., *The Person and the Human Mind: Issues in Ancient and Modern Philosophy*. Oxford: Oxford University Press, pp. 21–38.

———. 1994. 'The Hidden Politics of Cultural Identification'. *PT*, vol. 22, no. 1, pp. 152–66.

———. 1996. 'The Two Faces of Stoicism: Rousseau and Freud'. *JHP*, vol. 34, no. 3, pp. 335–56.

———. 1997. 'The Social and Political Sources of *Akrasia*'. *Ethics*, vol. 107, no. 4, pp. 644–57.

Rose, Jacqueline. 2005. 'John Locke, "Matters Indifferent", and the Restoration of the Church of England'. *HJ*, vol. 48, no. 3, pp. 601–21.

Rosen, Fred. 1992. *Bentham, Byron and Greece: Constitutionalism, Nationalism and Early Liberal Thought*. Oxford: Clarendon.

———. 1997. 'Liberalism and Nationalism in Early British Liberal Thought'. *Journal of Political Ideologies*, vol. 2, no. 2, pp. 177–88.

———. 2000. 'The Idea of Utility in Adam Smith's *The Theory of Moral Sentiments*'. *HEI*, vol. 26, pp. 79–103.

———. 2003. *Classical Utilitarianism from Hume to Mill*. London: Routledge.

———. 2004. 'J. S. Mill on Socrates, Pericles and the Fragility of Truth'. *JLH*, vol. 25, no. 2, pp. 181–94.

———. 2007. 'The Method of Reform'. In A. Zakaras and N. Urbinati, eds., *J. S. Mill's Political Thought*. Cambridge: Cambridge University Press, pp. 124–44.

Rosenblatt, Helena. 2008. *Liberal Values: Benjamin Constant and the Politics of Religion*. Cambridge: Cambridge University Press.

Ross, Ian Simpson. 2003. *The Life of Adam Smith*. Oxford: Oxford University Press.

Rothschild, Emma. 2001. *Economic Sentiments*. Cambridge MA: Harvard University Press.

———. 2004. 'Global Commerce and the Question of Sovereignty in the Eighteenth-Century Provinces'. *MIH*, vol. 1, no. 1, pp. 3–25.

———. 2005. 'David Hume and the Sea-Gods of the Atlantic'. Centre for History and Economics, University of Cambridge.

Runciman, David. 1997. *Pluralism and the Personality of the State*. Cambridge: Cambridge University Press.

———. 2000. 'What Kind of Person is Hobbes's State? A Reply to Skinner'. *JPP*, vol. 8, no. 2, pp. 268–78.

———. 2008. *Political Hypocrisy*. Princeton NJ: Princeton University Press.

Ryan, Alan. 1984. *Property and Political Theory*. Oxford: Blackwell.

———. 2007. 'Bureaucracy, Democracy, Liberty: Some Unanswered Questions in Mill's Politics'. In A. Zakaras and N. Urbinati, eds., *J. S. Mill's Political Thought*. Cambridge: Cambridge University Press, pp. 147–65.

Sabl, Andrew. 2002. *Ruling Passions: Political Offices and Democratic Ethics*. Princeton NJ: Princeton University Press.

———. 2006. 'Noble Infirmity: Love of Fame in Hume'. *PT*, vol. 34, no. 5, pp. 542–68.

Salingar, Leo. 1976. *Shakespeare and the Traditions of Comedy*. Cambridge: Cambridge University Press.

Salmon, J.H.M. 1959. *The French Wars of Religion in English Political Thought*. Cambridge: Cambridge University Press.

———. 1989. 'Stoicism and Roman Example: Seneca and Tacitus in Jacobean England'. *JHI*, vol. 50, no. 2, pp. 199–225.

Salter, John. 1999. 'Sympathy with the Poor: Theories of Punishment in Hugo Grotius and Adam Smith'. *HPT*, vol. 20, no. 2, pp. 205–24.

Saunders, David. 2003. 'The Natural Jurisprudence of Jean Barbeyrac: Translation as an Art of Political Adjustment'. *Eighteenth-Century Studies*, vol. 36, no. 4, pp. 473–90.

Savonius, Sami. 2004. 'Locke in French: The *Du Gouvernement Civil* of 1691 and its Readers'. *HJ*, vol. 47, no. 1, pp. 47–79.

Scanlon, Thomas M. 1988. 'The Significance of Choice'. In S. M. McMurrin, ed., *Tanner Lectures on Human Values*. Salt Lake City: University of Utah Press, vol. 8, pp. 149–216.

———. 1998. *What We Owe to Each Other*. Cambridge MA: Harvard University Press.

———. 2008. *Moral Dimensions: Permissibility, Meaning. Blame*, Cambridge MA: Harvard University Press.

Schabas, Margaret. 2003. 'Adam Smith's Debts to Nature'. *History of Political Economy*, vol. 35, pp. 262–81.

Schaub, Dina. 1995. *Erotic Liberalism: Women and Revolution in Montesquieu's Persian Letters*. Lanham MD: Rowman & Littlefield.

Reydams-Schils, Gretchen. 2002. 'Human Bonding and *oikeiōsis* in Roman Stoicism'. In *Oxford Studies in Ancient Philosophy*. Oxford: Clarendon, vol. 22, pp. 221–51.

———. 2005. *The Roman Stoics*. Chicago: University of Chicago Press.

Schliesser, Eric. 2005. 'Wonder in the Face of Scientific Revolutions: Adam Smith on Newton's "Proof" of Copernicanism'. *BJHP*, vol. 13, no. 4, pp. 697–732.

Schløsler, Jørn. 1994. 'Le *Christianisme Raisonnable* et le débat sur le "Socianianisme" de John Locke dans la presse Française de la première moitié du XVIIIᵉ siècle'. *LIAS*, vol. 21, no. 2, pp. 295–319.

Schneewind, Jerome. 1977. *Sidgwick's Ethics and Victorian Moral Philosophy*. Oxford: Oxford University Press.

———. 1998. *The Invention of Autonomy*. Cambridge: Cambridge University Press.

Schaffer, Simon. 1989. 'The Nebular Hypothesis and the Science of Progress'. In J. R. Moore, ed., *History, Humanity and Evolution: Essays for John C. Greene*. Cambridge: Cambridge University Press, pp. 131–53.

Schofield, Malcolm. 1998. 'Political Friendship and the Ideology of Reciprocity'. In P. Cartledge, P. Millett and S. von Reden, eds., *'Kosmos': Essays in Order, Conflict and Community in Classical Athens*. Cambridge: Cambridge University Press, pp. 37–51.

———. 2006. *Plato*. Oxford: Oxford University Press.

Schultz, Bart. 2004. *Henry Sidgwick, Eye of the Universe: An Intellectual Biography*. Cambridge: Cambridge University Press.

———. 2007. 'Mill and Sidgwick, Imperialism and Racism'. *Utilitas*, vol. 19, no. 1, pp. 104–30.

Schuurman, Paul. 2001. 'Locke's Logic of Ideas in Context: Content and Structure'. *BJHP*, vol. 9, no. 3, pp. 439–65.

———. 2003. *Ideas, Mental Faculties and Method: The Logic of Ideas of Descartes and Locke and Its Reception in the Dutch Republic*. Leiden: Brill.

Schwartzberg, Melissa. 2003. 'Rousseau on Fundamental Law'. *PS*, vol. 51, pp. 387–403.

Scott, Dominic. 1994. 'Reason, Recollection and the Cambridge Platonists'. In S. Hutton and A. Baldwin, eds., *Platonism and the English Imagination*. Cambridge: Cambridge University Press, pp. 139–50.

Scott, Jonathan. 1992. 'The Law of War: Grotius, Sidney, Locke and the Political Theory of Rebellion'. *HPT*, vol. 13, no. 4, pp. 565–85.

———. 2003. *England's Troubles*. Cambridge: Cambridge University Press.

Scott, W. R. 1937. *Adam Smith as Student and Professor*. Glasgow: Jackson & Co.

Scribner, Bob. 1998. *The German Reformation*. Basingstoke: Macmillan.

Seigel, Jerrold. 2005. *The Idea of the Self*. Cambridge: Cambridge University Press.

Semmel, Bernard. 1998. 'John Stuart Mill's Coleridgean Neoradicalism'. In Eldon Eisenach, ed., *Mill and the Moral Character of Liberalism*. University Park PA: Pennsylvania State University Press, pp. 49–76.

Semmel, Stuart. 2000. 'British Radicals and "Legitimacy": Napoleon in the Mirror of History'. *P&P*, no. 167, pp. 140–75.

Sen, Amartya. 1985. 'Well-Being, Agency and Freedom: The Dewey Lectures 1984'. *JoPh*, vol. 82, no. 4, pp. 169–221.

———. 1999. *Development as Freedom*. Oxford: Oxford University Press.

———. 2002. 'Open and Closed Impartiality'. *JoPh*, vol. 99, no. 9, pp. 445–69.

———. 2002a. *Rationality and Freedom*. Cambridge MA: Harvard University Press.

Senaralens, Vanessa de. 2003. *Montesquieu, historien de Rome*. Geneva: Librarie Droz.

Sennett, Richard. 1976. *The Fall of Public Man*. Cambridge: Cambridge University Press.

Shackleton, Robert. 1978. 'John Nourse and the London Edition *of l'Esprit des lois*'. In D. J. Mossop, G. E. Rodmell and D. B. Wilson, eds., *Studies in the French Eighteenth Century Presented to John Lough*. Durham: University of Durham, pp. 248–59.

———. 1979. 'Montesquieu, Suard and the *philosophes*'. In A. J. Bingham and V. W. Topazio, eds., *Enlightenment Essays in Honour of Lester G. Croker*. Oxford: Voltaire Foundation, 1979, pp. 309–14.

———. 1988. 'Montesquieu, Bolingbroke, and the Separation of Powers'. In his *Essays on Montesquieu and the Enlightenment*. Ed. D. Gilson and M. Smith. Oxford: Voltaire Foundation, pp. 3–15.

———. 1988a. 'La genèse de l'Esprit des lois'. In his *Essays on Montesquieu and the Enlightenment*. Ed. D. Gilson and M. Smith. Oxford: Voltaire Foundation, pp. 49–63.

Shackleton, Robert. 1988b. 'Les secretaires de Montesquieu'. In his *Essays on Montesquieu and the Enlightenment*. Ed. D. Gilson and M. Smith. Oxford: Voltaire Foundation, pp. 65–72.

———. 1988c. 'Montesquieu et les beaux-arts'. In his *Essays on Montesquieu and the Enlightenment*. Ed. D. Gilson and M. Smith. Oxford: Voltaire Foundation, pp. 103–7.

———. 1988d. 'Montesquieu and Machiavelli: A Reappraisal'. In his *Essays on Montesquieu and the Enlightenment*. Ed. David Gilson and Martin Smith. Oxford: Voltaire Foundation, pp. 116–31.

Shannon, Richard. 2000. *Gladstone: Heroic Minister*. London: Penguin.

Shapin, Stephen. 2000. 'Descartes the Doctor: Rationalism and its Therapies'. *British Journal for the History of Science*, vol. 33, no. 1, pp. 131–54.

Sheehan, Jonathan. 2005. *The Enlightenment Bible*. Princeton NJ: Princeton University Press.

Sheps, Arthur. 1975. 'The American Revolution and the Transformation of English Republicanism'. *Historical Reflections*, vol. 2, no. 1, pp. 3–28.

Sher, Richard B. 1994. 'From Troglodytes to Americans: Montesquieu and the Scottish Enlightenment on Liberty, Virtue and Commerce'. In D. Wootton, ed., *Republicanism, Liberty and Commercial Society*. Stanford CA: Stanford University Press, pp. 368–400.

Shklar, Judith. 1966. 'Rousseau's Two Models: Sparta and the Age of Gold'. *Political Science Quarterly*, vol. 81, no. 1, pp. 25–51.

———. 1979. 'Virtue in a Bad Climate: Good Men and Good Citizens in Montesquieu's *L'Esprit des lois*'. In A. J. Bingham and V. W. Topazio, eds., *Enlightenment Essays in Honour of Lester G. Croker*. Oxford: Voltaire Foundation, pp. 315–28.

———. 1984. *Ordinary Vices*. Cambridge: Harvard University Press.

———. 1985. *Men & Citizens: A Study of Rousseau's Social Theory*. Cambridge: Cambridge University Press.

———. 1987. *Montesquieu*. Oxford: Oxford University Press.

Simonutti, Luisa. 2007. '"Absolute, not Arbitrary, Power": Monarchism and Politics in the Thought of the Huguenots and Pierre Bayle'. In H. Blom, C. Laursen and L. Simonutti, eds. *Monarchies in the Age of Enlightenment*. Toronto: University of Toronto Press, pp. 45–59.

Simmons, A. John. 2000. *Justification and Legitimacy*. Cambridge: Cambridge University Press.

Skinner, Quentin. 1996. *Reason and Rhetoric in the Philosophy of Hobbes*. Cambridge: Cambridge University Press.

———. 1997. *Liberty before Liberalism*. Cambridge: Cambridge University Press.

———. 2002. 'A Third Concept of Liberty'. *PBA*, vol. 117, pp. 237–68.

———. 2002a. 'Classical Liberty and the Coming of the English Civil War'. In M. van Gelderen and Q. Skinner, eds., *Republicanism—A Shared European Heritage*. 2 vols. Cambridge: Cambridge University Press, vol. 2, pp. 9–28.

———. 2002b. 'Machiavelli on *virtù* and the Maintenance of Liberty'. In *Visions of Politics*, vol. 2: *Renaissance Virtues*. Cambridge: Cambridge University Press, pp. 160–85.

———. 2002c. 'Humanism, Scholasticism and Popular Sovereignty'. In *Visions of Politics*, vol. 2: *Renaissance Virtues*. Cambridge: Cambridge University Press, pp. 245–63.

———. 2002d. 'From the State of Princes to the Person of the State'. In *Visions of Politics*, vol. 2: *Renaissance Virtues*. Cambridge: Cambridge University Press, pp. 368–413.

———. 2002e. 'Augustan Party Politics and Renaissance Constitutional Thought'. In *Visions of Politics*, vol. 2: *Renaissance Virtues*. Cambridge: Cambridge University Press, pp. 344–67.

———. 2002f. 'Hobbes and the Classical Theory of Laughter'. In *Visions of Politics*, vol. 3: *Hobbes and Civil Science*. Cambridge: Cambridge University Press, pp. 142–76.

————. 2002g. 'Hobbes and the Purely Artificial Person of the State'. In *Visions of Politics*, vol. 3: *Hobbes and Civil Science*. Cambridge: Cambridge University Press, pp. 177–208.

————. 2006. 'Rethinking Political Liberty'. *HWJ*, no. 61, pp. 156–70.

————. 2008. *Hobbes and Republican Liberty*. Cambridge: Cambridge University Press.

————. 2009. 'On Trusting the Judgement of our Rulers'. In R. Bourke and R. Geuss, eds., *Political Judgement*. Cambridge: Cambridge University Press, pp. 115–33.

Smith, Alan. 1968. 'The Image of Cromwell in Folklore and Tradition'. *Folklore*, vol. 79, no. 1, pp. 17–39.

Smith, Eugene. 1995. 'The Commerce of Sympathy: Adam Smith on the Emergence of Morals'. *JHP*, vol. 33, no. 3, pp. 447–66.

Smith, G. W. 1980. 'The Logic of J. S. Mill on Freedom'. *PS*, vol. 28, no. 2, pp. 238–52.

————. 1980a. 'John Stuart Mill on Edger and Reville: An Episode in the Development of Mill's Conception of Freedom'. *JHI*, vol. 41, no. 3, pp. 433–49.

————. 1991. 'Social Liberty and Free Agency'. In J. Gray, ed., *J. S. Mill, 'On Liberty' in Focus*. London: Routledge, pp. 239–59.

————. 1993. 'Enlightenment Psychology and Individuality: The Roots of J. S. Mill's Conception of the Self'. *Enlightenment and Dissent*, vol. 12, pp. 70–86.

Smith, R. J. 1987. *The Gothic Bequest*. Cambridge: Cambridge University Press.

Soll, Jacob. 2003. 'Empirical History and the Transformation of Political Criticism in France from Bodin to Bayle'. *JHI*, vol. 64, no. 2, pp. 297–316.

————. 2005. *Publishing the Prince*. Ann Arbor MI: University of Michigan Press.

Somerville, Johann P. 1990. 'Oliver Cromwell and English Political Thought'. In J. Morrill, ed., *Oliver Cromwell and the English Revolution*. London: Longman, 1990, pp. 234–58.

Sonenscher, Michael. 2007. *Before the Deluge*. Princeton NJ: Princeton University Press.

————. 2008. *Sans-Culottes*. Princeton NJ: Princeton University Press.

Sorabji, Richard. 1999. *Emotion and Peace of Mind*. Oxford: Oxford University Press.

————. 2006. *Self: Ancient and Modern Insights about Individuality, Life, and Death*. Oxford: Oxford University Press.

Spadafora, David. 1990. *The Idea of Progress in Eighteenth-Century Britain*. New Haven CT: Yale University Press.

Spector, Céline. 1997. *Montesquieu, les 'Lettres persanes'. De l'anthropologie à la politique*. Paris: PUF.

————. 2001. *La vocabulaire de Montesquieu*. Paris: PUF.

————. 2003. 'Cupidité ou charité? L'ordre sans vertu, des moralistes du grand siècle à L'Esprit des lois de Montesquieu'. *Corpus*, no. 43, pp. 23–69.

————. 2005. 'Quelle justice, quelle rationalité? La mesure du droit dans "L'Esprit des Lois"'. In C. Volpilhac-Auger, ed., *Montesquieu en 2005* [= *SVEC* 2005:05]. Oxford: Voltaire Foundation, pp. 217–42.

————. 2006. *Montesquieu et l'émergence de l'Économie politique*. Paris: Honoré Champion Éditeur.

Stanton, Tim. 2006. 'Locke and the Politics and Theology of Toleration'. *PS*, vol. 54, no. 1, pp. 84–102.

———. 2007. 'The Name and Nature of Locke's "*Defence of Nonconformity*"'. *Locke Studies*, vol. 6, pp. 143–72.

Stapelbrook, Koen. 2008. *Love, Self-Deceit and Money: Commerce and Morality in the Early Neapolitan Enlightenment*. Toronto: University of Toronto Press.

Starobinski, Jean. 1953. *Montesquieu par lui-même*. Paris: Éditions du seuil.

———. 1993. *Blessings in Disguise; or, The Morality of Evil*. Trans. A. Goldhammer. Cambridge MA: Harvard University Press.

Steiner, Hillel. 1974–75. 'Individual Liberty'. *PAS*, vol. 75, pp. 33–50.

———. 1983. 'How Free? Computing Personal Liberty'. In A. Phillips-Griffiths, ed., *Of Liberty*. Cambridge: Cambridge University Press, pp. 73–83.

Stedman Jones, Gareth. 1982. 'The Language of Chartism'. In J. Epstein and D. Thompson, eds., *The Chartist Experience*. Basingstoke: Macmillan, pp. 3–58.

———. 1994. 'Kant, the French Revolution and the Definition of the Republic'. In B. Fontana, ed., *The Invention of the Modern Republic*. Cambridge: Cambridge University Press, pp. 154–72.

———. 2002. 'National Bankruptcy and Social Revolution: European Observers on Britain, 1813–1844'. In D. Winch and P. K. O'Brian, eds., *The Political Economy of British Historical Experience, 1688–1914*. Oxford: The British Academy/Oxford University Press, pp. 63–92.

Stein, Peter. 1980. *Legal Evolution*. Cambridge: Cambridge University Press.

Stewart, M. A. 1981. 'Locke's Professional Contacts with Robert Boyle'. *Locke Newsletter*, vol. 12, pp. 19–44.

———. 1991. 'The Stoic Legacy in the early Scottish Enlightenment'. In M. Osler, ed., *Atoms, 'Pneuma', and Tranquillity: Epicurean and Stoic Themes in European Thought*. Cambridge: Cambridge University Press, pp. 273–96.

Stimson Shannon, and Murray Milgate. 2001. 'Mill, Liberty and the Facts of Life'. *PS*, vol. 49, pp. 231–48.

Straumann, Benjamin. 2006. '"Ancient Caesarian Lawyers" in a State of Nature'. *PT*, vol. 24, no. 3, pp. 338–50.

Strawson, Peter F. 1968. 'Freedom and Resentment'. In P. F. Strawson, ed., *Studies in the Philosophy of Thought and Action*. Oxford: Oxford University Press, pp. 71–96.

Strong, Roy. 1978. *And When Did You Last See Your Father: The Victorian Painter and British History*. London: Thames & Clark.

Sullivan, Eileen P. 1983. 'Liberalism and Empire: J. S. Mill's Defence of the British Empire'. *JHI*, pp. 599–617.

Sullivan, Vickie B. 2004. *Machiavelli, Hobbes, and the Formation of a Liberal Republicanism in England*. Cambridge: Cambridge University Press.

———. 2006. 'Against the Despotism of a Republic: Montesquieu's Correction of Machiavelli in the Name of the Security of the Individual'. *HPT*, vol. 27, no. 2, pp. 263–89.

Takeda, Junko Thérèse. 2006. 'French Absolutism, Marsellais Civic Humanism, and Languages of Public Good'. *HJ*, vol. 49, no. 3, pp. 707–34.

Taylor, Antony. 1999. *'Down with the Crown': British Anti-Monarchism and Debates about Royalty Since 1790*. London: Reaktion Books.

Taylor, Charles. 1979. 'What's Wrong with Negative Liberty?' In A. Ryan, ed., *The Idea of Freedom*. Oxford: Clarendon, pp. 175–91.

———. 1996. *Sources of the Self: The Making of Modern Identity*. Cambridge: Cambridge University Press.

———. 2004. *Modern Social Imaginaries*. Durham NC: Duke University Press.

Taylor, Miles. 1992. 'John Bull and the Iconography of Public Opinion in England, *c.* 1712–1929'. *P&P*, no. 134, pp. 93–128.

———. 1996. 'The English Face of Karl Marx'. *Journal of Victorian Culture*, vol. 1, no. 2, pp. 227–53.

———. 2000. 'Republics versus Empires: Charles Dilke's Republicanism Reconsidered'. In G. Nash and A. Taylor, eds., *Republicanism in Victorian Society*. Stroud: Sutton, pp. 25–34.

Thiel, Udo. 2000. 'The Trinity and Human Personal Identity'. In M. A. Stewart, ed., *English Philosophy in the Age of Locke*. Oxford: Clarendon, pp. 217–43.

Thomas, Downing A. 2005. 'Negotiating Taste in Montesquieu'. *Eighteenth-Century Studies*, vol. 39, no. 1, pp. 71–90.

Thomas, Geoffrey. 1987. *The Moral Philosophy of T. H. Green*. Oxford: Clarendon.

Thomas, Keith. 2009. *The Ends of Life*. Oxford: Oxford University Press.

Thomas, William. 1979. *The Philosophic Radicals*. Oxford: Clarendon.

———. 1985. *Mill*. Oxford: Oxford University Press.

Thompson, Dennis F. 1976. *John Stuart Mill and Representative Government*. Princeton NJ: Princeton University Press.

———. 2005. *Restoring Responsibility*. Cambridge: Cambridge University Press.

———. 2007. 'Mill in Parliament: When Should a Philosopher Compromise?' In A. Zakaras and N. Urbinati, eds., *J. S. Mill's Political Thought*. Cambridge: Cambridge University Press, pp. 166–99.

Thompson, Martyn P. 1986. 'The History of Fundamental Law in Political Thought from the French Wars of Religion to the American Revolution'. *AHR*, vol. 91, pp. 1103–28.

———. 1987. *Ideas of Contract in English Political Thought in the Age of John Locke*. New York: Garland.

———. 1988. 'Significant Silences in Locke's *Two Treatises of Government*: Constitutional History, Contract and Law'. *HJ*, vol. 31, no. 2, pp. 275–94.

Thomson, Anne. 2008. *Bodies of Thought: Science, Religion and the Soul in the Early Enlightenment*. Oxford: Oxford University Press.

Thweatt, Vivien. 1980. *La Rochefoucauld and the Seventeenth Century Concept of the Self*. Geneva: Droz.

Trentmann, Frank. 2009. *Free-Trade Nation*. Oxford: Oxford University Press.

Trevor-Roper, Hugh. 1992. 'Hugo Grotius and England'. *From Counter-Reformation to Glorious Revolution*. London: Secker & Warburg, pp. 47–82.

Tribe, Keith. 1995. *Strategies of Economic Order*. Cambridge: Cambridge University Press.

———. 2008. '"Das Adam Smith Problem" and the Origins of Modern Smith Scholarship'. *HEI*, vol. 34, no. 4, pp. 514–25.

Tuck, Richard. 1974. 'Power and Authority in Seventeenth-Century England'. *HJ*, vol. 17, no. 1, pp. 43–61.

———. 1979. *Natural Rights Theories: Their Origin and Development*. Cambridge: Cambridge University Press.

———. 1986. 'A New Date for Filmer's *Patriarcha*'. *HJ*, vol. 29, no. 1, pp. 183–86.

———. 1990. 'The "Modern" Theory of Natural Law'. In A. Pagden, ed., *The Languages of Political Theory in Early-Modern Europe*. Cambridge: Cambridge University Press, pp. 99–122.

———. 1990a. 'Hobbes and Locke on Toleration'. In M. Dietz, ed., *Thomas Hobbes and Political Theory*. Lawrence KA: University Press of Kansas, pp. 153–71.

———. 1993. *Philosophy and Government 1572–1651*. Cambridge: Cambridge University Press.

———. 1999. *The Rights of War and Peace: Political Thought and the International Order from Grotius to Kant*. Oxford: Oxford University Press.

———. 2005. 'Introduction'. In Hugo Grotius, *The Rights of War and Peace* [1738 Jean Barbeyrac edn.], ed. Richard Tuck. 3 vols. Indianapolis IN: Liberty Fund, pp. ix–xxxiii.

———. 2008. *Free Riding*. Cambridge MA: Harvard University Press.

Tully, James. 1980. *A Discourse on Property*. Cambridge: Cambridge University Press.

———. 1993. *An Approach to Political Philosophy: Locke in Contexts*. Cambridge: Cambridge University Press.

Turner, Frank. 1981. *The Greek Heritage in Victorian Britain*. New Haven CT: Yale University Press.

———. 1986. 'British Politics and the Demise of the Roman Republic: 1700–1939'. *HJ*, vol. 29, no. 3, pp. 577–99.

Turner, Michael J. 1990. *British Politics in an Age of Reform*. Manchester: Manchester University Press.

———. 2001. 'Radical Opinion in an Age of Reform: Thomas Perronet Thompson and the *Westminster Review*'. *History*, vol. 86, pp. 18–40.

Tyler, Colin. 2003. 'T. H. Green, Advanced Liberalism and the Reform Question, 1865–1876'. *HEI*, vol. 29, no. 4, pp. 437–58.

———. 2006. 'Contesting the Common Good: T. H. Green and Contemporary Republicanism'. In W. Mander and M. Dimova-Cookson, eds., *T. H. Green: Ethics, Metaphysics and Political Philosophy*. Oxford: Oxford University Press, pp. 262–91.

Ullmann, W. 1975. *Law and Politics in the Middle Ages*. Cambridge: Cambridge University Press.

Urbinati, Nadia. 2002. *Mill on Democracy*. Chicago: University of Chicago Press.

———. 2006. *Representative Democracy*. Chicago: University of Chicago Press.

———. 2007. 'The Many Heads of the Hydra: J. S. Mill on Despotism'. In A. Zakaras and N. Urbinati, eds., *J. S. Mill's Political Thought*. Cambridge: Cambridge University Press, pp. 66–97.

Valihora, Karen. 2001. 'The Judgement of Judgement: Adam Smith's *Theory of Moral Sentiments*'. *British Journal of Aesthetics*, vol. 41, no. 2, pp. 138–61.

Vallance, Edward. 2000. '"An Holy and Sacramentall Paction": Federal Theology and the Solemn League and Covenant in England'. *EHR*, no. 116, pp. 50–75.

Vance, Norman. 1997. *The Victorians and Ancient Rome*. Oxford: Blackwell.

Varouxakis, Georgios. 1997. 'John Stuart Mill on Intervention and Non-Intervention'. *Millennium*, vol. 26, no. 1, pp. 57–76.

———. 1999. 'Guizot's Historical Works and J. S. Mill's Reception of Tocqueville'. *HPT*, vol. 20, no. 2, pp. 292–312.

———. 2002. *Victorian Political Thought on France and the French*. Basingstoke: Palgrave.

———. 2007. 'Cosmopolitan Patriotism in J. S. Mill's Political Thought'. In A. Zakaras and N. Urbinati, eds., *J. S. Mill's Political Thought*. Cambridge: Cambridge University Press, pp. 277–97.

Velema, W. E. 1997. 'Republican Readings of Montesquieu: *The Spirit of the Laws* in the Dutch Republic'. *HPT*, vol. 18, no. 1, pp. 44–63.

Venturi, Franco. 1963. 'Oriental Despotism'. *JHI*, vol. 24, no. 1, pp. 133–42.

Vernon, James. ed. 1997. *Re-reading the Constitution*. Cambridge: Cambridge University Press.

Vincent, Andrew. 1986. 'T. H. Green and the Religion of Citizenship'. In A. Vincent, ed., *The Philosophy of T. H. Green*. Aldershot: Ashgate, pp. 48–61.

———. 2004. s. v. 'T. H. Green'. *ODNB*. Oxford: Oxford University Press.

Vincent, Andrew, and Raymond Plant. 1984. *Philosophy, Politics and Citizenship: The Life and Thought of the British Idealists*. Oxford: Blackwell.

Vincent, John. 1966. *The Formation of the British Liberal Party, 1857–1868*. London: Penguin.

Vincent, Nicholas C. 1993. 'The Origins of the Chancellorship of the Exchequer'. *EHR*, vol. 108, no. 426, pp. 105–21.

Viner, Jacob. 1972. *The Role of Providence in the Social Order*. Philadelphia PA: American Philosophical Society.

Vivenza, Gloria. 2001. *Adam Smith and the Classics*. Oxford: Oxford University Press.

Volpilhac-Auger, Cathérine. 1985. *Tacite et Montesquieu* [= *SVEC*, no. 232]. Oxford: Voltaire Foundation.

———. 1993. *Tacite en France de Montesquieu à Chateaubriand* [= *SVEC*, no. 313]. Oxford: Voltaire Foundation.

Volpilhac-Auger, Cathérine. 2002. 'Montesquieu et l'impérialisme grec: Alexandre ou l'art de la conquête'. In D. W. Carrithers and P. Coleman, eds., *Montesquieu and the Spirit of Modernity* [= *SVEC*, 2002:09]. Oxford: Voltaire Foundation, pp. 49–60.

———. 2004. 'The Art of the Chapter Heading in Montesquieu or "*De la constitution d'Angleterre*"'. *JLH*, vol. 25, no. 2, pp. 169–79.

———. 2005. 'Une nouvelle "chaine secrete" de *L'Esprit des lois*: l'histoire du texte'. In C. Volpilhac-Auger, ed., *Montesquieu en 2005* [= *SVEC* 2005:5]. Oxford: Voltaire Foundation, pp. 83–216.

Wade, Ira O. 1977. *The Structure and Form of the French Enlightenment*. 2 vols. Princeton NJ: Princeton University Press.

Waddicor, Mark H. 1970. *Montesquieu and the Philosophy of Natural Law*. The Hague: Martinus Nijhoff.

Wahrman, Dror. 2004. *The Making of the Modern Self: Identity and Culture in Eighteenth-Century Britain*. New Haven CT: Yale University Press.

Waldron, Jeremy. 1988. *The Right to Private Property*. Oxford: Clarendon.

———. 1993. 'Mill and the Value of Moral Distress'. In *Liberal Rights: Collected Papers 1981–1991*. Cambridge: Cambridge University Press, pp. 115–33.

———. 2002. *God, Locke and Equality: Christian Foundations in Locke's Political Thought*. Cambridge: Cambridge University Press.

———. 2007. 'Pettit's Molecule'. In G. Brennan, R. Goodin, F. Jackson and M. Smith, eds., *Common Minds: Themes from the Philosophy of Philip Pettit*. Oxford: Oxford University Press, pp. 143–60.

Walker, D. P. 1964. *The Decline of Hell*. London: Routledge and Kegan Paul.

Walmsley, Jonathan Craig. 1998. 'John Locke's Natural Philosophy (1632–1671)'. PhD diss., King's College, London.

———. 2000. '*Morbus*—Locke's Early Essay on Disease'. *Early Science and Medicine*, vol. 5, pp. 366–93.

———. 2003. 'The Development of Locke's Mechanism in the Drafts of the *Essay*'. *BJHP*, vol. 11, no. 3, pp. 417–49.

———. 2006. 'Locke, Mechanism and Draft B: A Correction'. *BJHP*, vol. 14, no. 2, pp. 331–35.

Walsh, W. H. 1986. 'Green's Criticism of Hume'. In A. Vincent, ed., *The Philosophy of T. H. Green*. Aldershot: Ashgate, pp. 21–35.

Walzer, Michael. 1977. *Just and Unjust Wars*. New York: Boston Books.

———. 1994. *Spheres of Justice*. Oxford: Blackwell.

Waszeck, Norbert. 1984. 'Two Concepts of Morality: A Distinction of Adam Smith's Ethics and its Stoic Origin'. *JHI*, vol. 45, no. 4, pp. 591–606.

Watson, Gary. 2004. *Agency and Answerability*. Oxford: Clarendon.

Weil, E. 1998. *Hegel and the State*. Trans. M. A. Cohen. Baltimore MD: Johns Hopkins University Press.

Weinstein, David. 2007. *Utilitarianism and the New Liberalism*. Cambridge: Cambridge University Press.

Weinstein, W. L. 1965. 'The Concept of Liberty in Nineteenth Century English Political Thought'. *PS*, vol. 13, no. 2, pp. 145–62.

Wellek, René. 1931. *Immanuel Kant in England 1793–1838*. Princeton NJ: Princeton University Press.

Wendt, Alexander. 2004. 'The State as Person in International Theory'. *Review of International Studies*, vol. 30, pp. 289–316.

Whatmore, Richard. 2001. 'A "Gigantic Manliness": Paine's Republicanism in the 1790s'. In S. Collini, R. Whatmore and B. Young, eds., *Economy, Polity and Society*. Cambridge: Cambridge University Press, pp. 135–57.

———. 2002. 'Adam Smith's Role in the French Revolution'. *P&P*, no. 175, pp. 65–89.

———. 2009. '"Neither Masters nor Slaves": Small States and Empire in the Long Eighteenth Century'. In D. Kelly, ed., *Lineages of Empire: The Historical Roots of British Imperial Thought* [= *PBA*, vol. 155]. Oxford: Oxford University Press/The British Academy, pp. 53–81.

Whelan, Frederick G. 1988. 'Vattel's Doctrine of the State'. *HPT*, vol. 9, no. 1, pp. 59–90.

————. 2001. 'Oriental Despotism: Anquetil-Duperron's Response to Montesquieu'. *HPT*, vol. 22, no. 4, pp. 619–47.

Williams, Bernard. 1978. *Descartes: The Project of Pure Inquiry*. London: Penguin.

————. 1981. *Moral Luck*. Cambridge: Cambridge University Press.

————. 1993. *Shame and Necessity*. Berkeley CA: University of California Press.

————. 1995. 'The Point of View of the Universe: Sidgwick and the Ambitions of Ethics'. *Making Sense of Humanity*. Cambridge: Cambridge University Press, pp. 153–71.

————. 1999. 'Personal Identity and Individuation'. *Problems of the Self*. Cambridge: Cambridge University Press, pp. 1–18.

————. 2001. 'From Freedom to Liberty: The Construction of a Political Value'. *PPA*, vol. 30, no. 1, pp. 3–26.

————. 2006. 'Descartes' Use of Scepticism'. In M. Burnyeat, ed., *The Sense of the Past*. Princeton NJ: Princeton University Press, pp. 231–45.

Williams, Geraint. 1989. 'J. S. Mill and Political Violence'. *Utilitas*, vol. 1, no. 1, pp. 102–11.

————. 1996. 'The Greek Origins of Mill's Happiness'. *Utilitas*, vol. 8, no. 1, pp. 5–14.

Wilson, Margaret. 2008. *Epicureanism at the Origins of Modernity*. Oxford: Oxford University Press.

Winch, Donald. 1996. *Riches and Poverty: An Intellectual History of Political Economy in Britain, 1750–1834*. Cambridge: Cambridge University Press.

————. 2004. s. v. 'Adam Smith'. *ODNB*. Oxford: Oxford University Press.

Winkel, Laurens. 2000. 'Les origines antiques de l'*Appetitus Societatis* de Grotius'. *Legal History Review*, vol. 68, no. 3, pp. 393–403.

Wokler, Robert. 1975. 'The Influence of Diderot on the Political Theory of Rousseau: Two Aspects of a Relationship'. *SVEC*, no. 82, pp. 55–111.

————. 1994. 'Rousseau's Pufendorf: Natural Law and the Foundations of Commercial Society'. *HPT*, vol. 15, no. 3, pp. 373–402.

————. 1995. 'Review: Yves Glaziou, *Hobbes en France au XVIIIᵉ siècle*. Paris: PUF, 1993'. *HEI*, vol. 21, no. 3, pp. 473ff.

————. 1995. *Rousseau*. Oxford: Oxford University Press.

Wokler R., and M. Goldie, eds. 2006. *The Cambridge History of Eighteenth-Century Political Thought*. Cambridge: Cambridge University Press.

Wolffe, John. 1991. *The Protestant Crusade in Britain, 1829–1860*. Oxford: Oxford University Press.

————. 1998. 'A Transatlantic Perspective: Protestantism and National Identities in Mid-Nineteenth-Century Britain and the United States'. In T. Claydon and I. McBride, eds., *Protestantism and National Identity*. Cambridge: Cambridge University Press, pp. 291–309.

Wolin, Sheldon S. 2004. *Politics and Vision*. Expanded edn. Princeton NJ: Princeton University Press.

Wollheim, Richard. 1996. *Art and its Objects*. Cambridge: Cambridge University Press.

————. 1999. *On the Emotions*. New Haven CT: Yale University Press.

Wood, Neal. 1991. *Cicero's Social and Political Thought*. Berkeley CA: University of California Press.

Woolrych, Austin. 2000. *From Commonwealth to Protectorate*. New edn. London: Pimlico.

Wootton, David. 1989. 'John Locke, Socinian or Natural Law Theorist?' In J. Crimmins, ed., *Religion, Secularization and Political Thought*. London, pp. 39–67.

———. 1994. 'Ulysses Bound? Venice and the Idea of Liberty from Howell to Hume'. In D. Wootton, ed., *Republicanism, Liberty and Commercial Society*. Stanford CA: Stanford University Press, pp. 341–67.

———. 1997. 'Pierre Bayle, Libertine?' In M. A. Stewart, ed., *Studies in Seventeenth-Century Philosophy*. Oxford: Clarendon, pp. 197–226.

———. 2008. 'From Fortune to Feedback: Contingency and the Birth of Modern Political Science'. In I. Shapiro and S. Bedi, eds., *Political Contingency*. New York: New York University Press, pp. 21–53.

Worden, Blair. 2000. 'Thomas Carlyle and Oliver Cromwell'. *PBA*, vol. 105, pp. 131–70.

———. 2001. *Roundhead Reputations*. London: Penguin.

Wrigley, E. A. 2000. 'The Divergence of England: The Growth of the English Economy in the Seventeenth and Eighteenth Centuries'. *TRHS*, 6th series, vol. 10, pp. 117–41.

Yaffe, Gideon. 1999. *Liberty Worth the Name: Locke on Free Agency*. Princeton NJ: Princeton University Press.

Yolton, Jean. 2000. 'Introduction'. In Jean S. Yolton, ed., *John Locke as Translator: Three of the 'Essais' of Pierre Nicole in French and English* [= *SVEC*, no. 7]. Oxford: Voltaire Foundation, pp. 1–8.

Yolton, John. 1959. *John Locke and the Way of Ideas*. Cambridge: Cambridge University Press.

———. 1984. *Thinking Matter*. Oxford: Blackwell.

———. 1987. 'French Materialist Disciples of Locke'. *JHP*, vol. 25, no. 1, pp. 83–104.

Young, Brian. 1998. *Religion and Enlightenment in Eighteenth-Century Britain*. Oxford: Oxford University Press.

———. 2000. '"The Lust of Empire and Religious Hate": Christianity, History and India, 1790–1820'. In S. Collini, R. Whatmore, and B. Young, eds., *History, Religion and Culture: British Intellectual History 1750–1950*. Cambridge: Cambridge University Press, pp. 91–111.

Yousef, Nancy. 2001. 'Savage or Solitary: The Wild Child and Rousseau's Man of Nature'. *JHI*, vol. 62, no. 2, pp. 245–63.

Zastoupil, Lynn. 1994. *John Stuart Mill and India*. Stanford CA: Stanford University Press.

Zweig, Egon. 1904. *Die Lehre vom Pouvoir Constituant*. Tübingen: J. C. B. Mohr.

Index